Lecture Notes in Computer Science 11367

Commenced Publication in 1973
Founding and Former Series Editors:
Gerhard Goos, Juris Hartmanis, and Jan van Leeuwen

Editorial Board Members

David Hutchison
Lancaster University, Lancaster, UK
Takeo Kanade
Carnegie Mellon University, Pittsburgh, PA, USA
Josef Kittler
University of Surrey, Guildford, UK
Jon M. Kleinberg
Cornell University, Ithaca, NY, USA
Friedemann Mattern
ETH Zurich, Zurich, Switzerland
John C. Mitchell
Stanford University, Stanford, CA, USA
Moni Naor
Weizmann Institute of Science, Rehovot, Israel
C. Pandu Rangan
Indian Institute of Technology Madras, Chennai, India
Bernhard Steffen
TU Dortmund University, Dortmund, Germany
Demetri Terzopoulos
University of California, Los Angeles, CA, USA
Doug Tygar
University of California, Berkeley, CA, USA

More information about this series at http://www.springer.com/series/7412

Gustavo Carneiro · Shaodi You (Eds.)

Computer Vision – ACCV 2018 Workshops

14th Asian Conference on Computer Vision
Perth, Australia, December 2–6, 2018
Revised Selected Papers

Editors
Gustavo Carneiro
School of Computer Science
University of Adelaide
Adelaide, Australia

Shaodi You
Data61
Commonwealth Scientific and Industrial
Research Organization
Canberra, Australia

ISSN 0302-9743　　　　　　　ISSN 1611-3349　(electronic)
Lecture Notes in Computer Science
ISBN 978-3-030-21073-1　　　ISBN 978-3-030-21074-8　(eBook)
https://doi.org/10.1007/978-3-030-21074-8

LNCS Sublibrary: SL6 – Image Processing, Computer Vision, Pattern Recognition, and Graphics

© Springer Nature Switzerland AG 2019
This work is subject to copyright. All rights are reserved by the Publisher, whether the whole or part of the material is concerned, specifically the rights of translation, reprinting, reuse of illustrations, recitation, broadcasting, reproduction on microfilms or in any other physical way, and transmission or information storage and retrieval, electronic adaptation, computer software, or by similar or dissimilar methodology now known or hereafter developed.
The use of general descriptive names, registered names, trademarks, service marks, etc. in this publication does not imply, even in the absence of a specific statement, that such names are exempt from the relevant protective laws and regulations and therefore free for general use.
The publisher, the authors and the editors are safe to assume that the advice and information in this book are believed to be true and accurate at the date of publication. Neither the publisher nor the authors or the editors give a warranty, expressed or implied, with respect to the material contained herein or for any errors or omissions that may have been made. The publisher remains neutral with regard to jurisdictional claims in published maps and institutional affiliations.

This Springer imprint is published by the registered company Springer Nature Switzerland AG
The registered company address is: Gewerbestrasse 11, 6330 Cham, Switzerland

Preface

It is our great pleasure to present the workshop proceedings of the Asian Conference on Computer Vision (ACCV) that took place during December 2–6, 2018, in Perth, Australia. In total, ACCV 2018 hosted 11 workshops, each having different types of programs involving invited talks, challenges, and paper presentations. The ACCV 2018 workshops were the following:

- Scene Understanding and Modelling (SUMO) Challenge
- Learning and Inference Methods for High-Performance Imaging (LIMHPI)
- Attention/Intention Understanding (AIU)
- Museum Exhibit Identification Challenge (Open MIC) for Domain Adaptation and Few-Shot Learning
- RGB-D—Sensing and Understanding via Combined Color and Depth
- Dense 3D Reconstruction for Dynamic Scenes
- AI Aesthetics in Art and Media (AIAM)
- Third International Workshop on Robust Reading (IWRR)
- Artificial Intelligence for Retinal Image Analysis (AIRIA)
- Combining Vision and Language
- First International Workshop on Advanced Machine Vision for Real-Life and Industrially Relevant Applications (AMV)

The workshop topics are related to computer vision and its applications, interdisciplinary themes with other application areas, as well as challenges or competitions. Every workshop handles its own paper submission system, with each paper being reviewed by two to three reviewers. We thank all the workshop organizers for their fantastic efforts in holding these successful workshops. We also thank the publication chair for putting together the workshop proceedings.

April 2019

Gustavo Carneiro
Shaodi You

Organization

Scene Understanding and Modelling (SUMO) Challenge

Daniel Huber	Facebook, Carnegie Mellon University, USA
Lyne Tchapmi	Stanford University, USA
Frank Dellaert	Facebook, Georgia Tech, USA

Learning and Inference Methods for High-Performance Imaging (LIMHPI)

Antonio Robles-Kelly	Data61-CSIRO, Australia, Australian National University, Australia
Imari Sato	National Institute of Informatics, Japan

Attention/Intention Understanding (AIU)

Ikuhisa Mitsugami	Hiroshima City University, Japan
Ryo Yonetani	The University of Tokyo, Japan
Kris M. Kitani	Carnegie Mellon University, USA

Museum Exhibit Identification Challenge (Open MIC) for Domain Adaptation and Few-Shot Learning

Piotr Koniusz	ANU College of Engineering and Computer Science, Australia
Yusuf Tas	Data61/CSIRO and CECS/ANU, Australia
Hongguang Zhang	Data61/CSIRO and CECS/ANU, Australia
Samitha Herath	Data61/CSIRO and CECS/ANU, Australia
Mehrtash Harandi	Monash University, School of Engineering, Australia
Rui Zhang	Wuhan University of Technology, China

RGB-D—Sensing and Understanding via Combined Color and Depth

Paul L. Rosin	Cardiff University, UK
Toby Breckon	Durham University, UK
Yu-Kun Lai	Cardiff University, UK

Dense 3D Reconstruction for Dynamic Scenes

Yuchao Dai	Northwestern Polytechnical University, China
Yebin Liu	Tsinghua University, China

AI Aesthetics in Art and Media (AIAM)

Wen-Huang Cheng	Academia Sinica, Taiwan
Wei-Ta Chu	National Chung Cheng University, Taiwan
John See	Multimedia University, Malaysia
Lai-Kuan Wong	Multimedia University, Malaysia

Third International Workshop on Robust Reading (IWRR)

Lluis Gomez	Computer Vision Centre, Spain
Serge Belongie	Cornell University, USA
Masakazu Iwamura	Osaka Prefecture University, Japan
C. V. Jawahar	IIIT Hyderabad, India
Dimosthenis Karatzas	Computer Vision Centre, Spain
Jiri Matas	Czech Technical University, Czech Republic
Yash Patel	Carnegie Mellon University, USA
Marçal Russiñol	Computer Vision Centre, Spain

Artificial Intelligence for Retinal Image Analysis (AIRIA)

Philippe Burlina	The Johns Hopkins University, USA
Daniel Ting Shu Wei	Singapore Eye Research Institute, Singapore
	Singapore National Eye Center, Singapore
	Duke-NUS Medical School, Singapore
	A*STAR, Singapore
Wong Tien Yin	Singapore Eye Research Institute, Singapore
	Singapore National Eye Center, Singapore
	Duke-NUS Medical School, Singapore
Neil Bressler	The Johns Hopkins University, USA

Combining Vision and Language

Qi Wu	University of Adelaide, Australia
Fumin Shen	UESTC, China
Peng Wang	NWPU, China
Xiaodong He	JD AI Research, China
Chuang Gan	MIT-Watson Lab, USA
Anton van den Hengel	University of Adelaide, Australia

First International Workshop on Advanced Machine Vision for Real-Life and Industrially Relevant Applications (AMV)

Thomas B. Moeslund	Aalborg University, Denmark
Rikke Gade	Aalborg University, Denmark
Toon Goedeme	KU Leuven, Belgium
Steven Puttemans	KU Leuven, Belgium
Ajmal Mian	The University of Western Australia, Australia

Contents

Learning and Inference Methods for High-Performance Imaging (LIMHPI)

Anti-occlusion Light-Field Optical Flow Estimation
Using Light-Field Super-Pixels.................................... 3
    Hao Zhu, Xiaoming Sun, Qi Zhang, Qing Wang, Antonio Robles-Kelly, and Hongdong Li

Attention/Intention Understanding (AIU)

Localizing the Gaze Target of a Crowd of People.................... 15
    Yuki Kodama, Yasutomo Kawanishi, Takatsugu Hirayama, Daisuke Deguchi, Ichiro Ide, Hiroshi Murase, Hidehisa Nagano, and Kunio Kashino

A Thumb Tip Wearable Device Consisting of Multiple Cameras
to Measure Thumb Posture.. 31
    Naoto Ienaga, Wataru Kawai, Koji Fujita, Natsuki Miyata, Yuta Sugiura, and Hideo Saito

Summarizing Videos with Attention 39
    Jiri Fajtl, Hajar Sadeghi Sokeh, Vasileios Argyriou, Dorothy Monekosso, and Paolo Remagnino

Gait-Based Age Estimation Using a DenseNet 55
    Atsuya Sakata, Yasushi Makihara, Noriko Takemura, Daigo Muramatsu, and Yasushi Yagi

Human Action Recognition via Body Part Region Segmented
Dense Trajectories.. 64
    Kaho Yamada, Seiya Ito, Naoshi Kaneko, and Kazuhiko Sumi

AI Aesthetics in Art and Media (AIAM)

Let AI Clothe You: Diversified Fashion Generation.................. 75
    Rajdeep H. Banerjee, Anoop Rajagopal, Nilpa Jha, Arun Patro, and Aruna Rajan

Word-Conditioned Image Style Transfer 88
    Yu Sugiyama and Keiji Yanai

Font Style Transfer Using Neural Style Transfer and Unsupervised
Cross-domain Transfer.................................... 100
   Atsushi Narusawa, Wataru Shimoda, and Keiji Yanai

Paying Attention to Style: Recognizing Photo Styles
with Convolutional Attentional Units............................ 110
   John See, Lai-Kuan Wong, and Magzhan Kairanbay

Third International Workshop on Robust Reading (IWRR)

E2E-MLT - An Unconstrained End-to-End Method
for Multi-language Scene Text 127
   Michal Bušta, Yash Patel, and Jiri Matas

An Invoice Reading System Using a Graph Convolutional Network 144
   D. Lohani, A. Belaïd, and Y. Belaïd

Reading Industrial Inspection Sheets by Inferring Visual Relations 159
   Rohit Rahul, Arindam Chowdhury, Animesh, Samarth Mittal,
   and Lovekesh Vig

Learning to Clean: A GAN Perspective 174
   Monika Sharma, Abhishek Verma, and Lovekesh Vig

Deep Reader: Information Extraction from Document Images
via Relation Extraction and Natural Language 186
   D. Vishwanath, Rohit Rahul, Gunjan Sehgal, Swati,
   Arindam Chowdhury, Monika Sharma, Lovekesh Vig, Gautam Shroff,
   and Ashwin Srinivasan

Simultaneous Recognition of Horizontal and Vertical Text
in Natural Images 202
   Chankyu Choi, Youngmin Yoon, Junsu Lee, and Junseok Kim

Artificial Intelligence for Retinal Image Analysis (AIRIA)

Automatic Retinal and Choroidal Boundary Segmentation
in OCT Images Using Patch-Based Supervised
Machine Learning Methods 215
   David Alonso-Caneiro, Jason Kugelman, Jared Hamwood,
   Scott A. Read, Stephen J. Vincent, Fred K. Chen, and Michael J. Collins

Discrimination Ability of Glaucoma via DCNNs Models
from Ultra-Wide Angle Fundus Images Comparing Either
Full or Confined to the Optic Disc 229
   Hitoshi Tabuchi, Hiroki Masumoto, Shunsuke Nakakura,
   Asuka Noguchi, and Hirotaka Tanabe

Synthesizing New Retinal Symptom Images by Multiple
Generative Models 235
    Yi-Chieh Liu, Hao-Hsiang Yang, C.-H. Huck Yang, Jia-Hong Huang,
    Meng Tian, Hiromasa Morikawa, Yi-Chang James Tsai,
    and Jesper Tegnèr

Retinal Detachment Screening with Ensembles
of Neural Network Models...................................... 251
    Hiroki Masumoto, Hitoshi Tabuchi, Shoto Adachi, Shunsuke Nakakura,
    Hideharu Ohsugi, and Daisuke Nagasato

Recent Developments of Retinal Image Analysis in Alzheimer's Disease
and Potential AI Applications.................................. 261
    Delia Cabrera DeBuc and Edmund Arthur

Intermediate Goals in Deep Learning for Retinal Image Analysis 276
    Gilbert Lim, Wynne Hsu, and Mong Li Lee

Enhanced Detection of Referable Diabetic Retinopathy
via DCNNs and Transfer Learning 282
    Michelle Yuen Ting Yip, Zhan Wei Lim, Gilbert Lim,
    Nguyen Duc Quang, Haslina Hamzah, Jinyi Ho, Valentina Bellemo,
    Yuchen Xie, Xin Qi Lee, Mong Li Lee, Wynne Hsu, Tien Yin Wong,
    and Daniel Shu Wei Ting

Generative Adversarial Networks (GANs) for Retinal
Fundus Image Synthesis....................................... 289
    Valentina Bellemo, Philippe Burlina, Liu Yong, Tien Yin Wong,
    and Daniel Shu Wei Ting

AI-based AMD Analysis: A Review of Recent Progress 303
    P. Burlina, N. Joshi, and N. M. Bressler

Artificial Intelligence Using Deep Learning in Classifying Side
of the Eyes and Width of Field for Retinal Fundus Photographs 309
    Valentina Bellemo, Michelle Yuen Ting Yip, Yuchen Xie, Xin Qi Lee,
    Quang Duc Nguyen, Haslina Hamzah, Jinyi Ho, Gilbert Lim,
    Dejiang Xu, Mong Li Lee, Wynne Hsu, Renata Garcia-Franco,
    Geeta Menon, Ecosse Lamoureux, Ching-Yu Cheng, Tien Yin Wong,
    and Daniel Shu Wei Ting

OCT Segmentation via Deep Learning: A Review of Recent Work 316
    M. Pekala, N. Joshi, T. Y. Alvin Liu, N. M. Bressler, D. Cabrera DeBuc,
    and P. Burlina

Auto-classification of Retinal Diseases in the Limit of Sparse
Data Using a Two-Streams Machine Learning Model 323
    C.-H. Huck Yang, Fangyu Liu, Jia-Hong Huang, Meng Tian,
    M. D. I-Hung Lin, Yi Chieh Liu, Hiromasa Morikawa,
    Hao-Hsiang Yang, and Jesper Tegnèr

First International Workshop on Advanced Machine Vision for Real-Life and Industrially Relevant Applications (AMV)

LoANs: Weakly Supervised Object Detection
with Localizer Assessor Networks. 341
    Christian Bartz, Haojin Yang, Joseph Bethge, and Christoph Meinel

Reaching Behind Specular Highlights by Registration of Two Images
of Broiler Viscera. 357
    Anders Jørgensen, Malte Pedersen, Rikke Gade, Jens Fagertun,
    and Thomas B. Moeslund

Anomaly Detection Using GANs for Visual Inspection
in Noisy Training Data 373
    Masanari Kimura and Takashi Yanagihara

Integration of Driver Behavior into Emotion Recognition Systems:
A Preliminary Study on Steering Wheel and Vehicle Acceleration. 386
    Sina Shafaei, Tahir Hacizade, and Alois Knoll

Prediction Based Deep Autoencoding Model for Anomaly Detection. 402
    Zhanzhong Pang, Xiaoyi Yu, Jun Sun, and Inakoshi Hiroya

Multimodal Sensor Fusion in Single Thermal Image Super-Resolution. 418
    Feras Almasri and Olivier Debeir

PCA-RECT: An Energy-Efficient Object Detection Approach
for Event Cameras 434
    Bharath Ramesh, Andrés Ussa, Luca Della Vedova, Hong Yang,
    and Garrick Orchard

Unconstrained Iris Segmentation Using Convolutional Neural Networks. 450
    Sohaib Ahmad and Benjamin Fuller

Simultaneous Multi-view Relative Pose Estimation and 3D Reconstruction
from Planar Regions 467
    Robert Frohlich and Zoltan Kato

WNet: Joint Multiple Head Detection and Head Pose Estimation
from a Spectator Crowd Image. 484
    Yasir Jan, Ferdous Sohel, Mohd Fairuz Shiratuddin, and Kok Wai Wong

Markerless Augmented Advertising for Sports Videos 494
    Hallee E. Wong, Osman Akar, Emmanuel Antonio Cuevas,
    Iuliana Tabian, Divyaa Ravichandran, Iris Fu, and Cambron Carter

Visual Siamese Clustering for Cosmetic Product Recommendation 510
    Christopher J. Holder, Boguslaw Obara, and Stephen Ricketts

Multimodal Deep Neural Networks Based Ensemble Learning
for X-Ray Object Recognition 523
    Quan Kong, Naoto Akira, Bin Tong, Yuki Watanabe,
    Daisuke Matsubara, and Tomokazu Murakami

Author Index 539

Learning and Inference Methods for High-Performance Imaging (LIMHPI)

Anti-occlusion Light-Field Optical Flow Estimation Using Light-Field Super-Pixels

Hao Zhu[1], Xiaoming Sun[1], Qi Zhang[1], Qing Wang[1(✉)], Antonio Robles-Kelly[2], and Hongdong Li[3]

[1] Northwestern Polytechnical University, Xi'an 710072, China
qwang@nwpu.edu.cn
[2] Deakin University, Melbourne, Australia
[3] Australian National University, Canberra, ACT 0200, Australia

Abstract. Optical flow estimation is one of the most important problem in community. However, current methods still can not provide reliable results in occlusion boundary areas. Light field cameras provide hundred of views in a single shot, so the ambiguity can be better analysed using other views. In this paper, we present a novel method for anti-occlusion optical flow estimation in a dynamic light field. We first model the light field superpixel (LFSP) as a slanted plane in 3D. Then the motion of the occluded pixels in central view slice can be optimized by the un-occluded pixels in other views. Thus the optical flow in occlusion boundary areas can be well computed. Experimental results on both synthetic and real light fields demonstrate the advantages over state-of-the-arts and the performance on 4D optical flow computation.

Keywords: Light field · Optical flow

1 Introduction

Optical flow estimation is one of the most important problem in computer vision community and has been researched for decades. Due to the lack of views (2 views) in traditional optical flow methods, the optical flow in object boundaries (occlusion areas) are always over-smoothed. Light field [1,5,11] is a promising paradigm for describing complex 3D scene. Compared with traditional pinhole cameras, one most important benefit of light field cameras is that both spatial and angular information are recorded in a single shot (*e.g.*, there are 196 views extracted from the Lytro Illum camera). Thus, the occlusion problem in object boundaries can be better analysed using the provided other views in light field.

In the paper, we explore an optical flow estimation algorithm in the whole 4D light field using the most recently proposed light field superpixel (LFSP) [22] (or super-rays [7]). With the help of LFSP, the optical flow of occlusion

The work was supported in part by NSFC under Grant 61531014.

Fig. 1. Optical flow on real-world light-fields. First row, from left-to-right: central view images, target light-fields, depth and optical flow maps of the image, respectively. The top-right is the colour map of optical flow. Second row: enlarged versions of two regions of interest in the reference image marked with green and blue squares, respectively. In the bottom row, we also show the 4D light-field, depth and optical flow maps along the horizontal and vertical EPIs. (Color figure online)

areas in central view can be modelled using the 2D slice of 4D LFSP in other unoccluded views. Thus, the LFSP can benefit optical flow estimation on three aspects. First, the LFSP can be seen as a combination of the 2D superpixels in different views to describe the same object. In other words, the motion of a LFSP in another view can be equivalently represented by the one in the central view. Second, **piecewise** rigid optical flow map. The planarity of LFSP guarantees all pixels in a LFSP sharing the same motion model. Additionally the occlusion points in the object boundaries [21] can be better smoothed using other reliable un-occluded points in the LFSP. Apart from these, there is no blur effects [15,22] since each virtual camera in the light field has a small aperture [14] and can be regarded as a pinhole model.

The paper is organized as follows. In the following section we review recent progresses in light field optical flow estimation and clarifies the advantages or differences of our method compared with previous work. In Sect. 3, we first model the LFSP and derive the propagation method of motion vectors between different views in light field, then the proposed algorithm is described in details. In Sect. 4, extensive experiments are carried on both synthetic data and real scene light fields captured by a Lytro Illum [12]. Quantitative and qualitative comparisons verify the performance of our algorithm. We conclude on the work presented here in Sect. 5.

2 Related Work

2.1 Light Field and LFSP

Recall that a 4D light-field $L(u,v,x,y)$ describes the light rays between two parallel planes, namely the uv camera plane and the xy image plane. Here, we refer to these as angular and spatial spaces, respectively. In this manner, each (u,v) corresponds to the location of the viewpoint of light-field and each (x,y)

corresponds to a pixel location. Viewed in this way, the LFSP is a 4D light ray set, where all rays describe a proximately similar and continuous surface in 3D space [22]. In contrast with traditional 2D super-pixels, which are built on image pixels, each LFSP is defined in 4D space for each 2D slice in a fixed view corresponding to traditional 2D super-pixel. This is important, since, as a result, all 2D slices describing the same area captured from different views can be modeled using a plane or curved surface whereby the corresponding LFSP can be used to build the geometry distribution of the image region in 3D space.

2.2 Light Field Optical Flow

In light field area, as far as we know, there are two papers published for scene flow estimation. Heber et al. [6] formulated a convex global energy functional using the sub-aperture representations of light field and optimized it using a preconditioned primal-dual algorithm. Srinivasan et al. [16] pointed out the problem of defocus blur [15] and perspective in traditional pixel window based comparisons. They modeled the 4D oriented light field windows for scene flow estimation. These algorithms have the following disadvantages. First, common 2D or 4D patches limit the accuracy of optical flow estimation which has an over-smoothed depth or flow fields in object boundaries. Second, because the light field records the rays in the 3D space and each sub-aperture image can be seen as an all-in-focus image [14], it is unnecessary to consider blur effects in light field. Besides complexity increases when blindly introducing the 4D comparison. In contrast to these methods, the flow is computed over the LFSP which yields sharper object boundaries in our algorithm. Additionally, the whole 4D LFSP in light field is represented by its 2D superpixel slice in the central view which decreases the complexity.

3 The Proposed Method

The main advantages of light field in the proposed scene flow method, the depth and optical flow are optimized sequentially, whereby optimal techniques can be chosen for each task, *i.e.* the depth and the flow computation. This approach is specially suitable for light-field configurations due to the resulting cost function, where there are a large amount of data points in the depth term over the two images in the optical flow term. As a result, modern approaches have demonstrated surprising performance in depth estimation and the accuracy has achieved 0.02 sub-pixel [8,9]. However, the optical flow estimation still stays at pixel level accuracy [2].

3.1 Model

In the proposed solution, each LFSP s_i is modeled as a slanted-plane in the 3D space. Suppose that the normal of super-pixel slice $s_i^{0,0}$ in central view $(0,0)$ is

$\boldsymbol{n}_i^{0,0} = (a,b,c)^\top$ and the plane function is $\boldsymbol{n}_i^{0,0\top} \boldsymbol{X} = 1$ ($\boldsymbol{X} \in \mathbb{R}^3$), the normal of slice in the (u,v) view $s_i^{u,v}$ can be computed as,

$$\boldsymbol{n}_i^{u,v} = \frac{\boldsymbol{n}_i^{0,0}}{1 - a \cdot bl \cdot u - b \cdot bl \cdot v}, \quad (1)$$

where bl is the baseline in light-field camera. Following the slanted-plane assumption, the motion of each LFSP s_i can be described by a rotation matrix $\boldsymbol{R}_i \in \mathbb{R}^{3 \times 3}$ and a translation vector $\boldsymbol{t}_i \in \mathbb{R}^3$[1]. Given an equivalent intrinsic matrix $\boldsymbol{K}$ for the central view of light-field camera, for each pixel $p = (u,v,x,y) \in s_i$, the disparity $d(p,s_i)$ and optical flow $f(p,s_i)$ can be computed as,

$$\begin{aligned} d(p,s_i) &= bl \cdot fl \cdot \boldsymbol{n}_i^{u,v\top} \boldsymbol{K}^{-1}(x,y,1)^\top \\ f(p,s_i) &= \boldsymbol{K}(\boldsymbol{R}_i - \boldsymbol{t}_i \cdot \boldsymbol{n}_i^{u,v\top}) \boldsymbol{K}^{-1}(x,y,1)^\top - (x,y,1)^\top, \end{aligned} \quad (2)$$

where fl is the equivalent focal length of light-field camera.

3.2 Depth Recovery

Recall that a 4D light-field $L(u,v,x,y)$ can be sheared [14,17] using the expression

$$LF_d(u,v,x,y) = LF_0(u,v,x-ud,y-vd), \quad (3)$$

where LF_0 is the input 4D light-field and LF_d is the sheared light-field at the disparity d. For simplicity, the colour of pixel $p = (x,y)$ in the view (u,v) is denoted as $A_{p_d}(u,v)$ when the light-field is sheared at the disparity d, i.e. $A_{p_d}(u,v) := LF_d(u,v,x,y)$.

With this notation, we can write the energy function used here for the depth optimisation as follows

$$E(d) = \sum_{s_i \in S} E_{data}^d(s_i, \boldsymbol{n}_i) + \lambda_s^d \sum_{s_i \sim s_j \in S} E_{smo}^d(\boldsymbol{n}_i, \boldsymbol{n}_j), \quad (4)$$

where S is the LFSP set and s_i, s_j are the neighbouring LFSPs. ($\lambda_s^d = 2/7$). The data term is,

$$\begin{aligned} E_{data}^d(s_i, \boldsymbol{n}_i) &= 1 - e^{-\frac{C(s_i, \boldsymbol{n}_i)^2}{2\sigma_d^2}} \\ C(s_i, \boldsymbol{n}_i) &= \frac{1}{|s_i^{0,0}|} \sum_{p \in s_i^{0,0}} \frac{1}{|\Omega_p^{uocc}|} \sum_{(u,v) \in \Omega_p^{uocc}} |A_{p_{d(p,s_i)}}(u,v) - A_{p_{d(p,s_i)}}(0,0)|, \end{aligned} \quad (5)$$

where $|\cdot|$ denotes the size of the set $\cdot$, Ω_p^{uocc} denotes the un-occluded views for each pixel p in light-field and σ_d controls the sensitivity of the function to large distances. The main reason for choosing a Gaussian-like metric is that it is easier to escape a local minima than traditional L_2 norm in a global optimisation scheme [4]. Note that only the un-occluded views are selected for the cost computation. This is in contrast with [21], where the un-occluded views

---
[1] The motion $\boldsymbol{R}_i, \boldsymbol{t}_i$ are constants while the normal $\boldsymbol{n}_i^{u,v}$ changes with each view.

are selected by clustering pixel-by-pixel. Here we select the background areas for each boundary pixel according to the super-pixel segmentation in the central view and then obtain the un-occluded views using the light-field occlusion model in [19,21]. This approach also has the added advantage of speeding up the un-occluded view selection.

Following [13], the smoothness term in Eq. 5 is given by

$$E^d_{smo}(\boldsymbol{n}_i, \boldsymbol{n}_j) = \omega_{ij}(E_{orient}(\boldsymbol{n}_i, \boldsymbol{n}_j) + E_{depth}(\boldsymbol{n}_i, \boldsymbol{n}_j))$$

$$E_{orient}(\boldsymbol{n}_i, \boldsymbol{n}_j) = \theta_1 \rho_{\tau_1}(1 - \frac{|\boldsymbol{n}_i^T \boldsymbol{n}_j|}{\|\boldsymbol{n}_i\|\|\boldsymbol{n}_j\|}) \quad (6)$$

$$E_{depth}(\boldsymbol{n}_i, \boldsymbol{n}_j) = \theta_2 \frac{1}{|\mathcal{B}_{ij}|} \sum_{p \in \mathcal{B}_{ij}} \rho_{\tau_2}(d(p, s_i) - d(p, s_j)),$$

where $\omega_{ij} = e^{-\frac{[LF(s_i^{0,0}) - LF(s_j^{0,0})]^2}{2\sigma_c^2}}$, $LF(s_i^{0,0})$ denotes the mean colour of $s_i^{0,0}$ and σ_c controls the sensitivity between neighbouring super-pixels. In the equation above E_{orient} controls neighbouring LFSPs to orient in the same direction and E_{depth} controls shared boundaries co-aligned in the disparity space. Here, $\mathcal{B}_{ij}$ is the set of shared boundaries between the LFSP slices $s_i^{0,0}$ and $s_j^{0,0}$ and $\rho_\tau(x)$ denotes the truncated l_1 penalty function $\rho_\tau(x) = min(|x|, \tau)$.

3.3 Optical Flow Optimization

Based on the optimized normal $\boldsymbol{n}_i$ for each LFSP s_i in LF^1, the goal of optical flow optimization becomes that of finding the motion fields $\boldsymbol{R}_i$ and $\boldsymbol{t}_i$. To this end, we define the energy function as follows

$$E(f) = \sum_{s_i \in S} E_d^f(s_i, \boldsymbol{R}_i, \boldsymbol{t}_i) + \lambda_s^f \sum_{s_i \frown s_j \in S} E_s^f(\boldsymbol{R}_i, \boldsymbol{R}_j, \boldsymbol{t}_i, \boldsymbol{t}_j), \quad (7)$$

where λ_s^f is a parameter that controls the influence of the second term in the cost function.

The data term is hence given by,

$$E_d^f(s_i, \boldsymbol{R}_i, \boldsymbol{t}_i) = 1 - e^{-\frac{C(s_i, \boldsymbol{R}_i, \boldsymbol{t}_i)^2}{2\sigma_f^2}}$$

$$C(s_i, \boldsymbol{R}_i, \boldsymbol{t}_i) = \frac{1}{|s_i^{0,0}|} \sum_{p \in s_i^{0,0}} |LF^1(p) - LF^2(p + f(p, s_i))|, \quad (8)$$

where σ_f and other symbols have the same meaning as in Eq. 5. It is worth noticing that the cost function over the optical flow only considers the matching between the 2D central view slices across LF^1 and LF^2. The reasons for this are twofold. Firstly, the central view slices can represent the whole LFSP, as shown in [22]. Thus, adding more matches across other views can not improve the performance but only increase the running time. Secondly, the light-field camera has a low signal-to-noise ratio, especially in the boundary views, which can lead to unreliable matching results.

For our cost function, the smoothness term is

$$E_s^f(\boldsymbol{R}_i, \boldsymbol{R}_j, \boldsymbol{t}_i, \boldsymbol{t}_j) = \omega_{ij} \frac{1}{|\mathcal{B}_{ij}|} \sum_{p \in \mathcal{B}_{ij}} \rho_{\tau_3}(f(p, s_i) - f(p, s_j)), \tag{9}$$

where $\tau_3 = 150$. Noting that, the weight term ω_{ij} is determined by combining the colour and optimised disparity, we use

$$\omega_{ij} = e^{-\frac{[LF^1(s_i^{0,0}) - LF^1(s_j^{0,0})]^2 + [\bar{d}(s_i^{0,0}) - \bar{d}(s_j^{0,0})]^2}{2\sigma_c^2}}, \tag{10}$$

where σ_c and $\bar{d}(s_i^{0,0})$ denotes the normalised mean disparity of $s_i^{0,0}$. As a result, the depth term used here can decrease the weight when the foreground and background share similar textures and yield sharper optical flow fields on object boundary areas. This influence of the depth term in Eq. 10 is showed later on in Sect. 4, where we show real-world light-field experiments.

4 Experiments

4.1 Algorithm Stages

We compare our results with state-of-the-art algorithms both in light-field depth estimation and scene flow estimation. These include the globally consistent depth labeling (GCDL) method in [20], the phase-shift based depth estimation (PSD) approach in [10], the occlusion-aware depth estimation (OADE) method in [19], the large displacement optical flow (LDOF) approach in [3], the scene flow estimation with piecewise rigid scene model (PRSM) in [18], the object scene flow (OSF) algorithm in [13] and the oriented light-field window method for scene flow (OLFW) computation in [16]. It is worth noting that the PRSM and OSF are the two state-of-the-art methods on the Kitty Benchmark [2].

4.2 Results

Here, we have obtained all the results for the alternatives by using the code released by the authors[2]. Also, note that traditional methods such as PRSM and OSF are designed for wider baseline stereo configurations and, hence, for the sake of fairness, we have selected for the experiments pertaining these methods the central and the rightmost views of input light-fields (this implies the baseline is magnified by 4 times as compared to adjacent views).

Synthetic Data. In Table 1 and Fig. 2 we show the results and comparisons on optical flow computation on the synthetic light-fields. Our algorithm performs best on all of 10 light-fields. Compared with previous methods, our algorithm

---

[2] The code for the OSF yields a runtime error when processing the low resolution data for the "Drawing" scene and, as a result, has been omitted from the results shown here for that scene.

Table 1. Per-pixel endpoint errors of the estimated optical flows.

	Desktop		Mario		Drawing		Balls		NewBalls	
	Small	Big	Small	Big	Small	Big	Small	Big	Small	Big
PRSM [18]	1.261	1.809	1.120	1.395	1.257	3.093	0.289	0.495	0.670	0.892
OSF [13]	0.877	1.513	2.749	6.239	—	4.355	0.744	1.613	0.547	0.794
LDOF [3]	3.780	3.174	2.136	4.524	1.129	1.766	0.440	0.587	1.259	1.883
OLFW [16]	2.265	4.441	4.893	7.166	2.495	5.005	1.167	6.073	1.206	13.713
Ours	**0.781**	**1.393**	**0.826**	**1.012**	**0.928**	**1.324**	**0.284**	**0.481**	**0.496**	**0.693**

Table 2. Accuracy of optical flow estimation as a function of the number of views.

NumOfView	Desktop	Mario	Drawing	Balls	NewBalls
3 × 3	1.504	1.415	1.527	0.577	0.775
5 × 5	1.500	1.333	1.500	0.521	0.714
7 × 7	1.463	1.152	1.444	0.499	0.701
9 × 9	1.393	1.012	1.324	0.481	0.693

provides finer optical flow results. For example, there are three optical flow layers in the red box in the "Drawing" sequence, *i.e.*, the front and real legs of chair and the sofa. Only our algorithm can reconstruct these precisely whereas other methods tend to over-smooth them. In the green box of the "Mario" sequence, the dice is a continuous whole object where the motion vectors between the closest and farthest points have a smooth distribution. Previous methods either assign them the same motion vector (OSF and OLFW) or several discontinuous vectors (PRSM and LDOF). Only our method obtains continuous results. This may be the result of our method utilising multiview sub-apertures in the light-field, which provides more precise normals for each of the LFSPs.

Real Data. In Figs. 1 and 3 we show optical flow maps on the real-world light-fields. Due to the high-accuracy depth maps from the light-field, our algorithm generates fine optical flow maps, specially on the object boundaries, such as the slender leaves (both in red and yellow boxes in the "Plant1" imagery) and the gaps in the red box in the "Plant2" data. The 4D optical flow maps are also propagated well thanks to the LFSP (Table 2).

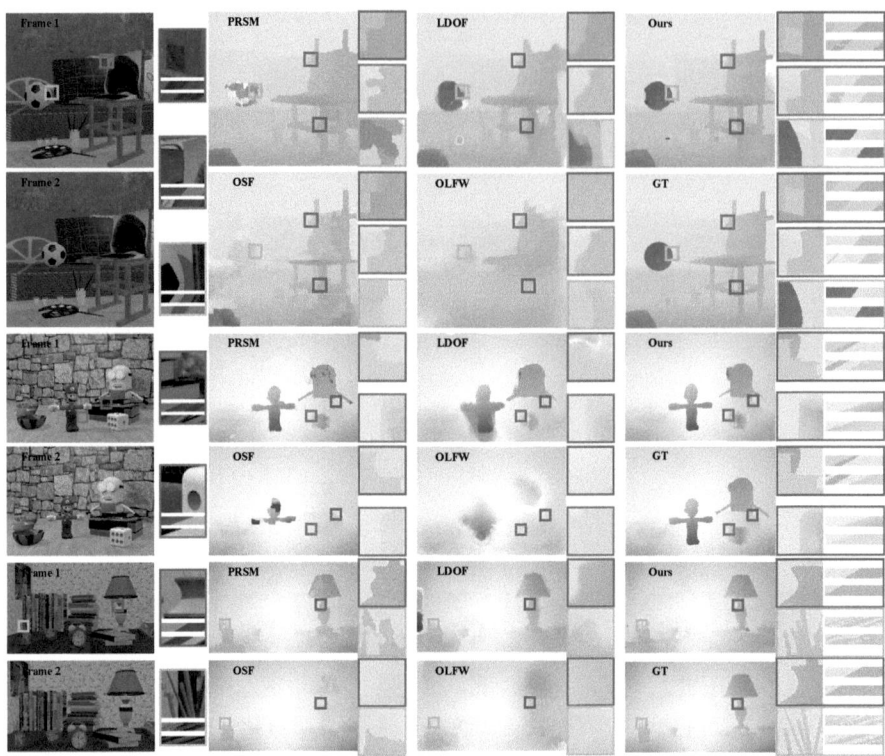

Fig. 2. Optical flow estimation results on the synthetic data for the "Drawing", "Mario" and "Desktop" sequences. For each box in our results and the GT (the rightmost column), the first and second rows show the 4D optical flow map in the horizontal and vertical EPIs, respectively. (Color figure online)

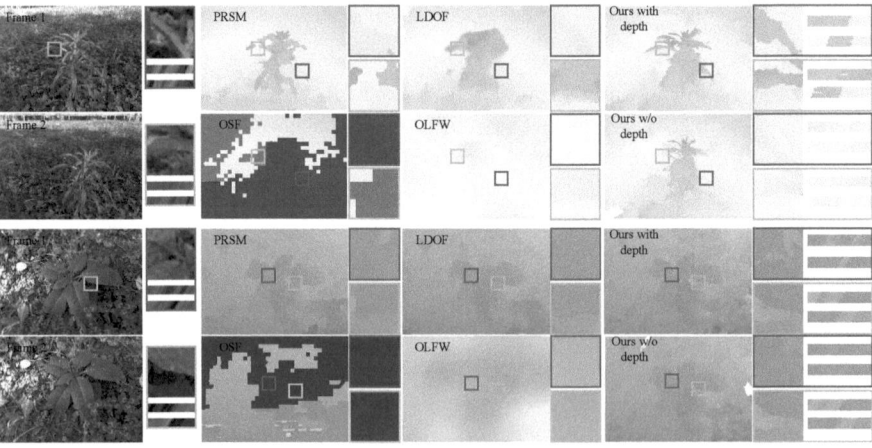

Fig. 3. Optical flow estimation results on the real-world light-fields "Plant1" and "Plant2". (Color figure online)

5 Conclusions

In this paper, we have presented a multi-view optical flow estimation for light-field imaging. Here, we have used the structure delivered by the 4D light-field using 4D LFSPs. We have shown how these LFSPs can be used to represent the objects in the scene as a set of slanted-planes in the 3D space so as to recover a piecewise rigid depth estimate. Moreover, we have shown how the optical flow can be effectively propagated from the central view to the other views in the imagery. The scene flow for the central view of light-field is estimated by sequentially optimizing the depth and optical flow. We have shown results that illustrate that the proposed algorithm not only obtains 4D optical flow for all views in light-fields, but also achieves better depth and flow maps than those delivered by a number of alternatives.

References

1. Adelson, E.H., Bergen, J.R.: The plenoptic function and the elements of early vision. Comput. Models Vis. Process. **1**(2), 3–20 (1991)
2. Andreas, G., Philip, L., Raquel, U., Moritz, M.: The kitti vision benchmark suite (2012). http://www.cvlibs.net/datasets/kitti/
3. Brox, T., Malik, J.: Large displacement optical flow: descriptor matching in variational motion estimation. IEEE T-PAMI **33**(3), 500–513 (2011). https://doi.org/10.1109/TPAMI.2010.143
4. Chen, C., Lin, H., Yu, Z., Kang, S., Yu, J.: Light field stereo matching using bilateral statistics of surface cameras. In: IEEE CVPR, pp. 1518–1525 (2014)
5. Gortler, S.J., Grzeszczuk, R., Szeliski, R., Cohen, M.F.: The lumigraph. In: SIGGRAPH, pp. 43–54. ACM (1996)
6. Heber, S., Pock, T.: Scene flow estimation from light fields via the preconditioned primal-dual algorithm. In: Jiang, X., Hornegger, J., Koch, R. (eds.) GCPR 2014. LNCS, vol. 8753, pp. 3–14. Springer, Cham (2014). https://doi.org/10.1007/978-3-319-11752-2_1
7. Hog, M., Sabater, N., Guillemot, C.: Super-rays for efficient light field processing. IEEE J-STSP (2017, in press). https://doi.org/10.1109/JSTSP.2017.2738619
8. Honauer, K., Johannsen, O., Kondermann, D., Goldluecke, B.: 4D light field dataset (2016). http://hci-lightfield.iwr.uni-heidelberg.de/
9. Honauer, K., Johannsen, O., Kondermann, D., Goldluecke, B.: A dataset and evaluation methodology for depth estimation on 4D light fields. In: Lai, S.-H., Lepetit, V., Nishino, K., Sato, Y. (eds.) ACCV 2016. LNCS, vol. 10113, pp. 19–34. Springer, Cham (2017). https://doi.org/10.1007/978-3-319-54187-7_2
10. Jeon, H.G., et al.: Accurate depth map estimation from a lenslet light field camera. In: IEEE CVPR, pp. 1547–1555 (2015)
11. Levoy, M., Hanrahan, P.: Light field rendering. In: SIGGRAPH, pp. 31–42. ACM (1996)
12. Lytro: The ultimate creative tool for cinema and broadcast (2016). http://blog.lytro.com/?s=cinema
13. Menze, M., Geiger, A.: Object scene flow for autonomous vehicles. In: IEEE CVPR, pp. 3061–3070, June 2015. https://doi.org/10.1109/CVPR.2015.7298925
14. Ng, R.: Digital light field photography. Ph.D. thesis, Stanford University (2006)

15. Pan, L., Dai, Y., Liu, M., Porikli, F.: Simultaneous stereo video deblurring and scene flow estimation. In: IEEE CVPR, July 2017
16. Srinivasan, P.P., Tao, M.W., Ng, R., Ramamoorthi, R.: Oriented light-field windows for scene flow. In: IEEE ICCV, pp. 3496–3504 (2015)
17. Tao, M., Hadap, S., Malik, J., Ramamoorthi, R.: Depth from combining defocus and correspondence using light-field cameras. In: IEEE ICCV, pp. 673–680 (2013)
18. Vogel, C., Schindler, K., Roth, S.: 3D scene flow estimation with a piecewise rigid scene model. IJCV **115**(1), 1–28 (2015)
19. Wang, T.C., Efros, A.A., Ramamoorthi, R.: Depth estimation with occlusion modeling using light-field cameras. IEEE T-PAMI **38**(11), 2170–2181 (2016)
20. Wanner, S., Goldluecke, B.: Variational light field analysis for disparity estimation and super-resolution. IEEE T-PAMI **36**(3), 606–619 (2014)
21. Zhu, H., Wang, Q., Yu, J.: Occlusion-model guided anti-occlusion depth estimation in light field. IEEE J-STSP **11**(7), 965–978 (2017). https://doi.org/10.1109/JSTSP.2017.2730818
22. Zhu, H., Zhang, Q., Wang, Q.: 4D light field superpixel and segmentation. In: IEEE CVPR, pp. 1–8. IEEE (2017)

Attention/Intention Understanding (AIU)

Localizing the Gaze Target of a Crowd of People

Yuki Kodama[1]([✉]), Yasutomo Kawanishi[1], Takatsugu Hirayama[2], Daisuke Deguchi[3], Ichiro Ide[1], Hiroshi Murase[1], Hidehisa Nagano[4], and Kunio Kashino[4]

[1] Graduate School of Informatics, Nagoya University, Aichi, Japan
kodamay2@murase.is.i.nagoya-u.ac.jp
[2] Institutes of Innovation for Future Society, Nagoya University, Aichi, Japan
[3] Information Strategy Office, Nagoya University, Aichi, Japan
[4] NTT Communication Science Laboratories, NTT Corporation, Chiyoda, Japan

Abstract. What target is focused on by many people? Analysis of the target is a crucial task, especially in a cinema, a stadium, and so on. However, it is very difficult to estimate the gaze of each person in a crowd accurately and simultaneously with existing image-based eye tracking methods, since the image resolution of each person becomes low when we capture the whole crowd with a distant camera. Therefore, we introduce a new approach for localizing the gaze target focused on by a crowd of people. The proposed framework aggregates the individually estimated results of each person's gaze. It enables us to localize the target being focused on by them even though each person's gaze localization from a low-resolution image is inaccurate. We analyze the effects of an aggregation method on the localization accuracy using images capturing a crowd of people in a tennis stadium under the assumption that all of the people are focusing on the same target, and also investigate the effect of the number of people involved in the aggregation on the localization accuracy. As a result, the proposed method showed the ability to improve the localization accuracy as it is applied to a larger crowd of people.

1 Introduction

Gaze estimation from an image is very useful for various applications. Gaze can tell us how a person looks into things to buy, which object s/he is interested in, and so on. Therefore, there are many studies focusing on human gaze estimation [1–5]. In a situation where many people gather in a space such as a cinema or a stadium, it is valuable to analyze where the people, i.e. a crowd of audience or spectators, are looking at. Here, each person's gaze is independent and there are many objects to be focused on by the people. So, we can assume that the more people look at a particular object simultaneously, the more potentially valuable, or interesting, the object is. Therefore, there is a strong demand to analyze a crowd of people looking at the same object simultaneously.

Fig. 1. Example of a situation that the proposed method assumes.

To analyze where a crowd of people is looking at, we need to observe all the members simultaneously. From the viewpoint of cost and convenience, rather than employing eye trackers, it is desired to estimate where they are looking at from an image capturing the whole crowd. One very simple solution is to capture each person in high-resolution from many cameras. However, this is difficult to implement. Instead, capturing the whole crowd by one camera is a more realistic solution. However, in this case, the face image of each person becomes small in size, so we can only obtain their face images in low-resolution.

Therefore, our goal is to localize a gaze target focused on by a crowd of people from one image captured from a distant camera position (Fig. 1). Since detailed information for each face or pair of eyes cannot be extracted from such an image, gaze estimation from the images with low-resolution will be inaccurate. Nevertheless, as shown in Fig. 2, when many people in the crowd are focusing on a common target, even if the gaze estimation result for each person is not accurate, their gaze target could be localized accurately by combining individual estimates. Based on this assumption, we propose a novel framework to localize the gaze target by aggregating the gaze estimation results of each person in the crowd.

For simplicity, in this paper, we will consider the simplest situation where all of the people in the crowd are focusing on a common object that exists on a two-dimensional space such as a screen or a ground.

Based on the analysis of the relationship between the number of people in a crowd and the localization accuracy, this paper reveals that this relationship has a positive correlation. Existing studies using the gazes of a group of people [6–8]

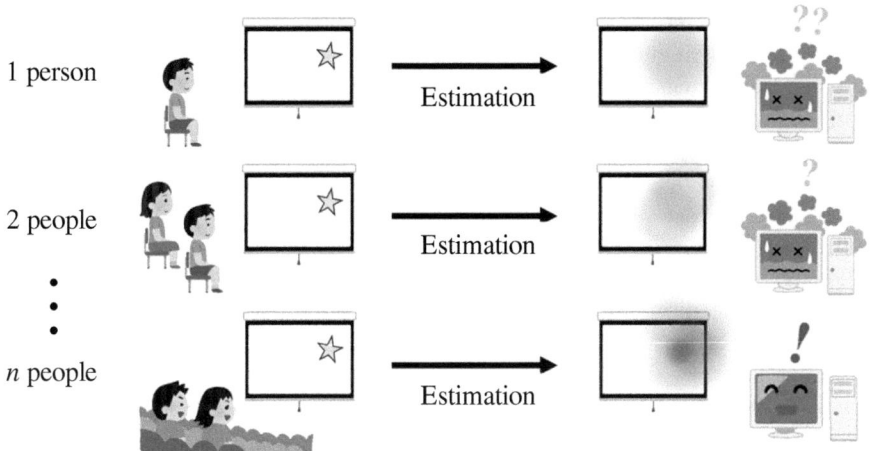

Fig. 2. Concept of improvement in the gaze localization accuracy by aggregating gaze estimations of a crowd of people.

have not analyzed this relationship, but this revelation shows that we can obtain more accurate results if we applied the method to a larger crowd.

Our contributions can be summarized in the following two folds:

1. Proposal of a novel method to localize a common gaze target focused on by a crowd of people.
2. Analysis on the relationship between the number of people involved in the aggregation and the localization accuracy in images capturing a crowd of people in a tennis stadium.

2 Related Works

2.1 Gaze Estimation Methods for One Person

There are many studies focusing on human gaze [1–3,9,10]. They improve localization accuracy, robustness for illuminative change, and so on. Most of these studies have focused on the gaze estimation for one person whose face image is captured in high-resolution. However, as we mentioned in Sect. 1, to analyze where a crowd of people is focusing on, it is necessary to observe all the members simultaneously, in which case, each person will be captured in low-resolution. Therefore, we cannot apply such gaze estimation methods for our purpose.

Meanwhile, some researchers have proposed gaze estimation methods for low-resolution images. Ono et al. focused on the gaze estimation from eye images [11]. In their case, the error in the position of a cropped eye region significantly increases the gaze estimation errors, which becomes more prominent with low-resolution images. To improve the estimation accuracy in such cases, they proposed a method considering the variations in the eye region's appearance related to three factors; gaze directions, positionings, and image pixels, by using 3-mode SVD (Singular Value Decomposition) [12]. Although this method improves the gaze estimation accuracy for low-resolution images, in their evaluation, eye regions in low-resolution images were detected based on the positions detected from high-resolution images capturing the same people. Hence, this method may not be able to estimate the gaze direction accurately directly from low-resolution images captured in our scenario because the eye region detection from low-resolution images is a very difficult task.

Meanwhile, Tawari et al. proposed a gaze estimation method which approximates the face direction as gaze direction based on the assumption that the gaze direction is distributed around the face direction [13]. Although this method improves the gaze estimation accuracy, the effect of approximation is limited; with extremely low-resolution images, the face direction estimation is also inaccurate.

2.2 Analysis on the Gazes of Many People

There are two types of existing studies that analyze the gazes of many people; One analyzes the gazes of many people sharing time and space and the other analyzes those of many people sharing only space.

For the former type, Park et al. focused on joint attention and estimated the objects focused on by a group of people [6]. They assume a situation when several people are wearing a head-mounted camera. Here, by using Structure from Motion (SfM) [14], each camera's position and pose are estimated. Then, each person's gaze is approximated by the camera's position and pose. However, this assumption is practically suited for only few people because of the requirement of the head-mounted cameras. Park et al. also attempted to reduce the number of people wearing the camera [7]. They estimate where the group of people are focussing on from only one head-mounted camera, by learning the relationships between the position of each person and his/her gaze target. In the estimation, the objects focused on by a group of people are estimated from the position of each person detected from the images captured by the head-mounted camera. It is very convenient since it only requires each person's position. However, when people follow an object with their head and eyes, without moving their positions, such as keep seating in a fixed position, this approach will not work properly.

Meanwhile, for the latter type, Sugano et al. proposed to estimate attention maps for videos displayed on a public display by aggregating people's gaze positions measured by a single fixed camera [8]. This approach can be applied for localizing where many people are focusing on in the display. However, it is difficult to be directly adopted to our research since they assume a situation where people approach the display, and thus high-resolution images of their faces can be collected. Also, it can accumulate the images many times and can improve the estimation accuracy by analyzing the accumulated gazes of many people because videos can be repeatedly displayed on a public display.

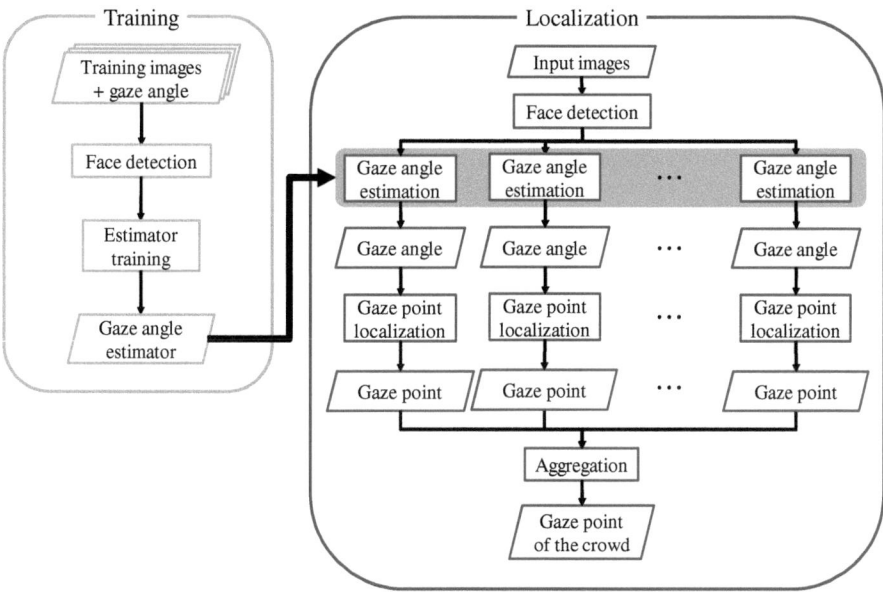

Fig. 3. Overview of the proposed method.

3 Gaze Target Localization for a Crowd of People

Hereafter, the locations of people and targets are represented in world coordinates. In the situation where many people gather in a space such as a cinema or a stadium, they are usually seated in a fixed position and observe some targets from there. In general, the positions of the seats in the world coordinate can be pre-measured. Also, each person's face usually exists above his/her seat. The region in the images captured by a fixed camera can also be pre-measured. Therefore, we assume if a person is detected from an image captured by a fixed camera, the position of his/her seat can be roughly specified. With this assumption, the detected face images can be mapped to the world coordinates.

Figure 3 shows the overview of the proposed method which consists of two phases; the training phase and the localization phase. In the training phase, a gaze angle estimator $f(x; \hat{\Theta})$ is trained. In the localization phase, the proposed method estimates the gaze angle a_j of each person j in a crowd, localizes the gaze point, aggregates them, and outputs the common gaze point $\hat{g}$ of the crowd. Before explaining the proposed method, we formulate the problem to localize a common gaze point $\hat{g}$ focused on by a crowd of people.

3.1 Formulation

Given a set of M face images $X = \{x_1, x_2, ..., x_M\}$ of a crowd, localizing their estimated gaze point $\hat{g}$ can be formulated as a problem finding g which maximizes $p(g|X; \Theta)$, where Θ represents the set of parameters of the gaze estimation.

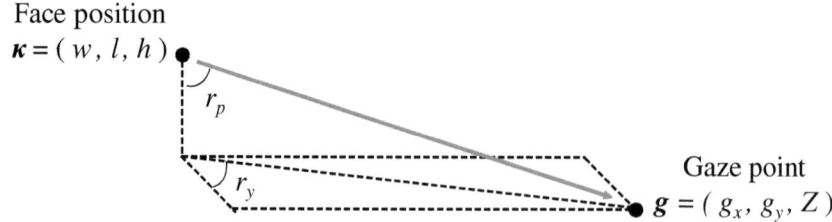

Fig. 4. Face and gaze positions in the world coordinate system.

By assuming that the prior probability $p(g)$ of the gaze point g follows a uniform distribution, it can be replaced by a constant C. We also assume that $p(g|x_i; \Theta)$, $x_i = 1...M$, are independent from each other. With these assumptions, Eq. (1) is derived from Bayes' theorem.

$$p(g|X; \Theta) = \frac{1}{C} \prod_i p(g|x_i; \Theta). \quad (1)$$

By taking the logarithm of this equation, the log likelihood of the gaze of the crowd can be calculated. Finally, localizing their gaze point $\hat{g}$ can be formulated as

$$\hat{g} = \arg\max_g \sum_i \log(p(g|x_i; \Theta)). \quad (2)$$

3.2 Training Phase

Firstly, from training images $\mathcal{I}_{\text{train}} = \{I_1, I_2, ...\}$, which are images capturing a crowd of people, faces are detected and cropped. For the face detection, we used a face detecter based on multi-task cascaded CNNs proposed by Zhang et al. [15]. The cropped face images are resized to $W \times H$ [pixels], and the resized face images $\{x_i\}_{i=1}^{Q}$ are used for training the gaze angle estimator. Q represents the number of the detected faces.

Then, the parameters Θ of the gaze angle estimator $f(x_i; \Theta)$ are learned by using training data $T = \{(x_i, r_i)\}$, where $r_i = (r_y, r_p)^T$ represents the gaze angle from the center of his/her face (face position κ_i) with the yaw angle r_y and the pitch angle r_p of the gaze angle, as shown in Fig. 4. Here, the gaze angle is calculated as the summation of face orientation and gaze direction angles. The function f is modeled as a Convolutional Neural Network (CNN) trained with this training data T. With regard to the loss function, we employ the mean squared error loss function defined as

$$L(\Theta) = \frac{1}{Q} \sum_{i=1}^{Q} (r_i - f(x_i; \Theta))^2. \quad (3)$$

In the training phase, parameters which minimizes $L(\Theta)$,

$$\hat{\Theta} = \arg\min_{\Theta} L(\Theta) \tag{4}$$

are searched as the optimal solution using the Adaptive Momentum (Adam) method [16].

3.3 Localization Phase

The localization phase commences in the same fashion as in the training phase, with M faces detected from an input image capturing a crowd of people. The detected faces $\{d_j\}_{j=1}^{M}$ are resized to $W \times H$ [pixels], and input to the trained gaze angle estimator $f(x_i; \hat{\Theta})$. Then, a gaze angle

$$\boldsymbol{a}_j = (a_{jy}, a_{jp})^T = f(d_j; \hat{\Theta}) \tag{5}$$

is calculated for each face image. Here, a_{jy} represents the yaw angle of his/her gaze, and a_{jp} the pitch angle of his/her gaze. As a result, a gaze point $\boldsymbol{g}_j = (g_{jx}, g_{jy}, Z)^T$ can be calculated based on the gaze angle $\boldsymbol{a}_j$ and the face position $\boldsymbol{\kappa}_j = (w_j, l_j, h_j)$ of each person as the point where the vector from the position of the face center and the plane with height Z crosses.

In general, even if the result of the gaze angle estimation is not correct, the true angle is likely to be nearby the result. Therefore, we assume that $p(\boldsymbol{g}|d_j; \hat{\Theta})$ follows the normal distribution $\mathcal{N}(\boldsymbol{g}_j, \sigma^2)$. By assuming this, Eq. (2) is equivalent to

$$\hat{\boldsymbol{g}} = \arg\max_{\boldsymbol{g}} \left(-\sum_{j=1}^{M} \frac{(\boldsymbol{g} - \boldsymbol{g}_j)^2}{2\sigma^2} - \log\sqrt{2\pi\sigma^2} \right) = \arg\min_{\boldsymbol{g}} \sum_{j=1}^{M} (\boldsymbol{g} - \boldsymbol{g}_j)^2, \tag{6}$$

where M is the number of the detected faces. Then, it can be solved as

$$\hat{\boldsymbol{g}} = \frac{1}{M} \sum_{j=1}^{M} \boldsymbol{g}_j = \overline{\boldsymbol{g}}. \tag{7}$$

As a result, a common gaze point of the crowd $\overline{\boldsymbol{g}} = (\overline{g}_x, \overline{g}_y, Z)^T$ is output.

4 Evaluation

4.1 Dataset Construction

Although there are some public datasets including face images with the ground truth of the gaze direction [9,17–20], most of them were recorded under controlled laboratory conditions, and there is also no dataset including images capturing many people in a frame. Therefore, we constructed a dataset by capturing 96 participants including men/women with/without glasses in a tennis stadium.

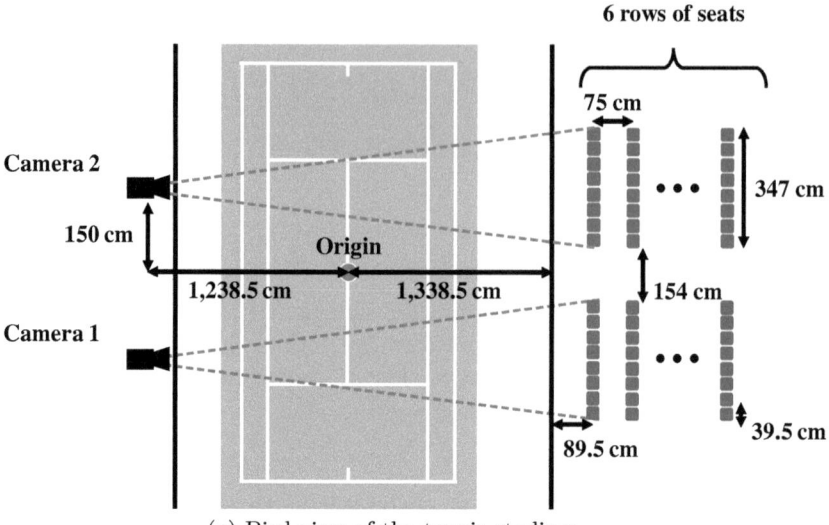

(a) Bird-view of the tennis stadium.

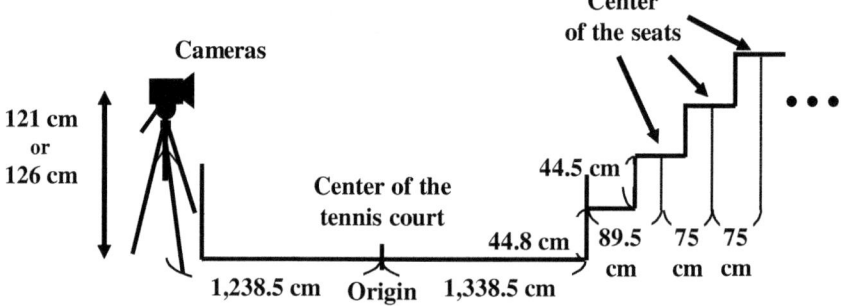

(b) Side view of the tennis stadium.

Fig. 5. Capture setting.

The ratio of both conditions were half and half. All participants signed an agreement form that allows us to use the images capturing them for research purpose. Each participant sat on one of the predefined spectator seats and was requested to focus on the same target on the tennis court ($Z = 0$) following instructions from a facilitator. These instructions did not include any restriction except for the focus target. All participants focused on the target in a natural way. Figure 5 shows the capture setting. We defined the center of the tennis court as the origin of the world coordinates, the Y-axis directing to the spectator seats, and the Z-axis directing upwards from the origin, in a right-handed coordinate system.

Figure 6 shows the positions of the gaze targets, and Fig. 7 shows the series of identification numbers assigned to the targets. The spectator seats are located toward the upper side of the figures. We defined 22 targets on the tennis court ($Z = 0$) distributed over the area where tennis players usually play.

Table 1. Number of images in the dataset.

Target ID	Camera 1	Camera 2	Target ID	Camera 1	Camera 2
1	269	270	12	306	304
2	313	314	13	319	319
3	297	297	14	259	256
4	293	294	15	290	289
5	302	302	16	286	288
6	301	301	17	313	313
7	261	262	18	293	293
8	272	272	19	296	296
9	295	296	20	273	272
10	297	299	21	281	279
11	286	287	22	293	294
			Total	6,395	6,397

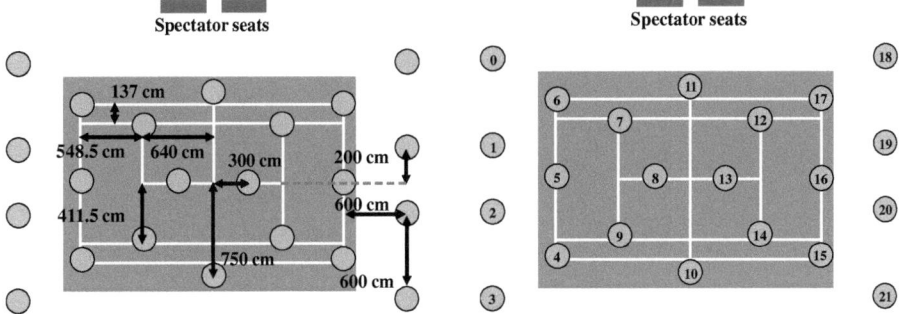

Fig. 6. Positions of the gaze targets.   **Fig. 7.** Identification numbers of targets.

The target was actually a box with a size of 16 cm long, 16 cm wide, and 15 cm high. We captured participants focussing on a target with two cameras fixed on the opposite side of the spectator seat. Each camera[1] was fixed at a height of 121 cm and 126 cm from the ground, respectively. One captured 48 participants and the other one captured the other 48 participants. There was no overlap in the participants captured by each camera. Camera parameters were as follows: 1,280 × 1,024 pixels, 15 fps, 8 bits color, and the focal length of the lens was 138 mm in the 35 mm equivalent focal length. Figure 8 is an example of the captured images. Table 1 shows the number of images in the constructed dataset.

---

[1] We used Flea3 (FL3-U3-13E4C-C) cameras produced by Point Grey Research.

4.2 Dataset Analysis

Every image in the dataset includes 48 people. Figure 9 shows the number of faces detected from each image in the dataset. This revealed that at least 24 faces could be detected from each image. The range of horizontal and vertical sizes of the detected faces were between 20 and 68 pixels, and 24 and 95 pixels, respectively. In total, 226,298 face images were detected from images captured by camera 1, and 228,441 by camera 2.

We annotated the face images with gaze angles based on the position of the detected face and the location of the target focussed on by them. The range of the annotated gaze angle was $[-74.02, 74.02]$ in yaw angle, and $[-20.09, -3.01]$ in pitch angle.

Fig. 8. Example of the captured image (camera 1).

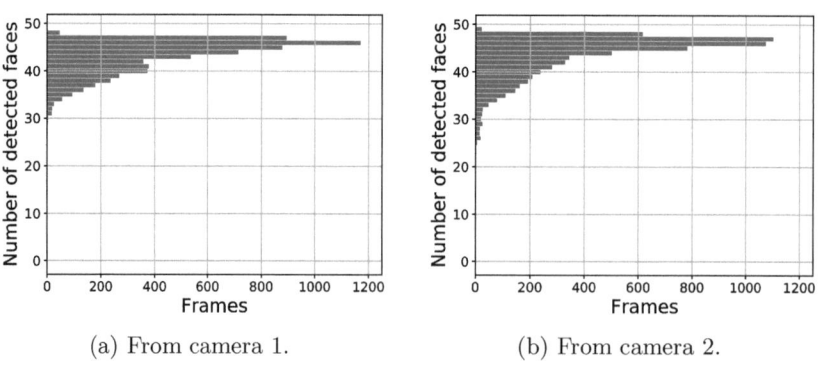

(a) From camera 1. (b) From camera 2.

Fig. 9. Histograms of the number of detected faces per frame.

4.3 Experimental Settings

First, we separated the images into two groups: images captured by camera 1, and images captured by camera 2. One group was used for training, and the other was used for evaluation, alternately. There was no overlap in the participants and they were cross-validated.

In the training phase, all pairs of detected face images and their gaze angles in the training data were used. All pairs of mirrored face images and their gaze angles were also used for training. Specifically, 552,596 pairs for camera 1 and 556,882 pairs for camera 2 were used. Considering that if the people are sufficiently far from the cameras, the gaze angle of every person in each captured image can be approximated as the same, since in our dataset, the distances between participants and cameras were quite far compared with the distance between participants, we trained only one estimator to estimate the gaze angle of all the participants.

As the gaze angle estimator, we used LeNet-5 [21], which was originally designed for the classification of very low-resolution images. To change the task from classification to gaze angle estimation, the number of units in the output layer was modified to two units corresponding to $\boldsymbol{a}_j = (a_{jy}, a_{jp})^T$ and also the activation layer of the output was changed to hyperbolic tangent. The gaze angles were normalized to the range [0, 1].

In the evaluation phase, all images capturing a crowd of people in the evaluation data were used. From each evaluation image, face images of many people are detected, and the trained gaze angle estimator outputs the gaze angle for each face image. The position of each participant's seat can be calculated from the capture settings. With an assumption that each person's face is positioned 75 cm above the seat level, the face position $\boldsymbol{\kappa}_j$ can also be calculated in the world coordinate system. Therefore, gaze points of all the face images are estimated based on the geometry in Fig. 4, and are aggregated by the proposed method.

We analyzed the relationship between the number of people involved in the aggregation and the localization error. Concretely, we aggregated the estimated gaze points while increasing the number of face images from 1 to 24. If more than 24 face images were detected, those with higher scores in the face detection were preferentially selected. We evaluated the method by the Mean Absolute Error (MAE), which is calculated as the distance between the estimated gaze point of the crowd and the position of the ground-truth target.

In the evaluation, we chose the result without aggregation (equivalent to the case when the number of people involved in the aggregation is only one) as the baseline. As a comparison method, we chose an aggregation method using median instead of average as in Eq. (7). By assuming that $p(\boldsymbol{g}|d_j; \hat{\Theta})$ follows the Laplace distribution, the solution of Eq. (2) can be calculated by the median of the estimated gaze points $\boldsymbol{g}_j$ for the detected face images d_j as similar to Eq. (6),

$$\hat{\boldsymbol{g}} = \underset{j=1,\ldots,M}{\text{median}}\, \boldsymbol{g}_j = \acute{\boldsymbol{g}}, \tag{8}$$

where the median is calculated as vector median [22]. As a result, a common gaze point of the crowd $\acute{\boldsymbol{g}} = (\acute{g}_x, \acute{g}_y, Z)^T$ is output.

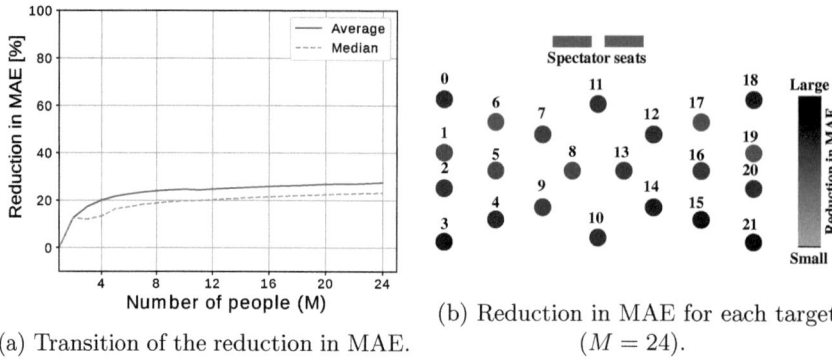

(a) Transition of the reduction in MAE.

(b) Reduction in MAE for each target ($M = 24$).

Fig. 10. Results of the proposed aggregation method.

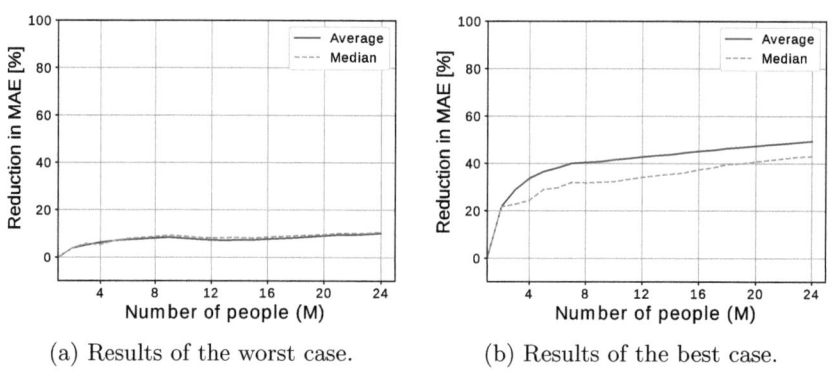

(a) Results of the worst case.

(b) Results of the best case.

Fig. 11. Results of the worst and the best reduction in MAE.

4.4 Results

Figure 10(a) shows the transition of reduction in MAE while increasing the number of people involved in the aggregation. The score shows the reduction rate from the case where the number of people is one (baseline). The results reveal that both aggregation methods based on Eqs. (7) and (8) improved the gaze localization accuracy by increasing the number of people, but the proposed method showed a larger reduction in MAE than the comparison method. The reduction in MAE from the baseline was 25.73% by aggregating the estimation results from 24 people. In particular, while the MAE was 13.99 m for the baseline, it decreased to 10.39 m by aggregating the estimation results from 24 people.

Figure 10(b) visualizes the reduction in MAE per target by aggregating the estimation results from 24 people. The color of each target indicates the reduction in MAE. Note that before the visualization, the reduction in MAE were normalized to the range [0, 1]. The worst reduction in MAE was obtained for target 21. Even so, the reduction in MAE reached 10.27% by aggregating the estimation results from 24 people. Moreover, the best reduction in MAE which

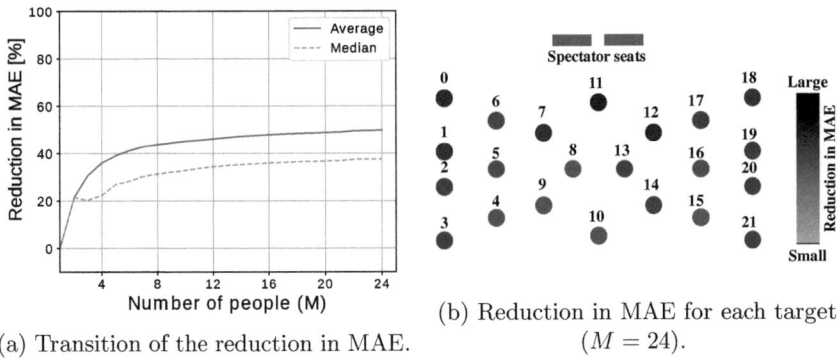

Fig. 12. Results along the X-axis.

was obtained for target 19 reached as high as 49.33% from the baseline. Figure 11 shows the results which showed the worst and the best reduction in MAE.

5 Discussions

Figure 10 revealed that the gaze localization accuracy was improved by increasing the number of people involved in the aggregation. In this section, we confirm the details of the results.

5.1 Number of People Involved in the Aggregation

Although Fig. 10 shows that the reduction in MAE increases in proportion to the number of people involved in the aggregation, the gain saturates at around 10 people. We consider that this is caused by the distribution of the gaze estimation results; although the proposed method expects that the estimation results isotropically distribute around the ground truth, this may not be true. In such a case, the aggregated results will not approach the ground truth but rather approach a biased center of the distribution. We will need to improve the aggregation method considering this problem in order to further improve the results.

5.2 Results Along Each Axis

The reduction in MAE for each target showed different behaviors along each axis. Figures 12(a) and 13(a) show the results along the X-axis and the Y-axis of the world coordinates, respectively. The reduction in MAE for the X-axis and the Y-axis were 49.78% and 18.95% by aggregating the estimation results from 24 people, respectively. We consider that the difference was caused by the significant difference of the ranges of the gaze angle; while the range of the yaw angle (corresponds to the estimation accuracy of the X-axis) was $[-74.02, 74.02]$, the range of the pitch angle (corresponds to the estimation accuracy of the

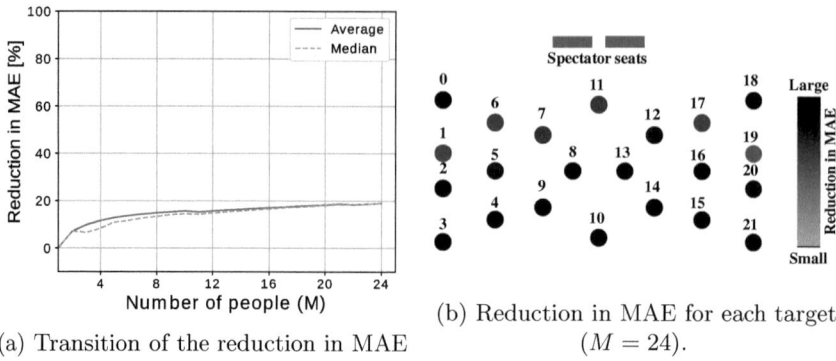

(a) Transition of the reduction in MAE

(b) Reduction in MAE for each target ($M = 24$).

Fig. 13. Results along the Y-axis.

Y-axis) was only between $[-20.09, -3.01]$, the latter being eight times smaller than the former. The appearance of the faces along the Y-axis changes little and the estimation is more difficult than that along the X-axis. Therefore, the estimation along the Y-axis had larger bias than that along the X-axis.

Figures 12(b) and 13(b) visualize the reduction in MAE for each target along the X-axis and the Y-axis by aggregating the estimation results from 24 people, respectively. These figures show that the reduction in MAE of the farther targets behave differently along the X-axis and the Y-axis; along the Y-axis, the reduction in MAE of the farther targets were low, while along the X-axis, the proposed method also improved that of the farther targets. We consider that this difference occurred since the proposed method is robust to the variance of gaze estimation results but not to the bias; along the Y-axis, the bias of the estimation results was too large to approach the ground truth, while along the X-axis, the proposed method could approach the ground truth.

In summary, if the estimation results have a too large bias, the proposed method could hardly approach the ground truth, since the proposed aggregation method did not have sufficient robustness to deal with it. An aggregation method with a higher robustness to a large bias should increase the reduction in MAE.

6 Conclusion

In this paper, we proposed a novel method for localizing a common gaze point focused on by a crowd of people. We also constructed a dataset including images capturing many people looking at a target. An evaluation using the dataset showed that the proposed method could improve the localization accuracy by aggregating the gaze estimation results from a crowd of people.

In future work, we plan to propose an aggregation method more robust to the estimation results with larger bias by employing a machine learning framework, and also deal with situations where multiple gaze targets exist. We also plan to extend the method to localize the gaze targets in the three-dimensional space.

References

1. Okamoto, K., et al.: Classification of pedestrian behavior in a shopping mall based on LRF and camera observations. In: Proceedings of the 12th IAPR Conference on Machine Vision Applications, pp. 1–5 (2011)
2. Fridman, L., Langhans, P., Lee, J., Reimer, B.: Driver gaze region estimation without use of eye movement. IEEE Intell. Syst. **31**, 49–56 (2016)
3. Yonetani, R., Kawashima, H., Hirayama, T., Matsuyama, T.: Gaze probing: event-based estimation of objects being focused on. In: Proceedings of the 20th IAPR International Conference on Pattern Recognition, pp. 101–104 (2010)
4. Hirayama, T., Sumi, Y., Kawahara, T., Matsuyama, T.: Info-concierge: proactive multi-modal interaction through mind probing. In: Proceedings of the 3rd Asia-Pacific Signal and Information Processing Association Annual Summit and Conference, pp. 1–10 (2011)
5. Recasens, A., Khosla, A., Vondrick, C., Torralba, A.: Where are they looking? In: Proceedings of the 28th International Conference on Neural Information Processing Systems, pp. 199–207 (2015)
6. Park, H.S., Jain, E., Sheikh, Y.: 3D gaze concurrences from head-mounted cameras. In: Proceedings of the 25th International Conference on Neural Information Processing Systems, pp. 422–430 (2012)
7. Park, H.S., Shi, J.: Social saliency prediction. In: Proceedings of the 2015 IEEE Conference on Computer Vision and Pattern Recognition, pp. 4777–4785 (2015)
8. Sugano, Y., Zhang, X., Bulling, A.: Aggregaze: collective estimation of audience attention on public displays. Proceedings of the 29th ACM Symposium on User Interface Software and Technology, pp. 821–831 (2016)
9. Zhang, X., Sugano, Y., Fritz, M., Bulling, A.: It's written all over your face: full-face appearance-based gaze estimation. In: Proceedings of the 2017 IEEE Conference on Computer Vision and Pattern Recognition Workshops, pp. 2299–2308 (2017)
10. Krafka, K., et al.: Eye tracking for everyone. In: Proceedings of the 2016 IEEE Conference on Computer Vision and Pattern Recognition, pp. 2176–2184 (2016)
11. Ono, Y., Okabe, T., Sato, Y.: Gaze estimation from low resolution images. In: Chang, L.-W., Lie, W.-N. (eds.) PSIVT 2006. LNCS, vol. 4319, pp. 178–188. Springer, Heidelberg (2006). https://doi.org/10.1007/11949534_18
12. Vasilescu, M.A.O., Terzopoulos, D.: Multilinear analysis of image ensembles: TensorFaces. In: Heyden, A., Sparr, G., Nielsen, M., Johansen, P. (eds.) ECCV 2002. LNCS, vol. 2350, pp. 447–460. Springer, Heidelberg (2002). https://doi.org/10.1007/3-540-47969-4_30
13. Tawari, A., Møgelmose, A., Martin, S., Moeslund, T.B., Trivedi, M.M.: Attention estimation by simultaneous analysis of viewer and view. In: Proceedings of the 17th IEEE International Conference on Intelligent Transportation Systems, pp. 1381–1387 (2014)
14. Agarwal, S., Furukawa, Y., Snavely, N., Simon, I., Curless, B., Seitz, S.M., Szeliski, R.: Building rome in a day. Comm. ACM **54**, 105–112 (2011)
15. Zhang, K., Zhang, Z., Li, Z., Qiao, Y.: Joint face detection and alignment using multitask cascaded convolutional networks. IEEE Signal Process. Lett. **23**, 1499–1503 (2016)
16. Kingma, D.P., Ba, J.: Adam: a method for stochastic optimization. In: Proceedings of the 3rd International Conference on for Learning Representations, pp. 1–15 (2015)

17. Zhang, X., Sugano, Y., Fritz, M., Bulling, A.: Appearance-based gaze estimation in the wild. In: Proceedings of the 2015 IEEE Conference on Computer Vision and Pattern Recognition, pp. 4511–4520 (2015)
18. Ariz, M., Bengoechea, J., Villanueva, A., Cabeza, R.: A novel 2D/3D database with automatic face annotation for head tracking and pose estimation. Comput. Vis. Image Underst. **148**, 201–210 (2016)
19. He, Q., et al.: OMEG: oulu multi-pose eye gaze dataset. In: Paulsen, R.R., Pedersen, K.S. (eds.) SCIA 2015. LNCS, vol. 9127, pp. 418–427. Springer, Cham (2015). https://doi.org/10.1007/978-3-319-19665-7_35
20. Funes Mora, K.A., Monay, F., Odobez, J.M.: EYEDIAP database: data description and gaze tracking evaluation benchmarks. In: Proceedings of the 2014 Symposium on Eye Tracking Research and Applications, pp. 255–258 (2014)
21. Le Cun, Y., Bottou, L., Bengio, Y., Haffner, P.: Gradient-based learning applied to document recognition. Proc. IEEE **86**, 2278–2324 (1998)
22. Astola, J., Haavisto, P., Neuvo, Y.: Vector median filters. Proc. IEEE **78**, 678–689 (1990)

A Thumb Tip Wearable Device Consisting of Multiple Cameras to Measure Thumb Posture

Naoto Ienaga[1(✉)], Wataru Kawai[2], Koji Fujita[3], Natsuki Miyata[4], Yuta Sugiura[1], and Hideo Saito[1]

[1] Keio University, Yokohama, Japan
ienaga@hvrl.ics.keio.ac.jp
[2] The University of Tokyo, Tokyo, Japan
[3] Tokyo Medical and Dental University, Tokyo, Japan
[4] National Institute of Advanced Industrial Science and Technology, Tokyo, Japan

Abstract. Today, cameras have become smaller and cheaper and can be utilized in various scenes. We took advantage of that to develop a thumb tip wearable device to estimate joint angles of a thumb as measuring human finger postures is important in terms of human-computer interface and to analyze human behavior. The device we developed consists of three small cameras attached at different angles so the cameras can capture the four fingers. We assumed that the appearance of the four fingers would change depending on the joint angles of the thumb. We made a convolutional neural network learn a regression relationship between the joint angles of the thumb and the images taken by the cameras. In this paper, we captured the keypoint positions of the thumb with a USB sensor device and calculated the joint angles to construct a dataset. The root mean squared error of the test data was 6.23° and 4.75°.

Keywords: Wearable device · Human computer interaction · Pose estimation

1 Introduction

Human sensing has become an increasingly indispensable technology in recent years. Contributions to promoting human health by measuring and analyzing human behavior is needed in the world where the number of aging individuals is increasing. In addition, human-computer interfaces are becoming essential as many people use multiple computers. In particular, finger posture measurement is important in designs for people to make devices that are easy to use and virtual reality which has become popular in recent years.

Methods for measuring finger posture can be roughly divided into three categories depending on where a sensor is attached: the environment, specific object, or the hand itself.

Environment. A convolutional neural network (CNN) achieves amazing results in various areas of computer vision, including hand keypoint detection. Methods were proposed to improve the detector by reconstructing three-dimensional (3D) hand keypoints and reprojecting them when generating training data [8], and to estimate the 3D hand keypoints from RGB images [11] and from RGB-D images [6]. There is also a hand pose estimation method using RGB-D images and a machine learning method other than CNN [9]. These methods do not require attaching the sensor to the hand, but the measurement could fail if the hand hides from the sensor.

Specific object. Studies have measured hand motion with a sensor attached to a specific object. For instance, a fisheye camera was fixed to the top of a bottle to estimate how the hand grips the bottle [3], and a band sensor was developed to estimate the grasping hand posture [5]. Although the sensor is robust against occlusion when the sensor is attached to a specific object, the sensor can measure only when a human is interacting with the object.

Hand itself. Many wearable devices were proposed since they are robust to the occlusion. A typical wearable sensor is a data glove. It is possible to calculate the joint angles of the hand with a sensor embedded in the glove. Data gloves need to cover the whole hand, wrist-worn sensors [2,4,7] and a camera [10] were developed to classify the hand pose. A fisheye camera ring was also developed to estimated hand gestures and palm writing by acquiring an image of a hand inside [1].

Our device is also attached to the hand itself. However, unlike previous studies, we utilize multiple cameras in this research. Today, cameras have become smaller and cheaper and can be expected to be utilized in various scenes. We take advantage of that to develop a thumb tip wearable device to measure joint angles of a thumb. The device consists of three small cameras attached at different angles so that the cameras can capture the four fingers. We assume that the appearance of the four fingers will change depending on the joint angles of the thumb.

With the advent of CNNs, it is possible to link input images and their labels automatically as long as there is a large amount of training data. The regression relationship between the joint angles and the images taken by the cameras is learned by the CNN. In this paper, we conduct an initial experiment to assess the effectiveness of the developed device. We captured the keypoint positions of the thumb with the Leap Motion (Leap Motion, https://www.leapmotion.com, last accessed: May 5, 2018) and calculated the joint angles of the thumb.

Our contributions are summarized as follows:

- We develop a thumb tip wearable device that use multiple small and inexpensive cameras. It can be easily attached to the thumb and used to estimate the thumb posture.
- We suggest that the finger joint angles can be estimated from the appearance of the fingers with the CNN.

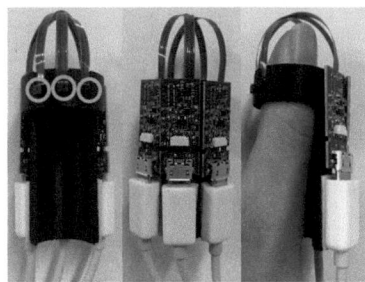
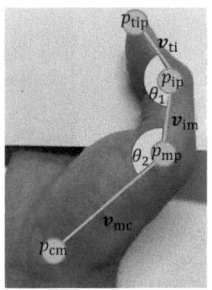

Fig. 1. The thumb tip wearable device we developed. Three cameras (left, circled) and their driving circuits are fixed to the device (center). The device can be attached to the thumb as shown on the right.

Fig. 2. θ_1 and θ_2 are calculated by finding the inner product of three vectors $\boldsymbol{v}_{\text{ti}}$, $\boldsymbol{v}_{\text{im}}$ and $\boldsymbol{v}_{\text{mc}}$ from the 3D positions of the four thumb keypoints; p_{tip}, p_{ip}, p_{mp} and p_{cm}.

2 Methodology

First, we describe the device we developed. We then explain the constructed dataset. Afterward, we describe the CNN architecture.

2.1 Device

We developed the thumb tip wearable device shown in Fig. 1. We use three small cameras which are arranged at 30° intervals to capture the four fingers. The cameras are IU233N2-Z manufactured by Sony Semiconductor Solutions Corporation (IU233N2-Z/IU233N5-Z, https://www.sony-semicon.co.jp/products_en/new_pro/december_2016/iu233_e.html, last accessed: May 5, 2018). The driving circuits are also fixed to the device.

2.2 Dataset

In this research, a dataset is constructed by using the images captured by the cameras as input data and the joint angles of the thumb acquired by the Leap Motion as the outputs. Figure 3 shows the scenes building the dataset. The acquired image and the 3D positions of the hand keypoints change according to the hand shape. Three captured images are converted to grayscale, resized to 1/8 in height and width, and then connected in the vertical direction to make a single grayscale image of 80 × 180 pixels (examples are in Fig. 3(b), (b')). The Leap Motion can easily acquire the 3D positions of the hand keypoints, but the accuracy is inferior to motion capture. Therefore, data is acquired only at the frame when the two joint angles θ_1 and θ_2 of the thumb are larger than 0° and smaller than 120°. θ_1 and θ_2 are calculated by finding the inner product of three vectors $\boldsymbol{v}_{\text{ti}}$, $\boldsymbol{v}_{\text{im}}$ and $\boldsymbol{v}_{\text{mc}}$ from the 3D positions of the four thumb keypoints; tip p_{tip}, interphalangeal joint p_{ip}, metacarpophalangeal joint p_{mp} and carpometacarpal joint p_{cm}. These relationships are shown in Fig. 2.

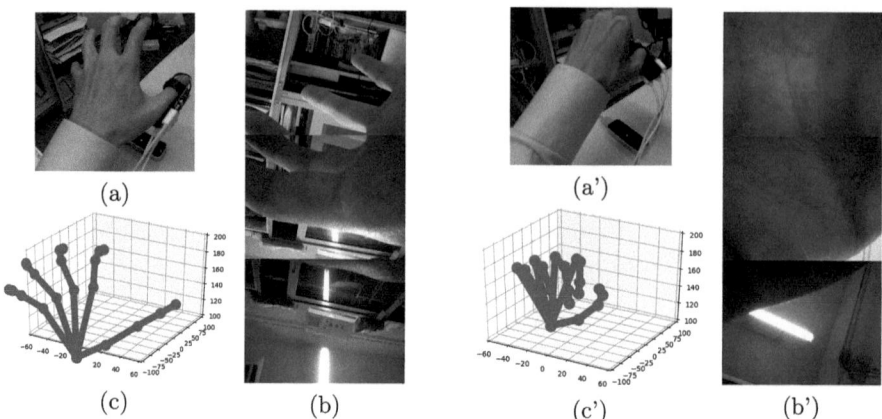

Fig. 3. Examples of the data collection. We used the device consisting of three cameras and the Leap Motion (a) and (a'). Three captured images are converted to grayscale, and then connected in the vertical direction to make a single image (b) and (b'). The Leap Motion provides the 3D positions of the hand keypoints (c) and (c').

Table 1. The CNN architecture. We repeat the first part three times and double the number of filters of the convolutional layer at each time. The activation function, ReLU, is used after all convolutional and fully connected layers. The batch normalization is used before all max pooling layers. After the first two fully connected layers, the dropout is 50%.

Layer	Filter size, strides or number of units
Input	80 × 180 × 1
Convolutional	3 × 3 × (1st:32, 2nd:64, 3rd:128), 1
Convolutional	3 × 3 × (1st:32, 2nd:64, 3rd:128), 1
Max pooling	2 × 2, 2
Fully connected	1024
Fully connected	1024
Fully connected	2

2.3 Network

The regression relationship for predicting the output value θ_1 and θ_2 estimated from the input image is learned by the CNN. The architecture of the CNN is shown in Table 1.

3 Experiment

The input image was scaled so that each pixel value falls within the range of [0, 1]. Then the average of all input data was subtracted from the input data

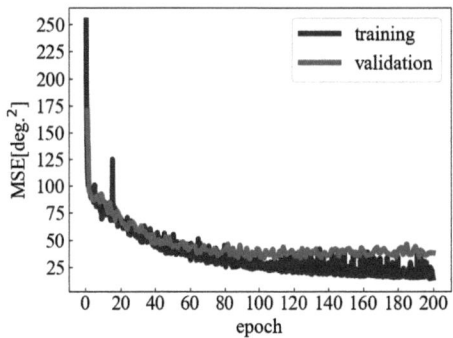

Table 2. MSE and RMSE of the testing.

Thumb angle	θ_1	θ_2
MSE[deg.^{2}]	38.83	22.52
RMSE[deg.]	6.23	4.75

Fig. 4. Training and validation loss.

Table 3. Correct and predicted joint angles of the thumb, and the MSE and RMSE of Fig. 5's *scene 1* and *scene 2*.

	Correct θ_1, θ_2		Predicted θ_1, θ_2		MSE[deg.^{2}]		RMSE[deg.]	
scene 1	2.58	4.27	15.69	8.68	171.70	19.42	13.10	4.41
scene 2	30.12	21.14	20.19	16.00	98.57	26.47	9.93	5.14

and divided by the standard deviation of all input data. The training data was shuffled randomly. The input data was augmented by random flipping (left to right) and random rotation by a random angle (max angle is 25). We used the Adam optimizer ($\beta_1 = 0.9, \beta_2 = 0.999, \epsilon = 1.0$). The learning rate was 0.03, and the batch size was 256. Loss function was the mean squared error (MSE). One male subject gathered a dataset while moving his hands randomly and keeping the palm level with the Leap Motion; 17931 frames were collected at around 30 fps (8997 frames with the right hand and 8934 frames with the left hand). Of those, 12553 frames were used for training, and 2689 frames were used for validation and testing. The training curve is illustrated in Fig. 4.

As the result of the validation because the loss of 95 epochs was the smallest (MSE: 31.93), we tested using the CNN learned with 95 epochs. The results of the MSE and the root mean squared error (RMSE) of the testing are shown in Table 2. Two testing examples and the results are shown in Table 3 and Fig. 5.

4 Discussion

Figure 6 shows a breakdown of the angle of the dataset. It is understood that most data is less than 40°. There are some possible reasons for this.

The first is that it is difficult to move one's hand completely randomly. If we moved our hands randomly, we would not cover the inner range of the motion. To solve this problem, it is necessary to first generate movements that uniformly cover the inner motion range and to have the subjects imitate the movements as much as possible to create a dataset.

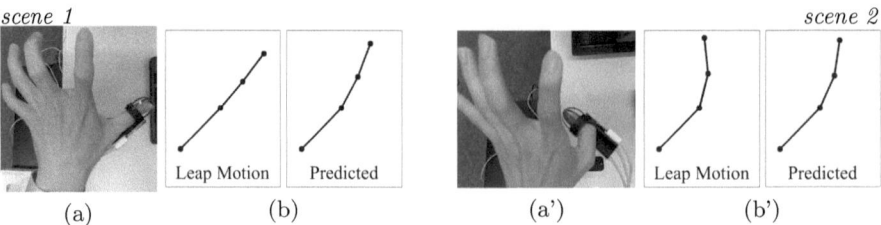

scene 1 (a) | Leap Motion / Predicted (b) | *scene 2* (a') | Leap Motion / Predicted (b')

Fig. 5. Two specific examples of testing, *scene 1* and *scene 2*. the hand states (a) and (a'), and the states of the thumb are reconstructed by θ_1 and θ_2 (b) and (b'). The left of (b) and (b') was created based on θ_1 and θ_2 acquired by the Leap Motion, and the right was created based on the predicted θ_1 and θ_2. Note that other parameters (e.g., finger length) are appropriate values because only angles were estimated.

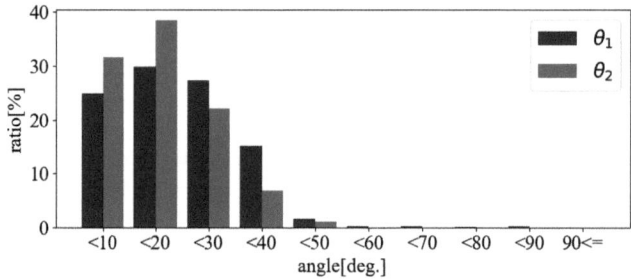

Fig. 6. A breakdown of the angle of the dataset. For example, about 25% of the dataset is data with θ_1 less than $10°$.

The next reason is the accuracy limit of the Leap Motion. This time, we used the Leap Motion because it is easy to use. However, especially when the thumb was bent deeply (θ_1 and θ_2 are large), we could not measure it properly. In *scene 1* of Fig. 5, the thumb is straight (a), and the illustration of the thumb created based on the thumb angles acquired by the Leap Motion (the left of (b)) is almost straight. However, in *scene 2*, the thumb actually (a') bends much more than the illustration (the left of (b')). To build a more accurate dataset, we have to use motion capture.

The limited accuracy may be caused by the device. The part that integrates the driving circuits with the device was large and hard, and cables between the cameras and the driving circuits were at the tip of the thumb. This design hindered the thumb movement. Again, cameras have become smaller and cheaper recently. We believe that this trend will continue. Camera images could be available via Wi-Fi or Bluetooth. Thus, these camera problems will be solved someday. Although we used three cameras this time, we are considering using more cameras to acquire more information in the future.

5 Conclusions

Taking advantage of the fact that cameras have become smaller and cheaper recently, we developed a thumb tip wearable device that can be easily attached to a thumb tip to measure the joint angles of the thumb as measuring finger movements has become an important technique especially in recent years. We proposed a method using a CNN to estimate the joint angles. We experimentally suggested that the finger joint angles wearing the device could be estimated by the state of the fingers.

We ignored the background of the input image; its influence was unknown (e.g., when the background changes). It may be necessary to incorporate some foreground (e.g., the hand) segmentation process into our deep learning framework.

In the future, we would like to propose a device and a method that can estimate joint angles other than the finger to which the device is attached by increasing the number of cameras and devising their arrangement. Furthermore, the device and the construction method of the dataset will be also improved.

Acknowledgements. This work was supported by JST AIP-PRISM Grant Number JPMJCR18Y2, Grant-in-Aid for JSPS Research Fellow Grant Number JP17J05489.

References

1. Chan, L., Chen, Y.L., Hsieh, C.H., Liang, R.H., Chen, B.Y.: CyclopsRing: enabling whole-hand and context-aware interactions through a fisheye ring. In: Proceedings of UIST, pp. 549–556 (2015)
2. Fukui, R., Watanabe, M., Shimosaka, M., Sato, T.: Hand shape classification with a wrist contour sensor. In: Proceedings of Experimental Robotics, pp. 939–949 (2013)
3. Kashiwagi, N., Sugiura, Y., Miyata, N., Tada, M., Sugimoto, M., Saito, H.: Measuring grasp posture using an embedded camera. In: Proceedings of WACVW, pp. 42–47 (2017)
4. Kim, D., et al.: Digits: freehand 3D interactions anywhere using a wrist-worn gloveless sensor. In: Proceedings of UIST, pp. 167–176 (2012)
5. Miyata, N., Honoki, T., Maeda, Y., Endo, Y., Tada, M., Sugiura, Y.: Wrap & sense: grasp capture by a band sensor. In: Proceedings of UIST, pp. 87–89 (2016)
6. Mueller, F., Mehta, D., Sotnychenko, O., Sridhar, S., Casas, D., Theobalt, C.: Real-time hand tracking under occlusion from an egocentric RGB-D sensor. In: Proceedings of ICCVW, pp. 1284–1293 (2017)
7. Rekimoto, J.: Gesturewrist and gesturepad: unobtrusive wearable interaction devices. In: Proceedings of ISWC, pp. 21–27 (2001)
8. Simon, T., Joo, H., Matthews, I., Sheikh, Y.: Hand keypoint detection in single images using multiview bootstrapping. In: Proceedings of CVPR, pp. 1145–1153 (2017)
9. Sridhar, S., Mueller, F., Oulasvirta, A., Theobalt, C.: Fast and robust hand tracking using detection-guided optimization. In: Proceedings of CVPR, pp. 3213–3221 (2015)

10. Vardy, A., Robinson, J., Cheng, L.T.: The WristCam as input device. In: Proceedings of ISWC (1999)
11. Zimmermann, C., Brox, T.: Learning to estimate 3D hand pose from single RGB images. In: Proceedings of ICCV, pp. 4903–4911 (2017)

Summarizing Videos with Attention

Jiri Fajtl[1(✉)], Hajar Sadeghi Sokeh[1], Vasileios Argyriou[1],
Dorothy Monekosso[2], and Paolo Remagnino[1]

[1] Robot Vision Team RoVit, Kingston University, London, UK
J.Fajtl@kingston.ac.uk
[2] Leeds Beckett University, Leeds, UK

Abstract. In this work we propose a novel method for supervised, keyshots based video summarization by applying a conceptually simple and computationally efficient soft, self-attention mechanism. Current state of the art methods leverage bi-directional recurrent networks such as BiLSTM combined with attention. These networks are complex to implement and computationally demanding compared to fully connected networks. To that end we propose a simple, self-attention based network for video summarization which performs the entire sequence to sequence transformation in a single feed forward pass and single backward pass during training. Our method sets a new state of the art results on two benchmarks TvSum and SumMe, commonly used in this domain.

Keywords: Video summarization · Self-attention · Sequence to sequence

1 Introduction

Personal videos, video lectures, video diaries, video messages on social networks and videos in many other domains are becoming to dominate other forms of information exchange. According to Cisco Visual Networking Index: Forecast and Methodology, 2016–2021[1], by 2019 video will account for 80% of all global Internet traffic, excluding P2P channels. Consequently, better methods for video management, such as video summarization, are needed.

Video summarization is a task where a video sequence is reduced to a small number of still images called keyframes, sometimes called storyboard or thumbnails extraction, or a shorter video sequence composed of keyshots, also called video skim or dynamic summaries. The keyframes or keyshots need to convey most of key information contained in the original video. This task is similar to a

---

This research was funded by the H2020 MONICA European project 732350 and by the NATO within the WITNESS project under grant agreement number G5437 and within the MIDAS G5381. We gratefully acknowledge the support of NVIDIA Corporation with the donation of the Titan Xp GPU used for this research.

[1] https://www.cisco.com/c/en/us/solutions/collateral/service-provider/visual-networking-index-vni/complete-white-paper-c11-481360.html.

lossy video compression, where the building block is a video frame. In this paper we focus solely on the keyshots based video summarization.

Video summarization is an inherently difficult task even for us people. In order to identify the most important segments one needs to view the entire video content and then make the selection, subject to the desired summary length. Naturally, one could define the keyshots as segments that carry mutually diverse information while also being highly representative of the video source. There are methods that formulate the summarization task as a clustering with cost functions based on exactly these criteria. Unfortunately, to define how well chosen keyshots represent the video source as well as the diversity between them is extremely difficult since this needs to reflect the information level perceived by the user. Common techniques analyze motion features, measure the distance between color histograms, image entropy or in the 2/3D CNN feature space [1,2,18,25], reflecting semantic similarities. However, none of these approaches can truly capture the information in the video context. We believe that to automatically generate high quality summaries, similar to what we are capable of, a machine should learn from us humans by means of a behavioral cloning or supervision.

Early video summarization methods were based on unsupervised methods, leveraging low level spatio-temporal features and dimensionality reduction with clustering techniques. Success of these methods solely stands on the ability to define distance/cost functions between the keyshots/frames with respect to the original video. As discussed above, this is very difficult to achieve as well as it introduces a strong bias in the summarization given by the type of used features such as semantic and pixel intensities. In contrast, models trained with supervision learn the transformation that produces summaries similar to those manually produced. Currently, there are two datasets with such annotations, TvSum [32] and SumMe [12], where each video is annotated by 15–20 users. The annotations vary between users with consistency expressed by a pairwise F-score ∼0.34. This fact reveals that the video annotation is a rather subjective task. We argue that under these circumstances it may be extremely difficult to craft a metric that would accurately express how to cluster video frames into keyshots, similar to human annotation. On this premise, we decided to adopt the supervised video summarization for our work.

Current state of the art methods for video summarization are based on recurrent encoder-decoder architectures, usually with bi-directional LSTM [14] or GRU [6] and soft attention [4]. While these models are remarkably powerful in many domains, such as machine translation and image/video captioning, they are computationally demanding, especially in the bi-directional configuration. Recently Vaswani et al. [34] demonstrated that it is possible to perform sequence to sequence transformation only with the attention. Along similar lines, we propose a pure attention, sequence to sequence network VASNet for video keyshots summarization and demonstrate its performance on TvSum and SumMe benchmarks. Architecture of this model does not employ recurrent or sequential processing and can be implemented with conventional matrix/vector operations

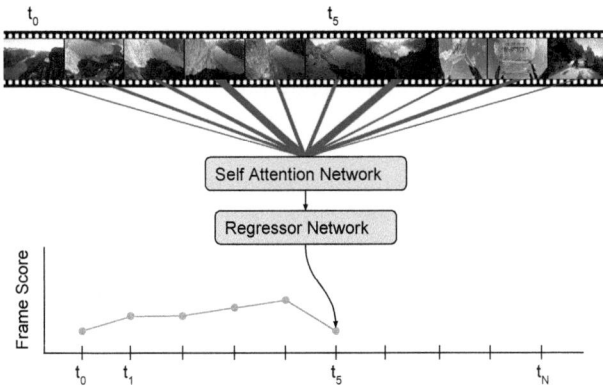

Fig. 1. For each output the self-attention network generates weights for all input features. Average of the input features, weighted by this attention, is regressed by a fully connected neural network to the frame importance score.

and run in a single forward/backward pass during inference/training, even for sequences with variable length. The architecture is centered around two key operations, attention weights calculation and frame level score regression. An overview of this model is shown in Fig. 1. Frame score at every step t is estimated from a weighted average of all input features. The weights are calculated with the self-attention algorithm. Given the generic architecture of our model we believe that it could be successfully used in other domains requiring sequence to sequence transformation. Our contributions are:

1. A novel approach to sequence to sequence transformation for video summarization based on soft, self-attention mechanism. In contrast, current state of the art relies on complex LSTM/GRU encoder-decoder methods.
2. A demonstration that a recurrent network can be successfully replaced with simpler, attention mechanism for the video summarization.

2 Related Work

Recent advancements in deep learning were rapidly adapted by researches focusing on video summarization, particularly encoder-decoder networks with attention for sequence to sequence transformation. In this section we will discuss several existing methods related to our work.

Zhang et al. [40] pioneered the application of LSTM for supervised video summarization to model the variable-range temporal dependency among video frames to derive both representative and compact video summaries. They enhance the strength of the LSTM with the determinantal point process which is a probabilistic model for diverse subset selection. Another sequence to sequence method for supervised video summarization was introduced by Ji et al. [15]. Their deep attention-based framework uses a bi-directional LSTM to encode the contextual information among input video frames. Mahasseni et al. [23] propose an adversarial network to summarize the video by minimizing the distance between the video and its summary. They predict video keyframes distribution with a sequential generative adversarial network. A deep summarization network in an encoder-decoder architecture via an end-to-end reinforcement learning has been proposed by Zhou et al. [42] to achieve state of the art results in unsupervised video summarization. They design a novel reward function that jointly takes diversity and representativeness of generated summaries into account. A hierarchical LSTM is constructed to deal with the long temporal dependencies among video frames by [41], but it fails to capture the video structure information, where the shots are generated by fixed length segmentation.

Some works use side semantic information associated with a video along with visual features, like surrounding text such as titles, queries, descriptions, comments, unpaired training data and so on. Rochan et al. in [29], proposed deep learning video summaries from unpaired training data, which means they learn from available videos summaries without their corresponding raw input videos. Yuan et al. [39], proposed a deep side semantic embedding model which uses both side semantic information and visual content in the video. Similarly Wei et al. [35] propose a supervised, deep learning method trained with manually created text descriptions as ground truth. At the heart of this method is the LSTM encode-decoder network. Wei achieves competitive results with this approach, however, more complex labels are required for the training. Fei et al. [9] complemented visual features with video frame memorability, predicted by a separate model such as [16] or [8].

Other approaches, like the one described in [31], use an unsupervised method by clustering some features extracted from the video, delete the similar frames, and select the rest of the frames as keyframe of the video. In fact, they used a hierarchical clustering method to generate a weight map from the frame similarity graph in which the clusters can easily be inferred. Another clustering method is proposed by Otani et al. [26], in which they use deep video features to encode various levels of content including objects, actions, and scenes. They extract the deep features from each segment of the original video and apply a clustering-based summarization technique on them.

2.1 Attention Techniques

The fundamental concept of attention mechanism for neural networks was laid by Bahdanau et al. [4] for the task of machine translation. This attention is based on an idea that the neural network can learn how important various samples in a sequence, or image regions, are with respect to the desired output state. These importance values are defined as attention weights and are commonly estimated simultaneously with other model parameters trained for a specific objective. There are two main distinct attention algorithms, hard and soft.

Hard attention produces a binary attention mask, thus making a 'hard' decision on which samples to consider. This technique was successfully used by Xu et al. [37] for image caption generation. Hard attention models use stochastic sampling during the training; consequently, backpropagation cannot be employed due to the non-differentiable nature of the stochastic processes. REINFORCE learning rule [36] is regularly used to train such models. This task is similar to learning an attention policy introduced by Mnih et al. [24].

In this work we exclusively focus on soft attention. In contrast to the hard attention, soft attention generates weights as true probabilities. These weights are calculated in a deterministic fashion using a process that is differentiable. This means that we can use backpropagation and train the entire model end-to-end. Along with the LSTM, soft attention is currently employed in the majority of sequence to sequence models used in machine translation [22], image/video caption generation [37,38], addressing neural memory [11] and other. Soft attention weights are usually calculated as a function of the input features and the current encoder or decoder state. The attention is global if at each step t all input features are considered or local where the attention has access to only limited number of local neighbors.

If the attention model does not consider the decoder state, the model is called self-attention or intra-attention. In this case the attention reflects the relation of an input sample t with respect to other input samples given the optimization objective. Self-attention models were successfully used in tasks such as reading comprehension, summarization and in general for task-independent sequence representations [5,20,27]. The self-attention is easy and fast to calculate with matrix multiplication in a single pass for entire sequence since at each step we do not need the result of past state.

3 Model Architecture

Common approach to supervised video summarization and other sequence to sequence transformations, is an application of a LSTM or GRU encoder-decoder network with attention. Forward LSTM is usually replaced with bi-directional BiLSTM since keyshots in the summary have relation to future video frames in the sequence. Unlike the RNN based networks, our method does not need to reach for special techniques, such as BiLSTM, to achieve non-causal behavior. The vanilla attention model has equal access to all past and future inputs. This aperture can be, however, easily modified and it can even be asymmetric, dilated, or exclude the current time step t.

The hidden state passed from encoder to decoder has always fixed length, however, it needs to encode information representing sequences with variable lengths. This means that there is a higher information loss for longer sequences. The proposed attention mechanism does not suffer from such loss since it accesses the input sequence directly without an intermediate embedding.

Architecture proposed in this work replaces entirely the LSTM encoder-decoder network with the soft, self-attention and a two layer, fully connected network for regression of the frame importance score. Our model takes an input sequence $\boldsymbol{X} = (\boldsymbol{x}_0, \ldots, \boldsymbol{x}_N)$, $\boldsymbol{x} \in \mathbb{R}^D$ and produces an output sequence

$Y = (y_0, \ldots, y_N)$, $y = [0, 1)$, both of length N. The input is a sequences of CNN feature vectors with dimensions D, extracted for each video frame. Figure 2 shows the entire network in detail.

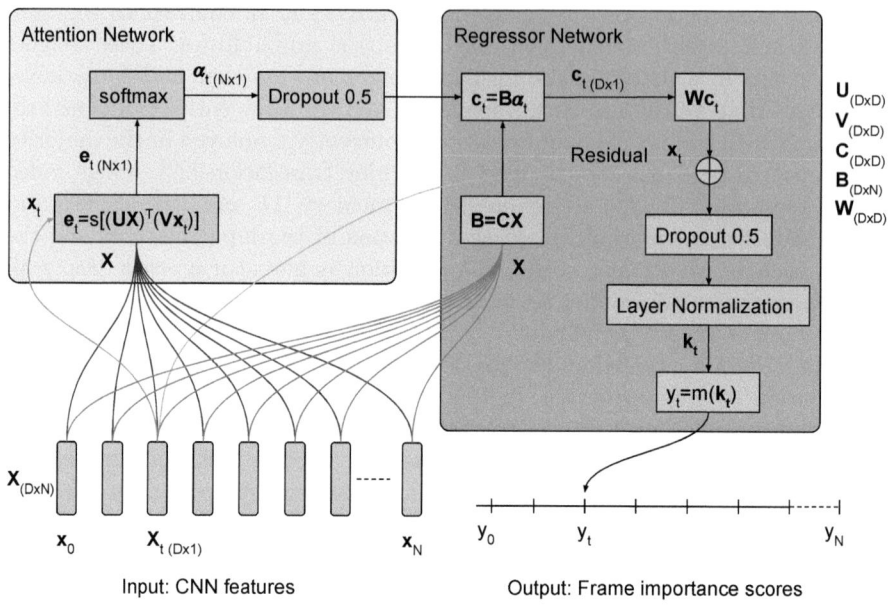

Fig. 2. Diagram of VASNet network attending sample x_t.

Unnormalized self-attention weight $e_{t,i}$ is calculated as an alignment between input feature $\mathbf{x}_t$ and the entire input sequence according to Luong et al. [21].

$$e_{t,i} = s[(\boldsymbol{U}\boldsymbol{x}_i)^T(\boldsymbol{V}\boldsymbol{x}_t)] \quad t = [0, N), \quad i = [0, N) \tag{1}$$

Here, N is the number of video frames, $\boldsymbol{U}$ and $\boldsymbol{V}$ are network weight matrices estimated together with other parameters of the network during optimization and s is a scale parameter that reduces values of the dot product between $\boldsymbol{U}\boldsymbol{x}_i$ and $\boldsymbol{V}\boldsymbol{x}_t$. We set the scale s to value 0.06, determined experimentally. Impact of the scale on the model performance was, however, minimal. Alternatively, the attention vector could be also realized by an additive function as shown by Bahdanou et al. [4].

$$e_{t,i} = \boldsymbol{M}\tanh(\boldsymbol{U}\boldsymbol{x}_i + \boldsymbol{V}\boldsymbol{x}_t) \tag{2}$$

where $\boldsymbol{M}$ are additional network weights learned during training. Both formulas have shown similar performance, however, the multiplicative attention is easier to parallelise since it can be entirely implemented as a matrix multiplication which can be highly optimized. The attention vector $\boldsymbol{e}_t$ is then converted to the attention weights $\boldsymbol{\alpha}_t$ with softmax.

$$\alpha_{t,i} = \frac{\exp(e_{t,i})}{\sum_{k=1}^{N} \exp(e_{t,k})} \tag{3}$$

The attention weights $\boldsymbol{\alpha}_t$ are true probabilities representing the importance of input features with respect to the desired frame level score at the time t. Linear transformation $\boldsymbol{C}$ is then applied to each input and the results then weighted with attention vector $\boldsymbol{\alpha}_t$ and averaged. The output is a context vector $\boldsymbol{c}_t$ which is used for the final frame score regression.

$$\boldsymbol{b}_i = \boldsymbol{C}\boldsymbol{x}_i \tag{4}$$

$$\boldsymbol{c}_t = \sum_{i=1}^{N} \alpha_{t,i} \boldsymbol{b}_i \qquad \boldsymbol{c}_t \in \mathbb{R}^D \tag{5}$$

The context vector $\boldsymbol{c}_t$ is then projected by a single layer, fully connected network with linear activation and residual sum followed by dropout and layer normalization.

$$\boldsymbol{k}_t = norm(dropout(\boldsymbol{W}\boldsymbol{c}_t + \boldsymbol{x}_t)) \tag{6}$$

The $\boldsymbol{C}$ and $\boldsymbol{W}$ are network weight matrices learned during the network training. To regularize the network we also add a dropout for attention weights as shown in Fig. 2. We found it to be beneficial, especially for small training datasets such as in the canonical setting for TvSum (40 videos) and SumMe (20 videos).

By design, the attention network discards the temporal order in the sequence. This is due to the fact that the context vector $\boldsymbol{c}_t$ is calculated as a weighted average of input features without any order information. The order of the output sequence is still preserved. The positional order for the frame score prediction is not important in the video summarization task, as has been shown in the past work utilizing clustering techniques that also discard the input frame order. For other tasks, such as machine translation or captioning, the order is essential. In these cases every prediction at time t, including attention weights, could be conditioned on state at $t-1$. Alternatively, a positional encoding could be injected to the input as proposed by [10,34].

Finally, a two layer neural network performs the frame score regression $y_t = m(\boldsymbol{k}_t)$. First layer has a ReLU activation followed by dropout and layer normalization [3], while the second layer has a single hidden unit with sigmoid activation.

3.1 Frame Scores to Keyshot Summaries

The model outputs frame-level scores that are then converted to keyshots. Following [40], this is done in two steps. First, we detect scene change points where each represents a potential keyshot segment. Second, we select a subset of these keyshots by maximizing the total frame score within these keyshots while constraining the total summary length to 15% of the original video length as per [12]. The scene change points are detected by Kernel Temporal Segmentation (KTS) method [28] as shown in Fig. 3. For each detected shot $i \in K$ we calculate score s_i.

$$s_i = \frac{1}{l_i} \sum_{a=1}^{l_i} y_{i,a} \tag{7}$$

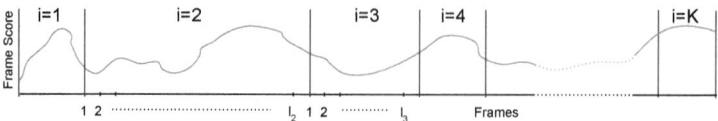

Fig. 3. Temporal segmentation with KTS.

where $y_{i,a}$ is score of a-th frame within shot i and l_i is the length of i-th shot. Keyshots are then selected with the Knapsack algorithm Eq. 8 according to [32].

$$\max \sum_{i=1}^{K} u_i s_i, \quad \text{s. t.} \quad \sum_{i=1}^{K} u_i l_i \leq L, u_i \in 0, 1 \tag{8}$$

Keyshots with $u_i = 1$ are then concatenated to produce the final video summary. For evaluation we create a binary summary vector where each frame in shot ($u_i = 1$) is set to one.

3.2 Model Training

To train our model we use the ADAM optimizer [17] with learning rate $5 \cdot 10^{-5}$ This low learning rate is used as a result of having a batch with single sample, where the sample is an entire video sequence. We use 50% dropout and $L2 = 10^{-5}$ regularization. Training is done over 200 epochs. Model with the highest validation F-score is then selected.

3.3 Computation Complexity

The self-attention requires a constant number of operations at each step for all input features N, each of size D. The complexity is thus $O(N^2 D)$. The recurrent layer, on the other hand, requires $O(N)$ sequential operations, each of complexity $O(ND^2)$. Self-attention needs less computation when the sequence length N is shorter than the feature size D. For longer videos, a local attention would be used rather then the global one.

4 Evaluation

4.1 Datasets Overview

In order to directly compare our method with the previous work we conducted all experiments on four datasets, TvSum [32], SumMe [12], OVP [7] and YouTube [7]. OVP and YouTube were used only to augment the training dataset. TvSum and SumMe are currently the only datasets suitably labeled for keyshots video summarization, albeit still small for training deep models. Table 1 provides an overview of the main datasets properties.

Table 1. Overview of the TvSum and SumMe properties.

Dataset	Videos	User annotations	Annotation type	Video length (sec)		
				Min	Max	Avg
SumMe	25	15–18	keyshots	32	324	146
TvSum	50	20	frame-level importance scores	83	647	235
OVP	50	5	keyframes	46	209	98
YouTube	39	5	keyframes	9	572	196

The TvSum dataset is annotated by frame-level importance scores, while the SumMe with binary keyshot summaries. OVP and YouTube are annotated with keyframes and need to be converted to the frame-level scores and binary keyshot summaries, following the protocol discussed in the following Sect. 4.2.

4.2 Ground Truth Preparation

Our model is trained using frame-level scores, while the evaluation is performed with the binary keyshot summaries. The SumMe dataset comes with keyshot annotations, as well as frame-level scores calculated as an average of the keyshot user summaries per frame. In the case of TvSum we convert the frame-level scores to keyshots following the protocol described in Sect. 3.1. Keyframe annotations in OVP and YouTube are converted to frame-level scores by temporarily segmenting the video into shots with KTS and then selecting shots that contain the keyframes. Knapsack is then used to constrain the total summary length, however in this case the keyshot score s_i (Eq. 8) is calculated as a ratio of number of keyframes within the keyshot and the keyshot length.

To make the comparison even more direct, we adopt identical training and testing ground truth data used by [23,40,42]. This represents CNN embeddings, scene change points, and generated frame-level scores and keyshot labels for all datasets. The preprocessed data are publicly available (Zhou et al. [42][2] and Zhang et al. [40][3]). CNN embeddings used in this preprocessed dataset have 1024 dimensions and were extracted from the pool5 layer of the GoogLeNet network [33] trained on ImageNet [30].

We use a 5-fold cross validation for both, canonical and augmented settings as suggested by [40]. In the canonical setting, we generate 5 random train/test splits for the TvSum and SumMe datasets individually. 80% samples are used for training and the rest for testing. In the augmented setting we also maintain the 5-fold cross validation with the 80/20 train/test, but add the other datasets to the training split. For example, to train the SumMe in the augmented setting we take all samples from TvSum, OVP and YouTube and 80% of the SumMe as the training dataset and the remaining 20% for evaluation.

---
[2] http://www.eecs.qmul.ac.uk/~kz303/vsumm-reinforce/datasets.tar.gz.
[3] https://www.dropbox.com/s/ynl4jsa2mxohs16/data.zip?dl=0.

4.3 Evaluation Protocol

To provide a fair comparison with the state of the art, we follow evaluation protocol from [23,40,42]. To asses the similarity between the machine and user summaries we use the harmonic mean of precision and recall expressed as the F-score in percentages.

$$F = 2 \times \frac{\text{precision} \times \text{recall}}{\text{precision} + \text{recall}} \times 100 \qquad (9)$$

True and false positives and false negatives for the F-score are calculated per-frame as the overlap between the ground truth and machine summaries, as shown in Fig. 4.

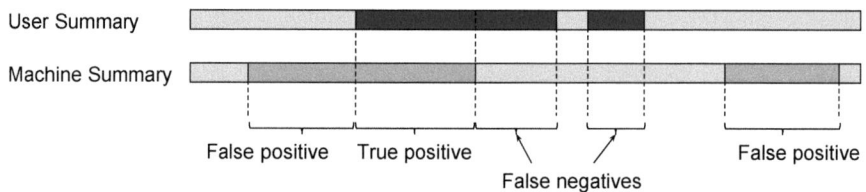

Fig. 4. True positives, False positives and False negatives are calculated per-frame between the ground truth and machine binary keyshot summaries.

Following [12], the machine summary is limited to 15% of the original video length and then evaluated against multiple user summaries according to [40]. Precisely, on the TvSum benchmark, for each video, the F-score is calculated as an average between the machine summary and each of the user summaries as suggested by [32]. Average F-score over videos in the dataset is then reported. On the SumMe benchmark, for each video, a user summary most similar to the machine summary is selected. This approach is proposed by [13] and also used in the work of Lin and Chin-Yew [19].

5 Experiments and Results

Results of the VASNet evaluation on TvSum and SumMe datasets, compared with the most recent state of the art methods are presented in Table 3. To illustrate how well the methods learned from the user annotations we show a human performance, which is calculated as pairwise F-scores between the ground truth and all user summaries. In Table 2 we also compare the human performance with F-scores calculated among the user summaries themselves.

We can see that the human performance is higher than the F-score among the user summaries which is likely caused by the fact that the training ground truth is calculated as an average of all user summaries and then converted to the keyshots, which are aligned on the scene change-points. These keyshots are

Table 2. Average pairwise F-scores calculated among user summaries and between ground truth (GT) and users summaries.

Dataset	Pairwise F score	
	Among users annotations	Training GT w.r.t. users annotations (human performance)
SumMe	31.1	64.2
TvSum	53.8	63.7

likely to be longer than the discrete user summaries, thus having higher mutual overlap. The pairwise F-score 53.8 for TvSum dataset is higher than the F-score 36 reported by the authors [32]. This is because we convert each user summary to keyshots with KTS and limit the duration to 15% of the video length and then calculate the pairwise F-scores. Authors of the dataset [32] calculate the F-score from *gold standard labels*, that is, from keyshots of length 2 seconds, a length used by users during the frame-level score annotation. We chose to follow the former procedure which is maintained in all evaluations in this work to make the results directly comparable.

Table 3. Comparison of our method VASNet with the state of the art methods for canonical and augmented settings. For a reference we add human performance measured as pairwise F-score between training ground truth and user summaries.

Method	SumMe		TvSum	
	Canonical	Augmented	Canonical	Augmented
dppLSTM [40]	38.6	42.9	54.7	59.6
M-AVS [15]	44.4	46.1	61.0	61.8
DR-DSN$_{sup}$ [42]	42.1	43.9	58.1	59.8
SUM-GAN$_{sup}$ [23]	41.7	43.6	56.3	61.2
SASUM$_{sup}$ [35]	45.3	-	58.2	-
Human	64.2	-	63.7	-
VASNet (proposed method)	**49.71**	**51.09**	**61.42**	**62.37**

In Table 3 we can see that our method outperforms all previous work in both canonical and augmented settings. On the TvSum benchmark the improvement is by 0.7% and 1% in the canonical and augmented settings respectively and 2% lower than the human performance. On the SumMe this is 12% and 11% in the canonical and augmented settings respectively and 21% below the human performance. In Fig. 5 we show this improvements visually.

The higher performance gain on the SumMe dataset is very likely caused by the fact that our attention model can extract more information from the ground truth compared to the TvSum, where most methods already closely approach the human performance. It is conceivable to assume that the small gain on the TvSum is caused by the negative effect of the global attention on long sequences. TvSum videos are comparatively longer than the SumMe as seen in Table 1. At every prediction step the global attention 'looks' at all video frames. For long video sequences frames from temporally distant scenes are likely less relevant than the local ones, but the global attention still needs to explore them. We believe that this increases variance in the attention weights, which negatively impacts the prediction accuracy. We hypothesize that this could be mitigated by the introduction of local attention.

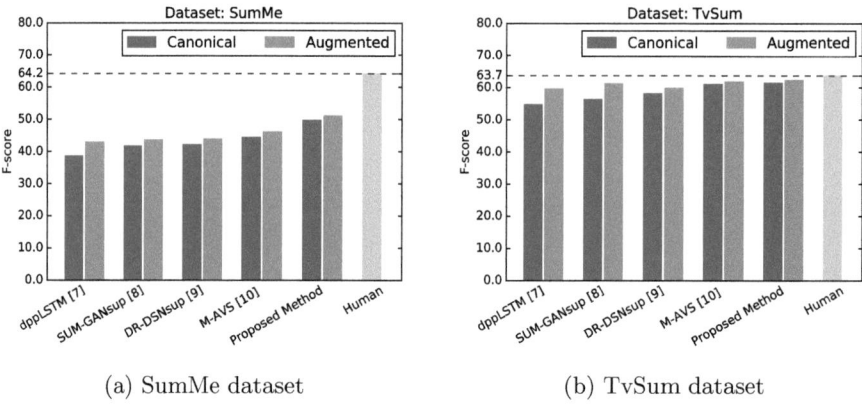

Fig. 5. VASNet performance gain compared to the state of the art and human performance.

5.1 Qualitative Results

To show the quality of the machine summaries produced by our method we plot the ground truth and predicted scores for two videos from TvSum in Fig. 6. We selected videos 10 and 11, since they are also used in previous work [42], thus enabling a direct comparison. We can see a clear correlation between the ground

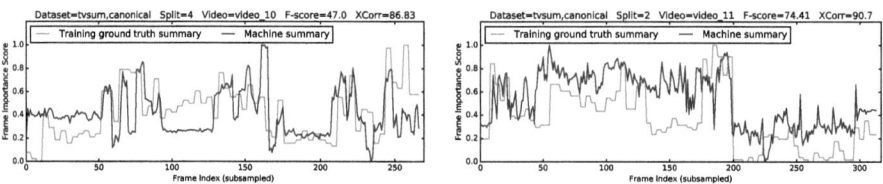

Fig. 6. Correlation between ground truth and machine summaries produced by VASNet for test videos 10 and 11 from TvSum dataset, also evaluated in [42].

truth and machine summary, confirming the quality of our method. Original videos and their summaries are available on YouTube.[4]

Fig. 7. Ground truth frame scores (gray), machine summary (blue) and corresponding keyframes for test video 7 from TvSum dataset. (Color figure online)

We also compare the final, binary keyshot summary with the ground truth. In Fig. 7 we show machine generated keyshots in light blue color over the ground truth importance scores shown in gray. We can see that the selected keyshots

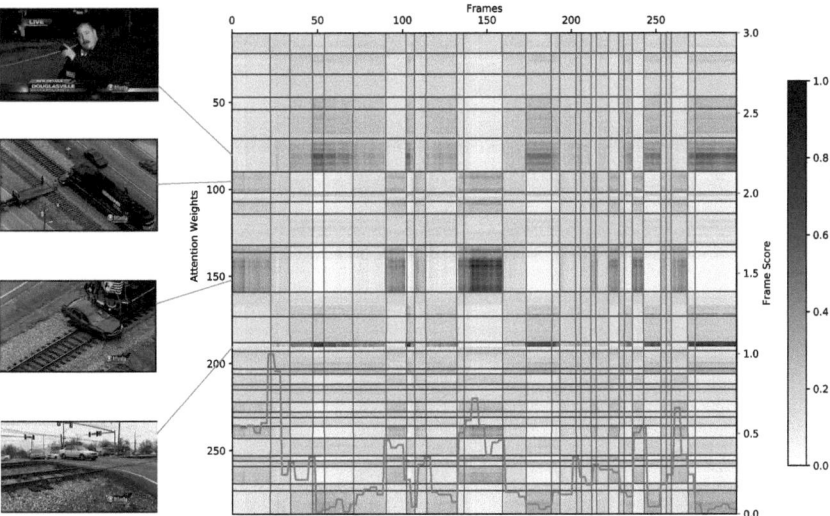

Fig. 8. Confusion matrix of attention weights for TvSum video 7 from test split 2. Green plot at the bottom shows the GT frame scores. Green and red horizontal and vertical lines show scene change points. Values were normalized to range 0–1 across the matrix. Frames are sub-sampled to 2 fps. (Color figure online)

---

[4] https://www.youtube.com/playlist?list=PLEdpjt8KmmQMfQEat4HvuIxORwiO9q9DB.

align with most of the peaks in the ground truth and that they cover the entire length of the video. The confusion matrix in Fig. 8 shows attention weights produced during evaluation of TvSum video 7. We can see that the attention strongly focuses on frames either correlated with low frame scores (top and bottom image in Fig. 8, attention weights for frames $\sim$80 and $\sim$190) or high scores (second and third image, frames $\sim$95 and $\sim$150). It is conceivable to assume that the network learns to associate every video frame with other frames of similar score levels.

Another interesting observation to make is that the transitions between the high and low attention weights in the confusion matrix highly correlate with the scene change points, shown as green and red horizontal and vertical lines. It is important to note that the change points, detected with KTS algorithm, were not provided to the model during learning or inference, nor were used to process the training GT. Thus, we believe that this model could be also applied to scene segmentation, removing the need for the KTS post-processing step. We will explore this possibility in our future work.

6 Conclusions

In this work propose a novel deep neural network for keyshot video summarization based on pure soft, self-attention. This network performs a sequence to sequence transformation without recurrent networks such as LSTM based encoder-decoder models. We show that on the supervised, keyhost video summarization task our model outperforms the existing state of the art methods on the TvSum and SumMe benchmarks. Given the simplicity of our model it is easier to implement and less resource demanding to run than LSTM encoder-decoder based methods, making it suitable for application on embedded or low power platforms.

Our model is based on a single, global, self-attention layer followed by two, fully connected network layers. We intentionally designed and tested the simplest architecture with global attention, and without positional encoding to establish a baseline method for such architectures. Limiting the aperture of the attention to a local region as well as adding the positional encoding are simple modifications that are likely to further improve the performance. We are considering these extensions for our future work.

The complete PyTorch 0.4 source code to train and evaluate our model, as well as trained weights to reproduce results in this paper, will be publicly available on https://github.com/ok1zjf/VASNet.

References

1. Argyriou, V.: Sub-hexagonal phase correlation for motion estimation. IEEE Trans. Image Process. **20**(1), 110–120 (2011)
2. Athiwaratkun, B., Kang, K.: Feature representation in convolutional neural networks. arXiv preprint arXiv:1507.02313 (2015)

3. Ba, J.L., Kiros, J.R., Hinton, G.E.: Layer normalization. arXiv preprint arXiv:1607.06450 (2016)
4. Bahdanau, D., Cho, K., Bengio, Y.: Neural machine translation by jointly learning to align and translate. arXiv preprint arXiv:1409.0473 (2014)
5. Cheng, J., Dong, L., Lapata, M.: Long short-term memory-networks for machine reading. In: Proceedings of the EMNLP, pp. 551–561 (2016)
6. Cho, K., Merrienboer, B., Gulcehre, C., Bougares, F., Schwenk, H., Bengio, Y.: Learning phrase representations using RNN encoder-decoder for statistical machine translation. In: Proceedings of the EMNLP (2014)
7. De Avila, S.E.F., Lopes, A.P.B., da Luz Jr., A., de Albuquerque Araújo, A.: VSUMM: a mechanism designed to produce static video summaries and a novel evaluation. Pattern Recogn. Lett. **32**(1), 56–68 (2011)
8. Fajtl, J., Argyriou, V., Monekosso, D., Remagnino, P.: AMNet: memorability estimation with attention. In: Proceedings of the IEEE CVPR, pp. 6363–6372 (2018)
9. Fei, M., Jiang, W., Mao, W.: Memorable and rich video summarization. J. Vis. Commun. Image Represent. **42**(C), 207–217 (2017)
10. Gehring, J., et al.: Convolutional sequence to sequence learning. In: Proceedings of the ICML, pp. 1243–1252, 06–11 August 2017
11. Graves, A., et al.: Hybrid computing using a neural network with dynamic external memory. Nature **538**(7626), 471 (2016)
12. Gygli, M., Grabner, H., Riemenschneider, H., Van Gool, L.: Creating summaries from user videos. In: Fleet, D., Pajdla, T., Schiele, B., Tuytelaars, T. (eds.) ECCV 2014. LNCS, vol. 8695, pp. 505–520. Springer, Cham (2014). https://doi.org/10.1007/978-3-319-10584-0_33
13. Gygli, M., et al.: Video summarization by learning submodular mixtures of objectives. In: Proceedings of the IEEE CVPR, pp. 3090–3098 (2015)
14. Hochreiter, S., Schmidhuber, J.: Long short-term memory. Neural Comput. **9**(8), 1735–1780 (1997)
15. Ji, Z., Xiong, K., Pang, Y., Li, X.: Video summarization with attention-based encoder-decoder networks. arXiv preprint arXiv:1708.09545 (2017)
16. Khosla, A., Raju, A.S., Torralba, A., Oliva, A.: Understanding and predicting image memorability at a large scale. In: Proceedings of the IEEE ICCV, pp. 2390–2398 (2015)
17. Kingma, D., Ba, J.: Adam: a method for stochastic optimization. In: Proceedings of the ICLR, vol. 5 (2015)
18. Larkin, K.G.: Reflections on Shannon information: in search of a natural information-entropy for images. CoRR abs/1609.01117 (2016)
19. Lin, C.Y.: ROUGE: a package for automatic evaluation of summaries. In: Text Summarization Branches Out: Proceedings of the ACL-2004 Workshop, pp. 74–81. Association for Computational Linguistics, Barcelona, July 2004
20. Lin, Z., et al.: A structured self-attentive sentence embedding. In: Proceedings of the ICLR (2017)
21. Luong, M.T., Pham, H., Manning, C.D.: Effective approaches to attention-based neural machine translation. arXiv preprint arXiv:1508.04025 (2015)
22. Luong, T., Pham, H., Manning, C.D.: Effective approaches to attention-based neural machine translation. In: Proceedings of the EMNLP (2015)
23. Mahasseni, B., Lam, M., Todorovic, S.: Unsupervised video summarization with adversarial LSTM networks. In: Proceedings of the IEEE CVPR, pp. 2982–2991 (2017)
24. Mnih, V., Heess, N., Graves, A., et al.: Recurrent models of visual attention. In: Proceedings of the NIPS, pp. 2204–2212 (2014)

25. Novak, C.L., Shafer, S.A.: Anatomy of a color histogram. In: Proceedings of the IEEE CVPR, pp. 599–605. IEEE (1992)
26. Otani, M., et al.: Video summarization using deep semantic features. In: Proceedings of the ACCV, pp. 361–377 (2016)
27. Parikh, A., et al.: A decomposable attention model for natural language inference. In: Proceedings of the EMNLP, pp. 2249–2255 (2016)
28. Potapov, D., Douze, M., Harchaoui, Z., Schmid, C.: Category-specific video summarization. In: Fleet, D., Pajdla, T., Schiele, B., Tuytelaars, T. (eds.) ECCV 2014. LNCS, vol. 8694, pp. 540–555. Springer, Cham (2014). https://doi.org/10.1007/978-3-319-10599-4_35
29. Rochan, M., Wang, Y.: Learning video summarization using unpaired data. arXiv preprint arXiv:1805.12174 (2018)
30. Russakovsky, O., Deng, J., Su, H., Krause, J., Satheesh, S., Ma, S., Huang, Z., Karpathy, A., Khosla, A., Bernstein, M.: Others: imagenet large scale visual recognition challenge. Int. J. Comput. Vision **115**(3), 211–252 (2015)
31. dos Santos Belo, L., Caetano Jr., C.A., do Patrocínio Jr., Z.K.G., Guimarães, S.J.F.: Summarizing video sequence using a graph-based hierarchical approach. Neurocomputing **173**, 1001–1016 (2016)
32. Song, Y., Vallmitjana, J., Stent, A., Jaimes, A.: TVSum: summarizing web videos using titles. In: Proceedings of the IEEE CVPR, pp. 5179–5187 (2015)
33. Szegedy, C., et al.: Going deeper with convolutions. In: Proceedings of the IEEE CVPR, pp. 1–9 (2015)
34. Vaswani, A., et al.: Attention is all you need. In: Proceedings of the NIPS, pp. 5998–6008. Curran Associates, Inc. (2017)
35. Wei, H., Ni, B., Yan, Y., Yu, H., Yang, X., Yao, C.: Video summarization via semantic attended networks. In: Proceedings of the AAAI (2018)
36. Williams, R.J.: Simple statistical gradient-following algorithms for connectionist reinforcement learning. In: Sutton, R.S. (ed.) Reinforcement Learning, pp. 5–32. Springer, Boston (1992). https://doi.org/10.1007/978-1-4615-3618-5_2
37. Xu, K., et al.: Show, attend and tell: neural image caption generation with visual attention. In: Proceedings of the ICML, pp. 2048–2057 (2015)
38. Yao, L., et al.: Describing videos by exploiting temporal structure. In: Proceedings of the IEEE ICCV, pp. 4507–4515 (2015)
39. Yuan, Y., Mei, T., Cui, P., Zhu, W.: Video summarization by learning deep side semantic embedding. IEEE Trans. Circuits Syst. Video Technol. **29**(1), 226–237 (2017). https://doi.org/10.1109/TCSVT.2017.2771247
40. Zhang, K., Chao, W.-L., Sha, F., Grauman, K.: Video summarization with long short-term memory. In: Leibe, B., Matas, J., Sebe, N., Welling, M. (eds.) ECCV 2016. LNCS, vol. 9911, pp. 766–782. Springer, Cham (2016). https://doi.org/10.1007/978-3-319-46478-7_47
41. Zhao, B., Li, X., Lu, X.: Hierarchical recurrent neural network for video summarization. In: Proceedings of the ACM Multimedia Conference, pp. 863–871 (2017)
42. Zhou, K., Qiao, Y., Xiang, T.: Deep reinforcement learning for unsupervised video summarization with diversity-representativeness reward. In: Proceedings of the AAAI (2018)

Gait-Based Age Estimation Using a DenseNet

Atsuya Sakata, Yasushi Makihara[✉], Noriko Takemura, Daigo Muramatsu, and Yasushi Yagi

Osaka University, Osaka, Japan
{sakata,makihara,muramatsu,yagi}@am.sanken.osaka-u.ac.jp,
takemura@ids.osaka-u.ac.jp

Abstract. Human age is one of important attributes for many potential applications such as digital signage, customer analysis, and gait-based age estimation is promising particularly for surveillance scenarios since it can be available at a distance from a camera. We therefore proposed a method of gait-based age estimation using a deep learning framework to advance the state-of-the-art accuracy. Specifically, we employed DenseNet as one of state-of-the-art network architectures. While the previous method of gait-based age estimation using a deep learning framework was evaluated only with a small-scale gait database, we evaluated the proposed method with OULP-Age, the world's largest gait database comprising more than 60,000 subjects with age range from 2 to 90 years old. Consequently, we demonstrated that the proposed method outperform existing methods based on both conventional machine learning frameworks for gait-based age estimation and a deep learning framework for gait recognition.

Keywords: Gait · Age · DenseNet

1 Introduction

Image-based human age estimation has recently become an attractive research topic in computer vision, pattern recognition, and biometrics, since there are many potential applications. For example, once a target person's age is estimated, an advertiser can change a content of a digital signage into more suitable one for the estimated age, and a shop manager may arrange goods based on customer's age statistics. It is also possible to prevent that people under age buy alcohol or cigarette based on the estimated age.

Most of the image-based human age estimation relies on facial image analysis [1–4] as we human also do so. In addition to the facial image analysis, gait video analysis for age estimation is promising, since it does not require as high

---

Supported by JST-Mirai Program JPMJMI17DH and JSPS Grant-in-aid for Scientific Research (B) 16H02848.

© Springer Nature Switzerland AG 2019
G. Carneiro and S. You (Eds.): ACCV 2018 Workshops, LNCS 11367, pp. 55–63, 2019.
https://doi.org/10.1007/978-3-030-21074-8_5

image resolutions as the facial image analysis. Therefore, it can be available even at a distance from a camera without subject cooperation [5,6], and which makes it much wider an application range of the image-based human age estimation, e.g., getting customer's age statistics from a wider area than a shop (e.g., the whole shopping mall), finding a lost child in a shopping mall, finding suspect candidates based on witness about his/her age.

In the early stage, research on gait-based age analysis started with age group classification such as classification of children and adults using representation of point light sources attached to some body joints [7], or classification of the younger and the elderly using minimum foot clearance from the ground [8]. Subsequently, an image analysis-based approach to classification of children, adults, and the elderly has been proposed in [9]. Thereafter, studies on gait-based age estimation has been started since 2010, by using an appearance-based gait feature such as gait energy image (GEI) [10] (a.k.a. averaged silhouette [11]), frequency-domain feature [12], or depth gradient histogram energy image (DGHEI) [13] in conjunction with machine learning techniques, for example, multi-label guided (MLG) subspace learning [14], ordinary preserving manifold learning [15], Gaussian process regression [16], ordinary preserving linear discriminant analysis (OPLDA) and ordinary preserving margin Fisher analysis (OPMFA) [17], support vector regression (SVR) [18], and age group-dependent manifold learning and regression [19].

In addition to the above-mentioned conventional machine learning-based approaches, Marin-Jimenez et al. [20] proposed a deep learning-based gait-based age estimation. More specifically, the authors design a multi-task deep model which outputs age as well as identity and gender. The model is, however, trained and tested only with small-scale gait database, i.e., TUM-GAID [21], which composed of 305 subjects almost in their twenties. Since a deep learning-based approach generally requires a huge number of training samples to reach a satisfactory accuracy, and also reasonable evaluation of gait-based age estimation requires a wide age range, we would say that the method [20] is not fully validated.

We therefore want to validate a deep learning-based approach to gait-based age estimation in this paper. Specifically, we designs a model for gait-based age estimation based on DenseNet [22], a state-of-the-art network architecture so far, and also train and test the model using the world largest gait database, OULP-Age [18], which comprising over 60,000 subjects with wide age range.

2 Proposed Method

2.1 Input Data

As appearance-based gait features [10–12,23,24] are more often used than the model-based gait features [25,26] in the gait recognition community. In particular, silhouette-based representation is dominant in the gait recognition community, since it can avoid being affected by clothes colors and textures, unlike the person re-identification task. We therefore adopt GEI [10] as the most widely used silhouette-based gait representation as input data for our deep learning model. We set the GEI size as 88 by 128 pixels.

2.2 Network Structure

We employ DenseNet [22] as a state-of-the-art network structure for our gait-based age estimation task. While the residual network (ResNet) [27] exploits a skip connection from a single previous layer, DenseNet exploits skip connections from all the preceding layers as shown in Fig. 1. DenseNet achieves the state-of-the-art accuracies with less parameters thanks to the dense connectivity, on object classification tasks as well as other tasks such as optical flow estimation [28] and saliency map estimation [29]. We briefly describe the network structure below and may refer the readers to [22] for more details.

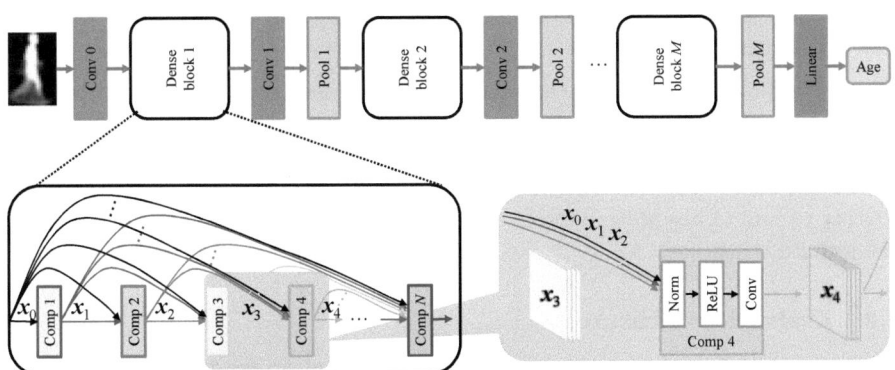

Fig. 1. An illustration of network architecture with M dense blocks, M composite layers, and growth rate $k = 4$.

DenseNet is mainly composed of multiple dense blocks and in-between transition layers including a pair of 1×1 convolution layer and a 2×2 average pooling layer with stride 2. Each dense block is then composed of multiple composite layers with dense connection, where each composite layer comprises a triplet of a 1×1 batch normalization layer, a rectified linear unit (ReLU) [30], and a 3×3 convolution layer. Here, we consider M dense blocks, and each dense block is composed of N composite layers. Given an input x_0 to a dense block whose number of feature maps is k_0, it is fed into the following composite layers (i.e., Comp 1, Comp 2, ..., Comp N) as shown in Fig. 1. The l-th composite layer receives feature maps from all the preceding composite layers, i.e., $[x_0, x_1, \ldots, x_{l-1}]$, and then output x_l whoes number of feature maps is k, which is so-called growth rate. In summary, the number of feature maps which the l-th composite layer receives, sums up to $k_0 + k(l-1)$, and hence each composite layer enjoys a sort of collective knowledge from the preceding layers. Specifically, we experimentally used $M = 5$ dense blocks and each dense blocks has $N = 5$ composite layers with $k = 12$ growth rate.

In addition to the above-mentioned main part, we insert a 7×7 convolution layer with stride 2 (Conv 0) before the first dense block, and also a 7×7 global average pooling layer followed by a one-dimensional full connection layer to output an age.

3 Experiments

3.1 Data Set

We employed OULP-Age [18] as the world's largest gait database for gait-based age estimation. OULP-Age was collected in conjunction with long-run exhibition of experience-based gait analysis demo in a science museum for an approx one year [31]. It consists of 63,846 (31,093 males and 32,753 females) with age ranging from 2 to 90 years old. The database is divided into a training set composed of 31,923 subjects (15,596 males and 16,327 females) and a test set composed of 31,923 subjects (15,497 males and 16,426 females).

3.2 Training

The network was trained using stochastic gradient descent (SGD) [32] with batch size 64 and 100 epochs. An initial learning rate was set to 0.1 and divided by 10 at epoch 50 and 75. We use a Nesterof momentum [33] of 0.9 without dampening. We adopt the weight initialization introduced by He et al. [34]. A loss function was set to sum of absolute difference between an output (i.e., estimated) age and the ground truth age.

3.3 Evaluation Measure

We evaluated the accuracy of gait-based age estimation using a mean absolute error (MAE). MAE is computed by comparing the estimated age $\hat{a}_i$ for the i-th test sample with its corresponding ground truth age a_i as

$$M = \frac{1}{n}\sum_{i=1}^{n} |\hat{a}_i - a_i|, \tag{1}$$

where n is the number of the test samples. In addition, we employed a cumulative score (CS) for evaluating gait-based age estimation. Specifically, we define the number of test samples whose absolute difference between an estimated age and the ground truth age is less than or equal to y as $n(y)$, and then CS of the y-year absolute error as

$$\text{CS}(y) = \frac{n(y)}{n}. \tag{2}$$

3.4 Sensitivity Analysis

Since the number of blocks M and the number of composite layers N are two key hyper-parameters for DenseNet, we analyze the sensitivity of these two hyper-parameters on gait-based age estimation accuracy. Specifically, we set $M \in \{2, 3, 4, 5, 6, 7\}$ and $N \in \{4, 5, 6\}$ and then evaluate an MAE for each parameter combination as shown in Fig. 2. As result, we can see that the number of dense blocks has an impact on the accuracy, namely, the accuracy significantly drop if the number of dense blocks is less than 5. On the other hand, the number of composite layers does not have much impact on the accuracy, at least within the range from 4 to 6.

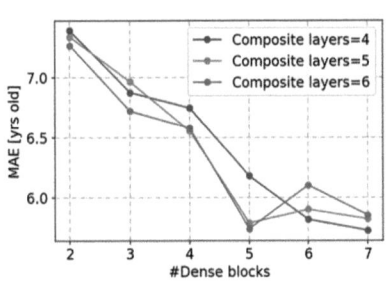
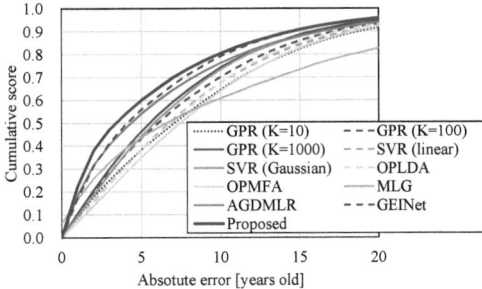

Fig. 2. Sensitivity analysis of the number of dense blocks and composite layers on MAE.

Fig. 3. Cumulative score.

Table 1. MAE [%] and cumulative score at 1, 5, and 10 years absolute errors. Bold and italic bold indicate the best and the second best performances, respectively.

Method	MAE	CS(1) [%]	CS(5) [%]	CS(10) [%]
MLG [14]	10.98	16.7	43.4	60.8
GPR ($k = 10$) [16]	8.83	9.1	38.5	64.7
GPR ($k = 100$) [16]	7.94	10.5	43.3	70.2
GPR ($k = 1000$) [16]	7.30	10.7	46.3	74.2
SVR (linear)	8.73	7.9	38.2	67.6
SVR (Gaussian)	7.66	9.4	44.2	73.4
OPLDA [17]	8.45	7.7	37.9	67.6
OPMFA [17]	9.08	7.0	34.9	64.1
ADGMLR [19]	6.78	*18.4*	54.0	76.2
GEINet [35]	*6.22*	17.2	*55.9*	*79.2*
Proposed method	**5.79**	**22.5**	**55.9**	**80.4**

3.5 Comparison with State-of-the-Arts

Finally, we compared the proposed method with benchmarks. As a baseline algorithm, a method using GPR with radial basis function [16] was adopted. More specifically, it requires huge computation on a gram matrix and its inverse matrix if all the training samples are used, we employ an active set method in the same way as in [31], where k nearest neighbors for each test sample are used for GPR and $k = 10, 100, 1000$ were evaluated. We also tested support vector regression (SVR) with linear and Gaussian kernels, denoted as SVR (linear) and SVR (Gaussian). We also evaluated existing methods of gait-based age estimation using conventional machine learning techniques such as MLG [14], OPLDA [17], OPMFA [17], and AGDMLR [19]. In addition, we employed a slightly modified version of GEINet [35] as a deep learning-based approach to age estimation. More specifically, the original GEINet outputs class (i.e., subject) likelihoods

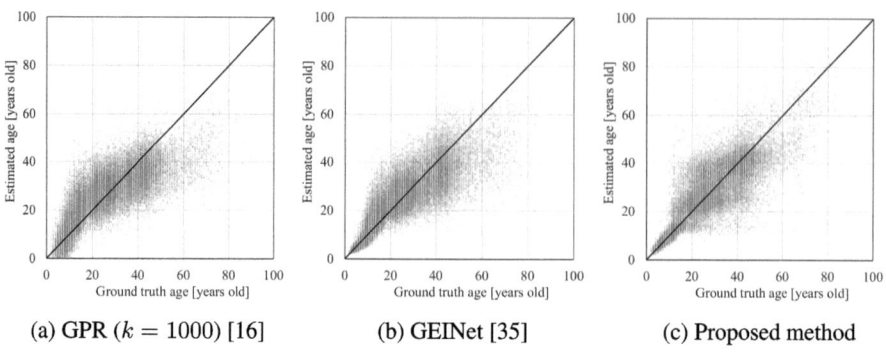

Fig. 4. Scatter plot between ground truth age and estimated age. Diagonal lines show equal lines of ground truth age and estimated age.

and hence the number of nodes at the last layer is equal to the number of subjects. On the other hand, the modified version of GEINet outputs an age and hence the last layer has just a single node.

CSs for the benchmarks and the proposed method are shown in Fig. 3. Also, MAEs and CSs for 1, 5, and 10 years tolerance are summarized in Table 1. As a result, deep learning-based methods (i.e., GEINet [35] and the proposed method) significantly outperform the other methods without deep learning. In addition, the proposed method outperforms GEINet. This is because the proposed method exploit more collective information by dense connectivity while a basic structure of GEINet is derived from AlexNet [36] without such a dense connectivity.

Moreover, scatter plots between the ground truth age and the estimated ages are shown for the baseline GPR ($k = 100$) as a non-deep learning-based method [16], GEINet [35] as a deep learning-based method, and the proposed method in Fig. 4. While the estimated ages for the baseline algorithm (Fig. 4(a)) is largely deviated for all the age range, GEINet (Fig. 4(b)) suppressed such a deviation, particularly, for the children under 15 years old. The proposed method further suppress the deviation for the children and then yielded the best accuracy as a result.

4 Conclusions

In this paper, we proposed a method of gait-based age estimation using a deep learning framework. Specifically, we employed DenseNet as a state-of-the-art network architecture for gait-based age estimation, and demonstrated its effectiveness with OULP-Age, the world's largest gait database comprising more than 60,000 subjects with age range from 2 to 90 years old.

One of future research avenues is further investigating suitable network architectures for gait-based age estimation, e.g., ResNet [27], PyramidNet [37], and ShakeNet [38]. In addition, it is also worth investigating multi-task learning framework, e.g., [20].

References

1. Kwon, Y.H., Lobo, N.V.: Age classification from facial images. Comput. Vis. Image Underst. **74**, 1–21 (1999)
2. Zhang, Y., Yeung, D.Y.: Multi-task warped Gaussian process for personalized age estimation. In: Proceedings of IEEE Computer Society Conference on Computer Vision and Pattern Recognition, San Francisco, CA, USA, pp. 1–8 (2010)
3. Lanitis, A., Draganova, C., Christodoulou, C.: Comparing different classifiers for automatic age estimation. IEEE Trans. Syst. Man Cybern. Part B **34**, 621–628 (2004)
4. Lanitis, A., Taylor, C.J., Cootes, T.F.: Toward automatic simulation of aging effects on face images. IEEE Trans. Pattern Anal. Mach. Intell. **24**, 442–455 (2002)
5. Bashir, K., Xiang, T., Gong, S.: Gait recognition without subject cooperation. Pattern Recogn. Lett. **31**, 2052–2060 (2010)
6. Martin-Felez, R., Xiang, T.: Uncooperative gait recognition by learning to rank. Pattern Recogn. **47**, 3793–3806 (2014)
7. Davis, J.W.: Visual categorization of children and adult walking styles. In: Bigun, J., Smeraldi, F. (eds.) AVBPA 2001. LNCS, vol. 2091, pp. 295–300. Springer, Heidelberg (2001). https://doi.org/10.1007/3-540-45344-X_43
8. Begg, R.: Support vector machines for automated gait classification. IEEE Trans. Biomed. Eng. **52**, 828–838 (2005)
9. Makihara, Y., Mannami, H., Yagi, Y.: Gait analysis of gender and age using a large-scale multi-view gait database. In: Kimmel, R., Klette, R., Sugimoto, A. (eds.) ACCV 2010. LNCS, vol. 6493, pp. 440–451. Springer, Heidelberg (2011). https://doi.org/10.1007/978-3-642-19309-5_34
10. Han, J., Bhanu, B.: Individual recognition using gait energy image. IEEE Trans. Pattern Anal. Mach. Intell. **28**, 316–322 (2006)
11. Liu, Z., Sarkar, S.: Simplest representation yet for gait recognition: averaged silhouette. In: Proceedings of the 17th International Conference on Pattern Recognition, vol. 1, pp. 211–214 (2004)
12. Makihara, Y., Sagawa, R., Mukaigawa, Y., Echigo, T., Yagi, Y.: Gait recognition using a view transformation model in the frequency domain. In: Leonardis, A., Bischof, H., Pinz, A. (eds.) ECCV 2006. LNCS, vol. 3953, pp. 151–163. Springer, Heidelberg (2006). https://doi.org/10.1007/11744078_12
13. Hofmann, M., Bachmann, S., Rigoll, G.: 2.5D gait biometrics using the depth gradient histogram energy image. In: Proceedings of the 5th IEEE International Conference on Biometrics Theory, Applications, and Systems, Washington D.C., USA, pp. 1–5 (2012). Paper ID 172
14. Lu, J., Tan, Y.P.: Gait-based human age estimation. IEEE Trans. Inf. Forensics Secur. **5**, 761–770 (2010)
15. Lu, J., Tan, Y.P.: Ordinary preserving manifold analysis for human age estimation. In: IEEE Computer Society and IEEE Biometrics Council Workshop on Biometrics, San Francisco, CA, USA, pp. 1–6 (2010)
16. Makihara, Y., Okumura, M., Iwama, H., Yagi, Y.: Gait-based age estimation using a whole-generation gait database. In: Proceedings of the International Joint Conference on Biometrics (IJCB 2011), Washington D.C., USA, pp. 1–6 (2011)
17. Lu, J., Tan, Y.P.: Ordinary preserving manifold analysis for human age and head pose estimation. IEEE Trans. Hum. Mach. Syst. **43**, 249–258 (2013)
18. Xu, C., Makihara, Y., Ogi, G., Li, X., Yagi, Y., Lu, J.: The OU-ISIR gait database comprising the large population dataset with age and performance evaluation of age estimation. IPSJ Trans. Comput. Vis. Appl. **9**, 24 (2017)

19. Li, X., Makihara, Y., Xu, C., Yagi, Y., Ren, M.: Gait-based human age estimation using age group-dependent manifold learning and regression. Multimed. Tools Appl. **77**, 28333–28354 (2018)
20. Marin-Jimenez, M., Castro, F., de la Torre, N.G.F., Medina-Carnicer, R.: Deep multi-task learning for gait-based biometrics. In: Proceedings of 2017 IEEE International Conference on Image Processing, pp. 106–110 (2017)
21. Hofmann, M., Geiger, J., Bachmann, S., Schuller, B., Rigoll, G.: The tum gait from audio, image and depth (gaid) database: multimodal recognition of subjects and traits. J. Vis. Comun. Image Represent. **25**, 195–206 (2014)
22. Huang, G., Liu, Z., van der Maaten, L., Weinberger, K.Q.: Densely connected convolutional networks. In: IEEE Conference on Computer Vision and Pattern Recognition (CVPR), pp. 2261–2269 (2017)
23. Wang, C., Zhang, J., Wang, L., Pu, J., Yuan, X.: Human identification using temporal information preserving gait template. IEEE Trans. Pattern Anal. Mach. Intell. **34**, 2164–2176 (2012)
24. Lam, T.H.W., Cheung, K.H., Liu, J.N.K.: Gait flow image: a silhouette-based gait representation for human identification. Pattern Recogn. **44**, 973–987 (2011)
25. Johnson, A.Y., Bobick, A.F.: A multi-view method for gait recognition using static body parameters. In: Bigun, J., Smeraldi, F. (eds.) AVBPA 2001. LNCS, vol. 2091, pp. 301–311. Springer, Heidelberg (2001). https://doi.org/10.1007/3-540-45344-X_44
26. Ariyanto, G., Nixon, M.: Marionette mass-spring model for 3D gait biometrics. In: Proceedings of the 5th IAPR International Conference on Biometrics, pp. 354–359 (2012)
27. He, K., Zhang, X., Ren, S., Sun, J.: Deep residual learning for image recognition. In: IEEE Conference on Computer Vision and Pattern Recognition (CVPR), pp. 770–778 (2016)
28. Zhu, Y., Newsam, S.D.: Densenet for dense flow. In: IEEE International Conference on Image Processing (ICIP), pp. 790–794 (2017)
29. Oyama, T., Yamanaka, T.: Influence of image classification accuracy on saliency map estimation. CAAI Trans. Intell. Technol. **3**(12), 140–152 (2018)
30. Nair, V., Hinton, G.E.: Rectified linear units improve restricted Boltzmann machines. In: Furnkranz, J., Joachims, T., (eds.) Proceedings of the 27th International Conference on Machine Learning (ICML-2010), pp. 807–814. Omnipress (2010)
31. Makihara, Y., et al.: Gait collector: an automatic gait data collection system in conjunction with an experience-based long-run exhibition. In: Proceedings of the 8th IAPR International Conference on Biometrics (ICB 2016). Number O17, Halmstad, Sweden, pp. 1–8 (2016)
32. Bousquet, O., Bottou, L.: The tradeoffs of large scale learning. In: Platt, J., Koller, D., Singer, Y., Roweis, S. (eds.) Advances in Neural Information Processing Systems 20, pp. 161–168. Curran Associates, Inc. (2008)
33. Sutskever, I., Martens, J., Dahl, G., Hinton, G.: On the importance of initialization and momentum in deep learning. In: Proceedings of the 30th International Conference on International Conference on Machine Learning, ICML 2013, vol. 28, pp. III-1139–III-1147. JMLR.org (2013)
34. He, K., Zhang, X., Ren, S., Sun, J.: Delving deep into rectifiers: surpassing human-level performance on imagenet classification. In: IEEE International Conference on Computer Vision (ICCV), pp. 1026–1034 (2015)

35. Shiraga, K., Makihara, Y., Muramatsu, D., Echigo, T., Yagi, Y.: Geinet: view-invariant gait recognition using a convolutional neural network. In: Proceedings of the 8th IAPR International Conference on Biometrics (ICB 2016). Number O19, Halmstad, Sweden, pp. 1–8 (2016)
36. Krizhevsky, A., Sutskever, I., Hinton, G.E.: Imagenet classification with deep convolutional neural networks. In: Pereira, F., Burges, C., Bottou, L., Weinberger, K. (eds.) Advances in Neural Information Processing Systems 25, pp. 1097–1105. Curran Associates, Inc. (2012)
37. Han, D., Kim, J., Kim, J.: Deep pyramidal residual networks. In: IEEE Conference on Computer Vision and Pattern Recognition (CVPR), pp. 6307–6315 (2017)
38. Gastaldi, X.: Shake-shake regularization of 3-branch residual networks. In: 5th International Conference on Learning Representations, Workshop Track, pp. 1–5 (2017)

Human Action Recognition via Body Part Region Segmented Dense Trajectories

Kaho Yamada[✉], Seiya Ito, Naoshi Kaneko, and Kazuhiko Sumi

Aoyama Gakuin University, Kanagawa, Japan
{yamada.kaho,ito.seiya}@vss.it.aoyama.ac.jp,
{kaneko,sumi}@it.aoyama.ac.jp

Abstract. We propose a novel action recognition framework based on trajectory features with human-aware spatial segmentation. Our insight is that the critical features for recognition are appeared in the partial regions of human, thus we segment a video frame into spatial regions based on the human body parts to enhance feature representation. We utilize an object detector and a pose estimator to segment four regions, namely full body, left/right arm, and upper body. From these regions, we extract dense trajectory features and feed them into a shallow RNN to effectively consider the long-term relationships. The evaluation result shows that our framework outperforms previous approaches on the standard two benchmarks, i.e. J-HMDB and MPII Cooking Activities.

Keywords: Action recognition · Body parts · Dense Trajectories

1 Introduction

Human action recognition is the task of classifying human activities performed in image sequences into meaningful action categories. It has been broadly studied in computer vision and video analysis fields with various potential applications such as security, surveillance, and human-computer interaction.

The effective representation of human motion is one of the critical aspects in action recognition. The traditional family of video representations is the handcrafted local features which have been extended from image features. In particular, trajectories around humans have shown to be efficient representation to recognize human activities and have been studied extensively in the past decade [10,15–18]. Among these trajectory-based local features, Dense Trajectories and its variants [17,18] have shown prominent performance on a variety of challenging datasets. They compute rich descriptors of HOG, HOF, and MBH along the trajectories of densely sampled and tracked key points to convey critical information about human behaviour.

Recently, as in the other problems in computer vision, deep neural networks have been applied to pursue the performance improvement of the task. One of the most successful architectures is two-stream Convolutional Network (ConvNet) [14] which consists of two ConvNets named spatial network and temporal network. The two separate networks respectively capture appearance and motion features from RGB and optical flow inputs for effective classification. Subsequent studies [19,20] have proposed improved architectures to achieve better performances. However, the unique research by He et al. [5] reported that the classifications of these approaches rely on the background information of a scene. In other words, the classification results may be affected when the same action is performed in different backgrounds, and vice versa. Meanwhile, most deep learning based methods employ the elaborate network architecture with the vast number of parameters to learn, which requires large-scale labelled datasets and substantial memory footprints for training. From a practical point of view, these shortcomings are critical for several real-world applications such as surveillance cameras, which are required to deal with various environments.

In this paper, we revisit the hand-crafted trajectory features and propose a novel action recognition framework with human-aware spatial segmentation. Our insight is that the critical features for recognition are appeared in the partial regions of human, therefore, we segment a video frame into spatial regions based on the human pose to enhance feature representation. While human-aware spatial segmentation was used in few works [18,21], we will show that our segmentation scheme is more effective and outperforms these methods on the two standard action recognition benchmarks. Furthermore, we will also demonstrate that a simple, shallow Recurrent Neural Network (RNN) improves the classification accuracy, especially for transitional actions, over commonly used Support Vector Machine (SVM) classifier.

2 Related Work

Matikainen et al. [10] used a simple Kanade-Lucas-Tomasi (KLT) tracker to produce feature trajectories over image sequence. They applied k-means clustering to the trajectories and computed an affine transformation matrix for each cluster centre. The elements of the matrix were used as feature dictionary which named Trajecton. Sun et al. [16] extracted trajectories by matching Scale-Invariant Feature Transform (SIFT) descriptors between two consecutive frames. The authors later proposed the improved method [15] by combining KLT with SIFT to extract long-term trajectories while increasing their density.

Among these trajectory-based methods, Dense Trajectories proposed by Wang et al. [17] have been shown to be an efficient representation for action recognition. In Dense Trajectories, feature points are sampled on spatial image grids and are tracked in multiple scales based on dense optical flow field [3]. Then, tracked points in consecutive frames are concatenated to form a trajectory. They computed multiple descriptors along the trajectories, i.e. Histogram of Gradient (HOG), Histogram of Optical Flow (HOF), and Motion Boundary Histogram (MBH), to capture the shape, appearance, and motion information. Later, the authors extended the work to Improved Trajectories [18], which considers camera motion to correct trajectories. They also found that using Fisher Vector (FV) [12] instead of Bag of Visual Words (BoVW) achieves better performance. Peng et al. [11] proposed a multi-layer nested FV encoding called Stacked

Fisher Vectors (SFV) and showed that the combination of FV and SFV increases classification accuracy. Zhou et al. [22] focused on human-object interaction and proposed a fine-grained action recognition method by linking object proposals. Although the authors also used spatial segmentation and trajectory-based features, our approach focuses on pure human motions to cope with more general cases.

Recently, methods based on deep neural networks have been actively studied. Simonyan et al. [14] proposed a successful action recognition method using two-stream ConvNets, which consists of spatial and temporal ConvNets arranged in parallel. It respectively processes RGB and optical flow images by the spatial and the temporal ConvNets followed by a class score fusion which produces the final prediction. Subsequent studies improved performance by combining the network with Improved Trajectories [19] or sparse temporal sampling strategy [20].

In the literature, the method closest to our approach was proposed by Yamada et al. [21]. They first performed human pose estimation to segment human body parts and then extract Dense Trajectories from the segmented regions. Compared to [21], our architecture has two improvements. First, we investigate the region segmentation scheme and propose a novel segmentation pipeline, which improves performance while reducing the number of regions. Second, we show that an RNN performs better than commonly used SVM, even using a shallow, two-layered network.

3 Method

This section presents the details of the proposed action recognition architecture. Figure 1 shows an overview of the proposed method. Taking a single video as an input, we first segment each video frame into spatial regions to focus on the action performed by a human. For each frame, we detect the full body region of the human using an object detection algorithm. We apply human pose estimation to the detected region to localize 2D joint positions. Using the 2D joint positions, we set more detailed regions for the right arm, left arm, and upper body. Then, we extract trajectory features from the four segmented regions (fully body, both arms, and upper body) in each time step. Before feeding the extracted features into a recurrent network, we encode them into fixed dimensions and stack the encoded features into a single vector. Lastly, the shallow recurrent network takes the stacked feature vector as an input to infer the action class.

3.1 Body Part Region Segmentation

In the proposed method, we segment each video frame into four spatial regions to focus on the actions performed by a human. The first region, or full body region, is segmented by the human bounding box produced by object detection algorithm. We utilize Single Shot Multibox Detector (SSD) [9] as a detector. We select a human bounding box with the highest class probability and use it as a full body region. The latter three regions, namely left arm, right arm,

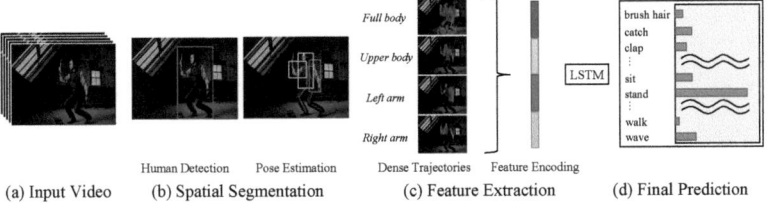

Human Detection	Pose Estimation	Dense Trajectories	Feature Encoding	
(a) Input Video	(b) Spatial Segmentation	(c) Feature Extraction	(d) Final Prediction

Fig. 1. Proposed action recognition architecture. First, an input video is fed into a human detector followed by a pose estimation algorithm to estimate a human location and 2D joint positions. We segment each frame into four spatial regions; full body, left/right arm, and upper body, by using the estimated location and joint positions. Then, dense trajectory features are extracted from each of the four regions over fixed time step and are encoded into fixed dimensional vectors. Lastly, the LSTM network takes the encoded features as inputs to infer the action class.

and upper body, are segmented based on the human pose. Taking the full body region as an input, we apply human pose estimation method [1] to acquire 2D joint positions. For left/right arm regions, we respectively compute two bounding boxes enclosing left/right wrist and shoulder joints. Lastly, the upper body region is computed to enclose both shoulders and both hips.

Through preliminary experiments, we found that enlarging the spatial regions before feature extraction yields better performance. The intuitive interpretation is that since the human joints are represented as skeletons, the regions computed from joint positions are narrower than the actual body parts. We empirically enlarge the full body, left/right arm, and upper body regions by 30%, 60%, and 60%, respectively. Note that we fix the lower base of the upper body region and enlarge only in the upper and horizontal directions. Figure 1(b) shows the segmented four spatial regions where colours of bounding boxes represent body parts (red: full body, yellow: upper body, magenta: left arm, cyan: right arm).

3.2 Feature Extraction

Using the segmented regions, we extract body part region segmented trajectory features from the input image sequences. First, we extract trajectories from the entire image region using Improved Trajectories [18]. Following [18], we densely sample a set of points on 8 spatial scales on a grid of size $W = 5$ pixels. The sampled points are tracked by dense optical flow [3]. For each frame I_t, we compute its dense optical flow field $\omega_t = (u_t, v_t)$ between I_{t+1}, where u_t and v_t are the horizontal and vertical component of the optical flow, respectively. Given each sampled point $P_t = (x_t, y_t)$ at I_t, its tracked position P_{t+1} at I_{t+1} is derived by:

$$P_{t+1} = (x_{t+1}, y_{t+1}) = (x_t, y_t) + (M * \omega_t)|_{(\bar{x}_t, \bar{y}_t)}, \tag{1}$$

where M is a median filter kernel and $(\bar{x}_t, \bar{y}_t)$ is the rounded position of (x_t, y_t). Then, we respectively select the trajectories inside the four segmented regions as depicted in Fig. 1(c). Along the selected trajectories, we compute descriptors, i.e. trajectory descriptor [18], HOG, HOF, and MBH. As a result, we acquire four sets of trajectory features corresponding to the body part regions.

3.3 Classification

To encode the extracted features, we utilize the Fisher Vector (FV) [12]. First, we reduce the dimensions of the descriptor by half using Principal Component Analysis (PCA), as in [18]. Then, we randomly select 256,000 features from the training set and estimate Gaussian Mixture Model (GMM) with the number of components $K = 256$. Finally, we apply power and L2 normalization to the FV and concatenate the normalized FV to combine different descriptor types. Note that the trajectory features from the four regions are individually encoded to FV and are concatenated in the fixed order, as shown in Fig. 2.

Using the encoded features as inputs, we employ a Recurrent Neural Network (RNN) as a classifier. Although most trajectory-based approaches [17,18] employ Support Vector Machine (SVM), it cannot hold long-term transition of actions. This is critical for the action such as *take put in oven*, which contains multiple sub-actions (open the oven door, put food in the oven, close the oven door). To cope with the long-term transition, we built the network with Long Short-Term Memory (LSTM) [6] which remembers the state over arbitrary time intervals. The proposed network consists of two layers, both of which are LSTM layers. As illustrated in Fig. 2, for each frame at t_n, we feed the encoded feature vector to the LSTM network. After network takes all feature vectors of a video clip of N frames, it outputs final prediction score. We take the action class with the highest probability as a prediction.

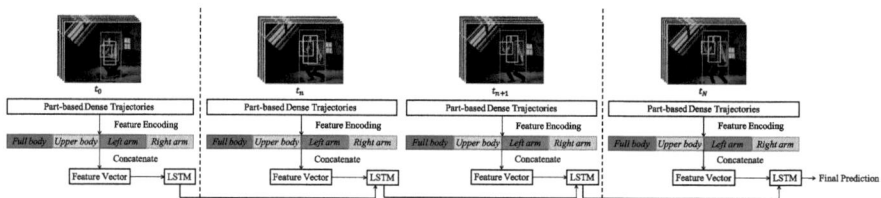

Fig. 2. Conceptual diagram of the classification pipeline. The LSTM network takes the encoded features over sequential video frames and provides class probabilities.

4 Experiments

4.1 Datasets

We conduct experiments on two popular action recognition datasets, namely J-HMDB [7] and MPII Cooking Activities [13], both of which have ground truth annotations for 2D human joint positions.

J-HMDB (stands for Joint-annotated HMDB) [7] is a subset of challenging HMDB51 dataset [8] which contains 928 video clips of 21 actions out of 6.8 K clips of 51 actions in HMDB51. The 21 categories including *brush hair, pick, golf, run, sit*, etc., are selected by excluding categories that contain facial expressions, interactions with others, and several special actions (e.g. *smiling, shaking hands*, or *cartwheel*). The dataset consists of 36–55 video clips per action class with each clip containing 15–40 frames of spatial resolution 320 × 240.

MPII Cooking Activities [13] contains 5,609 high-resolution video clips (1624 × 1224) of 64 fine-grained actions such as *cut dice, cut slices, cut stripes, wash hands, wash objects*. All clips are taken in a kitchen with a fixed camera, therefore there is no background variation. As in the original paper, we exclude the extra *background activity* class for classification.

We compare our framework with the published results of trajectory-based methods [11,17,18,21] as well as deep learning-based approaches [2,4]. For quantitative evaluation, we report the mean accuracy for both datasets.

Table 1. Quantitative comparison against previous approaches on the J-HMDB and the MPII Cooking Activities. * indicates our own implementation.

Method	J-HMDB	MPII Cook.
DT-BoVW [7,13]	56.6	59.2
IDT-FV [2]	65.9	67.6
IDT-(FV+SFV) [11]	69.0	-
(R-segmented+DT)-BoVW* [21]	60.6	-
Action Tubes [4]	62.5	-
P-CNN [2]	61.1	62.3
Ours	**69.8**	**68.2**

4.2 Results

Table 1 shows the quantitative comparison of the proposed architecture against previous approaches on the J-HMDB [7] and the MPII Cooking Activities [13] benchmarks. Note that Dense Trajectories [17] and Improved Trajectories [18] are abbreviated to "DT" and "IDT", respectively. Comparing to the baseline (IDT-FV), which our method is built upon, we achieve consistent improvements on all benchmarks. Moreover, the proposed method performs even better than the deep learning-based methods [2,4] which employ far deeper network architectures. Figure 3 shows per class classification accuracy comparison against the baseline on the J-HMDB dataset. We found that the proposed method is more robust to the arm-dominant actions, such as *throw, shoot ball, clap*, and *wave*. We obtain similar effects on the MPII Cooking Activities, where the accuracy for *wash hands* and *wash objects* are improved by over 20%. These results show that the proposed body part region segmentation contributes to the accuracy improvement for detailed actions. We also found that our method improves the

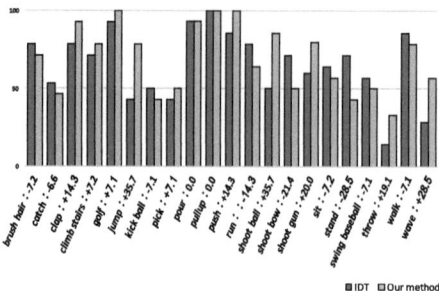

Fig. 3. Per class classification accuracy for J-HMDB dataset.

Table 2. Performance comparison of the proposed method in different settings.

Method	JHMDB	MPII
IDT-FV-LSTM	61.4	
Joint-FV-LSTM		63.4
(R-segmented+IDT)-FV-LSTM	**69.8**	**68.2**
(R-segmented with GT pose+IDT)-FV-LSTM	**73.5**	-

accuracy for transitional actions such as *open close cupboard* and *take put in oven* by over 10%. This shows the effectiveness of the LSTM for such challenging actions containing multiple sub-actions.

To evaluate the proposed method in detail, we conduct experiments in several settings. As shown in Table 2, using the body part region segmentation (R-segmented+IDT) improves the performance by a large margin. In addition, one can see the region segmentation with ground truth pose (R-segmented with GT pose+IDT) performs even better. This shows that the region segmentation has the potential for improvement if we can apply more precise pose estimation method. To compare with pose-based features, we also test the case using 2D joint positions themselves as features (Joint). The result shows the effectiveness of the proposed region segmentation over the pose-based representation.

5 Conclusions

We have proposed a novel action recognition framework based on trajectory features with body part region segmentation. Four body part regions (i.e. full body, left/right arm, and upper body) are segmented by the object detector and the pose estimator to enhance feature representation. From the segmented regions, we extract trajectory features using Improved Trajectories and encode them by Fisher Vector. The LSTM network takes the encoded features and provides class probabilities while considering long-term transitions. We evaluated the proposed framework on the J-HMDB and the MPII Cooking Activities benchmarks and showed performance improvements over previous approaches.

Acknowledgments. This work was partially supported by Aoyama Gakuin University-Supported Program "Early Eagle Program".

References

1. Cao, Z., Simon, T., Wei, S.E., Sheikh, Y.: Realtime multi-person 2D pose estimation using part affinity fields. In: CVPR (2017)
2. Chéron, G., Laptev, I., Schmid, C.: P-CNN: pose-based CNN features for action recognition. In: ICCV (2015)
3. Farnebäck, G.: Two-frame motion estimation based on polynomial expansion. In: Bigun, J., Gustavsson, T. (eds.) SCIA 2003. LNCS, vol. 2749, pp. 363–370. Springer, Heidelberg (2003). https://doi.org/10.1007/3-540-45103-X_50
4. Gkioxari, G., Malik, J.: Finding action tubes. In: CVPR (2015)
5. He, Y., Shirakabe, S., Satoh, Y., Kataoka, H.: Human action recognition without human. In: Hua, G., Jégou, H. (eds.) ECCV 2016. LNCS, vol. 9915, pp. 11–17. Springer, Cham (2016). https://doi.org/10.1007/978-3-319-49409-8_2
6. Hochreiter, S., Schmidhuber, J.: Long short-term memory. Neural Comput. **9**(8), 1735–1780 (1997)
7. Jhuang, H., Gall, J., Zuffi, S., Schmid, C., Black, M.J.: Towards understanding action recognition. In: ICCV (2013)
8. Kuehne, H., Jhuang, H., Garrote, E., Poggio, T., Serre, T.: HMDB: a large video database for human motion recognition. In: ICCV (2011)
9. Liu, W., et al.: SSD: single shot multibox detector. In: Leibe, B., Matas, J., Sebe, N., Welling, M. (eds.) ECCV 2016. LNCS, vol. 9905, pp. 21–37. Springer, Cham (2016). https://doi.org/10.1007/978-3-319-46448-0_2
10. Matikainen, P., Hebert, M., Sukthankar, R.: Trajectons: action recognition through the motion analysis of tracked features. In: ICCV Workshop (2009)
11. Peng, X., Zou, C., Qiao, Y., Peng, Q.: Action recognition with stacked fisher vectors. In: Fleet, D., Pajdla, T., Schiele, B., Tuytelaars, T. (eds.) ECCV 2014. LNCS, vol. 8693, pp. 581–595. Springer, Cham (2014). https://doi.org/10.1007/978-3-319-10602-1_38
12. Perronnin, F., Sánchez, J., Mensink, T.: Improving the fisher kernel for large-scale image classification. In: Daniilidis, K., Maragos, P., Paragios, N. (eds.) ECCV 2010. LNCS, vol. 6314, pp. 143–156. Springer, Heidelberg (2010). https://doi.org/10.1007/978-3-642-15561-1_11
13. Rohrbach, M., Amin, S., Andriluka, M., Schiele, B.: A database for fine grained activity detection of cooking activities. In: CVPR (2012)
14. Simonyan, K., Zisserman, A.: Two-stream convolutional networks for action recognition in videos. In: NIPS (2014)
15. Sun, J., Mu, Y., Yan, S., Cheong, L.F.: Activity recognition using dense long-duration trajectories. In: ICME (2010)
16. Sun, J., Wu, X., Yan, S., Cheong, L.F., Chua, T.S., Li, J.: Hierarchical spatio-temporal context modeling for action recognition. In: CVPR (2009)
17. Wang, H., Kläser, A., Schmid, C., Liu, C.L.: Action recognition by dense trajectories. In: CVPR (2011)
18. Wang, H., Schmid, C.: Action recognition with improved trajectories. In: ICCV (2013)
19. Wang, L., Qiao, Y., Tang, X.: Action recognition with trajectory-pooled deep-convolutional descriptors. In: CVPR (2015)

20. Wang, L., et al.: Temporal segment networks: towards good practices for deep action recognition. In: Leibe, B., Matas, J., Sebe, N., Welling, M. (eds.) ECCV 2016. LNCS, vol. 9912, pp. 20–36. Springer, Cham (2016). https://doi.org/10.1007/978-3-319-46484-8_2
21. Yamada, K., Yoshida, T., Sumi, K., Habe, H., Mitsugami, I.: Spatial and temporal segmented dense trajectories for gesture recognition. In: QCAV (2017)
22. Zhou, Y., Ni, B., Hong, R., Wang, M., Tian, Q.: Interaction part mining: a mid-level approach for fine-grained action recognition. In: CVPR (2015)

AI Aesthetics in Art and Media (AIAM)

Let AI Clothe You: Diversified Fashion Generation

Rajdeep H. Banerjee[✉], Anoop Rajagopal, Nilpa Jha, Arun Patro, and Aruna Rajan

Myntra Designs Pvt. Ltd., Bengaluru, India
{rajdeep.banerjee,anoop.kr,nilpa.jha,arun.patro,aruna.rajan}@myntra.com

Abstract. In this paper, we demonstrate automation of fashion assortment generation that appeals widely to consumer tastes given context in terms of attributes. We show how we trained generative adversarial networks to automatically generate an assortment given a fashion category (such as dresses and tops etc.) and its context (neck type, shape, color etc.), and describe the practical challenges we faced in terms of increasing assortment diversity. We explore different GAN architectures in context based fashion generation. We show that by providing context better quality images can be generated. Examples of taxonomy of design given a fashion article and finally automate generation of new designs that span the created taxonomy is shown. We also show a designer-in-loop process of taking a generated image to production level design templates (tech-packs). Here the designers bring their own creativity by adding elements, suggestive from the generated image, to accentuate the overall aesthetics of the final design.

Keywords: Fashion · GAN · Context

1 Introduction

Fashion is an interesting interplay of art and science - where science (data) informs us as to the customer's choice, art aims to create aesthetics with wide appeal that has relevance to the times we live in. Building fashion merchandise involves stocking customer needs and keeping a healthy long tail of merchandise that appeals to diverse aesthetics. Therefore, it is not enough to merely study what sells more to exploit the design process into making more of it, but also explore and create a diverse range of styles.

To appeal to a wide range of tastes in fashion - of the masses, as well as of fashionistas, fashion catalogs need week on week revisions, given the ephemeral nature of trends, and shifting consumer habits. How can we achieve this at scale, in a completely data driven way? Can we automate the process of design selection, and allow our human designers to focus on creative exploration over sorting through what has been done before to borrow elements? How can we inspire our designers by creating a base template of diverse designs, and allow them to innovate on top? We show how automated clothes design using generative adversarial networks (GANs) [3] - the promise of AI [6,12] - can be realised to the fullest to solve these problems.

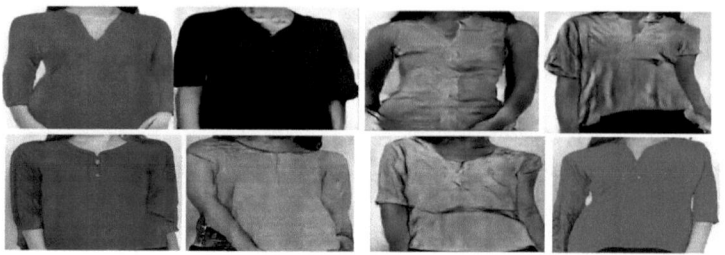

Fig. 1. Fashion generation with DC-GAN (Color figure online)

Tops:
{"type":["regular","bardot","tank",...."a-line"] , "length":["cropped","regular","longline"] , "neck":["round","v-neck","boat","polo"] , "pattern":["checked","solid","printed","stripes"], "sleeve length": ["short", "long", "sleeveless" , "three-quarter"]}

Dresses:
{"shape":["a-line","fit and flare","bodycon",....] , "length":["mini","maxi","midi"] , "neck":["round","v-neck","boat","halter"] , "pattern":["checked","solid","printed","stripes"], "sleeve length": ["short", "long", "sleeveless" , "three-quarter"]}

Fig. 2. Tops & Dresses taxonomy

To begin with, we use DC-GAN framework [6,7] and train with our catalogue images to produce images of fashion articles shown in Fig. 1. Many duplicates were observed, and also GAN generated images resembled our existing catalog too closely. For example (see Fig. 1), we observe many red/pink outfits in similar neck type and sleeve lengths. This resulted in producing more of what we already have, and added less diversity to our mix of fashion assortment. Also most of the images generated were hard to interpret by designers. For instance in second row third image from left of Fig. 1 shows a style with half sleeves on right hand and short/cap sleeves on the left. This leads to an ambiguity in designers mind on what sleeves should be used. Hence, can we make the design process efficient in capturing both the popular elements of fashion through some context and the longer tail of diverse tastes?

In this work, we explore fashion generation with context (in terms of class attributes/text) to address this problem of generating a wider taxonomy of designs. We come out with an exhaustive list of taxonomy of design attributes curated by fashion designers. We use this taxonomy as context and explore two approaches: (1) AC-GAN [5] modified for multi-label classification and (2) Attention-GAN [14] where we use these attributes as text input to the network.

Approach (1) provided good results for coarse attributes present in Fig. 2. However, it is observed that fine grained attributes in a fashion image is most often present in the accompanying text description. Hence we use approach (2) to generate fashion images with fine grained text appended with coarse attributes present in the catalog.

We propose to use a conditional and Attention GAN [14] framework using the fashion attributes/text for every fashion article type, so that we maintain the diversity of the catalogued assortment by providing context in the generation process. We exploit descriptive text to generate a diverse assortment, by focussing the generative network onto important (attention) regions in the input images. This is a powerful technique as we demonstrate, because together with our work described in the later sections, it can be used to create a rich corpus of text to image mappings, and learn regions of interest that descriptive text of images refer to, eventually enabling text based generation of images. Visualize a scenario where a consumer of fashion can specify their wish as: "I want to wear a classy dress to attend a business dinner, the neckline should be conservative, yet not boring - and the prints and pattern should represent *bhil art* [1] - from

Fig. 3. Tops types examples.

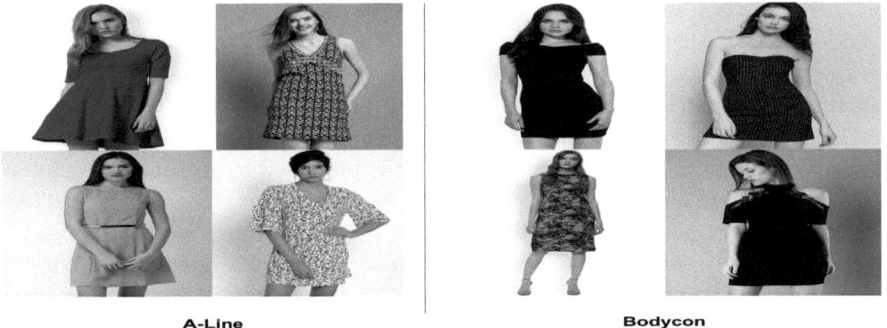

Fig. 4. Dress shapes examples.

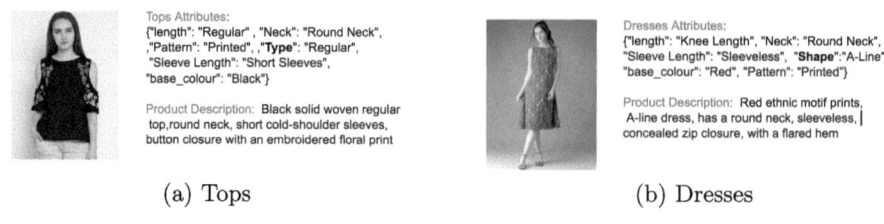

(a) Tops (b) Dresses

Fig. 5. Sample text description for tops and dresses (Color figure online)

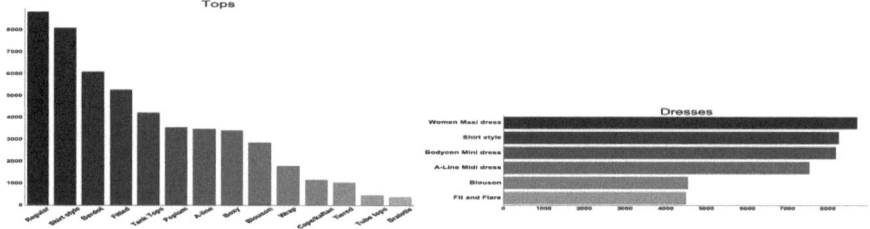

Fig. 6. Data distribution by taxonomy.

the region I belong to," and our fashion generation model can generate images of possible interest to the consumer given her description. This would not only solve the discovery problem in fashion retail for consumers, but also greatly simplify supply chain processes, that need a 3–6 month long predictive planning process and rely on a customer getting interested in a garment over mapping what the customer has in mind and manufacturing exactly that.

2 Related Work

Generation of fashion articles using generative models has generated a lot of interest [6,12]. In [12] a VAE/GAN is proposed to generate article types wherein the fashion image is first encoded using Variational Auto Encoders (VAE) and encoded data is then passed as input to GAN to learn its distribution.

In [6], DCGAN [7] was used to generate clothes and a practical system of taking it to production was evaluated with a human in-loop. [15] explores generation by separating components of a fashion article into texture, colour, and shape. In [2] a neural-style transfer approach is proposed to personalize and generate new fashion clothes. A system used to recommend styles to users and also aid the design of new products that matches user preferences is proposed in [4]. In [18] a two stage approach is proposed to generate new fashion based on design coding (using text) and a segmentation map. GANs have shown great results in generating sharper context through text. New image generation conditioned on text descriptions is explored in [10]. In [8,9,16,17] have encoded the whole text description into a global sentence vector as the condition for GAN-based image generation. This lacks in encoding fine grained information at the word level, which AttnGAN [14] addresses.

In our work, we propose to use a conditional and Attention GAN [14] framework using the fashion attributes/text for every fashion article type so that we maintain the practicality of the catalog assortment by providing context in the generation process.

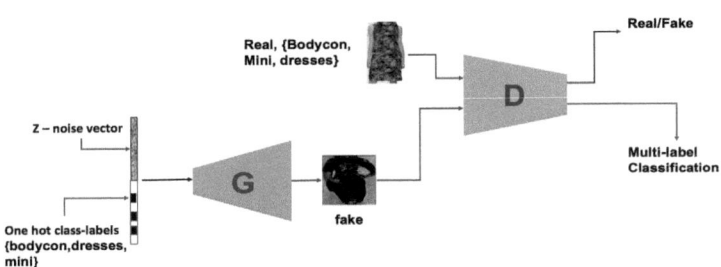

Fig. 7. Multi-label AC-GAN network.

3 Fashion Generation Using Taxonomy

Our dataset consists of images taken from a fashion e-commerce catalog for 2 major categories, women's tops and dresses. There are 50,630 images from Tops category and 62,236 images from Dresses category, all are front poses. The images are high resolution and are photographed under studio conditions. Additionally we have product descriptions and attribute provided for each image by an internal design team. We come up with a modified AC-GAN [5] which uses multi labeleled attribute tags for each image. For getting richer context through taxonomy we use product description along with the tags in the AttnGAN [14] framework. We talk more about the tags and description related taxonomy in the next section.

The term *fashion* encompasses substantial diversity in clothing apparel and accessories limited only by the stretch of imagination. Expressing this enormous complexity of visual experience in terms of well articulated distinctive classes is a challenging problem. In Fig. 2 we present the taxonomies of dresses and tops respectively. The tagged attributes represent high level features for the apparels as shown in Figs. 3 and 4, whereas the description has more fine grained details about the apparel. For example in Fig. 5, the description for the Tops image additionally tells it has *cold shouldered sleeves with a floral print*, whereas the tagged attribute *pattern* just tells us it is printed. For the red dress, we know from the description that the print is *ethnic motifs* and it has a *flared hemline*. Attribute tags usually contain a long tail, Fig. 6 shows the distribution of tops type and dress shape.

In our work, we explore attribute classes and text description as context using generative adversarial network (GAN) for fashion generation. For fashion generation with attribute classes we use the popular AC-GAN [5]. However, as a fashion image always come with multiple attributes (like round neck, printed, bardot Tops) we modify the AC-GAN softmax loss (for multi-class classification) with a multi-label soft margin loss for training that optimizes a multi-label one-versus-all loss based on max-entropy. Let x be an image and y_i^C be the one-hot encoding of multi-label representation where C is the total number of classes. Then loss function is given by

$$loss(x,y) = -\sum_i y_i \log((1+exp(-x_i))^{-1}) + (1-y_i)\log\left(\frac{exp(-x_i)}{1+exp(-x_i)}\right) \quad (1)$$

We then use this Multi-label AC-GAN (network architecture in Fig. 7) for fashion generation using attributes. However, as mentioned earlier, attribute tagging is a cumbersome process and most e-commerce sites only give coarse attributes. Hence we use the fine grained descriptions often provided in the text additionally with attributes (used as text instead of classes) to generate fashion images. To this end, we use Attn-GAN [14]. Attentional Generative Adversarial Network (AttnGAN) allows attention-driven, multi-stage refinement for fine-grained text-to-image generation. We describe how we create dataset to run AttnGAN in the next section.

4 Experiments

For a robust learning of the generative network we do augmentation of the training images, artificially creating more samples through scale change, adding noise etc. In all our experiments, we generate images of size 256 × 256.

In the multi-label AC-GAN network we use DC-GAN network architecture [7] for the generator and discriminator adding more up-sampling and down-sampling blocks to generate images at 256 × 256 pixels. We trained our network with an ADAM optimizer with learning rate = 0.0008, $\beta_1 = 0.9$ and one sided label smoothing [11] in the discriminator.

For fine grained image to text synthesis we use product descriptions in addition to coarse attribute tags in the AttnGAN [14] framework. As we had only one caption (description) per image, we augmented the descriptions per image. Within a category (for eg., dresses) for each image we take its coarse attribute key-value (see Fig. 2) combinations to form *attribute-classes*. Among all possible such classes we consider those with at least 3 images. Then for an image we randomly sample descriptions from the *attribute class* corresponding to that image, thus ensuring we augment descriptions including color from related images as in Fig. 8.

Original Description: (1 caption)
off-white and black striped top has a v-neck three-quarter sleeves with lace detail

Post augmentation: (3 captions)
1. off- white v-neck regular horizontal stripe regular regular sleeve three-quarter sleeve off-white black stripe top v-neck three-quarter sleeve lace detail
2. white v-neck regular stripe regular regular sleeve three-quarter sleeve white navy knit stripe top v-neck three-quarter sleeve
3. white v-neck regular horizontal stripe regular regular sleeve three-quarter sleeve white navy knit top stylised stripe v-neck three-quarter sleeve

Fig. 8. Augmented image captions

For the attention model we use a 3 stage Generator-Discriminator architecture as in [14]. For the DAMSM loss [14] we use $\lambda = 10$, image and text embedding dimension as 256 and 3 captions per image.

For a quantitative evaluation of our models we use Inception Score [11]. The intuition behind this metric is that good models should generate diverse but meaningful images. We compare outputs of the two generative models (sample images in Figs. 9, 10 and 11) using Inception Score [11], see Table 1. We see that multi-label AC-GAN even with coarse attributes has scores similar to AttnGAN, indicating a multi-label classifier in the discriminator is a good approach for context based generation.

To quantitatively evaluate image similarity we use multiscale structural similarity (MS-SSIM) [13]. MS-SSIM is a multi-scale variant of a well-characterized perceptual similarity metric that attempts to discount aspects of an image that are not important for human perception. MS-SSIM values range between 0.0 and 1.0; higher MS-SSIM values correspond to 'perceptually more similar images. We measure the MS-SSIM scores between 50 randomly chosen pairs of images within a given class for Multi-Label ACGAN model and same text attributes for the AttnGAN model, see Table 1. Figure 11 shows samples of image variants generated using the same fine grained text attribute. We also experiment to see how interpolating, as in [7], between 2 generated images helps in synthesizing new designs as shown in Fig. 12. The results in general are aesthetically well formed and additionally add to the variability of the generated outputs.

The above evaluations though talk about diversity and quality of data generated, they are not of use much in practice. In order to manufacture these type of newly generated styles, they need to be converted into what is called a "Tech pack". A tech pack is vital to production and a fashion designer spends good amount of time generating them. Tech pack contains sketches of the actual design and also some design elements added. This is where designer brings his inspiration and creativity to convert a generated image into an aesthetic sketch that can be taken to production.

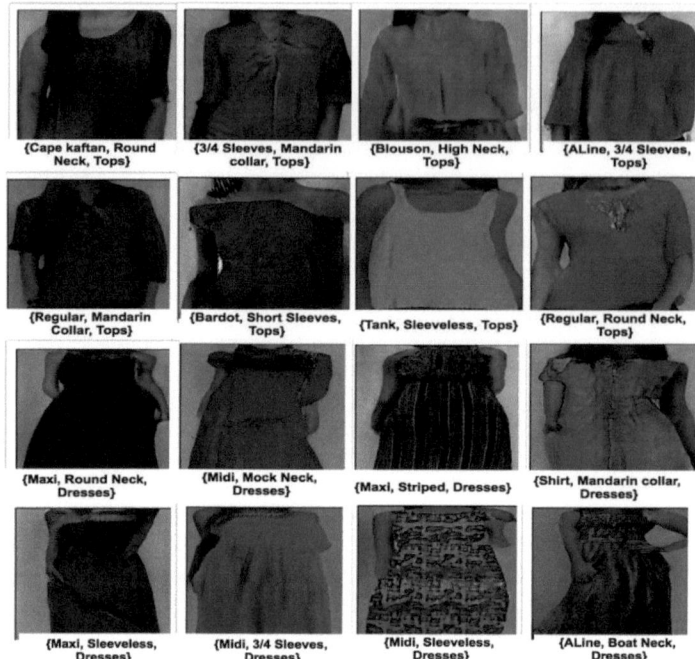

Fig. 9. MultiLabel-ACGAN Generation. Labels used for generation shown below images

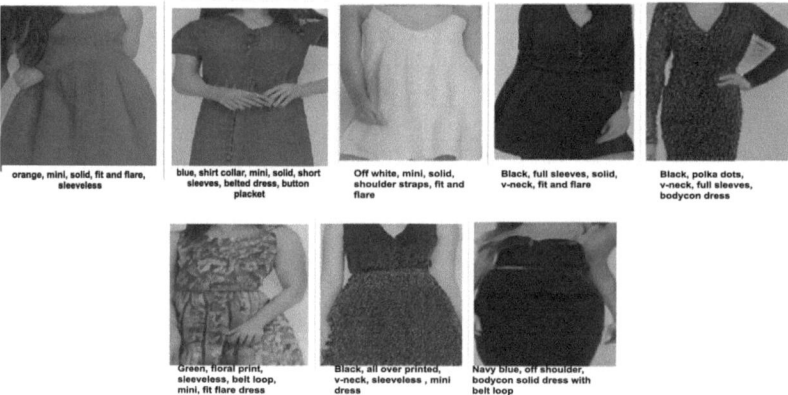

Fig. 10. Attention GAN Generation. Captions used for generation shown for above images

Figures 13 and 14 shows instances wherein the generated reference image is taken to a sketch detail and physical aesthetics are added in accordance with generated image by designers thought and inspiration. In Fig. 13 we a contrast center patch is added in accordance with reference image and in Fig. 14 a front

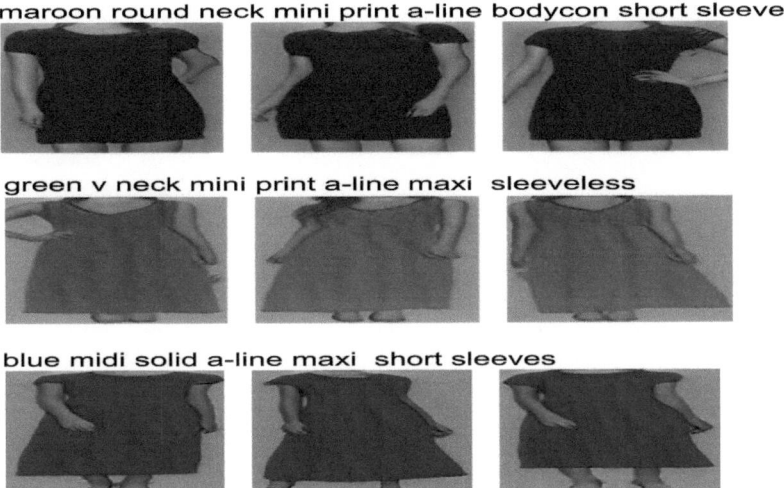

Fig. 11. Attention GAN Generation. Image variants generated with the same set of captions

Table 1. Inception and MSSIM score

Model	Inception score	MS-SSIM score
Multi-label AC-GAN	2.86 ± 0.133	0.15 ± 0.004
AttnGAN	2.96 ± 0.306	0.37 ± 0.007
Training dataset	3.46 ± 0.134	0.22 ± 0.006

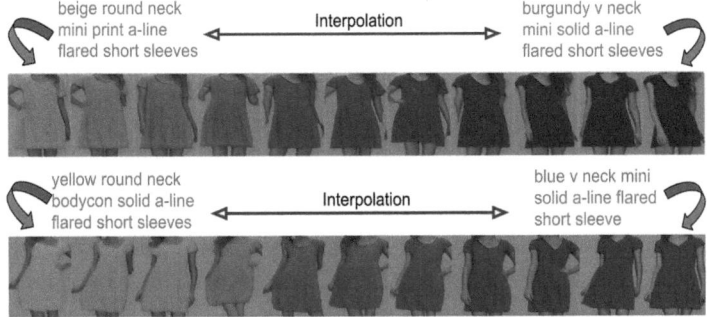

Fig. 12. Interpolation results between first and last images of each row

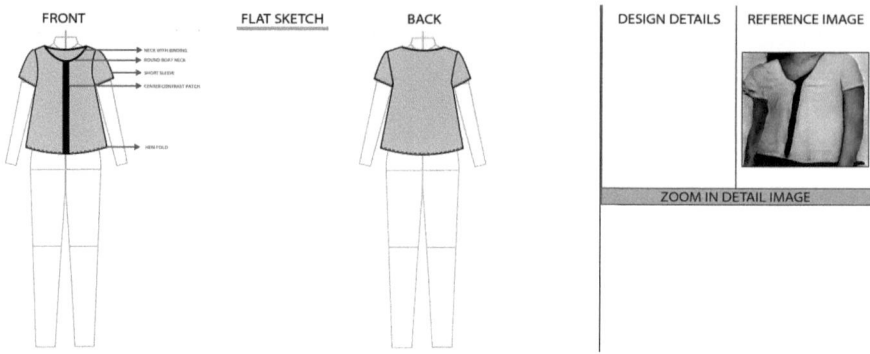

Fig. 13. Tech pack for Tops. The reference image refers to generated images from our approach. Flat sketch is the actual image which goes for manufacturing. We observe the interpretation of center patch adding to the aesthetics

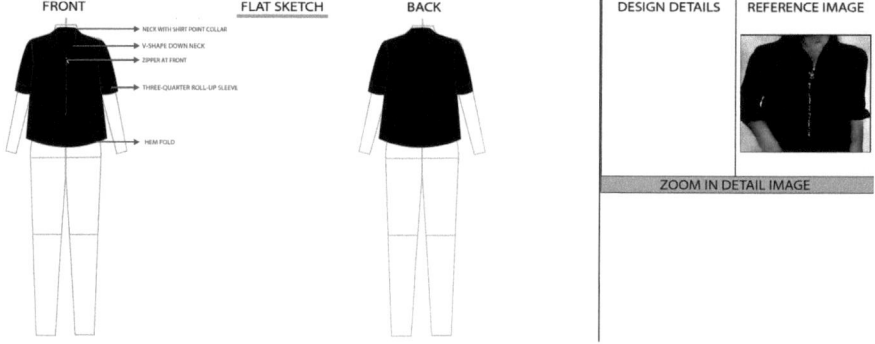

Fig. 14. Tech pack for Tops. The reference image refers to generated images from our approach. Flat sketch is the actual image which goes for manufacturing. The aesthetics is improved by the adding of zipper at the front which is indicative from the reference images.

zipper is added as a design element. Similarly in Figs. 15 and 16 we see tech packs for dresses. Notice the elasticated belt in Fig. 15 added by the designer to accentuate the looks which is vaguely indicated in the reference generated image. On the other hand in Fig. 16 there is a concealed zip added which is not visible. These calls on emphasizing the looks of the reference image is purely a designer call based on their experience but suggestive from the generated reference images. Thus it can be easily emphasized that Fashion generation with generative models enhances and eases the inspiration that a designer can obtain in creating aesthetic tech packs for manufacturing in fashion domain.

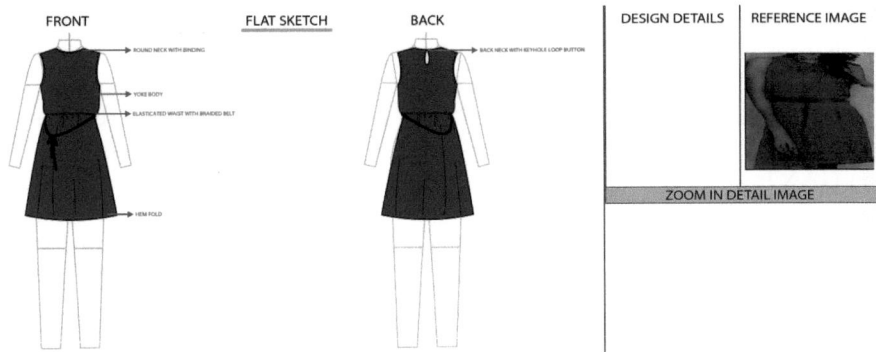

Fig. 15. Tech pack for dress. The reference image refers to generated images from our approach. Flat sketch is the actual image which goes for manufacturing. We observe the how the elasticated belt is added making the generated image aesthetic.

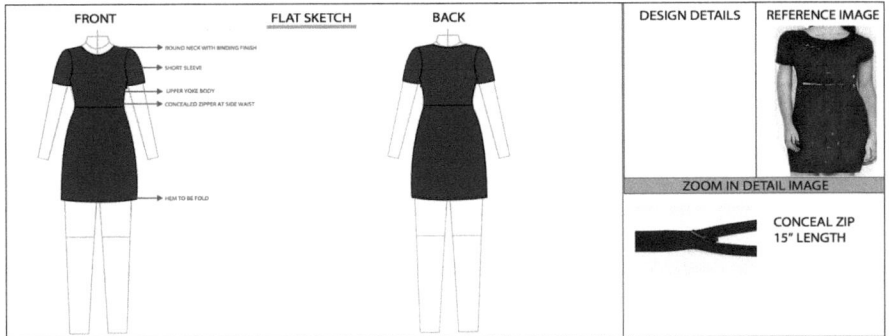

Fig. 16. Tech pack for dress. The reference image refers to generated images from our approach. Flat sketch is the actual image which goes for manufacturing. Addition of concealed zip (not visible) adds to aesthetics of style.

5 Conclusion

In this work, we have propose a contextual way of generating fashion articles using taxonomy/text. We have explored generation using coarse high level attributes in a multi-label setting as well as fine grained text descriptions in an attention setting. Both approaches aid in providing a better assortment in terms of addressing popular demand and the longer tail of diverse tastes and have an interesting byproduct of generating text to regions of interest mapping in images that can be further exploited for automated generation. We use the inception score as a metric for model evaluation and note that both models are close, with the attention model performing slightly better in some cases where the articles needed design details.

Our work has far reaching consequences for automated design generation, which has so far focused on automatically generating by training on given images as in [6], or training by separating components of a fashion article into texture, colour, and shape as in [15]. We exploit all fashion descriptions to auto generate images by following a region of interest detection based attention GAN framework. We plan to extend our mapping to include other crawled images/descriptors, social media content, and other user generated content on our platform to make the mappings richer, and the generative process catering to a wide range of fashion tastes.

References

1. The bhils - bhil art. http://bhilart.com/
2. Date, P., Ganesan, A., Oates, T.: Fashioning with networks: neural style transfer to design clothes. Machine Learning meets fashion, KDD (2017)
3. Goodfellow, I., et al.: Generative adversarial nets. In: Advances in Neural Information Processing Systems, pp. 2672–2680 (2014)
4. Kang, W.C., Fang, C., Wang, Z., McAuley, J.: Visually-aware fashion recommendation and design with generative image models. In: ICDM (2017)
5. Odena, A., Olah, C., Shlens, J.: Conditional image synthesis with auxiliary classifier GANs. In: Proceedings of the 34th International Conference on Machine Learning, vol. 70, pp. 2642–2651 (2017)
6. Osone, H., Kato, N., Sato, D., Muramatsu, N., Ochiai, Y.: Crowdsourcing clothes design directed by adversarial neural networks. In: 2017 Workshop Machine Learning for Creativity and Design. NIPS (2017)
7. Radford, A., Metz, L., Chintala, S.: Unsupervised representation learning with deep convolutional generative adversarial networks. arXiv preprint arXiv:1511.06434 (2015)
8. Reed, S., Akata, Z., Yan, X., Logeswaran, L., Schiele, B., Lee, H.: Generative adversarial text to image synthesis. arXiv preprint arXiv:1605.05396 (2016)
9. Reed, S.E., Akata, Z., Mohan, S., Tenka, S., Schiele, B., Lee, H.: Learning what and where to draw. In: Advances in Neural Information Processing Systems, pp. 217–225 (2016)
10. Rostamzadeh, N., et al.: Fashion-Gen: the generative fashion dataset and challenge. arXiv preprint arXiv:1806.08317 (2018)
11. Salimans, T., Goodfellow, I., Zaremba, W., Cheung, V., Radford, A., Chen, X.: Improved techniques for training GANs. In: Advances in Neural Information Processing Systems, pp. 2234–2242 (2016)
12. Torres, TJ.: Deep style: inferring the unknown to predict the future of fashion (2015). https://multithreaded.stitchfix.com/blog/2015/09/17/deep-style/
13. Wang, Z., Bovik, A.C., Sheikh, H.R., Simoncelli, E.P.: Image quality assessment: from error visibility to structural similarity. IEEE Trans. Image Process. **13**(4), 600–612 (2004)
14. Xu, T., et al.: AttnGAN: fine-grained text to image generation with attentional generative adversarial networks. In: ICCV (2017)
15. Yildirim, G., Seward, C., Bergmann, U.: Disentangling multiple conditional inputs in GANs. arXiv preprint arXiv:1806.07819 (2018)

16. Zhang, H., et al.: StackGAN: text to photo-realistic image synthesis with stacked generative adversarial networks. arXiv preprint (2017)
17. Zhang, H., et al.: StackGAN++: realistic image synthesis with stacked generative adversarial networks. arXiv preprint arXiv:1710.10916 (2017)
18. Zhu, S., Fidler, S., Urtasun, R., Lin, D., Loy, C.C.: Be your own prada: fashion synthesis with structural coherence. arXiv preprint arXiv:1710.07346 (2017)

Word-Conditioned Image Style Transfer

Yu Sugiyama and Keiji Yanai[✉]

Department of Informatics, The University of Electro-Communications, Tokyo,
1-5-1 Chofugaoka, Chofu-shi, Tokyo 182-8585, Japan
{sugiya-y,yanai}@mm.inf.uec.ac.jp

Abstract. In recent years, deep learning has attracted attention not only as a method on image recognition but also as a technique for image generation and transformation. Above all, a method called Style Transfer is drawing much attention which can integrate two photos into one integrated photo regarding their content and style. Although many extended works including Fast Style Transfer have been proposed so far, all the extended methods including original one require a style image to modify the style of an input image. In this paper, we propose to use words expressing photo styles instead of using style images for neural image style transfer. In our method, we take into account the content of an input image to be stylized to decide a style for style transfer in addition to a given word. We implemented the propose method by modifying the network for arbitrary neural artistic stylization. By the experiments, we show that the proposed method has ability to change the style of an input image taking account of both a given word.

1 Introduction

In recent years, deep learning has attracted attention not only as a method on image recognition but also as a technique for image generation and transformation. Above all, a technology called Neural Style Transfer proposed by Gatys et al. [3] is drawing much attention as a method to synthesize an image which has the style of a given style image and the content of a given content image using a Convolutional Neural Network (CNN). However, the original method takes relatively longer time (typically several minutes) for stylizing images. Thus, many extended methods of Neural Style Transfer for fast stylization have been proposed so far. The most representative one is Fast Style Transfer proposed by Johnson et al. [7] which employs an encoder-decoder network with residual blocks for real-time image transfer instead of an optimization-based method of the original one. However, all the extended methods including both original one and fast one require to prepare a style image for image stylization.

For practical point of view, preparing style images are not always easy for every user, especially on the setting of using for smart-phone applications. A user usually have to selects a style from limited numbers of the images pre-registered in the system. Instead, words can be easily provided to the system, even when using smartphone applications, via on-screen keyboards or voice recognition.

Then, in this paper, we propose to use words representing photo styles instead of using style images for neural image style transfer. In our method, we take into account the content of an input image to decide a transferred style in addition to a given word. We implemented the propose method by modifying the network for arbitrary neural artistic stylization [4] which enabled real-time arbitrary style transfer. We added a new sub-network which generates a style conditional vector from a given word. To train a sub-network, we used adversarial training instead of using a standard L2 loss. By the experiments, we show that the proposed method has ability to change the style of an input image according to given words.

Note that the combination of text-based style image search and an arbitrary style transfer network can possibly achieve the same objective of ours. The advantage of our method over it is expected that a mixed style can be transferred automatically when an unknown style word which is not included in the training dataset is given.

2 Related Work

Many works on neural style transfer have been proposed so far. In this section, we explain the original method [3] and the fast-version of neural style transfer [7]. In addition, we describe some multiple style methods and fast arbitrary style methods including arbitrary neural artistic stylization [4] which is a base method we extend in this paper.

Fig. 1. An example of style transfer which integrates the content of a content image and the style of a style image.

2.1 Neural Style Transfer

Neural Image Style Transfer using Convolutional Neural Networks (CNN) proposed by Gatys et al. [3] is the first method of CNN-based image style transfer.

In this method, given a style image and a content image, they generate a stylized image by optimizing an output image by minimizing the loss functions regarding both CNN activations of a content image and Gram matrix of a style image. It generates a stylized image by keeping the content of a content image and the style of a style image. For example, by integrating the content of a night church photo and the style of Gogh's starry night, we obtain a church painting in the style of Gogh as shown in Fig. 1. This method enables us to modify the style of an image keeping the content of the image easily. It replaces the information which are degraded while the signal of the content image goes forward through the CNN layers with style information extracted from the style image, and reconstructs a new image which has the same content as a given content images and the same style as a given style image.

In this method, they introduced "style matrix" which was presented by Gram matrix of CNN activations, that is, correlation matrix between feature maps in CNN. Recently, it is indicated that a style feature which represents the style of an image is not only a Gram matrix of feature maps but also various kinds of statistics which represents the distributions of feature maps such as a combination of a mean and variance of each element of feature maps [8]. Since the original method proposed by Gatys et al. employs an optimization-based method for image generation, and requires both forward and backward computation iteratively to synthesize a stylized image, the processing time tends to be longer (several minutes) even using a GPU.

In this method, they optimized the sum of the content loss function (Eq. 1) and the style loss function (Eq. 4) by iteratively updating an output image. They calculated losses with VGG19 [10] without FC layers as a CNN feature extractor. The content loss function is shown below. $\boldsymbol{x}_c$ and $\boldsymbol{x}_o$ represents CNN feature vectors of an original input image and a generated image, and $F^l(\boldsymbol{x})$ are the feature representation of $\boldsymbol{x}$ in Layer l of the VGG network.

$$L_{content}(\boldsymbol{x}_c, \boldsymbol{x}_o, l) = \frac{1}{2}||F^l(\boldsymbol{x}_c) - F^l(\boldsymbol{x}_o)||^2 \tag{1}$$

We define a Gram matrix of a CNN feature vector, F^l, as G^l which represents the style of an image. The style loss function is the sum of L2 losses between a gram matrix of a given style image and a gram matrix of the generated image over multiple layers.

$$G^l(\boldsymbol{x}) = (F^l(\boldsymbol{x}))(F^l(\boldsymbol{x}))^T \tag{2}$$

$$E_l(\boldsymbol{x}_s, \boldsymbol{x}_o) = \frac{1}{4N_l^2 M_l^2} \sum_{i,j} (G^l(\boldsymbol{x}_s) - G^l(\boldsymbol{x}_o))^2 \tag{3}$$

$$L_{style}(\boldsymbol{x}_s, \boldsymbol{x}_o) = \sum_{l=0}^{L} E_l(\boldsymbol{x}_s, \boldsymbol{x}_o) \tag{4}$$

$$L_{total}(\boldsymbol{x}_c, \boldsymbol{x}_s, \boldsymbol{x}_o) = \alpha L_{content}(\boldsymbol{x}_c, \boldsymbol{x}_o) + \beta L_{style}(\boldsymbol{x}_s, \boldsymbol{x}_o) \tag{5}$$

It requires long time to optimize the pair of content image and style image. It is impossible to generate an image in instantly. The solution of this problem is Fast Style Transfer which employs an encoder-decoder network.

2.2 Fast Style Transfer

Fast Neural Style Transfer [7] achieved an instant style transfer with a pre-trained encoder-decoder network which enables real-time style transfer by one-time feed-forward computation. Basically the loss functions are the same as optimization-based method by Gatys et al. [3]. In fast style transfer, an encoder-decoder network is optimized instead of optimizing output images.

To accelerate neural style transfer, several works using feed-forward style transfer networks which require only one-time feed-forward computation to realize style transfer have been published so far [7,13].

Johnson et al. proposed a perceptual loss to train a encoder-decoder network as a feed-forward style transfer network [7]. Their network can generate a stylized image for a given content image regarding consists of down-sampling layers, convolutional layers and up-sampling layers, which accepts an content image and outputs an synthesized image integrated with a fixed pre-trained style in real-time.

2.3 Multiple Style Transfer

Although Johnson et al.'s feed-forward network can treat only one fixed style, recently Dumoulin et al. [2] proposed a method to learn multiple styles with an encoder-decoder fast style transfer network. They used conditional version of Instance Normalization [14] instead of Batch Normalization [6] for normalization of activation signals, and they proposed to replace scale and bias parameters of instance normalization layers depending on the styles. They call this as "conditional instance normalization". Although they showed that the fast style network where all the batch normalization layers were replaced with the conditional instance normalization layers had ability to learn 32 artistic styles at the same time, the transferable styles are limited to trained styles and their mixtures.

The other approach on multiple style transfer is "Conditional Fast Style Neural Network" proposed by Yanai [15]. The idea on introducing conditions for style selection is similar to Demoulin et al. Dumoulin et al. introduced a new special layer, "conditional instance normalization" layer, while Yanai added an additional input signal which is concatenated with an internal activation signal and we introduced one additional 1×1 convolution layer to integrate an internal signal and a style signal. They use only common layers in the proposed networks. In addition, in their method, to mix multiple styles, they just assign weight values to the multiple elements of the conditional input vector such as $(0.2, 0.3, 0.1, 0.4)$.

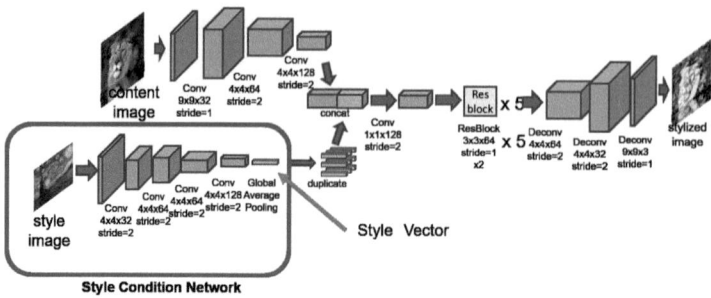

Fig. 2. Unseen Style Transfer Network [15].

2.4 Unseen/Arbitrary Style Transfer

More recently, a fast arbitrary style transfer method which can transfer even untrained styles has been proposed by Chen et al. [1]. They obtained feature map activations of a given content image and a given style image by VGG16, modify the feature maps by swapping each content activation patch with its closet-matching style patch, and generate a stylized image using the pre-trained inverse network which reconstructs a stylized image from the feature maps of the swapped activations. Their method is much faster than the original method by Gatys et al. [3]. However, it takes more than one second to generate a stylized image, since style swapping is a little bit complicated processing.

Yanai [15] propose a feed-forward network for arbitrary style transfer by extending "conditional fast style transfer network" (Fig. 2). In his method, mixing of trained multiple styles is possible by providing mixed conditional weights of the different styles. From these characteristics of the conditional style transfer, he came up with the idea that training of many styles and mixing of them might bring arbitrary style transfer. To do that, a conditional network is suitable, since it can accept a real-value conditional input the dimension of which can be fixed regardless of the number of training styles.

They found that it was possible by connecting a network which generates a conditional signal from a style image directly to the conditional input of a conditional style transfer network. They trained the conditional style transfer network with a style condition generator network in an end-to-end manner, and showed that it worked as arbitrary style network. The basic idea for arbitrary style transfer is different from [1]. The architecture is simpler than theirs, since the network is trained in an end-to-end manner and generates a stylized image from a content image and a style image directly by one-time feed-forward computation.

Ghiasi et al. proposed an arbitrary neural artistic stylization network [4] (Fig. 3). The idea of this network is similar to [15]. The difference is that this network generates parameters of instance normalization layers directly by a style condition generator network. This can be regarded as an extension of the multiple style network employing conditional instance normalization [2]. The quality of

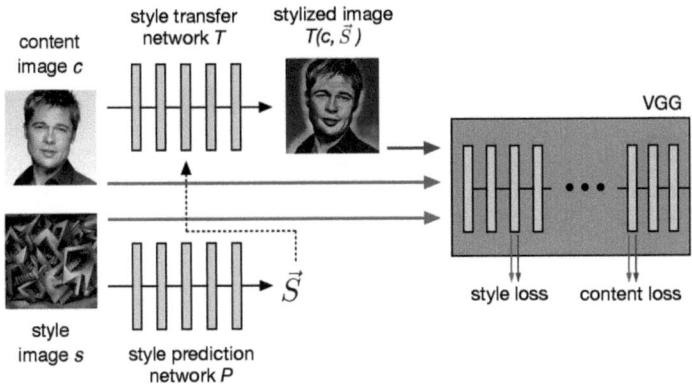

Fig. 3. Arbitrary neural artistic stylization network [4].

stylization is superior to "Unseen Style Network" [15] since it generates all the instance normalization parameters depending on given style images instead of simple concatenation of conditional vectors.

In this paper, we use an arbitrary neural artistic stylization network [4] as a base network, and extend it so as to achieve word-based style transfer. To say it concretely, we replace the part of a Style Prediction Network (SPN) in the network with a Style Selector Network (SSN) which generates a conditional signal from a given word. Note that we made pre-liminary experiments with "Unseen Style Transfer Network" [15] as well. It turned out that the arbitrary neural artistic stylization network [4] was more appropriate for our purpose.

3 Proposed Method

3.1 Overview

In the proposed method, we replace the part of a Style Prediction Network (SPN) in the arbitrary neural artistic stylization network [4] with a newly-introduced Word-based Style Selector Network (SSN) as shown in Fig. 4.

We use the arbitrary stylization network pre-trained with various kinds of content images and style images according to [4] as a base network. The arbitrary stylization network consists two networks: The main network is a style transfer network which is based on Conv-Deconv network with Residual Block proposed by Johnson et al. [7]. Note that all the batch normalization layers in the Johnson-style network were replaced with conditional instance normalization layers. The additional one is a style prediction network (SPN) which generates parameters of instance normalization layers. Conditional instance normalization normalizes each unit's activation z as

$$z = \gamma_s \frac{z - \mu}{\sigma} + \beta_s \qquad (6)$$

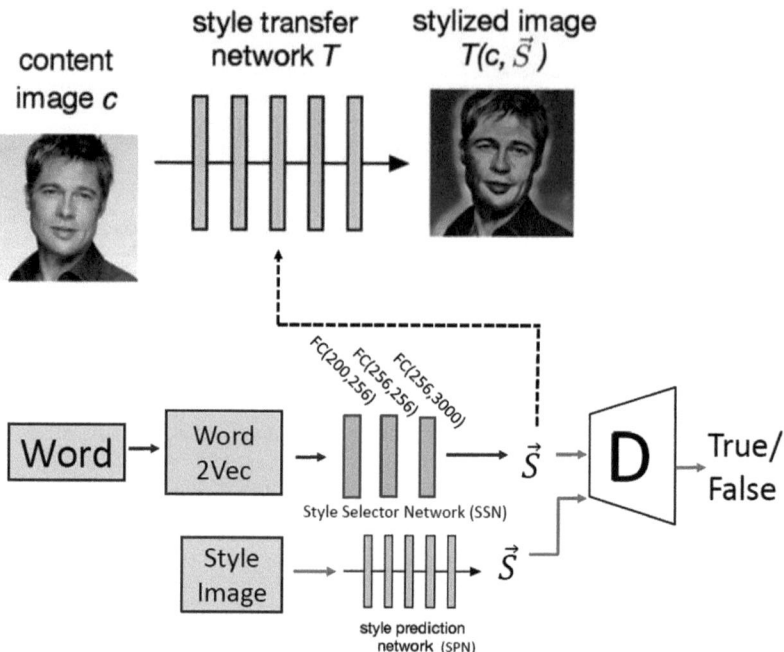

Fig. 4. The arbitrary stylization network with Style Selector Network (SSN) with adversarial training. In the figure, D represents the discriminator which classifies style vectors generated from SSN from style vectors generated from SPN.

where μ and σ are the mean and standard deviation across the spatial axes in an activation map [2]. γ_s and β_s constitute a linear transformation that specify the learned mean (β_s) and learned standard deviation (γ_s) of the unit. This linear transformation is unique to each style s. In particular, the concatenation $\tilde{S} = \gamma_s, \beta_s$ constitutes a roughly 3000-d embedding vector, a style vector, representing the style. SPN consists of a pre-trained Inception-v3 [11] and two additional fully-connected layers.

In the proposed network, we introduce Word-based Style Selector Network (SSN). We train the SSN using word-annotated style training images so that the output signal of the SSN approximates the output of the pre-trained SPN. To make the distribution of the output of SSN closer to the one of the output of SPN, we use adversarial training [5] instead of standard L2 minimization. An input of the SSN is a word embedding vector of a given word represented by Word2Vec, and the output is a style vector the dimension of which is roughly 3000.

3.2 Word Embedding

In the proposed method, we need to convert a word to a vector to provide it into the Style Selector Network. To do that, we use Word2Vec [9]. In the experiments, we used Japanese adjective words for representing Photo Style. Therefore we trained the Word2Vec model using open Japanese WikiPedia data containing many Japanese adjective expressions after pre-processing including removing low-frequency words and non-independent words which are neither nouns, adjectives nor verbs. We convert a given input word into a 200-dim word embedding vector with the trained Word2Vec model.

3.3 Style Selector Network

The Style Selector Network (SSN) (Fig. 4) generates a style vector corresponding to a given word expressing an image style instead of the Style Prediction Network (Fig. 3) which generates a style vector from a style input image in the original arbitrary stylization network.

The SSN takes a 200-d work embedding vector of a given word as an input. SSN consists of three fully-connected (FC) layers in Fig. 4. Note that each of the FC layers has a ReLU activation function and a Batch Normalization layer after it.

For training the SSN, we use the trained Style Prediction Network (SPN) which is originally a part of the arbitrary stylization network to generate ground-truth style vectors of training samples as shown in Fig. 4. For all the training word-annotated style images, we extract style vectors, s_i, using the trained SPN, and we obtain a 200-d word embedding vector, w_i, by Word2Vec. An input of the SSN is a word embedding vector of a given word represented by Word2Vec, and the output is a style vector the dimension of which is roughly 3000.

Although we can train the SSN by minimize a L2 loss function, to make the distribution of the output of SSN closer to the one of the output of SPN, we use adversarial training [5]. For adversarial training, we prepare a discriminator, D, which classifies style vectors generated from SSN from style vectors generated from SPN. SSN and D are trained alternatively so that D can discriminate them correctly and SSN can generate word-based style vectors which D classifies as image-based style vectors SPN generated. D consists of four FC layers each of which has batch normalization layers and ReLU after it except the last layer. The adversarial loss function is as follows:

$$L_{adv} = \mathbb{E}_{x \sim P_{data}(x)}[\log D(SPN(x))] + \mathbb{E}_{w \sim P_{data}(w)}[\log(1 - D(SSN(w)))] \quad (7)$$

where x and w represent a style image and a style word, respectively. We minimize this loss function for training of SSN, while we maximize this for training of the discriminator, D, i.e. $\min_{SSN} \max_D L_{adv}$. Note that SPN is the pre-trained model and kept fixed while training.

At the time of transformation of images, we remove SPN and the discriminator, and insert the SSN instead. We use the whole network as a word-based style transfer network which takes a word and an image as inputs.

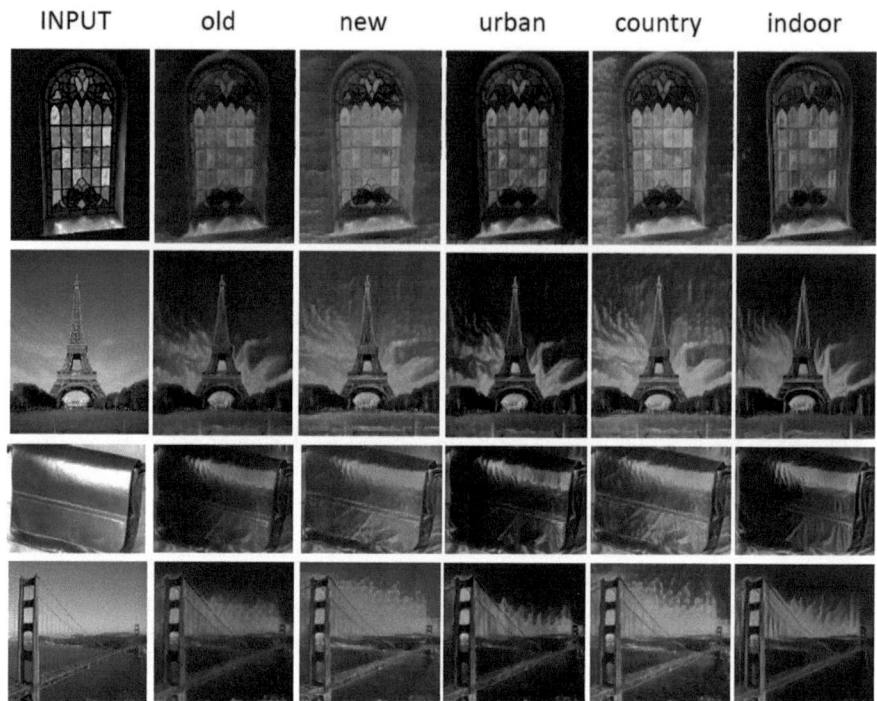

Fig. 5. The word-based stylized results with adversarial training.

4 Experiments

To train the Style Selector Network, we need to prepare style images with words expressing their styles. We select 500,000 images annotated with adjective words randomly from the Yahoo Flickr Creative Commons 100 Million Dataset (YFCC100M) [12] which are made of Creative Commoms images in the Flickr database. Note that we used the official pre-trained model of the arbitrary stylization network including the trained parameters of both a style transfer network and a style prediction network (SPN) available from the GitHub[1].

We made experiments with the trained network. Figure 5 shows the results by the model trained with 500,000 YFCC100M images for five words, "old", "new", "urban", "country" and "indoor". The styles were changed depending on style words, and all the images were stylized in the same way for the same word. In fact, we generated style vectors directly from only words. Therefore, the correspondence between a word and a style vector is one-to-one. To make results more diverse, one of the possible solutions is introducing small randomness by adding a random variable like a standard GAN for image generation. Among opposite meaning word pairs such as "old" and "new", their styles were largely

---
[1] https://github.com/tensorflow/magenta/.

Fig. 6. The word-based stylized results without adversarial training using L2 loss minimization.

different. However, both styles were relatively dark styles. The possible reason of this might be that mixing many styles or colors brings darker styles and colors in general.

Figure 6 shows the results with the model trained with L2 loss instead of adversarial loss. The differences of the styles among different words were very small, which indicated that the training of SSN did not succeed. Adversarial training was more effective for training of SSN than the standard L2 minimization.

As additional experiments, we trained the proposed model with Web image data we gathered by ourselves. We limited adjective words to ones related to "leather" for query words for Web image search. We picked up 84 highly-frequent adjective words with "leather" using Web search engines, and gathered 32,898 images with the combined query words of "leather" and one of the 84 adjective words using Web image search engines. Figure 7 shows the results generated by the model trained with word-associated Web images of only leather-related adjective words. Since "elderly", "fossil" and "old" were synonyms, the stylized images tends to be similar each other. On the other hand, among other three words the results are different.

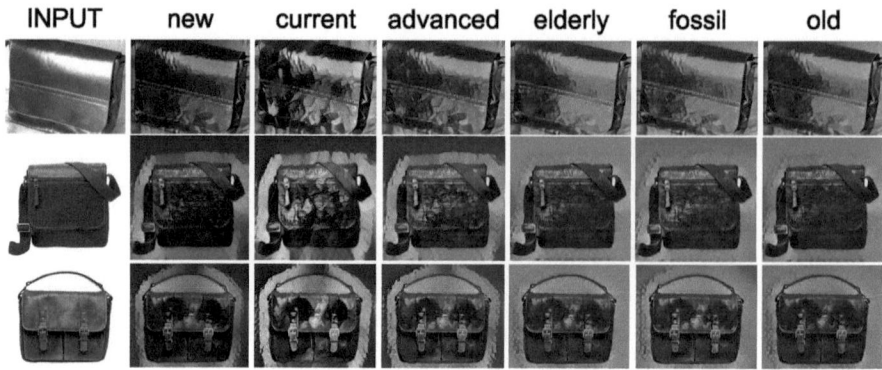

Fig. 7. The word-based stylized results with adjective-associated images gathered from the web.

5 Conclusions

In this paper, we proposed the fast style transfer network which modify the style of a given image based on a given word expressing image styles. By the proposed method, we have achieved word-based image style transfer which accepts any words as an input. In the experiments, we confirmed that different words generate different stylized images. In addition, the results with adversarial training seems to be superior to ones with L2 loss.

The results shown in this paper was still preliminary, and we just confirmed the proposed method worked. Comprehensive evaluation including evaluation by subjects is needed for future work. In addition, because in the current network one word corresponds to one style and the diversity was limited, we plan to introduce randomness by adding random variable to the input of SSN, or take into account the content of given images by adding image feature vectors of the given images to the input of SSN as additional information.

In this work, we extended a style transfer method which keeps content vectors of a content image and style vectors of a style image represented by Gram matrix. As results, the obtained results look like the images stylized by the average of many images associated with given adjective words. For future work, we plan to introduce more generic image transformation methods such as CycleGAN [16] for word-based image transformation.

Acknowledgments. This work was supported by JSPS KAKENHI Grant Number 15H05915, 17H01745, 17H05972, 17H06026 and 17H06100.

References

1. Chen, T.Q., Schmidt, M.: Fast patch-based style transfer of arbitrary style. arXiv preprint arXiv:1612.04337 (2016)
2. Dumoulin, V., Shlens, J., Kudlur, M.: A learned representation for artistic style. In: Proceedings of the ICLR (2017)

3. Gatys, L.A., Ecker, A.S., Bethge., M.: Image style transfer using convolutional neural networks. In: Proceedings of the IEEE Computer Vision and Pattern Recognition, pp. 2414–2423 (2016)
4. Ghiasi, G., Lee, H., Kudlur, M., Dumoulin, V., Shlens, J.: Exploring the structure of a real-time, arbitrary neural artistic stylization network. arXiv preprint arXiv:1705.06830 (2017)
5. Goodfellow, I., et al.: Generative adversarial nets. In: Proceedings of Advances in Neural Information Processing Systems, vol. 25, pp. 2672–2680 (2014)
6. Ioffe, S., Szegedy, C.: Batch normalization: accelerating deep network training by reducing internal covariate shift. arXiv preprint arXiv:1502.03167 (2015)
7. Johnson, J., Alahi, A., Fei-Fei, L.: Perceptual losses for real-time style transfer and super-resolution. In: Leibe, B., Matas, J., Sebe, N., Welling, M. (eds.) ECCV 2016. LNCS, vol. 9906, pp. 694–711. Springer, Cham (2016). https://doi.org/10.1007/978-3-319-46475-6_43
8. Li, Y., Wang, N., Liu, J., Hou, X.: Demystifying neural style transfer. arXiv preprint arXiv:1701.01036 (2017)
9. Mikolov, T., Sutskever, I., Chen, K., Corrado, G., Dean, J.: Distributed representations of words and phrases and their compositionality. In: Proceedings of Advances in Neural Information Processing Systems, vol. 25, pp. 3111–3119 (2013)
10. Simonyan, K., Vedaldi, A., Zisserman, A.: Very deep convolutional networks for large-scale image recognition. In: Proceedings of International Conference on Learning Representation (2015)
11. Szegedy, C., Vanhoucke, V., Ioffe, S., Shlens, J., Wojna, Z.: Rethinking the inception architecture for computer vision. In: Proceedings of the IEEE Conference on Computer Vision and Pattern Recognition, pp. 2818–2826 (2016)
12. Thomee, B., et al.: YFCC100M: the new data in multimedia research. Commun. ACM **59**(2), 64–73
13. Ulyanov, D., Lebedev, V., Vedaldi, A., Lempitsky, V.S.: Texture networks: feed-forward synthesis of textures and stylized images. In: ICML, pp. 1349–1357 (2016)
14. Ulyanov, D., Vedaldi, A., Lempitsky, V.: Instance normalization: the missing ingredient for fast stylization (2016)
15. Yanai, K.: Unseen style transfer based on a conditional fast style transfer network. In: Proceedings of International Conference on Learning Representation Workshop Track (ICLR WS) (2017)
16. Zhu, J.Y., Park, T., Isola, P., Efros, A.A.: Unpaired image-to-image translation using cycle-consistent adversarial networks. In: IEEE International Conference on Computer Vision (2017)

Font Style Transfer Using Neural Style Transfer and Unsupervised Cross-domain Transfer

Atsushi Narusawa, Wataru Shimoda, and Keiji Yanai[✉]

Department of Informatics, The University of Electro-Communications, Tokyo,
1-5-1 Chofugaoka, Chofu-shi, Tokyo 182-8585, Japan
{narusawa-a,shimoda-k,yanai}@mm.inf.uec.ac.jp

Abstract. In this paper, we study about font generation and conversion. The previous methods dealt with characters as ones made of strokes. On the contrary, we extract features, which are equivalent to the strokes, from font images and texture or pattern images using deep learning, and transform the design pattern of font images. We expect that generation of original font such as hand written characters will be generated automatically by the proposed approach. In the experiments, we have created unique datasets such as a ketchup character image dataset and improve image generation quality and readability of character by combining neural style transfer with unsupervised cross-domain learning.

1 Introduction

Recently, in the research field of character recognition, various tasks come to be studied according to the progress of deep learning. For example, scene character recognition, analysis of ancient document and image captioning are widely and actively studied at present. On the other hand, an image generation task using generative adversarial network has drawn a lot of attention. In the field of character recognition, image generation is also considered as a method for applications such as shape change of character font and generation of new fonts, which are beneficial in the languages having a large number of characters such as Chinese and Japanese. Several researchers have already been studying about font generation and font transformation using deep learning methods. In this paper, we also focus on transformation of character fonts and tackle a novel paradigm to transfer unique features obtained from images, which have specific patterns or designs to font images. Our work is different from traditional character recognition, which aims to simply recognize character of images, and our work is classified as kinds of "character engineering".

Generating new fonts for Japanese and Chinese requires large cost because they have over thousand kinds of character. It is needed to generate new Japanese fonts automatically using image generation techniques from several design patterns. However, problems still remain in adaptation of generative adversarial network to character images such as improvement of readability and training

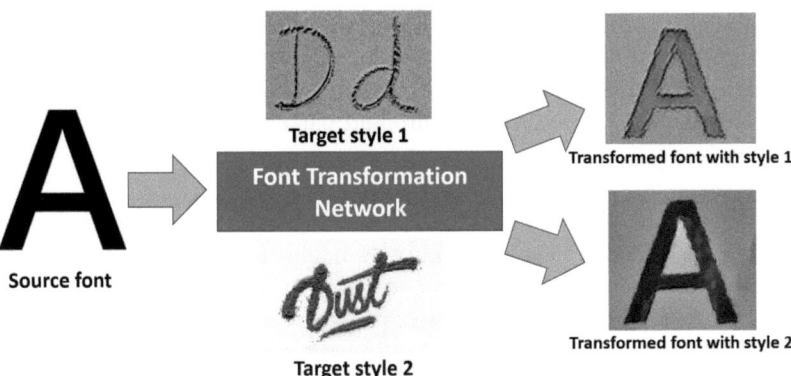

Fig. 1. Font transformation from a source font to the fonts stylized with the target styles.

with small dataset. Especially, the problem is widely known that we need a variety large scale dataset for high quality image generation tasks using deep learning. However, preparing the dataset for learning transferring patterns from same characters is difficult. To solve the problems, we focus on learning transferring patterns from images which do not have correspondence of character. That is, it is unsupervised character transformation where target domain patterns are not limited to characters but to an assembly of stoke patterns.

Our objective in this paper is to train a font transformation network by unsupervised domain transfer which needs no corresponding image pairs over two domains as shown in Fig. 1. In this figure, the source font, "A" was transformed into two kinds of fonts with two kinds of the target sand styles.

2 Related Works

2.1 Existing Font Image Generation Methods

We have two kinds of fonts: vector fonts and bitmap fonts. In general, regarding vector fonts generation, a character is considered as combination of set of stroke such as curve and upward brush-stroke and several components such as unit of radical. Zong et al. and Miyazaki et al. [9,15] decomposed characters into strokes and assigned them to corresponding transferred strokes. Lin et al. and Songhua et al. [8,12] generated Kanji by combining strokes and radicals.

Previous approaches make skeletons using vector information in advance for decomposing characters into strokes and generate fonts automatically by estimating and extracting strokes for the reconstruction of Kanji. Preparing description of stroke for every Kanji requires large annotation cost. On the contrary, we can extract strokes automatically using deep learning from font images and train networks for the correspondence of transformation automatically. On the other hand, generation of artistic character image such as ornamental writing including typography [11] has drawn attention. Methods for transferring texture and patterns images to fonts are needed. In this work we try to train deep neural transformation networks by learning the correspondence between strokes of character image for transferring texture and patterns.

2.2 Font Image Generation Using Deep Neural Network

"Rewrite"[1] and "Zi2Zi"[2] are notable works in character image generation using deep learning. "Rewrite" is a project to modify Neural Style Transfer [3] for adapting it to the font image generation. Neural Style Transfer is a method to mix two types of images. There are several reports [2] to use neural style transfer for the font image generation. "Zi2Zi" is a project based on Pix2Pix [10] to transform an image to another-domain image using generative adversarial network for character image. They used an encoder network for representing features of an image and a decoder network for reconstruction from the features. They concatenated both networks as a transformation network for learning the correspondence between pair of images. In this work, we extend the project "Zi2Zi" by adapting cross domain learning without pair of images.

3 Method

3.1 Overview of the Proposed Method

We propose a method to combine Fast Style Transfer [1,4] with unsupervised cross-domain learning using generative adversarial network [5,6,13,14]. The overall architecture of the proposed transformation network is shown in Fig. 2.

The networks for cross-domain learning consists of two transformation networks Fig. 3 and a discriminator networks Fig. 4. In cross-domain learning, we use two independent networks to convert the domain both directions. We define two transformation networks as G, F and two discriminator networks as D_x, D_y, respectively. Note that the transformation network, F, carries out inverse transformation of G. The transformation networks are trained with cycle loss, L_{cycle}, which enforces that any image applied with F and G goes back to the original image, i.e. $x = G(F(x))$. In addition, the transformation network is also trained with Adversarial Loss, $L_{adversarial}$, which enforces that the images transformed with G belong to the domain X and the images transformed with F belong to the domain Y. By optimizing these loss functions, all the networks are trained, and we obtain the transformation network which transform source fonts to the fonts stylized with the target style.

To improve readability in cross domain learning, we focus on losses of style transfer: content loss, $L_{content}$, and style Loss, L_{style}. In the standard style transfer, we extract features from per-trained model of VGG16 and the content features are extracted from one layer and style features are extracted from four

---
[1] https://github.com/kaonashi-tyc/Rewrite.
[2] https://kaonashi-tyc.github.io/2017/04/06/zi2zi.html.

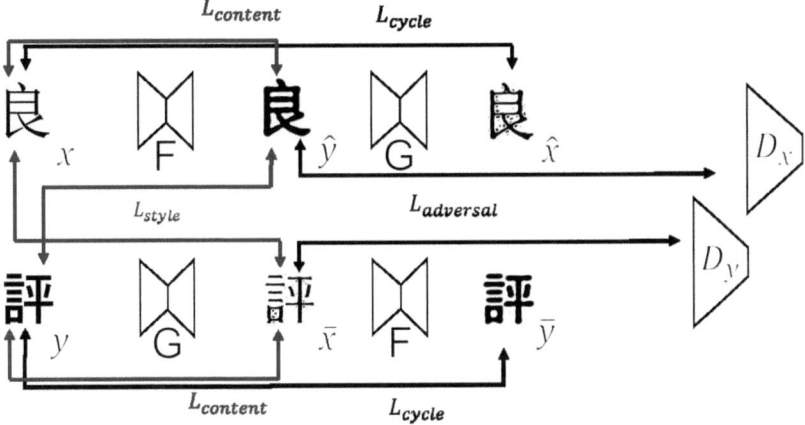

Fig. 2. The overall architecture of CycleGAN with neural style transfer.

Table 1. Configuration of the weight of loss.

Style weight	3.00E+05
Content weight	1.50E+00
Adversarial weight	4.50E+08
Cycle weight	3.50E+12

layers as shown in Fig. 5. In the proposed method, we combine four kinds of loss functions, and the transformation network is trained by optimizing an Eq. 1. Each of the weights for the loss functions is defined by grid search, and the values are indicated in Table 1.

$$L_{total} = \alpha L_{style} + \beta L_{content} + \gamma L_{adversarial} + \delta L_{cycle} \tag{1}$$

4 Experiments

4.1 Datasets

In this paper we transform font images to three kinds of texture pattern image dataset ketchup character, sand character and rope character images as shown in Fig. 6. The number of samples of each of the fonts are shown in Table 2. The ketchup character image dataset consists of many character images, while the sand character dataset includes several English words and handwritten arts images. The rope pattern dataset does not include any character images so that the dataset is constructed by cropping rope art images by hand manual operation. Therefore, we select 16 images from each dataset and locate them in a square to obtain enough style features. We prepare the 500 arranged images respectively.

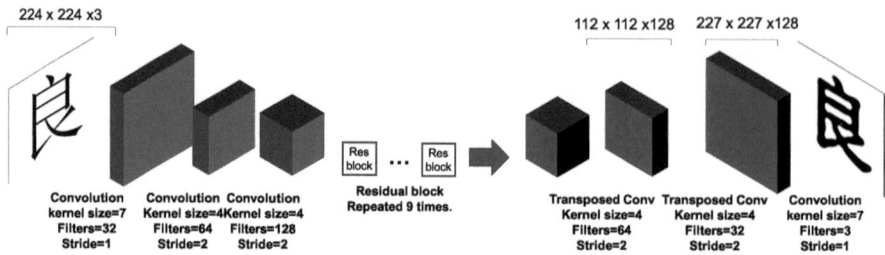

Fig. 3. The detail of encoder-decoder network.

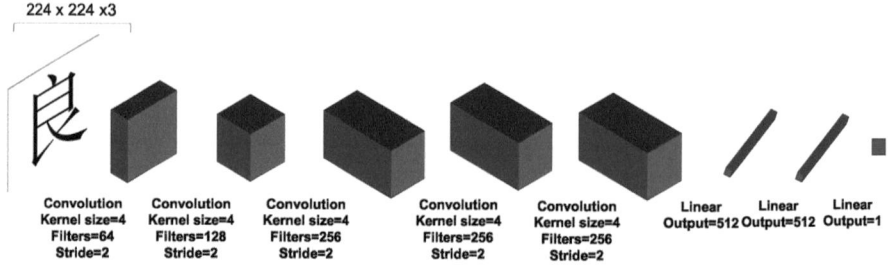

Fig. 4. The detail of discriminator.

4.2 Example of Image Generation

We show the image generation results of neural style transfer, CycleGAN and the proposed methods in Fig. 7. The results include only one direction so that a purpose of the purposed method is to transfer texture to font images. Note that in this case the networks are trained with larger weights value of content loss than indicated in Table 1. From the results, we observe that character shape of generated images become clearer than CycleGAN. Especially, in case of the sand character dataset, the results of neural style transfer (style loss + content loss) does not keep readability, while the proposed method keeps the readability. In addition, though there is a trade off between style loss and content loss, adversarial loss and cycle loss complement readability and transferring texture in several cases.

4.3 Objective Evaluation and Subjective Evaluation

In this subsection, we explore combination of the losses to show effect of style loss and content loss. According to Fig. 8, we can confirm that the readability is improved by content loss and adversarial loss leads natural texture of generated images visually.

Table 2. Texture character and pattern dataset

Dataset	Number
Ketchup character	445
Sand character	483
Rope pattern	796

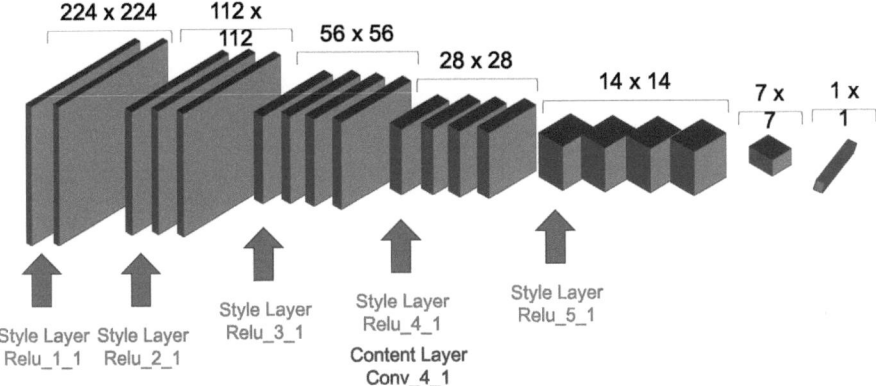

Fig. 5. Choice of layer for style features and content features.

Fig. 6. Examples of texture character and pattern dataset (From the left we show the examples of ketchup character, sand character and rope pattern images)

Furthermore, we compared mean of style loss to evaluate transferring texture of the transformation networks. We pick up a style image from each dataset and compute style loss for every generated image. We show mean of style losses in Table 3. Results of neural style transfer should show best performance so that optimize this style loss to be small during image generation. The proposed method aims to close the mean of style loss to the performance of neural style

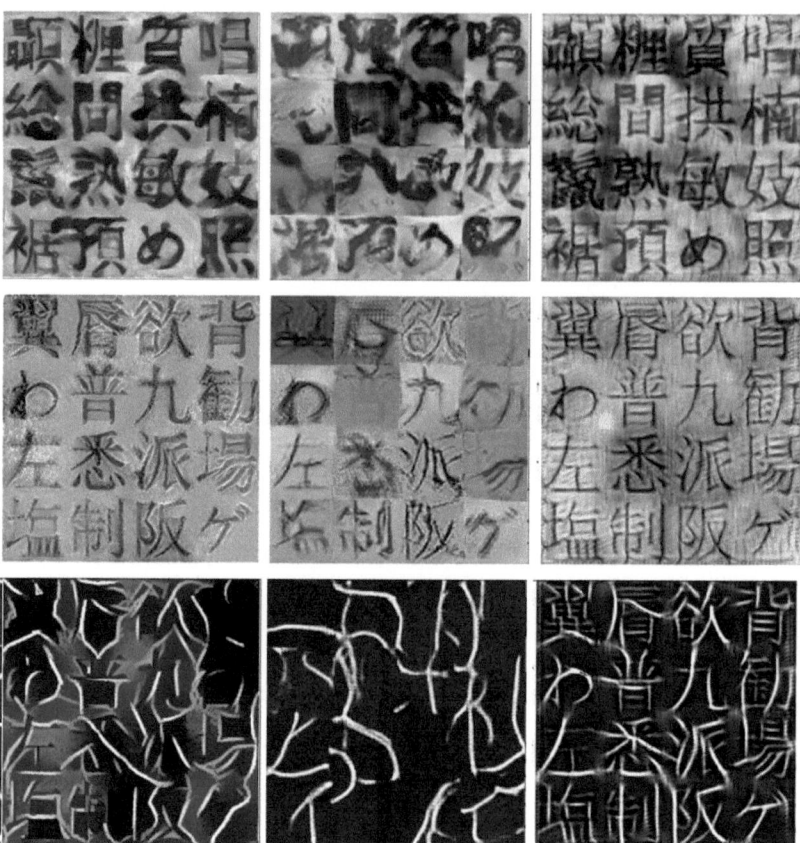

Fig. 7. From the left, we demonstrate the results of the neural style transfer, CycleGAN and the proposed method.

transfer. In the ketchup character image dataset, the combination of style loss, cycle loss and content loss achieved best performance. If adversarial loss is added to the combination, the mean of loss become worse than the CycleGAN. On the contrary, in the sand character image dataset there are little difference between neural style transfer and CycleGAN. In the proposed method results style loss does not work well, while adversarial loss show improvements. Finally, in the case of rope pattern image dataset, the tendency is similar to the case of ketchup dataset and all losses contribute the performance.

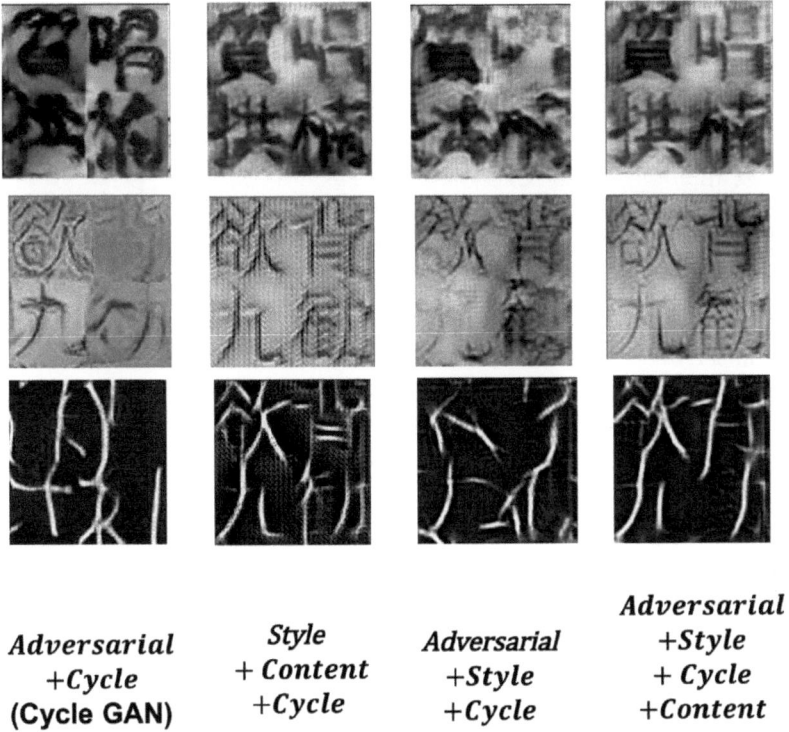

Fig. 8. The comparison of combination of the loss.

Table 3. The mean of the style loss.

	Ketchup character	Sand character	Rope pattern
Style + Content (Neural Style)	5.17E+06	2.77E+06	2.03E+07
Adversarial + Cycle (CycleGAN)	6.03E+06	3.11E+06	2.74E+07
Style + Cycle + Content	5.66E+06	3.36E+06	2.17E+07
Adversarial + Style + Cycle	5.98E+06	2.69E+06	2.06E+07
Adversarial + Style + Cycle + Content	6.00E+06	2.71E+06	1.99E+07

From the experimental results, combination of style loss, content loss and cycle loss or combination of all the losses is the better choice. Figure 9 shows the results of both simple and complicated characters with the model trained with all the losses. Compared with both, the results of the simpler samples were better in the quality, and the complicated characters were harder to transform, especially for the rope style.

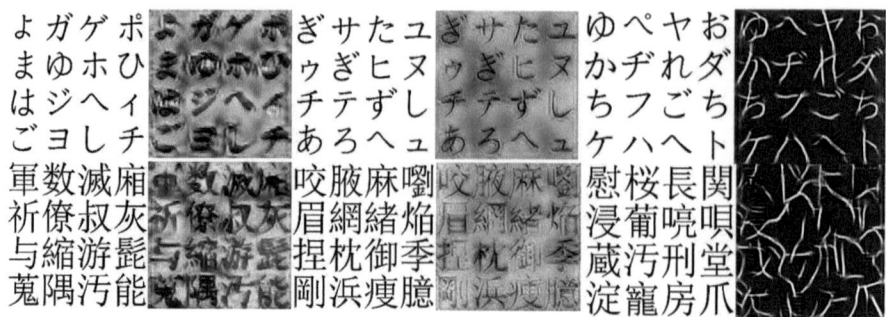

Fig. 9. (upper row) The results of simple characters, "Hiragana". (lower row) The results of complicated characters, "Kanji". For both, we used all the losses (style, content, cycle, and adversarial losses).

5 Conclusions

In this paper, we proposed a method to combine neural style network with CycleGAN by adding style loss and content loss to the CycleGAN model. We optimize four types of loss adversarial loss, cycle loss, style loss and content loss in the proposed method. These losses compete with each other, and we have explored the combination of the loss. We observed that the effective combinations differed in each dataset. The finding in the experiments over all the dataset is that content loss keeps original image character structure. The combination of content loss and style loss sometimes did not work, though there were also cases that show improvement by adding cycle loss. We consider that there are difference between Gram matrices obtained from the font images include many straight line and distortion in the shape. We also considered that the difference is relaxed by cycle loss and adversarial loss so that the losses sometimes cause distortion in straight line parts and it has potential to generate co-occurrence in the different domain data.

Currently, it is difficult to estimate patch-level correspondence on complicated patterns such as Kanji letters between source and target images. In general, the readability will not be changed if the shape of characters is changed but the structure is not changed. As future works, we consider to perturb the shape of input image to make it easy to find correspondence between sources and targets. In addition, we plan to introduce a patch-based approach [7] which used not Gram matrix which forced global consistency but only patch-based correspondences.

Acknowledgments. We would like to express great thanks to Prof. Seichi Uchida, Kyushu University, for the insightful and helpful comments. This work was supported by JSPS KAKENHI Grant Number 15H05915, 17H01745, 17H05972, 17H06026 and 17H06100.

References

1. Ulyanov, D., Lebedev, V., Lempitsky, A.V.: Texture networks: feed-forward synthesis of textures and stylized images. In: arXiv:1603.03417v1 (2016)
2. Gantugs, A., Iwana, B.K., Narusawa, A., Yanai, K., Uchida, S.: Neural font style transfer. In: International Conference on Document Analysis and Recognition (2017)
3. Gatys, L.A., Ecker, A.S., Bethge, M.: Image style transfer using convolutional neural networks. In: Proceedings of IEEE Computer Vision and Pattern Recognition (2016)
4. Johnson, J., Alahi, A., Fei-Fei, L.: Perceptual losses for real-time style transfer and super-resolution. In: Proceedings of European Conference on Computer Vision (2016)
5. Jun-Yan, Z., Taesung, P., Phillip, I., Alexei, E.: Unpaired image-to-image translation using cycle-consistent adversarial networks. In: Proceedings of IEEE International Conference on Computer Vision (2017)
6. Kim, T., Cha, M., Kim, M., Lee, J.K., Kim, J.: Learning to discover cross-domain relations with generative adversarial networks. In: International Conference on Machine Learning (2017). http://arxiv.org/abs/1703.05192
7. Li, C., Wand, M.: Combining Markov random fields and convolutional neural networks for image synthesis. In: Proceedings of IEEE Computer Vision and Pattern Recognition (2016)
8. Lin, J., Hong, C., Chang, R., Wang, Y., Lin, S., Ho, J.: Complete font generation of Chinese characters in personal handwriting style. In: 2015 IEEE 34th International Performance Computing and Communications Conference (IPCCC), pp. 1–5. IEEE (2015)
9. Miyazaki, T., et al.: Automatic generation of typographic font from a small font subset. In: arXiv preprint arXiv:1701.05703 (2017)
10. Phillip, I., Jun-Yan, Z., Tinghui, Z., Alexei, E.: Image-to-image translation with conditional adversarial networks. In: Proceedings of IEEE Computer Vision and Pattern Recognition (2017)
11. Shuai, Y., Jiaying, L., Zhouhui, L., Zongming, G.: Awesome typography: statistics-based text effects transfer. In: Proceedings of IEEE Computer Vision and Pattern Recognition (2016)
12. Songhua, X., Lau, F.C.M., Kwok-Wai, C., Yunhe, P.: Automatic generation of artistic Chinese calligraphy. In: IEEE Intelligent Systems (2005)
13. Taigman, Y., Polyak, A., Wolf, L.: Unsupervised cross-domain image generation. In: International Conference on Learning Representation (2017)
14. Yi, Z., Zhang, H., Tan, P., Gong, M.: DualGAN: unsupervised dual learning for image-to-image translation. In: Proceedings of IEEE International Conference on Computer Vision, pp. 2849–2857 (2017)
15. Zong, A., Zhu, Y.: StrokeBank: automating personalized Chinese handwriting generation. In: Advancement of Artificial Intelligence, pp. 3024–3030 (2014)

Paying Attention to Style: Recognizing Photo Styles with Convolutional Attentional Units

John See[1,2](✉), Lai-Kuan Wong[1], and Magzhan Kairanbay[1]

[1] Faculty of Computing and Informatics, Multimedia University,
Persiaran Multimedia, 63100 Cyberjaya, Selangor, Malaysia
{johnsee,lkwong}@mmu.edu.my, magzhan.kairanbay@gmail.com
http://viprlab.github.io
[2] Shanghai Jiao Tong University, Shanghai 200240, China

Abstract. The notion of style in photographs is one that is highly subjective, and often difficult to characterize computationally. Recent advances in learning techniques for visual recognition have encouraged new possibilities for computing aesthetics and other related concepts in images. In this paper, we design an approach for recognizing styles in photographs by introducing adapted deep convolutional neural networks that are attentive towards strong neural activations. The proposed convolutional attentional units act as a filtering mechanism that conserves activations in convolutional blocks in order to contribute more meaningfully towards the visual style classes. State-of-the-art results were achieved on two large image style datasets, demonstrating the effectiveness of our method.

1 Introduction

"A photograph is usually looked at – seldom looked into"

— Ansel Adams

Photography is both an artistic and technical process. Although photography styles are recognizable to humans to a certain degree of success with minimal transfer of knowledge, it is not a trivial problem that computers can encode well. In fact, a particular style or stylistic idea that is used in a photograph is neither mutually exclusive, nor interpreted to perfect confidence. Photographers, in general, do not only focus on one particular style of photo-taking or make strict decisions and compositions in a mechanical manner. In short, understanding photo style is a subjective process that is also inclined to a variety of interpretation.

Automatic interpretation and assessment of the aesthetic quality (or similar terms, the *beauty* and *appeal*) in images have seen an increase in interest from

---

This work is supported in part by Shanghai 'Belt and Road' Young Scholar Exchange Grant (17510740100), Shanghai Jiao Tong University and Multimedia University.

© Springer Nature Switzerland AG 2019
G. Carneiro and S. You (Eds.): ACCV 2018 Workshops, LNCS 11367, pp. 110–124, 2019.
https://doi.org/10.1007/978-3-030-21074-8_10

the computer vision community [10,11,16,19], particularly with the advent of deep learning techniques [8,14,22] that revolutionized the way how machines learn. A number of auxiliary and related tasks that are aesthetically motivated have also emerged in recent years, i.e. photo cropping [6], photo composition [15], photo enhancement [4]. Whilst these photo manipulation tasks have garnered a wide usability in tools and applications, researchers have ventured out less in the more challenging task of recognizing photo styles although there is clearly no lack of datasets [12,19] that can be utilized. Recently, the notion of style has also been explored in the areas of fashion [13] and paintings/artworks [20], an indication of an increase in attention towards more subjective domains. The task of classifying photo styles can contribute broadly to a wide range of applications such as photo search and semantic retrieval, and potentially, further capabilities for image synthesis and captioning.

In this paper, we describe an approach to recognizing photograph styles by introducing an attention-aware adaptation to standard deep convolutional neural networks (CNN). This filtering mechanism, named *convolutional attentional units*, acts to preserve activations in specific convolutional layers that contribute meaningfully towards certain style classes. Using the popular Residual Networks (ResNet) as our base network, we perform a thorough evaluation of our proposed method on two photo style datasets. Further class-activated heatmap visualizations provide additional evidence as to what has been learned in the network and which regions have been "attended to".

2 Related Works

Historically, distinct visual styles are apparent in art since the era of Renaissance art and is becoming increasingly popular in photography in the recent years. Mobile applications such as Instagram and Prisma have spurred growth in the research on style transfer, whereby the style of a painting or an image can be transferred automatically to a new image [7]. With more images being made available in various artistic or photographic style, understanding and recognizing styles is becoming a crucial task. Therefore, it is not surprising that there is a growing interest in image style analysis, covering a wide range of both artistic and photographic styles.

Image Style Classification. Aesthetics Visual Analysis (AVA) dataset [19] is one of the earliest photo datasets that contain style annotations. It is constructed entirely from DPChallenge website, a popular collection of digital photography contests. A subset of images from this large dataset contained multiple tags from 14 different photographic styles. The authors trained 14 one-versus-all linear SVMs using a variety of generic descriptors or low-level features such as color histograms, SIFT, Local Binary Patterns (LBP) features. Interestingly, color histograms was shown to perform well for the "Duotones", "Complementary Colors", "Light on White" and "Negative Image" styles while SIFT and

LBP features performed better for the "Shallow Depth-of-Field" and "Vanishing Point" categories. This indicated that handcrafted features tend to struggle with discriminating across distinct visual styles.

Following that, Karayev et al. [12] introduced two new datasets; Flickr Style and Wikipaintings for the purpose of style analysis and classification. In particular, the Flickr Style dataset contains 80,000 images and 20 style categories which embodies several different aspects of visual style, including photographic techniques, composition styles, moods, genres and types of scenes. The authors explored the effectiveness of various feature extraction methods, ranging from single features such as color histogram to deep CNN features (DeCAF6) and feature fusion. The feature fusion variation achieved the best mAP of 0.473 and 0.581 for the Flickr Style and AVA-Style dataset respectively. Lu et al. [16] proposed a single-column style CNN, which consists of 6 convolution layers followed by 3 fully-connected layers, achieving an mAP of 0.56 on the AVA-Style dataset. Notably, the network was also utilized to regularize feature learning for the aesthetic classification task. The authors later hypothesize that style attributes from the entire image may not represent the fine-grained information very well, and proposed a deep multi-patch aggregation network (DMA-Net) [17], using multiple patches cropped from one image. They adopted this approach for style, aesthetics and quality estimation. Specifically, their style classification achieve a good mAP of 0.64, significantly outperforming prior works.

A few other works focused on the classification of paintings and artworks into specific styles, genres and artists. Bar et al. [3] recognized the style of paintings using a combination of features extracted from deep neural networks, picture codes and low-level visual descriptors. One-vs-all SVMs were trained for each category of WikiArt dataset [20] (previously known as WikiPaintings in [12]). Chu et al. [5] classified oil painting images according to various styles (Academicism, Baroque, Cubism etc.), using an adapted VGG-19 CNN [22] model. For specific convolutional layers, the inner product between pairs of vectorized feature maps is used to construct the feature vector, which are then classified by an SVM classifier. Tan et al. [24] fine-tuned an AlexNet CNN [14] for large-scale style, genre and artist classification of fine-art paintings from the Wikiart dataset, achieving reasonably good results on all three tasks.

Other interesting datasets that would be useful for in-depth style analysis include the JenAesthetics subjective dataset [1] and Behance Artistic Media (BAM) dataset [25]. The JenAesthetics subjective dataset presents the subjective ratings for five different properties of the paintings (aesthetic, beauty, color, composition, and content), of the previously introduced JenAesthetics dataset, a colored oil paintings dataset that covers a wide range of different styles, art periods, and subject matters. On the other hand, the BAM dataset contains a set of binary attribute scores for over 2.5 million images from Behance, a portfolio website for professional and commercial artists. Each image in BAM is annotated with 20 rich attribute labels for content, emotions, and artistic media.

Attentional Mechanisms. The idea of attention models, which was first proposed for natural language processing (NLP) tasks such as machine translation [2] and question answering [9], have been recently proposed in various forms for use in images and videos. From training data, these models learn what to "attend to" based on the input sentence and the model outputs.

An alternative approach to attention [18] applies reinforcement learning to predict an approximate location to focus to. A Recurrent Neural Network (RNN) processes inputs sequentially, attending to different locations within the images to incrementally combine information from these fixations or "glimpses". In similar fashion, [26] also used a RNN with attention mechanisms to generate image captions, taking in CNN encodings of the input image. Attention weights can be visualized to provide interpretation into what the model is looking at while generating a word.

3 Adapting Networks with Attention Units

In this section we describe a method of allowing residual blocks from residual based networks to be equipped with convolutional attention units (CAU). These CAUs allow these residual blocks to focus their activations without needing to add further overhead into the number of learnable weights.

3.1 Residual Networks

Deep Residual Networks [8], or ResNets in short, was the winner of the ILSVRC 2015 challenge (3.57% error rate), which built upon its predecessors by introducing shortcut connections across stacks of layers, allowing the optimizer to handle convergence issues in very deeply stacked networks which are caused by vanishing/exploding gradients. The robustness of ResNets have been proven by its successful adaptation for other visual tasks [23,27].

He et al. [8] showed that it is easier to optimize the residual mapping $\mathcal{H}(\mathbf{x})$ by letting the layers fit a new mapping denoted by

$$\mathcal{F}(\mathbf{x}) := \mathcal{H}(\mathbf{x}) - \mathbf{x} \tag{1}$$

by recasting the original mapping to $\mathcal{F}(\mathbf{x}) + \mathbf{x}$, which is simply adding the layers copied from the learned shallower model, i.e. the identity mapping $\mathbf{x}$. The concept of residuals is motivated by the fact it is easier to find changes with respect to an identity mapping (from earlier layers) than a zero mapping (from scratch). In true hierarchical fashion, subsequent blocks fine-tune the output of a previous block, rather than generating the mapping from scratch. In such a case where an identity mapping is already optimal, the residual in Eq. 1 can be close to zero. This mechanism also safeguards the model from training error degradation resulting from additional layers.

These shortcut connections, or "skip connections" add neither extra parameters nor computational complexity to the network, while still trainable end-to-end with back-propagation. Computationally, a ResNet-50 (3.8 billion FLOPS) is only about a fifth of that of VGG-19 (19.6 billion FLOPs), despite having more than double the number of layers.

We opt to use the 50-layer residual network (ResNet-50 in short), which is a mid-length choice among the ResNet variants available at our disposal (34, 50, 101, 152 layers), which strikes a reasonable balance between network length and complexity. For simplicity in elaboration, the description of methods from here on will be referred entirely to the ResNet-50.

Table 1 depicts the building blocks of the ResNet-50 architecture, with each *stage* comprising of a number of stacked layers. Downsampling occurs at the end of each stage by connecting to a subsequent convolutional layer of stride 2, without the need of a pooling operation. Stages 2, 3, 4 and 5 contain a specific number of building blocks (each uniquely represented by suffixes $\beta = \{\text{'a'}, \text{'b'}, \ldots\}$).

Table 1. Architecture of a 50-layer ResNet, with layer configurations.

Layer stages	Output size	Configuration
conv1	112×112	7×7, 64, stride 2
conv2β	56×56	3×3 max pool, stride 2
		$\begin{bmatrix} 1 \times 1, 64 \\ 3 \times 3, 64 \\ 1 \times 1, 256 \end{bmatrix} \times 3$
conv3β	28×28	$\begin{bmatrix} 1 \times 1, 128 \\ 3 \times 3, 128 \\ 1 \times 1, 512 \end{bmatrix} \times 4$
conv4β	14×14	$\begin{bmatrix} 1 \times 1, 256 \\ 3 \times 3, 256 \\ 1 \times 1, 1024 \end{bmatrix} \times 6$
conv5β	7×7	$\begin{bmatrix} 1 \times 1, 512 \\ 3 \times 3, 512 \\ 1 \times 1, 2048 \end{bmatrix} \times 3$
Final	1×1	Average pool, 1000-d fc, softmax

3.2 Convolutional Attention Units

The attentional mechanisms introduced for sequential data [2,26] provide strong motivations for simplification on a single image. Our adaptation aims to create a soft attentional mask that acts as a "filter" for activations in specific convolutional layers. This approximates to object saliency, but rather, in the form of a *soft* kind of network memory that encodes a weighted contribution of all locations in the convolutional output. This is also beneficial in the sense that a soft attentional mask can be easily computed with only minimal additional parameters incurred to the existing backbone network.

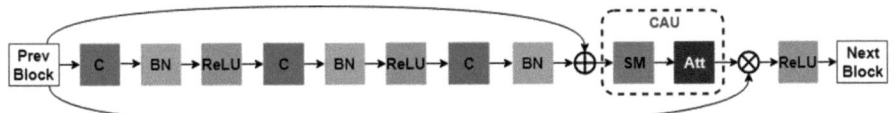

Fig. 1. Convolutional attentional units (CAU) attached to the end of a ResNet block.

Given an input image $\mathbf{x}$, a deep representation $\mathcal{D}_s \in \mathbb{R}^d$ at a particular block b of a residual network can be denoted as

$$\mathcal{D}_b = f(\mathbf{W}_b * \mathbf{x}) \qquad (2)$$

where $*$ denotes a set of layer operations consisting of 2D convolution, batch-normalization and activation, and $\mathbf{W}$ denotes the learnable parameters. A function $f(\cdot)$, typically non-linear, operates on these deep features (of essential dimension d, i.e. the depth). The soft attentional activations can be computed as follows:

$$\mathcal{A}(\mathbf{x}) = \text{softmax}([\mathcal{D}_b]) \qquad (3)$$

where $[\cdot]$ denotes an operation that prepares the features into a N-by-d matrix, with $N = w * h$ representing the number of output pixels. Specifically, each (i,j)-th *convolutional attentional unit* is determined as:

$$a_{ij} = \frac{\exp(f_{ij})}{\sum_{c=1}^{C}(f_{ic})} \qquad (4)$$

for $i = \{1 \ldots N\}, j = \{1 \ldots C\}$. C is the number of style classes.

The soft attentional map $\mathcal{S}$ is obtained by performing depth-wise mean for all N attentional activations in $\mathcal{A}$, before scaling by sum-normalization. This can be understood as averaging the class contributions to arrive at a score that depicts the importance of each spatial location.

Finally, we "attend" to the deep features from an earlier block $\widehat{\mathcal{D}}_b$ by the Hadamard product of the feature and the soft attentional map:

$$\mathcal{D}' = (\widehat{\mathcal{D}}_b \circ \mathcal{S})_i \qquad (5)$$

Convolutional attention units are fully differentiable that they can be appended into any existing end-to-end network, allowing gradients to propagate through the attention mechanism together with the rest of the network.

3.3 Framework

In this paper, we demonstrate how this can be done on ResNet blocks. Figure 1 shows how convolutional attentional units can be appended to the end of a ResNet block (this example shows the last block of stage 5 named '5c'). By design, the CAU module is placed after all residual units (convolution-batch

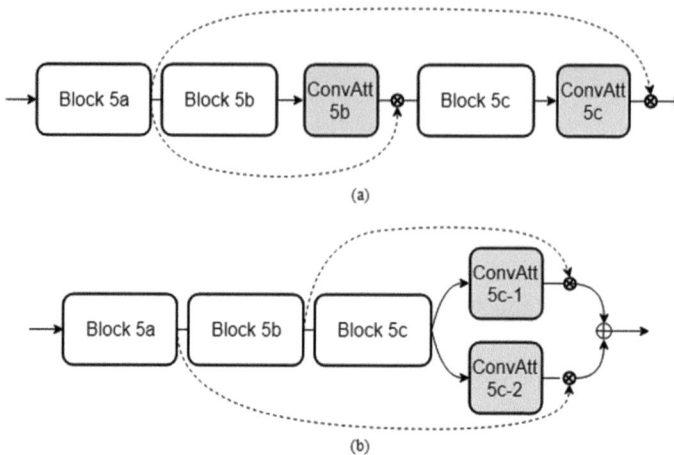

Fig. 2. Configurations to attach two CAUs to the last ResNet stage (a) in serial, (b) in parallel.

normalization-activation), but before the final activation layer. This ensures the new attention-aware neurons are mapped non-linearly before moving on to the next block.

The CAU module can be appended in a variety of ways. For clarity in notation, we define each CAU module as a function of two convolutional features ($w \times h \times d$ cubes), i.e. $CAU(\mathcal{D}_{b1}, \mathcal{D}_{b2})$, where $b1$ and $b2$ denote the attention-aware block and an earlier merging block respectively, constrained by $b1 \neq b2$ and $b1$ must be above or similar level with $b2$ in hierarchy terms. For simplicity, we can abuse this notation as $CAU(b1, b2)$.

Figure 2 illustrates two examples of how multiple CAU modules can be inserted into the ResNet architecture: (a) serially, and (b) parallelly. In the first setup, the $CAU(5b, 5a)$ module attends to the features originating from the '5a' block, followed by $CAU(5c, 5a)$ which in turn, attends to the earlier attention-aware output. In the second configuration, two CAU modules – $CAU(5c, 5b)$ and $CAU(5c, 5a)$, are attending separately to earlier blocks ('5a' and '5b'). Their respective outputs are then aggregated by simple summation.

4 Experiments

In our experiments, we focus our attention on photo-based image style datasets, rather than artwork/painting-based datasets [1,20]. We leave these for future exploration.

4.1 Datasets

Aesthetic Visual Analysis (AVA) [19]. This is the largest dataset to date for evaluating the aesthetic quality of photographs. The dataset contains more than

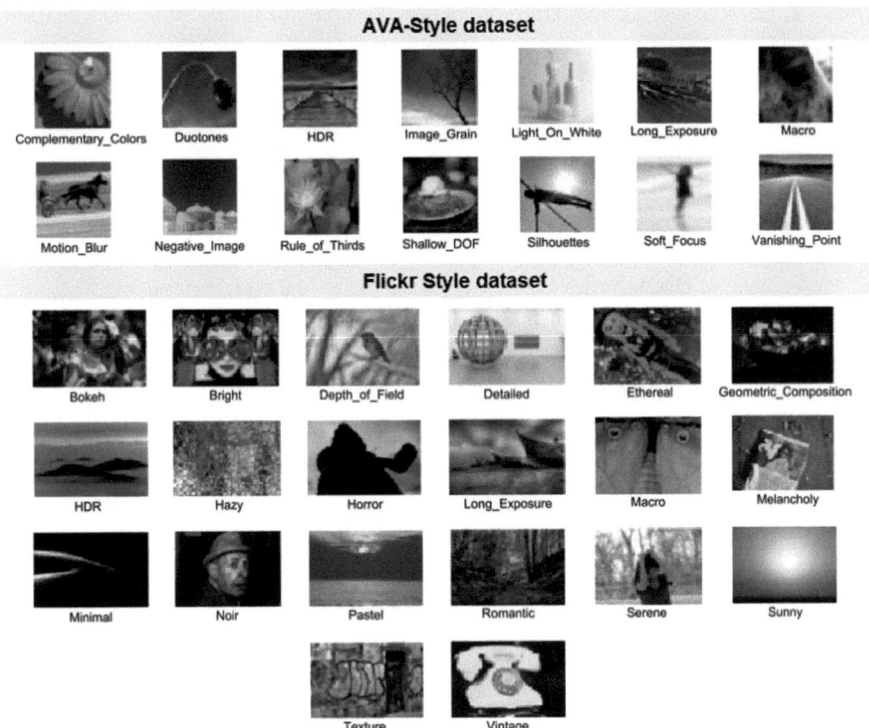

Fig. 3. Visual style categories of the AVA-Style and Flickr Style datasets

250K images (each evaluated by an average of 210 professional photographers). The AVA dataset contains semantic and style tags, the latter consisting of 14 unique styles, available in 14,079 images. The authors provide specific training (11,270 images) and test (2,809 images) partitions. Images in the training partition have only a single ground truth label, while images in the test partition can have several ground truth labels. Figure 3 shows a sample image from each style category of the AVA-Style dataset. A majority of these categories describe well-known photographic rules and techniques that are widely used by photographers.

Flickr Style [12]. This dataset consists of 20 visual styles collected from Flickr Groups, which are community-curated collections of visual concepts. Although Flickr users provide free-form tags for their uploaded images, their tags tend to be noisy and unreliable. The visual styles were carefully selected from a wide range of technical concepts such as optical techniques and composition styles, and also concepts that depict atmosphere, mood, color and genre. For each style, 4,000 images were collected from one dedicated Flickr Group, resulting in a total of 80,000 images which forms the Flickr Style dataset. A sample image for each visual style is shown in Fig. 3. The authors proposed for 20% of the data to be

Table 2. Comparison against state-of-the-art methods for image style classification.

Type	Methods	AVA-Style	Flickr Style
Baselines	Murray et al. [19]	0.538	-
	Karayev et al. [12]	0.581	0.368
Recent works	RAPID [16]	0.568	-
	StyleNet [6]	0.560	0.372
	DMA-Net$_{fc}$ [17]	0.600	-
	DMA-Net (with external data) [17]	0.641	-
	JAM [25]	0.615	0.389
Competing methods	ResNet50 (avgpool) features + SVM	0.636	0.398
	ResNet50 (f/t)	0.633	0.403
	ResNet50-CAU (best)	**0.671**	**0.430**

set aside for testing, and another 20% for validation. The rest of the data will be used for training. The data is stratified to provide class-balanced training and testing.

Performance Metrics. To measure the performance of our method, we consider the *mean Average Precision* (mAP), which is a typical overall metric for multi-label classification. We use this for both datasets, although test samples in the Flickr Style dataset contains only a single label. We also compute *per-class Average Precision* (AP) which gives us a reflection of how precise each class performs separately.

The baseline method for the AVA-Style dataset [19] reported the highest mAP of 0.538 by combining Fisher Vector (FV) signatures, color histogram and Local Binary Patterns (LBP) features by late fusion. Karayev et al. [12] reported a best mAP of 0.368 on the Flickr Style dataset, with features obtained using a outer product combination of late fusion features and high-level content classifier features. Their best mAP on the AVA-Style is 0.581, also using these similar features.

4.2 Results and Analysis

To demonstrate the feasibility of our proposed approach, we benchmark our results against a number of previous works from literature. We also report competing variants tested on the base network ResNet. Table 2 show that the proposed approach can yield state-of-the-art results (it is shown later in Table 3 that this is regardless of the CAU configuration used). We also show that a

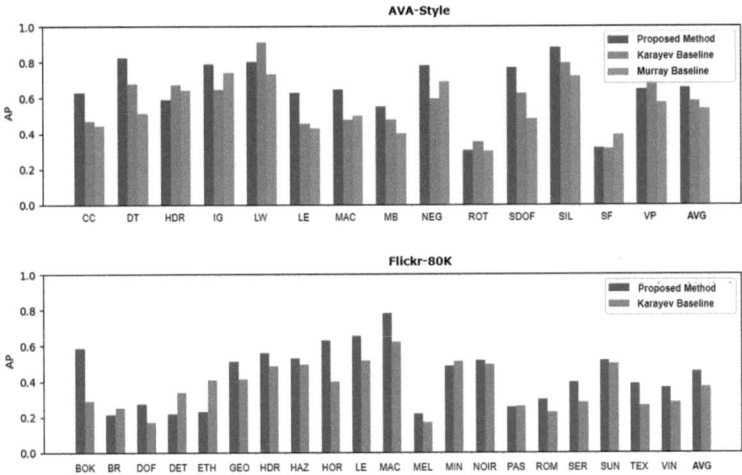

Fig. 4. Comparing Per-class Average Precision (AP) of our best method against the baseline(s) for AVA-Style and Flickr Style datasets. The style classes are abbreviated as per Fig. 3.

Table 3. Ablation study of attaching CAUs to different residual blocks in stage 5 of ResNet-50.

Type	abbrv	Configuration	AVA-Style	Flickr Style
Single	-	$CAU(5b, 5a)$	0.641	0.414
		$CAU(5c, 5a)$	0.659	0.419
		$CAU(5c, 5b)$	0.652	0.423
Double	serial-1	$CAU(5b, 5a) + CAU(5c, 5b)$	0.643	0.417
	serial-2	$CAU(5b, 5a) + CAU(5c, 5a)$	0.647	**0.430**
	parallel	$CAU(5c, 5a) + CAU(5c, 5b)$	**0.671**	0.428

basic ResNet-50 model with careful normalization procedures[1], can performed relatively well compared to more sophisticated models that have been previously proposed for this task.

Taking a closer look at per-class average precision (AP) scores (see Fig. 4), we can observe that the proposed method is superior to their respective dataset baselines in a majority of categories, i.e. 9 out of 14 categories for AVA-Style, and 15 out of 20 categories for Flickr Style. On our proposed method, the *Silhouette* and *Macro* photo styles are the most distinguishable concept for the AVA-Style and Flickr Style dataset respectively.

---

[1] (a) For pre-trained ResNet-50, we perform sample normalization on the extracted `avg_pool` features. (b) For fine-tuning ResNet-50, samples are mean subtracted.

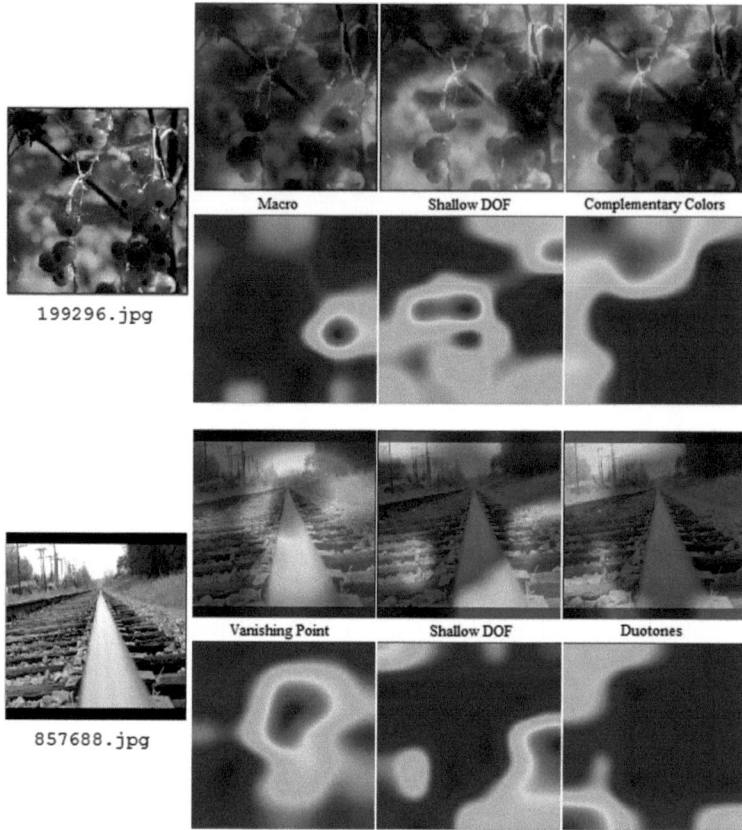

Fig. 5. Sample test images from AVA-Style and their respective Grad-CAM heatmaps condition upon certain target classes. All three ground-truth labels were correctly predicted by our model.

Ablation Study. To further investigate possible variability in the network architecture design, we conduct an ablation study into the various ways CAUs can be added to the ResNet. Experiments were performed only on the residual blocks in stage 5 (the final stage) of ResNet-50.

Table 3 summarizes the results on various configurations (single and double CAUs). Results show that the use of double CAUs can yield better performance than appending only single CAUs. We observe a leap in performance in the parallel design (method *parallel*) particularly on the AVA-Style dataset. The *serial-1* design, which relies on the same merging layer ('5a'), is marginally more robust on the Flickr Style dataset. It is important to note that attaching the CAU at the end of the residual stage ('5c') seems to produce slightly better results, even more so in the *parallel* setting.

Difficult Concepts. Generally, composition-based concepts like *Rules of Thirds* and emotion-based concepts like *Melancholy* are difficult to classify regardless of the method used. *Rules of Thirds* is a popular "rule of thumb" in photography used while composing the photo, which may not be easily characterized by appearance or content of the image, but rather the spatial placing of objects-of-interest. On the other hand, *Melancholy* is a highly subjective concept which relates closer to the emotion that is invoked from the image itself; hence, its poor precision is much expected.

4.3 Visualizations

To better visualize what the proposed network is learning, we picked a couple of example test images from the AVA-Style dataset, which is contains multiple labels, i.e. image '199296.jpg' and '857688.jpg'. We apply Gradient-based Class Activation Maps (Grad-CAM) [21] on the convolutional features of the final residual block based on the predicted labels. Figure 5 shows the Grad-CAMs (overlaid over original image) of two sample test images during prediction with our best model. Locations that are red indicate strong neural activations arising from a particular area in the image. The use of CAUs are pivotal at focusing attention at specific portions of the image as learned from training process.

Interestingly, we find that many of these areas of attention correspond closely to the stylistic concepts that the model intends to classify. For instance, the top image in Fig. 5 was classified as *Macro* owing to attention paid to the nearest bunch of grapes that are in zoomed focus. The bottom image which contains a low perspective view of railway tracks was best exemplified by the network picking up on the area corresponding to a *Vanishing Point*. These images were also correctly labeled as *Shallow DOF* where the Grad-CAM shows that the network relied on activations from areas with a strong background-foreground difference in focus.

Fig. 6. Changes to the Grad-CAM (on the *Vanishing Point* class) of the convolutional features of the final residual block after applying the two CAUs used in the parallel configuration.

Using an example, Fig. 6 illustrates the transition undergone by the Grad-CAM heatmaps of the two CAUs used in the parallel configuration, which were generated at each training step. We make two interesting observations here. Firstly, the attentive areas of both CAUs are slightly different, an indication that aggregating these features would ensure better coverage. Secondly, the convolutional features were able to converge very quickly to the important area of interest within a few iterations.

4.4 Future Directions

In this preliminary work, we have explored the use of CAUs in a limited way, but to an extent that it is worth investigating further. The following extensions are possible:

1. CAUs can be applied to other stages in a ResNet architecture. The impact of such attachments have not been experimented on. In this work, the penultimate stage was used since features tend to be richer and more definitive towards the top.
2. Image styles are not restricted to only photographs. The notion of *style* (and to some extent of relatedness, *emotion*) is very broad in which our proposed method can also be useful for artwork/painting genres [1,20] and fashion styles [13]. We leave these for future work.

5 Conclusions

This paper presents a fresh approach to photograph style classification by attending to salient neural activations, which leads to a more focused set of deeply learned features. Experimental results on two large image style datasets have demonstrated great potential in the use of convolutional attention units for deep CNNs. This mechanism could be particularly useful for coping with classification of subjective concepts such as image style, genre and emotion, where the underlying fixation of spatial locations could provide clues towards better understanding. We hope the findings in this work will serve to spur further research in this direction.

References

1. Amirshahi, S.A., Hayn-Leichsenring, G.U., Denzler, J., Redies, C.: JenAesthetics subjective dataset: analyzing paintings by subjective scores. In: Agapito, L., Bronstein, M.M., Rother, C. (eds.) ECCV 2014. LNCS, vol. 8925, pp. 3–19. Springer, Cham (2015). https://doi.org/10.1007/978-3-319-16178-5_1
2. Bahdanau, D., Cho, K., Bengio, Y.: Neural machine translation by jointly learning to align and translate. arXiv preprint arXiv:1409.0473 (2014)
3. Bar, Y., Levy, N., Wolf, L.: Classification of artistic styles using binarized features derived from a deep neural network. In: Agapito, L., Bronstein, M.M., Rother, C. (eds.) ECCV 2014. LNCS, vol. 8925, pp. 71–84. Springer, Cham (2015). https://doi.org/10.1007/978-3-319-16178-5_5

4. Bhattacharya, S., Sukthankar, R., Shah, M.: A framework for photo-quality assessment and enhancement based on visual aesthetics. In: Proceedings of the 18th ACM International Conference on Multimedia, pp. 271–280. ACM (2010)
5. Chu, W.T., Wu, Y.L.: Deep correlation features for image style classification. In: Proceedings of the 2016 ACM on Multimedia Conference, pp. 402–406. ACM (2016)
6. Fang, C., Lin, Z., Mech, R., Shen, X.: Automatic image cropping using visual composition, boundary simplicity and content preservation models. In: Proceedings of the 22nd ACM International Conference on Multimedia, pp. 1105–1108. ACM (2014)
7. Gatys, L.A., Ecker, A.S., Bethge, M.: Image style transfer using convolutional neural networks. In: Proceedings of the IEEE Conference on Computer Vision and Pattern Recognition, pp. 2414–2423 (2016)
8. He, K., Zhang, X., Ren, S., Sun, J.: Deep residual learning for image recognition. In: Proceedings of the IEEE Conference on Computer Vision and Pattern Recognition, pp. 770–778 (2016)
9. Hermann, K.M., et al.: Teaching machines to read and comprehend. In: Advances in Neural Information Processing Systems, pp. 1693–1701 (2015)
10. Hii, Y.L., See, J., Kairanbay, M., Wong, L.K.: Multigap: multi-pooled inception network with text augmentation for aesthetic prediction of photographs. In: 2017 IEEE International Conference on Image Processing (ICIP), pp. 1722–1726. IEEE (2017)
11. Kairanbay, M., See, J., Wong, L.-K.: Aesthetic evaluation of facial portraits using compositional augmentation for deep CNNs. In: Chen, C.-S., Lu, J., Ma, K.-K. (eds.) ACCV 2016. LNCS, vol. 10117, pp. 462–474. Springer, Cham (2017). https://doi.org/10.1007/978-3-319-54427-4_34
12. Karayev, S., et al.: Recognizing image style. arXiv preprint arXiv:1311.3715 (2013)
13. Kiapour, M.H., Yamaguchi, K., Berg, A.C., Berg, T.L.: Hipster wars: discovering elements of fashion styles. In: Fleet, D., Pajdla, T., Schiele, B., Tuytelaars, T. (eds.) ECCV 2014. LNCS, vol. 8689, pp. 472–488. Springer, Cham (2014). https://doi.org/10.1007/978-3-319-10590-1_31
14. Krizhevsky, A., Sutskever, I., Hinton, G.E.: Imagenet classification with deep convolutional neural networks. In: Advances in Neural Information Processing Systems, pp. 1097–1105 (2012)
15. Liu, L., Chen, R., Wolf, L., Cohen-Or, D.: Optimizing photo composition. Comput. Graph. Forum **29**(2), 469–478 (2010)
16. Lu, X., Lin, Z., Jin, H., Yang, J., Wang, J.Z.: Rapid: rating pictorial aesthetics using deep learning. In: Proceedings of the 22nd ACM International Conference on Multimedia, pp. 457–466. ACM (2014)
17. Lu, X., Lin, Z., Shen, X., Mech, R., Wang, J.Z.: Deep multi-patch aggregation network for image style, aesthetics, and quality estimation. In: International Conference on Computer Vision, pp. 990–998 (2015)
18. Mnih, V., Heess, N., Graves, A., et al.: Recurrent models of visual attention. In: Advances in Neural Information Processing Systems, pp. 2204–2212 (2014)
19. Murray, N., Marchesotti, L., Perronnin, F.: AVA: a large-scale database for aesthetic visual analysis. In: 2012 IEEE Conference on Computer Vision and Pattern Recognition (CVPR), pp. 2408–2415. IEEE (2012)
20. Saleh, B., Elgammal, A.: Large-scale classification of fine-art paintings: learning the right metric on the right feature. arXiv preprint arXiv:1505.00855 (2015)
21. Selvaraju, R.R., Cogswell, M., Das, A., Vedantam, R., Parikh, D., Batra, D.: Grad-CAM: visual explanations from deep networks via gradient-based localization. In: International Conference on Computer Vision, pp. 618–626. IEEE (2017)

22. Simonyan, K., Zisserman, A.: Very deep convolutional networks for large-scale image recognition. arXiv preprint arXiv:1409.1556 (2014)
23. Tai, Y., Yang, J., Liu, X.: Image super-resolution via deep recursive residual network. In: 2017 IEEE Conference on Computer Vision and Pattern Recognition (CVPR), pp. 2790–2798. IEEE (2017)
24. Tan, W.R., Chan, C.S., Aguirre, H.E., Tanaka, K.: Ceci n'est pas une pipe: a deep convolutional network for fine-art paintings classification. In: 2016 IEEE International Conference on Image Processing (ICIP), pp. 3703–3707. IEEE (2016)
25. Wilber, M.J., Fang, C., Jin, H., Hertzmann, A., Collomosse, J., Belongie, S.J.: BAM! The behance artistic media dataset for recognition beyond photography. In: International Conference on Computer Vision, pp. 1211–1220 (2017)
26. Xu, K., et al.: Show, attend and tell: neural image caption generation with visual attention. In: International Conference on Machine Learning, pp. 2048–2057 (2015)
27. Zhang, K., Zuo, W., Chen, Y., Meng, D., Zhang, L.: Beyond a Gaussian denoiser: residual learning of deep CNN for image denoising. IEEE Trans. Image Process. **26**(7), 3142–3155 (2017)

Third International Workshop on Robust Reading (IWRR)

E2E-MLT - An Unconstrained End-to-End Method for Multi-language Scene Text

Michal Bušta[1], Yash Patel[2(✉)], and Jiri Matas[1]

[1] Center for Machine Perception, Department of Cybernetics,
Czech Technical University, Prague, Czech Republic
`bustam@fel.cvut.cz, matas@cmp.felk.cvut.cz`
[2] Robotics Institute, Carnegie Mellon University, Pittsburgh, USA
`yashp@andrew.cmu.edu`

Abstract. An end-to-end trainable (fully differentiable) method for multi-language scene text localization and recognition is proposed. The approach is based on a single fully convolutional network (FCN) with shared layers for both tasks.

E2E-MLT is the first published multi-language OCR for scene text. While trained in multi-language setup, E2E-MLT demonstrates competitive performance when compared to other methods trained for English scene text alone. The experiments show that obtaining accurate multi-language multi-script annotations is a challenging problem. Code and trained models are released publicly at https://github.com/MichalBusta/E2E-MLT.

1 Introduction

Scene text localization and recognition, a.k.a. photo OCR or text detection and recognition in the wild, is a challenging open computer vision problem. Applications of photo OCR are diverse, from helping the visually impaired to data mining of street-view-like images for information used in map services and geographic information systems. Scene text recognition finds its use as a component in larger integrated systems such as those for autonomous driving, indoor navigations and visual search engines.

The growing cosmopolitan culture in modern cities often generates environments where multi-language text co-appears in the same scene (Fig. 1), triggering a demand for a unified multi-language scene text system. The need is also evident from the high interest in the ICDAR competition on multi-language text [33].

Recent advances in deep learning methods have helped in improving both the text localization [14,26,31,43] and text recognition [5,18,39] methods significantly. However, from the point of view of multi-language capabilities, these methods fall short in following aspects: (1) the evaluation is limited to English text only and the methods are not trained in a multi-language setup, (2) they solve text localization and recognition as two independent problems [14,16] or

Fig. 1. Text in multiple languages appearing in a scene. The proposed E2E-MLT method localizes words, predicts the scripts and generates a text transcription for each bounding box.

make use of multiple networks to solve individual problems [5,30] and (3) the existing OCR methods are lacking the ability to handle rotated or vertical text instances.

Multi-language scene text poses specific challenges. Firstly, the data currently publicly available for non-English scene text recognition is insufficient for training deep architectures. Individual languages have specific challenges, for example, CHINESE and JAPANESE have a high number of characters and there is a substantial number of instances where the text is vertical. BANGLA scene text is mostly hand written.

In this paper, we introduce E2E-MLT, an end-to-end trainable FCN based method with shared convolutional layers for multi-language scene text. E2E-MLT handles multi-language scene text localization, text recognition and script identification using a single fully convolutional network. The method has been trained for the following languages: ARABIC, BANGLA, CHINESE, JAPANESE, KOREAN, LATIN and is capable of recognizing 7,500 characters (compared to less than 100 in English [5,16,39]) and does not make use of any fixed dictionary of words [16,36]. With E2E-MLT, we make the following contributions:

– We experimentally demonstrate that script identification is not required to recognize multi-language text. Unlike competing methods [12,33], E2E-MLT performs script identification from the OCR output using a simple majority voting mechanism over the predicted characters.
– E2E-MLT is capable of recognizing highly rotated and vertical text instances, which is achieved by using a $cos(x) - sin(x)$ representation of the angle.
– We validate that FCN based architecture is capable of handling multi-language text detection and recognition. E2E-MLT is the first published multi-language OCR which works well across six languages.
– We provide the statistics of co-occurring languages at the image level and word level on the ICDAR RRC-MLT 2017 [33] dataset. These statistics

demonstrate that characters from different languages can not only co-occur in same image, but also co-occur within the same word.
- We publicly release a large scale synthetically generated dataset for training multi-language scene text detection, recognition and script identification methods.

The rest of the paper is structured as follows. In Sect. 2, previous work is reviewed. The method is described in Sect. 3 and experimentally evaluated in Sect. 4. Finally, conclusions are drawn is Sect. 5.

2 Related Work

2.1 Scene Text Localization

Scene text localization is the first step in standard text-spotting pipelines. Given a natural scene image, the objective is to obtain precise word level bounding boxes or segmentation maps.

Conventional methods such as [8,34,35] rely on manually designed features to capture the properties of scene text. Generally these methods seek character candidates via extremal region extraction or edge detection. Character-centric deep learning based method [18] makes use of a CNN [23] for image patches (obtained by sliding window) to predict text/no-text score, a character and a bi-gram class.

Jaderberg et al. [16] proposed a multi-stage word-centric method where horizontal bounding box proposals are obtained by aggregating the output of Edge Boxes [45] and Aggregate Channel Features [7]. The proposals are filtered using a Random Forest [4] classifier. As post-processing a CNN regressor is used to obtain fine-grained bounding boxes. Gupta et al. [14] drew inspiration from YOLO object detector [37] and proposed a fully-convolutional regression network trained on synthetic data for performing detection and regression at multiple scales in an image.

Tian et al. [43] use a CNN-RNN joint model to predict the text/no-text score, the y-axis coordinates and the anchor side-refinement. A similar approach [26] adapts the SSD object detector [29] to detect horizontal bounding boxes. Ma et al. [31] detects text of different orientations by adapting the Faster-RCNN [10] architecture and adding 6 hand-crafted rotations and 3 aspects.

A two-staged method for word or line level localization is proposed by Zhou et al. [44]. Following the architecture design principle of *U-Shape* [38] (a fully convolutional network with gradually merged features from different layers) is used. The text proposals obtained are then processed using NMS for final output.

As mentioned earlier, all of these methods deal with English text only. Methods trained for multi-language setup are described in ICDAR RRC-MLT 2017 [33]. *SCUT-DLVClab* trains two models separately, the first model predicts bounding box detections and second model classifies the detected bounding box into one of the script classes or background. *TH-DL* use a modified FCN with residual connections for generating text-proposals and a Fast-RCNN [10] for detection. GoogleLeNet architecture [42] is used for script-identification.

2.2 Scene Text Recognition

The objective of text recognition methods is to take the cropped word image and generate the transcription of the word present. Scene text recognition has been widely studied for English text. Jaderberg et al. [16] train a VGG-16 [41] based CNN on 9 million synthetic images to classify a cropped word image as one of the words in a dictionary. The dictionary contains roughly 90 000 English words and the words of the training and test set. Any word outside the dictionary is ignored.

Shi et al. [39] generates one sequence of characters per image by training a fully-convolutional network with a bidirectional LSTM using the Connectionist Temporal Classification (CTC) [13]. Unlike the OCR of proposed E2E-MLT, both [16,39] resize the source cropped word image to the fixed-sized matrix of 100×32 pixels regardless of the number of characters present or original aspect ratio.

Lee et al. [24] present a recursive recurrent network with soft-attention mechanism for lexicon-free scene text recognition. This method makes use of recursive CNNs with weight sharing to reduce the number of parameters. A RNN is used on top of convolutional features to automatically learn character level language model.

The aforementioned methods only deal with English text, where the number of characters is limited. Methods like [16,18] approach the problem from close dictionary perspective where any word outside the dictionary is ignored. Such setting is not feasible in multi-language scenario where the number of characters and possible set of words are very high. Text recognition in E2E-MLT is open-dictionary (in terms of set of words) and does not require any language specific information.

2.3 End-to-End Scene Text Methods

Recent end-to-end methods address both detection and recognition in a single pipeline. Given an image, the objective is to predict precise word level bounding boxes and corresponding text transcriptions.

Li et al. [25] make use of convolutional recurrent network to concurrently generate text bounding boxes and corresponding transcriptions. An approach similar to [31] was presented by Busta et al. [5], where the rotation is a continuous parameter and optimal anchor box dimensions are found using clustering on training set. The image crops obtained from predicted bounding boxes are transcribed using another fully convolutional network.

Liu et al. [30] introduce ROIRotate to extract the high-level features from shared convolutional layers and feed it to two separate branches for performing localization and recognition. The text localization branch utilizes the features

Fig. 2. Images from the synthetic multi-language in natural scenes dataset.

from lower level and higher level layers to incorporate small text regions. The text recognition branch consists of multiple convolutional layers followed by bi-directional LSTM. The base network and the two branches are optimized jointly.

The idea of our approach for scene text detection and recognition is inspired by that of Busta *et al.* [5]: that is take the state of the art object detector, modify it to handle specifics of scene text and address both localization and recognition using a single pipeline. Unlike [5], E2E-MLT does not make use of multiple networks, is end-to-end trainable, shares convolutional features for both tasks and is trained in a multi-language setup for six languages.

3 Method

Given a scene image containing instances of multi-language text, E2E-MLT obtains text localizations, generates text transcription and script class for each detected region. The structure of E2E-MLT is shown in Fig. 3. The model is optimized in an end-to-end fashion.

3.1 Multi-language Synthetic Data Generation

As mentioned earlier, existing multi-language scene text datasets do not provide sufficient data for deep network training. The largest such dataset is presented in ICDAR RRC-MLT 2017 [33]. This dataset consists of 7,200 training and 1,800 validation images for six languages. To overcome the problem of limited training data, we generate a synthetic multi-language text in natural scene dataset.

We adapt the framework proposed by Gupta *et al.* [14] to a multi-language setup. The framework generates realistic images by overlaying synthetic text over existing natural background images and it accounts for 3D scene geometry. Gupta *et al.* [14] proposed the following approach for scene-text image synthesis:

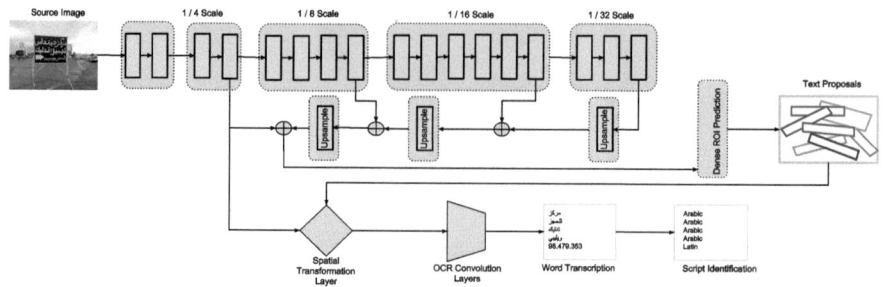

Fig. 3. E2E-MLT overview: Dense text proposals are generated and filtered by the text localization branch of E2E-MLT. Preserving the aspect ratio at bounding box level, features from shared layers are extracted. The OCR branch of E2E-MLT takes these pooled features and generates a character sequence or discards the bounding box as no-text.

- Text in the real world usually appears in well-defined regions, which can be characterized by uniform color and texture. This is achieved by thresholding gPb-UCM contour hierarchies [2] using efficient graph-cut implementation [3]. This provides prospective segmented regions for rendering text.
- Dense estimate of depth maps of segmented regions are then obtained using [28] and then planar facets are fitted to maps using RANSAC [9]. This way normals to prospective regions for text rendering is estimated.
- Finally, the text is aligned to prospective image region for rendering. This is achieved by warping the image region to frontal-parallel view using the estimated region normals, then a rectangle is fitted to this region, and finally, the text is aligned to the larger side of this rectangle.

The generated dataset contains the same set of language classes as ICDAR RRC-MLT 2017 [33]: ARABIC, BANGLA, CHINESE, JAPANESE, KOREAN, LATIN. The **Synthetic Multi-Language in Natural Scene Dataset** contains text rendered over natural scene images selected from the set of 8,000 background images collected by [14]. Annotations include word level and character level text bounding boxes along with the corresponding transcription and language/script class. The dataset has 245,000 images with thousands of images for each language. Sample examples are shown in Fig. 2.

Note: The pipeline presented in [14] renders text in a character by character manner, which breaks down the ligature of ARABIC and BANGLA words. We made appropriate changes in the pipeline to handle these language specific cases. Further, in order to incorporate real world samples of highly-rotated and vertical text instances, we preserve the reading direction at the word level.

3.2 Overall Architecture

An overview of the E2E-MLT model is shown in Fig. 3. We make use of the FPN object detector [27] with ResNet-34 [15] as the backbone of E2E-MLT. Text in natural scene images is often relatively small compared to the entire image size so we replace the first layer of ResNet-34 with a set of 3 × 3 convolutions with stride 2. Similar to [27], the proposed detector works on 1/4 scale of the original image due its high memory consumption.

The architecture along with dimensionality of activation maps after different layers is detailed in Table 1. $\overline{W}$ and $\overline{H}$ are the width and height respectively of the input image. ResN-B represents ResNet block [15], IN represents Instance-Normalization [6]. $|\hat{\mathcal{A}}|$ are the number of characters that can be recognized (the union of characters in all languages, 7500 is our setup). The initial convolutional layers are shared between the both localization and recognition tasks.

Table 1. FCN based E2E-MLT architecture for multi-language scene text localization and recognition.

Type	Channels	Size/Stride	Dim
Con2D, IN, CReLU	16	3 × 3	$\overline{W} \times \overline{H}$
Con2D, IN, CReLU	32	3 × 3/2	$\overline{W}/2 \times \overline{H}/2$
Con2D, IN, ReLU	64	3 × 3	
Con2D, IN, ReLU	64	3 × 3/2	$\overline{W}/4 \times \overline{H}/4$

OCR branch				Localization branch			
Type	Chn.	Size/Stride	Dim	Type	Chn.	Size/Stride	Dim
Con2D, IN, ReLU	128	3 × 3	$\overline{W}/4$ ×10	ResN-B x3	64	3 × 3	
Con2D, IN, ReLU	128	3 × 3		ResN-B x4	128	3 × 3/2	$\frac{\overline{W}}{8} \times \frac{\overline{H}}{8}$
maxpool		2 × 2/2 × 1	$\overline{W}/4 \times 5$	ResN-B x6	256	3 × 3/2	$\frac{\overline{W}}{16} \times \frac{\overline{H}}{16}$
Con2D, IN, ReLU	256	3 × 3		ResN-B x4	512	3 × 3/2	$\frac{\overline{W}}{32} \times \frac{\overline{H}}{32}$
Con2D, IN, ReLU	256			FPN lat. con.	256	1 × 1	$\frac{\overline{W}}{16} \times \frac{\overline{H}}{16}$
maxpool		2 × 2/2 × 1	$\overline{W}/4 \times 2$	FPN lat. con.	256	1 × 1	$\frac{\overline{W}}{8} \times \frac{\overline{H}}{8}$
Con2D, IN, ReLU×2	256	3 × 3		FPN lat. con.	256	1 × 1	$\frac{\overline{W}}{4} \times \frac{\overline{H}}{4}$
Dropout (0.2)				Dropout (0.2)			
Con2D	$|\hat{\mathcal{A}}|$	1 × 1	$\overline{W}/4 \times 1$	Con2D	7	1 × 1	
log softmax							

3.3 Text Localization

The natural scene image is fed into the E2E-MLT architecture and multiple levels of per-pixel text score and geometries are generated. The prediction output consists of seven channels: per-feature text/no-text confidence score r_p, distances to the top, left, bottom and right sides of the bounding box that contains this pixel and the orientation angle parameters as r_θ. To overcome the discontinuity in angle prediction, we represent it by $\sin(r_\theta)$ and $\cos(r_\theta)$. A shrunken version of the ground truth bounding box is considered as positive text region.

The joint loss function used for both localization and recognition in E2E-MLT is a linear combination of multiple loss functions: IoU loss proposed in [44], dice loss proposed in [32], CTC loss function proposed in [13] and mean squared error based loss for learning rotations (represented by L_{angle}). The overall loss function for end-to-end training is given by:

$$L_{final} = L_{geo} + \lambda_1 L_{angle} + \lambda_2 L_{dice} + \lambda_3 L_{CTC} \tag{1}$$

where L_{geo} is the IoU loss function and is invariant against text-regions of different scales. The CTC loss term denoted by L_{CTC} is for word level text recognition (details in Sect. 3.4). L_{angle} is a sum over mean squared loss obtained over $\sin(r_\theta)$ and $\cos(r_\theta)$ representations of rotation angle. We empirically observe that making use of two independent channels to predict the sin and cos of bounding box rotation angle helps with the localization of highly rotated and vertical text instances. Examples of generated bounding box outputs is shown in Table 2.

Since the text regions are relatively small compared to the entire image size, there is a high class imbalance between foreground (text-region) and background class. The dice loss term helps the network to overcome this class imbalance. The dice loss as defined in [32]:

$$L_{dice} = \frac{2\sum_i^N r_{p_i} g_i}{\sum_i^N r_{p_i}^2 + \sum_i^N q_i^2} \qquad (2)$$

where the summation in Eq. 2 runs over all the feature points in last convolutional layer. $g_i \in \{0, 1\}$ is the ground truth label for a given feature point with index i and $p_i \in (0, 1)$ is the corresponding from the network. For all our experimental setup, we keep $\lambda_1 = \lambda_2 = \lambda_3 = 1$ in Eq. 1.

Table 2. Example of learned proposal representation (actual output of the learned network): the red line is the top line, the green circle is start of reading direction - best viewed in zoom and color

The dense proposals from the network are then filtered based on the text confidence score r_p with the threshold value 0.9. Only the proposals with $r_p > 0.9$ are considered for further processing. Finally, locality aware NMS [44] is performed on filtered proposals to generate the final bounding box predictions.

3.4 Text Recognition

OCR branch of E2E-MLT is a FCN module for multi-language text recognition. The word level bounding boxes are predicted (as explained in Sect. 3.3) are compared against the ground truth bounding boxes. The predictions with the IoU of higher than 0.9 are used for training of the OCR branch of E2E-MLT.

These selected predictions are then used to estimate the warp parameters of the spatial transformer layer [17]. Note that the spatial transformer operation is applied on input image and not on the feature representation. Text recognition is highly rotation dependent. We handle rotation in separate step and make use of the spatial transformer to normalize image to scale and rotation, and thus making the learning task easier. Similar to [20], we make use of the bi-linear interpolation to compute the output values as it avoids misalignment and makes the input to the OCR module fixed height and variable width, while preserving the aspect ratio at word level.

The fully convolutional OCR module takes a variable-width feature tensor $\overline{W} \times 40 \times C$ as an input and outputs a matrix $\frac{\overline{W}}{4} \times |\hat{\mathcal{A}}|$, where $\mathcal{A}$ is the alphabet – the union of characters of all languages (= 7500 log-Softmax outputs), and $\overline{W} = \frac{wH'}{h}$ (where w, h are the width and height respectively of the text region, we fix $H' = 40$). The full network definition is provided in Table 1. The loss from text recognition in E2E-MLT architecture is computed using the Connectionist Temporal Classification (CTC) [13].

During all the experiments we use greedy decoding of network output. An alternative could be the use of, task and language specific techniques such as prefix decoding or decoding with language models (for the word spotting task). However, our OCR is generalized, open-dictionary and language independent.

3.5 Training Details

Both the text localization and OCR branches of E2E-MLT are trained together in an end-to-end fashion. A union of the ICDAR RRC-MLT 2017 [33] train dataset, the ICDAR RCTW 2017 [40] train dataset, the ICDAR 2015 [21] train dataset and Synthetic Multi-Language in Natural Scene Dataset (explained in Sect. 3.1) is used for training.

We make use of Adam [22] (base learning rate = 0.0001, $\beta_1 = 0.9$, $\beta_2 = 0.999$, weight decay = 0) for optimizing over joint loss for text localization and recognition (Eq. 1) and train until the validation error converges.

4 Experiments

Throughout our experimental analysis, we evaluate a single model trained in multi-language setup as explained in Sect. 3. We do not fine-tune the model for specific datasets or task while reporting the results. Unlike [30], we evaluate the performance using a single-scale. Further, the text recognition results are reported in an unconstrained setup, that is, without making the use of any predefined lexicon (set of words).

4.1 Multi-language Scene Text Recognition

First we run the analysis of the scripts co-occurrence in individual images (Table 3) and the scripts co-occurrence in words (Table 4). The script of the character is defined by the Unicode table [1]. Each character has its unique name (for example character 'A' has unicode name 'Latin Capital Letter A' therefore its script is Latin). The scripts which occur in the ICDAR MLT 2017 dataset [33] are LATin, ARabic, BENGali, HANGul, CJK, HIRagana, KATakana and DIGit. The rest of characters are considered to be SYMBOLS (SYM). The abbreviation CKH marks the group of CJK, HIRAGANA AND KATAKANA scripts. Table 4 shows that the script co-occurrence is non-trivial even on the word level. The OCR module in a practical application should satisfactorily handle at least the common combination of scripts of non-Latin script and Latin, Digit, and Symbols script.

The OCR accuracy on cropped words and the confusion matrix for individual script of the E2E-MLT is shown in Table 5. In this evaluation, the ground truth

Table 3. Script co-occurrence at image level on the ICDAR MLT-RRC 2017 [33] validation dataset. The row-column entry is incremented for all pairs of scripts present in an image.

	SYM	DIG	LAT	ARA	BENG	HANG	CJK	HIR	KAT
SYM	4361	2285	3264	400	482	652	903	378	312
DIG	2285	2838	2166	205	136	460	758	274	219
LAT	3264	2166	5047	501	150	443	876	299	258
ARA	400	205	501	797	0	0	0	0	0
BENG	482	136	150	0	795	0	0	0	0
HANG	652	460	443	0	0	847	81	32	28
CJK	903	758	876	0	0	81	1615	447	355
HIR	378	274	299	0	0	32	447	462	300
KAT	312	219	258	0	0	28	355	300	374

Table 4. Script co-occurrence in words in the ICDAR MLT-RRC 2017 validation dataset [33]. Column: script of a character. Row: script/script group of the word the character appeared in. If multiple scripts are present in the word, the row-column entry is incremented for each script.

	SYM	DIG	LAT	ARA	BENG	HANG	CJK	HIR	KAT
LAT	1046	635	52050	0	0	0	36	0	0
ARA	20	13	0	4881	0	0	0	0	0
BENG	63	5	0	0	3688	0	0	0	0
HANG	118	84	0	0	0	3767	0	0	0
CKH	416	499	21	0	0	0	7265	1424	1037

for a word is defined as the most frequent script. Confusion matrix shows that E2E-MLT does not make many mistakes due to confusing script confusion.

Table 5. E2E-MLT OCR accuracy on the ICDAR MLT-RRC 2017 validation dataset [33] and confusion matrix (GT script is in row, the recognized script in columns)

Script	Acc	$\frac{Edits}{len(GT)}$	Characters	Images	SYM	DIG	LAT	ARA	BENG	HAN	CJK	HIR	KAT
SYM	0.416	0.472	926	541	338	85	90	5	2	1	8	1	0
DIGIT	0.705	0.146	7027	1864	57	1695	87	9	4	1	6	1	2
LATIN	0.744	0.111	52708	9280	172	92	8946	27	2	4	36	3	3
ARA	0.462	0.250	4892	951	28	13	61	843	2	1	2	1	0
BENG	0.342	0.314	3781	673	17	9	19	4	615	4	5	0	0
HAN	0.652	0.217	3853	1164	47	27	37	1	6	1013	34	2	1
CJK	0.446	0.295	7771	1375	47	13	14	0	0	3	1281	8	10
HIR	0.317	0.268	1678	230	19	5	12	2	0	3	25	159	5
KAT	0.130	0.434	1011	177	12	2	7	0	0	1	18	6	131
Total	0.651	0.164	83647	16255									

In Table 6 we show some difficult cases for multi-language text recognition and demonstrate that some of the mistakes are non-trivial for a human reader as well.

Table 6. Difficult cases (for Latin-script native readers). Transcription errors, shown in red, which require close inspection - (a), (g), (h), (i). Note that for (i), the error is also in the ground truth. We were not able to establish a clear GT for (e) and (f). For (b), the transcription is 70004 in Bangla. In the context of Latin scripts, this same image will be interpreted as 900 08. Note the errors related to ":" and —, there are multiple types of colons and dashes in UTF.

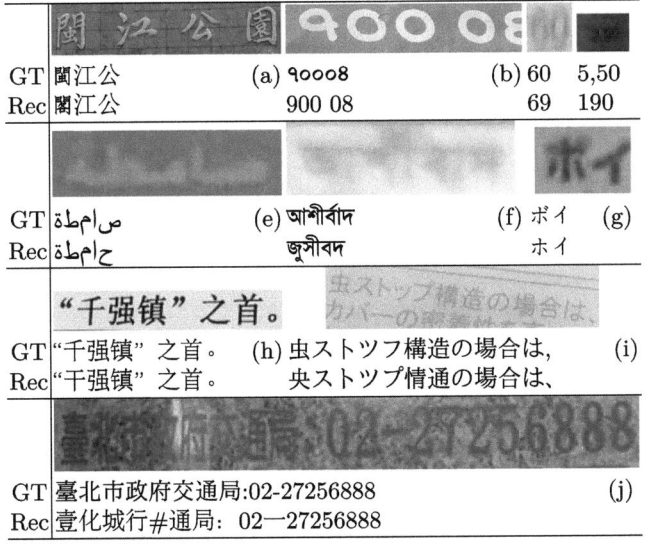

Table 7. Errors in the GT of the ICDAR MLT-RRC 2017 validation dataset [33]. Incorrect transcriptions are highlighted in red. Note that some errors lead to very large edit distances, e.g. in (f) and (h). GT errors effect both training and evaluation of the method. We estimate that at least 10% of errors on non-latin words reported for E2E-MLT on the ICDAR MLT dataset are due to GT mistakes.

Mistakes in the ground truth annotations adds to the challenge, see Table 7. For Latin-script native readers, they are hard to identify. Another common source of error is caused by GT bounding boxes that are incorrectly axis-aligned bounding.

4.2 End-to-End Scene Text on the ICDAR 2015 Dataset

The ICDAR 2015 dataset was introduced in the ICDAR 2015 Robust Reading Competition [21]. This dataset consists of 500 images taken from Google Glass device of people walking in city. Note that this dataset was not made with text in mind and thus adequately captures the real world scene text scenario. The dataset is referred as Incidental text and the text instances are small compared to entire image size. Unlike ICDAR RRC-MLT [33], the images in this dataset contain only English text.

Here we experimentally evaluate E2E-MLT on ICDAR 2015 [21] dataset. Note that E2E-MLT is trained to handle multi-language text and the same is capable of handling text instances from other languages (we do not train a different model for English).

E2E-MLT is a unconstrained multi-language scene text method. We do not make use of any per-image lexicon or dictionary. Thus, we evaluate E2E-MLT only for generic category where no per-image lexicon is available. Quantitative results are shown in Table 8.

4.3 End-to-End Multi-language Scene Text on the ICDAR MLT

We evaluate the performance of E2E-MLT on the validation set of ICDAR MLT 2017 [33] dataset. The dataset [33] comprises 7,200 training, 1,800 validation and 9,000 testing natural scene images. The ground truth annotations include

Table 8. End-to-end evaluation on generic setting (no lexicon) of ICDAR 2015 [21] dataset. The methods marked with asterisk are trained only for English scene text. E2E-MLT has a single unconstrained (no dictionary) model for six languages (7,500 characters). Further, the testing of E2E-MLT is done using a single-scale of input images. The low precision of E2E-MLT is partially because the ICDAR 2015 dataset contains non-latin text as well.

Method	Recall	Precision	F1-score	Recall ED1
TextProposals + DictNet* [11,16]	33.61%	79.14%	47.18%	-
DeepTextSpotter* [5]	-	-	47.0%	-
FOTS-Real time* [30]	-	-	51.40%	-
FOTS-multi-scale* [30]	53.20%	84.61%	65.33%	-
E2E-MLT	44.9%	71.4%	55.1%	59.6%

bounding box coordinates, the script class and text-transcription. The dataset deals with the following 6 languages: ARABIC, LATIN, CHINESE, JAPANESE, KOREAN, BANGLA. Additionally, punctuation and some math symbols sometimes appear as separate words and are assigned a special script class called SYMBOLS, hence 7 script classes are considered. Quantitative evaluation of end-to-end recognition (localization and recognition) is shown in Table 9. Qualitative results are demonstrated in Table 10.

Table 9. E2E-MLT end-To-end recognition results on ICDAR MLT 2017 [33] validation set.

Text length	E2E Recall	Precision	E2E Recall ED1	Loc. Recall IoU 0.5
2+	42.9%	53.7%	55.5%	68.4%
3+	43.3%	59.7%	59.9%	69.5%

Table 10. Example E2E-MLT results on the ICDAR MLT 2017 dataset [33]

4.4 Joint Multi-language Text Localization and Script Identification on the ICDAR RRC-MLT 2017

The objective of this task is to predict precise word level bounding boxes and the corresponding script class for each word. Existing text recognition algorithms [18, 19, 39] are language-dependent which makes script identification a prerequisite task for the other methods. In Sect. 4.3, we experimentally demonstrated that script identification is not required for multi-language text recognition. In E2E-MLT, once we transcribe the text, we make use of a simple majority voting from each character to predict the final script class.

In Table 11, we provide quantitative evaluation on joint text localization and script identification task of ICDAR MLT 2017 [33]. Note that unlike other methods in Table 11, we do not solve script identification as a separate task. Rather, we make use of transcribed text output of E2E-MLT.

Table 11. Joint text localization and script identification on the ICDAR RRC-MLT [33] test data.

Method	F-Measure	Recall	Precision
SCUT-DLVClab2	58.08%	48.77%	71.78%
TH-DL	39.37%	29.65%	58.58%
E2E-MLT	48.00%	45.98%	50.20%

5 Conclusion

E2E-MLT, an end-to-end trainable unconstrained method for multi-language scene text localization and recognition, was introduced. It is the first published multi-language OCR for scene text capable of recognizing highly rotated and vertical text instances.

Experimentally, we demonstrate that a single FCN based model is capable of jointly solving multi-language scene text localization and recognition tasks. Although E2E-MLT is trained to work across six languages, it demonstrates competitive performance on ICDAR 2015 [21] dataset compared to the methods trained on English data alone.

With the paper we will publish a large scale synthetically generated dataset for training multi-language scene text detection, recognition and script identification methods. The code and trained model will be released.

Acknowledgement. The research was supported by the Czech Science Foundation Project GACR P103/12/G084.

References

1. Unicode table. https://unicode-table.com/. Accessed 30 Sept 2017
2. Arbelaez, P., Maire, M., Fowlkes, C., Malik, J.: Contour detection and hierarchical image segmentation. PAMI **33**(5), 898–916 (2011)
3. Arbeláez, P., Pont-Tuset, J., Barron, J.T., Marques, F., Malik, J.: Multiscale combinatorial grouping. In: Proceedings of the IEEE Conference on Computer Vision and Pattern Recognition (2014)
4. Bosch, A., Zisserman, A., Munoz, X.: Image classification using random forests and ferns. In: CVPR (2007)
5. Bušta, M., Neumann, L., Matas, J.: Deep TextSpotter: an end-to-end trainable scene text localization and recognition framework. In: 2017 IEEE International Conference on Computer Vision (ICCV), pp. 2223–2231. IEEE (2017)
6. Chen, T.Q., Schmidt, M.: Fast patch-based style transfer of arbitrary style. arXiv preprint arXiv:1612.04337 (2016)
7. Dollár, P., Appel, R., Belongie, S., Perona, P.: Fast feature pyramids for object detection. PAMI **36**(8), 1532–1545 (2014)
8. Epshtein, B., Ofek, E., Wexler, Y.: Detecting text in natural scenes with stroke width transform. In: CVPR (2010)
9. Fischler, M.A., Bolles, R.C.: Random sample consensus: a paradigm for model fitting with applications to image analysis and automated cartography. Commun. ACM **24**(6), 381–395 (1981)
10. Girshick, R.: Fast R-CNN. In: ICCV (2015)
11. Gómez, L., Karatzas, D.: Textproposals: a text-specific selective search algorithm for word spotting in the wild. Pattern Recognit. **70**, 60–74 (2017)
12. Gomez, L., Nicolaou, A., Karatzas, D.: Improving patch-based scene text script identification with ensembles of conjoined networks. Pattern Recognit. **67**, 85–96 (2017)
13. Graves, A., Fernández, S., Gomez, F., Schmidhuber, J.: Connectionist temporal classification: labelling unsegmented sequence data with recurrent neural networks. In: ICML (2006)
14. Gupta, A., Vedaldi, A., Zisserman, A.: Synthetic data for text localisation in natural images. In: CVPR (2016)
15. He, K., Zhang, X., Ren, S., Sun, J.: Deep residual learning for image recognition. In: CVPR (2016)
16. Jaderberg, M., Simonyan, K., Vedaldi, A., Zisserman, A.: Reading text in the wild with convolutional neural networks. IJCV **116**(1), 1–20 (2016)
17. Jaderberg, M., Simonyan, K., Zisserman, A., et al.: Spatial transformer networks. In: NIPS (2015)
18. Jaderberg, M., Vedaldi, A., Zisserman, A.: Deep features for text spotting. In: Fleet, D., Pajdla, T., Schiele, B., Tuytelaars, T. (eds.) ECCV 2014. LNCS, vol. 8692, pp. 512–528. Springer, Cham (2014). https://doi.org/10.1007/978-3-319-10593-2_34
19. Jain, M., Mathew, M., Jawahar, C.: Unconstrained scene text and video text recognition for Arabic script. In: ASAR (2017)
20. Johnson, J., Karpathy, A., Fei-Fei, L.: Densecap: fully convolutional localization networks for dense captioning. In: CVPR (2016)
21. Karatzas, D., et al.: ICDAR 2015 competition on robust reading. In: ICDAR (2015)
22. Kingma, D., Ba, J.: Adam: a method for stochastic optimization. arXiv preprint arXiv:1412.6980 (2014)

23. LeCun, Y., Bottou, L., Bengio, Y., Haffner, P.: Gradient-based learning applied to document recognition. Proc. IEEE **86**(11), 2278–2324 (1998)
24. Lee, C.Y., Osindero, S.: Recursive recurrent nets with attention modeling for OCR in the wild. In: CVPR (2016)
25. Li, H., Wang, P., Shen, C.: Towards end-to-end text spotting with convolutional recurrent neural networks. In: ICCV (2017)
26. Liao, M., Shi, B., Bai, X., Wang, X., Liu, W.: Textboxes: a fast text detector with a single deep neural network. In: AAAI (2017)
27. Lin, T.Y., Dollár, P., Girshick, R., He, K., Hariharan, B., Belongie, S.: Feature pyramid networks for object detection. In: CVPR (2017)
28. Liu, F., Shen, C., Lin, G.: Deep convolutional neural fields for depth estimation from a single image. In: CVPR (2015)
29. Liu, W., et al.: SSD: single shot MultiBox detector. In: Leibe, B., Matas, J., Sebe, N., Welling, M. (eds.) ECCV 2016. LNCS, vol. 9905, pp. 21–37. Springer, Cham (2016). https://doi.org/10.1007/978-3-319-46448-0_2
30. Liu, X., Liang, D., Yan, S., Chen, D., Qiao, Y., Yan, J.: FOTS: fast oriented text spotting with a unified network. In: CVPR (2018)
31. Ma, J., et al.: Arbitrary-oriented scene text detection via rotation proposals. arXiv preprint arXiv:1703.01086 (2017)
32. Milletari, F., Navab, N., Ahmadi, S.A.: V-net: fully convolutional neural networks for volumetric medical image segmentation. In: 3DV (2016)
33. Nayef, N.: ICDAR 2017 competition on multi-lingual scene text detection and script identification (2017)
34. Neumann, L., Matas, J.: A method for text localization and recognition in real-world images. In: Kimmel, R., Klette, R., Sugimoto, A. (eds.) ACCV 2010. LNCS, vol. 6494, pp. 770–783. Springer, Heidelberg (2011). https://doi.org/10.1007/978-3-642-19318-7_60
35. Neumann, L., Matas, J.: Real-time scene text localization and recognition. In: CVPR (2012)
36. Patel, Y., Gomez, L., Rusiñol, M., Karatzas, D.: Dynamic lexicon generation for natural scene images. In: Hua, G., Jégou, H. (eds.) ECCV 2016. LNCS, vol. 9913, pp. 395–410. Springer, Cham (2016). https://doi.org/10.1007/978-3-319-46604-0_29
37. Redmon, J., Divvala, S., Girshick, R., Farhadi, A.: You only look once: unified, real-time object detection. In: CVPR (2016)
38. Ronneberger, O., Fischer, P., Brox, T.: U-Net: convolutional networks for biomedical image segmentation. In: Navab, N., Hornegger, J., Wells, W.M., Frangi, A.F. (eds.) MICCAI 2015. LNCS, vol. 9351, pp. 234–241. Springer, Cham (2015). https://doi.org/10.1007/978-3-319-24574-4_28
39. Shi, B., Bai, X., Yao, C.: An end-to-end trainable neural network for image-based sequence recognition and its application to scene text recognition. PAMI **39**(11), 2298–2304 (2017)
40. Shi, B., et al.: ICDAR 2017 competition on reading Chinese text in the wild (RCTW-17). arXiv preprint arXiv:1708.09585 (2017)
41. Simonyan, K., Zisserman, A.: Very deep convolutional networks for large-scale image recognition. arXiv preprint arXiv:1409.1556 (2014)
42. Szegedy, C., et al.: Going deeper with convolutions. In: CVPR (2015)
43. Tian, Z., Huang, W., He, T., He, P., Qiao, Y.: Detecting text in natural image with connectionist text proposal network. In: Leibe, B., Matas, J., Sebe, N., Welling, M. (eds.) ECCV 2016. LNCS, vol. 9912, pp. 56–72. Springer, Cham (2016). https://doi.org/10.1007/978-3-319-46484-8_4

44. Zhou, X., et al.: East: an efficient and accurate scene text detector. In: CVPR (2017)
45. Zitnick, C.L., Dollár, P.: Edge boxes: locating object proposals from edges. In: Fleet, D., Pajdla, T., Schiele, B., Tuytelaars, T. (eds.) ECCV 2014. LNCS, vol. 8693, pp. 391–405. Springer, Cham (2014). https://doi.org/10.1007/978-3-319-10602-1_26

An Invoice Reading System Using a Graph Convolutional Network

D. Lohani[1], A. Belaïd[2(✉)], and Y. Belaïd[2]

[1] MOSIG program, GVR, INP, 38000 Grenoble, France
devashishlohani@gmail.com
[2] Université de Lorraine-CNRS-LORIA,
Campus scientifique, 54500 Vandoeuvre-lès-Nancy, France
{abdel.belaid,yolande.belaid}@loria.fr

Abstract. In this paper, we present a model-free system for reading digitized invoice images, which highlights the most useful billing entities and does not require any particular parameterization. The power of the system lies in the fact that it generalizes to both seen and unseen layouts of invoice. The system first breaks down the invoice data into various set of entities to extract and then learns structural and semantic information for each entity to extract via a graph structure, which is later generalized to the whole invoice structure. This local neighborhood exploitation is accomplished via a Graph Convolutional Network (GCN). The system digs deep to extract table information and provide complete invoice reading upto 27 entities of interest without any template information or configuration with an excellent overall F-measure score of 0.93.

1 Introduction

We seek to set up a platform for managing personal data, which complies with the European recommendations on data security [1]. This platform must offer everyone the opportunity to manage his data, to secure, update, consolidate and evolve it. If the feeding of recent data does not pose too many problems, that of the old data requires careful digitization and retro-conversion. The data referred is mainly of the administrative document type and concerns contracts, invoices, pay slips, etc. The scanning is done by the customer and sent to the platform which retrieves the relevant information and provides services to the customers.

The work focused on the processing of invoice images. Invoices broadly contain two types of information: information relating to the issuing company and the receiving customer (generally corresponding to named entities of address type, numbers and billing dates, etc.) and information relating to the products ordered (containing labels, taxes and amounts). Several methods exist for information extration in invoices. Most of them are based on comparing the input document with an already observed template, e.g. rule, keyword or layout based techniques. Many systems first classify the templates, e.g. Intellix [2], ITE-SOFT [3,4], smartFIX [5] and others [6,7]. Due to their dependence on seeing the template beforehand, these systems cannot accurately extract information from unseen layouts of invoices. CloudScan [8] is perhaps the only model so far which can handle unseen layout invoices quite well. It is based on classification of word n-grams into entities of interest instead of mapping of words to fields. Even though their system performed quite well for simpler entities like date and invoice number, they were not able to extract complex multi-dimensional entities like company or client addresses. It is due to the fact that their system works linearly due to n-grams but invoices also have 2-dimensional relations within entities like in tables and addresses.

The extraction of information inside table is itself a very complicated research topic and has a very related limited work [4, 9, 10]. Authors in [9, 10] have similar approach where an input pattern in table is provided by the client for fields to extract. This pattern is modeled as a graph, which is used to mine similar graphs from a document image in order to produce a model. The biggest problem here is that the client needs to intervene in each invoice and draw a pattern to extract. Furthermore, the results show that it is difficult to adapt to new structures of table and we need to have more or less similar images for proper extraction, which is not the real world case.

Hamza et al. [4] have so far developed the most comprehensive system which deals with both entities inside and outside table. It analyses a document by retrieving and analyzing similar documents or elements of documents (cases) stored in a database. The retrieval step is performed using graph probing. The analysis step is done to the information found in the nearest retrieved cases. The problem with this system is that it is similar to template model as it has to store various cases and solutions but not every time the solution can fit the real world case.

We propose a generic approach to deal with all the information in the invoice in and outside table. We model the whole invoice document as a document graph of words, then we classify each word in the document into classes of interest to extract through a graph convolutional network (GCN) and finally we group the words of same classes together to obtain the final entities. The power of our system lies in the graph modeling using GCN which takes into account the features of its neighboring words and their interrelationships to decide the class of a word. The system automatically generalizes to various structures of entities to extract and learns their characteristics. We evaluate our model on a large dataset and provide very detailed and competitive results.

The paper is organized as follows: Sect. 2 presents our approach, Sect. 3 shows the experiments and results. Finally Sect. 4 concludes the work and provides future guidelines.

2 Approach

2.1 System Overview

Our system consists of four major steps as shown in Fig. 1. The system starts by extracting only words from the image. Features are calculated for each one of them by word embedding. The resulting vectors are used to model the complete document as a graph with words as nodes and edges depicting neighborhood relationships. This document graph is fed to a graph node classifier which classifies each word into classes of interest. Finally words belonging to same classes are grouped together to form entities.

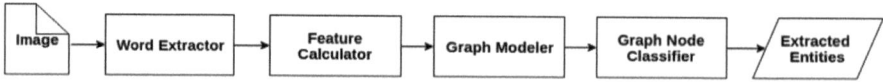

Fig. 1. Schema of our proposed approach

2.2 Word Modeling

Word modeling consists of two steps: word extraction and feature calculation with word representation, which will be detailed in the following.

Word Extraction: The invoice image is run through an OCR engine and the output is retrieved in HOCR format. From this output, we only take word zones (word id, content and bounding box) and ignore all other zones such as graphic lines, photos, blobs, etc., because the higher up zones are composed of word zones and accumulate more OCR segmentation errors. We perform the noise removal on word zones by simply avoiding words with extra big or extra small sizes, words without any content (usually table border and margin lines) and words with erroneous non-alphanumeric contents (prominent when salt and pepper noise is present). The output of this step is a collection of "good" words with their id, content and bounding box information.

Feature Calculation: For each word, we calculate boolean, numeric and text features as follows:

1. Boolean features are calculated as follows:
    (a) **isDate**: a parser to check whether a word or part of word could be a date.
    (b) **isZipCode:** checks if a 6 digit zipcode belongs to a small database of zip codes.
    (c) **isKnownCity, (d) isKnownDept, (e) isKnownCountry**: checks the word in a small database of known cities, departments and countries.
    (f) **nature**: an 8 dimensional binary vector which denotes the presence of a specific nature of the word. It includes: isAlphabetic, isNumeric, isAlphaNumeric, isNumberwithDecimal, isRealNumber, isCurrency, hasRealandCurrency, mix (except these categories), mixc (mix and currency word).
    We get a 13 dimensional boolean vector as output.

2. Numeric features of a word consists of its relative distance to its nearest neighbors (refer to Sect. 2.4 for more details) in 4 major directions (left, right, top and bottom) (refer to Fig. 2). Relative distances are calculated as follows:

$$RD_L = (Right(Word_{Left}) - Left(Word_{Source}))/Width_{Page} \quad (1a)$$

$$RD_T = (Bottom(Word_{Top}) - Top(Word_{Source}))/Height_{Page} \quad (1b)$$

$$RD_R = (Left(Word_{Right}) - Right(Word_{Source}))/Width_{Page} \quad (1c)$$

$$RD_B = (Top(Word_{Bottom}) - Bottom(Word_{Source}))/Height_{Page} \quad (1d)$$

Since the values are increasing from left to right and from top to bottom, so RD_L and RD_T are negative while RD_R and RD_B are positive. Each value is normalized with the highest possible value, so absolute value for each of four variables is always less than 1.

3. Text feature calculation is basically converting the word text into a meaningful vector representation. For this task, we use Byte Pair Encoding (BPE) [11] over Glove or Word2Vec because of its ability to deal with out of vocabulary words. This approach breaks the word into subwords to deduce the meaning of the complete word. BPE is an unsupervised subword segmentation method which starts with a sequence of symbols, for example characters, and iteratively merges the most frequent symbol pair into a new symbol. This proved out to be very useful in OCRed invoice images as we were able to deduce the meaning of a word correctly even in the presence of OCR errors due to its subwords.

Word Representation: We use BPEmb [12], a recent collection of pre-trained BPE vectors. We break the input word into maximum of 3 subwords if possible, using the French and English learned vocabulary. Then, we fetch for each subword a 100 dimensional embedding vector. As an output, for each word of the document, we get a 300 dimensional embedding vector.

Finally, we obtain a 317 dimensional feature vector of every word in the document.

2.3 Graph Modeler

In this step, the whole document is modeled as a graph with words as nodes and edges denoting nearest neighbors of a word in 4 major directions.

Algorithm 1. Line Formation

1: Sort words based on Top coordinate
2: Form lines as group of words which obeys the following:
    Two words (W_a and W_b) are in same line if:
        $Top(W_a) \leq Bottom(W_b)$ and $Bottom(W_a) \geq Top(W_b)$
3: Sort words in each line based on $Left$ coordinate

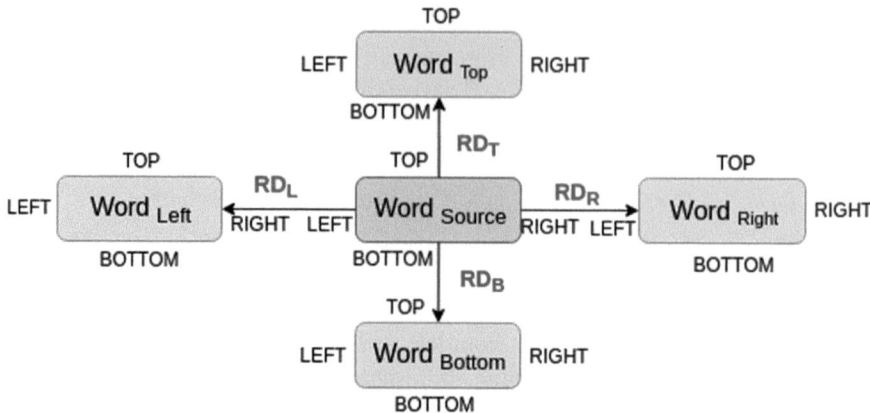

Fig. 2. Nearest neighbors of the source word, $Word_{Source}$ are $Word_{Left}$, $Word_{Top}$, $Word_{Right}$ and $Word_{Bottom}$. Each of the word has four bounding box coordinates: *Left, Top, Right, Bottom* depicting its extreme coordinates in 4 directions. Relative distances of $Word_{Source}$ with neighboring 4 words are designated as RD_L, RD_T, RD_R, RD_B for $Word_{Left}$, $Word_{Top}$, $Word_{Right}$ and $Word_{Bottom}$ respectively.

We first run the Line Formation algorithm as defined in Algorithm 1. As a result we get lines as array of words where within each line words are sorted from left to right and lines themselves are read from top to bottom. This ensures that words are read from top left corner of the image first, going line by line from left to right and at last the final bottom right word of the page is read. Note that here notion of line is just a group of words which are well aligned horizontally and we are not forming an actual line rectangle because in our case, lines are used just to read words in right order to build the document graph. Let W_{doc} denote the set of all words in the document. Mathematically, we define the undirected document graph as $G_{doc} = (W_{doc}, E)$, where each $v \in W_{doc}$ corresponds to a word and each edge $e \in E$, follows the Algorithm 2. The graph structure is stored in an unweighted adjacency matrix A which denotes nearest neighbor relationships of all words in a document. We can see in Fig. 3(B) that this approach provides generic graph for complete document without any user intervention and due to its low degree, it is computationally efficient unlike star graph for every entity in ITESOFT system as shown in Fig. 3(A). One can also observe in Fig. 3(B) that each word can have atmost 4° and only one edge in each direction. Words that are read before are given the priority in case of ambiguity. Eg: Word "le" at bottom left of Fig. 3(B) has no top edge connecting it to word "anticipe" because word "anticipe" was read before and it chose word "fois" as bottom edge rather than word "le" even though they had the same distance because left word is preferred in ambiguity as described in Algorithm 2.

Algorithm 2. Graph Modeling Algorithm

1: Read words from each line starting from topmost line going towards bottommost line
2: For each word, perform following:
   2.1 Check words which are in vertical projection with it:
   2.2 Calculate RD_L and RD_R for each of them (refer Sect. 2.3)
   2.3 Select nearest neighbour words in horizontal direction which have least magnititude of RD_L and RD_R, provided that those words do not have an edge in that direction
        2.3.1 In case, two words have same RD_L or RD_R, the word having higher top coordinate is chosen
   2.4 Repeat steps from 2.1 to 2.3 similarly for retrieving nearest neighbour words in vertical direction by taking horizontal projection, calculating RD_T and RD_B and choosing words having higher left coordinate incase of ambiguity
   2.5 Draw edges between word and its 4 nearest neighbours if they are available

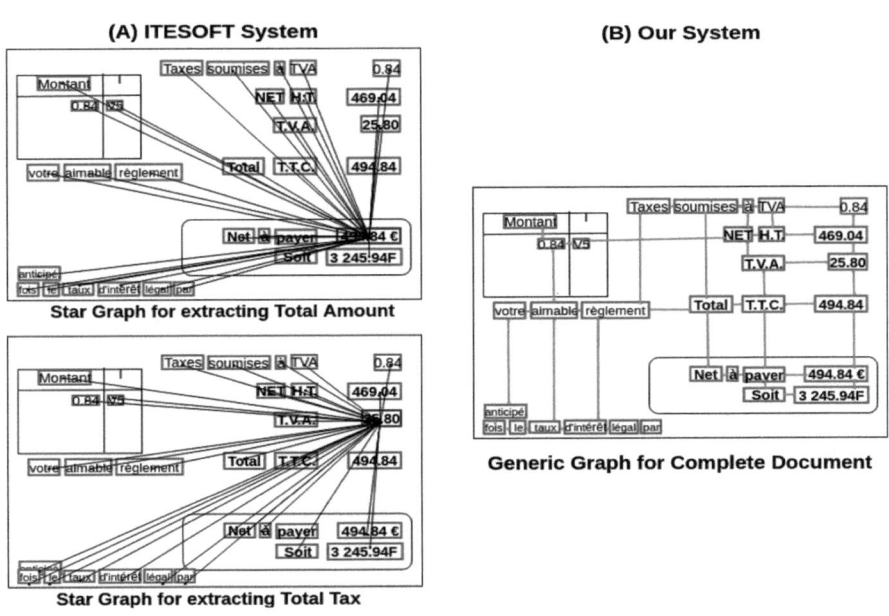

Fig. 3. Graph modeling: (A) ITESOFT system [3] with star graph for each entity to extract (B) Our System with one generic graph for complete document

2.4 Graph Node Classifier

In this step, we consider the problem of classifying nodes (words in our case) in a graph (such as a document graph), where class labels are available for some documents. The problem is basically graph node classification. In our context, it is very important to classify a node by looking into its neighborhood attributes in the graph. To solve this problem, recently [13] used multilayer neural networks operating on graphs called Graph Convolutional Networks (GCN). GCNs are neural networks operating on graphs and inducing features of nodes (i.e. real-valued vectors/embeddings) based on properties of their neighborhoods. In [13], authors show GCN to be very effective for the node classification task: the classifier was estimated jointly with a GCN, so that the induced node features were informative for the node classification problem. Depending on how many layers of convolution are used, GCNs can capture information only about immediate neighbors (with one layer of convolution) or any nodes at most K hops aways (if K layers are stacked on top of each other).

The basic idea is based on spectral graph theory that the graph convolutions can be dealt as multiplications in the graph spectral domain. The feature maps can be obtained by inverse transform from the graph spectral domain to original graph domain.

In our paper, the word features are learnt by GCN given the graph representation of the document. Given an invoice document, we define its input graph feature vector by F_{in} and we denote the output feature vector after graph convolution by F_{out}. Firstly, F_{in} is transformed to the spectral domain via graph Fourier transform. This transform is based on the normalized graph Laplacian, defined as $L = I_N - D^{-1/2} A D^{-1/2}$, where I_N and D are respectively the identity matrix and the diagonal degree matrix of the graph structure G. Then, L can be eigendecomposed as $L = U \Lambda U^T$, where U is a matrix of eigenvectors and Λ is a diagonal matrix whose diagonal elements are eigenvalues of L. The Fourier transform of F_{in} is a function of U defined as:

$$\hat{F}_{in} = U^T \times F_{in} \quad (2)$$

while the inverse transform is defined as:

$$F_{in} = U \times \hat{F}_{in} \quad (3)$$

The convolution of F_{in} with a spectral filter g_θ is given by:

$$F_{out} = g_\theta * F_{in} = U * g_\theta * U^T * F_{in} \quad (4)$$

where parameter θ is a vector to learn. In order to keep the filter K-localized in space and computationally efficient, [14] proposes an approximated polynomial filter defined as:

$$g_\theta = \sum_{k=0}^{K-1} \theta_k T_k(\tilde{L}) \quad (5)$$

where $T_k(x) = 2x T_{k-1}(x) - T_{k-2}(x)$ with $T_0(x) = 1$ and $T_1(x) = x$, $\tilde{L} = \frac{2}{\lambda_{max}} L - I_N$ and λ_{max} denotes the largest eigenvalue of L. $T_k(x)$ is the Chebyshev polynomial of x upto k order. The filtering operation can then be written as $F_{out} = g_\theta F_{in}$. In our model, we use the same filter as in [14] (Fig. 4).

For the graph representation of an invoice document, the ith input graph feature $f_{in,i} \in F_{in}$ of word node v_i is the 317 dimensional feature vector as calculated in Sect. 2.3. Then, the ith output feature $f_{out,i} \in F_{out}$ is:

$$f_{out,i} = \sum_{k=0}^{K-1} \theta_k T_k(\tilde{L}) f_{in,i} \quad (6)$$

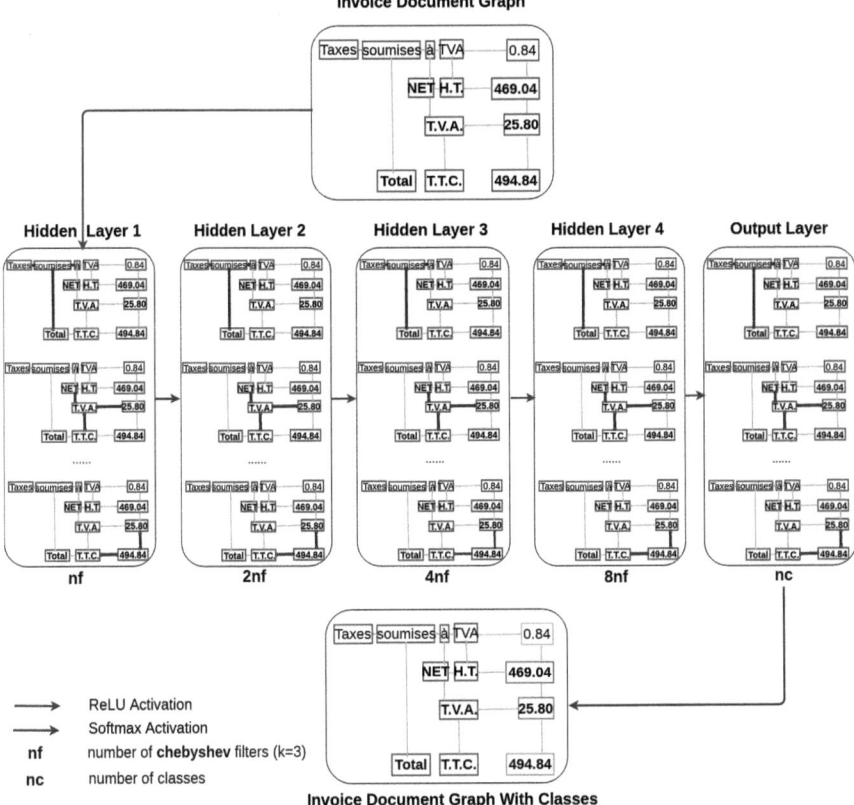

Fig. 4. Proposed 5 layer GCN architecture for graph node classification. Input document graph is passed through 4 hidden layers, each followed by ReLU (shown in green arrows) for non-linearity. We start initially with 16 Chebyshev filters (nf = 16). At last layer, we use the Softmax activation (shown in purple arrow) for classifying each word node into one of 28 classes (nc = 28). Predicted classes are shown in different colors. (Color figure online)

where we set $K = 3$ in the experiments to keep each convolution at most 3-steps away from a center vertex. Our GCN architecture contains 4 layers of graph convolutions with filters increasing by a factor of 2 per layer, starting from 16 filters in 1st layer, each followed by a Rectified Linear Unit (ReLU) activation to increase non-linearity. The output layer is passed through the Softmax activation function which provides a class label to each word of the document. We have 27 classes of interest plus an "undefined" class for not important words. For multi-class classification, we evaluate the cross-entropy error over all the words (as we have labels of all words in supervised training). Dataset has n number of invoice documents and each document has its own graph with labels and no document is linked to other documents in the graph. We perform batch gradient descent using the full dataset for every training iteration, i.e. we feed n non-linked independent graphs together in each iteration.

Finally, to extract entities, we group words belonging to the same entity class like all seller address class words, all shipping address class words, etc., to form entities while checking through some parsers and conditionals for date, invoice number, etc. to form entities and we follow left to right ordering for it.

3 Experiments

We perform the experiment of entity extraction as an entity classification in an invoice where entity could be in or outside table.

3.1 Dataset and Metric

We have a private dataset of 3100 invoices which is accumulated as a result of collaboration with a company. In current system, we scan each image in 300 dpi. The invoices are annotated at word level by providing each word a ground truth class from one of the 27 entity classes to extract (see Table 2 for detailed class types) plus an undefined class for not important words.

We use Tesseract OCR [15] for text extraction. Each word in the invoice is identified by its word id, location, content and ground truth class. Note that not all invoices had all the entities class present. Also, we have a fixed classes to extract inside a table like *product description, unit price, quantity, total*, etc. and if some other columns are present, then we label them *undefined*. This will be further illustrated with examples in coming sections.

For the experiment, we split the invoice dataset into a training, validation and testing set randomly, using 50%, 20% and 30% respectively. We also ensured that the entity class distribution remains the same in all the three sets. We intentionally kept only 50% for training and big set of 30% for testing because we want to see how well the GCN is able to generalize even with a small training set.

We measure the performance at a very strict way upto the word level. Even after the entities are extracted, the classification errors at the word level help us to point out where exactly the system is lacking and improvement is needed. This way, we can focus on improving that particular class of entity. We compare the predicted entity classes of words with their ground truth classes. We provide the performance per class in terms of precision, recall and F-measure. The overall system performance is the micro average precision, recall and F-measure as it unbiased in multi-class classification.

3.2 Experimental Setup

We train our 5 layer GCN model in a supervised scheme on the architecture described in Sect. 2.4 and evaluate on a test set of 930 randomly chosen invoices. We use the Chebyshev filters of order 3 ($k = 3$) and initial number of filters are 16 ($nf = 16$). The number of classes are 28 ($nc = 28$). We use the L2 regularization factor of 5.10^{-4} for the GCN layer and number of hidden units but we do not use any dropout. We train the model as a single big graph batch for a maximum of 2000 epochs using the Adam optimizer [16] with a learning rate of 0.001 and early stopping with a window size of 50, i.e. we stop training if the validation loss does not decrease for 50 consecutive epochs.

3.3 Results and Discussion

We present in Table 2 the extracted entity results for 27 classes of interest. Before analyzing the system, let us first look at the running time of the system as shown in Table 1. We can see that the OCR (in our case Tesseract OCR) took a big time of 3.5 s. The most time taking step is Feature Calculator because in this step, we have to calculate essential word features like nature, isZipCode, isKnownCity, etc. Also, fetching word embedding from BPE for each word of the image is time taking. We can see that core of the system, i.e., graph modeling and essentially graph node classifying is very quick and takes less than a second. The overall average time for an image to process is 15 s which still needs a big improvement.

Table 1. Running time of our system.

Step	Average running time (in seconds)
Word extractor	3.5
Feature calculator	9.8
Graph modeler	0.8
Graph node classifier	0.9
Total running time	15

The results can be analyzed in 4 broad categories. Words of each invoice falls in one of these 4 categories (refer to Table 2): General invoice entities (rows 1 to 4), company information entities (rows 5 to 13), client information entities (row 14 to 18) and table information entities (rows 19 to 27).

Let us analyze the results category-wise:

1. **General Invoice Entities:** Invoice number and invoice date are very well extracted with F1 0.95 and 0.90, even when sometimes the words are split into 2 or 3 parts (see Fig. 5). Payment mode has good recognition of 0.94 as it is usually preceded by few words and our GCN model easily captures it. Order number however has little low F-measure of 0.80 because it is usually confused with client number and is present very low in the invoices as shown in Fig. 5.
2. **Company Information Entities:** We provide detailed information about company as shown in examples of Fig. 6. Company address is recognized very well with 0.94 F1 score while company name is recognized with a lower 0.84 F1 score because many times the company name is recognized as company

address as they follow together. This infact is not a big error as company name can be part of address. Company identifiers like siret number, vat number, ape code(type of activity a company does) are extracted with more than 0.91 F1 score.

The reason of company siren number score to be 0.86 is that it is usually confused with siret number and they do share similar characteristics in a very condensed context. Company registration city is one of the lowest present entities in the invoices, still a good recognition is obtained. Phone number and fax are recognized very well with almost 0.90 F1 score even though they are quite close in structure.

3. **Client Information Entities:** Like company information, we provide indepth information about the invoice client. Client number is usually confused with order number as discussed above. We provide separate classes for client shipping and billing details as shown in examples of Fig. 7. We assume that when only one client address or client name is present, then it is billing name or billing address. When two client addresses are there, then it is very difficult to distinguish which address is shipping or which address is billing. The billing and shipping address words are mostly similar, i.e., they contain a proper name, a street number and name, a city name, zipcode and sometimes the country name. The only distinguishing feature is the header of addresses. Shipping and billing addresses have some specific headings (see (a) and (c) in Fig. 7). Our model automatically learns these heading representations and propagates this information to other nodes of the graph locally. From top of address like shipping name to bottom of address like country. The result clearly shows that our model extracts both shipping and billing entities very well with over 0.90 F1 score, depicting its power to segregate very closely related multi node entities through neighborhood features learned via convolutions.

4. **Extracted Table Entities:** We can easily observe through Table 2 that our model performs excellent table extraction. System like CloudScan [8] fails to deal with table entities as their approach was heavily dependent on linear neighborhood due to n-grams. Due to excellent feature calculation for price with nature like number with decimal, real values, real values with currency, currency, etc. as discussed in Sect. 2.2, we had a very specific feature representation for various table price related entities. Further, the 4 nearest graph modeling further connected these prices to form a structure. With extraction results of over 0.98 F1 score for table price entities (unit price, price without tax, tax rate, total without tax, total tax amount, net payable amount) (refer to Fig. 8), it is clear that our model is extremely good for table extraction. Further product description which contains different kinds of words like model numbers, guarantee, etc., also has a very good score of 0.95 F1.

The micro averaged overall invoice entity extraction performance of our system is excellent with 0.93 F1 score.

Table 2. Performance of our model on various classes to extract.

Row	Extracted entity	F1	Precision	Recall
1	Invoice number	**0.90**	**0.92**	0.88
2	Invoice date	**0.95**	**0.94**	**0.96**
3	Order number	0.80	0.82	0.78
4	Payment mode	**0.94**	**0.95**	**0.93**
5	Company name	0.85	0.87	0.84
6	Company address	**0.94**	**0.94**	**0.94**
7	Company siren number	0.86	0.87	0.86
8	Company siret number	**0.91**	**0.91**	**0.92**
9	Company vat number	**0.94**	**0.94**	**0.95**
10	Company APE code	**0.95**	**0.95**	**0.95**
11	Company registration city	0.82	0.88	0.77
12	Company phone number	0.89	**0.90**	0.89
13	Company fax number	**0.90**	**0.90**	**0.90**
14	Client number	0.79	0.81	0.79
15	Client billing name	**0.91**	**0.91**	**0.92**
16	Client billing address	**0.90**	**0.90**	**0.91**
17	Client shipping name	**0.93**	**0.94**	**0.92**
18	Client shipping address	**0.90**	**0.91**	0.89
20	Product serial number	0.87	0.87	0.87
21	Product description	**0.95**	**0.95**	**0.96**
22	Product unit price	**0.99**	**0.99**	**0.99**
23	Product Quantity	**0.92**	**0.91**	**0.93**
24	Product price without tax	**0.98**	**0.98**	**0.98**
25	Tax rate	**0.99**	**0.99**	**0.99**
26	Total without tax	**0.98**	**0.99**	**0.98**
27	Total tax amount	**0.99**	**0.99**	**0.99**
28	Net payable amount	**0.99**	**0.99**	**0.99**
	Micro average	**0.93**	**0.93**	**0.929**

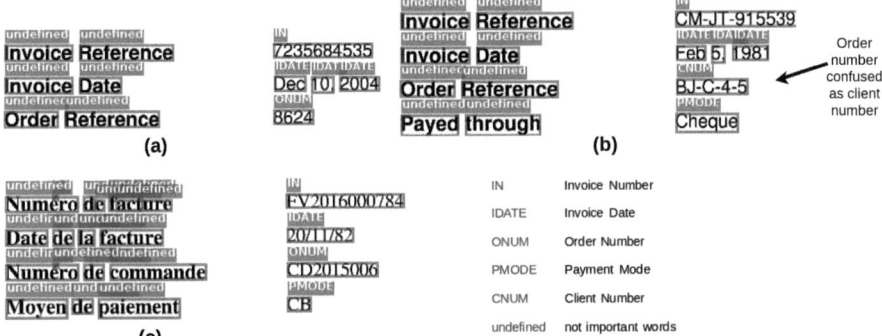

Fig. 5. Example: general invoice entities extraction.

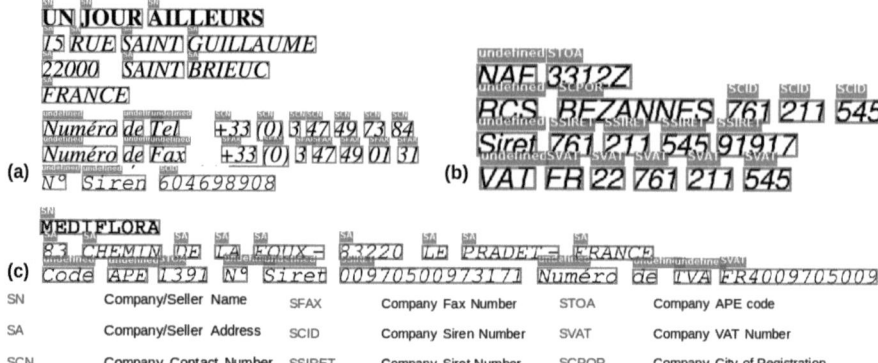

Fig. 6. Example: company entities extraction

Fig. 7. Example: client entities extraction

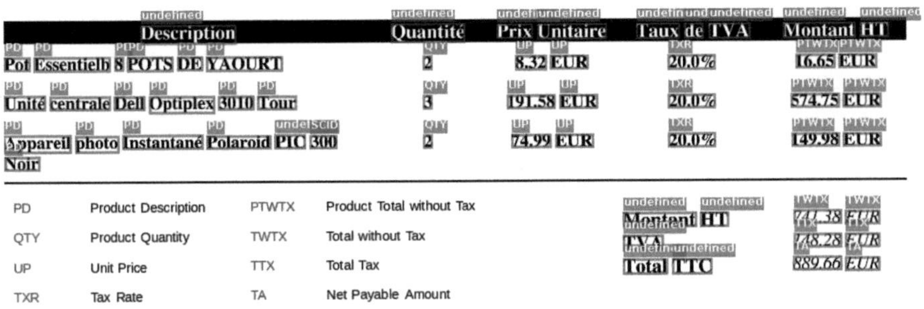

Fig. 8. Example: table extraction

4 Conclusion

In this paper, we proposed a novel and generic approach to extract invoice entities from printed invoice documents. We proved that our approach using localized Graph Convolutional Networks is template independent and effective. It is a complete invoice reading system which extracts entities both inside and outside the table. We extracted 27 very fine entities from the document with an excellent extraction rate of 0.93 F1 score, which is also the best score so far in any IAS available. It is unfortunate that we cannot directly compare our results with the existing systems as there is still no public dataset available in invoices due to their sensitive nature. We sincerely wish such a dataset will be published soon and it would drive the field forward significantly. Unfortunately, we cannot release our own dataset due to privacy restrictions. We showed through various categories of result that our system is able to model entity relations very effectively and is able to generalize the whole invoice document through a graph structure. In our future works, we would like to focus more on the architecture of graph convolutional network, on pre-processing of mobile captured image, on improving the running time of the system, on post processing and on incorporating user feedback in the system.

References

1. Nadeau, D., Sekine, S.: A survey of named entity recognition and classification. Lingvist. Invest. **30**, 3–26 (2007)
2. Schuster, D., et al.: Intellix-end-user trained information extraction for document archiving. In: 2013 12th International Conference on Document Analysis and Recognition (ICDAR), pp. 101–105. IEEE (2013)
3. Rusinol, M., Benkhelfallah, T., Poulain dAndecy, V.: Field extraction from administrative documents by incremental structural templates. In: 2013 12th International Conference on Document Analysis and Recognition (ICDAR), pp. 1100–1104. IEEE (2013)
4. Hamza, H., Belaïd, Y., Belaïd, A.: A case-based reasoning approach for invoice structure extraction. In: Ninth International Conference on Document Analysis and Recognition, ICDAR 2007, vol. 1, 327–331. IEEE (2007)

5. Dengel, A.R., Klein, B.: smartFIX: a requirements-driven system for document analysis and understanding. In: Lopresti, D., Hu, J., Kashi, R. (eds.) DAS 2002. LNCS, vol. 2423, pp. 433–444. Springer, Heidelberg (2002). https://doi.org/10.1007/3-540-45869-7_47
6. Cesarini, F., Francesconi, E., Gori, M., Soda, G.: Analysis and understanding of multi-class invoices. Doc. Anal. Recogn. **6**, 102–114 (2003)
7. d'Andecy, V.P., Hartmann, E., Rusiñol, M.: Field extraction by hybrid incremental and a-priori structural templates. In: 2018 13th IAPR International Workshop on Document Analysis Systems (DAS), pp. 251–256. IEEE (2018)
8. Palm, R.B., Winther, O., Laws, F.: Cloudscan-a configuration-free invoice analysis system using recurrent neural networks. In: 2017 14th IAPR International Conference on Document Analysis and Recognition (ICDAR), pp. 406–413. IEEE (2017)
9. Kasar, T., Bhowmik, T.K., Belaid, A.: Table information extraction and structure recognition using query patterns. In: 2015 13th International Conference on Document Analysis and Recognition (ICDAR), pp. 1086–1090. IEEE (2015)
10. Santosh, K., Belaïd, A.: Document information extraction and its evaluation based on client's relevance. In: 2013 12th International Conference on Document Analysis and Recognition (ICDAR), pp. 35–39. IEEE (2013)
11. Sennrich, R., Haddow, B., Birch, A.: Neural machine translation of rare words with subword units. In: 54th Annual Meeting of the Association for Computational Linguistics, pp. 1715–1725 (2016)
12. Heinzerling, B., Strube, M.: BPEmb: tokenization-free pre-trained subword embeddings in 275 languages. In: Proceedings of the Eleventh International Conference on Language Resources and Evaluation (LREC 2018). European Language Resources Association (ELRA), Miyazaki (2018)
13. Kipf, T.N., Welling, M.: Semi-supervised classification with graph convolutional networks. In: ICLR (2017)
14. Defferrard, M., Bresson, X., Vandergheynst, P.: Convolutional neural networks on graphs with fast localized spectral filtering. In: Advances in Neural Information Processing Systems, pp. 3844–3852 (2016)
15. Smith, R.: An overview of the tesseract OCR engine. In: Ninth International Conference on Document Analysis and Recognition, ICDAR 2007, vol. 2, pp. 629–633. IEEE (2007)
16. Kingma, D.P., Ba, J.: Adam: a method for stochastic optimization. arXiv preprint arXiv:1412.6980 (2014)

Reading Industrial Inspection Sheets by Inferring Visual Relations

Rohit Rahul[1]([✉]), Arindam Chowdhury[1], Animesh[1], Samarth Mittal[2], and Lovekesh Vig[1]

[1] TCS Research, Delhi, India
rohit.rahul@tcs.com
[2] BITS Pilani, Goa Campus, Pilani, India

Abstract. The traditional mode of recording faults in heavy factory equipment has been via handmarked inspection sheets, wherein a machine engineer manually marks the faulty machine regions on a paper outline of the machine. Over the years, millions of such inspection sheets have been recorded and the data within these sheets has remained inaccessible. However, with industries going digital and waking up to the potential value of fault data for machine health monitoring, there is an increased impetus towards digitization of these handmarked inspection records. To target this digitization, we propose a novel visual pipeline combining state of the art deep learning models, with domain knowledge and low level vision techniques, followed by inference of visual relationships. Our framework is robust to the presence of both static and non-static background in the document, variability in the machine template diagrams, unstructured shape of graphical objects to be identified and variability in the strokes of handwritten text. The proposed pipeline incorporates a capsule and spatial transformer network based classifier for accurate text reading, and a customized CTPN [15] network for text detection in addition to hybrid techniques for arrow detection and dialogue cloud removal. We have tested our approach on a real world dataset of 50 inspection sheets for large containers and boilers. The results are visually appealing and the pipeline achieved an accuracy of **87.1%** for text detection and **94.6%** for text reading.

1 Introduction

Industrial inspection of factory equipment is a common process in factory settings, involving inspection engineers conducting a physical examination of the equipment and subsequently marking faults on paper based inspection sheets. While many industries have digitized the inspection process [1,5,11], paper based inspection is still widely practiced, frequently followed by a digital scanning process. These paper based scans have data pertaining to millions of faults detected over several decades of inspections. Given the tremendous value of fault data for predictive maintenance, industries are keen to tap into the vast reservoir of fault data stored in the form of highly unstructured scanned inspection sheets and generate structured reports from them.

However, there are several challenges associated with digitizing these reports ranging from image preprocessing and layout analysis to word and graphic item recognition [10]. There has been plenty of work in document digitization in general but very little prior work on digitization of inspection documents. In this paper, we have addressed the problem of information extraction from boiler and container inspection documents. The target document, as shown in Fig. 1, has multiple types of printed machine line diagrams, where each diagram is split into multiple zones corresponding to different components of the machine. The inspection engineer marks handwritten damage codes and comments against each component of the machine (machine zone). These comments are connected via a line or an arrow to a particular zone. Thus, the arrow acts as a connector that establishes the relationship between a text cloud containing fault codes, and a machine zone.

2 Problem Description

In this work, we strive to extract relevant information from industrial inspection sheets which contain multiple 3D orthogonal machine diagrams. Figure 1(A) shows one such inspection sheet consisting of 7 machine diagrams. We define a *set* as a collection of inspection sheets which contain identical machine diagrams while the individual machine diagrams in an inspection sheet are called *templates*, as shown in Fig. 4. Each template consists of multiple zones. In Fig. 1(B) we mark individual zones with different colors. In industrial setting, an inspector goes around examining each machine. If he detects any damage in a machine then he identifies the zone where the damage has occurred. He then draws an entity which we call as *connector* as shown in Fig. 1(B) and writes a damage code at the tail of the connector. Each code corresponds to one of the predefined damages that could occur in the machine. This damage code is shown as text in Fig. 1(B). Often, the text is enclosed in a bubble or a cloud structure that carry no additional information of relevance but adds to the overall complexity of the

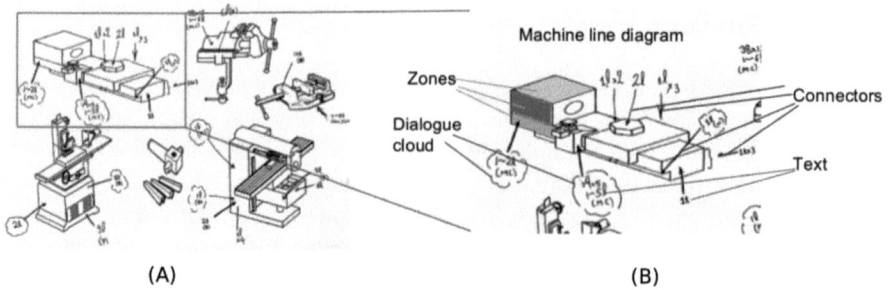

Fig. 1. (A) Overview of an inspection sheet (B) Essential components of the sheet. (Color figure online)

problem. Our task is to localize and read the damage codes that are written on the inspection sheet and associate each damage code with the zone against which it is marked and store the information in a digital document. This allows firms to analyze data on their machines, that was collected over the years, with minimum efforts.

3 Proposed Method

We propose a novel framework for extracting damage codes, handwritten by a user on an inspection sheet and then associating the same with corresponding zones, as shown in Fig. 2. The major components of our model are described in detail in this section. We first remove the templates and the clouds. Then, we localize the text patches and the connectors. Further, we combine the information on the connectors and text patches for more accurate localization and extraction of the text. This is followed by reading of the damage codes. Finally, we associate the damage codes with the zones, leaveraging the knowledge about the connectors. This process successfully establishes a one-to-one mapping between the zones and corresponding damage codes.

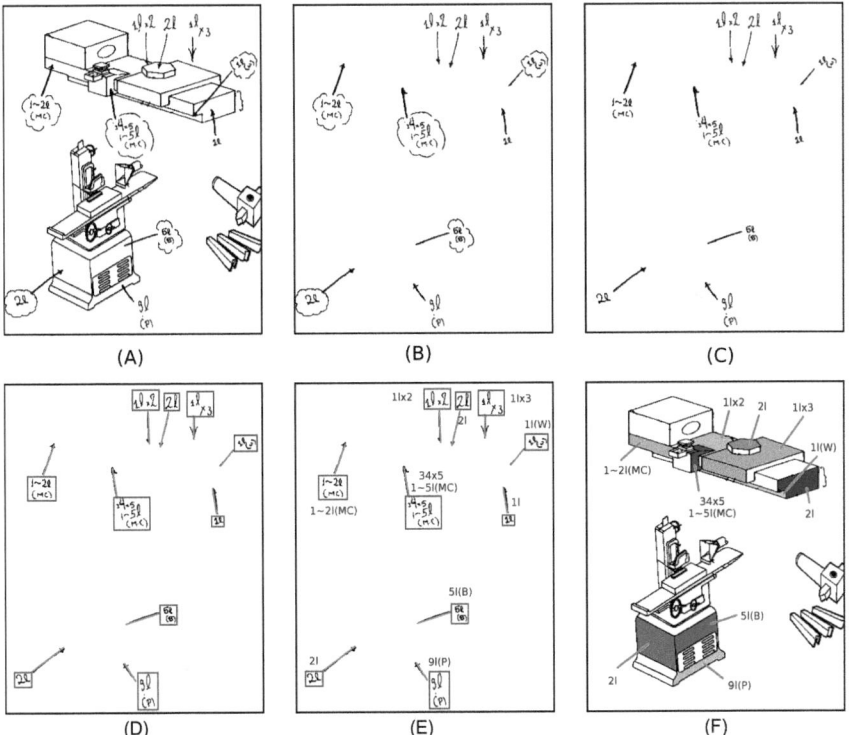

Fig. 2. Overview of the framework: (A) Original input image (B) Template removal (C) Cloud removal (D) Text and arrow localization (E) Text reading (F) Text-to-zone association

3.1 Template Extraction and Removal

An inspection sheet is essentially composed of a static and a dynamic part. The static part is the 3D orthogonal view of a machine that remains constant over a set of inspection sheets. On the other hand, the dynamic part consists of arrows, clouds and text that is added by the user on top of the static part, as shown in Fig. 3. Our goal is to find specific components of the dynamic part and to identify relationships among those parts. We have found that at times static part interferes with the detection of the dynamic part and therefore, as a first step, we remove the static part from the input images.

Template Extraction: Having established the presence of static and dynamic parts in a particular set of sheets, we automate the process of extracting the templates in the sheet. The process involves inversion of the images followed by depthwise averaging and a final step of adaptive thresholding. This generates an image containing just the template. We have noticed that though there are multiple sheets with similar templates, the relative start point of each template is not consistent among the sheets. Hence there is a need to find the individual templates and localize them in the input image. To this end, we find contours on the depth averaged image and then arrange all the detected contours in a tree structure with the page being the root node. In such an arrangement, all nodes at depth 1 are the templates.

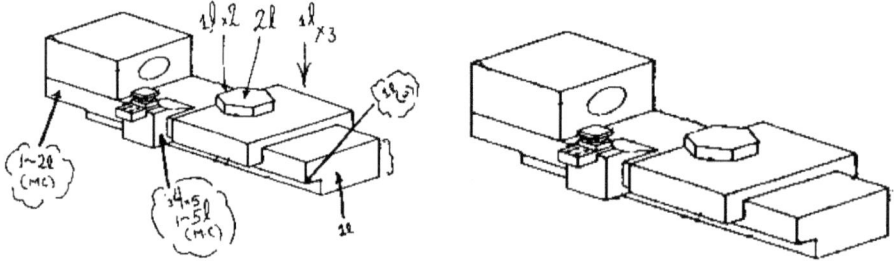

Fig. 3. Original image   **Fig. 4.** Template in the image

Template Localization: Now that we have the templates, we use *Normalized Cross Correlation* [16] to match the templates with input sheets. This gives us the correlation at each point in the image. By taking the point exhibiting maximum correlation, we can find the location of the template present in the image.

$$R(x,y) = \frac{\sum_{x',y'}(T(x',y') * I(x+x',y+y'))}{\sqrt{\sum_{x',y'} T(x',y')^2 * \sum_{x',y'} I(x+x',y+y')^2}}$$

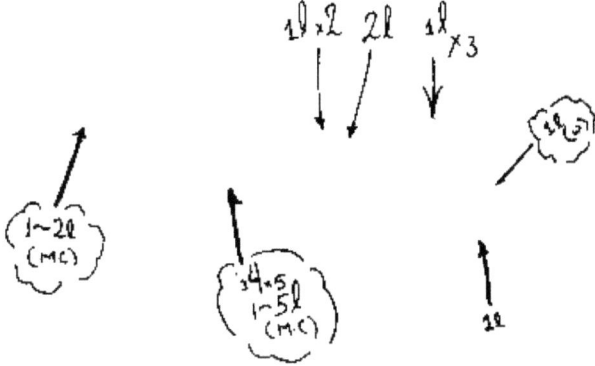

Fig. 5. Image with template removed

Template Subtraction: To remove the template that was localized in the previous step we use the operator Not(T(i, j)) and R(i, j) on two images T and R, where T is the template image and R is the input image. The resulting image after template subtraction is shown in Fig. 5.

3.2 Dialogue Cloud Segmentation and Removal

Dialogue cloud contains the text/comment in documents as shown in Fig. 6. They are present sporadically in the inspection sheet and interfere with the detection of dynamic parts like connectors and text. We have used the encoder-decoder based *SegNet* [2] architecture for segmenting out dialogue clouds. It was trained on a dataset of 200 cloud images to distinguish 3 classes namely background, boundary and cloud. Generally, it was able to learn the structure of the cloud. At times, the segnet would classify a few pixels as background which would lead to introduction of salt and pepper noise around the place where the cloud was present, but we address this issue while text reading by performing median filtering.

3.3 Connector Detection and Classification

Connectors established a one-to-one relationship between text and its corresponding zone. They sometimes manifest as arrows with a prominent head but often they are just lines or multiple broken pieces of a line, as shown in the image, making the automation process far more complex. We tackle this problem using two approaches:

1. CNN to detect the arrows with prominent heads
2. Detection of Lines

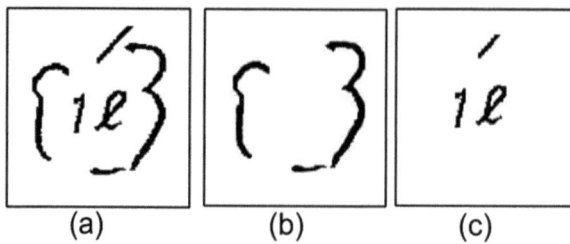

Fig. 6. Cloud segmentation a. input image b. mask generated by segnet c. mask removed

Arrow Classification: As the first step we extract all the connected components from the image to send them to our classifier. We train the *Convolutional Neural Network* (CNN) on 2 classes which are Arrow and background. We modified the architecture of *Zeiler-Fergus* Network (ZF) [17] and show that our network outperforms ZF network in the task of arrow classification by a considerable margin. We trained the classifier to learn the features of the connectors which have a prominent arrow like head. We observed that including the connectors which do not have a prominent head (i.e they are just a line) confuses all CNN models and the precision falls dramatically. To detect arrows in the input image, we feed each connected component found after the template removal to the CNN classifier. All the connected components that are arrows and have a prominent head are classified as such, subsequently, we use the information of the text patches to find out the head and tail point of the arrow.

Line Detection: Most of the arrows having a prominent head would be, at this point, detected by the arrow CNN. Here, we describe the process of detecting arrows that have been drawn as a line (i.e. without a prominent head). To this end, we use a three-step approach. The first step involves detection of various lines that were present in the input image after the removal of templates through hough lines. This is followed by line merging and line filtering where we filter the lines based on the association with the text patch. The filtering step is required because a lot of noise would also be detected as lines which can be filtered leveraging the knowledge gained after text patch detection and association. We further elaborate on the filtering step in Sect. 3.5.

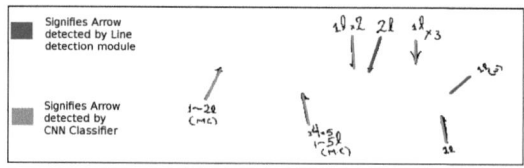

Fig. 7. Arrow detection

Line Merging: As can be seen in Fig. 5 that after template removal a lot of arrows are broken into segments and hence for each segment a separate line would be detected. As a result there would be multiple lines for a single arrow. Therefore we merge the lines if they have the same slope and the euclidean distance between them is within 50 px. The resulting image after arrow classification and line detection and merging is shown in Fig. 7.

3.4 Text Patch Detection

The text patches in the input image is usually present in the vicinity of a template. To detect these text patches, we employ *Connectionist Text Proposal Network* (CTPN) [15] which has proven to be quite effective in localizing text lines in scene images. With a bit of fine-tuning the same model was able to locate text boxes in the input images. Initially, we trained the CTPN on full size images but it failed to produce desired results. It captured multiple text patches, that occur colinearly, in a single box. This anomaly resulted from the low visual resolution of the individual text patches when looked at from a global context which is the entire image. The network simply captured any relevant text as a single item if they are horizontally close. As a resolution of the same, we sample 480 × 360 px windows from the input image with overlap. These windows offer better visual separation between two colinear text patches, resulting in superior localization. Nevertheless, not all text boxes that contained more than one text patch can not be eliminated by the same, as shown in Fig. 8(A).

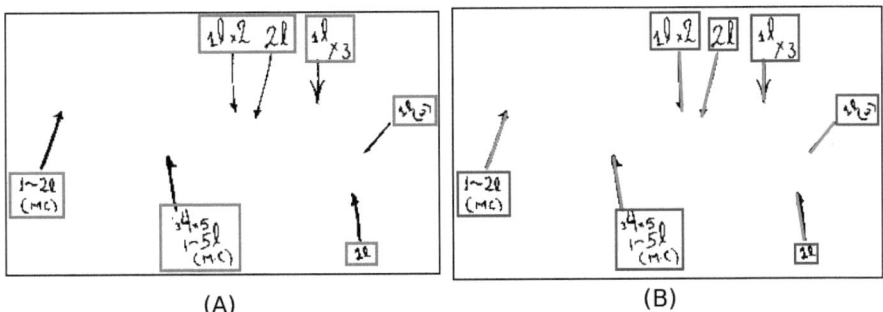

Fig. 8. (A) Text boxes detected by CTPN (B) Final text boxes after association with connectors

3.5 Connector Filtering and Text Patch Association

For complete resolution of the problem discussed in last section, we use the available information from the detected arrows, as each text patch must have a corresponding arrow tail pointing to it. We associate each arrow to one of the bounding boxes by extrapolating the arrow tails. Once all the detected arrows are associated to a bounding box, we cluster the text patches present, with the number of clusters being equal to the number of arrows associated to that bounding box. This means that if there exists a bounding box that has two or more arrows associated to it, we will obtain the same number of text patches as the number of arrows. We use K-means clustering for this purpose, where K is the number of arrows associated to a CTPN bounding box. This ensures that there will always be only one text patch associated to a single arrow, as shown in Fig. 8(B). Once we have the bounding boxes of the text patches, we extract them and send them to the reading pipeline.

3.6 Text Reading

This section describes the text reading component of our model. Input to this system is a set of text patches extracted from the inspection sheets. Each patch contains handwritten alpha-numeric codes corresponding to a particular kind of physical damage. Major challenges arise from the fact that these damage codes are not always structured horizontally in a straight line but consist of multiple lines with non-uniform alignments, depending on the space available to write on the inspection sheets, as shown in Fig. 9. Moreover, the orientation of the characters in these codes are often irregular making the task of reading them even more difficult.

Due to these irregularities, it was difficult to read an entire text sequence as a whole. Instead, we designed our model to recognize one character at a time and then arrange them in proper order to generate the final sequence. The model consists of a segmentation module that generates a set of symbols from the parent image in no particular order, followed by a ranking mechanism to arrange them in standard human readable form. We then employ two deep neural networks to recognize the characters in the sequence. The final component is a correction module that exploits the underlying syntax of the codes to rectify any character level mistake in the sequence.

Segmentation of individual characters in the image patch is performed using *Connected Component Analysis* (CCA). As CCA uses a region growing approach, it can only segment out characters that neither overlap nor have any boundary pixels in common. So, the CCA output may have one or more than one characters in a segment. In our experiments, we found that the segments had a maximum of two characters in them.

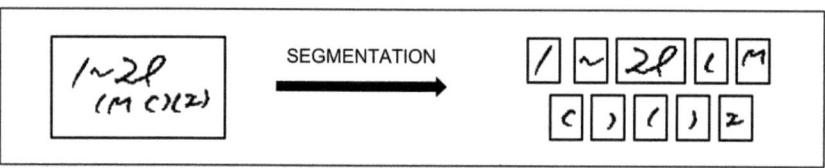

Fig. 9. Segmentation output of text patch

Ranking of segmented characters is described in Algorithm 1. It takes a list of unordered segments and returns another that has the characters arranged in a human readable form i.e. left-to-right & top-to-bottom, as shown in Fig. 10.

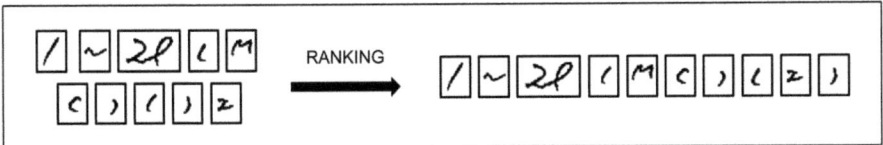

Fig. 10. Segmented output of text patch ranked in human readable format

Character Recognition is implemented as a two-step process. First step is to determine whether a segment contains one or two characters. Towards this end, we use *Capsule Network* (CapsNet) [12] which performs remarkably well in classifying multiple characters with considerable overlap. We modified the standard formulation of CapsNet by introducing a new output class, *None* representing the absence of any character in the image. Therefore, in case there is only a single character present in the segment, CapsNet predicts *None* as one of the two classes. In spite of being a powerful classification model, the performance of CapsNet on the test data was limited. This necessitated the second step in which we use a *Spatial Transformer Network* (STN) [7] to recognize single character segments. STN consists of a differentiable module that can be inserted anywhere in CNN architecture to increase its geometric invariance. As a result, STN proved to be more effective in addressing randomness in the spatial orientation of characters in the images, thereby boosting the recognition performance. Finally, in case of segments that had two characters, we take the CapsNet predictions as the output as STN cannot classify overlapping characters. This scheme is described in Fig. 11.

Correction module incorporates domain knowledge to augment neural network predictions. It has two parts. First, a *rule-based system* that uses the grammar of the damage codes to rectify predictions of the networks. For example, as per the grammar, an upper case "B" can only be present between a pair of parenthesis, i.e. "(B)". If the networks predict "1B)", then our correction module would

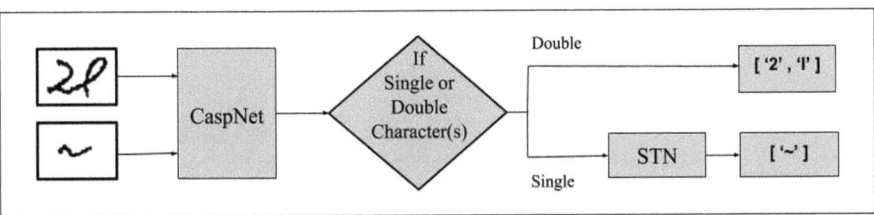

Fig. 11. Capsnet and STN

correct this part of the sequence by replacing the "1" by a "(". On top of it is an *edit-distance based* module which finds the closest sequence to the predicted damage sequence from an exhaustive list of possible damage codes. An example is shown in Fig. 12.

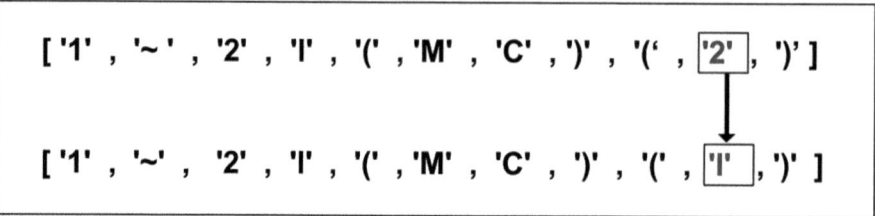

Fig. 12. Correction made in the CapsNet and STN predictions based on the grammar of the defect codes

3.7 Zone Mapping

After getting the location of the arrows and associating them with the corresponding text, we now have to map the damage codes to the zone. A sample machine part with different zones are shown in Fig. 13. Here, arrows are used to describe this relationship as the head of an arrow points to the relevant zone and the tail of the same points to the text patch that is to be associated with the corresponding zone. We have already done the latter in the previous section and now we are left with the task of finding out the relevant zone to which the arrow is pointing. We observed that this problem can be easily solved by ray casting algorithm [14]. If we extend a ray from the head of the arrow, the zone that it intersects first is the relevant zone and can be mapped to the text patch (Fig. 14).

We summarize the proposed method in the following flow diagram:

Algorithm 1. Ranking

Require: $seg\_list[s_1, s_2, s_3, ..., s_n]$: Segment $s_i = [(x_1 : x_{m_i}), (y_1 : y_{m_i})]$, a collection of pixel coordinates.
1: **procedure** RANKING(seg_list)
2:     using s_i, calculate extremes and centroid of segmented images, $y_{i\_top}, y_{i\_bottom}, x_{i\_left}, x_{i\_right}, y_{i\_cen}$ and the x_{i_cen}
3:     sort seg_list in ascending order of y_{i_cen} parts
4:     $line\_bottom \leftarrow y_{i\_top}$; $line\_begin\_Idx \leftarrow 0$
5:     **for** i in (1,len(seg_list)) **do**
6:         **if** $y_{i\_top} >$ overlap_thresh **then**
7:             sort previous line based on x_{i_left} ; $line\_begin\_Idx \leftarrow i$
8:         $line\_begin\_Idx = \max(y_{i\_top}$, line_bottom$)$
9:     sort last line based on x_{i_left}
10:    **return** seg_list

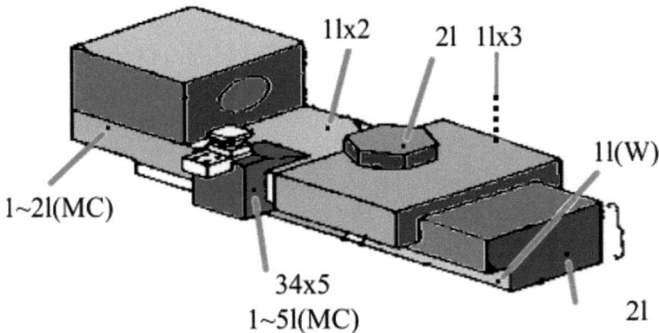

Fig. 13. In this example, different zones of a subassembly are shown with different colors and the rays are shown as dotted red lines extending from the arrow head (Color figure online)

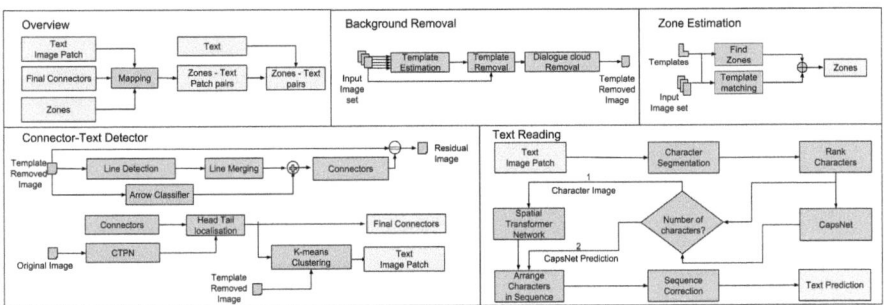

Fig. 14. Flow diagram of the proposed framework. Each component represents a set of operations that extract a particular information from the input images.

4 Experiments

4.1 Implementation Details

We have a confidential dataset provided by a firm. It has 72 different kinds of machine structures distributed across 10 sets of images. There were 50 equally distributed images for testing. This implies that a particular set has same machine line diagrams forming the static background. For training purpose, a separate set of 450 images are kept with same distribution of background machine line diagram sets. All the sheets are in JPEG format with resolution of 3500×2400 sq. px. They have been converted into inverted binarized version where the foreground is white and background is black. The conversion is done by Otsu's binarisation.

Dialogue Cloud Segmentation: For this process, we have used the SegNet [2] model to train on 200 images. Two classes are cloud pixels and background. As there is an imbalance, the classes are weighted by 8.72 for the foreground and 0.13 for the background.

Arrow Classifier: The classifier is inspired from [13]. It includes 6 convolution layers and 2 fully connected layer with ReLU [9] activation. Max pool and dropout (with 0.5 probability) were used for regularization. We set the learning rate of 0.001 and used the Adam [8] optimizer with cross entropy loss to train it on 800 images with equal number of images per class. We initialized the network using Xavier initializer [4] and trained the model till best validation accuracy achieved after 50 epochs. We used *Batch Normalization* [6] with every convolution layer so as to make the network converge faster. The network is 99.7% accurate on a balanced test set of 400 images. The input images are resized to (128×128) with padding such that the aspect ratio of the images is undisturbed (Fig. 15).

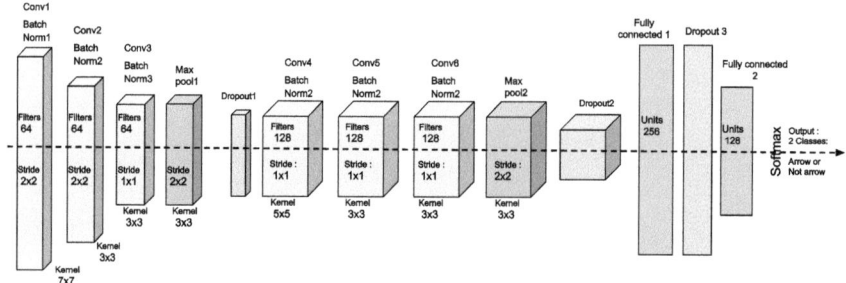

Fig. 15. Architecture of CNN used for the arrow classification

Capsule Network: We have used this network as it has proven to be effective in classifying overlapping characters on the MNIST [3] dataset. We set the learning rate to 0.0005 and use the Adam Optimizer to train our model on all the single characters as well as on all the possible pairs of characters touching each other.

Spatial Transformer Network (STN): These are convolutional neural networks, containing one or several Spatial Transformer Modules. These modules try to make the network spatially invariant to its input data, in a computationally efficient manner, leading to more accurate object classification results. We have taken the architecture from [7]. All the input images are padded and resized to 32×32 so that they do not loose their original aspect ratio. We trained this network on images of all the 31 characters.

4.2 Results

We present results for individual components as well as the overall performance of the model.

The results of Connector Detection is shown in Table 1. A total of 385 arrows were correctly localized out of 429 arrows present. The detection was performed on the sheets where the templates were removed. Majority of the false negatives

Table 1. Accuracy of individual components for text extraction and association

Component	Accuracy
Connector detection	89.7%
CTPN	91.6%
Patch association	95.1%
Clustering	95.6%
Zone mapping	96.4%

Table 2. Accuracy of individual components for text reading

Component	Accuracy
CCA	97.54%
Ranking	98.08%
CapsNet (Overlap)	66.11%
CapsNet (Non-Overlap)	89.59%
STN	95.06%
Sequence reading	94.63%

Table 3. Cumulative accuracy for the complete framework

Component	Individual accuracy	Cumulative accuracy
Text association	87.1%	87.1%
Text reading	94.63%	82.3%

occured as a result of probabilistic hough lines missing the entire line or most of the line, resulting in its removal during the arrow filtering stage.

The result of text patch detection using CTPN is shown in Table 1. It detected 392 text patches out of a total of 429 text patches correctly. It missed a few patches entirely and it resulted in a few false negatives in which it was generating a bounding box enclosing more than a single text patch inside it.

Out of the 392 text patches that the CTPN detected, 374 were correctly associated with the correct arrow, giving us the Patch Association accuracy as shown in Table 1.

And for the boxes which were associated with multiple arrows (false negative of CTPN enclosing more than a single text patch), we applied k-means clustering on the connected components present inside the CTPN boxes. It resulted in clusters of connected components belonging to the same text patch. Out of 23 such text patches which asked for clustering, k-means clustering 22 of them correctly yielding an overall accuracy of 95.6% as shown in Table 1.

We present the results of the text reading module in Table 2. We performed our experiments on 349 image patches. The accuracy of the CCA is calculated as the percentage of correct characters outputs in the total number of outputs. Ranking accuracy is calculated as a percentage of correct rankings done by the total number of images patches. The performance of the capsule network has been measured for two tasks (mentioned in the Table 2 above), one being the recognition of the overlapping characters and second, character level recognition in cases of non-overlapping characters. And at last the STN accuracy shows the character level accuracy which is better than the character level accuracy of the Capsule Network, justifying the reason why STN was used in the first place. Now the sequence level recognition's accuracy can be measured by measuring the ground-truth as well as the final predictions of the networks passing through both the correction modules, which is shown in the Table 2. The way we consider a prediction correct is if and only if all the characters in the predicted string matches with the ground-truth in the correct order.

The cumulative accuracy of the framework is provided in Table 3.

5 Conclusion

The proposed framework has given a detection accuracy of 87.1% for detection and 94.63% for reading. It manages to achieve high accuracy and is robust to different types of noise in arrow/cloud/text detection and character recognition. While it may be possible to train a deep system or model to learn this task in an end to end fashion given a very large set of cleanly annotated documents, but with the limited data at our disposal, incorporation of domain information was mandatory. As the entire pipeline is dedicated to a given layout, we plan to formulate an approach that is customizable with different layout types in future.

References

1. Agin, G.J.: Computer vision systems for industrial inspection and assembly. Computer **5**, 11–20 (1980)
2. Badrinarayanan, V., Kendall, A., Cipolla, R.: SegNet: a deep convolutional encoder-decoder architecture for image segmentation. IEEE Trans. Pattern Anal. Mach. Intell. **39**(12), 2481–2495 (2017)
3. Deng, L.: The MNIST database of handwritten digit images for machine learning research [best of the web]. IEEE Signal Process. Mag. **29**(6), 141–142 (2012)
4. Glorot, X., Bengio, Y.: Understanding the difficulty of training deep feedforward neural networks. In: Proceedings of the Thirteenth International Conference on Artificial Intelligence and Statistics, pp. 249–256 (2010)
5. Golnabi, H., Asadpour, A.: Design and application of industrial machine vision systems. Robot. Comput.-Integr. Manuf. **23**(6), 630–637 (2007)
6. Ioffe, S., Szegedy, C.: Batch normalization: accelerating deep network training by reducing internal covariate shift. arXiv preprint arXiv:1502.03167 (2015)
7. Jaderberg, M., Simonyan, K., Zisserman, A., et al.: Spatial transformer networks. In: Advances in Neural Information Processing Systems, pp. 2017–2025 (2015)
8. Kingma, D.P., Ba, J.: Adam: a method for stochastic optimization. arXiv preprint arXiv:1412.6980 (2014)
9. Krizhevsky, A., Sutskever, I., Hinton, G.E.: Imagenet classification with deep convolutional neural networks. In: Advances in Neural Information Processing Systems, pp. 1097–1105 (2012)
10. Marinai, S.: Introduction to document analysis and recognition. In: Marinai, S., Fujisawa, H. (eds.) Machine Learning in Document Analysis and Recognition. Studies in Computational Intelligence, vol. 90, pp. 1–20. Springer, Heidelberg (2008). https://doi.org/10.1007/978-3-540-76280-5_1
11. Ramakrishna, P., et al.: An AR inspection framework: feasibility study with multiple AR devices. In: 2016 IEEE International Symposium on Mixed and Augmented Reality (ISMAR-Adjunct), pp. 221–226, September 2016. https://doi.org/10.1109/ISMAR-Adjunct.2016.0080

12. Sabour, S., Frosst, N., Hinton, G.E.: Dynamic routing between capsules. In: Advances in Neural Information Processing Systems, pp. 3859–3869 (2017)
13. Seddati, O., Dupont, S., Mahmoudi, S.: Deepsketch: deep convolutional neural networks for sketch recognition and similarity search. In: 2015 13th International Workshop on Content-Based Multimedia Indexing (CBMI), pp. 1–6. IEEE (2015)
14. Shimrat, M.: Algorithm 112: position of point relative to polygon. Commun. ACM **5**(8), 434 (1962)
15. Tian, Z., Huang, W., He, T., He, P., Qiao, Y.: Detecting text in natural image with connectionist text proposal network. In: Leibe, B., Matas, J., Sebe, N., Welling, M. (eds.) ECCV 2016. LNCS, vol. 9912, pp. 56–72. Springer, Cham (2016). https://doi.org/10.1007/978-3-319-46484-8_4
16. Yoo, J.C., Han, T.H.: Fast normalized cross-correlation. Circuits Syst. Signal Process. **28**(6), 819–843 (2009). https://doi.org/10.1007/s00034-009-9130-7
17. Zeiler, M.D., Fergus, R.: Visualizing and understanding convolutional networks. In: Fleet, D., Pajdla, T., Schiele, B., Tuytelaars, T. (eds.) ECCV 2014. LNCS, vol. 8689, pp. 818–833. Springer, Cham (2014). https://doi.org/10.1007/978-3-319-10590-1_53

Learning to Clean: A GAN Perspective

Monika Sharma[(✉)], Abhishek Verma, and Lovekesh Vig

TCS Research, New Delhi, India
{monika.sharma1,verma.abhishek7,lovekesh.vig}@tcs.com

Abstract. In the big data era, the impetus to digitize the vast reservoirs of data trapped in unstructured scanned documents such as invoices, bank documents, courier receipts and contracts has gained fresh momentum. The scanning process often results in the introduction of artifacts such as salt-and-pepper/background noise, blur due to camera motion or shake, watermarkings, coffee stains, wrinkles, or faded text. These artifacts pose many readability challenges to current text recognition algorithms and significantly degrade their performance. Existing learning based denoising techniques require a dataset comprising of noisy documents paired with cleaned versions of the same document. In such scenarios, a model can be trained to generate clean documents from noisy versions. However, very often in the real world such a paired dataset is not available, and all we have for training our denoising model are unpaired sets of noisy and clean images. This paper explores the use of Generative Adversarial Networks (GAN) to generate denoised versions of the noisy documents. In particular, where paired information is available, we formulate the problem as an image-to-image translation task i.e, translating a document from noisy domain (i.e., background noise, blurred, faded, watermarked) to a target clean document using Generative Adversarial Networks (GAN). However, in the absence of paired images for training, we employed CycleGAN which is known to learn a mapping between the distributions of the noisy images to the denoised images using unpaired data to achieve image-to-image translation for cleaning the noisy documents. We compare the performance of CycleGAN for document cleaning tasks using unpaired images with a Conditional GAN trained on paired data from the same dataset. Experiments were performed on a public document dataset on which different types of noise were artificially induced, results demonstrate that CycleGAN learns a more robust mapping from the space of noisy to clean documents.

Keywords: Document cleaning suite · CycleGAN · Unpaired data · Deblurring · Denoising · Defading · Watermark removal

1 Introduction

The advent of industry 4.0 calls for the digitization of every aspect of industry, which includes automation of business processes, business analytics and phasing out of manually driven processes. While business processes have evolved to store large volumes of scanned digital copies of paper documents, however for many such documents the information stored needs to be extracted via text recognition techniques. While capturing these images via camera or scanner, artifacts tend to creep into the images such as background noise, blurred and faded text. In some scenarios, companies insert a watermark in the documents which poses readability issues after scanning. Text recognition engines often suffer due to the low quality of scanned documents and are not able to read the documents properly and hence, fail to correctly digitize the information present in the documents. In this paper, we attempt to perform denoising of the documents before the document is being sent to text recognition network for reading and propose a document cleaning suite based on generative adversarial training. This suite is trained for background noise removal, deblurring, watermark removal and defading and learns a mapping from the distribution of noisy documents to the distribution of clean documents.

Background noise removal is the process of removing the background noise, such as uneven contrast, see through effects, interfering strokes, and background spots on the documents. The background noise presents a problem to the performance of OCR as it is difficult to differentiate the text and background [3,5,9,14]. De-blurring is the process of removal of blur from an image. Blur is defined as distortion in the image due to various factors such as shaking of camera, improper focus of camera etc. which decreases the readability of the text in the document image and hence, deteriorates the performance of OCR. Recent works for deblurring have focused on estimating blur kernels using techniques such as GAN [6], CNN [10], dictionary-based prior [12], sparsity-inducing prior [15] and hybrid non-convex regularizer [24]. Watermark removal aims at removing the watermark from an image while preserving the text in the image. Watermarks are low-intensity images printed on photographs and books in order to prevent copying of the material. But this watermark post scanning creates hinderance in reading the text of interest from documents. Inpainting [20,23] techniques are used in the literature to recover the original image after detecting watermarks statistically. Defading is the process of recovering text that has lightened/faded over time, which usually happens in old books and documents. This is also detrimental to the OCR performance. To remove all these artifacts that degrade the quality of documents and create hinderance in readability, we formulate the document cleaning process as an image-to-image translation task at which Generative Adversarial Networks (GANs) [6] are known to give excellent performance.

However, with the limited availability of paired data i.e., noisy and corresponding cleaned documents, we proposed to train CycleGAN [26] for unpaired datasets of noisy documents. We train CycleGAN for denoising/background noise removal, deblurring, watermark removal and defading tasks. CycleGAN eliminates the need for one-to-one mapping between images of source and target domains by a two-step transformation of source image i.e., first source image is mapped to an image in target domain and then back to source again. We evaluate the performance of our document cleaning suite on synthetic and publicly available datasets and compare them against state-of-the-art methods. We use

Kaggle's document dataset for denoising/background noise removal [4], the BMVC document deblurring dataset [7] which are publicly available online. There does not exist any document dataset for watermark removal and defading online. Therefore, we have synthetically generated document datasets for watermark removal and defading tasks, and have also made these public for the benefit of research community. Overall, our contributions in this paper are as follows:

- We proposed a Document Cleaning Suite which is capable of cleaning documents via denoising/background noise removal, deblurring, watermark removal and defading for improving readability.
- We proposed the application of CycleGAN [26] for translating a document from a noisy document distribution (e.g. with background noise, blurred, watermarked and faded) to a clean document distribution in the situations where there is shortage of paired dataset.
- We synthetically created a document dataset for watermark removal and defading by inserting logos as watermarks and applying fading techniques on Google News dataset [1] of documents, respectively.
- We evaluate CycleGAN for background noise removal, deblurring, watermark removal and defading on publicly available kaggle document dataset [4], BMVC deblurring document dataset [7] and synthetically created watermarked and defading document datasets, respectively.

The remaining parts of the paper are organized as follows. Section 2 reviews the related work. Section 3 introduces CycleGAN and explains its architecture. Section 4 provides details of datasets, training, evaluation metric used and also discusses experimental results and comparisons to evaluate the effectiveness and superiority of CycleGAN for cleaning the noisy documents. Section 5 concludes the paper.

2 Related Work

Generative adversarial Network (GAN) [6] is the idea that has taken deep learning by storm. It employs adversarial training which essentially means pitting two neural networks against each other. One is a generator while the other is a discriminator, where the former aims at producing data that are indistinguishable from real data while the latter tries to distinguish between real and fake data. The process eventually yields a generator with the ability to do a plethora of tasks efficiently such as image-to-image generation. Other notable applications where GANs have established their supremacy are representation learning, image editing, art generation, music generation etc. [2,13,19,21,22].

Image-to-image translation is the task of mapping images in source domain to images in target domain such as converting sketches into photographs, grayscale images to color images etc. The aim is to generate the target distribution given the source distribution. Prior work in the field of GANs such as Conditional GAN [17] forces the image produced by generator to be conditioned on the output which allows for optimal translations. However, earlier GANs require one-to-one mapping of images between source and target domain i.e., a paired dataset. In case of documents, it is not possible to always have cleaned documents corresponding to each noisy document. This persuaded us to explore unpaired image-to-image translation methods, e.g. Dual-GAN [25] which uses dual learning and CycleGAN [26] which makes use of cyclic-consistency loss to achieve unpaired image-to-image translation.

In this paper, we propose to apply CycleGAN for document cleaning task. It has two pairs of generators and discriminators. One pair focuses on converting source domain to target domain while the other pair focuses on converting target domain to source domain. This bi-directional conversion process allows for a cyclic consistency loss for CycleGAN which ensures the effective conversion of an image from source to target and then back to source again. The transitivity property of cyclic-consistency loss allows CycleGAN to perform well on unpaired image-to-image translation.

Existing methods for removing background noise from document images consist of binarization and thresholding techniques, fuzzy logic, histogram, morphology and genetic algorithm based methods [3,5]. An automatic method for color noise estimation from a single image using Noise Level Function (NLF) and a Gaussian Conditional Random Field (GCRF) based removal technique was proposed in [14] for producing a clean image from noisy input. Sobia et al. [9] employs a technique for removing background and punch-hole noise from handwritten Urdu text. We observed that deep learning has not been applied in literature for removing noise from document images.

There exists quite a lot of work on deblurring of images. For example, Deblur-GAN [11] uses conditional GANs to deblur images, [18] uses a multi-scale CNN to create an end-to-end system for deblurring. Ljubenovic et al. proposed class-adapted dictionary-based prior for the image [16]. There also exists method of sparsity-inducing prior on the blurring filter, which allows for deblurring images containing different classes of images such as faces, text etc. [15] when they co-occur in a document. A non-convex regularization method was developed by Yao et al. [24] which leveraged the non-convex sparsity constraints on image gradients and blur kernels for improving the kernel estimation accuracy. [10] uses a CNN to classify the image into one of the degradative sub-spaces and the corresponding blur kernel is then used for deblurring.

Very few attempts have been made in past for removing watermarks from images. Authors in [20] proposed to use image inpainting to recover the original image. However, the method developed by Xu et al. [23] detects the watermark using statistical methods and subsequently, removes it using image inpainting. To the best of our knowledge, we did not find any work on defading of images.

3 CycleGAN

CycleGAN [26] has shown its worth in scenarios where there is paucity of paired dataset, i.e., image in source domain and corresponding image in target domain.

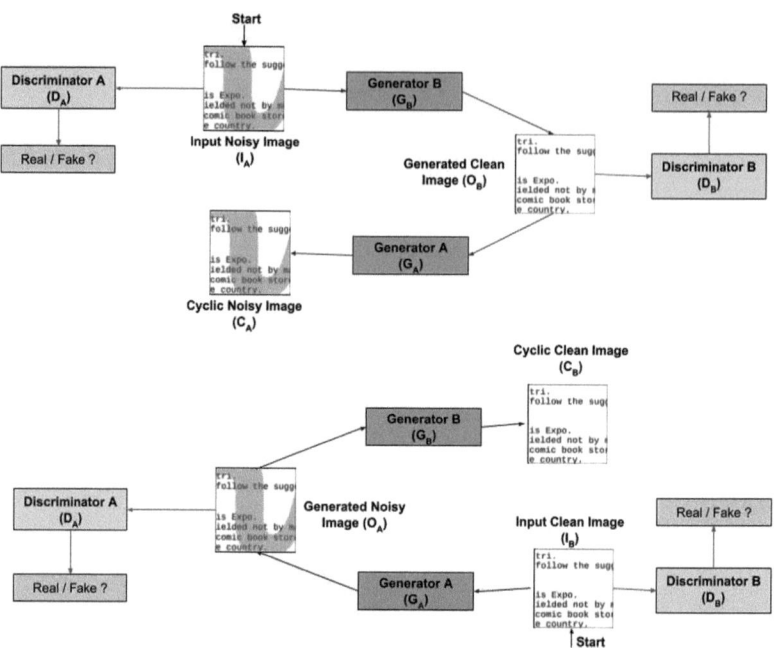

Fig. 1. Overview of CycleGAN - It consists of two generators, G_A and G_B which map noisy images to clean images and clean to noisy images, respectively using cycle-consistency loss [26]. It also contains two discriminators D_A and D_B which acts as adversary and rejects images generated by generators.

This property of CycleGAN, of working without the need of one-to-one mapping between input domain and target domain and still being able to learn such image-to-image translations, persuades us to use them for document cleaning suite where there is always limited availability of clean documents corresponding to noisy documents. To circumvent the issue of learning meaningful transformations in case of unpaired dataset, CycleGAN uses cycle-consistency loss which says that if an image is transformed from source distribution to target distribution and back again to source distribution, then we should get samples from source distribution. This loss is incorporated in CycleGAN by using two generators and two discriminators, as shown in Fig. 1. The first generator G_B maps the image from noisy domain A (I_A) to an output image in target clean domain B (O_B). To make sure that there exists a meaningful relation between I_A and O_B, they must learn some features which can be used to map back O_B to original noisy input domain. This reverse transformation is carried out by second generator G_A which takes as input O_B and converts it back into an image C_A in noisy domain. Similar process of transformation is carried out for converting images in clean domain B to noise domain A as well. It is evident in the Fig. 1 that each discriminator takes two inputs - original image in source domain and generated image via a generator. The task of the discriminator is to distinguish between them so that discriminator is able to defeat generator by rejecting images generated by it. While competing against discriminator so that it stops rejecting its images, the generator learns to produce images very close to the original input images.

We use the same network of CycleGAN as proposed in [26]. The generator network consists of two convolutional layers of stride 2, several residual blocks, two layers of transposed convolutions with stride 1. The discriminator network uses 70×70 PatchGANs [8] to classify the 70×70 overlapping patches of images as real or fake.

4 Experimental Results and Discussion

This section is divided into the following subsections: Sect. 4.1 provides details of the datasets used for the document cleaning suite. In Sect. 4.2, we elaborate on the training details utilized to perform our experiments. Next, we give the performance evaluation metric in Sect. 4.3. Subsequently, Sect. 4.4 discusses the results obtained from the experiments we conducted and provides comparison with the baseline model i.e., Conditional GAN [17].

Table 1. Performance comparison of Conditional GAN and CycleGAN based on PSNR

Task	PSNR (in dB)	
	ConditionalGAN	CycleGAN
Background removal	27.624	**31.774**
Deblurring	19.195	**30.293**
Watermark removal	29.736	**34.404**
Defading	28.157	**34.403**

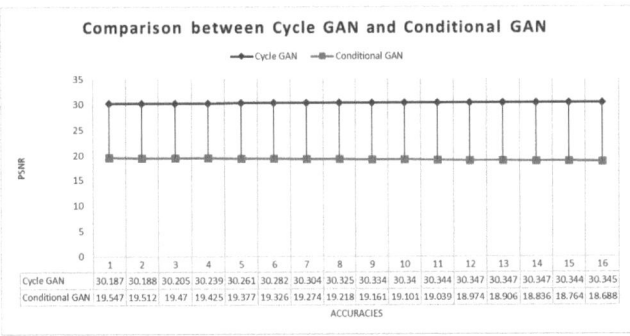

Fig. 2. Plot showing comparison between PSNR of images produced by CycleGAN [26] and ConditionalGAN [17] on test-set of deblurring document dataset [7]. The test-set consists of 16 sets of 100 documents each, where each set is blurred with one of the 16 different blur kernels used for creating the training dataset.

4.1 Dataset Details

We used 4 separate document datasets, one each for background noise removal, deblurring, watermark removal and defading. Their details are given below:

- **Kaggle Document Denoising Dataset**: This document denoising dataset hosted by Kaggle [4] consists of noisy documents with noise in various forms such as coffee stains, faded sun spots, dog-eared pages, and lot of wrinkles etc. We use this dataset for training and evaluating CycleGAN for removing background noise from document images. We have used a training set of 144 noisy documents to train CycleGAN and tested the trained network on a test dataset of 72 document images.
- **Document Deblurring Dataset**: We used artificial deblurring dataset of documents [7] available online for training CycleGANs to deblur the blurred documents. This dataset was created by taking documents from the CiteSeerX repository and were further processed via various geometric transformations and two types of blur i.e., motion blur and de-focus blur, on them to make the noise look more realistic. We have used only a subset of this dataset by random sampling of 2000 documents for training CycleGAN. For evaluation, this deblurring dataset has a test-set which consists of 16 sets of 100 documents, with each set blurred with one of the 16 different blur kernels used for creating the training dataset.
- **Watermark Removal Dataset**: As there exists no publicly available dataset for watermarked document images, we generated our own synthetic watermark removal document dataset. To create the dataset, we first obtained text documents from Google News Dataset [1] and approx. 21 logos from the Internet for inserting watermarks. Then, we pasted the logos on the documents by making logos transparent with varying values of alpha channel. We used variations in the position of logo, size of logo and transparency factor for creating randomness in the watermarked documents and to make them realistic. The training set of 2000 images and test set of 200 images from this synthetic dataset was used for experimental purposes.
- **Document Defading Dataset**: Similar to watermark removal dataset, we artificially generated faded documents from Google News Dataset [1] by applying various dilation operations on document images. Here again, the train and test set consisted of 2000 and 200 document images, respectively for training and evaluating the performance of CycleGAN for defading purposes.

4.2 Training Details

We use the same training procedure as adopted for CycleGan in paper [26]. Least-squares loss is used to train the network as this loss is more stable and produces better quality images. We update the discriminators by using a history of generated images rather than the ones produced by latest generator to reduce model oscillations. We use Adam optimizer with learning rate of 0.0002 and momentum of 0.5 for training CycleGAN on noisy images of size 200×200. The network is trained for 12, 30, 12 and 8 epochs for background noise removal, deblurring, watermark removal and defading, respectively.

For Conditional GAN [17], we use kernel size of 3×3 with a stride 1 and zero-padding by 1 for all convolutional and deconvolutional layers of generator network. In case of discriminator network, the first three convolutional and deconvolutional layers were composed of kernels of size 4×4 with a stride 2 and zero-padding by 1. However, the last two layers in discriminator network uses kernel of size 4×4 with stride of size 1. The network is trained on input images of size 200×200 using Adam Optimizer with a learning rate of 2×10^{-3}. We use 6.6×10^{-3} and 1 as values of weights for adversarial loss and perceptual loss, respectively. The network is trained for 5 epochs for each of the document cleaning tasks i.e., background noise removal, deblurring, watermark removal and defading.

4.3 Evaluation Metric

We evaluate the performance of CycleGAN using Peak Signal-to-Noise Ratio (PSNR)[1] as an image quality metric. PSNR is defined as ratio of the maximum possible power of a signal and the power of distorting noise which deteriorates the quality of its representation. PSNR is usually expressed in terms of Mean-squared error (MSE). Given a denoised image (D) of size $m \times n$ and its corresponding noisy image (I) of same size, PSNR is given as follows :

$$PSNR = 20 \times \log 10(\frac{Max_D}{MSE}) \qquad (1)$$

where Max_D represents the maximum pixel intensity value of image D. Higher the PSNR value, better is the image quality.

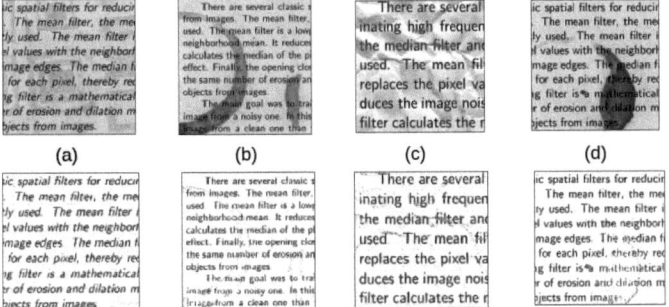

Fig. 3. Examples of sample noisy images (upper row) cleaned by CycleGAN and their corresponding cleaned images (bottom row) from Kaggle Document Denoising Dataset [4]

---

[1] Peak Signal-to-Noise Ratio: http://www.ni.com/white-paper/13306/en/.

4.4 Results

Now, we present the results obtained on document datasets using CycleGAN for document cleaning purposes. Table 1 gives the comparison of Conditional GAN and CycleGAN for denoising, deblurring, watermark removal and defading tasks. We observe that CycleGAN beats Conditional GAN on all these document cleaning tasks as shown in Table 1. Row 1 of Table 1 gives mean PSNR values of images deblurred using Conditional GAN and CycleGAN. CycleGAN obtains higher PSNR value of 31.774 dB as compared to that of Conditional GAN's PSNR (27.624 dB) on Kaggle Document Denoising dataset [4]. Similarly, PSNR value of CycleGAN (19.195 dB) is better than Conditional GAN for deblurring dataset [7]. We have also shown the PSNR comparison for deblurring test-set using a plot, as given in Fig. 2 which shows the superiority of CycleGAN over Conditional GAN. Row 3 and 4 gives the PSNR values for watermark removal and defading task. Here again, CycleGAN gives better image quality.

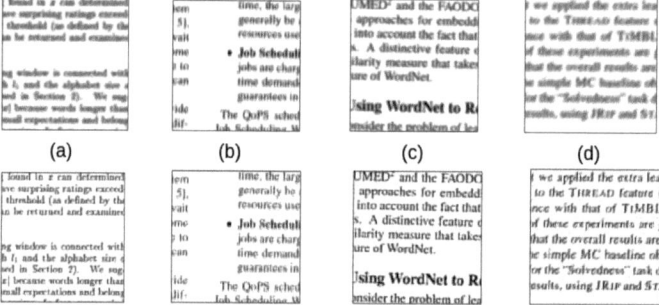

Fig. 4. Results of CycleGAN on deblurring document dataset [7]. Top row shows the blurred images and bottom row shows their corresponding deblurred images.

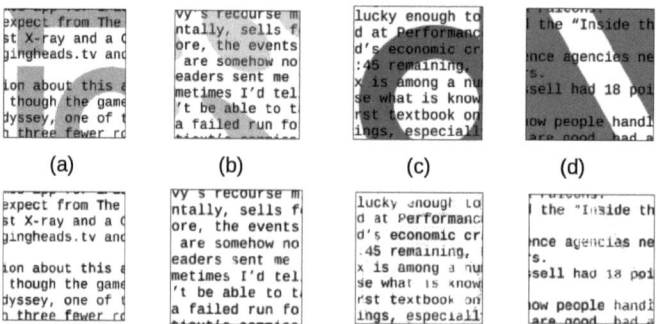

Fig. 5. Samples of watermarked images (first row) and their respective cleaned images (second row) produced by CycleGAN.

Fig. 6. Figure showing example images of faded (top row) and corresponding defaded images (bottom row) with recovered text by CycleGAN.

We also show some sample examples of clean images produced after the application of CycleGAN for all four tasks - background noise removal, deblurring, watermark removal and defading, as given in Figs. 3, 4, 5 and 6, respectively.

5 Conclusion

In this paper, we proposed and developed Document Cleaning Suite which is based on the application of CycleGAN and is responsible for performing various document cleaning tasks such as background noise removal, deblurring, watermark removal and defading. Very often it is difficult to obtain clean images corresponding to a noisy image, and simulation of noise for training image-to-image translators does not adequately generalize to the real world. Instead, we trained a model to learn the mapping from an input distribution to an output distribution of images, while preserving the essence of the image. We used CycleGAN because it has been seen to provide good results for such domain adaptation scenarios where there is limited availability of paired datasets i.e., noisy and corresponding cleaned image. We demonstrated the effectiveness of CycleGAN on publicly available and synthetic document datasets, and the results demonstrate that it can clean up a variety of noise effectively.

References

1. Google news dataset: EMNLP 2011 Sixth Workshop on Statistical Machine Translation (2011). http://www.statmt.org/wmt11/translation-task.html#download
2. Chen, X., Duan, Y., Houthooft, R., Schulman, J., Sutskever, I., Abbeel, P.: Info-GAN: Interpretable representation learning by information maximizing generative adversarial nets. CoRR **abs/1606.03657** (2016). http://arxiv.org/abs/1606.03657
3. Farahmand, A., Sarrafzadeh, A., Shanbehzadeh, J.: Document image noises and removal methods. In: Proceedings of the International MultiConference of Engineers and Computer Scientists 2013, vol. 1 (2013). http://www.iaeng.org/publication/IMECS2013/IMECS2013_pp436-440.pdf

4. Frank, A.: UCI machine learning repository. University of California, School of information and computer science, Irvine, CA (2010). http://archive.ics.uci.edu/ml
5. Ganbold, G.: History document image background noise and removal methods. Int. J. Knowl. Content Dev. Technol. **5**, 11 (2015). http://ijkcdt.net/xml/05531/05531.pdf
6. Goodfellow, I.J., et al.: Generative Adversarial Networks. ArXiv e-prints, June 2014
7. Hradiš, M., Kotera, J., Zemčík, P., Šroubek, F.: Convolutional neural networks for direct text deblurring. In: Proceedings of BMVC 2015. The British Machine Vision Association and Society for Pattern Recognition (2015). http://www.fit.vutbr.cz/research/view_pub.php?id=10922
8. Isola, P., Zhu, J., Zhou, T., Efros, A.A.: Image-to-image translation with conditional adversarial networks. CoRR **abs/1611.07004** (2016). http://arxiv.org/abs/1611.07004
9. Javed, S.T., Fasihi, M.M., Khan, A., Ashraf, U.: Background and punch-hole noise removal from handwritten urdu text. In: 2017 International Multi-topic Conference (INMIC), pp. 1–6, November 2017. https://doi.org/10.1109/INMIC.2017.8289451
10. Jiao, J., Sun, J., Satoshi, N.: A convolutional neural network based two-stage document deblurring. In: 2017 14th IAPR International Conference on Document Analysis and Recognition (ICDAR), vol. 01, pp. 703–707, November 2017. https://doi.org/10.1109/ICDAR.2017.120
11. Kupyn, O., Budzan, V., Mykhailych, M., Mishkin, D., Matas, J.: DeblurGAN: Blind motion deblurring using conditional adversarial networks. CoRR **abs/1711.07064** (2017). http://arxiv.org/abs/1711.07064
12. Li, H., Zhang, Y., Zhang, H., Zhu, Y., Sun, J.: Blind image deblurring based on sparse prior of dictionary pair. In: Proceedings of the 21st International Conference on Pattern Recognition (ICPR2012), pp. 3054–3057, November 2012
13. Lin, D., Fu, K., Wang, Y., Xu, G., Sun, X.: MARTA GANs: unsupervised representation learning for remote sensing image classification. IEEE Geosci. Remote Sens. Lett. **14**(11), 2092–2096 (2017). https://doi.org/10.1109/LGRS.2017.2752750
14. Liu, C., Szeliski, R., Kang, S.B., Zitnick, C.L., Freeman, W.T.: Automatic estimation and removal of noise from a single image. IEEE Trans. Pattern Anal. Mach. Intell. **30**(2), 299-314 (2006). http://people.csail.mit.edu/celiu/denoise/denoise_pami.pdf
15. Liu, R.W., Li, Y., Liu, Y., Duan, J., Xu, T., Liu, J.: Single-image blind deblurring with hybrid sparsity regularization. In: 2017 20th International Conference on Information Fusion (Fusion), pp. 1–8, July 2017. https://doi.org/10.23919/ICIF.2017.8009659
16. Ljubenovic, M., Zhuang, L., Figueiredo, M.A.T.: Class-adapted blind deblurring of document images. In: 2017 14th IAPR International Conference on Document Analysis and Recognition (ICDAR), vol. 01, pp. 721–726, November 2017. https://doi.org/10.1109/ICDAR.2017.123
17. Mirza, M., Osindero, S.: Conditional generative adversarial nets. CoRR **abs/1411.1784** (2014). http://arxiv.org/abs/1411.1784
18. Nah, S., Kim, T.H., Lee, K.M.: Deep multi-scale convolutional neural network for dynamic scene deblurring. CoRR **abs/1612.02177** (2016). http://arxiv.org/abs/1612.02177
19. Peng, Y., Qi, J., Yuan, Y.: CM-GANs: Cross-modal generative adversarial networks for common representation learning. CoRR **abs/1710.05106** (2017). http://arxiv.org/abs/1710.05106

20. Qin, C., He, Z., Yao, H., Cao, F., Gao, L.: Visible watermark removal scheme based on reversible data hiding and image inpainting. Sig. Process. Image Commun. **60**, 160–172 (2018). https://doi.org/10.1016/j.image.2017.10.003, http://www.sciencedirect.com/science/article/pii/S0923596517301868
21. Radford, A., Metz, L., Chintala, S.: Unsupervised representation learning with deep convolutional generative adversarial networks. CoRR **abs/1511.06434** (2015). http://arxiv.org/abs/1511.06434
22. Wang, L., Gao, C., Yang, L., Zhao, Y., Zuo, W., Meng, D.: PM-GANs: Discriminative representation learning for action recognition using partial-modalities. CoRR **abs/1804.06248** (2018). http://arxiv.org/abs/1804.06248
23. Xu, C., Lu, Y., Zhou, Y.: An automatic visible watermark removal technique using image inpainting algorithms. In: 2017 4th International Conference on Systems and Informatics (ICSAI), pp. 1152–1157, November 2017. https://doi.org/10.1109/ICSAI.2017.8248459
24. Yao, Q., Kwok, J.T.: Efficient Learning with a Family of Nonconvex Regularizers by Redistributing Nonconvexity. ArXiv e-prints, June 2016
25. Yi, Z., Zhang, H., Tan, P., Gong, M.: DualGAN: Unsupervised dual learning for image-to-image translation. CoRR **abs/1704.02510** (2017). http://arxiv.org/abs/1704.02510
26. Zhu, J., Park, T., Isola, P., Efros, A.A.: Unpaired image-to-image translation using cycle-consistent adversarial networks. CoRR **abs/1703.10593** (2017). http://arxiv.org/abs/1703.10593

Deep Reader: Information Extraction from Document Images via Relation Extraction and Natural Language

D. Vishwanath[1], Rohit Rahul[1(✉)], Gunjan Sehgal[1(✉)], Swati[1(✉)], Arindam Chowdhury[1(✉)], Monika Sharma[1(✉)], Lovekesh Vig[1(✉)], Gautam Shroff[1(✉)], and Ashwin Srinivasan[2(✉)]

[1] TCS Research, New Delhi, India
{vishwanath.d2,rohit.rahul,sehgal.gunjan,j.swati,chowdhury.arindam1,
monika.sharma1,lovekesh.vig,gautam.shroff}@tcs.com
[2] BITS Pilani, Goa Campus, Pilani, India
ashwin@goa.bits-pilani.ac.in

Abstract. Recent advancements in the area of Computer Vision with state-of-art Neural Networks has given a boost to Optical Character Recognition (OCR) accuracies. However, extracting characters/text alone is often insufficient for relevant information extraction as documents also have a visual structure that is not captured by OCR. Extracting information from tables, charts, footnotes, boxes, headings and retrieving the corresponding structured representation for the document remains a challenge and finds application in a large number of real-world use cases. In this paper, we propose a novel enterprise based end-to-end framework called DeepReader which facilitates information extraction from document images via identification of visual entities and populating a meta relational model across different entities in the document image. The model schema allows for an easy to understand abstraction of the entities detected by the deep vision models and the relationships between them. DeepReader has a suite of state-of-the-art vision algorithms which are applied to recognize handwritten and printed text, eliminate noisy effects, identify the type of documents and detect visual entities like tables, lines and boxes. Deep Reader maps the extracted entities into a rich relational schema so as to capture all the relevant relationships between entities (words, textboxes, lines etc.) detected in the document. Relevant information and fields can then be extracted from the document by writing SQL queries on top of the relationship tables. A natural language based interface is added on top of the relationship schema so that a non-technical user, specifying the queries in natural language, can fetch the information with minimal effort. In this paper, we also demonstrate many different capabilities of Deep Reader and report results on a real-world use case.

D. Vishwanath and R. Rahul have contributed equally.

1 Introduction

With the proliferation of cameras and scanning software on mobile devices, users are frequently uploading a variety of scanned images of documents such as invoices, passports and contracts to application servers on the cloud. Currently, much of the processing of these documents is at least partially done manually owing to the critical nature of the transactions involved. However, with recent advancements in deep learning for vision applications, it has become possible to further automate this process. The problem falls under the realm of information extraction from images and has been a longstanding research problem for vision researchers [1].

While OCR accuracies have significantly improved, thanks to advancement in deep learning, these alone are insufficient for effective extraction of visual information from scanned documents. Most documents have a rich set of visual entities in the form of tables, text-boxes, blocks, charts, and arrows. Until recently, vision algorithms were not powerful enough to accurately identify and extract these visual entities, which resulted in errors being propagated downstream in the extraction pipeline. Real world documents often have a combination of both handwritten and printed text which makes text harder to localize and identify. Additionally, the scanning process can often introduce noise in the documents which confuses the text recognition algorithms. Therefore, any real world deployment has to address these vision challenges in order to be effective.

In addition to address the vision problems mentioned above, there are challenges involved in understanding the complex visual structure between the entities in the document. The visual relationships between the different entities detected in an image are often critical to understanding and reasoning over the information present prior to extraction. For example a text label might only make sense if viewed in the context of the entity it is connected to via an arrow.

Humans utilize a lot of universal background knowledge while reading documents, and this needs to be incorporated into any extraction engine. For example, we know that an address comprises of a city and country name. This knowledge needs to be captured and embedded into the system. Also, very often incorporation of domain knowledge or business rules can often boost the extraction performance and enable validation and correction of extracted data.

In this paper we present Deep Reader, a platform for information extraction from images which attempts to incorporate these salient relationships prior to information extraction. The platform utilizes state of the art deep learning based vision algorithms for denoising the image documents and identifying entities such as tables, printed and handwritten text, text blocks, boxes and lines. The spatial relationships between these entities are then recorded and used to populate a high level relational schema. The relational schema in question is designed to be as generic and exhaustive as possible. Users are allowed to filter and retrieve relevant data from the populated schema either via SQL queries, or via a conversational interface. This allows users to incorporate domain specific information and business rules in their queries, for example SWIFT address must comprise of 8 alphanumeric characters, drawer name always occurs before drawee etc. Once the user is satisfied with the results of their queries, the queries are stored and may be applied to other documents sharing the same template.

2 Related Work

Extracting text from images have been an active field of research for several decades. With the advent of deep neural networks, OCR engines have become very powerful with opensource offerings like Tesseract [2], and cloud API based solutions like Google Text Vision API. Interpreting documents with a relatively simple textual layout and good quality scans is now reasonably straightforward thanks to these advancements. However, when dealing with documents following several different templates with diverse visual layouts, retrieving semantically accurate information can be very challenging. There has been extensive line of work towards solving this problem.

Yshitani [18] developed an information extraction system wherein a document instance is matched with a set of pre-stored models which define categories of documents. The extracted document text is compared against a pre-compiled list of keywords and their spelling variants. The results are matched with each document in a database of word models and their logical relationships.

Cesarini [3] requires user to build a conceptual model of the document, which is then used to match, interpret and extract contents from the document. The work places more emphasis on the classification and organization of the documents rather than extraction of key fields. Both Cesarani [3] and Peanho [1] build an Attribute Relational Graph based representation of the document to capture relationships between entities in an image, however their system relies on considerable expertise from user to create suitable template document models.

[4] propose a system for extracting field information from administrative documents using a document model for extracting structural relationships between words. As the system processes more documents, it refines its structural model. More recently, [5] proposed a technique to extract data from colored documents by extracting rectangles and modeling the topological relationship between them as a graph. The technique was generalized to extraction from new cases based on topological and context similarity. An Entity Recognition model was proposed in [6], using geometrical relationships between entities. [7] propose a system for automatic separation of static and variable content in Administrative Document Images using a probabilistic model for determining whether a pixel is static or dynamic.

A relevant problem for extraction is that of document template identification for which several techniques have been proposed. Bruel developed a matching technique that was more robust to noise in the template instance [8], and subsequently to capture the layout of a complex document [9]. In [9], the authors generate a hierarchical representation of documents and templates using XY-trees and utilize tree edit distance to identify the correct template for a new instance. Hamza [10] utilize a bottom-up approach which involves keyword extraction followed by clustering to generate high level structures. The document is represented as a graph with these high level structures as nodes and edges indicative of spatial relationships. Documents are mapped via graph probing, which is an approximation of graph edit distance. Schultz et al. [11] have developed an invoice reading system, where documents are again represented by a graph but nodes are split into key-nodes and data-nodes, corresponding to keywords and values (numbers, dates etc.). Graph probing is used to find the correct template. Extraction is done by examining the nearby words of every data-node.

In fact, in many of these works approximate solutions to known hard problems (such as graph distance, tree edit distance and maximum cliques) have been used to match an input document with a document model. In DeepReader, we utilize a combination of visual structure similarity and textual similarity (captured by a deep Siamese network) to classify documents to the appropriate template.

Information Extraction from documents remains an open problem in general and in this paper we attempt to revisit this problem armed with a suite of state of the art deep learning vision APIs and deep learning based text processing solutions. These include utilization of generative adversarial networks [12] for image denoising, Siamese networks [13] for document template identification and sequence to sequence models for handwritten text recognition [14]. DeepReader also utilizes low-level vision routines that are extremely useful for identifying text based entities in an image and populating a pre-defined relational schema. This relational schema can then be queried using standard SQL.

The advent of sequence to sequence models has allowed for significant advancement in several text modeling tasks and these models play a crucial role in several state of the art conversational systems [15]. DeepReader utilizes a sequence to sequence model to provide users with the ability to query the system via a natural language conversational interface. The interface builds on prior work that utilizes seq2seq models for learning an NL to SQL query mapping [16] The motivation is to allow non-technical users to efficiently utilize the system for efficient data extraction from images.

3 DeepReader Architecture

DeepReader processes documents in several stages as shown in Fig. 1. Initially a raw document image which may be blurred, noisy or faded is input to the system. A denoising suite is employed to clean the image prior to data extraction. The clean image is then sent for document identification to ascertain the correct template for the document. DeepReader vision APIs are subsequently employed for entity extraction followed by a schema mapping layer to populate a relational database that adheres to the DeepReader schema. The user may retrieve contents from the database either via SQL or via a Conversational Interface.

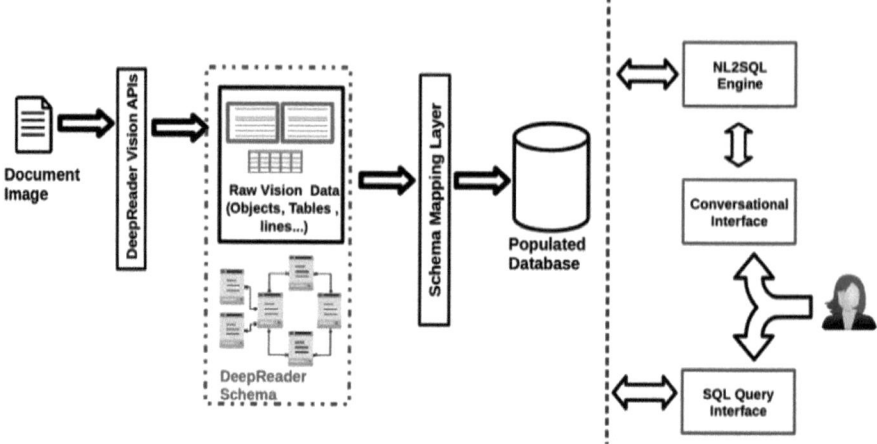

Fig. 1. Deep Reader workflow for writing rules for a query

4 Computer Vision Components of Deep Reader

To pre-process a document for information extraction, a number of visual elements need to be identified. These include printed and handwritten text, text lines, clusters of text lines (also referred to as textblocks), boxes, and tables. DeepReader leverages a number of deep vision APIs in order to identify the different visual elements present in the document. Additionally, a document cleaning suite based on generative adversarial networks is developed and is a vital pre processing step as described below.

4.1 Image De-noising

In this section, we address the issue of degradation in quality of images due to camera shake, improper focus, imaging noise, coffee stains, wrinkles, low resolution, poor lighting, or reflections. These kind of problems drastically affect the performance of many computer vision algorithms like text detection, OCR and localization. The objective here is to reconstruct high-quality images directly from noisy inputs and also to preserve the highly structured data in the images.

Text document images are markedly different from natural scene images as text documents contain more detailed information and are therefore more sensitive to noise. Thus, we propose a denoising method by utilizing generative adversarial networks (GANs) [12]. Generative Adversarial Networks have been applied to different image-to-image translation problems, such as super resolution [17], style transfer [18], and product photo generation [19]. In DeepReader, we have implemented conditional generative adversarial networks (cGANs) in which both the generator and discriminator are conditioned on extra information $\mathbf{y}$ as described in [20]. In our case, the variable $\mathbf{y}$ is represented by a class label i.e., the cleaned image. We have conditioned only on the discriminator by feeding **y** as an extra input layer. The cGANs network is trained using the following minimax objective function:

$$\min_G \max_D E_{x \sim P_r}[log(D(x|y))] + E_{\widetilde{x} \sim P_g}[log(1 - D(\widetilde{x}|y))] \quad (1)$$

where P_r is data distribution and P_g is model distribution defined by $\widetilde{x} = G(z)$, $z = P(z)$ and z is one of the samples from the noisy images dataset.

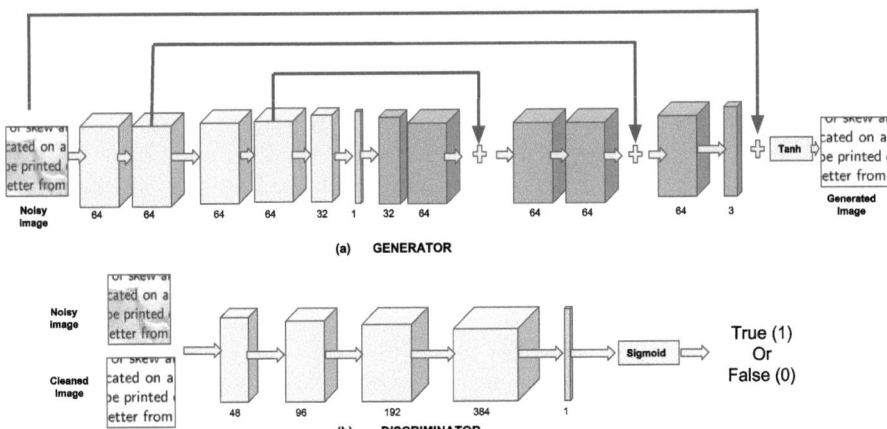

Fig. 2. The architecture of cGANs for denoising images. The upper figure shows the generator model and the lower figure shows the discriminator model. The generator model takes noisy images as input and generates a high-quality image while the discriminator takes both clean and noisy images and learns to differentiate between them. Reproduced from [20]. (Color figure online)

Generator: The architecture of our network is shown in Fig. 2. The generator network consists of a combination of convolutional layers (represented by grey color blocks) and deconvolutional layers (represented by blue color blocks). Each of the blocks is followed by batch normalization and the activation used in the convolutional layer is PReLU while for deconvolutional layer, ReLU activation is employed. For all the layers, the stride is set to be 1. In order to maintain the dimension of each feature map to be the same as that of the input, we use zero padding. For efficient network training and better convergence performance, symmetric skip connections are used as shown in the generator network.

Discriminator: The discriminator is used to classify each input image into two labels - real or fake. The discriminator network consists of convolutional layers each having batch normalization and PReLU activation. A sigmoid function is stacked at the top to map the output to a probability score between [0, 1].

The loss function used for the cGAN network is same as define in [20]:

$$L = L_E + \lambda_a L_A + \lambda_p L_P \quad (2)$$

where, L_E is per-pixel loss function, L_P is perceptual loss and L_A is adversarial loss (loss from the discriminator). λ_a and λ_p are pre-defined weights for adversarial loss and perceptual loss, respectively.

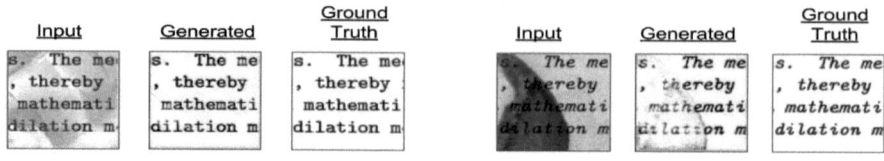

Fig. 3. Sample output after de-noising the image

Peformance Evaluation: We have evaluated our model on a public kaggle document dataset[1] hosted by [21]. The performance measure used for the evaluation of the model are Peak Signal to Noise Ratio (PSNR) and Structural Similarity Index (SSIM) [22]. The value of PSNR and SSIM obtained are **17.85 dB** and **0.946**, respectively. Some of the output images obtained from generator model are shown in Fig. 3.

4.2 Document Identification

One of the more pressing challenges in the pipeline is determining the correct template in which to classify the test document. We utilize a deep Siamese network for this [13]:

The base of our Siamese network consists of a traditional Convolutional Neural Network (CNN). It consists of two convolutional layers with 64 and 128 filter size respectively. Each convolutional layer operates on stride of 1 and is followed by a max pool layer of size 2×2, which is also operating at a stride of 1. All convolutional layers in our base CNN have Rectified Linear Units (ReLU) as an activation function. The output of the final max pool layer is flattened into a vector and is passed into the succeeding fully connected dense layer having 512 hidden units and sigmoid activation. This dense layer is followed by the computation of an energy function over the feature representations at the highest level. The Siamese network is learnt using a contrastive loss function [23]. We trained the siamese network on an image size of 500×400. While training, the optimizer used is Stochastic Gradient Descent (SGD) with learning rate of 10^{-2}, Nestrov momentum value was set to 0.99 and weight decay was set to 10^{-6}. We evaluated the performance of our model on a dataset containing 9 types of bank documents and the model yielded an accuracy of **88.89%**.

4.3 Processing Handwritten Text

A major challenge in extracting useful information from scanned text documents is the recognition of handwritten text (HTR) in addition to printed text. It is an important problem for an enterprises attempting to digitize large volumes of handmarked scanned documents. Towards this end, we use the HTR system proposed in [24] which uses a convolutional feature extractor followed by a recurrent

---

[1] https://www.kaggle.com/c/denoising-dirty-documents.

encoder-decoder model for mapping the visual features to a set of characters in the image. A general overview of the model is provided in [14].

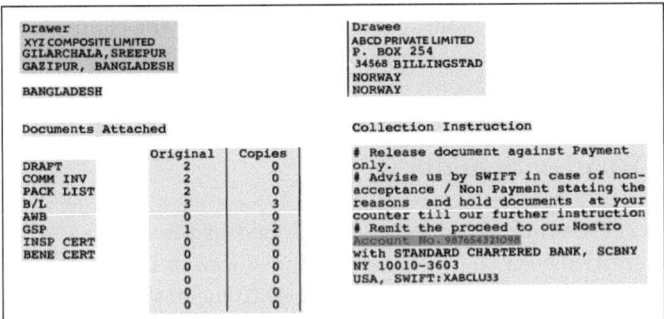

Fig. 4. Sample bank document

5 Extracting Different Text Entities from the Document

A document has many entities like words, lines, text blocks, and text boxes. The information of interest may involve one or several of these entities, which makes it imperative to detect all of the entities present in the document.

5.1 Detecting Textual Entities

We utilize a combination of connected components, and spatial clustering to identify and cluster text characters in the image into words, lines and blocks. For scene text or colored images present in the document, we use the connectionist text proposal network (CTPN) [25]. The objective is to get the location of the different textual entities present in the image.

5.2 Entities

The following high level entities were extracted:

1. **Page lines:** To get the page lines we perform horizontal clustering on the words based on the Euclidean Distance between connected component clusters. After we localize the page lines, each page line patch is sent through a standard OCR engine (such as Tesseract, Google Vision or Abby FineReader) to get the text corresponding to that line. We noticed that sending smaller patches resulted in higher accuracy from the OCR engine.
2. **Text Block:** A text block is a set of lines which begin at approximately the same x coordinate and the vertical distance between them is not more than twice the height of the line. Figure 4 shows a highlighted block.

3. **Lines of the Text Block or Box:** The lines that lie inside a particular textblock or box are also identified seperately as block or box lines.
4. **Boxes:** To find the Boxes, we first erode the image followed by the thresholding and inversion. After that we compare the area of each connected component with the area of its bounding box. If the area of the connected component is within a percent of the area of bounding box then we deem that connected component as a box.

6 Deep Reader Schema

Once all the entities are identified as mentioned in the above section, relations between the entities need to be populated and stored in the database. The corresponding database schema should be designed to facilitate the subsequent information extraction. All the entities are associated with their spatial coordinates and this information conveys the whereabouts of the neighbouring text entities. This information is then used to infer different logical and spatial relationships (Figs. 5 and 6).

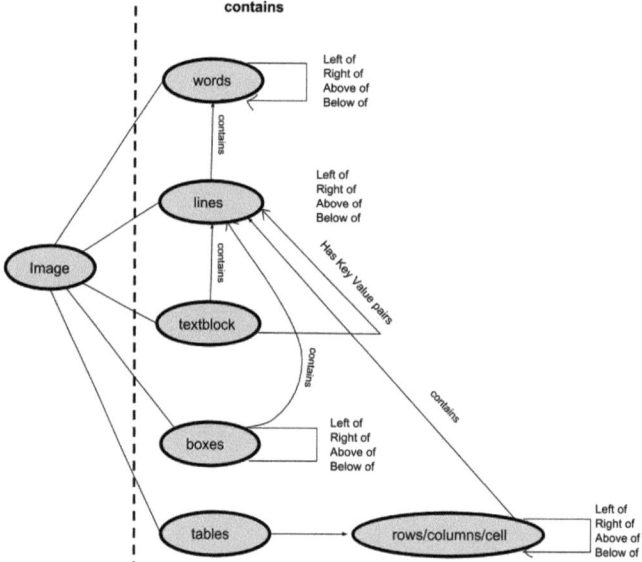

Fig. 5. Deep Reader schema

The line entities identified from the vision components includes information about the line text, individual words in the line along with the line and word coordinates. Using the coordinate position of words, DeepReader extracts words to the left/right/above/below of other words and maintains it in the schema. Similarly it uses the raw vision data to maintain the words and the lines in which they occur in the schema as a separate table. As shown in the Fig. 4, the word 'SREEPUR' will be detected by the vision components along with the associated coordinates. The word to the left is 'GILARCHALA', right is 'null', above is 'COMPOSITE' and below is 'BANGLADESH'. In this way deep reader maintains the relative spatial position of each word/line/block etc.

The text block entities identified includes attributes in a similar fashion. The line id, word id, word text, line text of every word and line in the text block, along with coordinates for each word and line as well as the text of the individual lines identified in the block is populated in the database. Additional relationships such as lines below/above a word in the text block are also maintained. For example 'DRAWEE' can be extracted from the document using the line below word relationship. The line below the word DRAWEE in the textblock is 'ABCD PRIVATE LIMITED'.

7 Incorporation of Universal and Domain Specific Background Knowledge

It has been observed that most of the documents such as bank receipts, invoices, etc. in the real world have certain universal patterns that humans implicitly utilize while reading them. In DeepReader universal background knowledge is incorporated in four different ways:

1. Via the use of universal abstract data types such as city, country, date, phone number. This greatly aids extraction as the relevant field can often be retrieved just by looking up the type information.
2. Via universal validation rules enforcing well known patterns. For example an address must contain a country, city and zip code and every amount or price field must be a real number with an associated currency. These rules help the system validate and refine the resulting extractions.
3. Via well known aliases or semantically similar entities such as Amount, Amnt, Amt.
4. Via commonly occuring visual/text patterns: For example phrases seperated by a colon or different fonts in a box normally constitute a key value pair. In Fig. 4 "SWIFT: SCBLUS33" is an example of a key value pair. Using the key SWIFT its value can be directly fetched by querying on this relationship table.

In addition to universal background knowledge, domain specific background knowledge is incorporated into the system to correct for OCR spelling mistakes, and for further data typing. For example it may make sense to add a data type called designation for resumes, whereas it may make sense to add a SWIFT number as a data type for financial documents. Users of DeepReader have the flexibility to add this knowledge into their extraction application.

8 SQL Queries to Extract Useful Fields

Once the relational schema is populated with data from the document, it can now be queried like a regular database schema using SQL. Thus the original problem of information extraction from images has been abstracted to the problem of simply querying on a set of tables. This allows for a wider audience that may not be familiar with Vision but is familiar with SQL to specify extraction rules/steps.

9 Natural Language Interface to Deep Reader

While querying in SQL certainly makes the information extraction solutions more accessible to a wider range of programmers, it may be possible to reach an even wider audience if the system had a conversational interface, obviating the need for familiarity with SQL. There has recently been good progress in converting natural language queries into SQL [16] using sequence to sequence models. Deep Reader builds on this work to offer users a conversational interface that maps NL utterances internally into an SQL query, and extracts the relevant information.

While sometimes a simple SQL query will be sufficient to fetch the required information from the database. Many times, a complex query or a sequence of simple queries has to be executed in a pipeline to get the correct information. These complex queries can be broken up into multiple simple queries, storing and building upon the intermediate results. For this to happen, the intermediate results are saved and fed as a data table into the subsequent query. This way a sequence of queries will get executed and result in a workflow which can be saved and applied on other similar documents in one shot to get the required information. This is explained in more detail in the subsequent sections.

9.1 Intent Identification

The user when interacting with Deep Reader through Natural Language, can ask for a variety of different fields. An intent identifier is necessary to classify the NL-Query and ascertain the intention. We will categorize the given NL-utterances into 3 classes. These are (1) extraction queries, (2) request for creating or saving a workflow & (3) book-keeping. Once the intent is known, the NL-Query is passed to its respective model for further processing. All the three models are explained in further sections.

We formulate the intent identification as a classification problem with each NL-utterance being fed as input to a sequential neural model with a softmax output over the possible intents. Recurrent Neural Networks (RNN) [26] offer state of the art results for finding patterns in sequential data. We use Long Short Term Memory (LSTMs) [27] which is a flavour of RNN and captures important experiences that have very long time lags in between.

9.2 Processing Extraction Queries

Once the intent identifier classifies the given NL-Query as an extraction query, an NL-Query is sent to this model for further processing. The corresponding SQL-Query is structured as follows:

SELECT $SELECT\_COL$ **FROM** $TABLE$
WHERE $COND\_COL$ OP $COND\_VAL$

To map an NL utterance to an SQL query we need to perform the following steps:

1. **Entity Recognition:** $COND_VAL as shown above is an entity which is document specific and the same has to be extracted from the NL sentence. This corresponds to the Named Entity Recognition (NER) problem and here we utilize Conditional Random Fields (CRFs) [28] to solve this problem.
   During training, each word in the NL-query is tagged as either an entity or a non-entity and a CRF is trained on this encoding. Once we get the $COND_VAL, using the CRF, the same will be replaced with a standard word in the dictionary. For example, 'SWIFT' will be identified as an entity by CRFs in the sentence "Please get me the word towards right of SWIFT" and will be replaced with "Please get me the word towards right of <COND_VAL>". This will help in processing the NL-query by subsequent models in the pipeline.

2. **Template Mapping:** We employ a template-based approach to the generation of SQL-Queries and formulate it as a slot filling problem. All simple NL-queries will be mapped to one of the templates in our template pool. We formulate this as a classification problem with the modified NL-Query being classified by a deep sequential model. Below are a few sample SQL templates used.

SELECT * FROM TABLE
WHERE id=(SELECT id FROM TABLE WHERE string="VALUE")

SELECT * FROM TABLE WHERE primary_str="VALUE"

SELECT SUBSTR(line, pos(VALUE),) FROM TEMP

SELECT SUBSTR(line, pos(VALUE1), pos(VALUE2)-pos(VALUE1)) FROM TEMP

3. **Table Mapping:** Once the correct template is identified, slots for TABLE and VALUE are required to be filled. The VALUE is readily obtained from the Entity Recognition model. The NL-Query has words with many linguistic variants which can map to the same relevant table. For example, the sentences "get me the word towards the right of SWIFT" and "get me the word immediately next to SWIFT" will map to the same table "rightof". This mapping is done using an LSTM model trained to classify on these variations (Table 1).

Table 1. Results for different LSTM models

Model	No. of training samples	No. of testing samples	Accuracy
Intent Identification	250	31	100%
Entity Recognition	130	130	96.3%
Template Mapping	160	44	90.2%
Table Mapping	160	44	100%

9.3 Creating a Workflow: Sequence of Extraction Queries

Simple extraction queries will only fetch information which is readily available from the database. Often complex queries need to be executed to extract relevant information. Designing complex queries for every possible use case would blow up the SQL-template space and would inhibit query reuse. However, complex queries can be broken down into multiple simple queries, allowing for storing and building upon the intermediate results.

For example, as shown in the Fig. 4, to get the "Account" information, below are the set of NL-Queries needs that to be executed in a sequence.

- "Kindly get the block information for the block containing the word remit"
- "Please get the line which has word Account in it from the previous result"
- "Get substring which is towards right of Account from the previous result"

Different combinations of simple queries executed in sequence will fetch the complex entity. By default, the output of any intermediate result is stored in a temporary table which can be queried further.

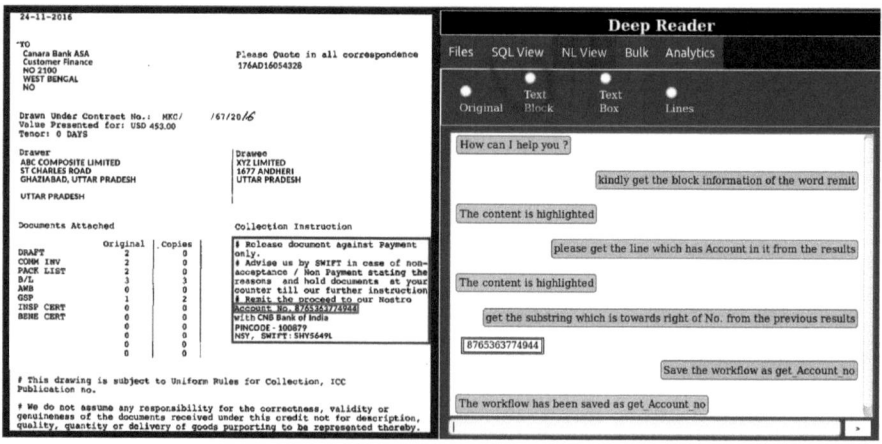

Fig. 6. Graphical user interface

9.4 Book-Keeping

A sequence of meaningful NL-Queries will fetch the required information. Once saved, this workflow can be applied to a new document with a similar template. A simple framework using queues has been built in order to store the recent set of commands in a sequence. Once the user fetches a meaningful information, the workflow is saved. Simple NL-Queries like "clear the workflow", "save the workflow", "apply the workflow on this document" etc. are used for book-keeping.

10 Conclusions and Future Work

This paper introduces DeepReader, a framework for the extraction of relevant data from image documents. We have elaborated on the vision challenges involved in processing real documents such as removal of background noise and hand written text recognition. We proposed a GAN based architecture for noise removal and a state of the art sequence-to-sequence attention model for handwritten text recognition. In addition, the spatial relationships between visual entities are captured via a rich predefined relational schema. A Siamese Network was used to identify the template of a document. A NL Interface has been integrated to allow novice users to converse with the system for rapid and easy data extraction.

The current DeepReader framework can be used to process a wide variety of real world documents that adhere to a finite number of templates, however several enhancements are required for better generalization. Organizing universal background knowledge by developing a framework for prioritizing rules for a particular context, and allowing for easy inter-operability to domain ontologies for easy integration of domain specific knowledge are part of the future plans. An aspect that is being explored is learning the rules for extraction automatically via examples. This would allow users to specify the extraction fields automatically without writing down elaborate extraction rules. The underlying philosophy is that while the innate human ability to see and discriminate objects in the real world is not yet fully understood, the ability to read and understand documents can be performed via a combination of background knowledge and visual/textual cues. With the progress of deep learning in being able to capture the visual elements more accurately, perhaps document understanding can now be accomplished to a much more satisfactory degree.

References

1. Peanho, C.A., Stagni, H., da Silva, F.S.C.: Semantic information extraction from images of complex documents. Appl. Intell. **37**, 543–557 (2012)
2. Smith, R.: An overview of the tesseract OCR engine. In: Ninth International Conference on Document Analysis and Recognition, ICDAR 2007, vol. 2, pp. 629–633. IEEE (2007)
3. Cesarini, F., Gori, M., Marinai, S., Soda, G.: Informys: a flexible invoice-like form-reader system. IEEE Trans. Pattern Anal. Mach. Intell. **20**, 730–745 (1998)

4. Rusinol, M., Benkhelfallah, T., Poulain dAndecy, V.: Field extraction from administrative documents by incremental structural templates. In: 12th International Conference on Document Analysis and Recognition (ICDAR), pp. 1100–1104. IEEE (2013)
5. Hammami, M., Héroux, P., Adam, S., d'Andecy, V.P.: One-shot field spotting on colored forms using subgraph isomorphism. In: International Conference on Document Analysis and Recognition (2015)
6. Kooli, N., Belaïd, A.: Semantic label and structure model based approach for entity recognition in database context. In: 13th International Conference on Document Analysis and Recognition (ICDAR), pp. 301–305. IEEE (2015)
7. Aldavert, D., Rusinol, M., Toledo, R.: Automatic static/variable content separation in administrative document images. In: 14th IAPR International Conference on Document Analysis and Recognition (ICDAR), pp. 87–92. IEEE (2017)
8. Breuel, T.M.: A practical, globally optimal algorithm for geometric matching under uncertainty. Electron. Notes Theor. Comput. Sci. **46**, 188–202 (2001)
9. Breuel, T.M.: High performance document layout analysis. In: Proceedings of the Symposium on Document Image Understanding Technology, pp. 209–218 (2003)
10. Hamza, H., Belaïd, Y., Belaïd, A.: A case-based reasoning approach for invoice structure extraction. In: Ninth International Conference on Document Analysis and Recognition, ICDAR 2007, vol. 1, pp. 327–331. IEEE (2007)
11. Schulz, F., Ebbecke, M., Gillmann, M., Adrian, B., Agne, S., Dengel, A.: Seizing the treasure: transferring knowledge in invoice analysis. In: 10th International Conference on Document Analysis and Recognition, ICDAR 2009, pp. 848–852. IEEE (2009)
12. Goodfellow, I., et al.: arxiv: 1406.2661 (2014)
13. Koch, G., Zemel, R., Salakhutdinov, R.: Siamese neural networks for one-shot image recognition. In: ICML Deep Learning Workshop, vol. 2 (2015)
14. Chowdhury, A., Vig, L.: An efficient end-to-end neural model for handwritten text recognition. arXiv preprint arXiv:1807.07965 (2018)
15. Vinyals, O., Le, Q.: A neural conversational model. arXiv preprint arXiv:1506.05869 (2015)
16. Yu, T., Li, Z., Zhang, Z., Zhang, R., Radev, D.: TypeSQL: knowledge-based type-aware neural text-to-SQL generation. arXiv preprint arXiv:1804.09769 (2018)
17. Ledig, C., et al.: Photo-realistic single image super-resolution using a generative adversarial network. arXiv preprint (2017)
18. Li, C., Wand, M.: Precomputed real-time texture synthesis with Markovian generative adversarial networks. In: Leibe, B., Matas, J., Sebe, N., Welling, M. (eds.) ECCV 2016. LNCS, vol. 9907, pp. 702–716. Springer, Cham (2016). https://doi.org/10.1007/978-3-319-46487-9_43
19. Bousmalis, K., Silberman, N., Dohan, D., Erhan, D., Krishnan, D.: Unsupervised pixel-level domain adaptation with generative adversarial networks. In: The IEEE Conference on Computer Vision and Pattern Recognition (CVPR), vol. 1, p. 7 (2017)
20. Zhang, H., Sindagi, V., Patel, V.M.: Image de-raining using a conditional generative adversarial network. arXiv preprint arXiv:1701.05957 (2017)
21. Frank, A.: UCI machine learning repository. University of California, School of Information and Computer Science, Irvine (2010). http://archive.ics.uci.edu/ml
22. Wang, Z., Bovik, A.C., Sheikh, H.R., Simoncelli, E.P.: Image quality assessment: from error visibility to structural similarity. IEEE Trans. Image Process. **13**, 600–612 (2004)

23. Chopra, S., Hadsell, R., LeCun, Y.: Learning a similarity metric discriminatively, with application to face verification. In: IEEE Computer Society Conference on Computer Vision and Pattern Recognition, vol. 1, pp. 539–546 (2005)
24. Chowdhury, A., Lovekesh, V.: An efficient end-to-end neural model for handwritten text recognition (2018)
25. Tian, Z., Huang, W., He, T., He, P., Qiao, Y.: Detecting text in natural image with connectionist text proposal network. In: Leibe, B., Matas, J., Sebe, N., Welling, M. (eds.) ECCV 2016. LNCS, vol. 9912, pp. 56–72. Springer, Cham (2016). https://doi.org/10.1007/978-3-319-46484-8_4
26. Mikolov, T., Karafiát, M., Burget, L., Černocký, J., Khudanpur, S.: Recurrent neural network based language model. In: Eleventh Annual Conference of the International Speech Communication Association (2010)
27. Hochreiter, S., Schmidhuber, J.: Long short-term memory. Neural Comput. **9**, 1735–1780 (1997)
28. Lafferty, J., McCallum, A., Pereira, F.C.: Conditional random fields: probabilistic models for segmenting and labeling sequence data (2001)

Simultaneous Recognition of Horizontal and Vertical Text in Natural Images

Chankyu Choi[✉], Youngmin Yoon, Junsu Lee, and Junseok Kim

NAVER Corporation, Seongnam-si, South Korea
{chankyu.choi,youngmin.yoon,junsu.lee,jun.seok}@navercorp.com

Abstract. Recent state-of-the-art scene text recognition methods have primarily focused on horizontal text in images. However, in several Asian countries, including China, large amounts of text in signs, books, and TV commercials are vertically directed. Because the horizontal and vertical texts exhibit different characteristics, developing an algorithm that can simultaneously recognize both types of text in real environments is necessary. To address this problem, we adopted the direction encoding mask (DEM) and selective attention network (SAN) methods based on supervised learning. DEM contains directional information to compensate in cases that lack text direction; therefore, our network is trained using this information to handle the vertical text. The SAN method is designed to work individually for both types of text. To train the network to recognize both types of text and to evaluate the effectiveness of the designed model, we prepared a new synthetic vertical text dataset and collected an actual vertical text dataset (VTD142) from the Web. Using these datasets, we proved that our proposed model can accurately recognize both vertical and horizontal text and can achieve state-of-the-art results in experiments using benchmark datasets, including the street view test (SVT), IIIT-5k, and ICDAR. Although our model is relatively simple as compared to its predecessors, it maintains the accuracy and is trained in an end-to-end manner.

Keywords: Horizontal and vertical text recognition ·
Directional encoding mask · Selective attention network ·
Supervised learning

1 Introduction

Optical character recognition (OCR) in the wild is a challenging problem in computer-vision research, and several approaches have been studied to perform OCR on images acquired from various environments such as documents or natural scenes. OCR is usually segmented into separate modules such as scene text detection and scene text recognition. The scene text detection module identifies the regions of interest in images that contain text; various algorithms handle this task. Subsequently, the scene text recognition module translates these regions into labeled text. This study presents a novel method to perform scene text recognition.

Majority of the prior scene text recognition algorithms only attempted to cover the horizontal text. However, in several Asian countries, including China, large amounts of text in signs, books, and TV commercials are vertically oriented. Horizontal and vertical texts exhibit different characteristics that should be simultaneously solved for. They occupied different aspect ratio text region in image. Therefore, a clever algorithm must be developed to deal with both types of text. Figure 1 depicts the reason due to which the OCR algorithm is able to handle the vertically directed text in real environments. A recent study used arbitrarily oriented text recognition (AON) [5] encoded image input in four directions (top-to-bottom, bottom-to-top, left-to-right, and right-to-left) to detect a freely rotated word. AON can, therefore, adapt in an unsupervised manner to tackle the rotated text using four orientations of directional information.

In this study, inspired by the AON method, we simultaneously recognize the horizontal and vertical texts. Our method uses carefully designed information formulated via the directional encoding mask (DEM) and selective attention network (SAN) methods. Both the modules help the network to learn quickly and accurately. DEM is designed to extract the direction of a text region before it is passed to the text recognition model. Therefore, it should be created in advance during the preparation time of the ground truth data. It encapsulates the directional information for the text region. An advantage of DEM is that it helps the network to quickly and accurately learn to distinguish between vertical and horizontal text in a supervised manner. Our contributions are as follows.

(1) We created two alternative methods, namely, DEM and SAN that can simultaneously deal with both horizontal and vertical characters.
(2) To train for vertical text, we generated a synthetic vertical text dataset (SVTD). In addition, to evaluate the performance with respect to the vertical text, we collected an actual vertical text dataset (VTD142), including building signs and titles. All the real data were collected from the webpages.
(3) Our model achieves state-of-the-art results with respect to various benchmark datasets.

2 Related Work

Previously, the development of OCR algorithms mostly used handcrafted features, which are difficult to design and exhibit limited performance in specific areas; however, currently, neural networks offer a promising alternative for powerful OCR algorithms [9,10,15,26]. Convolutional recurrent neural network (CRNN) [23] encode the input images using convolutional neural network (CNN) and further decode the encoded features using recurrent neural network (RNN) by connectionist temporal classification (CTC). Recurrent and recursive convolution network [16,17] improve the representational power and efficiency of the encoders. Attention OCR [30] improves the overall performance using positional encoding and attention mechanisms. Gated recurrent convolutional neural

Fig. 1. Majority of the prior scene text recognition algorithms only attempted to cover the horizontal text. However, in several Asian countries, including China, large amounts of text in signs, books, and TV commercials are vertically directed.

network (GRCN) [27] adopt gated recurrent CNNs to further improve the performance. Currently, even though there are several deep neural network (DNN) [4,5,24] in use, only a few studies that focus on the vertical and horizontal texts have been conducted. FOTS [18] handles oriented text, which is essentially different from recognizing characters the in vertical direction. The results also exhibited lower performance as compared to the attention-based decoder because they have experimented with a CTC-based decoder. AON [5] is an unsupervised learning method that learns a character's direction by network oneself. Conversely, we examine the orientation of a word during the training stage and add this feature to the network so that the network can be learned in a supervised manner. We extended the AON to a supervised learning method to recognize the horizontal and vertical texts.

3 Proposed Method

We begin by explaining the manner in which a unified network can be designed to simultaneously handle the horizontal and vertical texts using an image's aspect ratio. We examine the direction of a word during the training stage and add this feature to the network so that the network can be learned in a supervised manner. To explain it more clearly, our methods determine the direction of the text after checking the width-to-height ratio of the input image. Further, the vertical text is rotated by 90° and input to the network. In this study, we introduce the two methods that are required to achieve this.

3.1 Directional Encoding Mask

DEM combines the input image and the directional information of the characters, which are further encoded by the CNN encoder. Because DEM contains the directional information of the text, the network uses this information while training. In this study, we encode the directional information in cosine for the horizontal text and in sine for the vertical text. The equation below describes the DEM.

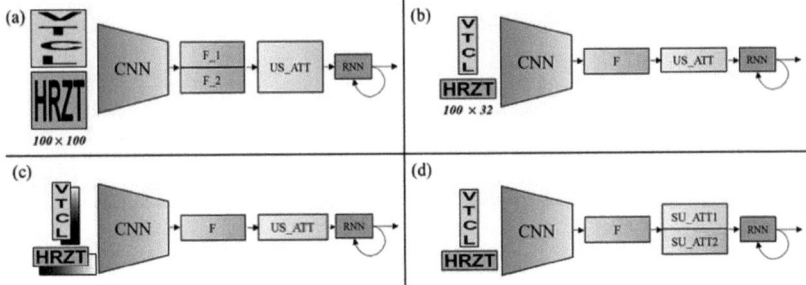

Fig. 2. Various models for recognizing the horizontal and vertical text: (a) AON style [5] with 2-directional clue network, (b) Baseline, (c) DEM, (d) SAN. F means features, SU_ATT means supervised attention and US_ATT means unsupervised attention mechanism respectively.

$$\text{DEM} = \begin{cases} \{y \mid y = \sin(0.5 * normalized\_width * \pi)\}, & \text{if width} > \text{height} \\ \{y \mid y = \cos(0.5 * normalized\_width * \pi)\}, & \text{otherwise} \end{cases} \quad (1)$$

In the Eq. (1), the normalized width is the x coordinate in normalized space [0, 1]. As can be observed from the equation, we encode DEM for the horizontal text using a cosine function. The DEM for vertical text is encoded using a sine function. The kernel function of DEM can be replaced by similar functions; therefore, we chose it experimentally.

$$X = concat(I, DEM) \quad (2)$$

DEM is not a single value, but a two-dimensional image of the same size as the input image. DEM and the input image are concatenated and entered into the CNN. X is used as the input of the CNN.

3.2 Selective Attention Network

SAN is another supervised learning method. It has two attention masks, each of which reacts according to the corresponding text direction; therefore, they work separately. SAN can turn its own attention weight on and off depending on the direction of the text. This differs from AON's clue network because it is based on supervised learning. The *character feature vector* for the RNN is defined as:

$$x_t^c = W_c c_{t-1}^{OneHot} \quad (3)$$

where c_{t-1} is one hot encoding of the previous letter (ground truth during training and predicted during test time).

Let s_t be the hidden state of the LSTM at time t. Further, we compute the output and the subsequent state of the LSTM, as shown

$$(y_t, s_t) = LSTM_{step}(x_t, s_{t-1}) \quad (4)$$

SVTD   VTD142

Fig. 3. SVTD is a new synthetic vertical text dataset in a similar fashion as [1]. VTD142 is real vertical text dataset, which was collected from web.

Let us denote the cnn features as $f = f_{i,j,c}$ where i, j are the index locations in the feature map and c indexes the channels. We verified the aspect ratios of the image inputs and created two attention modules. These attention masks are denoted as $\alpha_t^{(h,v)}$, where h and v indicate the horizontal and vertical texts, respectively. We name this as *selective attention network* because it responds to the text direction (Fig. 3).

$$\alpha_t^{(h,v)} = softmax(V_a^T \circ tanh(W_s^{(h,v)} s_t + W_f f_{i,j})) \quad (5)$$

SAN comprises only one set of attention weights for each horizontal and vertical text. In the Eq. (5), $\circ$ is the Hadamard product and $tanh$ is applied element-wise to its vector argument. Further, the *visual feature vector* (also known as the *context vector*), x_t^v is computed as the weighted image features based on the attention at time step t as shown:

$$x_t^v = \sum_{i,j} \alpha_{t,i,j}^{(h,v)} f_{i,j,c} \quad (6)$$

We can define x_t as the input of LSTM, as depicted bellow.

$$x_t = x_t^c + x_t^v \quad (7)$$

The final predicted distribution over the letters at time t is described as shown.

$$\tilde{y}_t = W_{\tilde{o}} y_t + b_{\tilde{o}} \quad (8)$$

$$\tilde{Y} = \{\tilde{y}_0, ..., \tilde{y}_t, ..., \tilde{y_{T-1}}\} \quad (9)$$

In the equations, T is the sequence length of the RNN and $\tilde{Y}$ is the result of our LSTM decoder.

4 Experiments

4.1 Dataset

A range of datasets of images of words are used to train and test the model.

SVT [28] includes cropped images, including 257 training images and 647 test images, captured from Google Street View

IIIT5k [20] contains 2000 cropped training images and 3000 testing images downloaded from the Google image search engine

ICDAR 2003 [19] (IC03 in short) contains 258 full-scene and 936 cropped images for training, and 251 full-scene and 860 cropped images for testing.

ICDAR 2013 [14] (IC13 in short) contains 1015 cropped text images, but no lexicon is associated.

ICDAR 2015 [13] (IC15 in short) contains 2077 cropped text images without lexicon.

SVTD is a new synthetic vertical text dataset in a similar fashion as [1]. It includes 1 million training word images and 3,000 testing word images.

VTD142 is real vertical text dataset including 142 word images. We collect it from web.

Large amounts of datasets are needed to create a good-performance, deep-learning model. However, producing annotated training data requires considerable time and effort. Compared to other tasks in computer vision, generating high-quality synthetic data using various font files in optical character recognition (OCR) is easy. In previous studies, millions of synthetic images were created for recognition [12] and they have been further developed for use in detectors [8]. However, those studies only dealt with horizontal characters, not vertical ones, which could not be directly used. We applied the method described in [8] to find the area in which the letters were rendered. The depth and segmentation maps were estimated from the background image to be synthesized, and the vertical characters were rendered in the homogeneous regions. We also applied augmentation techniques, such as affine transformations, contrast changes, and certain noises, to generate various images. To our knowledge, there are no publicly available vertical-text datasets that can be used for evaluation; hence, we had to collect new data to properly evaluate our proposed method. To this end, we chose several appropriate keywords (e.g., vertical sign, building's sign, and vertical text) and used them in the web. We usually gathered vertical signs on the buildings because that is the way they are mostly seen in real environments, such as streets, shops, and buildings.

We follow the evaluation protocol of [28], which is set to recognize words, that include only alphanumeric characters (0–9 and A–Z) and are at least three characters long. Results are not case-sensitive.

4.2 Exploring Various Models

To recognize the vertical and horizontal texts, we consider various models in Fig. 2. (a) depicts a network based on AON. It is an unsupervised method that

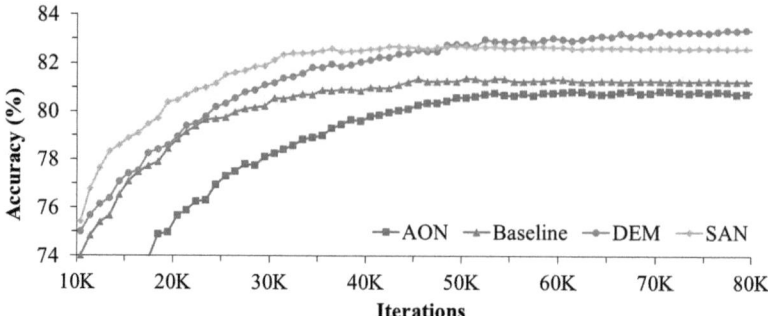

Fig. 4. Comparison of the performance of the baseline and the proposed method. The x-axis represents the number of iterations and the y-axis represents the average accuracy of the test DB.

learns the text direction without using any relevant information. The input image has a square ratio and is encoded with respect to two directions (top-to-bottom and left-to-right). The clue network (CN) identifies the text direction and focuses on that direction. (b) depicts an unsupervised method, which is our baseline network. It differs from AON because the input image is observed to be rectangular. We hypothesized that a rectangle would be more efficient than a square because we only need to consider two directions, i.e., horizontal and vertical. In fact, the vertical text images are transposed. This hypothesis was proved via experiments that depicted an approximate performance improvement of 2–3%p. (c) depicts that DEM (S), our proposed supervised module, provides the text direction to the network. (d) depicts that SAN, our second proposed supervised network, works selectively depending on the text direction.

4.3 Implementation Details

The input images in our experiment are resized to 100×32 for VGG or 256×32 for ResNet [4] and have one channel (gray-scale). The pixel values are normalized to the range $(-0.5, 0.5)$ before they are provided as input to the network. All the LSTM cells used in our experiments have 512 memory units, and the dropouts are not used. The RMSProp method is used to conduct training with a batch size of 512. The initial learning rate is 0.001 and decreases by a factor of 0.9 as the validation errors stop decreasing for 10 iterations. Gradient clipping is applied at a magnitude of 5, and training is terminated after 100,000 iterations. To train our network, 8 million synthetic data released by [12] and 4 million synthetic instances (excluding images that contain non-alphanumeric characters) cropped from 90,000 images [8] were used. In addition, we modified the open source by [8] to generate 1 million synthetic vertical data for training and 3000 data for testing. We did not apply any data augmentation processes to the training dataset. Because we implemented our method using TensorFlow v1.6, CUDA9.0, and cuDNN v7.0, the proposed model can be GPU-accelerated. The experiments

Table 1. Results of recognition accuracy on general benchmarks. "50" are lexicon sizes, "None" means lexicon-free.

Method	IIIT5k		SVT		IC03		IC13	IC15	SVTD	VTD
	50	None	50	None	50	None	None	None	None	None
ABBYY [28]	24.3	-	35.0	-	56.0	-	-	-	-	-
Wang et al. [28]	-	-	57.0	-	76.0	-	-	-	-	-
Mishra et al. [20]	64.1	-	73.2	-	81.8	-	-	-	-	-
Novikova et al. [21]	64.1	-	72.9	82.8	-	-	-	-	-	-
Wang et al. [29]	-	-	70.0	-	90.0	-	-	-	-	-
Bissacco et al. [3]	-	-	90.4	-	-	-	87.6	-	-	-
Goel et al. [6]	-	-	77.3	-	89.7	-	-	-	-	-
Alsharif et al. [2]	-	-	74.3	-	93.1	-	-	-	-	-
Almazan et al. [1]	91.2	-	89.2	-	-	-	-	-	-	-
Yao et al. [31]	80.2	-	75.9	-	88.5	-	-	-	-	-
Su and Lu et al. [25]	-	-	83.0	-	92.0	-	-	-	-	-
Jaderberg et al. [11]	95.5	-	93.2	71.7	97.8	89.6	81.8	-	-	-
Rodriguez et al. [22]	76.1	-	-	70.0	-	-	-	-	-	-
Gordo et al. [7]	93.3	-	91.8	-	-	-	-	-	-	-
Lee et al. [16]	96.8	78.4	96.3	80.7	97.9	88.7	90.0	-	-	-
Shi et al. [23]	97.6	78.2	96.4	80.8	98.7	93.1	90.8	-	-	-
Shi et al. [24]	96.2	81.9	95.5	81.9	98.3	90.1	88.6	-	-	-
Baoguang et al. [24]	96.2	81.9	95.5	81.9	98.3	90.1	88.6	-	-	-
Chen-Yu et al. [16]	96.8	78.4	**96.3**	80.7	97.9	88.7	90.0	-	-	-
Cheng et al. [5]	**99.6**	**87.0**	96.0	82.8	98.5	91.5	92.3	68.2	-	-
Baseline	96.5	82.3	93.3	83.4	96.5	93.1	91.5	67.9	87.0	62.0
DEM	97.5	83.3	93.8	83.6	98.1	93.5	92.7	69.7	87.9	65.2
SAN	97.1	83.0	93.7	85.5	98.5	93.3	92.5	68.0	87.6	64.8
ResNet+DEM	98.6	85.8	94.1	86.7	98.3	94.0	93.7	73.1	**90.5**	**70.9**
ResNet+SAN	98.0	86.0	94.6	**87.4**	**98.5**	**94.1**	**94.2**	**73.5**	89.6	66.9

were performed on a workstation with one Intel Xeon(R) E5-2650 2.20 GHz CPU and one NVIDIA Tesla M40 GPU.

5 Results

Figure 4 compares the performance of the baseline with that of the proposed method. As exhibited by the results, our baseline performed better than the AON-based method in terms of speed and accuracy. This is because an input image of 100 × 32 is effective while recognizing the horizontal and vertical characters that maintain an image input of 100 × 100. Additionally, it was better at recognizing characters while using the DEM and SAN methods of supervised learning than while using the baseline of unsupervised learning. In most of the benchmark datasets, DEM performed slightly better than SAN.

Fig. 5. Results of attention and recognition for horizontal and vertical characters.

Table 1 compares the performance of the state-of-the-art method and the proposed method. The combination of a ResNet-based CNN backbone exhibits the same effect as that exhibited by DEM and SAN. We achieved state-of-the-art performance for SVT, IC13, IC15, SVDT, and VDT142 based on a lexicon-free evaluation protocol. This exhibits that our algorithm works better in real world environments when there is no lexicon. Figure 5 depicts the results of attention and recognition for horizontal and vertical characters, both of which confirm that the method works well. The main purpose of our study is to compare the performance between a supervised proposed method and an unsupervised baseline method for text direction. We would like to emphasize that our model not only recognizes vertical text but also recognizes horizontal text as compared with existing methods.

6 Conclusions

We presented a unified network to simultaneously deal with the horizontal and vertical texts. Our proposed DEM and SAN modules are supervised methods and exhibit better perceived performances than those exhibited by the previous methods. We achieved state-of-the-art results with respect to popular benchmark datasets and verified that our model works for a real vertical text dataset (VTD142).

References

1. Almazán, J., Gordo, A., Fornés, A., Valveny, E.: Word spotting and recognition with embedded attributes. IEEE Trans. Pattern Anal. Mach. Intell. **36**(12), 2552–2566 (2014)
2. Alsharif, O., Pineau, J.: End-to-end text recognition with hybrid HMM maxout models. arXiv preprint arXiv:1310.1811 (2013)
3. Bissacco, A., Cummins, M., Netzer, Y., Neven, H.: PhotoOCR: reading text in uncontrolled conditions. In: Proceedings of the IEEE International Conference on Computer Vision, pp. 785–792 (2013)
4. Cheng, Z., Bai, F., Xu, Y., Zheng, G., Pu, S., Zhou, S.: Focusing attention: towards accurate text recognition in natural images. CoRR abs/1709.02054 (2017). http://arxiv.org/abs/1709.02054

5. Cheng, Z., Liu, X., Bai, F., Niu, Y., Pu, S., Zhou, S.: Arbitrarily-oriented text recognition. CoRR abs/1711.04226 (2017). http://arxiv.org/abs/1711.04226
6. Goel, V., Mishra, A., Alahari, K., Jawahar, C.: Whole is greater than sum of parts: recognizing scene text words. In: 2013 12th International Conference on Document Analysis and Recognition (ICDAR), pp. 398–402. IEEE (2013)
7. Gordo, A.: Supervised mid-level features for word image representation. In: Proceedings of the IEEE Conference on Computer Vision and Pattern Recognition, pp. 2956–2964 (2015)
8. Gupta, A., Vedaldi, A., Zisserman, A.: Synthetic data for text localisation in natural images. In: Proceedings of the IEEE Conference on Computer Vision and Pattern Recognition, pp. 2315–2324 (2016)
9. He, K., Zhang, X., Ren, S., Sun, J.: Deep residual learning for image recognition. In: Proceedings of the IEEE Conference on Computer Vision and Pattern Recognition, pp. 770–778 (2016)
10. He, K., Zhang, X., Ren, S., Sun, J.: Identity mappings in deep residual networks. In: Leibe, B., Matas, J., Sebe, N., Welling, M. (eds.) ECCV 2016. LNCS, vol. 9908, pp. 630–645. Springer, Cham (2016). https://doi.org/10.1007/978-3-319-46493-0_38
11. Jaderberg, M., Simonyan, K., Vedaldi, A., Zisserman, A.: Deep structured output learning for unconstrained text recognition. arXiv preprint arXiv:1412.5903 (2014)
12. Jaderberg, M., Simonyan, K., Vedaldi, A., Zisserman, A.: Synthetic data and artificial neural networks for natural scene text recognition. CoRR abs/1406.2227 (2014). http://arxiv.org/abs/1406.2227
13. Karatzas, D., et al.: ICDAR 2015 competition on robust reading. In: 2015 13th International Conference on Document Analysis and Recognition (ICDAR), pp. 1156–1160. IEEE (2015)
14. Karatzas, D., et al.: ICDAR 2013 robust reading competition. In: Document Analysis and Recognition (ICDAR), pp. 1484–1493 (2013)
15. Krizhevsky, A., Sutskever, I., Hinton, G.E.: Imagenet classification with deep convolutional neural networks. In: Advances in Neural Information Processing Systems, pp. 1097–1105 (2012)
16. Lee, C.Y., Osindero, S.: Recursive recurrent nets with attention modeling for OCR in the wild. In: Proceedings of the IEEE Conference on Computer Vision and Pattern Recognition, pp. 2231–2239 (2016)
17. Liang, M., Hu, X.: Recurrent convolutional neural network for object recognition. In: Proceedings of the IEEE Conference on Computer Vision and Pattern Recognition, pp. 3367–3375 (2015)
18. Liu, X., Liang, D., Yan, S., Chen, D., Qiao, Y., Yan, J.: FOTS: fast oriented text spotting with a unified network. In: Proceedings of the IEEE Conference on Computer Vision and Pattern Recognition, pp. 5676–5685 (2018)
19. Lucas, S.M., et al.: ICDAR 2003 robust reading competitions, p. 682. IEEE (2003)
20. Mishra, A., Alahari, K., Jawahar, C.: Scene text recognition using higher order language priors. In: BMVC-British Machine Vision Conference. BMVA (2012)
21. Novikova, T., Barinova, O., Kohli, P., Lempitsky, V.: Large-lexicon attribute-consistent text recognition in natural images. In: Fitzgibbon, A., Lazebnik, S., Perona, P., Sato, Y., Schmid, C. (eds.) ECCV 2012. LNCS, vol. 7577, pp. 752–765. Springer, Heidelberg (2012). https://doi.org/10.1007/978-3-642-33783-3_54
22. Rodriguez-Serrano, J.A., Gordo, A., Perronnin, F.: Label embedding: a frugal baseline for text recognition. Int. J. Comput. Vis. **113**(3), 193–207 (2015)

23. Shi, B., Bai, X., Yao, C.: An end-to-end trainable neural network for image-based sequence recognition and its application to scene text recognition. IEEE Trans. Pattern Anal. Mach. Intell. **39**(11), 2298–2304 (2017)
24. Shi, B., Wang, X., Lv, P., Yao, C., Bai, X.: Robust scene text recognition with automatic rectification. CoRR abs/1603.03915 (2016). http://arxiv.org/abs/1603.03915
25. Su, B., Lu, S.: Accurate scene text recognition based on recurrent neural network. In: Cremers, D., Reid, I., Saito, H., Yang, M.-H. (eds.) ACCV 2014. LNCS, vol. 9003, pp. 35–48. Springer, Cham (2015). https://doi.org/10.1007/978-3-319-16865-4_3
26. Szegedy, C., et al.: Going deeper with convolutions. In: Proceedings of the IEEE Conference on Computer Vision and Pattern Recognition, pp. 1–9 (2015)
27. Wang, J., Hu, X.: Gated recurrent convolution neural network for OCR. In: Advances in Neural Information Processing Systems, pp. 335–344 (2017)
28. Wang, K., Babenko, B., Belongie, S.: End-to-end scene text recognition. In: 2011 IEEE International Conference on Computer Vision (ICCV), pp. 1457–1464. IEEE (2011)
29. Wang, T., Wu, D.J., Coates, A., Ng, A.Y.: End-to-end text recognition with convolutional neural networks. In: 2012 21st International Conference on Pattern Recognition (ICPR), pp. 3304–3308. IEEE (2012)
30. Wojna, Z., et al.: Attention-based extraction of structured information from street view imagery. arXiv preprint arXiv:1704.03549 (2017)
31. Yao, C., Bai, X., Shi, B., Liu, W.: Strokelets: a learned multi-scale representation for scene text recognition. In: Proceedings of the IEEE Conference on Computer Vision and Pattern Recognition, pp. 4042–4049 (2014)

Artificial Intelligence for Retinal Image Analysis (AIRIA)

Automatic Retinal and Choroidal Boundary Segmentation in OCT Images Using Patch-Based Supervised Machine Learning Methods

David Alonso-Caneiro[1,2(✉)], Jason Kugelman[1], Jared Hamwood[1], Scott A. Read[1], Stephen J. Vincent[1], Fred K. Chen[2,3,4], and Michael J. Collins[1]

[1] Contact Lens and Visual Optics Laboratory, School of Optometry and Vision Science, Queensland University of Technology, Brisbane, QLD, Australia
d.alonsocaneiro@qut.edu.au
[2] Centre for Ophthalmology and Visual Science, The University of Western Australia, Perth, Australia
[3] Ocular Tissue Engineering Laboratory, Lions Eye Institute, Perth, Australia
[4] Department of Ophthalmology, Royal Perth Hospital, Perth, Australia

Abstract. The assessment of retinal and choroidal thickness derived from spectral domain optical coherence tomography (SD-OCT) images is an important clinical and research task. Current OCT instruments allow the capture of densely sampled, high-resolution cross-sectional images of ocular tissues. The extensive nature of such datasets makes the manual delineation of tissue boundaries time-consuming and impractical, especially for large datasets of images. Therefore, the development of reliable and accurate methods to automatically segment tissue boundaries in OCT images is fundamental. In this work, two different deep learning methods; convolutional neural networks (CNN) and recurrent neural networks (RNN) are evaluated to calculate the probability of the retinal and choroidal boundaries of interest to be located in a specific position within the SD-OCT images. The method is initially trained using small image patches centred around the three boundaries of interest. After that, the method can be used to provide a per-layer probability map that marks the most likely location of the boundaries. To convert each layer-probability map into a boundary position, the map is subsequently traced using a graph-search method. The effect of the network architecture (CNN vs RNN), patch size, and image intensity compensation on the performance and subsequent boundary segmentation is presented. The results are compared with manual boundary segmentation as well as a previously proposed method based on standard image analysis techniques.

1 Introduction

Optical coherence tomography (OCT) has become one of the key methodologies for imaging the eye [1,2] since it provides dense and high-resolution cross-sectional images of the retina, and choroid (the vascular tissue which lies posterior to the retina), both of which cannot be obtained from other clinical imaging modalities used to assess the health of the posterior segment (e.g. fundus photography). Thickness data extracted from OCT images can be used to expand our knowledge of the ocular tissue changes that occur during normal development [3,4], with age [5,6], during the development and progression of refractive error [7,8], and with the onset and treatment of a variety of ocular diseases [9–13]. Consequently, the reliable segmentation of tissue boundaries is a fundamental task for both research purposes and the clinical assessment of the eye.

Initial methods proposed for the segmentation of retinal and choroidal boundaries relied on standard image processing methods [14,15]. In recent years, machine learning techniques have become more popular for OCT image analysis, with a number of different methods proposed for the segmentation of OCT data in healthy and diseased eyes, including support vector machine [16], CNN and graph-search method [17], random forest classifier [18] and semantic segmentation using fully-convolutional networks [19,20]. Fang et al. [17] proposed a convolutional neural network (CNN) and graph-search method (termed as CNN-GS) for the automatic segmentation of nine retinal layer boundaries in OCT retinal images of patients with non-exudative age-related macular degeneration. The supervised machine learning method (CNN network) is used to predict the boundary location and outputs a per-layer probability image. This probability image is then used to trace the boundary using graph-search methods. The method of Fang et al. [17] runs a square input patch size of 33 × 33 pixels (window) through the image, and later work by Hamwood et al. [21] demonstrated that patch size and network complexity can be modified to improve the performance of the retinal layer segmentation technique.

Within medical image analysis, recurrent neural networks (RNNs) have been widely applied to image sequences and volumetric data in a temporal manner [22,23]. However, there is little exploration into their ability to extract spatial features from individual images. For automatic OCT retinal segmentation, Kugelman et al. [24] proposed the use of a recurrent neural network (RNN) in place of the previously proposed CNN. The authors highlighted the usefulness of RNNs for such a task and noted the highly sequential layer structure of the OCT images as a reason for this.

This study examines the effect of using different supervised machine learning methods (RNN vs CNN), as well as the effect of patch sizes and image preprocessing on retinal and choroidal boundary segmentation in spectral domain OCT (SD-OCT) images. Although some aspects of this work have been explored previously for retinal boundary analysis, the segmentation of the choroid using machine learning methods remains largely unexplored. The aim of this work is to better understand the optimal architecture for choroidal boundary detection and subsequent layer segmentation. This study provides a step towards understanding and improving the performance of the classification and optimization of OCT chorio-retinal layer segmentation. The findings of this work may inform future machine learning method development in OCT imaging analysis using deep learning strategies.

2 Methods

The automatic segmentation process used here involves a number of methods. Firstly, a neural network is trained as a patch-based classifier with patches centred on the boundaries of interest on one set of OCT B-scans (set A). Next, a second set of OCT B-scans is used to evaluate the network (set B). Sets A and B have data from different subjects. For each scan in set B, per-class probability maps are constructed. Each probability map is then used to construct a graph, and a boundary position prediction is obtained by performing a shortest-path graph search. The following sections provide greater detail of the methods involved. Table 1 summarises the data used for training, validation and evaluation.

Table 1. Summary of data used for training, validation and evaluation

Set	Data	Participants	Images	Total patches
A	Training	40	240	1,167,600
A	Validation	10	60	292,800
B	Evaluation	49	294	761,856 per image

2.1 OCT Data

The dataset used consists of SD-OCT scans from a longitudinal study that has been described in detail in a number of previous publications [3,4]. In this study, SD-OCT scans for 101 children were collected at four different visits over an 18-month period. At each visit, two sets of six foveal centred radial retinal scans were taken on each subject, however, only the data from the first visit is used throughout this paper. The acquired images measure 1536 pixels wide and 496 pixels deep with a vertical scale of 3.9 microns per pixel and a horizontal scale of 5.7 microns per pixel. These were exported and analysed using custom software where an automated graph based method was used to segment three layer boundaries for each image. This segmented data was then assessed by an expert human observer who manually corrected any segmentation errors. The three layer boundaries within the labelled data include the outer boundary of the retinal pigment epithelium (RPE), the inner boundary of the inner limiting membrane (ILM), and the choroid/scleral boundary (CHR).

2.2 Neural Network Models

Convolutional Neural Networks (CNN). Convolutional neural networks (CNNs) have shown considerable success for image based tasks and state-of-the-art results for a variety of problems. In contrast to the fully-connected layers within multi-layer perceptron (MLP) neural networks, the neurons in a layer within CNNs are only connected to a local region of neurons in the previous layer. The motivation here is that, within an image, local context can provide more useful information than global context. The resulting benefit, particularly for large images, is that such networks are generally much sparser and therefore much more efficient to train when compared with MLPs which possess a much larger number of connections and parameters for the same sized input.

CNNs consist of a number of different layers with a set of associated parameters for each layer. Convolutional layers take a number of equal sized kernels (filters) which are convolved with the input and concatenated together to produce an output. The parameters include: the kernel size (height × width), the stride lengths (vertical, horizontal), the quantity of zero-padding (top, bottom, left, right) applied to the input, and the number of kernels. Pooling layers take a single window sliding over the input. At each step, an operation is performed to pool the input to a smaller size. Such operations include max pooling (where the maximum value is taken from within the window), and average pooling (where the average of the values is taken). The parameters here include: the window size (height × width), the stride lengths (vertical, horizontal), the quantity of zero-padding applied to the input (top, bottom, left, right) and the pooling operation (max or average). Activation layers can be used to introduce non-linearity into neural networks. For CNNs, the rectified linear unit (ReLU) is a common choice. Two CNNs with different patch sizes and complexity are used within this work with the architectures listed in Table 2. These include: the Cifar CNN (CNN 1) introduced by Fang et al. [17] and the Complex CNN (CNN 2) presented by Hamwood et al. [21] with variants for both a 64 × 32 and 64 × 64 sized patch.

Table 2. CNN architectures used within this work. Fully-connected (FC) layers are equivalent to convolutional layers where the kernel size is equal to the spatial size of the input and there is no zero-padding applied to the input. #F represents the number of filters, (#,#)S is the stride lengths (horizontal, vertical), and (#,#,#,#)P is the zero-padding applied to the input (top, bottom, left, right).

CIFAR CNN (CNN 1)		Complex CNN (CNN 2)	
32 × 64	64 × 64	32 × 64	64 × 64
5 × 5 Convolutional 32F (1,1)S (2,2,2,2)P		5 × 5 Convolutional 32F (1,1)S (0,0,0,0)P	
3 × 3 Max Pooling (2,2)S (0,1,0,1)P		ReLU	
ReLU		3 × 3 Convolutional 32F (1,1)S (0,0,0,0)P	
5 × 5 Convolutional 32F (1,1)S (0,0,0,0)P		ReLU	
ReLU		3 × 3 Convolutional 64F (1,1)S (0,0,0,0)P	
3 × 3 Average Pooling (2,2)S (0,1,0,1)P		2 × 2 Max Pooling (2,2)S (1,1,1,1)P	
5 × 5 Convolutional 64F (1,1)S (0,0,0,0)P		3 × 3 Convolutional 64F (1,1)S (0,0,0,0)P	
ReLU		ReLU	
3 × 3 Average Pooling (2,2)S (0,1,0,1)P		3 × 3 Convolutional 128F (1,1)S (0,0,0,0)P	
8 × 4 FC 64F	8 × 8 FC 64F	2 × 2 Max Pooling (2,2)S (1,1,1,1)P	
ReLU		13 × 5 FC 128F	13 × 13 FC 128F
1 × 1 FC 4F			

Recurrent Neural Networks (RNN). Recurrent neural networks (RNNs) have been widely applied to, and have shown success for, problems involving sequential data such as speech recognition and translation. The main difference between these networks and multi-layer perceptron (MLP) variants is the addition of a feedback connection within each of the cells (neurons). These connections allow each cell's output to be calculated based on both the input and the previous state. Due to problems such as vanishing gradient, a variety of more complex cell types have been introduced including: the long short-term memory (LSTM) [25] and the gated recurrent unit (GRU) [26].

To perform image classification using a recurrent neural network, the architecture used is that presented by Kugelman et al. [24] which was inspired by the ReNet architecture [27]. Rather than using temporal operation on a sequence of images or volumetric data this RNN-based architecture processes each individual patch spatially by treating rows and columns of pixels as sequences. Parameters associated with each layer include: the direction of operation (vertical or horizontal), number of passes (1: unidirectional, 2: bidirectional), number of filters, and receptive field size (height, width). The size of the receptive field represents the size of the region of the input which is processed by the RNN at each step. The direction of operation corresponds to whether the RNN will process each row of a column (vertical) or each column of a row (horizontal) before moving to the next column and row respectively. A unidirectional layer will pass over the input only in a single direction whereas a bidirectional layer will additionally pass over the input in the opposite direction with the outputs for each pass concatenated. The number of filters in each layer indicates the depth of the output, with the addition of more filters enabling the network to learn an increased number of patterns from the input. The RNN architecture [24] used within this work is described in Table 3.

Table 3. RNN architecture used within this work. FC: fully-connected layer, #F: number of filters per pass, (#,#)R: receptive field size (height, width).

RNN	
64×32	64×64
Vertical Bidirectional 16F (1,1)R	
Horizontal Bidirectional 16F (1,1)R	
Vertical Bidirectional 16F (2,2)R	
Horizontal Bidirectional 16F (2,2)R	
16×8 FC 4F	16×16 FC 4F

2.3 Patch Classification and Image Pre-processing

The networks are trained for classification using small patches of the OCT images. Here, each patch is assigned to a class depending on the layer boundary that it is centred upon, with classes constructed for each of the three layer boundaries of interest (ILM, RPE and CHR) as well as an additional "background" class for patches that are not centred upon any of the three layer boundaries. Patches of size 64 × 32 and 64 × 64 (height × width pixels) are utilised with layer boundaries centred one pixel above and to the left of the central point.

All networks are trained using 1,460,400 patches using an 80/20 training (1,167,600 patches) and validation (292,800 patches) set split. These patches are constructed from each of 300 B-scans (240 for training and 60 for validation) (set A) which is comprised of six scans from 50 randomly selected participants (40 for training and 10 for validation). The scans are cropped a small amount on each side (approximately 100 pixels from the left and 250 pixels from the right) due to the presence of the optic nerve head and shadowing within this region. In each scan, three boundary patches and one random background patch are sampled from each column giving equal balance to the four classes. The Adam algorithm [28] with default parameters is used for training to minimise categorical cross-entropy loss with each network trained until convergence is observed with respect to the validation loss. Afterwards, the model with the greatest validation accuracy is chosen for evaluation.

The choroid is a pigmented vascular layer of the eye. Its vascular nature combined with the fact that is located behind a hyper-reflective layer (RPE) means that the contrast and visibility of the posterior boundary tends to be weak. Thus use of OCT contrast enhancement techniques [29], also known as attenuation coefficient [30], was considered in this work since it may improve the visibility of the boundaries, especially for the posterior choroid, and reduce the effect of shadows caused by the retinal blood vessels. The technique works under the assumption that local backscattering can be related to that of the corresponding attenuation, and therefore can be compensated. In this work the effect of the attenuation compensation will be tested with two different network-input options; the standard intensity and the contrast enhanced (attenuation coefficient) equivalent.

2.4 Boundary Delineation and Model Evaluation

Given a scan and a trained classification network, probability maps for each of the boundary classes may be constructed by classifying patches centred on each pixel in the scan (761,856 patches per scan). From such a probability map, the boundary positions may be delineated by performing a graph search using Dijkstra's shortest path algorithm [31] where each pixel in the map corresponds to a vertex in the graph. Directed edges associated with each vertex are connected to neighbouring vertices to the immediate right (horizontally, diagonally above and diagonally below). To remove the need for manual start and end point initialisation, columns of maximum probability vertices, connected top to bottom, are appended to each end of the graph, with additional left to right connections made to the existing graph. The edge weights between each pair of vertices are determined by the respective probabilities and are given by the following equation:

$$w_{sd} = 2 - (P_s + P_d) + w_{min} \tag{1}$$

where P_s and P_d are the probabilities (0-1) of the source and destination vertices respectively, and w_{min} is a small positive number added for system stability.

This step is performed using a set of 294 B-scans (set B) which is comprised of six scans from 49 randomly selected participants that were not used for training. Therefore, no overlap exists between the participants included in the evaluation and training data. To evaluate the performance, the delineated boundary positions for each image are compared to the true positions from which the Dice overlap percentage is calculated (for vitreous (top of the image to ILM), retina (ILM to RPE), choroid (RPE to CHR), and sclera (CHR to bottom of the image)) as well as the mean pixel error and mean absolute pixel error (for ILM, RPE and CHR) for each scan.

3 Results

Each of the architectures described in Sect. 2.2 were trained using 64 × 32 and 64 × 64 patch sizes as described in Sect. 2.3. For the 64 × 32 patch size, each network was also trained using images pre-processed using contrast enhancement for the choroid/scleral boundary. Evaluations were performed as described in Sect. 2.4 with results for the Dice overlap presented in Table 4 and the boundary position errors in Table 5. For reference to a baseline, the results are compared with an automatic non-machine learning graph-search image-processing segmentation method [32] evaluated on the same set of data (set B). Figure 1 shows example results from a single scan evaluated using an RNN.

The dice overlap results indicate a similar level of performance across all methods for the two top regions (vitreous and retina), in terms of both mean percentage and standard deviation. All methods yielded very similar high mean dice overlap percentages between 99.80 and 99.83 for the vitreous as well as

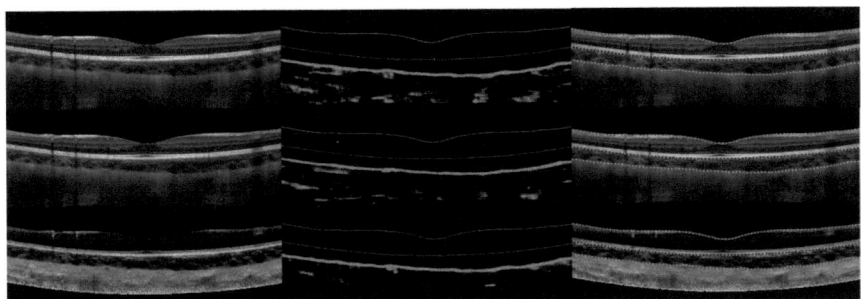

Fig. 1. Example results for segmentation of a single scan using the RNN 64 × 32 (top row), RNN 64 × 64 (middle row), and RNN 64 × 32 with contrast enhancement (bottom row). From left to right: raw image, combined probability maps of the three boundary classes, and boundary delineations where dotted lines are the predicted boundary locations and the solid lines indicates the true boundary locations. (red: ILM, blue: RPE, green: CHR). (Color figure online)

Table 4. Dice overlap for each of the networks. Mean percentage (%) and (standard deviation) are reported for each of the four segmented regions. [CE] indicates that the network was trained and tested with images pre-processed using contrast enhancement. CNN 1: Cifar CNN, CNN 2: Complex CNN. The best results for each region are highlighted bold text.

Method	Vitreous	Retinal	Choroid	Sclera
RNN (64 × 32)	**99.83** (0.08)	99.36 (0.13)	97.33 (1.55)	98.95 (0.78)
RNN (64 × 32) [CE]	99.82 (**0.05**)	99.36 (**0.10**)	**97.56 (1.09)**	99.05 (0.55)
RNN (64 × 64)	99.82 (**0.05**)	99.32 (0.11)	97.55 (1.39)	**99.08** (0.67)
CNN 1 (64 × 32)	99.81 (0.06)	99.33 (0.12)	96.89 (2.58)	98.73 (1.49)
CNN 1 (64 × 32) [CE]	**99.83** (**0.05**)	99.32 (0.12)	97.43 (1.12)	99.02 (**0.53**)
CNN 1 (64 × 64)	**99.83** (**0.05**)	**99.40** (**0.11**)	97.46 (1.89)	99.00 (0.92)
CNN 2 (64 × 32)	**99.83** (0.06)	99.34 (0.12)	96.97 (2.18)	98.78 (1.31)
CNN 2 (64 × 32) [CE]	99.82 (**0.05**)	99.19 (0.13)	97.29 (1.25)	99.02 (0.59)
CNN 2 (64 × 64)	99.81 (0.06)	99.30 (0.11)	97.04 (2.41)	98.88 (1.58)
Automatic baseline	99.80 (0.19)	98.87 (0.46)	95.93 (3.81)	98.40 (2.08)

low standard deviations of less than 0.20, indicating a high level of consistency between the segmentation results of each scan. In addition, all machine learning-based methods exhibited strong performance for the retina with mean percentages between 99.19 and 99.36. Again, standard deviations were low, with all method's respective results between 0.10 and 0.13. All machine learning based methods outperformed the baseline method in terms of mean and standard deviation. These results correspond to the results of boundary position error for the ILM with low mean error, mean absolute error and standard deviations across all methods (Table 5).

In contrast, the dice overlap results for the choroid region is more variable between methods. The automatic baseline method performed the poorest with a mean of 95.93 and standard deviation of 3.81. On the other hand, the RNN with a 64 × 32 patch size and contrast enhancement performed the best with a mean of 97.56 and a standard deviation almost four times lower at 1.09. Overall, it can be observed that contrast enhancement resulted in superior network performance in terms of both mean and standard deviation with an average increase in percentage of 0.36 and decrease in standard deviation of 0.95 indicating more accurate and consistent segmentation results. Increasing the patch size from 64 × 32 to 64 × 64 also showed improvement in performance, although this effect was less pronounced and consistent than for the contrast enhancement, with the Complex CNN showing little to no improvement (mean improvement of 0.29 and mean standard deviation improvement of 0.21). With respect to the network architectures, the RNN-based methods gave the best dice overlap results for the choroid with a mean dice overlap of 97.48 and corresponding standard deviation of 1.34, which marginally outperformed both the Cifar CNN (97.26 (1.86)) and the Complex CNN (97.10 (1.95)).

Table 5. Boundary position errors (in pixels) for each of the networks. Mean error (ME) and mean absolute error (MAE) are reported in terms of mean value and (standard deviation of the per-scan means) for each of the three boundaries. [CE] indicates that the network was trained and tested with images pre-processed using contrast enhancement. CNN 1: Cifar CNN, CNN 2: Complex CNN. The best results for each boundary are highlighted in bold text.

Method	ILM		RPE		CHR	
	ME	MAE	ME	MAE	ME	MAE
RNN (64 × 32)	−**0.08** (0.24)	**0.47** (0.12)	−0.35 (0.22)	0.54 (0.14)	0.35 (3.54)	3.80 (2.93)
RNN (64 × 32) [CE]	−0.22 (**0.23**)	0.52 (**0.09**)	−0.28 (0.22)	0.52 (**0.13**)	**0.13** (**2.57**)	3.43 (1.97)
RNN (64 × 64)	−0.19 (0.24)	0.51 (**0.09**)	−0.43 (**0.20**)	0.59 (0.14)	0.42 (3.03)	**3.36** (2.52)
CNN 1 (64 × 32)	−0.20 (0.25)	0.52 (**0.09**)	−0.30 (0.25)	0.54 (0.14)	0.78 (6.29)	4.67 (5.65)
CNN 1 (64 × 32) [CE]	−0.09 (0.25)	0.48 (0.10)	−0.40 (0.28)	0.61 (0.16)	−0.35 (2.68)	3.55 (**1.95**)
CNN 1 (64 × 64)	−0.09 (0.24)	0.49 (0.11)	0.14 (0.23)	**0.48** (**0.13**)	1.17 (4.01)	3.67 (3.51)
CNN 2 (64 × 32)	−0.12 (0.24)	0.49 (**0.09**)	−0.39 (**0.20**)	0.56 (0.14)	0.99 (5.36)	4.44 (4.84)
CNN 2 (64 × 32) [CE]	−0.26 (**0.23**)	0.53 (**0.09**)	−0.65 (0.25)	0.77 (0.18)	0.25 (2.86)	3.57 (2.14)
CNN 2 (64 × 64)	−0.30 (**0.23**)	0.55 (0.10)	−0.38 (**0.20**)	0.56 (**0.13**)	0.34 (6.00)	4.42 (5.43)
Automatic baseline	−0.27 (0.41)	0.58 (0.36)	−1.14 (0.65)	1.23 (0.60)	−3.64 (8.62)	5.82 (7.77)

Table 6. Layer thickness repeatability (in pixels) for each pair of scans across two sets for 31 participants. Mean error (ME) and mean absolute error (MAE) are reported in terms of mean value and (standard deviation of the per-scan means) for the retina (ILM to RPE) and choroid (RPE to CHR). [CE] indicates that the network was trained and tested with images pre-processed using contrast enhancement. CNN 1: Cifar CNN. The best results for each layer are highlighted in bold text.

Method	Retina		Choroid	
	ME	MAE	ME	MAE
CNN 1 64 × 32 [CE]	−0.01 (**0.39**)	1.14 (0.52)	−**0.04** (**1.38**)	2.82 (**1.56**)
RNN 64 × 32 [CE]	**0.00** (**0.39**)	**1.12** (0.51)	0.17 (1.83)	2.88 (1.96)
Manual	−0.01 (0.46)	1.32 (**0.48**)	−0.11 (2.04)	**2.32** (1.66)

These trends in dice overlap results for the choroid appear to be similar to those for the sclera but do not appear to translate to similar differences in the position errors for the RPE boundary. Indeed, the RPE boundary position errors for all machine learning-based methods were low, with mean absolute errors and corresponding standard deviations of less than 0.80 pixels and 0.20 pixels respectively. In contrast, the mean absolute error for the CHR boundary was significantly higher for all methods (between 3.36 and 4.67 pixels). Applying contrast enhancement to the images improved the performance of all networks significantly with an average decrease in mean absolute error of 0.79 pixels and standard deviation of 2.45 pixels. This is a similar result to that observed for the dice overlap. Likewise, increasing the patch size gave different outcomes depending on the network architecture with an improvement in mean absolute error and standard deviation for the RNN and Cifar CNN observed whereas there was little difference in the results for the Complex CNN as was observed in the previous Dice results. Of the tested network architectures, the RNN gave the lowest CHR mean absolute error and corresponding standard deviation with 3.53 pixels and 2.47 pixels respectively. These were superior to the results of the Cifar CNN (3.96 (3.71)) and the Complex CNN (4.14 (4.14)).

Repeatability error was calculated for the retina and choroid. This was calculated by comparing the thickness between each corresponding scan between two sets. This was only calculated for all participants in set B where all scans were available in both sets (31 participants, 186 scans). Table 6 compares the repeatability error of two of the automatic machine learning methods (CNN 64 × 32 and RNN 64 × 32, both with contrast enhancement) and the repeatability of the manual segmentations provided by an expert human observer. The results show the two machine learning methods to perform comparably to one another in terms of mean absolute repeatability error. However, in contrast to these methods, the error of the manual method was higher for the retina but lower for the choroid.

4 Discussion

This work has investigated a range of patch-based supervised machine learning methods for the segmentation of retinal and choroidal boundaries in OCT images. Here, the difference in network architecture (RNN vs. CNN), the effect of the patch size as well as the impact of contrast enhancement were explored. In the past, a number of patch-based CNN methods have been presented for the segmentation of OCT retinal layers. However, the application of RNNs to this problem is largely unexplored as is the use of machine learning techniques for the segmentation of the choroidal layer in OCT images.

Evaluation results showed that the mean absolute boundary error and standard deviation of the ILM exhibited consistent performance across all methods. For the RPE, all machine learning-based methods performed similarly but with a significant improvement in performance compared to the baseline method (which was based entirely on standard image analysis methods and a graph search method). Overall, the performance on these two boundaries for the machine learning methods is promising. In terms of total retinal thickness (ILM to RPE), the machine learning methods were observed to yield mean absolute repeatability errors lower than that of manual segmentation.

This overall similarity and level of performance was not evident for the CHR boundary with a much greater level of variability within the mean absolute errors and standard deviations across the methods. In addition, the CHR boundary proved much more difficult to segment with an average mean absolute error for all methods of 4.07 pixels, compared to 0.51 pixels for the ILM and 0.64 pixels for the RPE. There was also greater inconsistency in the segmentation performance with an average standard deviation of 3.87 pixels compared to 0.12 pixels for the ILM and 0.19 pixels for the RPE.

For the CHR boundary segmentation, contrast enhancement improved the results significantly with an average decrease in the mean absolute error and standard deviation of 0.79 and 2.45 pixels respectively. Increasing the patch size improved the segmentation performance for two of the networks while the other network's results remained largely unchanged. There was also a noticeable difference between the performance of the three different architectures for the CHR boundary segmentation. The RNN was observed to outperform the two CNN networks in terms of mean absolute error and standard deviation with an average of 3.53 pixels and 2.47 respectively compared to 3.96 pixels and 3.71 pixels for the best performing CNN. For the ILM and RPE boundaries, all three architectures gave a very similar level of performance. Here, the greater difficulty in segmenting the CHR boundary may be attributed to greater variability and richness of the features along the boundary compared to the ILM and RPE. This difficulty was also evident when observing the mean absolute repeatability of the machine learning methods with errors approximately 0.5 pixels higher compared to the manual segmentation.

The ability of the RNN method to perform competitively to a CNN-based one was highlighted by Kugelman et al. [24]. Here, it was noted that RNNs were suitable for classifying the OCT retinal image patches due the clear structure of the layers which the RNN operates on sequentially, pixel-by-pixel. Similar competitive performance is observed here for the choroid/scleral (CHR) boundary.

Although a variety of network configurations and methods have been explored, there are a number of combinations and ideas that have not been tested or considered here. In particular, future work may focus on semantic segmentation methods and how these compare to the patch-based ones presented here. Also, methods utilising volumetric data are of interest given the additional context that is potentially available between adjacent scans. As mentioned previously, such methods for medical image analysis have utilised RNNs to process the sequence of images in a volume. Additionally, there is room for investigation involving the graph-search component of the method. More sophisticated graph cut algorithms (e.g. normalised cut, heuristics) may help to provide improved accuracy. End-to-end machine learning approaches are also of interest. One such previous method [33] utilised a semantic segmentation network trained to output layer area masks which was then followed by a 'topology-aware' regression network to output each layer thickness as a numerical quantity. From here, the layer boundary positions were extracted and a graph-search was not required. The potential use of the proposed methods for the segmentation of other feature in the chorio-scleral interface should also be explored in the future [34].

Given the good performance of the methods on the ILM and RPE boundaries as shown here, the design and evaluation of such methods in the future could concentrate on boundaries such as the choroid/scleral boundary (CHR) which, as shown here, are much more challenging to segment. In this work, data from healthy children was utilised. Given the importance of automatic segmentation methods to the diagnosis and monitoring of ocular diseases, future work should also focus on validating these methods using pathological data as well as data from different age groups. Such pathologies cause changes in the topology of the layers potentially creating a more difficult segmentation problem. In addition, some pathologies (e.g. cataracts in elderly patients) can cause degradation of the OCT image quality [35]. For retinal segmentation, Kugelman et al. [24] showed that similar methods can be applied to data of AMD patients. However, for choroidal segmentation, the performance is relatively unexplored. The findings presented here may be used to inform the direction of future investigations into such methods for the segmentation of retinal and choroidal layers in OCT images.

References

1. Huang, D., et al.: Optical coherence tomography. Science **254**, 1178–1181 (1991)
2. de Boer, J.F., Leitgeb, R., Wojtkowski, M.: Twenty-five years of optical coherence tomography: the paradigm shift in sensitivity and speed provided by Fourier domain OCT. Biomed. Opt. Express **8**, 3248–3280 (2017)
3. Read, S.A., Collins, M.J., Vincent, S.J., Alonso-Caneiro, D.: Choroidal thickness in childhood. Invest. Ophthalmol. Vis. Sci. **54**, 3586 (2013)
4. Read, S.A., Collins, M.J., Vincent, S.J., Alonso-Caneiro, D.: Macular retinal layer thickness in childhood. Retina **35**, 1223–1233 (2015)
5. Grover, S., Murthy, R.K., Brar, V.S., Chalam, K.V.: Normative data for macular thickness by high-definition spectral-domain optical coherence tomography (spectralis). Am. J. Ophthalmol. **148**, 266–271 (2009)
6. Margolis, R., Spaide, R.F.: A pilot study of enhanced depth imaging optical coherence tomography of the choroid in normal eyes. Am. J. Ophthalmol. **147**, 811–815 (2009)
7. Harb, E., Hyman, L., Fazzari, M., Gwiazda, J., Marsh-Tootle, W.: Factors associated with macular thickness in the comet myopic cohort. Optom. Vis. Sci. **89**, 620–631 (2012)
8. Read, S.A., Collins, M.J., Vincent, S.J., Alonso-Caneiro, D.: Choroidal thickness in myopic and nonmyopic children assessed with enhanced depth imaging optical coherence tomography. Invest. Ophthalmol. Vis. Sci. **54**, 7578 (2013)
9. Sakamoto, A., et al.: Three-dimensional imaging of the macular retinal nerve fiber layer in glaucoma with spectral-domain optical coherence tomography. Invest. Ophthalmol. Vis. Sci. **51**, 5062 (2010)
10. Wood, A., Binns, A., Margrain, T., Drexler, W., Považay, B., Esmaeelpour, M., Sheen, N.: Retinal and choroidal thickness in early age-related macular degeneration. Am. J. Ophthalmol. **152**, 1030–1038.e2 (2011)
11. Bussel, I.I., Wollstein, G., Schuman, J.S.: OCT for glaucoma diagnosis, screening and detection of glaucoma progression. Br. J. Ophthalmol. **98**, ii15–ii19 (2014)
12. Medina, F.J.L., Callén, C.I., Rebolleda, G., Muñoz-Negrete, F.J., Callén, M.J.I., del Valle, F.G.: Use of nonmydriatic spectral-domain optical coherence tomography for diagnosing diabetic macular edema. Am. J. Ophthalmol. **153**, 536–543.e1 (2012)
13. Fung, A.E., et al.: An optical coherence tomography-guided, variable dosing regimen with intravitreal ranibizumab (lucentis) for neovascular age-related macular degeneration. Am. J. Ophthalmol. **143**, 566–583.e2 (2007)
14. Baghaie, A., Yu, Z., D'Souza, R.M.: State-of-the-art in retinal optical coherence tomography image analysis. Quant. Imaging Med. Surg. **5**, 603 (2015)
15. DeBuc, D.C.: A review of algorithms for segmentation of retinal image data using optical coherence tomography. In: Image Segmentation. InTech (2011)

16. Vermeer, K., Van der Schoot, J., Lemij, H., De Boer, J.: Automated segmentation by pixel classification of retinal layers in ophthalmic OCT images. Biomed. Opt. Express **2**, 1743–1756 (2011)
17. Fang, L., Cunefare, D., Wang, C., Guymer, R.H., Li, S., Farsiu, S.: Automatic segmentation of nine retinal layer boundaries in OCT images of non-exudative amd patients using deep learning and graph search. Biomed. Opt. Express **8**, 2732–2744 (2017)
18. Lang, A., et al.: Retinal layer segmentation of macular OCT images using boundary classification. Biomed. Opt. Express **4**, 1133–1152 (2013)
19. Ben-Cohen, A., et al.: Retinal layers segmentation using fully convolutional network in OCT images. RSIP Vision (2017)
20. Pekala, M., Joshi, N., Freund, D.E., Bressler, N.M., DeBuc, D.C., Burlina, P.M.: Deep learning based retinal OCT segmentation. CoRR abs/1801.09749 (2018)
21. Hamwood, J., Alonso-Caneiro, D., Read, S.A., Vincent, S.J., Collins, M.J.: Effect of patch size and network architecture on a convolutional neural network approach for automatic segmentation of OCT retinal layers. Biomed. Opt. Express **9**, 3049–3066 (2018)
22. Chen, J., Yang, L., Zhang, Y., Alber, M., Chen, D.Z.: Combining fully convolutional and recurrent neural networks for 3D biomedical image segmentation. In: Proceedings of the 30th International Conference on Neural Information Processing Systems, NIPS 2016, USA, pp. 3044–3052. Curran Associates Inc. (2016)
23. Chen, H., et al.: Automatic fetal ultrasound standard plane detection using knowledge transferred recurrent neural networks. In: Navab, N., Hornegger, J., Wells, W.M., Frangi, A.F. (eds.) MICCAI 2015. LNCS, vol. 9349, pp. 507–514. Springer, Cham (2015). https://doi.org/10.1007/978-3-319-24553-9_62
24. Kugelman, J., Alonso-Caneiro, D., Read, S.A., Vincent, S.J., Collins, M.J.: Automatic segmentation of OCT retinal boundaries using recurrent neural networks and graph search. Biomed. Opt. Express **9**, 5759–5777 (2018)
25. Hochreiter, S., Schmidhuber, J.: Long short-term memory. Neural Comput. **9**, 1735–1780 (1997)
26. Cho, K., et al.: Learning phrase representations using RNN encoder-decoder for statistical machine translation. arXiv preprint arXiv:1406.1078 (2014)
27. Visin, F., Kastner, K., Cho, K., Matteucci, M., Courville, A., Bengio, Y.: ReNet: a recurrent neural network based alternative to convolutional networks. arXiv preprint arXiv:1505.00393 (2015)
28. Kingma, D.P., Ba, J.: Adam: a method for stochastic optimization. arXiv preprint arXiv:1412.6980 (2014)
29. Girard, M.J., Strouthidis, N.G., Ethier, C.R., Mari, J.M.: Shadow removal and contrast enhancement in optical coherence tomography images of the human optic nerve head. Invest. Ophthalmol. Vis. Sci. **52**, 7738–7748 (2011)
30. Vermeer, K., Mo, J., Weda, J., Lemij, H., De Boer, J.: Depth-resolved model-based reconstruction of attenuation coefficients in optical coherence tomography. Biomed. Opt. Express **5**, 322–337 (2014)
31. Dijkstra, E.W.: A note on two problems in connexion with graphs. Numer. Math. **1**, 269–271 (1959)
32. Alonso-Caneiro, D., Read, S.A., Collins, M.J.: Automatic segmentation of choroidal thickness in optical coherence tomography. Biomed. Opt. Express **4**, 2795–2812 (2013)
33. He, Y., et al.: Topology guaranteed segmentation of the human retina from OCT using convolutional neural networks. CoRR abs/1803.05120 (2018)

34. Chandrasekera, E., Wong, E.N., Sampson, D.M., Alonso-Caneiro, D., Chen, F.K.: Posterior choroidal stroma reduces accuracy of automated segmentation of outer choroidal boundary in swept source optical coherence tomography. Invest. Ophthalmol. Vis. Sci. **59**, 4404–4412 (2018)
35. van Velthoven, M.E.J., van der Linden, M.H., de Smet, M.D., Faber, D.J., Verbraak, F.D.: Influence of cataract on optical coherence tomography image quality and retinal thickness. Br. J. Ophthalmol. **90**, 1259–1262 (2006)

Discrimination Ability of Glaucoma via DCNNs Models from Ultra-Wide Angle Fundus Images Comparing Either Full or Confined to the Optic Disc

Hitoshi Tabuchi[✉], Hiroki Masumoto, Shunsuke Nakakura, Asuka Noguchi, and Hirotaka Tanabe

Department of Ophthalmology, Tsukazaki Hospital, Himeji, Japan
h.tabuchi@tsukazaki-eye.net

Abstract. We examined the difference in ability to discriminate glaucoma among artificial intelligence models trained with partial area surrounding the optic disc (Cropped) and whole area of a ultra-wide angle ocular fundus camera (Full). 1677 normal fundus images and 950 glaucomatous fundus images of the Optos 200Tx (Optos PLC, Dunfermline, United Kingdom) images in the Tsukazaki Hospital ophthalmology database were included in the study. A k-fold method (k = 5) and a convolutional neural network (VGG16) were used. For the full data set, the area under the curve (AUC) was 0.987 (95% CI 0.983–0.991), sensitivity was 0.957 (95% CI 0.942–0.969), and specificity was 0.947 (95% CI 0.935–0.957). For the cropped data set, AUC was 0.937 (95% CI 0.927–0.949), sensitivity was 0.868 (95% CI 0.845–0.889), and specificity was 0.894 (95% CI 0.878–0.908). The values of AUC, sensitivity, and specificity for the cropped data set were lower than those for the full data set. Our results show that the whole ultra-wide angle fundus is more appropriate as the amount of information given to a neural network for the discrimination of glaucoma than only the range limited to the periphery of the optic disc.

1 Introduction

Ultra-wide angle ocular fundus cameras (Optos, Optos PLC, Dunfermline, United Kingdom) still present unique capabilities even ten years after their release. These non-mydriatic fundus camera have particular ability to identify retinal detachment in children [1], and can photograph 80% of the area of the fundus from a pupil of only 2 mm [2] and, the Optos' shooting range is unrivaled in this type of commercially available fundus camera [3]. Also, to the best of our knowledge, all previous studies on the identification of retinal detachment using artificial intelligence (AI) have used Optos cameras [4]. However, since this imaging device uses pseudo-color, it has many disadvantages. For example, it has been suggested that it is inferior to other imaging devices for detailed analysis [5]. Perhaps one of the most important functions of a fundus photographing device for remote diagnosis is the ability to detect retinal detachment [4]. A number of papers have reported on detecting several other diseases using AI in conjunction with a diagnostic device capable of detecting retinal detachment [6–8]. Among these, one report has suggested that the Optos could be used to identify glaucoma [7]. This is of particular interest as it is a rather common condition. Another interesting aspect of that report is that the Optos was able to detect early stage of glaucoma using images captured by Optos 200TX, which were considered to be low quality images [7]. Therefore, to investigate the possibility of improving the ability of deep convolutional neural networks (DCNNs) to diagnose glaucoma using Optos, we proposed two approaches/hypotheses. The first hypothesis is that, by using the whole wide-angle fundus image, the area ratio of the main lesion area in the image would decrease, which would result in decreased the diagnostic performance. The second contrary hypothesis is that information on the image other than the main lesion area is also useful for diagnosis.

In this study, we prepared two types of fundus photographs, a narrow range and a wide range, for training of DCNNs and examined the effect of such training on discrimination ability. In other words, we examined the difference in ability to discriminate glaucoma among DCNN models trained with partial area surrounding the optic disc and whole area of a ultra-wide angle ocular fundus camera Optos 200Tx.

2 Method

2.1 Cropping of the Image Surrounding the Optic Disc by AI

The original image of Optos was 3072×3900 pixels. First, the image of the right eye was flipped horizontally and aligned with the image of the left eye. Subsequently, the image was trimmed roughly to the area containing the optic disc, and this was performed using a U-Net network used for segmentation and localization of the papilla. The image output from U-Net was reformatted to its original size. The portion with the largest area in the image was extracted and the center of gravity of the extracted region was calculated. We calculated the center of gravity in the original image and cropped 400×400 pixels centered on the coordinates. The right eye was then flipped back to its original orientation.

2.2 Dataset

Hypothesis verification was performed using 1677 normal fundus images and 950 glaucoma fundus images among the Optos 200Tx images in the Tsukazaki Hospital ophthalmology database, which were photographed between December 1, 2011, and May 27, 2018. The glaucoma image data were approved by a glaucoma specialist whose diagnosis was confirmed comprehensively from visual field examination and OCT, among others. We prepared two data sets as follows: full data set, a data set of the whole image (3072×3900 pixels); and cropped data set, a data set of the image (400×400 pixels) cropped only around the optic disc by the above method (Fig. 1). For each data set, the neural network model was constructed and evaluated.

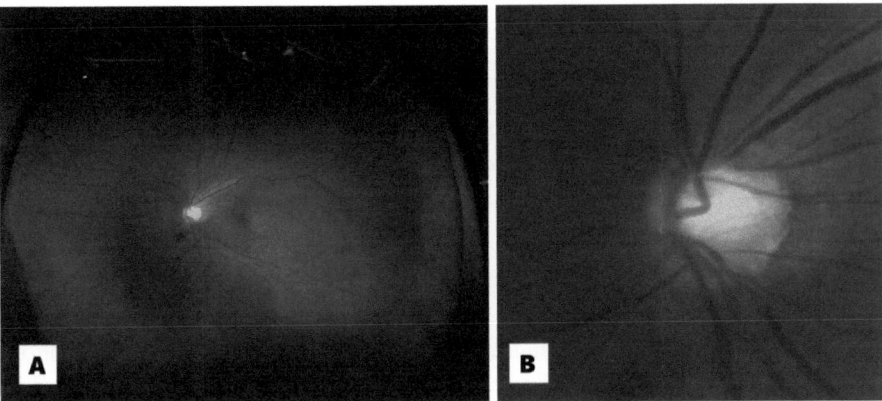

Fig. 1. Example images for the two data sets *(A)*: A whole image of Optos 200Tx for the full data set. *(B)*: An image cropped around the optic disc for the cropped data set. A and B are images of a glaucoma patient.

2.3 Processing Flow

In this study, a k-fold cross-validation method (k = 5) was used. Here, k − 1 groups were used as training data and the remaining group was used as test data. Regarding the training data, nine types of data augmentation were applied, namely, no conversion, increasing the contrast, lowering the contrast, γ correction (γ = 0.75, 1.5), smoothing, histogram flattening, Gaussian noise, and salt & pepper noise. For the normal images, three out of nine types of image augmentation were randomly performed to each image, and horizontal reversal was performed to increase the number of images six-fold. For the glaucoma images, six out of nine types of image augmentation were randomly performed; furthermore, the number of images was increased 12-fold when including the left/right inversion. Model training was conducted using data-extended training images and the performance of the model was evaluated using test images. These series of steps of data expansion, training, and performance evaluation were repeated k times, and all of the blocks were used as test images. Combinations of images divided into k blocks were the same for both the full data set and the cropped data set.

2.4 Building a Model

This study was conducted using VGG16 as DCNN, the details of which are described in [6]. VGG16 outputs the probability associated with the binary classification cases of healthy vs. glaucoma. An appropriate threshold was set, and images for which the probability of glaucoma exceeded the threshold were diagnosed as being associated with glaucoma. The construction and evaluation of the model were carried out using Keras (https://keras.io/en/), where Python's tensorflow (https://www.tensorflow.org/) was used as backend. Training and inference of this model were performed using an NVIDIA's GeForce GTX 1080 Ti GPU.

2.5 Performance Evaluation

When each k-fold model was used for the test data, the ROC curve was derived using the value output as the probability of glaucoma. Using the receiver operating characteristic (ROC) curve, the area under the curve (AUC) and the sensitivity/specificity were obtained to evaluate the ability to identify healthy and glaucoma cases.

2.6 Statistics

Based on the average and deviation of AUC of five models, the 95% confidence interval of AUC was calculated after assuming that AUC had a normal distribution. For sensitivity and specificity, the point at which both sensitivity and specificity on the ROC curve were closest to 100% was used for the representative values. Based on those values, the confidence interval was calculated using the Clopper–Pearson method. The ROC curve was calculated by using the Python Scikit-learn package, while AUC and the confidence interval of sensitivity/specificity were calculated using the Scipy Python package.

2.7 Enrollment and Ethical Statement

This research adhered to the Declaration of Helsinki and was approved by the ethics committee of Tsukazaki Hospital. This was a study that retrospectively reviewed the Optos® images and there were no issues with personally identifiable information involved, the Institutional Review Board of Tsukazaki Hospital waived the need for consent.

3 Results

For the full data set, AUC was 0.987 (95% CI 0.983–0.991), sensitivity was 0.957 (95% CI 0.942–0.969), and specificity was 0.947 (95% CI 0.935–0.957). For the cropped data set, AUC was 0.937 (95% CI 0.927–0.949), sensitivity was 0.868 (95% CI 0.845–0.889), and specificity was 0.894 (95% CI 0.878–0.908) (Fig. 2). The values of AUC, sensitivity, and specificity for the cropped data set were lower than those for the full data set.

These results demonstrated the ability of the two VGG16 s trained models with two different data sets (full and cropped) to distinguish between glaucoma and healthy cases. The full data set was composed of images using the full Optos image (3072 × 3900 pixels), and the cropped data set was composed of images (400 × 400 pixels) cropped around the optic disc.

4 Discussion

Our results found that the whole ultra-wide angle fundus images yield better discrimination performance as it provides more information to the DCNN for detecting glaucoma compared with the images with the range limited to the surrounding the optic

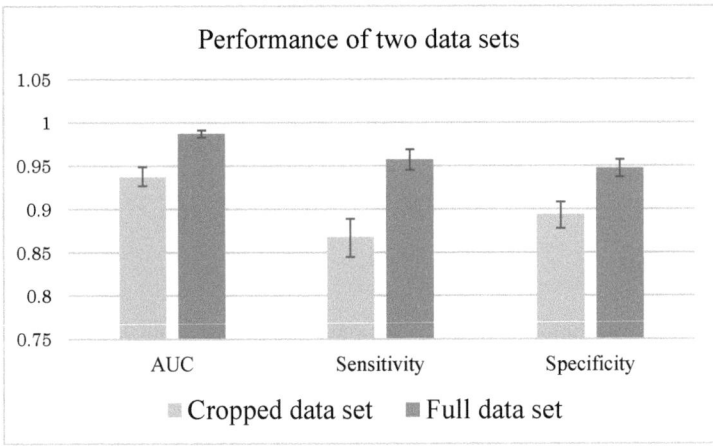

Fig. 2. Performance of two data sets

disc. This suggests that image information other than that on the optic disc may be used for artificial intelligence discrimination using Optos®.

In AI discrimination, deciding which part within the whole image should be used is important as it influences the discrimination performance. As Optos® has a relatively short history as a diagnostic device and there is no international image database, it is important requirement that the device requires fewer images to train. In this context, the result of the present study showing that the diagnostic efficiency declined when narrowing the region of interest was disappointing. However, we believe that the study provided important information for the future development of glaucoma discrimination based on DCNNs using this imaging device.

Our study results are limited to images of Optos® 200 Tx. There is a possibility that Optos' newer models, which is said to have higher resolution, and other imaging devices may show higher performance than what we found in this study using images containing only the optic disc area. Furthermore, based on this study design, it cannot be definitively asserted that a ultra-wide angle range is necessary for the AI-based identification of glaucoma. For example, studies have not been performed in the range inside the blood vessel arcade, where nerve fiber layer defect (NFLD) is assumed to be detectable, and the efficiency of the discrimination ability in that range may be higher than in the ultra-wide angle range.

We believe that retinal detachment, for which early diagnosis is directly linked to a complete cure, is the most important disease for AI-based remote diagnosis of the fundus. On the other hand, glaucoma is the most important eye disease as it is the number one cause of blindness in Japan, which is the first country exhibiting a super-aged society. And this would be applicable in other Asian countries, where aging is also progressing rapidly. This explains why we continue our efforts to further improve the ability to discriminate glaucoma by AI using this device.

This study revealed that learning efficiency becomes poor upon limiting the image range only to the optic disk area. Our next task is to extend the range to the vascular arcade range and compare its discrimination ability to the ultra-wide angle range. We considered that our approach has greater potential than other fundus diagnostic devices in automatically diagnosing fundus diseases by combining AI with Optos, which is a ultra-wide angle ocular fundus photographing device. We would like to extend the possibility of AI identification using Optos by accumulating methodological knowledge like that obtained in this study.

5 Conclusion

In this study, it was found that using the entire image as input for super wide-angle fundus imaging is more appropriate for DCNN based discrimination of glaucoma as the amount of information given to a neural network for discrimination was increased, when compared to the range limited to the periphery of the optic disc.

References

1. 1990-The Beginning. https://www.optos.com/en/about/
2. Products. https://www.optos.com/en/products/
3. Imaging ultra-wide without compromise ZEISS CLARUS 500. https://www.zeiss.com/meditec/int/products/ophthalmology-optometry/retina/diagnostics/fundus-imaging/clarus-500.html
4. Ohsugi, H., Tabuchi, H., Enno, H., Ishitobi, N.: Accuracy of deep learning, a machine-learning technology, using ultra–wide-field fundus ophthalmoscopy for detecting rhegmatogenous retinal detachment. Sci. Rep. **25**, 9425 (2017)
5. Meshi, A., et al.: Comparison of retinal pathology visualization in multispectral scanning laser imaging. Retina (2018). [Epub ahead of print]
6. Matsuba, S., et al.: Accuracy of ultra–wide-field fundus ophthalmoscopy-assisted deep learning, a machine-learning technology, for detecting age related macular degeneration. Int. Ophthal. (2018). https://doi.org/10.1007/s10792-018-0940-0
7. Masumoto, H., Tabuchi, H., Nakakura, S., Ishitobi, N., Miki, M., Enno, H.: Deep-learning classifier with an ultrawide-field scanning laser ophthalmoscope detects glaucoma visual field severity. J. Glaucoma **27**, 647–652 (2018)
8. Nagasawa, T., et al.: Accuracy of deep learning, a machine-learning technology, using ultra–widefield fundus ophthalmoscopy for detecting idiopathic macular holes. Peer J. **6**, e5696 (2018). https://doi.org/10.7717/peerj.5696.eCollection2018

Synthesizing New Retinal Symptom Images by Multiple Generative Models

Yi-Chieh Liu[1], Hao-Hsiang Yang[1], C.-H. Huck Yang[2,3], Jia-Hong Huang[1,2], Meng Tian[4], Hiromasa Morikawa[2], Yi-Chang James Tsai[3], and Jesper Tegnèr[2,5(✉)]

[1] National Taiwan University, Taipei, Taiwan
{b01310048,r05921014}@ntu.edu.tw
[2] Biological and Environmental Sciences and Engineering Division, Computer, Electrical and Mathematical Sciences and Engineering Division,
King Abdullah University of Science and Technology, Thuwal, Saudi Arabia
{chao-han.yang,jiahong.huang,hiromasa.morikawa,
jesper.tegner}@kaust.edu.sa
[3] Georgia Institute of Technology, Atlanta, GA, USA
james.tsai@ce.gatech.edu
[4] Department of Ophthalmology, Bern University Hospital, Bern, Switzerland
tianmeng1231@gmail.com
[5] Unit of Computational Medicine, Center for Molecular Medicine, Department of Medicine, Karolinska Institutet, Stockholm, Sweden

Abstract. Age-Related Macular Degeneration (AMD) is an asymptomatic retinal disease which may result in loss of vision. There is limited access to high-quality relevant retinal images and poor understanding of the features defining sub-classes of this disease. Motivated by recent advances in machine learning we specifically explore the potential of generative modeling, using Generative Adversarial Networks (GANs) and style transferring, to facilitate clinical diagnosis and disease understanding by feature extraction. We design an analytic pipeline which first generates synthetic retinal images from clinical images; a subsequent verification step is applied. In the synthesizing step we merge GANs (DCGANs and WGANs architectures) and style transferring for the image generation, whereas the verified step controls the accuracy of the generated images. We find that the generated images contain sufficient pathological details to facilitate ophthalmologists' task of disease classification and in discovery of disease relevant features. In particular, our system predicts the drusen and geographic atrophy sub-classes of AMD. Furthermore, the performance using CFP images for GANs outperforms the classification based on using only the original clinical dataset. Our results are evaluated using existing classifier of retinal diseases and class activated maps, supporting the predictive power of the synthetic images and their utility for feature extraction. Our code examples are available online. (https://github.com/huckiyang/EyeNet-GANs).

1 Introduction

As a rule, it is challenging to automatically diagnose retinal diseases from images, partly because of the difficulty of acquiring public data with a sufficient number of annotated images due to concerns of personal privacy. Meanwhile, different ophthalmologists may provide conflicting judgments about identical images; therefore, it can be arduous to reach consensus about a diagnosis. Thus, it is clear that a larger number of retinal images collected from a system with provided unbiased feature detection would be beneficial for ophthalmologists' clinical practice.

Generative models, such as Generative Adversarial Networks [1] (GANs), and style transferring [2] techniques, have achieved impressive results for generating sharp and realistic images. Therefore, these two methods are used to synthesize the disease images from healthy retinal images and diseased ones. Synthesized images not only impose high-level symptom features to the original ones but help ophthalmologists build the understanding of related diseases. The definition of image synthesis in [3] is seen as an image reconstruction process coupled with feature transformation. The synthesized part is responsible for inverting features back to the color space and the feature transformation matches certain statistics of a original image to a generated image [4].

We consider images with Age-Related Macular Degeneration (AMD) as an asymptomatic retinal disease and the leading cause of irreversible visual loss among the aged population. Despite the advances of therapeutics, there is still no satisfactory treatment. It raises the issue that diagnosing AMD from its early stage and having proper managing it properly are more important than ever. The development of AMD is classified as several stages that can be discerned by two explicit symptoms, drusen and Geographic Atrophy (GA). Drusen are one of the earliest clinical indications of AMD, which appears as focal, with yellow excrescences deep in the retina with extra-cellular deposits located beneath the retinal pigment, epithelium, and Bruch's membrane; the number, size and distribution of these deposits is highly variable. GA, symptomatic of a more advanced stage of AMD, is described as a well-demarcated area of decreased retinal thickness. Such areas have relative changes in color compared to surroundings allowing an increased visualization of the underlying choroidal vessels. The phenomenon is that less intense and more diffuse hyperfluorescence in which pigment clumping sometimes forms a microreticular pattern, is demonstrated [5–7]. To sum up, two symptoms (drusen and GA) are established clinical hallmarks of AMD. Drusen size and confluency have been historically associated with the progression of AMD, which also contributes to the development of GA. Our chief objective is to generate images equipped with a sufficient number of pathological features to capture the two different stages of AMD.

The contribution of this paper consists of two parts. First, style transferring, WGANs and DCGANs are used to build a new artificial neural network as the framework for the generation of synthetic pathologically relevant but detailed images. Second, after new images are obtained and diagnosed by ophthalmologists, we use Class Activation Maps (CAMs) [8] to locate the advanced features within the generated images. Finally, the EyeNet [9] is used to classify generated images according to the established labelling of diseases.

The paper is organized into five sections. Following this introduction, in the second section, we survey related work. In the third section, we present our analytic pipeline, including an account of how we fuse DCGANs, WGANs, style transferring, EyeNet, and CAMs. In the fourth section, we present and discuss computational experimental results. In the last section, we summarize conclusions and outline prospects the future work.

2 Related Work

Below, we survey previous work on GANs, from which we benefit, synthetic image generation, and computational retinal disease methods.

2.1 GANs

Since the pioneering formulation of GANs [1], there have been numerous studies of how to formulate the optimization problem of balancing on the one hand the training of a generative network **G** producing realistic synthetic samples, and on the other, a discriminator network **D** that distinguishes between real and synthetic (generated) data. We adopt an adversarial loss

$$min_G max_D L_{GANS} = E_{x \sim p_{data}(x)}[log D(x)] + E_{x \sim p_{prior}(z)}[log(1 - D(z))] \quad (1)$$

Yet, a major issue has been the stability and convergence of training a GAN. Recent work [10] demonstrated improved stability when using a Kantorovich-Rubinstein metric, which we have adopted in our training of the GAN for retinal images. Rapid advances have demonstrated that GANs generate realistic images, with a rich number of features. For example, GANs have been successfully applied for face generation [11], indoor scene reconstruction [12] and person re-identification [13]. Here we benefit from recent progress with GANs to generate new synthetic retinal disease images using both Deep Convolutional Generative Adversarial Networks (DCGANs) [14] and Wasserstein GANs (WGANs) [10]. These architectures utilize a convolutional decoder, and DCGAN enables the employment of large GANs using Convolutional Neural Networks (CNNs), resulting in stable training across various datasets. Finally, our use of WGANs improves the stability of learning, thereby avoiding known challenges such as model collapse [10].

2.2 Generation of Synthetic Images

Recently, researchers have used convolutional neural networks to generate images [15] with different given style. The method makes use of a pre-trained network to optimize the image and its features. However, this method operates as a global optimization; therefore, generated image exhibit distortions and detailed parts cannot be presented on the transferred images. Meeting this challenge, recent work [2] accomplished realistic image generation and style transferring. On the other hand, in [14], authors combined a convolutional neural network and GANs to generate new images, thus mitigating the impact of a limited number of features of pathological relevance in original images. While their work clearly improved the state-of-the-art methods, the technique may generate poor image samples or fails to converge. To ensure convergence and quality of generated images, we deploy a closed form solution for style transferring [16].

2.3 Computational Retinal Disease Methods

There is a challenge to build large high-quality medical databases despite massive investment in, for example, data collection, labeling, and data augmentation. Exceptions include the recently released ChestXray14 [17] dataset which contains 112,120 frontal-view chest radiographs with up to 14 thoracic pathological labels. Yet, in contrast, for retinal research, the DRIVE dataset [18], which contains only 40 retina images, has long been a standard. However, recently the Retina Image Bank (RIB) [19], containing a large number of different kinds of retinal images, is truly an enabler for the kind of work presented in our paper. Despite this, we still need techniques to augment such databases due to various challenges, such as the limited amount of annotation, thus effectively transforming a small dataset with low diversity into one that approximates the underlying data distribution. For example, in [20,21], GANs were used to generate a variety of retinal images and targeting control (healthy) images. Using the Retinal Image Bank, we aim to generate new retinal images that have a sufficient number of pathological details so that we have abundant and useful retinal images to train and build robust classifier. In [22], authors propose a method that implements automated segmentation of retina to facilitate the detection of disease. Article [9] uses the whole retinal images in [19] to train the classifier, which can discern multiple diseases with the extraction of visual traits. Our work depends on having a pre-trained network to test the quality of generated images and uses CAMs to present symptoms identified by the classifier.

3 Methodology

In this section, we describe different methods in our proposed pipeline. For generative models, GANs and style transferring based networks are discussed. For verification, we elaborate EyeNet and CAMs.

3.1 Style Transferring

The input contains two images: a content and a style image and pre-trained CNNs; the output is the synthesized image. In our case, the content image means the disease image with pathological details; the style image represents the healthy retinal image. When it comes to the existing style transferring methods, even though the style is changed, the content of the image can be seen in the new image. Thus, we expect generated images with pathological details, so content images are seen as disease images. For each image, the output from the CNNs classifier obtains various level features from many convolutional layers. Generated images preserve the original semantic content from the content image but look like a style image. For the content and the style part, loss functions that are computed from the similarity of images from convolutional layers can be defined; style transferring becomes an optimization problem when the optimal image is obtained with the least loss. The pixels in the image can be computed iteratively by gradient descent.

3.2 DCGANs and WGANs for Image Generation

Although original GANs provide an intriguing algorithm with surprising results, the instability is what we concern about when it comes to medical applications, which requires precision and detailed images for diagnosis. To improve the quality of generated images, we chose DCGANs and WGANs to establish our generative model. In this part, with a random initialized parameter, we build a generator of retinal diseases while the improving discriminator. For a specific symptom, generated images contain similar optical traits. Furthermore, high dimensional neural networks for computer vision sometimes materialize higher forms of neglected visual features. Therefore, generated retinal images not only become the aid of diagnosis and strategy to explore diseases, but also provide diverse computer training data.

3.3 Class Activation Maps

The class activation maps (CAMs) in [8] provide a method that localizes features on images. From localized features, the performance of the generated image can be evaluated and observed. As discussed in Sect. 3.1, convolutional layers of CNNs are used to extract the visual feature of images. Through this method, not only the similarity of images is tested with high-level disease features, but a series of pathological details is built.

3.4 EyeNet

Besides CAMs, EyeNet as proposed in [9] is used to evaluate the correctness of generated images. In [9], the authors trained a network that classifies different retinal diseases; 52 kinds of retinal diseases are labeled and classified. Proposed methods [23] include three frameworks: U-net, SVM and ResNet50; prediction by ResNet50 performs best. Therefore, ResNet50 is modified so that the generated images also can be classified to make sure of their correctness.

3.5 Pipeline

We propose a pipeline structure in Fig. 1. Initially, with feature extraction by style transferring and GANs, more images are generated. In order to verify the correctness, CAMs and EyeNet are used to compute the high level visual features and predict the diseases, respectively. Results from the CAMs present pathological details. Moreover, generated images can be applied to feed to other classifier to train the more accurate classifier. All researches benefits not only the newly trained network, but also ophthalmologists. Original retinal images give doctors an initial diagnosis, and the generated images provide them more clues. CAMs help ophthalmologists judge accurately, and they can reach the consensus with EyeNet. To sum up, our pipeline improves the efficiency and accuracy of the medical system and contributes to researchers.

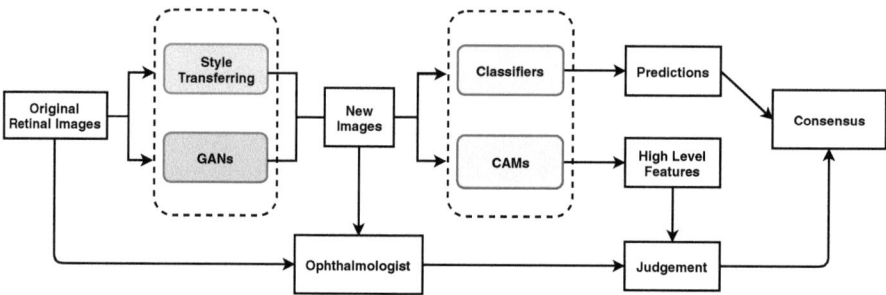

Fig. 1. Proposed pipeline to improve retinal diagnosis efficiency by combining GANs and EyeNet to assist ophthalmologists and doctors. EyeNet is used to check the performance. Finally, observation of similarities among some diseases are analyzed and described.

4 Experiments

In this section, we describe the implementation details and experiments we conduct to validate our proposed methods. Initially, the data collection and setup of experiments are emphasized. And generating images by style transferring, GANs are presented. Finally, generated images are diagnosed by doctors and EyeNet is used to check the performance. Furthermore, observation of similarity among some diseases are analyzed and described.

4.1 Dataset Collection

Experimental images come from the Retina Image Bank (RIB) [19]. Retinal image collection contains three types of photography that are fluorescein angiography (FA), optical coherence tomography (OCT) and color fundus photography (CFP). FA are gray-scale images and CFP are colorful images. CFP and FA imaging are reliable for whole fundus, and used as our dataset.

4.2 Setup

As discussed above, we use images with AMD for experiments. Images contain CFP and FA type, and present the symptom of drusen and GA. All DNNs were implemented in PyTorch, and we modified the publicly available PyTorch code for the neural network algorithm. Details of various methods are described later, respectively. The derivative of all generative models is sped in CUDA for gradient-based optimization.

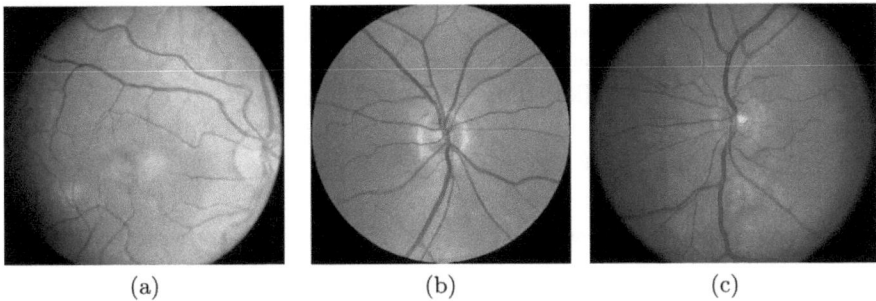

Fig. 2. Three CFP fundus images that are used to generate new images are seen as style images. (Color figure online)

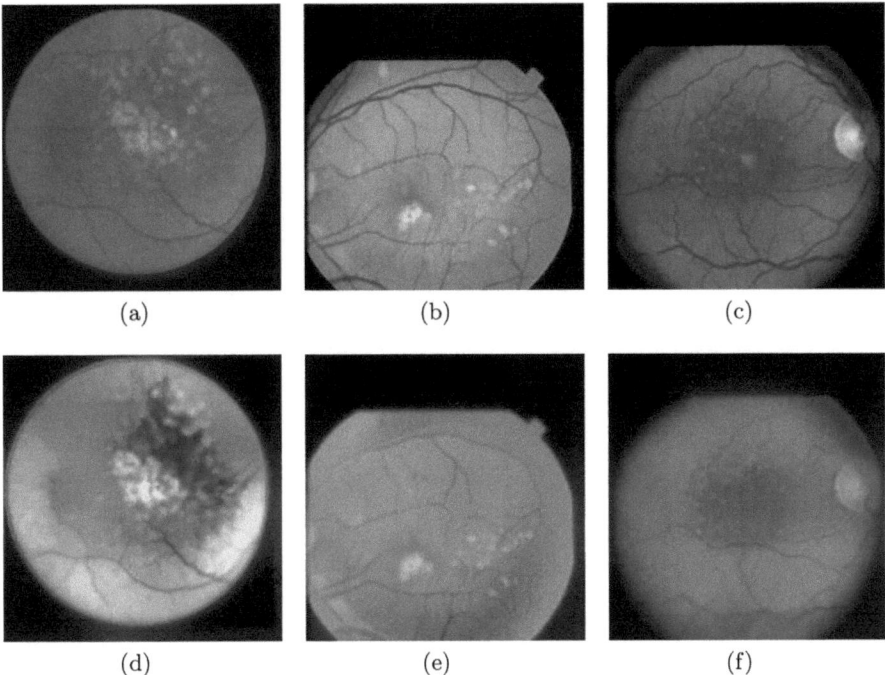

Fig. 3. Three CFP fundus images with symptom of drusen and corresponding generated images. (a), (b), (c) Original images. (d), (e), (f) Generated images. (Color figure online)

4.3 Style Transferring Neural Networks

Style transferring neural network in [16] was modified to generate new disease images. This network adopts layers from "conv1_1" to "conv4_1" in pre-trained VGG-19 [24] network for the encoder, whose weights are provided by ImageNet-pretrained weights. What's more, multi-level stylization strategy proposed in [16] is applied to optimize the VGG features in different layers. Input images are three CFP images and three FA images as style images shown in Figs. 2 and 5. Six CFP images with three drusen and three GA images in Figs. 3 and 4. Also, FA images are applied to generate new images in Figs. 6 and 7. For CFP images, six images are shown in Figs. 3 and in 4. In Fig. 3, generated images contain round, discrete yellow-white dots, which are the symptom of drusen. In the same way, in Fig. 4, well-demarcated areas appear on the three images. Therefore, style transferring can generate new retinal symptom images.

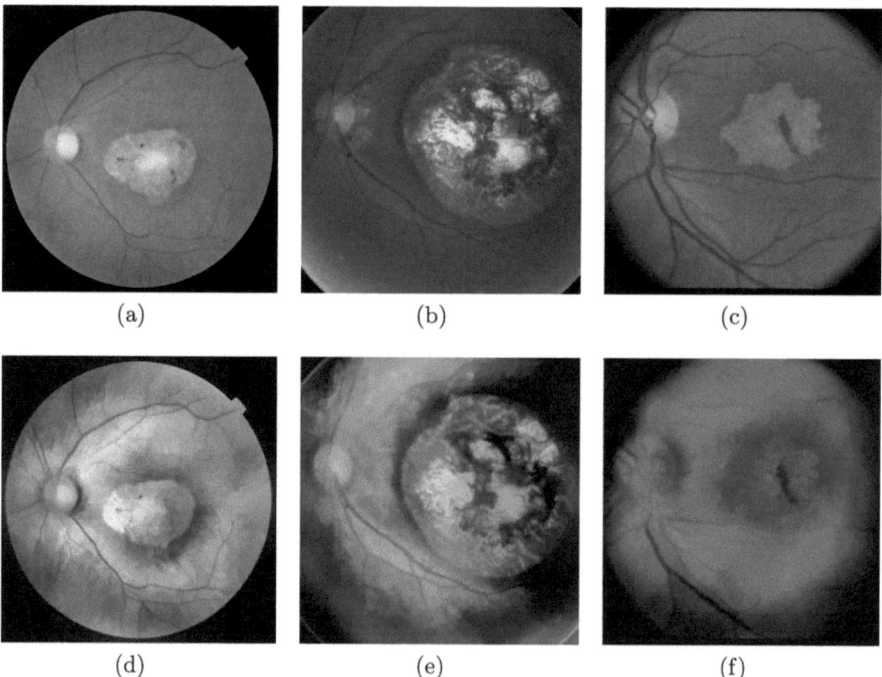

Fig. 4. Three CFP fundus images with symptom of GA and corresponding generated images. (a), (b), (c) Original images. (d), (e), (f) Generated images. (Color figure online)

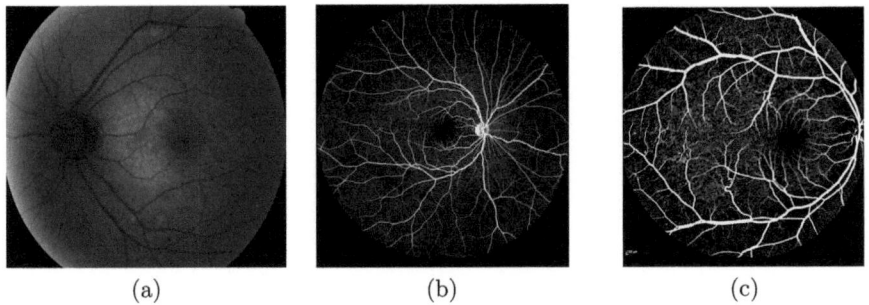

(a)   (b)   (c)

Fig. 5. Three AF fundus images that are used to generate new images are seen as style images.

Furthermore, generated images from FA images are presented in Figs. 6 and 7. Results in the images are nearly identical to the original images, because original networks are applied to stylize color images. However, six generated images contain more concise features than the original ones, which helps ophthalmologists make better judgments. Therefore, this style transferring networks can fulfill edge sharpening and enhancement of contrast. No matter which kinds of images are generated, advanced features in new disease images still exist. Furthermore, analyses of image performance by EyeNet and CAMs for prediction are presented in a later section.

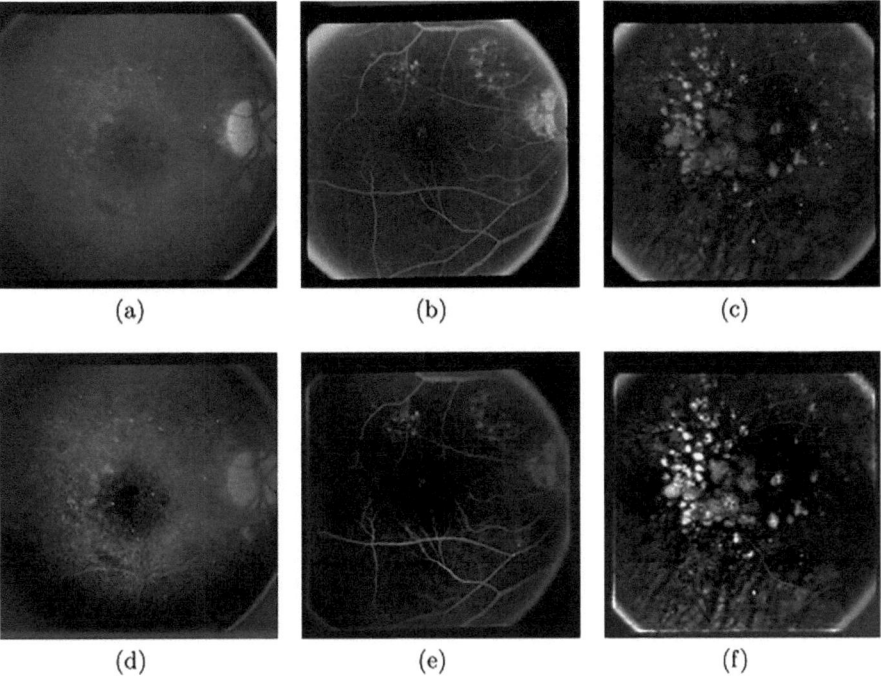

(a)   (b)   (c)

(d)   (e)   (f)

Fig. 6. Three FA fundus images with symptom of drusen and corresponding generated images. (a), (b), (c) Original images. (d), (e), (f) Generated images.

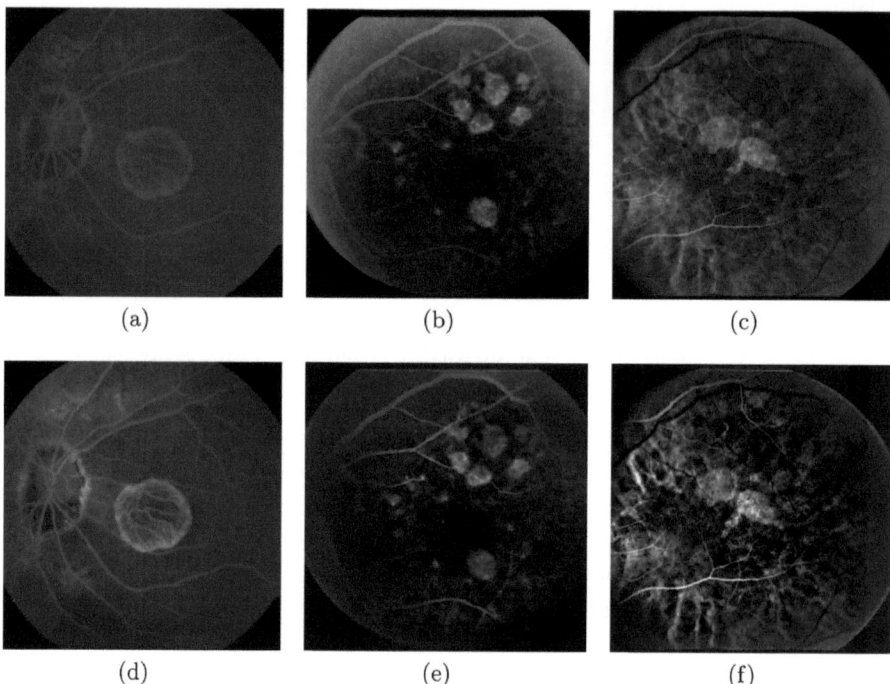

Fig. 7. Three FA fundus images with symptom of GA and corresponding generated images. (a), (b), (c) Original images. (d), (e), (f) Generated images.

4.4 DCGANs and WGANs

In this section, DCGANs and WGANs are trained with thousands of CFP and FA images that have symptoms of drusen and GA separately; both of the models require four to six hours to train. Generated images have been diagnosed by ophthalmologists for verification. Images generated by DCGANs, which are shown in Fig. 8, cannot be identified as a valid retinal image with symptom. However, drusen and GA images generated by WGANs can be used by ophthalmologists to diagnose. In Fig. 9, generated drusen images are diagnosed as insignificant of drusen but can be identified by EyeNet. As for generated GA images in Fig. 9, irregularly shaped macular atrophy can be identified by an ophthalmologist. Macular atrophy is a distinguishable trait of GA, which means WGANs indeed learn the symptoms of drusen and GA from specific AMD and generate new images. Thus, WGANs perform better than DCGANs because of resolution. Structure of DCGANs limits the size of generated images to be 64 × 64, so some pathological details are lost. We choose WGANs for following experiments.

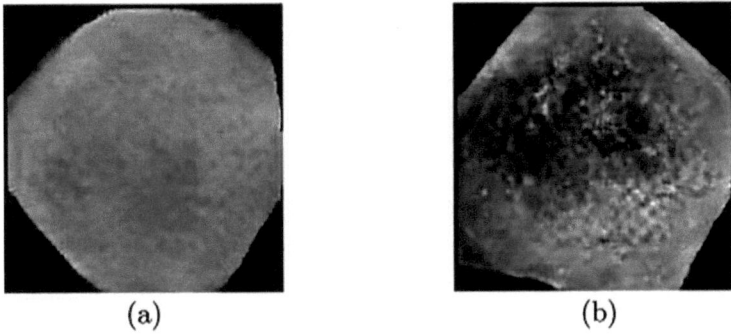

Fig. 8. Drusen images generated by DCGANs.(a) CFP image. (b) FA image.

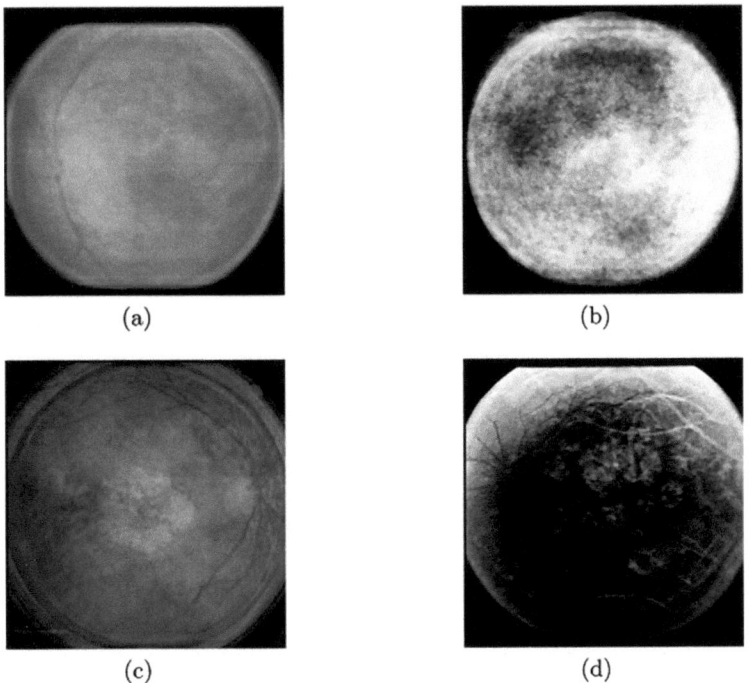

Fig. 9. Drusen and GA images generated by WGANs. (a) Generated drusen CFP image. (b) Generated drusen FA image. (c) Generated drusen CFP image. (d) Generated GA FA image.

4.5 EyeNet Results for Prediction

EyeNet in [9] is trained to predict the accuracy of images to accomplish the pipeline. Though ImageNet and our retinal dataset are much different, using pre-trained weights on ImageNet rather than random ones has boosted testing accuracy of any models with 5 to 15%. Besides, pre-trained models tend to converge much faster than random initialized. The training images encompass 52 kinds of fundus images, which are randomly divided into three parts: 70% for training, 10% for validation and 20% for testing. It is noted that synthesized images are not used to train this network. The training lasts 400 epochs. The first 200 epochs take a learning rate of 1e–4 and the second 200 take 1e–5. Besides, we apply random data augmentation during training. In every epoch, 70% probability for a training sample is affinely transformed. After EyeNet is trained, generated images are fed into it, and the average predicted probabilities are shown in Table 1. Compared to drusen, The accuracy declines when it comes to identifying generated geographic atrophy images. The lack of geographic atrophy images in the EyeNet dataset weaken the capability of the classifier to discern traits about geographic atrophy. Despite of the setback, there is a exciting exploration that the predictions are not randomly distributed but focus on particular diseases, which is likely caused by the high-dimensional features mentioned above.

Table 1. Average accuracy classified by EyeNet.

	Drusen-CFP	Drusen-FA	GA-CFP	GA-FA
Real Images	0.442	0.368	0.166	0.128
WGANs	**0.594**	0.374	0.254	0.291
Style Transferring	0.376	**0.657**	0.139	0.231

4.6 Image Sample Size Effect

Generative models are data-driven and the performance highly depending on the sample size. The EyeNet dataset we use contains 19496 retinal images with 1448 AMD images. In this section, We choose 338 drusen images as samples to test the size effect of GANs. Experiments show the difficulty of synthesizing high quality images rises along with the increase of the sample number. Figure 10 shows accuracy of successfully predicting synthesized images, but AMD slightly declines as the sample number increases. In general, the more samples used to train a generative, the harder it is to extract specific visual features for generative model, which requires images with similarity; this is difficult to achieve when it

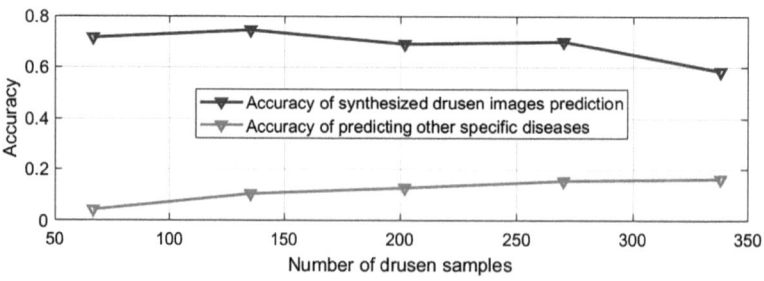

Fig. 10. Size effect of image samples and probability of predicting other specific diseases.

comes to biological traits. On the other hand, prediction error focuses on some specific diseases, and the probability of predicting these diseases rises when the sample number falls. The phenomenon implies that high dimensional features in the retinal images exist. Furthermore, with more sample images, we can more likely to detect the symptom. This is a pathological approach to reveal hidden relations among diseases.

4.7 Pathological Retinal Diseases Classification Inspired by Size Effect of GANs

With higher quality images and thriving computer vision skills, visible retinal disease symptoms can being detected and represented. Based on traditional classification, symptoms have pathological correlations among retinal diseases for ophthalmologist to use in diagnoses, as shown in Fig. 11. However, according to the discovery above, retinal diseases have hidden relation connected by invisible features. With GANs, we can propose a method to improve current classification. In this case, the classification could modified by the results of GANs as shown in Fig. 12.

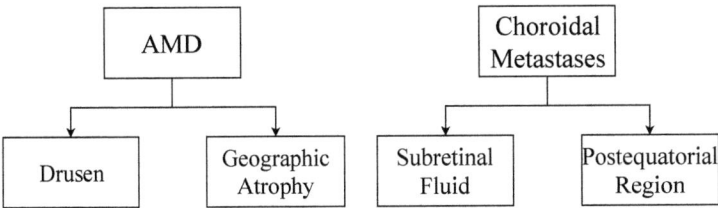

Fig. 11. Clinical hierarchical relationship of AMD and Choroidal metastases from [25, 26]. Drusen increase a person's risk of developing AMD; Geographic atrophy (GA) is an advanced form of age-related macular degeneration that can result in the progressive and irreversible loss of retina. Subretinal fluid and equatorial retina are significant features in choroidal metastases from clinical understanding.

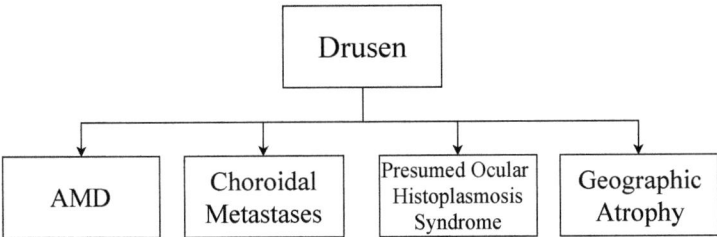

Fig. 12. Pathological Classification referring to GANs results. As a visual representation learned by deep network, Drusen are correlated to AMD (58.3%), Choroidal metastasis (5.12%), Presumed-ocular-histoplasmosis-syndrome (6.52%), and Pattern dystrophy (2.57%).

4.8 Neural Network Visualization for Retinal Images

Finally, we verified the hypothesis that vessel-based segmentation and contrast enhancement are two coherent features to decide the type of retinal diseases. Using techniques of generating CAMs introduced in [8], we visualized feature maps of the final convolutional layer of ResNet50 in Fig. 13. In our results, generated drusen images are well identified. However, generated GA images are not focused on the exact location of the symptom, but they are close. As discussed above, in the clinical diagnosis process, "vessel patterns" and "fundus structure"

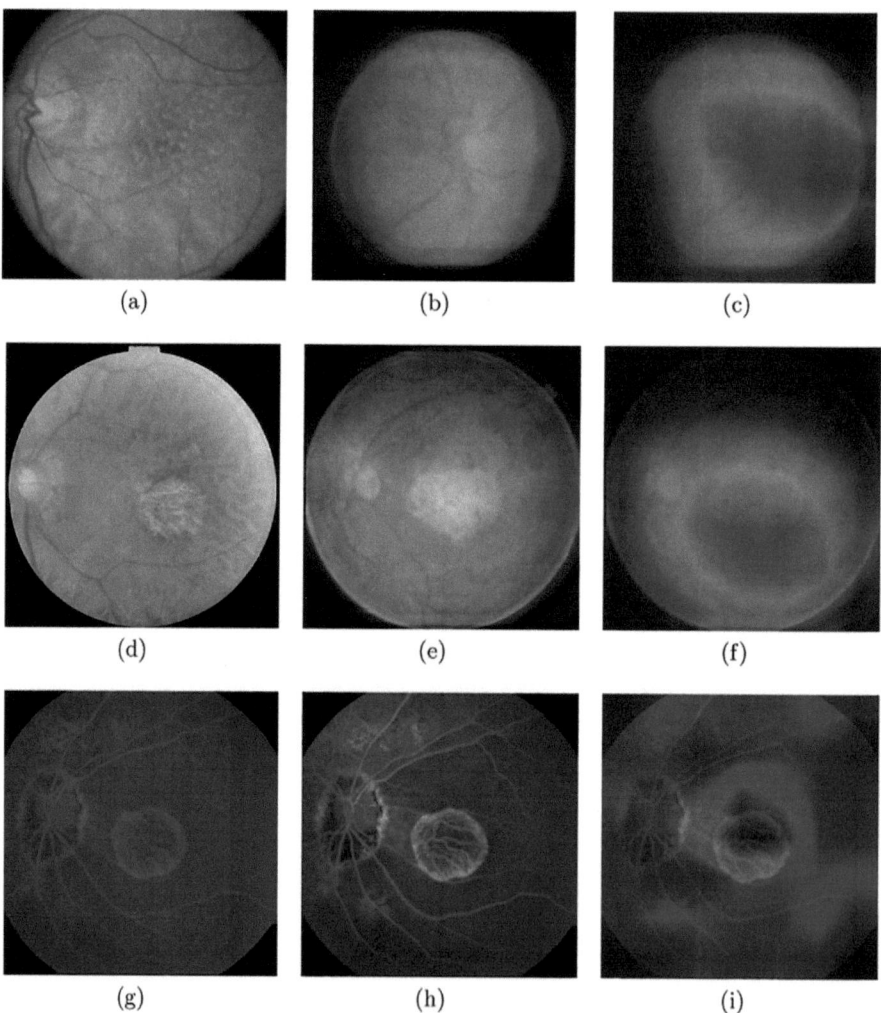

Fig. 13. Generated images and their CAMs. (a) Original drusen image (CFP). (b) Generated image of (a) by WGANs. (c) CAM of (b). (d) Original GA image (CFP). (e) Generated image of (d) by WGANs. (f) CAM of (e). (g) Original GA image (FA). (h) Generated image of (g) by style transferring. (i) CAM of (g).

are the most crucial features for identifying the symptoms of different diseases. These types of features cover more than 80% of retinal diseases [27,28].

5 Conclusions and Future Work

We have implemented style transferring, DCGANs and WGANs to generate disease images that are detailed to capture different stages of AMD. Symptoms of images are drusen and GA; both FA and CFP images are generated. Images from DCGANs are difficult to be identified due to limit of resolution. However, images from style transferring and WGANs are easier to identify by ophthalmologists, and generated images preserve pathological details. EyeNet is used to predict the disease label, and results of generated drusen images are similar to original images. However, generated GA images are more distant compared to original images, because of the small number of GA images used during training EyeNet. This phenomenon shows that generated new images can be fed into the classifier to improve it. Also, CAMs are useful for extracting label-specific features. In Fig. 13(c), (f) and (i), warmer color parts are located in the well-demarcated areas or spots, which represents disease features that are close to those parts.

In this paper, only a small number of disease images are synthesized and evaluated, so various images can be tested and enhanced further. Furthermore, different kinds of skills like semantic segmentation can be merged into the original GANs framework. With better and diverse generated images, classifier can be trained robustly and applied to predict the disease more precisely. Above all, a re-trained network discovers hidden relationships and provides ophthalmologists with useful disease features warranting further investigation.

References

1. Goodfellow, I., et al.: Generative adversarial nets. In: Advances in Neural Information Processing Systems, pp. 2672–2680 (2014)
2. Luan, F., Paris, S., Shechtman, E., Bala, K.: Deep photo style transfer. CoRR, abs/1703.07511 **2** (2017)
3. Li, Y., Fang, C., Yang, J., Wang, Z., Lu, X., Yang, M.H.: Universal style transfer via feature transforms. In: Guyon, I., Luxburg, U.V., Bengio, S., Wallach, H., Fergus, R., Vishwanathan, S., Garnett, R. (eds.) Advances in Neural Information Processing Systems 30, pp. 386–396. Curran Associates, Inc. (2017)
4. Salehinejad, H., Valaee, S., Dowdell, T., Colak, E., Barfett, J.: Generalization of deep neural networks for chest pathology classification in x-rays using generative adversarial networks. In: IEEE International Conference on Acoustics, Speech and Signal Processing (ICASSP), pp. 990–994. IEEE (2018)
5. Klein, R., Klein, B.E., Knudtson, M.D., Meuer, S.M., Swift, M., Gangnon, R.E.: Fifteen-year cumulative incidence of age-related macular degeneration: the beaver dam eye study. Ophthalmology **114**, 253–262 (2007)
6. Green, W.R., McDonnell, P.J., Yeo, J.H.: Pathologic features of senile macular degeneratlon. Ophthalmology **92**, 615–627 (1985)
7. Gheorghe, A., Mahdi, L., Musat, O.: Age-related macular degeneration. Rom. J. Ophthalmol. **59**, 74–77 (2015)

8. Zhou, B., Khosla, A., Lapedriza, À., Oliva, A., Torralba, A.: Learning deep features for discriminative localization. In: CVPR (2016)
9. Yang, C.H.H., et al.: A novel hybrid machine learning model for auto-classification of retinal diseases. arXiv preprint arXiv:1806.06423 (2018)
10. Arjovsky, M., Chintala, S., Bottou, L.: Wasserstein generative adversarial networks. In: International Conference on Machine Learning, pp. 214–223 (2017)
11. Pumarola, A., Agudo, A., Martinez, A.M., Sanfeliu, A., Moreno-Noguer, F.: GANimation: Anatomically-Aware Facial Animation from a Single Image. In: Ferrari, V., Hebert, M., Sminchisescu, C., Weiss, Y. (eds.) ECCV 2018. LNCS, vol. 11214, pp. 835–851. Springer, Cham (2018). https://doi.org/10.1007/978-3-030-01249-6_50
12. Fan, H., Su, H., Guibas, L.J.: A point set generation network for 3D object reconstruction from a single image. In: CVPR, vol. 2, p. 6 (2017)
13. Qian, X., et al.: Pose-normalized image generation for person re-identification. arXiv preprint arXiv:1712.02225 (2017)
14. Radford, A., Metz, L., Chintala, S.: Unsupervised representation learning with deep convolutional generative adversarial networks. arXiv preprint arXiv:1511.06434 (2015)
15. Gatys, L.A., Ecker, A.S., Bethge, M.: Image style transfer using convolutional neural networks. In: Proceedings of the IEEE Conference on Computer Vision and Pattern Recognition, pp. 2414–2423 (2016)
16. Li, Y., Liu, M.Y., Li, X., Yang, M.H., Kautz, J.: A closed-form solution to photorealistic image stylization. arXiv preprint arXiv:1802.06474 (2018)
17. Wang, X., Peng, Y., Lu, L., Lu, Z., Bagheri, M., Summers, R.M.: Chestx-ray8: hospital-scale chest x-ray database and benchmarks on weakly-supervised classification and localization of common thorax diseases. In: IEEE Conference on Computer Vision and Pattern Recognition (CVPR), pp. 3462–3471. IEEE (2017)
18. Staal, J., Abràmoff, M.D., Niemeijer, M., Viergever, M.A., Van Ginneken, B.: Ridge-based vessel segmentation in color images of the retina. TMI **23**, 501–509 (2004)
19. Retina Image Bank: A project from the American Society of Retina Specialists. http://imagebank.asrs.org/about. Accessed 30 June 2018
20. Beers, A., et al.: High-resolution medical image synthesis using progressively grown generative adversarial networks. arXiv preprint arXiv:1805.03144 (2018)
21. Guibas, J.T., Virdi, T.S., Li, P.S.: Synthetic medical images from dual generative adversarial networks. arXiv preprint arXiv:1709.01872 (2017)
22. Kaur, J., Mittal, D.: Segmentation and measurement of exudates in fundus images of the retina for detection of retinal disease. J. Biomed. Eng. Med. Imaging **2**, 27 (2015)
23. Yang, C.H.H., et al.: Auto-classification of retinal diseases in the limit of sparse data using a two-streams machine learning model. arXiv preprint arXiv:1808.05754 (2018)
24. Simonyan, K., Zisserman, A.: Very deep convolutional networks for large-scale image recognition. arXiv:1409.1556 (2014)
25. Coleman, H.R., Chan, C.C., Ferris, F.L., Chew, E.Y.: Age-related macular degeneration. Lancet **372**, 1835–1845 (2008)
26. Mewis, L., Young, S.E.: Breast carcinoma metastatic to the choroid: analysis of G7 patients. Ophthalmology **89**, 147–151 (1982)
27. Crick, R.P., Khaw, P.T.: A Textbook of Clinical Ophthalmology: A Practical Guide to Disorders of the Eyes and Their Management. World Scientific, Singapore (1998)
28. Akram, I., Rubinstein, A.: Common retinal signs. an overview. Optometry Today (2005)

Retinal Detachment Screening with Ensembles of Neural Network Models

Hiroki Masumoto(✉), Hitoshi Tabuchi, Shoto Adachi,
Shunsuke Nakakura, Hideharu Ohsugi, and Daisuke Nagasato

Department of Ophthalmology, Tsukazaki Hospital, Himeji, Japan
h.masumoto@tsukzaki-eye.net

Abstract. Rhegmatogenous retinal detachment is an important condition that should be diagnosed early. A previous study showed that normal eyes and eyes with rhegmatogenous retinal detachment could be distinguished using pseudo-ocular fundus color images obtained with the Optos camera. However, no study has used pseudo-ocular fundus color images to distinguish eyes without retinal detachment (not necessarily normal) and those with rhegmatogenous retinal detachment. Furthermore, the previous study used a single neural network with only three layers. In the current study, we trained and validated an ensemble model of a deep neural networks involving ultra-wide-field pseudocolor images to distinguish non-retinal detachment eyes (not necessarily normal) and rhegmatogenous retinal detachment eyes. The study included 600 non-retinal detachment, 693 bullous rhegmatogenous retinal detachment, and 125 non-bullous rhegmatogenous retinal detachment images. The sensitivity and specificity of the ensemble model (five models) were 97.3% and 91.5%, respectively. In sum, this study demonstrated promising results for a screening system for rhegmatogenous retinal detachment with high sensitivity and relatively high specificity.

Keywords: Retinal detachment · Neural network · Screening

1 Introduction

Rhegmatogenous retinal detachment (RRD) is an important concern in acute ophthalmologic clinics, and in the United States [1]. If the condition is treated early, the probability of successful treatment is high [2, 3]; however, if the condition is not treated early, proliferative vitreoretinopathy occurs, treatment becomes difficult, and the probability of cure remarkably reduces [4–6]. Early diagnosis of RRD leads to early treatment and greatly improves the chance of good visual function in the future.

RRD lesions do not occur in the macular region or vascular arcade, but in the periphery of the retina, unlike many retinal diseases [7]. Thus, a wide-range camera is required for the diagnosis of RRD. The Optos camera (Optos Co., Dunfermline, UK) is considered suitable for the diagnosis of RRD. A general non-mydriatic camera, such as AF-230 (Nidek Co., Aichi, Japan), obtains images at an angle of view of 45° and in the range of 100° to 120° using a panoramic image function. The Optos camera can obtain a pseudo-fundus color image in the range of 200° in a non-mydriatic state with a pupil diameter of 2 mm [8].

Many clinical applications of image diagnosis using machine learning have been reported. In the field of ophthalmology, work on fundus cameras and optical coherence tomography have been published [9–12].

A previous study [13] showed that normal and RRD eyes could be distinguished using pseudo-ocular fundus color images obtained with the Optos camera. However, no study has yet used pseudo-ocular fundus color images to distinguish non-retinal detachment (not necessarily normal) (non-RD) and RRD. Additionally, the previous study used a single neural network with three layers. The number of layers was lower in this network than in a network called AlexNet (five layers) reported in 2012 [14]. Moreover, a single model (not multiple models) was adopted, instead in this current study, we trained and validated an ensemble model of deep neural networks involving ultra-wide-field pseudocolor images to distinguish non-RD and RRD eyes.

2 Methods

2.1 Dataset

This study was performed in adherence to the guidelines of the Declaration of Helsinki. Ultra-wide-field pseudocolor images were obtained from the Tsukazaki Hospital Ophthalmologic Database between December 1, 2011 and July 8, 2018, and 600 other images randomly extracted from 3708 images were obtained between December 1, 2011 and May 27, 2018, all used in this study. Other images included images of eyes with age-related macular degeneration, retinal vein occlusion, glaucoma, a macular hole, and proliferative diabetic retinopathy.

For constructing the RD image screening system, the following three categories were set: non-RD, bullous rhegmatogenous retinal detachment (BRRD), and non-bullous rhegmatogenous retinal detachment (NBRRD). We used 600 non-RD, 693 BRRD, and 125 NBRRD images. A retinal specialist classified the RRD images into BRRD and NBRRD images (Fig. 1).

In this study, we performed verification using the k-fold method (k = 5). All data were classified into K groups. K-1 groups were used as training data, and the remaining group was used as test data. We applied a horizontal flip to all images and augmented the amount of training data by two times. Moreover, among nine types of image preprocesses (no conversion, no contrast, high contrast, low contrast, γ correction [$\gamma = 0.75, 1.5$], smoothing, histogram flattening, Gaussian noise, and salt and pepper noise), three preprocesses were randomly applied to the non-RD and BRRD images and the number of images eventually increased six times. All nine image preprocesses were applied to NBRRD images and the number of images eventually increased 18 times. Neural network models were then trained. Training of the neural network models was performed using augmented training images, and validation was performed using the test images. The processes of data augmentation, training, and validation were repeated k times, and all blocks were used as test data.

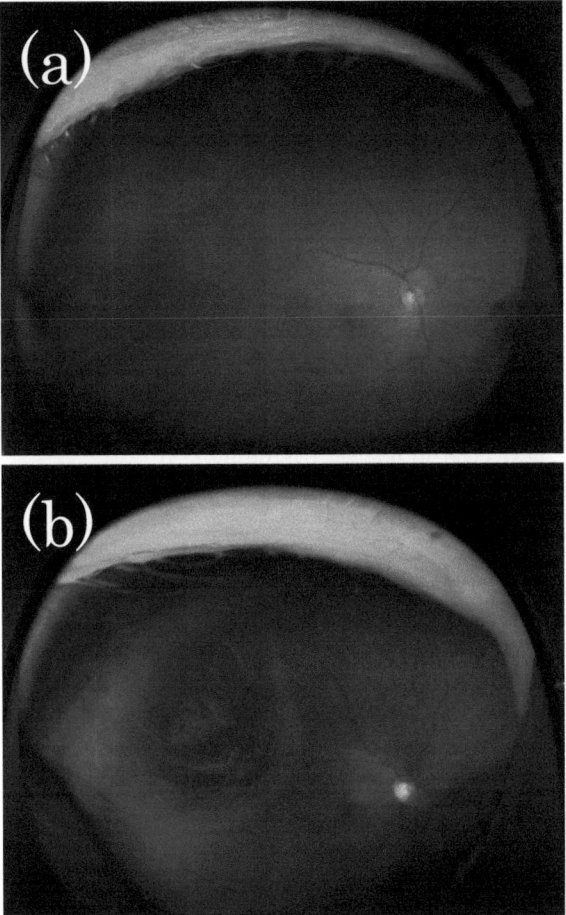

Fig. 1. Rhegmatogenous retinal detachment images. (a) Non-bullous rhegmatogenous retinal detachment. (b) Bullous rhegmatogenous retinal detachment

2.2 Model Construction

We constructed and trained nine different network structures (VGG16, VGG19, ResNet50, InceptionV3, InceptionResNetV2, Xception, DenseNet121, DenseNet169, and DenseNet201) [15–20]. We then validated each model with the test data. All models included layers that captured the features of images and layers that classified based on features. First, image files (3072 × 3900 pixels × 3 ch [RGB]) were converted to 192 × 256 pixels as input and saved as jpeg files. We read the jpeg files again and set them with a tensor of 192 × 256 pixel × 3 channels comprising an integer of 0–255. We then normalized the tensor from 0 to 1.

This work used an ensemble of models for deciding RRD. The final decision rule for the system with regard to deciding RRD was that it was considered that even when one of the n models identified an image as an RRD image, the diagnosis of the ensemble model was RRD.

The layers that captured the image features were mainly a convolutional layer and max-pooling layers [21–23]. Alternatively, by extracting the maximum value within the range of the kernel, the max-pooling layer helps with invariance [24]. Furthermore, in ResNet50 and other models, residual learning was performed so that the original features of the image can be retained even as the layer becomes deep [16].

The classification layer included a flatten operation, fully connected layer, and dropout layer. The flatten operation prepares for classification by flattening a three-dimensional tensor in a single dimension. The fully connected layer is a layer that implements classification logic from feature vectors already obtained from previous layers [14]. The dropout layer is a layer that drops a part of the information that is transferred to the next layer to prevent overfitting [25].

The training used momentum SGD (with learning coefficient = 0.001, inertia term = 0.9) [26, 27], which is one of the stochastic gradient descent methods. The loss function used was categorical-crossentropy.

We used fine-tuning, which uses different data and learned parameters in advance. This method increases the learning speed and makes it easy to achieve high performance even with limited data [28]. The parameters obtained by learning (Imagenet) were used as initial values of parameters, except the fully connected layer.

The construction and validation of the model were implemented using keras (https://keras.io/en/) with tensorflow (https://www.tensorflow.org/) as backend. Training and validation of the model were performed using an NVIDIA GeForce GTX 1080 Ti graphics-processing unit.

2.3 Performance Evaluation in a Single Model

In this study, the evaluation was based on whether non-RD and RRD could be discriminated (i.e., the difference between BRRD and NBRRD was not considered).

We calculated the sensitivity and specificity of each model. In addition, the sum of sensitivity and specificity was defined as model score (MS). We examined which model had the highest MS. The MS was calculated as follows:

$$MS = Sensitivity + Specificity. \tag{1}$$

2.4 Performance Evaluation in an Ensemble Model

We used a score of sensitivity called MS (for model score) originally created for this study, to measure the sensitivity of each model compared to the average of the other models (see below). N models were used in consecutive order from the highest MS model. Among the RRD images, the proportion of those correctly identified as RRD images was defined as sensitivity$_{(n)}$ (even by one of the n models). Additionally, among the non-RD images, the proportion of those identified as non-RD images was defined as specificity$_{(n)}$. Furthermore, MS$_{(n)}$ was calculated using the following equation:

$$MS_{(n)} = \frac{Sensitivity_{(n)} - Average(Sensitivity_{(n)})}{SE(Sensitivity_{(n)})} + \frac{Specificity_{(n)} - Average(Specificity_{(n)})}{SE(Specificity_{(n)})}. \quad (2)$$

$$Average(Sensitivity_{(n)}) = \frac{1}{8}\sum_{k=2}^{9} Sensitivity_{(k)}. \quad (3)$$

$$SE(Sensitivity_{(n)}) = \sqrt{\frac{1}{8}\sum_{k=2}^{9}(Sensitivity_{(k)} - Average(Sensitivity_{(n)}))^2}. \quad (4)$$

$$Average(Specificity_{(n)}) = \frac{1}{8}\sum_{k=2}^{9} Specificity_{(k)}. \quad (5)$$

$$SE(Specificity_{(n)}) = \sqrt{\frac{1}{8}\sum_{k=2}^{9}(Specificity_{(k)} - Average(Specificity_{(n)}))^2}. \quad (6)$$

2.5 Statistical Analysis

The confidence interval for the MS score was not reported here since it is relatively new. All statistical analyses were performed using Python Scipy and statsmodel library.

3 Results

3.1 Performance Evaluation of a Single Model

Table 1 shows the MS, sensitivity, and specificity in descending order of the MS. The DenseNet201 model was found to have the highest MS.

Table 1. The model score, sensitivity, and specificity of each model.

Model	Model score	Sensitivity	Specificity
DenseNet201	1.912318663	0.93398533	0.978333333
VGG19	1.905876121	0.942542787	0.963333333
DenseNet169	1.905207824	0.935207824	0.97
DenseNet121	1.898871231	0.920537897	0.978333333
VGG16	1.898096985	0.936430318	0.961666667
ResNet50	1.891984515	0.930317848	0.961666667
InceptionV3	1.870207824	0.935207824	0.935
InceptionResNetV2	1.830199674	0.898533007	0.931666667
Xception	1.817868786	0.909535452	0.908333333

The DenseNet201 model has the highest model score.

Table 2. Sensitivity for BRRD and NBRRD images in each model.

Model	BRRD	NBRRD
DenseNet121	0.962	0.688
DenseNet169	0.973	0.728
DenseNet201	0.968	0.744
InceptionResNetV2	0.941	0.664
InceptionV3	0.971	0.736
ResNet50	0.964	0.744
VGG16	0.974	0.728
VGG19	0.977	0.752
Xception	0.947	0.704

The sensitivity for BRRD images is higher than that for NBRRD images.

Table 2 shows the sensitivity on dividing RRD into BRRD and NBRRD in each model. We found that the sensitivity for BRRD images was higher than that for NBRRD images.

3.2 Performance Evaluation of Multiple Models

Table 3 and Fig. 2 present the models, $MS_{(n)}$, sensitivity$_{(n)}$, and specificity$_{(n)}$ at n = 2–9. The MS was the highest at n = 5, and the sensitivity and specificity were 97.3% and 91.5%, respectively.

Table 3. Sensitivity, specificity, and model score when using an ensemble of n models.

n	Model	Sensitivity	Specificity	Model score
2	['DenseNet201', 'VGG19']	0.963	0.950	−0.484
3	['DenseNet201', 'VGG19', 'DenseNet169']	0.967	0.935	−0.155
4	['DenseNet201', 'VGG19', 'DenseNet169', 'DenseNet121']	0.969	0.928	0.143
5	['DenseNet201', 'VGG19', 'DenseNet169', 'DenseNet121', 'VGG16']	0.973	0.915	0.510
6	['DenseNet201', 'VGG19', 'DenseNet169', 'DenseNet121', 'VGG16', 'ResNet50']	0.974	0.902	0.422
7	['DenseNet201', 'VGG19', 'DenseNet169', 'DenseNet121', 'VGG16', 'ResNet50', 'InceptionV3']	0.976	0.878	0.097
8	['DenseNet201', 'VGG19', 'DenseNet169', 'DenseNet121', 'VGG16', 'ResNet50', 'InceptionV3', 'InceptionResNetV2']	0.978	0.848	−0.158
9	['DenseNet201', 'VGG19', 'DenseNet169', 'DenseNet121', 'VGG16', 'ResNet50', 'InceptionV3', 'InceptionResNetV2', 'Xception']	0.980	0.820	−0.374

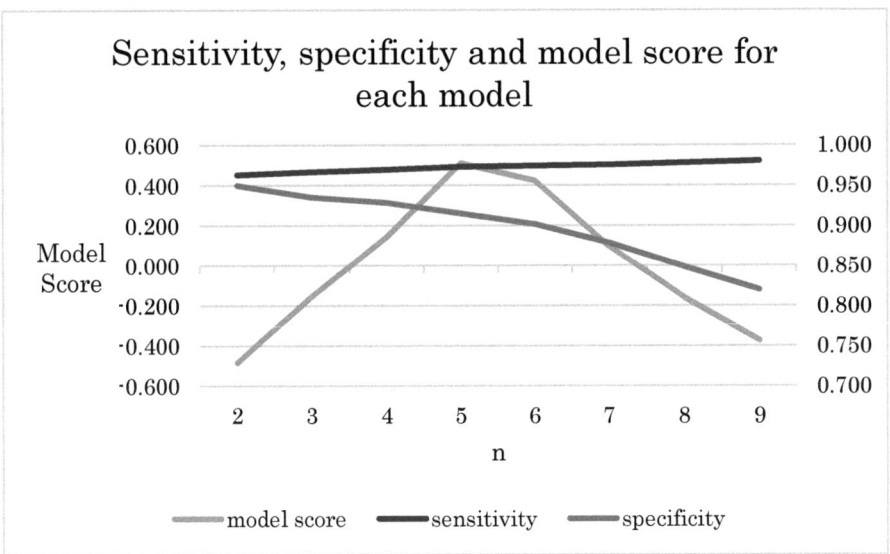

Fig. 2. Sensitivity, specificity, and model score when using n models. The *left* vertical axis shows the model score, while the *right* vertical axis shows the sensitivity and specificity. The model score is the highest at n = 5.

4 Discussion

We developed a RRD screening system involving ensembles of model. With regard to deciding RRD, it was considered that even when one of the n models identified an image as an RRD image, the diagnosis of the ensemble model was RRD. As this study attempted to construct a screening system, it was important for an ensemble model to identify RRD as easily as possible. Additionally, the specificity was required to be relatively high. As it is difficult to use the area under the receiver operating characteristic (ROC) curve as an evaluation approach for an ensemble model, we believe it important to used the MS described above. The use of the sum of sensitivity and specificity is an approach that has been adopted in a previous study that described a method to calculate the Youden Index from the ROC curve [29].

We initially classified BRRD, NBRRD, and non-RD and then considered NBRRD and BRRD as RRD. As there is no difference in the necessity of clinic visit between NBRRD and BRRD [30], there is no need to consider BRRD and NBRRD separately in a screening system. However, we thought that the diversity of images would be too large when considering NBRRD and BRRD together as one category (RRD). As shown in Fig. 1, BRRD had many green pixels at the lesion (pseudo-ocular fundus color image). The difference between an NBRRD lesion and a normal lesion is smaller than the difference between a BRRD lesion and a normal lesion. Additionally, the characteristics of RRD are diverse, and a neural network may not be able to capture the features of RD when NBRRD and BRRD are not considered together as an input. We assumed that the sensitivity for NBRRD would be lower than that for BRRD considering the small difference between an NBRRD lesion and a normal lesion, and in fact, we found that the sensitivity for NBRRD (72.1%) was lower than that for BRRD (96.4%).

The current study has some limitations. First, this study involved a retrospective data search in a single facility. Thus, it will be necessary in the future to evaluate the robustness of the model through prospective examination of data from other facilities. Second, based on work reported in the American Academy of Ophthalmology [1], the number of images in our study for testing was relatively modest (about 800) compared to other previous research which may have involved several hundreds of thousands of images [31]. Nevertheless, to our knowledge, no large-scale examinations have been performed during ultra-wide-field pseudocolor imaging and we believe that this number is adequate considering it is the first study of its kind. Third, the number of NBRRD images was particularly low, and the rate of overlooking NBRRD was high. This will have to be addressed in the future.

5 Conclusion

We developed a promising screening system for RRD with high sensitivity and relatively high specificity. In the future we will address limitations and disadvantages of this system and add necessary functions for utilization in actual clinical situations.

References

1. https://www.aao.org/eyenet/article/malpractice-risk-retinal-detachments
2. Miki, D., Hida, T., Hotta, K., Shinoda, K., Hirakata, A.: Comparison of scleral buckling and vitrectomy for retinal detachment resulting from flap tears in superior quadrants. Jpn. J. Ophthalmol. **45**, 187–191 (2001)
3. Heussen, N., Feltgen, N., Walter, P., Hoerauf, H., Hilgers, R.D., Heimann, H., SPR Study Group: Scleral buckling versus primary vitrectomy in rhegmatogenous retinal detachment study (SPR Study): predictive factors for functional outcome. Study report no. 6. Graefes Arch. Clin. Exp. Ophthalmol. **249**, 1129–1136 (2011)
4. Lean, J.S., Silicone Study Group, et al.: Vitrectomy with silicone oil or sulfur hexafluoride gas in eyes with severe proliferative vitreoretinopathy: results of a randomized clinical trial. Silicone Study Report 1. Arch. Ophthalmol. **110**, 770–779 (1992)
5. Azen, S., Silicone Study Group, et al.: Vitrectomy with silicone oil or sulfur hexafluoride gas in eyes with severe proliferative vitreoretinopathy: results of a randomized clinical trial. Silicone Study Report 2. Arch. Ophthalmol. **110**, 780–792 (1992)
6. Scott, I.U., Flynn Jr., H.W., Murray, T.G., Feuer, W.J., Perfluoron Study Group: Outcomes of surgery for retinal detachment associated with proliferative vitreoretinopathy using perfluoro-n-octane: a multicenter study. Am. J. Ophthalmol. **136**, 454–463 (2003)
7. Machemer, R., Aaberg, T.M., Freeman, H.M., Irvine, A.R., Lean, J.S., Michels, R.M.: An updated classification of retinal detachment with proliferative vitreoretinopathy. Am. J. Ophthalmol. **112**, 159–165 (1991)
8. Hu, Z., Liu, Q., Paulus, Y.M.: New Frontiers in retinal imaging. Int. J. Ophthalmic Res. **2**, 148–158 (2016)

9. Gulshan, V., et al.: Development and validation of a deep learning algorithm for detection of diabetic retinopathy in retinal fundus photographs. JAMA **316**, 2402–2410 (2016)
10. De Fauw, J., et al.: Clinically applicable deep learning for diagnosis and referral in retinal disease. Nat. Med. **24**, 1342 (2018)
11. Burlina, P.M., et al.: Automated grading of age-related macular degeneration from color fundus images using deep convolutional neural networks. JAMA ophthalmol. **135**(11), 1170–1176 (2017)
12. Burlina, P.M., Joshi, N., Pacheco, K.D., Freund, D.E., Kong, J., Bressler, N.M.: Use of deep learning for detailed severity characterization and estimation of 5-year risk among patients with age-related macular degeneration. JAMA ophthalmol. **136**, 1359–1366 (2018)
13. Ohsugi, H., Tabuchi, H., Enno, H., Ishitobi, N.: Accuracy of deep learning, a machine-learning technology, using ultra-wide-field fundus ophthalmoscopy for detecting rhegmatogenous retinal detachment. Sci. Rep. **7**, 9425 (2017)
14. Krizhevsky, A., Sutskever, I., Hinton, G.E.: ImageNet classification with deep convolutional neural networks. In: Advances in Neural Information Processing Systems, pp. 1097–1105 (2012)
15. Simonyan, K., Andrew, Z.: Very deep convolutional networks for large-scale image recognition. Preprint https://arxiv.org/pdf/1409.1556.pdf (2014)
16. He, K., Zhang, X., Ren, S., Sun, J.: Deep residual learning for image recognition. In: Proceedings of the IEEE Conference on Computer Vision and Pattern Recognition, pp. 770–778 (2016)
17. Huang, G., Liu, Z., Van Der Maaten, L., Weinberger, K.Q.: Densely connected convolutional networks. In: CVPR, vol. 1, p. 2 (2017)
18. Szegedy, C., Vanhoucke, V., Ioffe, S., Shlens, J., Wojna, Z.: Rethinking the inception architecture for computer vision. In: Proceedings of the IEEE Conference on Computer Vision and Pattern Recognition, pp. 2818–2826 (2016)
19. Szegedy, C., Ioffe, S., Vanhoucke, V., Alemi, A.A.: Inception-v4, inception-resnet and the impact of residual connections on learning. In: AAAI, vol. 4, p. 12 (2017)
20. Chollet, F.: Deep learning with depthwise separable convolutions. Preprint https://arxiv.org/pdf/1610.02357.pdf
21. Deng, J., Dong, W., Socher, R., Li, L.J., Li, K., Fei-Fei, L.: ImageNet: a large-scale hierarchical image database. In: CVPR, pp. 248–255 (2009)
22. Russakovsky, O., et al.: ImageNet large scale visual recognition challenge. Int. J. Comput. Vision **115**, 211–252 (2015)
23. Lee, C.Y., Xie, S., Gallagher, P., Zhang, Z., Tu, Z.: Deeply-supervised nets. In: AISTATS, vol. 2, p. 5 (2015)
24. Scherer, D., Müller, A., Behnke, S.: Evaluation of pooling operations in convolutional architectures for object recognition. In: Diamantaras, K., Duch, W., Iliadis, L.S. (eds.) ICANN 2010. LNCS, vol. 6354, pp. 92–101. Springer, Heidelberg (2010). https://doi.org/10.1007/978-3-642-15825-4_10
25. Srivastava, N., Hinton, G., Krizhevsky, A., Sutskever, I., Salakhutdinov, R.: Dropout: a simple way to prevent neural networks from overfitting. J. Mach. Learn. Res. **15**, 1929–1958 (2014)
26. Qian, N.: On the momentum term in gradient descent learning algorithms. Neural Netw. **12**, 145–151 (1999)
27. Nesterov, Y.: A method for unconstrained convex minimization problem with the rate of convergence $O(1/k^2)$. Doklady AN USSR. **269**, 543–547 (1983)

28. Agrawal, P., Girshick, R., Malik, J.: Analyzing the performance of multilayer neural networks for object recognition. In: Fleet, D., Pajdla, T., Schiele, B., Tuytelaars, T. (eds.) ECCV 2014. LNCS, vol. 8695, pp. 329–344. Springer, Cham (2014). https://doi.org/10.1007/978-3-319-10584-0_22
29. Schisterman, E.F., Faraggi, D., Reiser, B., Hu, J.: Youden index and the optimal threshold for markers with mass at zero. Stat. Med. **27**, 297–315 (2008)
30. Kang, H.K., Luff, A.J.: Management of retinal detachment: a guide for non-ophthalmologists. BMJ **336**, 1235–1240 (2008)
31. Grassmann, F., et al.: A deep learning algorithm for prediction of age-related eye disease study severity scale for age-related macular degeneration from color fundus photography. Ophthalmology **125**, 1410–1420 (2018)

Recent Developments of Retinal Image Analysis in Alzheimer's Disease and Potential AI Applications

Delia Cabrera DeBuc[✉] and Edmund Arthur

Bascom Palmer Eye Institute, University of Miami Miller School of Medicine, Miami, USA
dcabrera2@med.miami.edu

Abstract. Alzheimers disease (AD) is the most common progressive neurodegenerative illness and cause of dementia in the elderly. The critical barriers for primary prevention in AD are the lack of rapid, non-invasive, sensitive and low-cost biomarkers. As the eye and brain share essential structural and pathogenic pathways, non-invasive eye biomarkers could be identified to obtain new insights into the onset and progression of AD and its complications in the eye. In this short review, recent developments of retinal image analysis in AD and potential artificial intelligence (AI) applications are presented. Some approaches are still very much novel research techniques, others are more established and transitioning into the clinical diagnostic arena. Together they provide us with the capability to move AD detection research forwards by using novel peripheral biomarkers.

1 Introduction

Alzheimers disease (AD) is the most common progressive neurodegenerative illness and cause of dementia in the elderly [1]. The two most important causes of the progressive brain nerve cell death in AD are plaques and tangles that accumulate in the brain. The plaques are made of a protein known as beta-amyloid that accumulates between the dying brain cells. The tangles are made of another protein called tau that accumulates within the brain nerve cells. The critical barriers for primary prevention in AD are the lack of rapid, non-invasive, sensitive and low-cost biomarkers. Previous studies have suggested that AD initiates decades before it is clinically expressed [2]. Therefore, it would be possible to identify persons who will ultimately show the disease long before the early symptoms appear as well as to target potential interventions to prevent AD expression in such individuals at high risk.

The routine clinical detection of AD is based on cognitive measures used in neuropsychological tests. However, this type of clinical assessment is a limited approach for those people with considerable brain or cognitive reserve. Also, different biomarkers and imaging modalities have played a key role in increasing our knowledge of AD, its associated mechanisms, and pathways. However, measures of brain biochemistry and anatomy using molecular markers or advanced imaging techniques are not surrogates for cognitive processing and especially not for psychological function. Current procedures, such as neuroimaging methods (e.g., magnetic resonance imaging (MRI) and positron emission tomography (PET)), as well as protein levels (e.g., tau and amyloid) derived from cerebrospinal fluid (CSF) sampling tests, are very high-priced and extremely invasive. They also lack in specificity and are not readily accessible to most clinicians and affected individuals.

As the eye and brain share important structural and pathogenic pathways, non-invasive eye biomarkers could be identified to obtain new insights into the onset and progression of AD and its complications in the eye. The link between eye pathology and AD has been established in multiple studies [3]. The neuronal loss in AD associated with optic nerve parameters includes retinal ganglion cells (RGCs). These cells are like neurons in the cerebral cortex and have been correlated to neurodegeneration in AD. Patients with AD often have symptoms affecting visual function, including loss of best-corrected visual acuity (BCVA), reduced contrast sensitivity, ocular motility abnormalities, and color vision defects [3].

This short review offers an insight into the methodologies available for investigating AD detection using retinal image analysis as well as showcase potential AI applications. Some approaches are still very much novel research techniques, others are more established and transitioning into the clinical diagnostic arena. Together they provide us with the capability to move AD detection research forwards by using novel peripheral biomarkers. These approaches could allow us to further characterize eye-brain signatures that may facilitate a more comprehensive assessment of the effect of cognitive impairment on ocular and cerebral function at the early stage of AD.

2 The Role of the Retinal Tissue and Ophthalmic Imaging in Alzheimers Disease

The retina and optic nerve, considered to be part of the central nervous system (CNS), prolong from the diencephalon during their embryonic development [4,5]. The retina contains various neural elements, which are interconnected with each other and play a crucial role in visual processing. Also, the vasculature network of the retina shares certain features with the brain vasculature network because both complexes must provide sufficient levels of oxygen and substrates to the large demand of the tissues supplied [5]. Moreover, the blood-retina barrier is very like its cerebral counterpart. Lastly, both the retinal and cerebral microcirculation have an autoregulation mechanism that can control vascular resistance in face of changing systemic blood pressure to maintain constant blood flow [5].

Current techniques and imaging developments in ophthalmology have allowed a more precise visualization of the various retinal layers and its microcirculation noninvasively, providing a microscope to investigate the brain microcirculation [4,6]. Consequently, imaging of the eye is increasingly investigated as a potential tool for discovering ocular biomarkers of primarily non-ophthalmic disorders, ranging from neurovascular and neurodegenerative diseases to cardiovascular disease [4]. Numerous studies have revealed that many brain diseases like AD could be reflected in retinal alterations, and therefore could also be correlated with structural changes in the retinal neural layers and microvasculature [4]. It has been hypothesized that if an association can be made between the amyloid in the brain and the amyloid in the eye, then it would be feasible to diagnose AD by looking into the eye. This evidence has progressively accumulated, supporting the hypothesis that the retina may be a window to the brain [4,7,8].

The link between retina pathology and a variety of neurodegenerative and cerebrovascular diseases has been established in various studies [4]. Particularly, this link reinforces the use of retinal vessels as biomarkers to assess the condition of the cerebral vessels supplying the neurons in the brain. Therefore, examining pathologic alterations of the retinal tissue may be valuable for understanding the etiology of AD. Also, it has been shown that the initial pathology of AD may originate in the visual association area where visual function integrates with other areas of the brain [7]. In this perspective, retinal imaging can possibly provide an affordable and faster option, potentially replacing or complementing the current expensive neuroimaging methods.

3 Retinal Imaging Technologies and Applications in AD

The continuous innovations in optical imaging technologies have made it easier to obtain retinal images with high-quality, even without pupillary dilation. These developments have lately pointed to consider retinal imaging technology as a helpful tool for diagnosing acute medical, neuro-ophthalmologic, and neurologic conditions. As a result, several population-based studies have used retinal imaging to relate ophthalmic abnormalities to the risk of hypertension, subclinical and clinical stroke, renal dysfunction, cardiovascular mortality and cognitive impairment. These epidemiologic studies were generally based on the assessment of big retinal vessels with diameters greater than $70\,\mu$ using a conventional fundus camera. Nonetheless, recent advancements in optical imaging have increased the field of view of ocular fundus cameras, typically to capture an ultra-wide field (UWF) image (200°), and allow the evaluation of smaller retinal vessels. One of the current devices taking advantage of UWF imaging capabilities are the Optos (Marlborough, MA) retinal imaging devices and Heidelberg Engineering (Carlsbad, CA), which recently introduced a noncontact UWF module that attaches easily to any Spectralis or HRA2 camera head [9]. Furthermore, Optical coherence tomography (OCT), one of the most widely used ophthalmic decision-making technologies, has revolutionized the diagnosis and treatment of ocular disease [6]. This technology utilizes retro-reflected light to provide micron-resolution, cross-sectional scans of biological tissues.

One of the latest ophthalmic imaging developments, Optical coherence angiography (OCA), facilitates the assessment of small vessel abnormalities (capillary dropout) without the need for dye injection [10–13]. Also, imaging potentials of wide-field OCT-based microangiography (OMAG) have been reported for evaluating the intraretinal layers, retinal pigment epithelium, choriocapillaris and the vitreous cavity [14]. Adaptive optics retinal cameras and adaptive optics OCT can also facilitate the assessment of noninvasive imaging of the retinal capillary network and visualize both cone and rod photoreceptors [15–17]. In contrast to the conventional intensity-based OCT technology, Polarization-Sensitive Optical Coherence Tomography provides quantitative information of the retinal tissue by taking advantage of the tissue-specific contrast because of the light- polarization state changes [18].

3.1 Retinal Imaging in AD

Although dementia of Alzheimers type is a disease attributed to pathology observed in the brain, recent studies have shown that there is evidence of visual problems in the early stages of AD due to dysfunction in the visual cortex. This evidence has motivated clinicians working with ophthalmic imaging to explore the potential associations between the eye and brain in AD. Most cross-sectional and longitudinal studies have reported cognitive impairment consistently to be associated with retinal abnormalities [19–33]. Typical retinal abnormalities that have been correlated with worse cognitive functioning in MCI subjects and AD patients include arteriolar narrowing and venular widening, scarcer vasculature and suboptimal bifurcation angles as well as suboptimal junctional branching coefficients, thinning of the nerve fiber layer (NFL), changes in macular volume, degeneration of both the retinal ganglion cell (RGC) and optic nerve, and retinal angiopathy involving reduced blood flow and vascular structural alterations [20,34]. According to the reported studies, the retina may be used as an objective biomarker by which it is possible to assess early microvascular and neurodegenerative changes in dementias and it may also provide some clues regarding the microvascular mechanisms of the diseases. However, further investigation using larger cohorts with well-controlled confounding variables is still required to assess the potential use of retinal imaging for detecting and tracking the evolution of AD.

3.2 Novel Applications of Retinal Imaging in AD

A variety of novel applications of retinal imaging in AD have been reported. NeuroVision LLC., has been developing tests to detect amyloid beta plaques in the eye [35,36]. The Retinal Amyloid Index test (NeuroVision, LLC) utilizes a device that looks and functions similarly to a conventional retinal imaging scanner and a curcumin compound, administered orally to the patient, to detect amyloid plaques in the retina [37]. Optina Diagnostics has developed a hyperspectral retinal camera able to collect and process the light intensity for a large number (225) of contiguous spectral bands at very high speeds [38]. The collection of sequential images of the retina using this camera allows for an in-depth understanding of the retinal tissue using spectral signatures. This imaging application also takes advantage of deep learning architectures to predict cerebral amyloid positron emission tomography (PET) status [39]. NeuroVisions and Optina Diagnostics tests are promising, but they are not yet confirmed as accurate, useful and concrete using larger data. Also, inclusion bodies have been identified with Blue Peak Autofluorescence (BAF) in the preclinical stage of Alzheimers disease using spectral domain OCT (Fig. 1) [40]. In this study, the inclusion bodies surface area was found to be increased as a function of cortical amyloid burden. A recent study reported a decrease in the volumes of the macular nerve fiber layer, outer nuclear layer, and inner plexiform layer in individuals with preclinical AD relative to controls [41].

Additional applications take advantage of ultra-wide field (UWF) imaging, polarization-based techniques and confocal scanning laser ophthalmoscopy (cSLO) [42–48]. These advanced imaging modalities allow a more comprehensive view and quantification of the retina compared to the traditional fundus photography [29,42]. For example, a cSLO multi-wavelength imaging prototype that can detect fluorescent-labelled cells has been used to assessing phases of cell death in a triple transgenic AD model [47]. Also, a recent study identified drusen-like regions and pigment dispersion in individuals with mild and advanced cognitive impairment by using a cSLO device (EasyScan, i-Optics Corporation, The Netherlands) without the need of an injected dye (Fig. 2) [48]. Interestingly, this study was designed to simultaneously obtain multiple retinal measures, such as structural and functional indicators of the retina. This specific design provided an opportunity to find and study the relationship between various pieces of information, such as the caliber, tortuosity, and network complexity of the retinal microvasculature (arteries and veins) with respect to functional features (e.g., contrast sensitivity, electrical response through ERGs), concomitant to both fractal vascular and neural analysis [48]. Moreover, larger foveal avascular zones and decreased outer retinal and choroidal flow rates compared with controls was found in patients with AD [49]. In another study, a lower density was observed for the retinal vascular superficial and deep plexuses in AD than in MCI subjects [50]. Also, retinal oximetry abnormalities have been reported in individuals with MCI and AD compared with a healthy cohort [51,52]. As Berisha et al. show in [28], there is a significant reduction in the blood flow rate of the retina using Doppler OCT in patients with AD when compared with control subjects, confirming the possible association between blood flow changes in the retina and the brain. Although different studies using dissimilar OCT scanners have reported contrasting trends in the retinal cellular layers using different anatomical landmarks in manufacturer and custom-built segmentation algorithms, our intend in this section is by no means a complete review of current information on OCT changes reported in correlation with AD.

4 Challenges of AI-Based Retinal Imaging Applications in AD

A great challenge exists to understanding how changes in the retinal neurovascular unit reflect neurovascular pathology in the brain, which seems to play a critical role to understand cerebral neurovascular pathogenesis. Another challenge is the variations in retinal structural and vascular features between individuals due to aging along with the existing confounding variables that may also result in retinal changes. Also, it has been reported that amyloid deposition can be identified among cognitively normal elderly persons during life and the prevalence of asymptomatic amyloid deposition may be like that of symptomatic amyloid deposition. An early study has shown that in a group of participants without clinically significant impairment, amyloid deposition was not associated with worse cognitive function, suggesting that an elderly person with a significant amyloid burden can remain cognitively normal [36]. Therefore, AI algorithms for retinal classification tasks using neuroimaging indicators for training should carefully consider potential pitfalls related to both confounding factors and asymptomatic amyloid deposition features.

The use of different ophthalmic instruments or technologies to collect imaging data for AI applications is another major limitation affecting the integration of big data in ophthalmology [53,54]. To demonstrate this limitation, we obtained fundus images from five individuals with type 2 diabetes mellitus (DM) using two different fundus cameras, and calculated specific caliber parameters using images from both devices. The instruments used were the EasyScan (EasyScan, i-Optics Corporation, The Netherlands) and the Retinal Function Imager (RFI; Optical Imaging, Rehovot, Israel). The RFI is an adapted traditional fundus camera for blood flow analysis. The EasyScan is a confocal scanning laser ophthalmoscopy (SLO) based retinal imaging system that can deliver contrast-rich images with a much greater depth of field than a fundus camera, even when faced with media opacities. The RFI and EasyScan images were exported and analyzed with the Singapore I Vessel Assessment (SIVA) software [55]. SIVA uses a semi-automated computer assisted vascular assessment program. After images were segmented, 6 vessels (3 arteries, 3 veins) were selected from the collection of segmented vessels. Then, five parameters (mean width, standard deviation of width, length/diameter ratio, simple tortuosity, and curvature tortuosity) were measured for these vessels. The comparability results between these two instruments was relatively low. The only parameters measured that displayed strong correlation coefficients were the mean vessel width (0.65) and simple tortuosity (0.79) (Fig. 3). Therefore, it is clear after this simple illustrative example that improved software analysis considering different imaging technologies and magnification correction factors would allow for better data structure and standardization once an efficient strategy is in place for better comparability between different imaging instruments.

The quality assurance of the data and algorithms precision to extract image-based features are additional important factors to consider when using retinal imaging in AI applications. A final imperative consideration is to carefully collect retinal imaging data from healthy subjects without subtle brain abnormalities. In general, it is unknown whether healthy subjects included in normative databases of retinal imaging devices may have focal discrete lesions (i.e. mild signs) in the brain without visible or detectable ocular manifestations (Fig. 4). Thus, caution should be exercised when considering normative data from retinal imaging, particularly if considering them for AI applications of non-ocular disease.

Additional aspects to be considered in the detection and evaluation of features for AI applications using retinal imaging are the differences in phenotyping, the velocity of disease development in patients, the disease duration and impact of age, the subclinical retinal damage, and the practicality of features to be confirmed in independent populations. Also, we note that the predictors at the population level may not apply to all individuals and that large-scale studies are frequently needed.

5 Potential Applications of Retinal Imaging-Based AI in AD

Retinal imaging-based AI methods could offer further accuracy in measurements as well as consistent data mining tools. The AIs applications in ophthalmology predominantly focuses on the diseases with a high rate, such as age-related or congenital cataract, diabetic retinopathy, glaucoma, age-related macular degeneration, and retinopathy of prematurity. Furthermore, automated methods developed till date mostly perform single tasks targeting the segmentation and classification of retinal vessels or specific retinal lesions independently. Although AI has been widely studied in image processing associated to ophthalmic images, mainly based on the fundus photographs, AI-assisted methods based on retinal images from individuals with cognitive impairment and other neurodegenerative diseases are currently emerging. For example, a machine learning approach, based on a non-invasive amyloid ligand-free hyperspectral retinal imaging method, was used to identify biomarkers correlating with the cerebral load of amyloid plaques determined with PET imaging [56]. In this study, a classifier was trained using 102 datasets (1–3 per subject) to establish the predictive value of those texture features, based on the cerebral amyloid status determined from binary reads by an expert rater on $_{18}$F-Florbetaben PET studies. A leave-one-out approach determined the sensitivity and specificity values of the method. The estimated sensitivity and specificity values of 85% and 93% (respectively) were achieved independently of cognition after extracting texture features of the spatial and spectral dimensions in segmented retinal vascular areas in a cohort (n = 40) including individuals with probable AD (n = 15) and age-matched controls (53–85 years) with no concomitant retinal diseases and without significant ocular media opacity [56].

Another study, outlined a methodology using fixed-grid wavelet networks for segmentation of the peripapillary retinal nerve fiber layer in OCT images from subjects with AD and healthy individuals [57]. However, this study only reported the methods used without an in-depth analysis and report of potential results obtained with only 28 images segmented from an unknown number of patients. In this study, different features of OCT images were extracted using a wrapper model. The image classification task was performed using back propagation and radial basis function without a proper disclosure of results to allow us to document the efficacy of the methodology used to classify OCT images in AD patients [57]. However, a more recent study from this group, have reported the same segmentation methodology for both OCT and MRI images (n = 100, 50 healthy and 50 AD images) with an estimated sensitivity and specificity values of 94.32% and 99.82% respectively [58]. A variety of features were extracted from MRI and OCT images. These features included the ellipticity, ratio between thickness calculation, curvature variance, salience variance, average number of regional minima in the gradient image inside the object, perimeter, and area

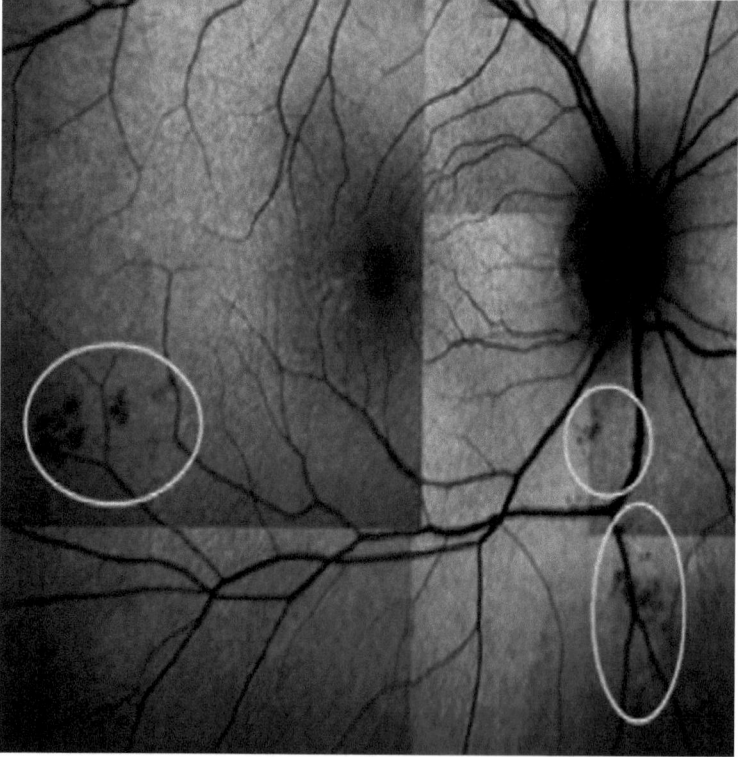

Fig. 1. Spectralis SD-OCT image showing inclusion bodies (circled in red ellipses) identified via Blue Peak autofluorescence (BAF) imaging in a high neocortical amyloid-beta load cognitively normal older adult [40]. (Color figure online)

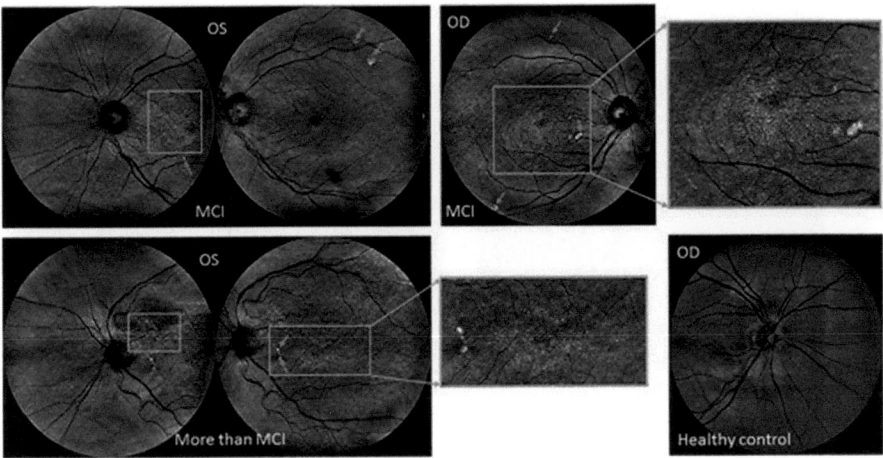

Fig. 2. Retinal topographical features observed in individuals with mild cognitive impairment. Top row: Central and nasal infrared light-images obtained from a female subject (79 years old) with MCI showing extramacular features such as drusen-like regions depicted by irregularly shaped bright spots in the periphery of the superior quadrant as well as with pigment dispersion in both eyes. Bottom image: Left- Central and nasal infrared light-images obtained from a female subject (81 years old) with MCI showing tortuous vessels, and extramacular features such as drusen-like regions along with pigment dispersion in the left eye. Right- Nasal infrared-light image obtained from a healthy control (71 years old). All images were acquired with the EasyScan Unit (i-Optics Corporation, The Netherlands). The red arrows indicate the location of the drusen and white spots observed at extramacular locations. The ROIs enclosed by the orange rectangles indicate the locations where pigment dispersion was observed. (Color figure online)

finding the second, third and fourth moments. The classification task rendered a true and false acceptance rate of 98.93% and 1.07% respectively [58].

There is no doubt that ophthalmic technologies could rely on artificial intelligence, and that a low-cost screening of AD using the eye could be introduced provided the methodology proves to be successful and scalable. However, the correct selection of the design for the AI applications utilizing either machine learning or deep learning approaches might offer some understanding into hidden configurations and features of the neurovascular retinal structures. This insight could not merely facilitate the automatic implementation of vessel segmentation, identification, and classification tasks but provide a more comprehensive pathophysiological information about the retinal changes concerning brain phenotypes in AD.

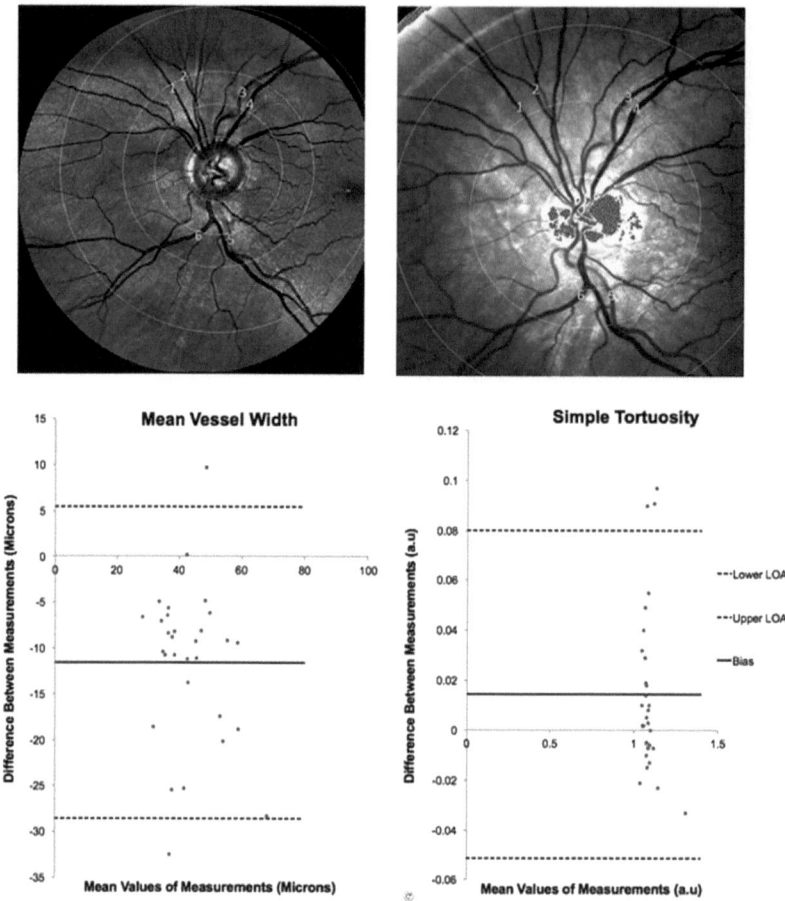

Fig. 3. Fundus images from a type 2 DM subject captured with two different ophthalmic instruments. Top Left: Image (FOV: 45°) obtained with the EasyScan (i-Optics Corporation, The Netherlands). Top Right: Image (FOV: 35°) obtained with the Retinal Function Imager (RFI; Optical Imaging, Rehovot, Israel). Bottom figures show the Bland-Altman plots for the only two parameters with strong correlation coefficients (i.e., mean vessel width and simple tortuosity). Arterioles are in red and venules are in blue. The SIVA software automatically detects the optic disc and traces vessels in a zone 0.5–2.0-disc diameter from the disc margin. Different circular ROIs (see the white concentric circles) with various radii around the optic disc center are superposed on the fundus images: Inner ring: 0.5–1.0 disc diameters away from the disc margin, and the Outer ring: 0.5–2.0 disc diameters away from the disc. The vessels used in the analysis are labeled with numbers from 1 to 6. Abbreviations: LOA (limits of agreement) (Color figure online)

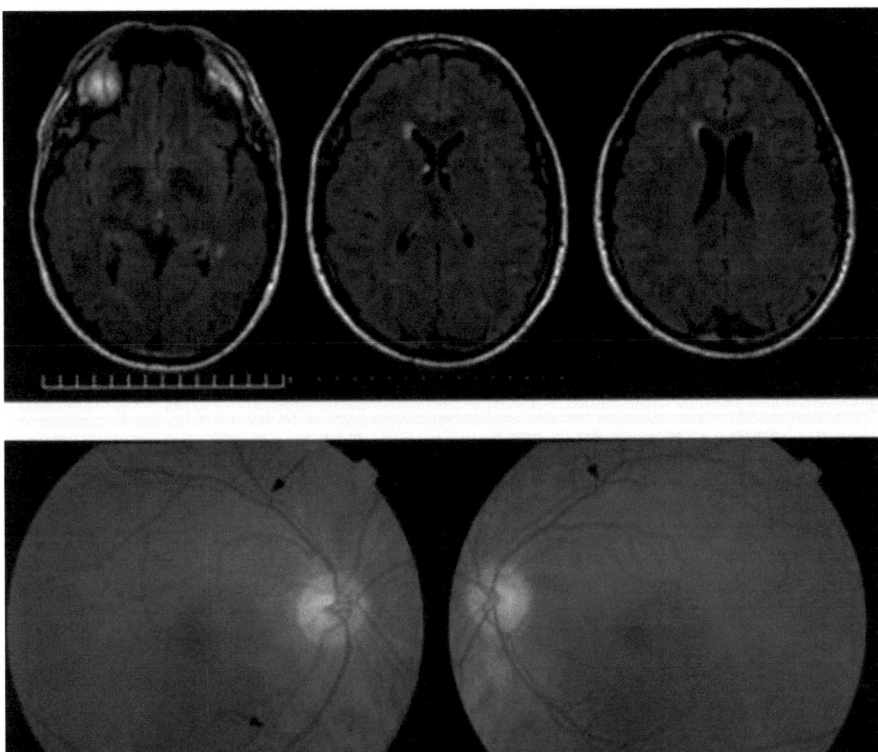

Fig. 4. Magnetic resonance images (MRI) and fundus images from a supposedly healthy subject (male, 51 years old) with focal discrete lesions in the brain without visible or detectable ocular manifestations. TOP: MRI images showing mild to moderate white matter (WM) disease in the MRI image. The images show focal discrete lesions in anterior and posterior WM, focal confluence in posterior WM and periventricular caps. BOTTOM: Fundus images annotated (see black arrows) showing arterio-venous crossings. The arterio-venous crossings are common in the normal healthy population. Reports in the literature have established that they are not correlated with any systemic factors (e.g. hypertension, diabetes) [29]. Image courtesy of Valia Rodriguez, M.D., Ph.D., Aston University

6 Conclusion

Artificial intelligence has become one of the most influential areas of computer science that can contribute significantly to the healthcare industry. The discovery of biomarkers in AD is a complicated process that demands considering multiple factors and approaches to obtain reliable biomarkers that could allow us to predict risk or response to treatment very early and with low false positive and false negative rates. The continuous development of medical technology and advanced methods to analyze and interpret ophthalmic data has facilitated the introduction of many retinal measures over time. These developments are helping to understand how changes in the retinal neurovascular unit reflect neurovascular pathology in the brain, and once integrated with AI applications could create an opportunity for individuals under the risk of AD to track their condition through the eye which could help doctors to make a diagnosis faster and more accurately, for early prevention and timely treatment.

Future studies are still needed to investigate the fundamental mechanisms involved in AD in relation to the ocular changes. Moreover, most of the biomarker identification methods and AI approaches are still under development and unresolved due to the need of big data and training experience to facilitate the transitioning into the clinical diagnostic arena. Together these advances once fully developed and tested could offer us with the ability to move the research on AI applications in AD forwards.

References

1. Goedert, M., Spillantini, M.G.: A century of Alzheimer's disease. Science **314**, 777–781 (2006)
2. Kawas, C.H., Corrada, M.M., Brookmeyer, R., et al.: Visual memory predicts Alzheimer's disease more than a decade before diagnosis. Neurology **60**, 1089–1093 (2003)
3. Katz, B., Rimmer, S.: Ophthalmologic manifestations of Alzheimer's disease. Surv. Ophthalmol. **34**, 31–43 (1989)
4. Cabrera DeBuc, D., Somfai, G.M., Koller, A.: Retinal microvascular network alterations: potential biomarkers of cerebrovascular and neural diseases. Am. J. Physiol. Heart Circ. Physiol. **312**, H201–H212 (2017)
5. Cogan, D.G., Kuwabara, T.: Comparison of retinal and cerebral vasculature in trypsin digest preparations. Br. J. Ophthalmol. **68**, 10–12 (1984)
6. Drexler, W., Liu, M., Kumar, A., Kamali, T., Unterhuber, A., Leitgeb, R.A.: Optical coherence tomography today: speed, contrast, and multimodality. J. Biomed. Opt. **19**, 071412 (2014)
7. London, A., Benhar, I., Schwartz, M.: The retina as a window to the brainfrom eye research to CNS disorders. Nat. Revi. Neurol. **9**, 44 (2013)
8. Cheung, A.T., Chen, P.C., Larkin, E.C., et al.: Microvascular abnormalities in sickle cell disease: a computer-assisted intravital microscopy study. Blood **99**, 3999–4005 (2002)
9. Optos Web site. www.optos.com. Accessed 27 Sept 2018
10. Makita, S., Hong, Y., Yamanari, M., Yatagai, T., Yasuno, Y.: Optical coherence angiography. Opt. Express **14**, 7821–7840 (2006)
11. Wang, R.K., Jacques, S.L., Ma, Z., Hurst, S., Hanson, S.R., Gruber, A.: Three dimensional optical angiography. Opt. Express **15**, 4083–4097 (2007)
12. Wang, Y., Fawzi, A., Tan, O., Gil-Flamer, J., Huang, D.: Retinal blood flow detection in diabetic patients by Doppler Fourier domain optical coherence tomography. Opt. Express **17**, 4061–4073 (2009)
13. Yasuno, Y., Hong, Y., Makita, S., et al.: In vivo high-contrast imaging of deep posterior eye by 1-mm swept source optical coherence tomography and scattering optical coherence angiography. Opt. Express **15**, 6121–6139 (2007)

14. Zhang, Q., Lee, C.S., Chao, J., et al.: Wide-field optical coherence tomography based microangiography for retinal imaging. Sci. Rep. **6**, 22017 (2016)
15. Rha, J., Jonnal, R.S., Thorn, K.E., Qu, J., Zhang, Y., Miller, D.T.: Adaptive optics flood-illumination camera for high speed retinal imaging. Opt. Express. **14**, 4552–4569 (2006)
16. Roorda, A., Romero-Borja, F., Donnelly III, W., Queener, H., Hebert, T., Campbell, M.: Adaptive optics scanning laser ophthalmoscopy. Opt. Express **10**, 405–412 (2002)
17. Kim, J.E., Chung, M.: Adaptive optics for retinal imaging. Retina **33**, 1483–1486 (2013)
18. Park, B.H., de Boer, J.F.: Polarization sensitive optical coherence tomography. In: Drexler, W., Fujimoto, J.G. (eds.) Optical Coherence Tomography - Technology and Applications, pp. 1055–1101. Springer, Cham (2015)
19. Ding, J., Strachan, M.W., Fowkes, F.G., et al.: Association of retinal arteriolar dilatation with lower verbal memory: the Edinburgh type 2 diabetes study. Diabetologia **54**, 1653–1662 (2011)
20. La Morgia, C., Ross-Cisneros, F.N., Koronyo, Y., et al.: Melanopsin retinal ganglion cell loss in Alzheimer disease. Ann. Neurol. **79**, 90–109 (2016)
21. Hart, N.J., Koronyo, Y., Black, K.L., Koronyo-Hamaoui, M.: Ocular indicators of Alzheimers: exploring disease in the retina. Acta Neuropathol. **132**, 767–787 (2016)
22. Blanks, J.C., Schmidt, S.Y., Torigoe, Y., Porrello, K.V., Hinton, D.R., Blanks, R.H.: Retinal pathology in Alzheimer's disease. II. Regional neuron loss and glial changes in GCL. Neurobiol. Aging. **17**, 385–395 (1996)
23. Feke, G.T., Hyman, B.T., Stern, R.A., Pasquale, L.R.: Retinal blood flow in mild cognitive impairment and Alzheimers disease. Alzheimers Dement. (Amst.) **1**, 144–151 (2015)
24. Frost, S., Kanagasingam, Y., Sohrabi, H., et al.: Retinal vascular biomarkers for early detection and monitoring of Alzheimers disease. Transl. Psychiatry **3**, e233 (2013)
25. Hinton, D.R., Sadun, A.A., Blanks, J.C., Miller, C.A.: Optic-nerve degeneration in Alzheimers disease. N. Engl. J. Med. **315**, 485–487 (1986)
26. Paquet, C., Boissonnot, M., Roger, F., Dighiero, P., Gil, R., Hugon, J.: Abnormal retinal thickness in patients with mild cognitive impairment and Alzheimers disease. Neurosci. Lett. **420**, 97–99 (2007)
27. Koronyo-Hamaoui, M., Koronyo, Y., Ljubimov, A.V., et al.: Identification of amyloid plaques in retinas from Alzheimers patients and noninvasive in vivo optical imaging of retinal plaques in a mouse model. Neuroimage **54**, S204–S217 (2011)
28. Berisha, F., Feke, G.T., Trempe, C.L., McMeel, J.W., Schepens, C.L.: Retinal abnormalities in early Alzheimers disease. Invest. Ophthalmol. Vis. Sci. **48**, 2285–2289 (2007)
29. Cheung, C.Y., Ong, Y.T., Ikram, M.K., et al.: Microvascular network alterations in the retina of patients with Alzheimers disease. Alzheimers Dement. **10**, 135–142 (2014)
30. Curcio, C.A., Drucker, D.N.: Retinal ganglion cells in Alzheimers disease and aging. Ann. Neurol. **33**, 248–257 (2004)
31. Frost, S., Martins, R.N., Kanagasingam, Y.: Ocular biomarkers for early detection of Alzheimers disease. J. Alzheimers Dis. **22**, 1–16 (2010)
32. Guo, L., Duggan, J., Cordeiro, M.: Alzheimers disease and retinal neurodegeneration. Curr. Alzheimer Res. **7**, 3–14 (2010)

33. Parisi, V., Restuccia, R., Fattapposta, F., Mina, C., Bucci, M.G., Pierelli, F.: Morphological and functional retinal impairment in Alzheimers disease patients. Clin. Neurophysiol. **112**, 1860–1867 (2001)
34. Hampel, H., Toschi, N., Babiloni, C., et al.: Revolution of Alzheimer precision neurology: passageway of systems biology and neurophysiology. J. Alzheimers Dis. **64**, S47–S105 (2018)
35. http://www.neurovisionimaging.com
36. Aizenstein, H.J., Nebes, R.D., Saxton, J.A., et al.: Frequent amyloid deposition without significant cognitive impairment among the elderly. Arch. Neurol. **65**, 1509–1517 (2008)
37. Koronyo, Y., Biggs, D., Barron, E., et al.: Retinal amyloid pathology and proof-of-concept imaging trial in Alzheimers disease. JCI Insight **2017**(2), 93621 (2017)
38. www.optinadx.com
39. https://www.newswire.ca/news-releases/optina-diagnostics-looks-to-advance-biomarker-discovery-through-collaboration-with-imagia-689742211.html
40. Snyder, P.J.: Alzheimer's & dementia: diagnosis. Assess. Dis. Monit. **4**, 169178 (2016)
41. Santos, C.Y., Johnson, L.N., Sinoff, S.E., Festa, E.K., Heindel, W.C., Snyder, P.J.: Change in retinal structural anatomy during the preclinical stage of Alzheimer's disease. Alzheimers Dement. (Amst.) **10**, 196–209 (2018)
42. Csincsik, L., MacGillivray, T.J., Flynn, E., et al.: Peripheral retinal imaging biomarkers for Alzheimers disease: a pilot study. Ophthalmic Res. **59**, 182192 (2018)
43. Campbell, M.C., Corapi, F., Emptage, L., et al.: The relationship between amyloid in the retina and a brain-based post-mortem diagnosis of alzheimers disease. Alzheimer's Dement.: J. Alzheimer's Assoc. **13**, P284–P285 (2017)
44. Baumann, B., Woehrer, A., Ricken, G., et al.: Visualization of neuritic plaques in Alzheimers disease by polarization-sensitive optical coherence microscopy. Sci. Rep. **7**, 43477 (2017)
45. Danesh-Meyer, H.V., Birch, H., Ku, J.F., Carroll, S., Gamble, G.: Reduction of optic nerve fibers in patients with Alzheimer disease identified by laser imaging. Neurology **67**, 1852–1854 (2006)
46. Kurna, S.A., Akar, G., Altun, A., Agirman, Y., Gozke, E., Sengor, T.: Confocal scanning laser tomography of the optic nerve head on the patients with Alzheimers disease compared to glaucoma and control. Int. Ophthalmol. **34**, 1203–1211 (2014)
47. Cordeiro, M.F., Guo, L., Coxon, K.M., et al.: Imaging multiple phases of neurodegeneration: a novel approach to assessing cell death in vivo. Cell Death Dis. **1**, e3 (2010)
48. DeBuc, D.C., Kostic, M., Oropesa, S., Somfai, G.M., Mendoza-Santiesteban, C.: Investigating multimodal diagnostic eye biomarkers of cognitive impairment by measuring vascular and neurogenic changes in the retina. Alzheimer's Dement.: J. Alzheimer's Assoc. **14**, P1095 (2018)
49. Bulut, M., Kurtulus, F., Gozkaya, O., et al.: Evaluation of optical coherence tomography angiographic findings in Alzheimers type dementia. Br. J. Ophthalmol. **102**, 233–237 (2018)
50. Jiang, H., Wei, Y., Shi, Y., et al.: Altered macular microvasculature in mild cognitive impairment and Alzheimer disease. J. Neuroophthalmol. **38**, 292–298 (2018)
51. Olafsdottir, O.B., Saevarsdottir, H.S., Hardarson, S.H., et al.: Retinal oxygen metabolism in patients with mild cognitive impairment. Alzheimers Dement. (Amst.) **10**, 340–345 (2018)

52. Stefnsson, E., Olafsdottir, O.B., Einarsdottir, A.B., et al.: Retinal oximetry discovers novel biomarkers in retinal and brain diseases. Invest. Ophthalmol. Vis. Sci. **58**, BIO227–BIO233 (2017)
53. Munk, M.R., Giannakaki-Zimmermann, H., Berger, L., et al.: OCT-angiography: a qualitative and quantitative comparison of 4 OCT-A devices. PLoS One **12**, e0177059 (2017)
54. Cosatto, V.F., Liew, G., Rochtchina, E., et al.: Retinal vascular fractal dimension measurement and its influence from imaging variation: results of two segmentation methods. Curr. Eye Res. **35**, 850–856 (2010)
55. Cheung, C.Y., Tay, W.T., Mitchell, P., et al.: Quantitative and qualitative retinal microvascular characteristics and blood pressure. J. Hypertens. **29**, 1380–1391 (2011)
56. Soucy, J.P., Chevrefils, C., Sylvestre, J.P., et al.: An amyloid ligand-free optical retinal imaging method to predict cerebral amyloid PET status. Alzheimer's Dement.: J. Alzheimer's Assoc. **14**, P771 (2018)
57. Sandeep, C.S., Kumar, A.S., Mahadevan, K., Manoj, P.: Classification of OCT images for the early diagnosis of Alzheimer's disease. In: 2017 International Conference on Intelligent Computing and Control (I2C2), Coimbatore, pp. 1–5 (2017)
58. Sandeep, C.S., Kumar, S.A., Mahadevan, K., Manoj, P.: Analysis of MRI and OCT images for early diagnosis of Alzheimers disease using wavelet networks. AMSE J. Lect. Model. Simul. 31–40 (2017). http://amsemodelling.com/publications/lectures_on_modelling_and_simulation.html

Intermediate Goals in Deep Learning for Retinal Image Analysis

Gilbert Lim[✉], Wynne Hsu, and Mong Li Lee

School of Computing, National University of Singapore, Singapore, Singapore
{limyongs,whsu,leeml}@comp.nus.edu.sg

Abstract. End-to-end deep learning has been demonstrated to exhibit human-level performance in many retinal image analysis tasks. However, such models' generalizability to data from new sources may be less than optimal. We highlight some benefits of introducing intermediate goals in deep learning-based models.

1 Introduction

Recent developments in the application of deep learning to retinal imaging have received much attention [1], with human-level performance achieved for the classification of diabetic retinopathy [2] and related conditions on large real-world datasets of retinal images [3–7]. A similar trend has also been observed in other medical imaging fields such as lymph node metastases detection in pathology [8], skin cancer classification in dermatology [9] and pneumonia detection with X-rays in radiology [10], etc.

We observe that such clinical implementations have typically adopted the following end-to-end methodology. A comprehensive dataset of images is first collected, with ground truth labels obtained from multiple human experts. This dataset of images is then split into a training set, and a (usually much smaller) validation set. The training set of images is then used to train deep learning models, usually of well-known architectures such as VGGNet [11], ResNet [12] and GoogleNet Inception [13] – often pretrained on ImageNet data [14]. The outputs of these models (possibly a mix of architectures) is then ensembled, and parameters such as class thresholds are then tuned on the held-out validation set of images. Finally, model performance is evaluated on the actual test dataset, accompanied by visualizations such as saliency heatmaps [15,16] and t-SNE projections [17] that demonstrate the plausibility of the model's internal workings.

In this paper, we discuss the limitations of such end-to-end methodology and review recent works in using intermediate goals for retina image analysis applications.

2 Limitations of End-to-End Learning

Existing deep neural networks, for all their vaunted performance, are not quite "intelligent" in the way that humans are. For example, a child may grasp the concept of a cup from a few images, by understanding it as a hollow vessel. Once this is established, novel images of cups can be identified as such, even if they vary heavily in orientation and ornamentation from the original examples. This is not the case for deep neural networks, which learn to distinguish cups from other objects using features that are not necessarily intuitive. If all available training images of cups happen to contain yellow cups, for instance, there may be no way for the neural network model to properly disentangle that colour property from the elemental "cup" concept.

An immediate problem for deep learning in medical imaging, then, is that the most useful data – usually where a particular condition is manifested – is often scarce. For instance, consider a diabetic retinopathy deep neural network model trained on a dataset, where virtually all images with proliferative diabetic retinopathy contain both haemorrhages and hard exudates. From this data, the model might consider merely haemorrhage features as sufficient for classification purposes. When confronted with a test image with extensive hard exudates, but without haemorrhages, the model could classify it as non-referable, despite this being an "unreasonable" diagnosis to a human grader. As such, it is important to include training examples with hard exudates for this task, but it is extremely difficult to acquire images with all possible combinations of features needed for training a robust classifier.

Further, deep neural network models are sensitive to factors that a human would subconsciously correct for. For example, this is demonstrated in [18], which applies deep learning to the classification of optical coherence tomography (OCT) images. The authors found that OCT scans from a different imaging device that they had used for the training set, produced poor segmentation maps when segmented with a model trained on that training set. While there exist numerous methods – such as soft attention [15], Grad-CAM [16] and Integrated Gradients [19] – for visualizing pixel-level contributions to the final end-to-end model output as a saliency map, it remains that such visualizations are retrospective. As such, they cannot automatically detect or handle cases where the input has become unsuitable for the end-to-end model, as observed in [18].

3 Usage of Intermediate Goals

Introducing a human-defined intermediate objective to the training process can mitigate some of the limitations of the end-to-end methodology. For example, the work in [18] trained separate segmentation models and required these models to demonstrate explicit knowledge about retinal tissue layer categorization. This can be regarded as a sanity checkpoint for medical imaging models. With this, a subsequent shared classification model, which took a segmentation map as input, was able to produce excellent results since diagnosis is supposed to be inferred from the tissue layers. Algorithms may then be designed to detect and flag out likely failed segmentations, for instance when there are noisy and/or disjoint tissue layer segmentations, possibly with reference to expected segmentation map pixel-level statistics.

We can employ intermediate objectives for other retinal image analysis tasks such as diabetic retinopathy screening. In the manual screening process, human graders are trained to follow established guidelines, which involve the identification and counting of specific lesion types. End-to-end deep learning models have no explicit knowledge of these guidelines, and instead implicitly learn the relationship between input images and guideline classification only through exposure to a large number of training examples. As such, their performance might be argued to be incidental, and vulnerable to relatively minor changes in the imaging procedure. For example, if we train an end-to-end deep learning model on a dataset of retinal images taken at a 40° field of view (FOV) and test it on images with a narrower FOV, then the model may mistake microaneurysms to be haemorrhages due to the magnification of the retinal features in the test images. Such failures are hidden in end-to-end deep learning models.

In the automated grading of diabetic retinopathy, the detection of microaneurysms (a biomarker [20]) as an intermediate goal had been a major focus of prior research [21–24], due to their relatively uniform appearance and the general correlation between quantity of microaneurysms and severity of diabetic retinopathy. A joint optimization of referable diabetic retinopathy and individual lesions has also been attempted with a custom backward-forward propagation method, in order to enhance the sparsity of intermediate filters, and thereby reduce the influence of lesion confounders [25]. Interestingly, it was discovered that different lesion classes were optimally detected at different stages in models trained under this procedure, with bright lesions (hard and soft exudates) optimally detected in the earlier stages, and dark lesions (microaneurysms and haemorrhages) in the later stages.

Similar imaging biomarkers, such as the progression of the optic cup-to-disc ratio in glaucoma, and drusen within the vicinity of the macula in age-related macular degeneration, have also been targeted as natural intermediate goals. For example, the explicit segmentation of the optic disc and optic cup had been recognized and targeted as an intermediate goal for glaucoma, much as microaneurysms and other lesions had been for diabetic retinopathy [26,27], and this segmentation task was also a natural candidate for the application of deep neural network models [28]. It should be noted that intermediate goals are not strictly restricted to image features. For example, a 9-class severity for age-related macular degeneration can first be predicted as an intermediate goal towards estimating 5-year progression risk [29], despite it of course being technically possible to predict the progression risk directly as the target labels. As with [18], this allows for the two parts of the algorithm to be assessed separately. This general principle may be applied whenever a visual symptom – e.g. change in vascular morphology for retinopathy of prematurity [30] – is known to be associated with the targeted condition.

Numerous computer vision methods have been applied to handle the object detection and segmentation tasks involved. Deep learning architectures such as convolutional neural networks (CNNs) have also been utilized, as with the FDA-approved IDx-DR system which incorporates CNNs for detecting various types of lesions, alongside a multiscale feature bank detector for microaneurysms [31]. However, such biomarker-based intermediate goals may be difficult to formulate given the lack of relevant ground truth, which usually involves fine-grained segmentation of lesions or structures. This is because manual segmentation is often time-consuming and somewhat orthogonal to the primary mission of medical institutions, since it is generally unnecessary for diagnoses to be made.

Other than this, there exists a further class of retinal image analysis tasks, where the mechanism of a condition is not known. The tasks covered thus far have all been performed by humans, and as such there exist objective criteria of what features to look out for. However, there may well exist many useful retinal image analysis tasks that humans are not capable of performing due to the features involved being too subtle, but which deep neural network models are able to execute. An example would be the prediction of cardiovascular risk factors from retinal fundus photographs [32]. It was found that risk factors such as age, gender, smoking status, HbA1c, body mass index and systolic blood pressure could be predicted to some extent using just fundus photographs, a feat that is beyond human graders as far as is known. Preliminary work likewise suggests that ischemic stroke risk might be predicted on fundus photographs with end-to-end deep learning [33], but again without established human-auditable features that might serve as intermediate goals. As such, the vascular tree segmentation was identified and examined as a potential intermediate goal in this case.

As discussed above, the lack of suitable fine-grained ground truth is one of the most common obstacles against implementing intermediate goals in practice. Towards this end, advances in the generation of saliency heatmaps from end-to-end deep learning systems may offer the possibility of the saliency heatmap features themselves being used as-is as the intermediate goal, possibly with some preprocessing. For example, annotated lesion data for diabetic retinopathy remains rare. However, it may be possible to filter saliency heatmaps so as to produce good-enough lesion-level ground truth with high probability. This methodology is especially applicable for retinal analysis tasks where saliency heatmaps and human judgment with domain knowledge can refine each other in an iterative development process, for example with clinical experts helping to "close the gap" between saliency heatmap ground truth, and gold standard ground truth. Additionally, it also can be applied when the proper intermediate goals are unknown.

4 Conclusion

In this paper, we have discussed the benefits of explicitly defining *intermediate goals* in the training and evaluation of deep learning models. The immediate benefit of breaking a retinal image analysis task into intermediate goals is twofold. It imposes a degree of *conceptual understanding* on the model, and introduces *modularity* into the model. We believe that there is much room for exploration, in how best to integrate intermediate goal-based models, with end-to-end deep learning models.

References

1. Ting, D.S.W., Pasquale, L.R., Peng, L., et al.: Artificial intelligence and deep learning in ophthalmology. Br. J. Ophthalmol. **103**, 167–175 (2018)
2. Wong, T.Y., Cheung, G.C., Larsen, M., et al.: Diabetic retinopathy. Nat. Rev. Dis. Primers **2** (2016). Article number 16012
3. Gulshan, V., Peng, L., Coram, M., et al.: Development and validation of a deep learning algorithm for detection of diabetic retinopathy in retinal fundus photographs. JAMA **316**, 2402–2410 (2016)
4. Gargeya, R., Leng, T.: Automated identification of diabetic retinopathy using deep learning. Ophthalmology **124**, 962–969 (2017)
5. Burlina, P.M., Joshi, N., Pekala, M., et al.: Automated grading of age-related macular degeneration from color fundus images using deep convolutional neural networks. JAMA Ophthalmol. **135**, 1170–1176 (2017)
6. Ting, D.S.W., Cheung, C.Y., Lim, G., et al.: Development and validation of a deep learning system for diabetic retinopathy and related eye diseases using retinal images from multiethnic populations with diabetes. JAMA **318**, 2211–2223 (2017)
7. Kermany, D.S., Goldbaum, M., Cai, W., et al.: Identifying medical diagnoses and treatable diseases by image-based deep learning. Cell **172**, 1122–1131 (2018)
8. Bejnordi, B.E., Veta, M., Van Diest, P.J., et al.: Diagnostic assessment of deep learning algorithms for detection of lymph node metastases in women with breast cancer. JAMA **318**, 2199–2210 (2017)
9. Esteva, A., Kuprel, B., Novoa, R.A., et al.: Dermatologist-level classification of skin cancer with deep neural networks. Nature **542**, 115 (2017)
10. Rajpurkar, P., Irvin, J., Zhu, K., et al.: Chexnet: radiologist-level pneumonia detection on chest x-rays with deep learning. arXiv preprint arXiv:1711.05225 (2017)
11. Simonyan, K., Vedaldi, A., Zisserman, A.: Very deep convolutional networks for large-scale image recognition. In: Proceedings of the International Conference on Learning Representations (2015)
12. He, K., Zhang, X., Ren, S., Sun, J.: Deep residual learning for image recognition. In: Proceedings of the IEEE Conference on Computer Vision and Pattern Recognition, pp. 770–778 (2016)
13. Szegedy, C., Liu, W., Jia, Y., et al.: Going deeper with convolutions. In: Proceedings of the IEEE Conference on Computer Vision and Pattern Recognition, pp. 1–9 (2015)
14. Burlina, P., Pacheco, K.D., Joshi, N., et al.: Comparing humans and deep learning performance for grading AMD: a study in using universal deep features and transfer learning for automated AMD analysis. Comput. Biol. Med. **82**, 80–86 (2017)
15. Xu, K., Ba, J., Kiros, R., et al.: Show, attend and tell: neural image caption generation with visual attention. In: Proceedings of the International Conference on Machine Learning, pp. 2048–2057 (2015)
16. Selvaraju, R.R., Cogswell, M., Das, A., et al.: Grad-CAM: visual explanations from deep networks via gradient-based localization. In: Proceedings of the IEEE International Conference on Computer Vision, pp. 618–626 (2017)
17. van der Maaten, L., Hinton, G.: Visualizing data using t-SNE. J. Mach. Learn. Res. **9**, 2579–2605 (2008)
18. De Fauw, J., Ledsam, J.R., Romera-Paredes, B., et al.: Clinically applicable deep learning for diagnosis and referral in retinal disease. Nat. Med. **24**, 1342 (2018)
19. Sundararajan, M., Taly, A., Yan, Q.: Axiomatic attribution for deep networks. In: Proceedings of the International Conference on Machine Learning, pp. 3319–3328 (2017)

20. Nunes, S., Pires, I., Rosa, A., et al.: Microaneurysm turnover is a biomarker for diabetic retinopathy progression to clinically significant macular edema: findings for type 2 diabetics with nonproliferative retinopathy. Ophthalmologica **223**, 292–297 (2009)
21. Quellec, G., Lamard, M., Josselin, P.M., et al.: Optimal wavelet transform for the detection of microaneurysms in retina photographs. IEEE Trans. Med. Imaging **27**, 1230–1241 (2008)
22. Niemeijer, M., Van Ginneken, B., Cree, M.J., et al.: Retinopathy online challenge: automatic detection of microaneurysms in digital color fundus photographs. IEEE Trans. Med. Imaging **29**, 185–195 (2010)
23. Lim, G., Lee, M.L., Hsu, W., Wong, T.Y.: Transformed representations for convolutional neural networks in diabetic retinopathy screening. In: Proceedings of the AAAI Workshop on Modern Artificial Intelligence for Health Analytics (MAIHA), AAAI, pp. 34–38 (2014)
24. Abràmoff, M.D., Lou, Y., Erginay, A., et al.: Improved automated detection of diabetic retinopathy on a publicly available dataset through integration of deep learning. Invest. Ophthalmol. Vis. Sci. **57**, 5200–5206 (2016)
25. Quellec, G., Charrière, K., Boudi, Y., et al.: Deep image mining for diabetic retinopathy screening. Med. Image Anal. **39**, 178–193 (2017)
26. Cheng, J., Liu, J., Xu, Y., et al.: Superpixel classification based optic disc and optic cup segmentation for glaucoma screening. IEEE Trans. Med. Imaging **32**, 1019–1032 (2013)
27. Xu, Y., Lin, S., Wong, D.W.K., Liu, J., Xu, D.: Efficient reconstruction-based optic cup localization for glaucoma screening. In: Mori, K., Sakuma, I., Sato, Y., Barillot, C., Navab, N. (eds.) MICCAI 2013. LNCS, vol. 8151, pp. 445–452. Springer, Heidelberg (2013). https://doi.org/10.1007/978-3-642-40760-4_56
28. Lim, G., Cheng, Y., Hsu, W., Lee, M.L.: Integrated optic disc and cup segmentation with deep learning. In: Proceedings of the International Conference on Tools with Artificial Intelligence, pp. 162–169. IEEE (2015)
29. Burlina, P.M., Joshi, N., Pacheco, K.D., et al.: Use of deep learning for detailed severity characterization and estimation of 5-year risk among patients with age-related macular degeneration. JAMA Ophthalmol. **136**, 1359–1366 (2018)
30. Niemeijer, M., Staal, J., van Ginneken, B., et al.: Comparative study of retinal vessel segmentation methods on a new publicly available database. In: Proceedings of Medical Imaging 2004: Image Processing, vol. 5370, pp. 648–657. International Society for Optics and Photonics (2004)
31. Abràmoff, M.D., Lavin, P.T., Birch, M., et al.: Pivotal trial of an autonomous AI-based diagnostic system for detection of diabetic retinopathy in primary care offices. npj Digit. Med. **1**, 39 (2018)
32. Poplin, R., Varadarajan, A.V., Blumer, K., et al.: Prediction of cardiovascular risk factors from retinal fundus photographs via deep learning. Nat. Biomed. Eng. **2**, 158 (2018)
33. Lim, G., Lim, Z.W., Xu, D., et al.: Feature isolation for hypothesis testing in retinal imaging: an ischemic stroke prediction case study. In: Proceedings of the Innovative Applications of Artificial Intelligence Conference (2019)

Enhanced Detection of Referable Diabetic Retinopathy via DCNNs and Transfer Learning

Michelle Yuen Ting Yip[1,2(✉)], Zhan Wei Lim[4], Gilbert Lim[4],
Nguyen Duc Quang[2], Haslina Hamzah[3], Jinyi Ho[3], Valentina Bellemo[2],
Yuchen Xie[2], Xin Qi Lee[2], Mong Li Lee[4], Wynne Hsu[4], Tien Yin Wong[1,2,3],
and Daniel Shu Wei Ting[1,2,3]

[1] Duke-NUS Medical School, National University of Singapore, Singapore, Singapore
michelle.yip@u.duke.nus.edu, daniel.ting.s.w@singhealth.com.sg
[2] Singapore Eye Research Institute, Singapore, Singapore
[3] Singapore National Eye Centre, Singapore, Singapore
[4] National University of Singapore, School of Computing, Singapore, Singapore

Abstract. A clinically acceptable deep learning system (DLS) has been developed for the detection of diabetic retinopathy by the Singapore Eye Research Institute. For its utility in a national screening programme, further enhancement was needed. With newer deep convolutional neural networks (DCNNs) being introduced and technological methodology such as transfer learning gaining recognition for better performance, this paper compared the performance of the DCNN used in the original DLS, VGGNet, with newer DCNNs, ResNet and Ensemble, with transfer learning. The DLS performance improved with higher AUC, sensitivity and specificity with the adoption of the newer DCNNs and transfer learning.

Keywords: Deep learning · Convolutional neural networks · Diabetic retinopathy

1 Introduction

1.1 Diabetic Retinopathy: A Global Problem

It is projected that by 2040, 600 million people will suffer from diabetes in the world [16]. Among these, one third are estimated to have one form of diabetic retinopathy (DR) although 80% of these individuals may be unaware of their condition [22]. Diagnosis is often late, with one-third of patients with DR presenting with vision-threatening DR. Early detection, referral and treatment will reduce the risk of blindness. Screening for DR will benefit from an automated system in terms of efficiency and reproducibility [8].

1.2 Prior Work of AI in Medicine

The medical arena has in recent years gradually welcomed the advantages of artificial intelligence (AI) systems [25]. One such application is in medical imaging, with specialities ranging from dermatology to radiology investing in this area of research [5,15,26].

In particular, ophthalmology has been at the forefront of innovations, with far-reaching implications in other systemic diseases beyond the eye [24]. Automated systems in detection of a range of ophthalmological pathologies have been developed and reported to have good performance with the adoption of DLSs, comparable to human assessment [23]. Detection of age-related macular degeneration (AMD) with a DLS was evaluated by Burlina and colleagues with a high AUC, ranging between 0.94 and 0.96, and accuracy between 88.4% and 91.6% [3]. Grassmann et al. further explored the use of multiple DCNNs in detection of AMD with similarly good results [7]. A DLS identifying glaucoma has also been attempted. Though various methods have been explored by multiple groups, Li et al. was successful at generating acceptable results with AUC, sensitivity and specificity for glaucoma detection exceeding 0.9. Retinopathy of prematurity is another area that has been targeted by groups such as Brown et al. [2] and Worrall et al. [27] in the effort to circumvent childhood blindness.

However, DR remains to be the main interest of many research groups due to its public health significance and high prevalence. Abràmoff et al. developed and evaluated a DLS for diagnosis of DR and was successful in obtaining approval from the US Food and Drug Administration (FDA) [1]. A group at Google AI Healthcare built upon this work with the same publicly available datasets to evaluate the Inception-v3 network which demonstrated consistency with a panel of board-certified ophthalmologists [8].

Although majority of the literature focuses on fundus photographs, other ophthalmology imaging modalities such as Optical Coherence Tomography (OCT) [19], OCT Angiography [17], slit lamp images [6] have also been capturing interest for the development of DLSs.

1.3 Preliminary Study

In 2017, Ting et al. published a DLS developed and tested using real-world DR screening cohorts with close to 500,000 retinal images, showing clinically acceptable performance (AUC, sensitivity and specificity of more than 90%) for simultaneous detection of common ophthalmological diseases, namely AMD, glaucoma and diabetic retinopathy [21]. This DLS system by Ting et al. had been developed using the DCNN VGGNet as the neural architecture and serves as a preliminary study. Since the release of VGGNet, newer DCNNs with more layers have been published which show better feature extractions and yield better results. ResNet in particular has been garnering attention for its accuracy secondary to its extreme depth, whilst still being easy to train [12]. An ensemble of the outputs of both ResNet and VGGNet has been found to perform better with higher accuracy by reducing false negative results [9,11]. In addition, transfer learning has been shown to improve performances of DLS and has been especially useful in medical image classification [13,18].

1.4 Study Aim

The primary aim of this study is to enhance this DLS with the use of newer DCNNs, with transfer learning, to improve its diagnostic performance in detecting diabetic retinopathy.

2 Methods

2.1 Training Dataset and Testing Dataset

Both the training and testing datasets were obtained from Singapore National Integrated Diabetic Retinopathy Screening Programme (SiDRP). The SiDRP was established from 2010, screening half of the diabetic population in Singapore by 2015. SiDRP uses digital retinal photography, a tele-ophthalmology platform for assessment of DR by a team of trained professional graders (>5 years of experience). For this study, 2 graders analysed each image and for discordant findings, a retinal specialist (PhD-trained with >5 years of experience in conducting DR assessment) would generate the final grading. The training dataset was taken from the SiDRP between 2010 and 2013. Once trained, the DCNNs were subsequently tested on images obtained from SiDRP between 2014 and 2015.

The International Clinical Diabetic Retinopathy Severity Scale (ICDRS) was utilised for DR classification. For the purpose of this paper, referable DR is defined as moderate non-proliferative DR or worse, including diabetic macular edema and ungradable images. Vision-threatening DR is defined as severe non-proliferative DR or proliferative DR.

2.2 Different Convolutional Neural Networks of the DLS

This study explored three different DCNNs, namely VGGNet, ResNet and Ensemble.

(a) VGGNet
VGGNet is a 16-layered network, designed by the Visual Geometry Group in Oxford in 2014 and won second place for image classification in the infamous ImageNet Large Scale Visual Recognition Challenge (ILSVRC) [20]. This competition evaluates many DCNNs on their speed and accuracy in object detection and image classification. An adapted VGGNet was the initial choice for the previous study by Ting et al. as it had been demonstrated to have excellent performance on the classification of retinal images [21]. VGGNet was trained on Caffe framework where no layers were frozen.

(b) ResNet
ResNet-50 was introduced in 2015 by the Microsoft group, comprising of 50 layers and won first place in ILSVRC 2015 [12]. It has been popular for its ability to

increase the depth of the network architecture and thus increasing accuracy, whilst still maintaining ease for training and optimisation. This is because it employs 'skip' residual connections that perform identity mappings. For this study, PyTorch was the framework for ResNet. Due to close association with the 1,000 classes in ImageNet, the last linear layer of the pre-trained model was discarded and replaced for purposes of DR classification.

(c) Ensemble

Ensemble is a DCNN made up of a combination of the 2 networks, VGGNet and ResNet, probability output scores, where performance is expected to match or exceed single DCNNs [10].

2.3 Transfer Learning

Using transfer learning, ResNet was pre-trained with the ImageNet database for weight initialisation and general-purpose features. ImageNet is one of the largest annotated databases. This comprehensive annotated dataset consists of more than 1.2 million natural images over 1,000 categories, the largest image dataset currently available. It has been accredited to advance image recognition in the deep learning field and has formed the basis of the benchmark to evaluate new DCNNs for image recognition in the annual ILSVRC [13].

2.4 Statistical Analysis

The primary outcome measures include area under the curve (AUC) of the receiver operating characteristic curve, specificity and sensitivity of the DLSs, developed using ResNet and Ensemble. The operating thresholds for the DLSs were selected to enable comparisons with the human graders' past performances (sensitivity of 90%) and criteria set forth by Singapore's Ministry of Health. The reference standard was set as the grading finalised by professional graders and retinal specialists.

3 Results

Details of the training and validation datasets used for the development and testing of the DLS in detection of referable DR and vision-threatening DR are outlined in Table 1. 148,266 images were used to train and validate the three different DLSs. 76,370 images (38,185 eyes) from SiDRP data from 2010 to 2013 were used in the training dataset and a separate, similar sized dataset of 71,896 images (35,948 eyes) from SiDRP 2014 to 2015 were allocated to evaluate the DLS. In the former, 8.4% (n = 3,192) were referable eyes and 1.4% eyes (n = 548) displayed vision-threatening DR in accordance with the finalized reference standard grading. Similar proportions are reflected in the validation dataset, encompassing 3.8% eyes (n = 1,373) with referable DR and 0.5% eyes (n = 194) with vision-threatening DR. The remaining balance were eyes that were non-referable.

The performance of the DLSs in detection of referable DR and vision-threatening DR are shown in Table 2.

Table 1. Training and validation datasets of diabetic retinopathy used to evaluate the DLSs.

Dataset	No.			No. of eyes		
	Patients	Images	Eyes	Non-referable	Referable DR	Vision-threatening DR
Training dataset (SiDRP 2010–13)	13,099	76,370	38,185	34,993	3,192	548
Validation dataset (SiDRP 2014–15)	14,880	71,896	35,948	34,575	1,373	194

Table 2. Results of DLS performance of three different DCNNs (VGGNet, ResNet and Ensemble).

	VGGNet	ResNet	Ensemble
Referable DR			
- AUC	0.936	0.969	0.970
- Sensitivity	90.5%	91.7%	92.2%
- Specificity	91.6%	93.1%	92.5%
Vision-threatening DR			
- AUC	0.958	0.994	0.987
- Sensitivity	100%	96.2%	96.2%
- Specificity	91.1%	98.5%	98.9%

4 Conclusion

Better performance of the DLS was reported with the use of newer DCNNs (ResNet and Ensemble) and transfer learning, with higher AUC, sensitivity and specificity for detection of both referable DR as well as vision-threatening DR.

With the rapidly evolving field of deep learning and AI, newer neural architectures and techniques advancing the performance of DCNNs are continuously being developed. For image recognition and classification, the aforementioned annual ILSVRC, and the subsequent succeeding Kaggle, serves as a platform to showcase the abilities of these novel developments such as DenseNet, Inception-v4, Dual Path Networks (DPN). DenseNet has been regarded by some as an extension of ResNet by allowing deeper layers to be feasible through the use of connections between layers in a feed-forward fashion [14]. The new DPN was designed to encompass the advantages of both ResNet and DenseNet and has shown success at the ILSVRC competition in 2017 [4].

There will undoubtedly be continued growth of the deep learning field and future work for medical image analysis will be warranted to keep pace. However, the rate at which these new techniques are translating to real-world applications, especially in the medical sector, often fails to catch up. Thus, further research is essential to evaluate the use of these models in prospective clinical trials.

References

1. Abràmoff, M.D., et al.: Improved automated detection of diabetic retinopathy on a publicly available dataset through integration of deep learning. Investig. Ophthalmol. Vis. Sci. **57**(13), 5200–5206 (2016)
2. Brown, J.M., et al.: Automated diagnosis of plus disease in retinopathy of prematurity using deep convolutional neural networks. JAMA Ophthalmol. **136**, 803–810 (2018)
3. Burlina, P.M., Joshi, N., Pekala, M., Pacheco, K.D., Freund, D.E., Bressler, N.M.: Automated grading of age-related macular degeneration from color fundus images using deep convolutional neural networks. JAMA Ophthalmol. **135**(11), 1170–1176 (2017)
4. Chen, Y., Li, J., Xiao, H., Jin, X., Yan, S., Feng, J.: Dual path networks. In: Advances in Neural Information Processing Systems, pp. 4467–4475 (2017)
5. Esteva, A., Kuprel, B., Novoa, R.A., Ko, J., Swetter, S.M., Blau, H.M., Thrun, S.: Dermatologist-level classification of skin cancer with deep neural networks. Nature **542**(7639), 115 (2017)
6. Gao, X., Lin, S., Wong, T.Y.: Automatic feature learning to grade nuclear cataracts based on deep learning. IEEE Trans. Biomed. Eng. **62**(11), 2693–2701 (2015)
7. Grassmann, F., et al.: A deep learning algorithm for prediction of age-related eye disease study severity scale for age-relatedmacular degeneration from color fundus photography. Ophthalmology **125**, 1410–1420 (2018)
8. Gulshan, V., et al.: Development and validation of a deep learning algorithm for detection of diabetic retinopathy in retinal fundus photographs. Jama **316**(22), 2402–2410 (2016)
9. Han, S.S., et al.: Deep neural networks show an equivalent and often superior performance to dermatologists in onychomycosis diagnosis: Automatic construction of onychomycosis datasets by region-based convolutional deep neural network. PloS one **13**(1), e0191493 (2018)
10. Hansen, L.K., Salamon, P.: Neural network ensembles. IEEE Trans. Pattern Anal. Mach. Intell. **12**(10), 993–1001 (1990)
11. Harangi, B.: Skin lesion detection based on an ensemble of deep convolutional neural network. arXiv preprint arXiv:1705.03360 (2017)
12. He, K., Zhang, X., Ren, S., Sun, J.: Deep residual learning for image recognition. In: Proceedings of the IEEE Conference on Computer Vision and Pattern Recognition, pp. 770–778 (2016)
13. Hoo-Chang, S., et al.: Deep convolutional neural networks for computer-aided detection: CNN architectures, dataset characteristics and transfer learning. IEEE Trans. Med. Imaging **35**(5), 1285 (2016)
14. Huang, G., Liu, Z., van der Maaten, L., Weinberger, K.Q.: Densely connected convolutional networks. In: CVPR, vol. 1, p. 3 (2017)
15. Litjens, G., et al.: A survey on deep learning in medical image analysis. Med. Image Anal. **42**, 60–88 (2017)
16. Moss, S.E., Klein, R., Klein, B.E.: The 14-year incidence of visual loss in a diabetic population1. Ophthalmology **105**(6), 998–1003 (1998)

17. Prentašić, P., et al.: Segmentation of the foveal microvasculature using deep learning networks. J. Biomed. Optics **21**(7), 075008 (2016)
18. Rampasek, L., Goldenberg, A.: Learning from everyday images enables expert-like diagnosis of retinal diseases. Cell **172**(5), 893–895 (2018)
19. Schlegl, T., Waldstein, S.M., Vogl, W.-D., Schmidt-Erfurth, U., Langs, G.: Predicting semantic descriptions from medical images with convolutional neural networks. In: Ourselin, S., Alexander, D.C., Westin, C.-F., Cardoso, M.J. (eds.) IPMI 2015. LNCS, vol. 9123, pp. 437–448. Springer, Cham (2015). https://doi.org/10.1007/978-3-319-19992-4_34
20. Simonyan, K., Zisserman, A.: Very deep convolutional networks for large-scale image recognition. arXiv preprint arXiv:1409.1556 (2014)
21. Ting, D.S.W., et al.: Development and validation of a deep learning system for diabetic retinopathy and related eye diseases using retinal images from multiethnic populations with diabetes. Jama **318**(22), 2211–2223 (2017)
22. Ting, D.S.W., Cheung, G.C.M., Wong, T.Y.: Diabetic retinopathy: global prevalence, major risk factors, screening practices and public health challenges: a review. Clin. Exp. Ophthalmol. **44**(4), 260–277 (2016)
23. Ting, D.S.W., et al.: Artificial intelligence and deep learning in ophthalmology. Br. J. Ophthalmol. **103**, 167–175 (2018)
24. Ting, D.S.W., Wong, T.Y.: Eyeing cardiovascular risk factors. Nat. Biomed. Eng. **2**(3), 140 (2018)
25. Ting, D.S., Liu, Y., Burlina, P., Xu, X., Bressler, N.M., Wong, T.Y.: AI for medical imaging goes deep. Nat. Med. **24**(5), 539 (2018)
26. Ting, D.S., Yi, P.H., Hui, F.: Clinical applicability of deep learning system in detecting tuberculosis with chest radiography. Radiology **286**(2), 729 (2018)
27. Worrall, D.E., Wilson, C.M., Brostow, G.J.: Automated retinopathy of prematurity case detection with convolutional neural networks. In: Carneiro, G., et al. (eds.) LABELS/DLMIA -2016. LNCS, vol. 10008, pp. 68–76. Springer, Cham (2016). https://doi.org/10.1007/978-3-319-46976-8_8

Generative Adversarial Networks (GANs) for Retinal Fundus Image Synthesis

Valentina Bellemo[1(✉)], Philippe Burlina[2], Liu Yong[3], Tien Yin Wong[1,4,5], and Daniel Shu Wei Ting[1,4,5]

[1] Singapore Eye Research Institute, Singapore, Singapore
bellemo.valentina@seri.com.sg, daniel.ting.s.w@singhealth.com.sg
[2] Johns Hopkins University, Baltimore, USA
[3] Institute of High Performance, A*Star, Singapore, Singapore
[4] Singapore National Eye Centre, Singapore, Singapore
[5] Duke-NUS Medical School, Singapore, Singapore

Abstract. The lack of access to large annotated datasets and legal concerns regarding patient privacy are limiting factors for many applications of deep learning in the retinal image analysis domain. Therefore the idea of generating synthetic retinal images, indiscernible from real data, has gained more interest. Generative adversarial networks (GANs) have proven to be a valuable framework for producing synthetic databases of anatomically consistent retinal fundus images. In Ophthalmology, GANs in particular have shown increased interest. We discuss here the potential advantages and limitations that need to be addressed before GANs can be widely adopted for retinal imaging.

Keywords: Retinal fundus images · Medical imaging · Generative adversarial networks · Deep learning · Survey

1 Introduction

Computer-aided medical diagnosis is of great interest for medical specialists to assist in the interpretation of biomedical images. Harnessing the power of artificial intelligence (AI) and machine learning (ML) algorithms has sparked tremendous attention over the past few years. Deep learning (DL) methods – in particular – have been demonstrated to perform remarkably well for medical images analysis tasks [33]. Specifically, in Ophthalmology, DL systems with clinically acceptable performance have been achieved, for different end goals, including detecting different eye diseases, such as diabetic retinopathy (DR) [18,23,31,52,53], glaucoma [32], and age-related macular degeneration (AMD) [7,21]. These results show substantial potential for health-care and retinal applications, and possible implementation in screening programs.

However, there is a considerable need for large, diverse and accurately annotated data for further development, training and validation of DL models.

High costs, in terms of money and time, are required to obtain high quality data from healthy and diseased subjects. Furthermore, as is the case for certain pathologies, the number of samples is often too limited to be statistically significant to conduct certain analyses. More importantly, legal concerns regarding patient privacy and anonymized medical records introduce critical limitations leading to possible bias to the research outcome, as seeking genuine patient consent is a fundamental ethical and legal requirement of all healthcare practitioners [12,56].

Nevertheless, one of the most interesting and innovative alternatives of using existing patient data, when dealing with medical images, is to artificially create new synthetic data, where generative models can potentially help overcome the aforementioned limitations. Here we focus on one of the recent breakthroughs in DL research, generative adversarial networks (GANs), and their applications in the field of retinal image synthesis. In particular, in this review paper, a broad overview of recent work (as of end of September 2018) on GANs for retinal images synthesis is provided. Potential clinical applications are also discussed.

2 Background

Synthesizing realistic images of the eye fundus is a challenging task since before the DL era. It was originally approached by formulating complex mathematical models of the anatomy of the eye [17,37]. Currently, the advances in technology have brought high computational power leading ML to neural networks with deep architectures. Considering recent progresses in DL algorithms, GAN represents a valuable framework. The rapid enhancement of GANs [15] facilitated the synthesis of realistic-looking images, leading to slightly anatomically consistent and reasonable visual quality colored retinal fundus images [5,13,14,22,24,60]. GAN is an unsupervised DL machine, introduced by Goodfellow et al. [20], based on two models: a generator and a discriminator. The generative model learns to capture the data distribution, taking random samples of noise, and generates plausible images from that distribution. The discriminative model estimates the probability that a sample comes from the data distribution rather than generator distribution, and therefore is tasked to discriminate between real and fake images (Fig. 1).

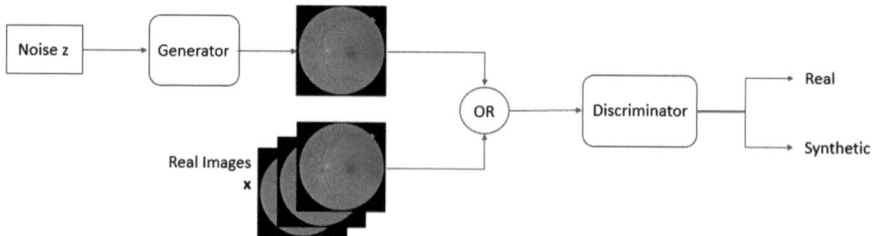

Fig. 1. GAN general scheme.

The performance of both networks simultaneously improves over time during the training process: while the generator tries to fool the discriminator by generating images as realistic as possible, the discriminator tries to not get fooled by the generator by improving its discriminative capability. Equation 1 represents one of the widely used GAN general loss function.

$$\min_G \max_D V(D,G) = \mathbf{E}_{x \sim p_{(data)}(x)}[log D(x)] + \mathbf{E}_{x \sim p_{(z)}(z)}[log(1 - D(G(z)))] \quad (1)$$

A variety of prominent extensions have been proposed, including DCGAN [42] and cGAN [38], to the most recent WGAN [3], LSGAN [36], AC-GAN [40], cycleGAN [62]. The adoption of GAN into medical imaging field covers applications such as denoising [57], reconstruction [48], detection [1], classification [46], segmentation [43], synthesis [4].

Concerning retinal fundus images field, GANs have been widely used for segmentation [30,35,47,49,50] purposes, and relatively less explored in synthesis [5,13,14,22,24,60] and super-resolution tasks [34].

3 Retinal Image Synthesis: Current Status

GANs have demonstrated capabilities to generate synthetic medical images with impressive realism. Existing work on GANs for the synthesis of colour retinal fundus images [5,13,14,22,24,60] is described in this section (Table 1).

Costa et al. [13] paired retinal fundus images with vessel tree segmentation. The binary maps of retinal vasculatures were obtained using U-Net [45] architecture. The pairs were used to learn a mapping from a binary vessel tree to a new retinal image (512×512 pixel), using image-to-image translation technique (Pix2Pix [25]). They used the general GAN adversarial loss and a global L1 loss, controlling low-frequency information in images generated by the generator. The training set consisted of 614 image pairs from the Messidor-1 dataset. For evaluation of their synthetic results, they adopted two no-reference retinal image quality metrics, Image structure clustering (ISC) [39], and Q_v [29] scores. While the latter score focused more on the assessment of contrast around vessel pixels, the former performed a more global evaluation.

Notably, Costa et al. proposed a follow-up work [14], where the authors trained jointly an Adversarial autoencoder (AAE) for retinal vascularity synthesis and a GAN for the generation of colour retinal images. Specifically, the VAE was used to learn a latent representation of retinal vessel trees and subsequently generate the corresponding retinal vessel tree masks, by sampling into a multi-variate Normal distribution. In turn, the adversarial learning mapped the vessel masks into colour fundus images, by sampling a multi-dimensional Gaussian distribution using the adversarial loss. The L1 loss promoted the consistency of global visual features, such as macula and optic disc. Again, 614 healthy macular-centered retinal images from Messidor-1 dataset were downscaled to 256×256 and used for the training phase. The authors performed qualitative and quantitative experiments comparing real and synthetic database containing the same number of pairs. They found that the model did not memorize the training data: the synthetic vessels resulted in images visually different from the closest on the real database. The authors decided to adopt again the ISC metric. Also, they evaluated U-Net [45] performance when trained to segment first real images only, and then synthetic data only. They found that training with only synthetic data lead to only slightly inferior AUCs values. However, combining synthetic and real images for training led to decreased performance. Some synthetic results are shown in Fig. 2.

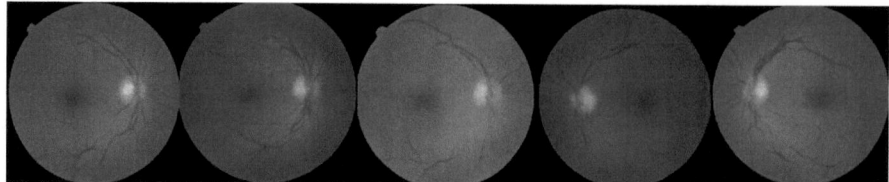

Fig. 2. Examples of synthetic images, reproduced with permission [14].

Similarly, Guibas et al. [22] proposed a two-stage pipeline, consisting of a DCGAN [42] architecture trained to synthesize retinal vasculature from noise, and a second cGAN (Pix2Pix [25]) to generate the corresponding colour fundus image, trained with Messidor fundus images. To evaluate the reliability of their synthetic data, the authors trained the same U-Net [45] with pairs of real images from DRIVE and pairs of synthetic samples. By computing F1 scores, they found that training with only synthetic data leads to only slightly inferior values. They also calculated the difference between the synthetic and real datasets with KL divergence score, to demonstrate that the synthetic data are diverse from the real sets and do not copy the original images. Some synthetic results are shown in Fig. 3.

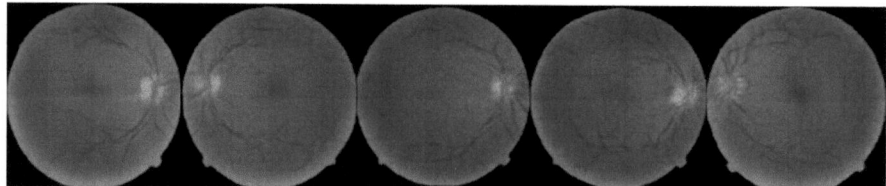

Fig. 3. Examples of synthetic images, reproduced with permission [22].

Zhao et al. [60] developed Tub-GAN, a framework capable of producing different outputs from the same binary vessel segmentation, by varying a latent code z. The model can learn from small training sets of 10–20 images. The authors deployed the method by Isola et al. [25] to generate retinal fundus images from binary segmentation masks. They built the generator with an encoder-decoder strategy allowing the introduction of latent code in a natural manner, without need of dropout. Along with this, they implemented a Tub-sGAN incorporating style transfer into the framework. This is made possible by introducing a style image as an additional training input. Thus, in terms of the optimization problem, the approach incorporates other two perceptual loss components [19]: style loss and content loss, as well as a total variation loss. The authors trained the models with 20 DRIVE images (resized to 512 × 512), 10 STARE images (resized to 512 × 512), 22 HRF images. As HRF raw images are of very large size (3304 × 2336), they resized the data to 2048 × 2048 instead. The authors extensively validated of the quality of their synthetic images and observed that 90% of the synthetic images are realistic looking. Zhao et al. carried out many experiments to evaluate the performance of different segmentation methods (a patch-based CNN and a re-implementation of DRIU [35]), demonstrating, from F1 scores, that by training the same model with both real and synthetic images, the segmentation performance improves (compared to Costa et al. work). They also considered an evaluation scheme in which the same trained segmentation model is applied on both synthetic and real images. Furthermore, to provide a quality assessment, the Structural similarity image quality metric (SSIM [55]) were applied, showing that SSIM scores were higher compared to Costa et al. results. Some synthetic results are shown in Fig. 4.

In another recent work, Zhao et al. [61] aimed at the generation of a synthetic fundus image dataset for vessels segmentation purposes. The authors explored a variant of gater recurrent unit [11], a recurrent neural network. Multiple styles of images can be reproduced taking advantage of recurrence.

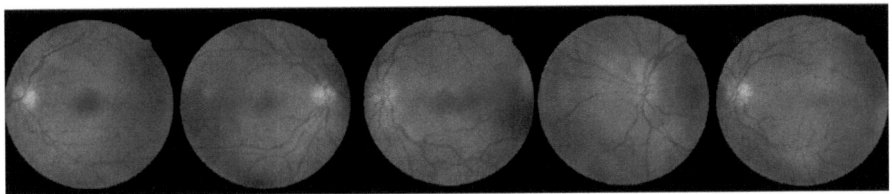

Fig. 4. Examples of synthetic images, reproduced with permission [60].

Similarly, Iqbal et al. [24] proposed MI-GAN for generating synthetic medical images and their segmented masks, from only tens of training samples. The authors proposed a variant of the style transfer, and considered DRIVE and STARE database. They updated the generator twice than discriminator to get faster convergence and overall training time was reduced significantly. The framework helped to enhance the image segmentation performance when used as additional training dataset.

Beers et al. [5] investigated the potential of progressive growing GANs (PGGANs [26]) for synthesizing fundus retinal images associated with retinopathy of prematurity. The GAN was trained in phases and the generator initially synthesized low resolution images (4 × 4 pixels). Additional convolutional layers were iteratively introduced to train the generator to produce images at twice the previous resolution, until the desired 512 × 512 pixels, considering interpolation between nearest neighbour upsampling. They deployed Wasserstein loss. The authors also showed that including segmentation maps as additional channels enhanced details; the segmentations were obtained with a pretrained U-Net [45]. They used 5,550 posterior pole retinal photographs, resized to 512 × 512, collected from the ongoing multi-centre Imaging and Informatics in Retinopathy of Prematurity (i-ROP) cohort study. The authors evaluated the vessels quality of the synthesized images considering a segmentation algorithm trained on real images and tested on real and generated images. Furthermore, to explore the variability of the synthetic results, they also trained a network for encoding synthetic images to predict the latent vector which produced them. They demonstrated that it was able to qualitatively approximate the global vessel structure. Some synthetic results are shown in Fig. 5.

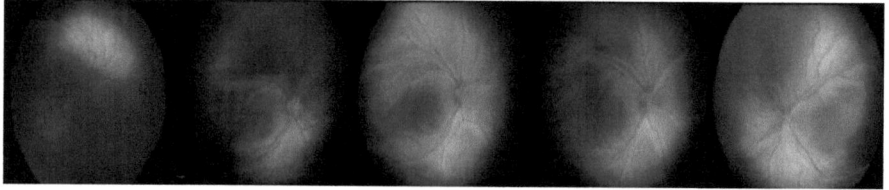

Fig. 5. Examples of synthetic images, reproduced with permission [5].

3.1 Limitations

In the AI field, the synthesis of medical images based on the general idea of adversarial learning has recently seen dramatic progress. Although adversarial techniques have achieved a great success in the generation of retinal fundus images, their application to retinal imaging is still very new and their adoption into clinical field is so far very limited or non-existent. There are many limitations concerning the proposed approaches that should be the subject of future research.

First, GAN can work with retinal images of size often lower than the resolution provided by current retinal fundus image acquisition systems. This can lead to a possible lack of quality of the synthesized datasets.

Second, it can be observed that the global consistency of the synthetic images is quite realistic-looking. Also, optic disc and fovea can be quite reasonably reconstructed, suggesting that GAN can automatically learn and reproduce intrinsic features, without any explicit human intervention. However, the consideration that optic disk and macula appear correctly located is a necessary but not sufficient condition: plausible diameter and geometry are critical in a clinical context. Important diseases are related to macula and optic disc, such as diabetic macular edema (DME) and glaucoma.

Table 1. List of papers on synthesis of coloured retinal fundus images.

	Datasets	Methods	Validation
Costa et al. [13]	-Messidor 512×512	-cGAN(Pix2Pix)	-ISC, Q_v
Costa et al. [14]	-Messidor 256×256	-AAE -cGAN(Pix2Pix)	-Segmentation -ISC
Guibas et al. [22]	-Messidor 512×512	-cGAN(Pix2Pix)	-Segmentation -KL divergence
Zhao et al. [60]	-Drive -Stare 512×512 -HRF 2048×2048 -Style references	-cGAN(Pix2Pix) -Style transfer	-Segmentation -SSIM
Iqbal et al. [24]	-Drive -Stare 512×512 -Style references	-cGAN(Pix2Pix) -Style transfer	-Segmentation
Beers et al. [5]	-i-ROP 4×4 ... 512×512	-PGANS	-Segmentation -Latent space espression

Third, all the existing approaches attach importance to retinal vascularity, showing that the generated images preserve the retinal vessels morphology. However, although high plausibility is shown, often the synthetic vessel networks are not clinically acceptable because of abnormal interruptions, unusual width variation along the same vessel, and lack of distinction between veins and arteries [14]. This could hinder the proper detection and preservation of retinal conditions such as arteries/vein occlusions and retinal emboli.

Fourth, while synthetic retinal images generated with GANs have overall consistent appearance, retinal lesions, instead, cannot be replicated properly. Zhao et al. examined some clinical pathological case (Fig. 6), using as style reference retinal images with DR, artery occlusion and cataract: the results are very far to be considered clinically acceptable. Also, the synthetic retinal images associated with retinopathy of prematurity by Beers et al. suffer of anatomical un-realism.

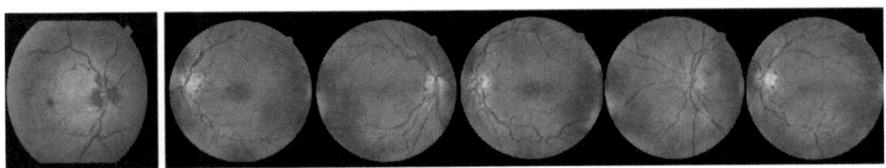

Fig. 6. Synthetic retinal images with pathology. The first image is style reference [60].

Fifth, although many quality evaluation approaches were explored, from segmentation methods to image quality metrics, they cannot be considered gold standard validation systems. In fact, first of all, realism and reliability of synthetic results should always be judged by retinal experts and ophthalmologists. Only after clinical assessment a synthetic retinal image can be considered clinically acceptable and then useful for further technical analysis purpose.

Appan et al. [2,41] have recently proposed novel solution for generating retinal images with hemorrhages using a GAN, obtain quite reliable results. The authors used both lesion and vessels annotations for training the model. Hence, they developed a DL system for the synthesis of retinal image with different severity, by providing their corresponding lesion masks, is feasible.

3.2 GAN and Variational Autoencoder

Along with GAN, another class of deep generative models to be explored for medical imaging tasks is Variational Autoencoder (VAE) [27]. The input for GAN is a latent (random) vector. It is not easy to manipulate the output of GAN to generate synthetic images with desired characteristics/features. VAE has been proposed to address this problem. There are two parts for a VAE, namely an encoder and a decoder. The encoder will encode input images by a multilayer convolutional neural network into a latent vector of random variables with corresponding mean and standard deviation. Unlike GAN starting with a random signal, VAE samples from the input-related latent vector and passes it to the decoder to reconstruct the original input image. Therefore, we can directly control VAEs to generate desired synthetic output images by selecting relevant input images. However, the output from original VAE may look blurry as the loss function to measure the similarity between input and output is mean squared error (MSE). In order to address this issue, Rezende et al. [44] add in adversarial network for similarity metrics, by combining both the merits of VAE and GAN. The use of VAE in medical imaging is very novel [8,54] and merits to be explored more fully for retinal image analysis.

4 Potential Clinical Applications

One of the most interesting application of GAN is image augmentation and the main motivation of existing work is the growing need for annotated data in medical image analysis area. Database of synthetic images could tremendously facilitate the development of robust DL systems. This is essential for the scenario of rare eye diseases: small population datasets with limited diversity could be amplified by approximating and sampling the underlying data distribution. Heterogeneity and size of training databases would dramatically increase with use of GANs. Several areas may potentially benefit from GANs, from common conditions with less severe spectrum, to less common conditions.

The common condition of DR has a wide spectrum of disease severity (Figs. 7, 8 and 9). Among patients with diabetes, approximately 70%–80% have no

DR and 10–20% have mild non-proliferative DR (NPDR) [16,59]. Mild NPDR (Fig. 7) is characterized by presence of microaneurysms (dilations of the retinal capillary) in the retina; given their variability in terms of locations and size, it is hard to obtain a diverse and large dataset to train algorithms dealing with mild NPDR. The application of GAN in this scenario may work if the artificially synthesized retinal images can simulate various examples of mild NPDR retinal images. Considering a more sever spectrum, within patients with diabetes, less than 5% have visual-threatening DR (VTDR), defined as proliferative DR (PDR, Fig. 10) and DME (Fig. 11) [16,59]. Although in the retinal fundus some changes can be quite obvious, they can also be quite variable, ranging from having the presence of new vessels at the optic disc to anywhere in the retina, presence of hard exudates at the centre of the macula and etc. Given the lack of prevalence, it is hard to build a robust model to detect these conditions and GAN could help to augment datasets of VTDR eyes.

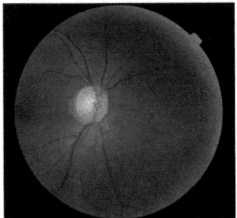 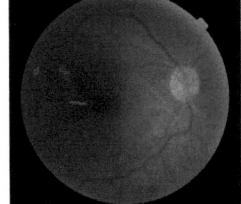 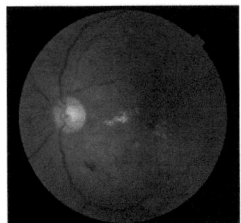

Fig. 7. Mild NPDR.   **Fig. 8.** Moderate NPDR.   **Fig. 9.** Severe NPDR.

Concerning AMD (Fig. 12), the diseases can be classified as early and late AMD. Specifically, the prevalence of early, late and any AMD is shown to be 8%, 0.4%, and 8.7% respectively [58]. While early disease is mainly defined as either any soft drusen and pigmentary abnormalities or large soft drusen, the late disease is defined as the presence of any of geographic atrophy or pigment epithelial detachment, subretinal haemorrhage or visible subretinal new vessel, or subretinal fibrous scar or laser treatment scar. Given the variety of manifestations and the lower prevalence, GAN could help to enhance database of AMD eyes.

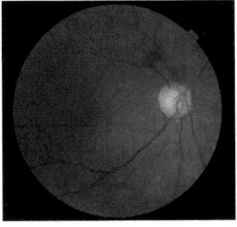 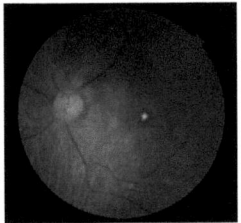

Fig. 10. PDR.   **Fig. 11.** DME.

Similarly, glaucoma (Fig. 13) is the leading cause of global irreversible blindness, with an overall global prevalence of 3.5% [51]. In details, while prevalence and risks vary among races and countries, prevalence is limited to 3% for primary open-angle glaucoma and 0.5% for primary angle-closure glaucoma. Glaucoma is associated with characteristic damage to the optic nerve and manifests itself in retinal images as optic disc dimension and shape variation and pixel level changes.

In the challenging case of rare diseases, GANs could potentially be functional in increasing the size of datasets of positive cases such as retinal vein occlusion (RVO) (Fig. 14) [28] and retinal emboli [10], where the prevalence is less than 1%. Also, epiretinal membrane (ERM) [9] disease could be considered.

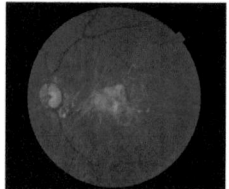
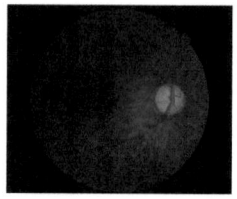
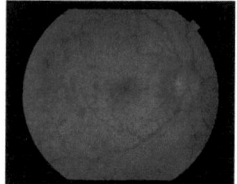

Fig. 12. AMD. **Fig. 13.** Glaucoma. **Fig. 14.** RVO.

It is quite common that a well-trained AI model for retinal images may not be able to generalize well and to achieve expected performance when being deployed on dataset collected from different devices, fields of view, resolutions, cohorts, ethnic groups, as in the case of retinal fundus images. This is commonly referred as domain adaption problem in ML [6]. GAN can be used to generate synthetic images with characteristics which are unique on target domain to achieve desired performance in this scenario.

5 Conclusion

GANs have seen tremendous progress over the past few years and the synthesis of retinal images via GANs has recently also seen increased interest. Limitations such as lack of large annotated datasets and high costs for high quality medical data collection may be overcome via these techniques. Also, legal concerns regarding patient privacy and anonymized medical records could be addressed via these generative approaches. However, GAN applications to medical imaging field are still growing and the results are far from clinically deployable still. In fact, retinal images provide vital information about the health of patients, therefore any synthetic generation has to be consistent carefully in the context of synthetic generation considering the special anatomy of colour retinal fundus images.

Existing approaches of retinal image synthesis attach importance to retinal vascularity and show that while optic disc and fovea can be reconstructed rather well, lesions must be replicated with high fidelity as well, which is a problem of continued investigation. Meaningful and appropriate assessment of the generated images degree of realism must be carried out by experts and ophthalmologists, in order to get efficient quality validation. Furthermore, as previous studies suggest, quantitative evaluation can be conducted by performing methods based on the problem domain. Therefore, in the future, the introduction of manual annotations for retinal lesions on training datasets of less than 50 images will be the first natural extension of the current models. This would have the goal to produce realistic-looking synthetic images and the new annotated data could be applied to develop novel retinal image analysis techniques, or to enhance existing database with meaningful data. Also, the flexibility of GAN suggests these can be used for deploying these methodologies used for retinal synthesis purpose to different medical images.

References

1. Alex, V., Mohammed Safwan, K.P., Chennamsetty, S.S., Krishnamurthi, G.: Generative adversarial networks for brain lesion detection. In: Medical Imaging 2017: Image Processing, vol. 10133, p. 101330G. International Society for Optics and Photonics (2017)
2. Appan, K.P., Sivaswamy, J.: Retinal image synthesis for CAD development. In: Campilho, A., Karray, F., ter Haar Romeny, B. (eds.) ICIAR 2018. LNCS, vol. 10882, pp. 613–621. Springer, Cham (2018). https://doi.org/10.1007/978-3-319-93000-8_70
3. Arjovsky, M., Chintala, S., Bottou, L.: Wasserstein GAN. arXiv preprint arXiv:1701.07875 (2017)
4. Baur, C., Albarqouni, S., Navab, N.: MelanoGANs: High resolution skin lesion synthesis with GANs. arXiv preprint arXiv:1804.04338 (2018)
5. Beers, A., et al.: High-resolution medical image synthesis using progressively grown generative adversarial networks. arXiv preprint arXiv:1805.03144 (2018)
6. Blitzer, J., McDonald, R., Pereira, F.: Domain adaptation with structural correspondence learning. In: Proceedings of the 2006 Conference on Empirical Methods in Natural Language Processing, pp. 120–128. Association for Computational Linguistics (2006)
7. Burlina, P.M., Joshi, N., Pekala, M., Pacheco, K.D., Freund, D.E., Bressler, N.M.: Automated grading of age-related macular degeneration from color fundus images using deep convolutional neural networks. JAMA Ophthalmol. **135**(11), 1170–1176 (2017)
8. Chen, X., Pawlowski, N., Rajchl, M., Glocker, B., Konukoglu, E.: Deep generative models in the real-world: an open challenge from medical imaging. arXiv preprint arXiv:1806.05452 (2018)
9. Cheung, N., et al.: Prevalence and risk factors for epiretinal membrane: the Singapore epidemiology of eye disease study. Br. J. Ophthalmol. **101**(3), 371–376 (2017)
10. Cheung, N., et al.: Prevalence and associations of retinal emboli with ethnicity, stroke, and renal disease in a multiethnic asian population: the Singapore epidemiology of eye disease study. JAMA Ophthalmol. **135**(10), 1023–1028 (2017)
11. Chung, J., Gulcehre, C., Cho, K., Bengio, Y.: Empirical evaluation of gated recurrent neural networks on sequence modeling. arXiv preprint arXiv:1412.3555 (2014)

12. Dysmorphology Subcommittee of the Clinical Practice Committee: informed consent for medical photographs. Genet. Med. **2**(6), 353 (2000)
13. Costa, P., et al.: Towards adversarial retinal image synthesis. arXiv preprint arXiv:1701.08974 (2017)
14. Costa, P., et al.: End-to-end adversarial retinal image synthesis. IEEE Trans. Med. Imaging **37**(3), 781–791 (2018)
15. Creswell, A., White, T., Dumoulin, V., Arulkumaran, K., Sengupta, B., Bharath, A.A.: Generative adversarial networks: an overview. IEEE Sig. Process. Mag. **35**(1), 53–65 (2018)
16. Ding, J., Wong, T.Y.: Current epidemiology of diabetic retinopathy and diabetic macular edema. Curr. Diab. Rep. **12**(4), 346–354 (2012)
17. Fiorini, S., Ballerini, L., Trucco, E., Ruggeri, A.: Automatic generation of synthetic retinal fundus images. In: Eurographics Italian Chapter Conference, pp. 41–44 (2014)
18. Gargeya, R., Leng, T.: Automated identification of diabetic retinopathy using deep learning. Ophthalmology **124**(7), 962–969 (2017)
19. Gatys, L.A., Ecker, A.S., Bethge, M.: Image style transfer using convolutional neural networks. In: Proceedings of the IEEE Conference on Computer Vision and Pattern Recognition, pp. 2414–2423 (2016)
20. Goodfellow, I., et al.: Generative adversarial nets. In: Advances in Neural Information Processing Systems, pp. 2672–2680 (2014)
21. Grassmann, F., et al.: A deep learning algorithm for prediction of age-related eye disease study severity scale for age-related macular degeneration from color fundus photography. Ophthalmology **125**(9), 1410–1420 (2018)
22. Guibas, J.T., Virdi, T.S., Li, P.S.: Synthetic medical images from dual generative adversarial networks. arXiv preprint arXiv:1709.01872 (2017)
23. Gulshan, V., et al.: Development and validation of a deep learning algorithm for detection of diabetic retinopathy in retinal fundus photographs. JAMA **316**(22), 2402–2410 (2016)
24. Iqbal, T., Ali, H.: Generative adversarial network for medical images (MI-GAN). J. Med. Syst. **42**(11), 231 (2018)
25. Isola, P., Zhu, J.Y., Zhou, T., Efros, A.A.: Image-to-image translation with conditional adversarial networks. arXiv preprint (2017)
26. Karras, T., Aila, T., Laine, S., Lehtinen, J.: Progressive growing of GANs for improved quality, stability, and variation. arXiv preprint arXiv:1710.10196 (2017)
27. Kingma, D.P., Welling, M.: Auto-encoding variational bayes. arXiv preprint arXiv:1312.6114 (2013)
28. Koh, V.K., et al.: Retinal vein occlusion in a multi-ethnic Asian population: the Singapore epidemiology of eye disease study. Ophthalmic Epidemiol. **23**(1), 6–13 (2016)
29. Köhler, T., Budai, A., Kraus, M.F., Odstrčilik, J., Michelson, G., Hornegger, J.: Automatic no-reference quality assessment for retinal fundus images using vessel segmentation. In: 2013 IEEE 26th International Symposium on Computer-Based Medical Systems (CBMS), pp. 95–100. IEEE (2013)
30. Lahiri, A., Ayush, K., Biswas, P.K., Mitra, P.: Generative adversarial learning for reducing manual annotation in semantic segmentation on large scale miscroscopy images: automated vessel segmentation in retinal fundus image as test case. In: Conference on Computer Vision and Pattern Recognition Workshops, pp. 42–48 (2017)

31. Lee, C.S., Tyring, A.J., Deruyter, N.P., Wu, Y., Rokem, A., Lee, A.Y.: Deep-learning based, automated segmentation of macular edema in optical coherence tomography. Biomed. Opt. Express **8**(7), 3440–3448 (2017)
32. Li, Z., He, Y., Keel, S., Meng, W., Chang, R.T., He, M.: Efficacy of a deep learning system for detecting glaucomatous optic neuropathy based on color fundus photographs. Ophthalmology **125**(8), 1199–1206 (2018)
33. Litjens, G., et al.: A survey on deep learning in medical image analysis. Med. Image Anal. **42**, 60–88 (2017)
34. Mahapatra, D.: Retinal vasculature segmentation using local saliency maps and generative adversarial networks for image super resolution. arXiv preprint arXiv:1710.04783 (2017)
35. Maninis, K.-K., Pont-Tuset, J., Arbeláez, P., Van Gool, L.: Deep retinal image understanding. In: Ourselin, S., Joskowicz, L., Sabuncu, M.R., Unal, G., Wells, W. (eds.) MICCAI 2016. LNCS, vol. 9901, pp. 140–148. Springer, Cham (2016). https://doi.org/10.1007/978-3-319-46723-8_17
36. Mao, X., Li, Q., Xie, H., Lau, R.Y., Wang, Z., Smolley, S.P.: Least squares generative adversarial networks. In: 2017 IEEE International Conference on Computer Vision (ICCV), pp. 2813–2821. IEEE (2017)
37. Menti, E., Bonaldi, L., Ballerini, L., Ruggeri, A., Trucco, E.: Automatic generation of synthetic retinal fundus images: vascular network. In: Tsaftaris, S.A., Gooya, A., Frangi, A.F., Prince, J.L. (eds.) SASHIMI 2016. LNCS, vol. 9968, pp. 167–176. Springer, Cham (2016). https://doi.org/10.1007/978-3-319-46630-9_17
38. Mirza, M., Osindero, S.: Conditional generative adversarial networks. https://arxiv.org/abs/1709.02023 (2014)
39. Niemeijer, M., Abramoff, M.D., van Ginneken, B.: Image structure clustering for image quality verification of color retina images in diabetic retinopathy screening. Med. Image Anal. **10**(6), 888–898 (2006)
40. Odena, A., Olah, C., Shlens, J.: Conditional image synthesis with auxiliary classifier GANs. arXiv preprint arXiv:1610.09585 (2016)
41. Pujitha, A.K., Sivaswamy, J.: Solution to overcome the sparsity issue of annotated data in medical domain. CAAI Trans. Intell. Technol. **3**(3), 153–160 (2018)
42. Radford, A., Metz, L., Chintala, S.: Unsupervised representation learning with deep convolutional generative adversarial networks. arXiv preprint arXiv:1511.06434 (2015)
43. Rezaei, M., Yang, H., Meinel, C.: Whole heart and great vessel segmentation with context-aware of generative adversarial networks. Bildverarbeitung für die Medizin 2018. I, pp. 353–358. Springer, Heidelberg (2018). https://doi.org/10.1007/978-3-662-56537-7_89
44. Rezende, D.J., Mohamed, S., Wierstra, D.: Stochastic backpropagation and approximate inference in deep generative models. arXiv preprint arXiv:1401.4082 (2014)
45. Ronneberger, O., Fischer, P., Brox, T.: U-Net: convolutional networks for biomedical image segmentation. In: Navab, N., Hornegger, J., Wells, W.M., Frangi, A.F. (eds.) MICCAI 2015. LNCS, vol. 9351, pp. 234–241. Springer, Cham (2015). https://doi.org/10.1007/978-3-319-24574-4_28
46. Salehinejad, H., Valaee, S., Dowdell, T., Colak, E., Barfett, J.: Generalization of deep neural networks for chest pathology classification in x-rays using generative adversarial networks. In: 2018 IEEE International Conference on Acoustics, Speech and Signal Processing (ICASSP), pp. 990–994. IEEE (2018)

47. Shankaranarayana, S.M., Ram, K., Mitra, K., Sivaprakasam, M.: Joint optic disc and cup segmentation using fully convolutional and adversarial networks. In: Cardoso, M.J., et al. (eds.) FIFI/OMIA -2017. LNCS, vol. 10554, pp. 168–176. Springer, Cham (2017). https://doi.org/10.1007/978-3-319-67561-9_19
48. Shitrit, O., Raviv, T.R.: Accelerated magnetic resonance imaging by adversarial neural network. In: Cardoso, M.J., et al. (eds.) DLMIA/ML-CDS -2017. LNCS, vol. 10553, pp. 30–38. Springer, Cham (2017). https://doi.org/10.1007/978-3-319-67558-9_4
49. Singh, V.K., et al.: Retinal optic disc segmentation using conditional generative adversarial network. arXiv preprint arXiv:1806.03905 (2018)
50. Son, J., Park, S.J., Jung, K.H.: Retinal vessel segmentation in fundoscopic images with generative adversarial networks. arXiv preprint arXiv:1706.09318 (2017)
51. Tham, Y.C., Li, X., Wong, T.Y., Quigley, H.A., Aung, T., Cheng, C.Y.: Global prevalence of glaucoma and projections of glaucoma burden through 2040: a systematic review and meta-analysis. Ophthalmology **121**(11), 2081–2090 (2014)
52. Ting, D.S.W., et al.: Development and validation of a deep learning system for diabetic retinopathy and related eye diseases using retinal images from multiethnic populations with diabetes. JAMA **318**(22), 2211–2223 (2017)
53. Ting, D.S., Liu, Y., Burlina, P., Xu, X., Bressler, N.M., Wong, T.Y.: AI for medical imaging goes deep. Nat. Med. **24**(5), 539 (2018)
54. Tomczak, J.M., Welling, M.: Improving variational auto-encoders using householder flow. arXiv preprint arXiv:1611.09630 (2016)
55. Wang, Z., Bovik, A.C., Sheikh, H.R., Simoncelli, E.P.: Image quality assessment: from error visibility to structural similarity. IEEE Trans. Image Process. **13**(4), 600–612 (2004)
56. Watt, G.: Using patient records for medical research. Br. J. Gen. Pract. **56**(529), 630–631 (2006)
57. Wolterink, J.M., Leiner, T., Viergever, M.A., Išgum, I.: Generative adversarial networks for noise reduction in low-dose ct. IEEE Trans. Med. Imaging **36**(12), 2536–2545 (2017)
58. Wong, W.L., et al.: Global prevalence of age-related macular degeneration and disease burden projection for 2020 and 2040: a systematic review and meta-analysis. Lancet Glob. Health **2**(2), e106–e116 (2014)
59. Yau, J.W., et al.: Global prevalence and major risk factors of diabetic retinopathy. Diab. care **35**(3), 556–564 (2012)
60. Zhao, H., Li, H., Maurer-Stroh, S., Cheng, L.: Synthesizing retinal and neuronal images with generative adversarial nets. Med. Image Anal. **49**, 14–26 (2018)
61. Zhao, H., Li, H., Maurer-Stroh, S., Guo, Y., Deng, Q., Cheng, L.: Supervised segmentation of un-annotated retinal fundus images by synthesis. IEEE Trans. Med. Imaging **38**(1), 46–56 (2018)
62. Zhu, J.Y., Park, T., Isola, P., Efros, A.A.: Unpaired image-to-image translation using cycle-consistent adversarial networks. arXiv preprint (2017)

AI-based AMD Analysis: A Review of Recent Progress

P. Burlina[1]([✉]), N. Joshi[1], and N. M. Bressler[2]

[1] Johns Hopkins University Applied Physics Laboratory, Laurel, MD, USA
pburlin2@jhu.edu
[2] Wilmer Eye Institute, Johns Hopkins University School of Medicine,
Baltimore, MD, USA

Abstract. Since 2016 much progress has been made in the automatic analysis of age related macular degeneration (AMD). Much of it was dedicated to the classification of referable vs. non-referable AMD, fine-grained AMD severity classification, and assessing the five-year risk of progression to the severe form of AMD. Here we review these developments, the main tasks that were addressed, and the main methods that were carried out.

Keywords: AMD diagnostics · Retinal diseases

1 The Importance of AMD and the Need for Automated Diagnostics

Age-related macular degeneration (AMD) is caused by damage to the macula. AMD affects millions of individuals in the US and is the main cause of irreversible central vision loss in the US and in developed countries in individuals over fifty [1,2]. AMD is associated with the presence of drusen. Drusen are long-spacing collagen and phospholipid vesicles located between the basement membrane of the retinal pigment epithelium (RPE) and the remainder of Bruch's membrane.

The intermediate stage AMD – often causing no visual deficit – is marked by the occurrence of many medium-sized drusen with a greatest linear dimension ranging from $63\,\mu$ to $125\,\mu$, or at least one large druse greater than 125μ, or geographic atrophy (GA) of the RPE not involving the fovea.

The intermediate stage of AMD often leads to the advanced stage, where more significant damage to the macula happens through either the choroidal neovascular (CNV) or "wet" advanced form, or GA involving the center of the macula or "dry" advanced form. The advanced stage AMD, when it is left untreated, can often lead to damage resulting in loss of central vision acuity affecting daily activities like reading, driving or recognizing objects, and consequently poses a substantial burden on affected individuals and socioeconomic burden on society.

Preferred practice recommends identifying at-risk individuals that have intermediate AMD and refer these to an ophthalmologist for follow up and potential treatment. Often choroidal neovascular AMD can be treated if caught before the disease progresses from the intermediate stage to the advanced stages where vision loss occurs. This fact has motivated several studies using machine learning to develop methods for automatically detecting referable AMD, which is defined as intermediate or above (advanced) stages of AMD, from fundus images. Additional endeavors looking at more granular classification of AMD have also emerged.

Manual screening of the entire at-risk population of individuals over fifty is not realistic because of the very large population at risk (for example the size is over 110 million in the US). Likewise, it is not feasible in all US healthcare environments to perform such screening because of varying or poor access to care. These issues are similar or often more prominent in low and middle income countries. Automated AMD diagnostic algorithms are therefore a critical area of research.

Additionally, while no treatment comparable to anti-VEGF currently exists for GA, clinical studies are now being pursued to identify treatments for slowing GA progression. Automated algorithms can therefore help in assessing treatment efficacy, where it is important to objectively quantify disease progression under therapy, and careful manual grading by clinicians is prohibitive.

Here we review recent or current investigations that are attempting endeavors in automated AMD analysis.

2 Recent Progress in AMD Analysis via DL

While work in automatic retinal image analysis (ARIA) has seen much progress in the past decades (e.g. [3–7]) it has remained limited by the use of classical image features and traditional machine learning techniques.

On the other hand, work in deep learning has recently led to significant progress in computer vision and medical image analysis in general [8,9]. In automated retinal image analysis in particular DL methods have been used to automatically detect patients with referable age related macular degeneration, doing fine grained AMD classification or risk assessment [10–15]. These different studies are reviewed below.

Deep Universal Features, Referability, and Multiclass Classification. The studies in [10,12] were the first (to the best of our knowledge) to use deep learning features to help in the automated classifications of AMD. Several binary and multiclass classification problems were considered including four-, three- and two-class (i.e. referable vs. not referable) classification problems. The referable problem consisted as that of finding individuals with AREDS grade 3 (intermediate) or 4 (advanced). The study made use of deep universal features and used the AREDS1 dataset which consisted of about five thousand high quality fundus images and resulted in accuracies of 79.4%, 81.5%, and 93.4% respectively for the above cited problems, and linear kappa values of 0.696, 0.722, 0.848. This performance was shown to be close to the physician performance.

Deep Convolutional Neural Networks and Referability Classification. The problem that was considered in [11] was again the binary problem consisting of discerning between referable and non-referable types of AMD. This study used the full AREDS dataset. Originally in the AREDS study, a 4-step scale classification scheme was used to categorize participants at enrollment time, this scale was not based on an analysis of outcome data, and it differentiated between the following types of AMD: no AMD (AMD-1), early AMD (AMD-2), intermediate AMD (AMD-3) and advanced AMD (AMD-4) [16]. This scale was reduced to a 2-class classification into non-referable AMD (AMD-1 and AMD-2) vs. referable AMD (AMD-3 and AMD-4). The case of AMD-3 (intermediate) was particularly interesting given that individuals could present no obvious signs of having it in terms of visual acuity loss, yet be at the threshold of developing the advanced form which could entail irremediable visual loss. In that work, using over 130 thousand images from AREDS, using AlexNet network resulted in classification accuracies between 88.4% and 91.6%, AUC between 0.94 and 0.96, and kappa between 0.764 and 0.829.

Application to Referability, Using Large Multi-ethnic Database. One potential limitation of those prior studies was the recognition that AREDS predominantly included mostly caucasian participants[1].

In the study [15,17] DL models were developed to adjudicate AMD referability as well as DR referability. The study used a large population of clinical data that consisted of a varied dataset with three ethnic groups comprising Malays, Chinese and Indian sub-populations [15].

Referability of both AMD and DR was studied, models were trained and tested on a dataset with more than 71 thousand images and more than 14 thousand multi-ethnic patients. It led to a performance for AMD referability classification of 93.2% sensitivity and 88.7% specificity, and AUC of 0.932.

Refined Referability. As a follow up to the work performed in [11], the study in [14] looked again at referability of AMD. Using AREDS as the dataset, and an approach that solved first a 4-class problem (from AREDS AMD-1 through AMD-4) that was fused down to the 2-class problem (referable vs. not) the study obtained an AUC of 0.972. This was compared to a direct 2-class classification approach using ResNet which gave an AUC of 0.970, in both cases improving on the original work in [11].

Fine Grained Classification and Risk Assessment. More complex and granular 4-, 9-, and 12-steps AMD severity classification problems were considered in [13] as well as [18]. The work in [13] solved both a 4-class classification problem and a detailed AREDS 9-step severity scale, using ResNet. It resulted in a performance measured via linearly weighted kappa equal to 0.77 for the 4-class problem, and a 9-class detailed severity performance with linear kappa of 0.74.

---

[1] Although it was also suggested that this may not necessarily have a substantial influence on the generalizability of the deep learning models.

Most notably the problem of estimating the probability that the eye would move to an advanced stage AMD within 5 year was estimated via DCNNs. This 5 year risk prediction led to a resulting performance, measured via the error on the probability of advancing to the most severe type of AMD in 5 years, ranging from 3.5% to 5.3%. The study used 3 different types of risk prediction methods based on either DL-based classification or regression. It used over 67 thousand images from AREDS. The significance of this was that it allowed a machine to perform tasks whose performance by human clinicians usually demands highly trained retinal specialists.

In [18] a related study was done but with different data partitioning and using over 120 thousand manually graded color fundus images from 3654 patients in the AREDS dataset. It performed a 12+1-class classification problem (including the 9 step scale previously described and 3 additional steps for the advanced neovascular or non-neovascular forms of AMD) and an additional 13th class corresponding to ungradeable images. This study used an ensemble of DCNNs resulting in improved performance. It led to a linear kappa value of 0.83, quadratic weighted kappa of 0.92 and accuracy of 63.3%. Generalizability was also tested by testing the DL models with another dataset (Augsburg Study KORA dataset) and led to linear kappa values of 0.19, and when evaluated for individuals over 55, kappa was found to be 0.58.

Data. With regards to data, AMD datasets have been less available and plentiful than their counterparts in DR (e.g. Messidor, EyePACS, etc.). However there is one exception to this, which is the NIH dataset developed under the AREDS (age related eye disease study) program which is available upon request to NIH [16]. Images in AREDS were procured from consented individuals over a 12-year longitudinal study which had over 130,000 field-2 stereoscopic color fundus photographs captured during the AREDS study from 4613 study participants at baseline and with follow-up visits.

Quantitative grading was done by certified graders (retinal specialists) at a fundus photograph reading center and were assigned to each image. These grades include multiple scaling systems which can be used as "reference standard" data set for the binary or multi-class classification problems that have been considered by several studies. Stereo images and bilateral right and left eyes were made available.

The 4-step AREDS scale mentioned earlier was used for eligibility criteria in AREDS. That scale was structured as follows: (i) eyes with no or only small drusen ($DS < 63\,\mu m$) and no pigmentation abnormalities were classified as normal and given a score of 1. (ii) eyes with multiple small drusen or medium-sized drusen ($63\,\mu m \leq DS < 125\,\mu m$) and/or pigmentation abnormalities related to AMD were classified as early stage AMD and given a score of 2. (iii) eyes with large drusen ($DS \geq 125\,\mu m$) or numerous medium-sized drusen and pigmentation abnormalities were classified as intermediate AMD and given a score of 3. (iv) eyes with lesions associated with CNV or GA (e.g. retinal pigment epithelial detachment, subretinal pigment epithelial hemorrhage) were classified as advanced AMD [3,6,9] and given a score of 4 if the fellow eye did not have central geographic atrophy or choroidal neovascular AMD. The more advanced 9 and 12 step severity scale is much more complex and is described in [13].

Looking Forward. Being able to monitor individuals for possible progression to advanced AMD and administration of AREDS-like supplements to reduce risk of progression to advanced AMD has been and remains a key endeavor.

Overall these studies show the promise of DL algorithms for public screening applications, an important endeavor considering that the number of individuals in the population at risk of intermediate or advanced AMD is expected to exceed 2.4 billion worldwide by 2050 [2].

Generally, these algorithms still have some limitations that will need to be addressed. They have not been very much validated in clinical environments, only on retrospective data. In particular, these algorithms need to be tested on newly acquired digital images, across a wide number of clinical centers, across a wide number of media (especially lens) opacities, various age groups, ethnicities, and with the number of false positives and false negative identified, before wide spread acceptance for screening can occur.

Also, considering that deep learning techniques are data driven and the quality of the models generated depends on the data itself, the availability of data often comes as a limiting factor. Therefore methods that use generative models are important to consider in the future development of DL models for AMD, specifically for augmenting datasets [19].

3 Conclusion

We reviewed DL-based methods for automated AMD diagnostics, which now demonstrate results that meet human clinical performance, a promising factor when considering the possible deploying these algorithms in clinical settings.

References

1. Klein, R., Klein, B.E.K.: The prevalence of age-related eye diseases and visual impairment in aging: current estimates. Investig. Ophthalmol. Vis. Sci. **54**(14) (2013)
2. Velez-Montoya, R., Oliver, S.C.N., Olson, J.L., Fine, S.L., Quiroz-Mercado, H., Mandava, N.: Current knowledge and trends in age-related macular degeneration: genetics, epidemiology, and prevention. Retina **34**(3), 423–441 (2014)
3. Burlina, P., Freund, D.E., Dupas, B., Bressler, N.: Automatic screening of age-related macular degeneration and retinal abnormalities. In: 2011 Annual International Conference of the IEEE Engineering in Medicine and Biology Society, EMBC, pp. 3962–3966. IEEE (2011)
4. Holz, F.G., Strauss, E.C., Schmitz-Valckenberg, S., van Lookeren Campagne, M.: Geographic atrophy: clinical features and potential therapeutic approaches. Ophthalmology **121**(5), 1079–1091 (2014)
5. Venhuizen, F.G., et al.: Automated staging of age-related macular degeneration using optical coherence tomography. Investig. Ophthalmol. Vis. Sci. **58**(4), 2318–2328 (2017)

6. Freund, D.E., Bressler, N., Burlina, P.: Automated detection of drusen in the macula. In: 2009 IEEE International Symposium on Biomedical Imaging: From Nano to Macro, ISBI 2009, pp. 61–64. IEEE (2009)
7. Feeny, A.K., Tadarati, M., Freund, D.E., Bressler, N.M., Burlina, P.: Automated segmentation of geographic atrophy of the retinal epithelium via random forests in AREDS color fundus images. Comput. Biol. Med. **65**, 124–136 (2015)
8. Esteva, A., et al.: Dermatologist-level classification of skin cancer with deep neural networks. Nature **542**(7639), 115–118 (2017)
9. Burlina, P., Billings, S., Joshi, N., Albayda, J.: Automated diagnosis of myositis from muscle ultrasound: exploring the use of machine learning and deep learning methods. PloS one **12**(8), e0184059 (2017)
10. Burlina, P., Freund, D.E., Joshi, N., Wolfson, Y., Bressler, N.M.: Detection of age-related macular degeneration via deep learning. In: 2016 IEEE 13th International Symposium on Biomedical Imaging (ISBI), pp. 184–188. IEEE (2016)
11. Burlina, P., Joshi, N., Pekala, M., Pacheco, K., Freund, D.E., Bressler, N.M.: Automated grading of age-related macular degeneration from color fundus images using deep convolutional neural networks. JAMA Ophtalmol. **135**, 1170–1176 (2017)
12. Burlina, P., Pacheco, K.D., Joshi, N., Freund, D.E., Bressler, N.M.: Comparing humans and deep learning performance for grading AMD: a study in using universal deep features and transfer learning for automated AMD analysis. Compu. Biol. Med. **82**, 80–86 (2017)
13. Burlina, P., Joshi, N., Pacheco, K.D., Freund, D.E., Kong, J., Bressler, N.M.: Use of deep learning for detailed severity characterization and estimation of 5-year risk among patients with age-related macular degeneration. JAMA Ophthalmol. **136**, 1359–1366 (2018)
14. Burlina, P., Joshi, N., Pacheco, K.D., Freund, D.E., Kong, J., Bressler, N.M.: Utility of deep learning methods for referability classification of age-related macular degeneration. JAMA Ophthalmol. **136**, 1305–1307 (2018)
15. Ting, D.S.W., et al.: Development and validation of a deep learning system for diabetic retinopathy and related eye diseases using retinal images from multiethnic populations with diabetes. JAMA **318**(22), 2211–2223 (2017)
16. Age-Related Eye Disease Study Research Group et al. The age-related eye disease study system for classifying age-related macular degeneration from stereoscopic color fundus photographs: the age-related eye disease study report number 6. Am. J. Ophthalmol. **132**(5), 668–681 (2001)
17. Ting, D.S.W., Liu, Y., Burlina, P., Xu, X., Bressler, N.M., Wong, T.Y.: AI for medical imaging goes deep. Nat. Med. **24**(5), 539 (2018)
18. Grassmann, F., et al.: A deep learning algorithm for prediction of age-related eye disease study severity scale for age-related macular degeneration from color fundus photography. Ophthalmology **125**, 1410–1420 (2018)
19. Burlina, P.M., Joshi, N., Pacheco, K.D., Liu, T.Y.A., Bressler, N.M.: Assessment of deep generative models for high-resolution synthetic retinal image generation of age-related macular degeneration. JAMA Ophthalmol. **137**(3), 258 (2019)

Artificial Intelligence Using Deep Learning in Classifying Side of the Eyes and Width of Field for Retinal Fundus Photographs

Valentina Bellemo[1(✉)], Michelle Yuen Ting Yip[2(✉)], Yuchen Xie[1(✉)], Xin Qi Lee[1], Quang Duc Nguyen[1], Haslina Hamzah[3], Jinyi Ho[3], Gilbert Lim[4], Dejiang Xu[4], Mong Li Lee[4], Wynne Hsu[4], Renata Garcia-Franco[5], Geeta Menon[6], Ecosse Lamoureux[1,2,3], Ching-Yu Cheng[1,2,3], Tien Yin Wong[1,2,3], and Daniel Shu Wei Ting[1,2,3]

[1] Singapore Eye Research Institute, Singapore, Singapore
bellemo.valentina@seri.com.sg
[2] Duke-NUS Medical School, Singapore, Singapore
[3] Singapore National Eye Centre, Singapore, Singapore
daniel.ting.s.w@singhealth.com.sg
[4] School of Computing, National University of Singapore, Singapore, Singapore
[5] Instituto Mexicano de Oftalmologia, IAP, Queretaro, Mexico
[6] Department of Ophthalmology, Frimley Park Hospital, Frimley, UK

Abstract. As the application of deep learning (DL) advances in the healthcare sector, the need for simultaneous, multi-annotated database of medical images for evaluations of novel DL systems grows. This study looked at DL algorithms that distinguish retinal images by the side of the eyes (Left and Right side) as well as the field positioning (Macular-centred or Optic Disc-centred) and evaluated these algorithms against a large dataset comprised of 7,953 images from multi-ethnic populations. For these convolutional neural networks, L/R model and Mac/OD model, a high AUC (0.978, 0.990), sensitivity (95.9%, 97.6%), specificity (95.5%, 96.7%) and accuracy (95.7%, 97.2%) were found, respectively, for the primary validation sets. The models presented high performance also using the external validation database.

Keywords: Retinal fundus images · Medical imaging · Deep learning

1 Introduction

Deep learning (DL) is a branch of artificial intelligence that comprises of multiple algorithms within the architecture of neural networks that enables data abstractions and is based on learning data representations. DL systems are particularly useful in automating predictive analysis. These benefits of DL systems have been applied to a plethora of medical fields including histopathology [10], radiology [6], dermatology [2], and ophthalmology [8]. These areas primarily capitalise on the DL systems' ability for medical image classification. Specifically in ophthalmology, clinically acceptable DL systems have been developed to detect different eye diseases, such as diabetic retinopathy, possible glaucoma, and age-related macular degeneration (AMD) [1,3,4,7–9].

Notably, there is a growing acknowledgement of the need for multiple annotations of retinal images to train and validate DL systems. To illustrate, categorising between Left and Right eyes will be critical in mapping image level data to eye level. In addition, differentiation of Macular-centred from Optic Disc-centred images (Fig. 1) may be useful in identifying site specific diseases such as AMD. This is an easy but time consuming task for grading technicians and ophthalmologists. Furthermore, these types of classifications are international and do not vary among the different retinal grading scales. DL frameworks may provide a solution to this challenge by automatically labelling retinal images, which may maximise efficiency in the classification process and furthering future machine learning efforts.

This paper focuses on the development and evaluation of two DL models. One model classifies retinal images into Left or Right eye (L/R) and the other classifies Macular-centred or Optic Disc-centred images (Mac/OD).

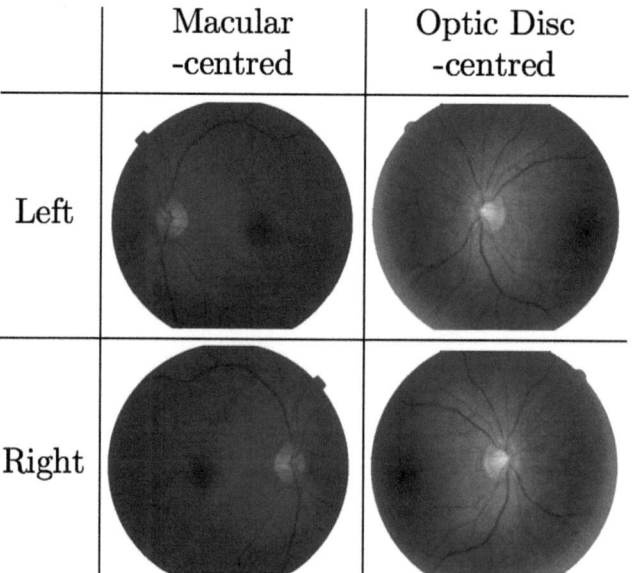

Fig. 1. Examples of left versus right and macular versus optic disc-centred fundus photographs.

2 Methods

2.1 Training and Testing Datasets

Data from the Singapore Epidemiology of Eye Disease (SEED) study was used for training and primary validation of the DL models. This is a population-based study of Singaporeans, 40 to 80 years of age, from the 3 major ethnic groups in Singapore: Malay (recruited from 2004 to 2006), Indian (recruited from 2007 to 2009) and Chinese (recruited from 2009 to 2011) [5]. Canon camera was used for capturing the fundus photographs.

Specifically for this study, 28,775 images from the Indian population-based study, Singapore Indian Eye Study (SINDI) and the Chinese population-based study, Singapore Chinese Eye Study (SCES) were used to train and develop the L/R DL model (n = 14,068 images of Left eye; 14,707 images of Right eye). These same images from SINDI and SCES trained the Mac/OD DL model (n = 12,654 Macular-centred images; 16,121 Optic Disc-centred images).

Subsequently, 6,811 images from SINDI and SCES, previously unseen by the model, were used for the primary validation of the DL model performance of the L/R DL model (n = 3,343 images of Left eye; 3,468 images of Right eye) and the Mac/OD DL model (n = 3,059 Macular-centred images; 3,752 Optic Disc-centred images). Each retinal image was graded by a senior non-medical professional grader and this grading was taken as the reference standard.

Similarly, both the models were also tested using external validation datasets from Mexican (338 images, clinical-based cohort), Zambian (419 images, population-based cohort), and Australian (387 images, clinical-based cohort) subjects. Specifically, Topcon camera was used for capturing fundus photographs from these Hispanic (n = 152 images of Left eye; 186 images of Right eye; n = 240 Macular-centred images; 98 Optic Disc-centred images), African (n = 208 images of Left eye; 211 images of Right eye; n = 304 Macular-centred images; 115 Optic Disc-centred images) and Caucasian (n = 190 images of Left eye; 197 images of Right eye; n = 205 Macular-centred images; 182 Optic Disc-centred images) communities.

2.2 L/R and Mac/OD Models

The DL models utilised an adapted VGGNet architecture for binary classification into Left or Right eye, and Macular or Optic Disc-centred image. This convolutional neural network (CNN) had been demonstrated previously to have state-of-the-art performance in retinal image analysis [8].

Image pre-processing represented the preliminary step. Firstly, each retinal photograph was automatic segmented in order to extract the Optic Disc, and subsequently uniformly rescaled to 512×512 pixels, the standardized square template. The first layer of the CNN was fed with input maps of RGB values of the template images. These pixel values were subsequently propagated to the following layers. The training was achieved by presenting the network with batches (size = 32) of labelled images from the training dataset, incrementally learning the key characteristics of the images belonging to each class. In fact, during this phase, the CNN gradually adapted its weights parameters to differentiate between L/R and Mac/OD images of the retina, with online backpropagation of errors using gradient descent, and max-pooling layers to select good invariant features. Model performance stabilized well reaching convergence before 100,000 batch iterations. In each model, the softmax output layer contained two output nodes, corresponding to the two classes (0 for R/Mac and 1 for L/OD). The output was thresholded at 0.50 for validation purpose, being adequate to L/R and Mac/OD binary classification.

2.3 Statistical Analysis

The outcome measures used to evaluate the performance of the DL models were area under the curve (AUC) of the receiver operating characteristic curve (ROC), sensitivity, specificity, and accuracy. Specifically, we considered L as positive case for L/R model and OD as positive case for Mac/OD model: sensitivity was the proportion of correctly detected L/OD (true positive) in Left/OD-centred retinal images; specificity was the proportion of correctly detected R/Mac (true negative) in Right/Mac-centred retinal images; accuracy was the proportion of true positive and true negative in all evaluated cases. The main analysis consisted of the classification of the retinal images from primary validation dataset and external validation datasets.

Bootstrapped and asymptotic 2-sided 95% CIs were calculated and presented for proportions (sensitivity, specificity) and AUC, respectively. The statistical analysis was performed using R Statistical Software (version 3.5.1; R Foundation for Statistical Computing, Vienna, Austria).

3 Results

The numerical results for primary validation dataset are summarised in Table 1. For the DL model on L/R classification, AUC of 0.978 (95% CI, 0.974–0.981), sensitivity of 95.9% (95.1%–96.5%), specificity of 95.5% (95% CI, 97.7%–96.1%) and accuracy of 95.7% (95% CI, 95.2%–96.1%) were achieved. The ROC plot is shown in Fig. 2. Similarly for the DL model on Mac/OD classification of images, AUC of 0.990 (95% CI, 0.988–0.992), sensitivity of 97.6% (97.1%–98.1%), specificity of 96.7% (95% CI, 96.1%–97.3%) and accuracy of 97.2% (95% CI, 96.8%–97.6%) were reported. The ROC plot is shown in Fig. 3.

The numerical results for external validation datasets are summarised in Table 2. For the DL model on L/R classification, an AUC of 0.973 (95% CI, 0.955–0.991), sensitivity of 96.7% (95% CI, 92.5%–98.9%), specificity of 96.8% (95% CI, 93.1%–98.8%) and accuracy of 96.7% (95% CI, 94.3%–98.4%) were achieved for the Hispanic population. Regarding African and Caucasian pulations, AUC, sensitivity, specificity, and accuracy were, respectively: 0.956 (95% CI, 0.933–0.976) and 0.976 (95% CI, 0.961–0.991), 94.3% (95% CI, 90.3%–97.0%) and 95.8 (95% CI, 91.9%–98.2%), 92.2%(95% CI, 92.7%–98.3%) and

91.9% (95% CI, 87.1%–95.3%), 95.2% (95% CI, 92.7%–97.1%) and 93.8% (95% CI, 90.9%–96.0%). The ROC plots are shown in Fig. 4. Equivalently for the DL model on Mac/OD classification of images, AUC of 0.993 (95% CI, 0.980–1.000), 0.955 (95% CI, 0.927–0.983), 0.957 (95% CI, 0.938–0.980), sensitivity of 99.0% (95% CI, 94.4%–100.0%), 92.2% (95% CI, 85.7%–96.4%), 90.1% (95% CI, 84.7%–94.0%), specificity of 99.6% (95% CI, 97.7%–100.0%), 98.7% (95% CI, 96.7%–99.6%), 97.1% (95% CI, 93.7%–98.9%) and accuracy of 99.4% (95% CI, 97.9%–99.9%), 96.9% (95% CI, 94.8%–98.3%), 93.8% (95% CI, 91.0%–96.0%) were reported for Mexico, Zambia and Australia datasets. The ROC plots are shown in Fig. 5.

Table 1. Results of performance of L/R model and Mac/OD model.

Primary validation	AUC	Sensitivity (%)	Specificity (%)	Accuracy (%)
L/R	0.978	95.9	95.5	95.7
Mac/OD	0.990	97.6	96.7	97.2

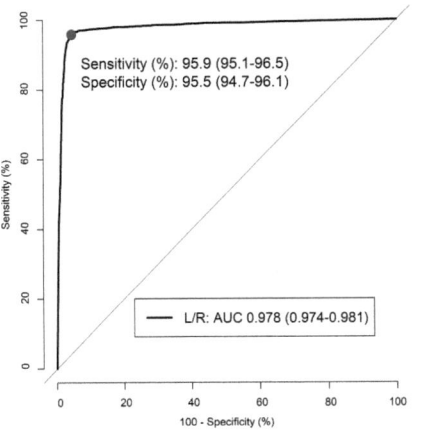

Fig. 2. Primary validation: ROC L/R

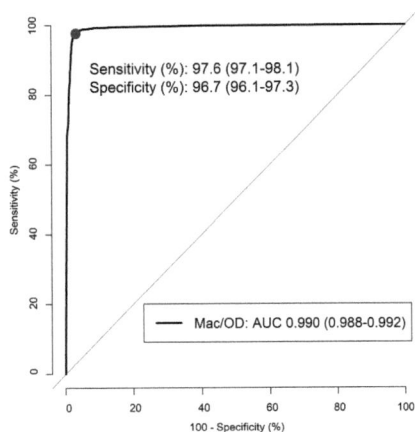

Fig. 3. Primary validation: ROC Mac/OD

Table 2. Results of performance of L/R model and Mac/OD model.

External validation	AUC	Sensitivity (%)	Specificity (%)	Accuracy (%)
L/R				
Hispanic	0.973	96.7	96.8	96.7
African	0.956	94.3	96.2	95.2
Caucasian	0.976	95.8	91.9	93.8
Mac/OD				
Hispanic	0.993	99.0	99.6	99.4
African	0.955	92.2	98.7	96.9
Caucasian	0.957	90.1	97.1	93.8

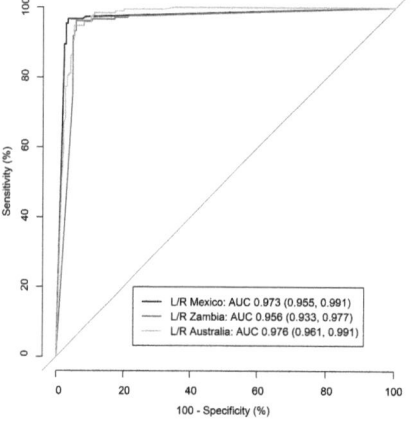
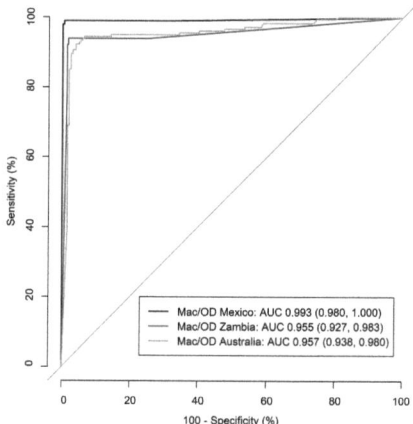

Fig. 4. External validation: ROC L/R

Fig. 5. External validation: ROC Mac/OD

4 Conclusions

This study showed that this DL model is highly accurate in classifying retinal images into categories of Left and Right images as well as categories of Macular and Optic Disc-centred images, reporting high sensitivities and specificities. The ability and flexibility of generalization for classification were proved by considering heterogeneous sources and settings for validation purpose, as well as multi-ethnic population datasets from different cohort studies. Consequently, this will enable the automation of this time-consuming and repetitive process and encourage the move towards simultaneous multi-labelling of images by artificial intelligence.

References

1. Burlina, P.M., Joshi, N., Pekala, M., Pacheco, K.D., Freund, D.E., Bressler, N.M.: Automated grading of age-related macular degeneration from color fundus images using deep convolutional neural networks. JAMA Ophthalmol. **135**(11), 1170–1176 (2017)
2. Esteva, A., et al.: Dermatologist-level classification of skin cancer with deep neural networks. Nature **542**(7639), 115 (2017)
3. Grassmann, F., et al.: A deep learning algorithm for prediction of age-related eye disease study severity scale for age-related macular degeneration from color fundus photography. Ophthalmology (2018)
4. Gulshan, V., et al.: Development and validation of a deep learning algorithm for detection of diabetic retinopathy in retinal fundus photographs. JAMA **316**(22), 2402–2410 (2016)
5. Ho, H., et al.: Association of systemic medication use with intraocular pressure in a multiethnic Asian population: the Singapore epidemiology of eye diseases study. JAMA Ophthalmol. **135**(3), 196–202 (2017)
6. Lakhani, P., Sundaram, B.: Deep learning at chest radiography: automated classification of pulmonary tuberculosis by using convolutional neural networks. Radiology **284**(2), 574–582 (2017)
7. Li, Z., He, Y., Keel, S., Meng, W., Chang, R.T., He, M.: Efficacy of a deep learning system for detecting glaucomatous optic neuropathy based on color fundus photographs. Ophthalmology (2018)
8. Ting, D.S.W., et al.: Development and validation of a deep learning system for diabetic retinopathy and related eye diseases using retinal images from multiethnic populations with diabetes. JAMA **318**(22), 2211–2223 (2017)
9. Wong, T.Y., Bressler, N.M.: Artificial intelligence with deep learning technology looks into diabetic retinopathy screening. JAMA **316**(22), 2366–2367 (2016)
10. Xu, Y., et al.: Large scale tissue histopathology image classification, segmentation, and visualization via deep convolutional activation features. BMC Bioinf. **18**(1), 281 (2017)

OCT Segmentation via Deep Learning: A Review of Recent Work

M. Pekala[1], N. Joshi[1], T. Y. Alvin Liu[2], N. M. Bressler[2], D. Cabrera DeBuc[3], and P. Burlina[1(✉)]

[1] Johns Hopkins University Applied Physics Laboratory, Laurel, MD, USA
pburlin2@jhu.edu
[2] Wilmer Eye Institute, Johns Hopkins University School of Medicine, Baltimore, MD, USA
[3] Bascom Palmer Eye Institute, University of Miami Miller School of Medicine, Miami, FL, USA

Abstract. Optical coherence tomography (OCT) is an important retinal imaging method since it is a non-invasive, high-resolution imaging technique and is able to reveal the fine structure within the human retina. It has applications for retinal as well as neurological disease characterization and diagnostics. The use of machine learning techniques for analyzing the retinal layers and lesions seen in OCT can greatly facilitate such diagnostics tasks. The use of deep learning (DL) methods principally using fully convolutional networks has recently resulted in significant progress in automated segmentation of optical coherence tomography. Recent work in that area is reviewed herein.

Keywords: OCT segmentation ·
Neurodegenerative, retinal and vascular diseases

1 The Importance of OCT and the Need for Automated Segmentation

Optical coherence tomography (OCT) is a non-invasive, high-resolution, imaging technique capable of capturing micron-scale structure within the human retina which is organized into layers (Fig. 1), and the invention of OCT has revolutionized the field of ophthalmology and neurology.

In ophthalmology, OCT is currently instrumental in the diagnosis, prognostication and treatment management of diabetic retinopathy (DR) and age related macular degeneration (AMD). This has far-reaching impact, as diabetic retinopathy is the leading cause of blindness in the developed world among the working-age population [1]; furthermore, AMD is the leading cause of central vision loss throughout North America [2] and other developed countries in patients aged 50 and over.

In terms of embryonic development, the retina is part of the central nervous system (CNS). In neurology, detailed cross-sectional imaging of the retina by

OCT has provided neurologists with a new biomarker, as it has been shown that retinal thinning, in particular thinning of the retinal nerve fiber layer (RNFL), is associated with various neurological disorders such as stroke, Parkinson's disease and Alzheimer's disease [3].

Different ophthalmic and neurological diseases affect different layers of the retina in various forms. For example, diabetic macular edema (DME) typically leads to fluid accumulation within the retina; neovascular AMD is usually characterized by fluid underneath the retina; multiple sclerosis can be associated with thinning of the RNFL. The diverse nature of OCT pathologies highlights the importance of accurate OCT segmentation. However, manual segmentation is labor and time intensive. Therefore, automatic, reliable, accurate OCT segmentation is crucial for further expanding the usefulness of the OCT technology.

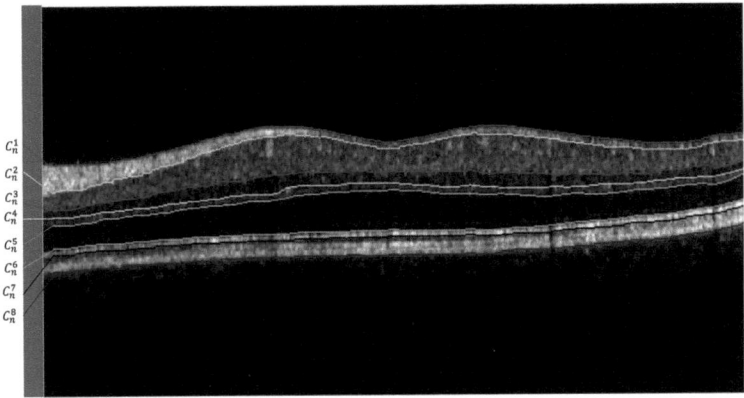

Fig. 1. SD-OCT scan showing the retinal structure (reproduced with permission from [4]). Eight intraretinal layers boundaries are shown in red, yellow, magenta, white, cyan, green, black and blue solid lines, where these are: red-internal limiting membrane (ILM), yellow-outer boundary of the retinal fiber layer (RNFLo), magenta-inner plexiform layer-inner nuclear layer (IPL-INL), white-inner nuclear layer-outer plexiform layer (INL-OPL), cyan-outer boundary of the outer plexiform layer (OPLo), green-inner segment-outer segment (IS-OS), black-outer segment-retinal pigment epithelium (OS-RPE), and blue-retinal pigment epithelium-choroid (RPE-CH). (Color figure online)

2 Automated Segmentation Methods

Automatic retinal image analysis (ARIA) has seen substantial progress in the past few decades as large datasets have been made publicly available and machine learning techniques have evolved (e.g. [5–10]). This progress has permeated work in automatic OCT segmentation. Much work has been done in classical methods for OCT segmentation, and it has been directed towards the use of graph based methods [11] as seen in [4,12–18]. A recent study, in [19] exemplifies these classical approaches: a 7 layer OCT segmentation using kernel regression (KR)-based classification was developed to estimate diabetic macular edema (DME) as well as OCT layer boundaries, a method which was then combined with an approach using graph theory and dynamic programming and validated on 110 B-scans and ten patients with severe DME pathology, yielding a DICE coefficient of 0.78. For an extensive review of classical methods see [17,18].

Recently, work in deep learning has had substantial impact on medical imaging (see examples such as [20,21]) and also ARIA, for instance to automatically detect patients with referable age related macular degeneration from fundus images [22,23], for AMD fine grained severity classification and assessment of 5 year risk of advancement to the advanced form of AMD [24–26], DR referability [27], cardiovascular risks factors estimation from retinal fundus imagery [28], or retinal OCT [29]. For OCT segmentation, recent studies have featured the use of convolutional neural networks (ConvNets) and FCNs. We review next some of the recent contributions using these techniques.

Most methods using DL for OCT segmentation consist of estimating the location of retinal surfaces and lesions (e.g. edema). These methods most often solve a per-pixel (or "dense") classification resulting in semantic segmentation, and most of these methods also use fully convolutional networks (FCNs) for labeling each pixel in the image with the most probable corresponding retinal layer label. Fully convolutional neural networks [30,31] are a subcategory of ConvNets that take tensor-like data as input and produce tensor-like output data. In particular these networks can be used to map 2D or 3D OCT to corresponding 2D or 3D labeled images where each pixel has a class estimate (i.e. per-pixel for 2D or per-voxel labels for 3D cubes).

Two recent widely used FCNs are U-Nets [32] and DenseNets [30]. Most recent FCN-based methods for OCT segmentation use these networks, with additional pre- and post-processing steps, or use modifications of these baseline networks architectures and loss functions. In particular, the U-Net architecture has been used recently for a number of medical image segmentation tasks. It consists of an encoder-like path and a decoder path, and interconnections (skip connections) between each level of the encoder and the decoder. DenseNets also make use of skip connections from each layer to each subsequent layers which permit each layer of the network to directly process the outputs from all previous layers. This approach therefore makes richer sets of features available at each layer of the network while also providing a mechanism to alleviate the vanishing gradient problem which can arise during training when back-propagating gradients. This is in contrast to more traditional networks which generate features in a strictly serial fashion (i.e. each layer operates solely upon the output of the previous layer). The details of the DenseNet-FCN architecture are described in [30]. Next we review specific studies using FCNs for OCT segmentation.

A recent study in [33] used a cascaded U-Net architecture [32] and compared performance to that of a classical approach based on random forests. [34] uses a hybrid ConvNets and graph based method to identify OCT boundary layers. The work in [35] was applied for both retinal layers and fluid segmentation. The architecture used is also related to the encoder and decoder structure of

U-Nets. One departure includes using a modified loss function that includes also the DICE coefficient in the loss. The method was evaluated on the Duke OCT dataset including DME patients. The dataset included 110 annotated SD-OCT B-scans of 512×740 images from 10 patients. The segmentation was done on 7 layers and includes one additional class for the fluid labeling. The study demonstrated improvement over baseline versions of FCNs including U-Nets. Distances in pixels from ground truth for the methods ranged from 0.16 to 0.34 for different zones in the retina, and compared favorably to the other methods. DICE metrics using leave one out experiments performed on 8 patients resulted in values from 0.77, for the fluid segmentation, to 0.99 for several other layers.

In another reported study, [36] used a variation of the baseline U-Net architecture to segment optic nerve head OCT. This study included 100 patients from the Singapore National Eye Center: 40 healthy patients and 60 glaucoma patients. This segmentation algorithm achieved a DICE coefficient of 0.84. In addition, it was found that that algorithm performed better in a statistically significant manner when compensated images were used for training. Adaptive compensation is a post-processing technique used to remove effects of light attenuation and has been shown to remove various artifacts, such as blood vessel shadows.

The work in [37] used ConvNets and a U-Net-like architecture to delineate intraretinal fluid on OCT. Using 1289 OCT images, the CNN obtained a maximal cross-validated DICE of 0.911, when compared with segmentation by human experts. The agreement between experts and between experts and CNN both reached a generally accepted value of excellent agreement, and there was no statistical difference between the two.

The work in [38] used the DenseNet architecture [30,31] and coupled it with post-processing that made use of a heuristic approach or an approach using Gaussian processes (GP) regression with a Radial Basis Function (RBF) kernel [39]. The RBF kernel had two hyper-parameters, a noise variance and a characteristic length scale. The method used a K-fold cross validation for performance evaluation. The performance was measured by computing the distance between gold standard and detected boundaries. Results showed mean unsigned errors of the order of 1.06 pixels for the best method using DenseNets and GP. This performance was better than the human interoperator error of 1.10 pixels. That method exceeded the performance of a number of classical methods of records it was compared to, and also exceeded the performance of the baseline DenseNet approach, showing the usefulness of GP.

3 Conclusion

We reviewed recent methods for segmenting OCT images using fully convolutional networks. These methods now demonstrate results with performance improving on classical segmentation methods and on par with human operators.

References

1. Wong, T.Y., Cheung, N., Mitchell, P.: Diabetic retinopathy. Lancet **376**(9735), 124–136 (2010)
2. Bressler, N.M.: Age-related macular degeneration is the leading cause of blindness. JAMA **291**(15), 1900–1901 (2004)
3. London, A., Benhar, I., Schwartz, M.: The retina as a window to the brain-from eye research to CNS disorders. Nat. Rev. Neurol. **9**(1), 44–53 (2013)
4. Tian, J., et al.: Performance evaluation of automated segmentation software on optical coherence tomography volume data. J. Biophoton. **9**(5), 478–489 (2016)
5. Burlina, P., Freund, D.E., Dupas, B., Bressler, N.: Automatic screening of age-related macular degeneration and retinal abnormalities. In: 2011 Annual International Conference of the IEEE Engineering in Medicine and Biology Society, EMBC, pp. 3962–3966. IEEE (2011)
6. Holz, F.G., Strauss, E.C., Schmitz-Valckenberg, S., van Lookeren Campagne, M.: Geographic atrophy: clinical features and potential therapeutic approaches. Ophthalmology **121**(5), 1079–1091 (2014)
7. Venhuizen, F.G., et al.: Automated staging of age-related macular degeneration using optical coherence tomography. Invest. Ophthalmol. Vis. Sci. **58**(4), 2318–2328 (2017)
8. Burlina, P., Freund, D.E., Joshi, N., Wolfson, Y., Bressler, N.M.: Detection of age-related macular degeneration via deep learning. In: 2016 IEEE 13th International Symposium on Biomedical Imaging (ISBI), pp. 184–188. IEEE (2016)
9. Freund, D.E., Bressler, N., Burlina, P.: Automated detection of drusen in the macula. In: 2009 IEEE International Symposium on Biomedical Imaging: From Nano to Macro, ISBI 2009, pp. 61–64. IEEE, 2009
10. Feeny, A.K., Tadarati, M., Freund, D.E., Bressler, N.M., Burlina, P.: Automated segmentation of geographic atrophy of the retinal epithelium via random forests in AREDS color fundus images. Comput. Biol. Med. **65**, 124–136 (2015)
11. Juang, R., McVeigh, E.R., Hoffmann, B., Yuh, D., Burlina, P.: Automatic segmentation of the left-ventricular cavity and atrium in 3D ultrasound using graph cuts and the radial symmetry transform. In: 2011 IEEE International Symposium on Biomedical Imaging: From Nano to Macro, pp. 606–609. IEEE (2011)
12. Cabrera DeBuc, D.: A review of algorithms for segmentation of retinal image data using optical coherence tomography. In: Image Segmentation, InTech (2011)
13. Heidelberg Engineering GmbH. Spectralis HRA+OCT user manual software (2014)
14. Lee, K., Abramoff, M.D., Garvin, M., Sonka, M.: The Iowa reference algorithms (retinal image analysis lab, Iowa institute for biomedical imaging, IA), (2014)
15. Lang, A., et al.: Retinal layer segmentation of macular OCT images using boundary classification. Biomed. Optics Express **4**(7), 1133–1152 (2013)
16. Dufour, P.A., et al.: Graph-based multi-surface segmentation of OCT data using trained hard and soft constraints. IEEE Trans. Med. Imag. **32**(3), 531–543 (2013)
17. Tian, J., et al.: Real-time automatic segmentation of optical coherence tomography volume data of the macular region. PLOS One **10**(8) (2015)
18. Breger, A., et al.: Supervised learning and dimension reduction techniques for quantification of retinal fluid in optical coherence tomography images. Eye **31**, 1212 (2017)
19. Chiu, S.J., Allingham, M.J., Mettu, P.S., Cousins, S.W., Izatt, J.A., Farsiu, S.: Kernel regression based segmentation of optical coherence tomography images with diabetic macular edema. Biomed. Opt. Express **6**(4), 1172–1194 (2015)

20. Esteva, A., et al.: Dermatologist-level classification of skin cancer with deep neural networks. Nature **542**(7639), 115–118 (2017)
21. Burlina, P., Billings, S., Joshi, N., Albayda, J.: Automated diagnosis of myositis from muscle ultrasound: exploring the use of machine learning and deep learning methods. PLOS One **12**(8) (2017)
22. Burlina, P., Joshi, N., Pekala, M., Pacheco, K., Freund, D.E., Bressler, N.M.: Automated grading of age-related macular degeneration from color fundus images using deep convolutional neural networks. JAMA Ophtalmol. **135**, 1170–1176 (2017)
23. Burlina, P., Pacheco, K.D., Joshi, N., Freund, D.E., Bressler, N.M.: Comparing humans and deep learning performance for grading AMD: a study in using universal deep features and transfer learning for automated AMD analysis. Comput. Biol. Med. **82**, 80–86 (2017)
24. Burlina, P., Joshi, N., Pacheco, K.D., Freund, D.E., Kong, J., Bressler, N.M.: Use of deep learning for detailed severity characterization and estimation of 5-year risk among patients with age-related macular degeneration. JAMA Ophthalmol. **136**, 1359–1366 (2018)
25. Burlina, P., Joshi, N., Pacheco, K.D., Freund, D.E., Kong, J., Bressler, N.M.: Utility of deep learning methods for referability classification of age-related macular degeneration. JAMA Ophtalmol. **136**, 1305–1307 (2018)
26. Ting, D.S.W., Liu, Y., Burlina, P., Xu, X., Bressler, N.M., Wong, T.Y.: AI for medical imaging goes deep. Nat. Med. **24**(5), 539 (2018)
27. Ting, D.S.W., et al.: Development and validation of a deep learning system for diabetic retinopathy and related eye diseases using retinal images from multiethnic populations with diabetes. JAMA **318**(22), 2211–2223 (2017)
28. Poplin, R., et al.: Prediction of cardiovascular risk factors from retinal fundus photographs via deep learning. Nat. Biomed. Eng. **2**(3), 158 (2018)
29. Lee, C.S., Baughman, D.M., Lee, A.Y.: Deep learning is effective for classifying normal versus age-related macular degeneration OCT images. Ophthalmol. Retina **1**(4), 322–327 (2017)
30. Jégou, S., Drozdzal, M., Vazquez, D., Romero, A., Bengio, Y.: The one hundred layers tiramisu: Fully convolutional densenets for semantic segmentation. In: 2017 IEEE Conference on Computer Vision and Pattern Recognition Workshops (CVPRW), pp. 1175–1183. IEEE (2017)
31. Huang, G., Liu, Z., Weinberger, K.Q., van der Maaten, L.: Densely connected convolutional networks. arXiv preprint arXiv:1608.06993 (2016)
32. Ronneberger, O., Fischer, P., Brox, T.: U-Net: convolutional networks for biomedical image segmentation. In: Navab, N., Hornegger, J., Wells, W.M., Frangi, A.F. (eds.) MICCAI 2015. LNCS, vol. 9351, pp. 234–241. Springer, Cham (2015). https://doi.org/10.1007/978-3-319-24574-4_28
33. He, Y., et al.: Towards topological correct segmentation of macular OCT from cascaded FCNs. In: Cardoso, M.J., et al. (eds.) FIFI/OMIA -2017. LNCS, vol. 10554, pp. 202–209. Springer, Cham (2017). https://doi.org/10.1007/978-3-319-67561-9_23
34. Fang, L., Cunefare, D., Wang, C., Guymer, R.H., Li, S., Farsiu, S.: Automatic segmentation of nine retinal layer boundaries in OCT images of non-exudative AMD patients using deep learning and graph search. Biomed. Opt. Express **8**(5), 2732–2744 (2017)
35. Roy, A.G., et al.: Relaynet: retinal layer and fluid segmentation of macular optical coherence tomography using fully convolutional networks. Biomed. Opt. Express **8**(8), 3627–3642 (2017)

36. Devalla, S.K., et al.: A deep learning approach to digitally stain optical coherence tomography images of the optic nerve head. Invest. Ophthalmol. Vis. Sci. **59**(1), 63–74 (2018)
37. Lee, C.S., Tyring, A.J., Deruyter, N.P., Wu, Y., Rokem, A., Lee, A.Y.: Deep-learning based, automated segmentation of macular edema in optical coherence tomography. bioRxiv, p. 135640 (2017)
38. Pekala, M., Joshi, N., Freund, D.E., Bressler, N.M., DeBuc, D.C., Burlina, P.M.: Deep learning based retinal OCT segmentation. arXiv preprint arXiv:1801.09749 (2018)
39. Rasmussen, C.E., Williams, C.K.: Gaussian Processes for Machine Learning, vol. 1. MIT press Cambridge, Cambridge (2006)

Auto-classification of Retinal Diseases in the Limit of Sparse Data Using a Two-Streams Machine Learning Model

C.-H. Huck Yang[1,2(✉)], Fangyu Liu[3(✉)], Jia-Hong Huang[1,6], Meng Tian[4], M.D. I-Hung Lin[5], Yi Chieh Liu[6], Hiromasa Morikawa[1], Hao-Hsiang Yang[6], and Jesper Tegnèr[1,7]

[1] Biological and Environmental Sciences and Engineering Division, Computer, Electrical and Mathematical Sciences and Engineering Division, King Abdullah University of Science and Technology, Thuwal, Saudi Arabia
{chao-han.yang,jiahong.huang,hiromasa.morikawa, jesper.tegner}@kaust.edu.sa
[2] Georgia Institute of Technology, Atlanta, GA, USA
[3] University of Waterloo, Waterloo, Canada
fangyu.liu@uwaterloo.ca
[4] Department of Ophthalmology, Bern University Hospital, Bern, Switzerland
[5] Department of Ophthalmology, Tri-Service General Hospital, Taipei, Taiwan
[6] National Taiwan University, Taipei, Taiwan
[7] Unit of Computational Medicine, Center for Molecular Medicine, Department of Medicine, Karolinska Institutet, Solna, Sweden

Abstract. Automatic clinical diagnosis of retinal diseases has emerged as a promising approach to facilitate discovery in areas with limited access to specialists. Based on the fact that fundus structure and vascular disorders are the main characteristics of retinal diseases, we propose a novel visual-assisted diagnosis hybrid model mixing the support vector machine (SVM) and deep neural networks (DNNs). Furthermore, we present a new clinical retina labels collection sorted by the professional ophthalmologist from the educational project Retina Image Bank, called EyeNet, for ophthalmology incorporating 52 retina diseases classes. Using EyeNet, our model achieves 90.40% diagnosis accuracy, and the model performance is comparable to the professional ophthalmologists (https://github.com/huckiyang/EyeNet2).

1 Introduction

Computational retinal disease methods [1,2] has been investigated extensively through different signal processing techniques. Retinal diseases are accessible to machine learning techniques due to their visual nature in contrast to other common human diseases requiring invasive techniques for diagnosis or treatments. Typically, the diagnosis accuracy of retinal diseases based on the clinical retinal images is highly dependent on the practical experience of a physician or ophthalmologist. However, training highly-skilled ophthalmologists usually take

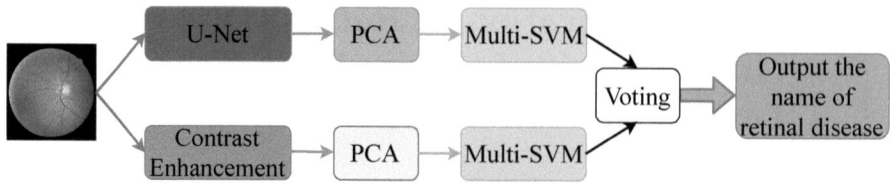

Fig. 1. This figure represents our proposed two-streams model. A raw retinal image as an input of DNNs, U-Net, and as the other input to a contrast enhancement algorithm. Then we pass the output of U-Net to two separated PCA processing. Finally, the output of these two PCA modules is sent as inputs to the retina disease classifier, SVM, which give the outcome of predicted retina disease.

years and the number of them, especially in the less-developed area, is still far from enough. Therefore, developing an automatic retinal diseases detection system is important, and it will broadly facilitate diagnostic accuracy of retinal diseases. Moreover, for remote rural areas, where there are even no ophthalmologists locally to screen retinal disease, the automatic retinal diseases detection system also helps non-ophthalmologists find the patient of the retinal disease, and further, refer them to the medical center for further treatment.

The development of automatic diseases detection (ADD) [3] alleviates enormous pressure from social healthcare systems. Retinal symptom analysis [4] is one of the important ADD applications given that it offers a unique opportunity to improve eye care on a global stage. The World Health Organization estimates that age-related macular degeneration (AMD) and Diabetic Retinopathy, which are two typical retinal diseases, are expected to affect over 500 million people worldwide by 2020 [5].

Moreover, the increasing number of cases of diabetic retinopathy globally requires extending efforts in developing visual tools to assist in the analytic of the series of retinal disease. These decision support systems for retinal ADD, as [6] for non-proliferative diabetic retinopathy have been improved from recent machine learning success on the high dimensional images processing by featuring details on the blood vessel. [7] demonstrated an automated technique for the segmentation of the blood vessels by tracking the center of the vessels on Kalman Filter. However, these pattern recognition based classification still rely on hand-crafted features and only specify for evaluating single retinal symptom. Despite extensive efforts using wavelet signal processing, retinal ADD remains a viable target for improved machine learning techniques applicable for point-of-care (POC) medical diagnosis and treatment in the aging society [8].

To the best of our knowledge, the amount of clinical retinal images are less compared to other cell imaging data, such as blood cell and a cancer cell. However, a vanilla deep learning based diseases diagnosis system requires large amounts of data. Therefore, we propose a novel visual-assisted diagnosis algorithm which is based on an integration of the support vector machine and deep neural networks. The primary goal of this work is to automatically classify 52 specific retinal diseases for human beings with the reliable clinical-assisted ability on the intelligent medicine approaches. To foster the long-term visual analytics research, we also present a visual clinical label collection, EyeNet, including several crucial symptoms as AMD, DR, uveitis, BRVO, BRAO.

Contributions

- We design a novel two-streams-based algorithm on the support vector machine and deep neural networks to facilitate medical diagnosis of retinal diseases.
- We present a new clinical labels collection, EyeNet, for Ophthalmology with 52 retina diseases classes as a crucial aid to the ophthalmologist and medical informatics community.
- Finally, we visualize the learned features inside the DNNs model by heat maps. The visualization helps in understanding the medical comprehensibility inside our DNNs model.

2 Related Work

In this section, we review some works related to our proposed method. We divide the related works into three parts including medical dataset comparison, dimension reduction by feature extraction, and image segmentation by neural networks.

2.1 Medical Dataset Comparison

Large-scale datasets help the performance of deep learning algorithms comparable to human-level on the tasks of speech recognition [9], image classification and recognition [10], and question answering [11–15]. In the medical community, large scale medical datasets also help algorithms achieve expert-level performance on detection of skin cancer [16], diabetic retinopathy [17], heart arrhythmias [18], pneumonia [19], brain hemorrhage [20], lymph node metastases [21], and hip fractures [22].

Recently, the number of openly available medical datasets is growing. In Table 1, we try to provide a summary of the publicly available medical image datasets related to ours. According to Table 1, we notice that the recently released ChestXray14 [23] is the largest medical dataset containing 112,120 frontal-view chest radiographs with up to 14 thoracic pathology labels. Moreover, the smallest medical dataset is DRIVE [24] containing 40 retina images. Regarding the openly available musculoskeletal radiograph databases, the Stanford Program for Artificial Intelligence in Medicine and Imaging has a medical dataset containing pediatric hand radiographs annotated with skeletal age (AIMI). The Digital Hand Atlas [25] includes the left-hand radiographs which are from children of various ages labeled with radiologist readings of bone age. Then, our proposed EyeNet contains 52 classes of diseases and 1747 images.

Table 1. Overview of available different types of medical label collection and image datasets.

Name of dataset	Study type	Label	Number of images
EyeNet	Retina	Labels mining of Retinal Diseases	1747
DRIVE [24]	Retina	Retinal Vessel Segmentation	40
MURA [26]	Musculoskeletal (Upper Extremity)	Abnormality	40,561
Digital Hand Atlas [25]	Musculoskeletal (Left Hand)	Bone Age	1,390
ChestX-ray14 [23]	Chest	Multiple Pathologies	112,120
DDSM [27]	Mammogram	Breast Cancer	10,239

2.2 Dimension Reduction by Feature Extraction

Feature extraction is a method to make the task of pattern classification or recognition easier. In image processing and pattern recognition, feature extraction is one of the special forms of dimensionality reduction [28] in some sense. The purpose of feature extraction is to exploit the most relevant information based on the original data and describe the information in a space with lower dimensions. For example, typically the size of original medical image data, such as functional magnetic resonance imaging (fMRI) scans, is very large and it causes algorithms computationally inefficient. In this case, we will transform the original data into a reduced representation set of features. That is, we exploit a set of feature vectors to describe the original data and the process is called image feature extraction. In [29], the authors mention that the representation by extracted feature vectors should have a dimensionality that corresponds to the intrinsic dimensionality of the original data. Then, the intrinsic dimensionality of data is the minimum number of parameters required to account for the properties of the original data. Moreover, the authors of [30] claim that dimensionality reduction mitigates the curse of dimensionality and the other undesired properties of spaces with high dimensions. The dimensionality reduction by feature extraction method has been used in many different application fields such as document verification [31], character recognition [32], extracting information from sentences [13,14,33], machine translation [34,35] and so on.

2.3 Image Segmentation by Neural Networks

Typically, researchers exploit the convolutional neural networks to do image classification tasks with a single class output label. However, in the biomedical image processing tasks, the output should contain localization. That is to say, a class label is assigned to each pixel. Furthermore, thousands of images in training set are typically beyond reach in the biomedical tasks. Therefore, the authors of [36] train a neural networks model, with sliding-window, to predict the output class label of each pixel by providing a sub-region, small patch, around that pixel as input.

In [36], we know that the neural network model can do localization and the number of training data, in the sense of patches, is much larger than the training images. Apparently, [36] has two drawbacks. First, there exists some trade-off between the use of context and localization accuracy. Then, since the model runs separately for each small patch and there is much redundancy due to overlapping patches, it is not efficient in the sense of computational speed. Recently, the authors of [37,38] have proposed an approach which can do the good localization and use of context at the same time.

In the U-Net paper [39], the authors build upon an even more elegant neural network architecture, the so-called fully convolutional network [40]. The authors modify the architecture such that it works with very few training images and produces even more accurate image segmentation. The main idea of [40] is to supplement a usual contracting neural network by the successive layers. Then, the authors exploit upsampling operators to replace pooling operators, so the resolution of output is enhanced by these layers. In order to do localization, the authors combine the upsampled output and high-resolution features from the contracting path. Furthermore, a successive convolutional layer learns

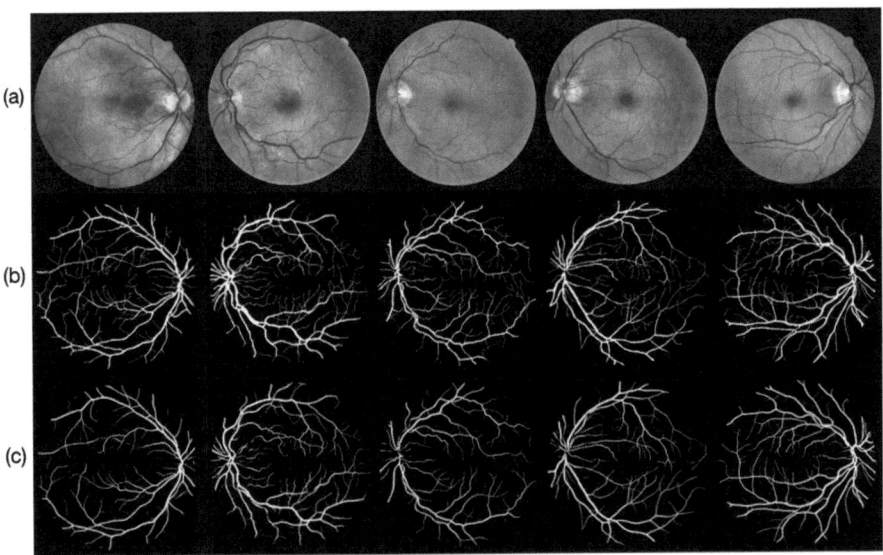

Fig. 2. The figure shows the result of U-Net effects on (a), unseen eyeball clinical images with different morphological shapes. (b) is the ground truth and (c) is the generated result of vessel-subtracted U-Net. Based on (b) and (c), we discover that the results are highly similar to the ground truth.

to assemble a more accurate output based on this information. Due to the advantages of U-Net mentioned above, we modify and incorporate the U-Net to our proposed method.

3 Methodology

In this section, we present the workflow of our proposed model, referring to Fig. 1.

3.1 U-Net

DNNs has greatly boosted the performance of image classification due to its power of image feature learning [41]. The active retinal disease is characterized by exudates around retinal vessels resulting in cuffing of the affected vessels [42]. However, ophthalmology images from clinical microscopy are often overlayed with white sheathing and minor features. Segmentation of retinal images has been investigated as a critical [43] visual-aid technique for ophthalmologists. U-Net [39] is a functional DNNs, especially for segmentation. Here, we proposed a modified version of U-Net by reducing the copy and crop processes with a factor of two. The adjustment could speed up the training process and have been verified as an adequate semantic effect on small size images. We use cross-entropy for evaluating the training processes as:

$$E = \sum_{x \in \Omega} w(x) log(p_l(x)) \qquad (1)$$

where p_l is the approximated maximum function, and the weight map is then computed as:

$$w(x) = w_c(x) + w_0 \cdot exp(\frac{-(d_{x1} + d_{x2})^2}{2\sigma^2}) \qquad (2)$$

d_{x1} designates the distance to the border of the nearest edges and d_{x2} designates the distance to the border of the second nearest edges. LB score is shown as [8]. We use the deep convolutional neural network (CNN) of two 3 × 3 convolutions. Each step followed by a rectified linear unit (ReLU) and a 2 × 2 max pooling operation with stride 2 for downsampling; a layer with an even x- and y-size is selected for each operation. For the U-Net model, we use existing DRIVE [24] dataset as the training segmentation mask. Then, we use Our proposed model converges at the 44th epoch when the error rate of the model is lower than 0.001. The Jaccard similarity of our U-Net model is 95.59% by validated on a 20% test set among EyeNet shown in Fig. 2. This model is robust and feasible for different retinal symptoms as illustrated in Fig. 3. The area under ROC curve is 0.979033 and the area under the Precision-Recall curve is 0.910335.

3.2 Principal Component Analysis as Eigenface in the limit of Sparse Data

$$\lambda_k = \frac{1}{M} \sum_{n=1}^{M} (u_k^T \Phi_n)^2 \qquad (3)$$

Eigenface [44] is classical and high-efficient image recognition technique derived from the covariance matrix of the probability distribution over the high-dimensional vector space of face images. Even with a single training image, previous works [45,46] of eigenface already established robust automatic classification with confident accuracy (85.6%) by combined principal component analysis (PCA) and SVM classifiers. As a biological feature, retinal images share similar properties with the human face for a potential with eigenface recognition [47] included finite semantic layout between facial features and ophthalmological features [48]. The eigenface could be calculated [44] by maximizing the equivalent (3), where Φ_n represent the face differ, u_k is a chosen k_{th} vector, λ_k is the

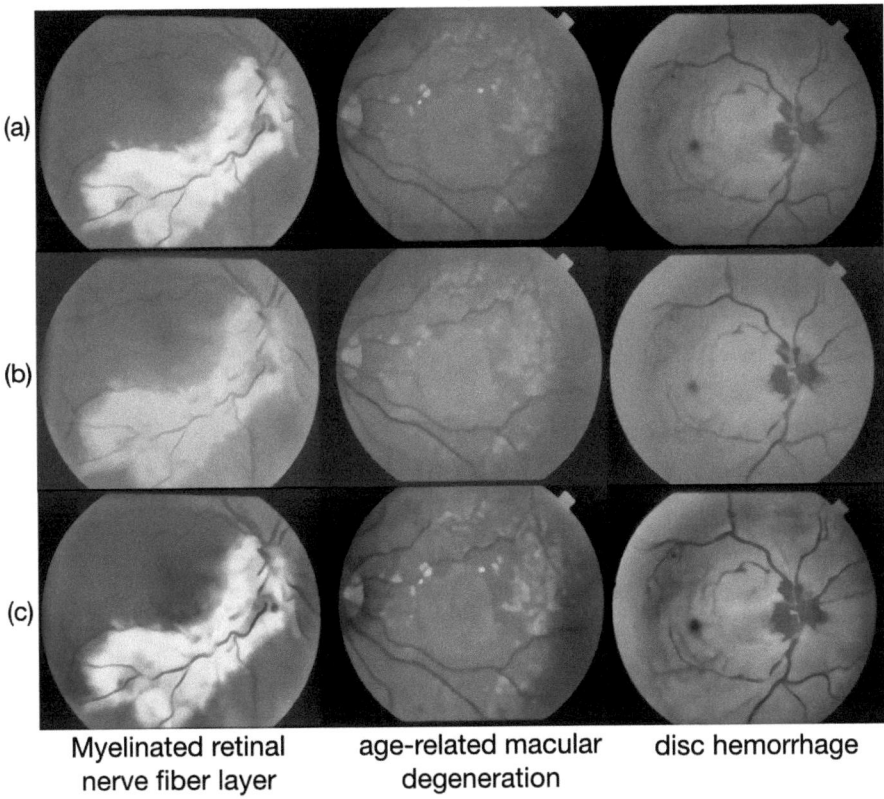

Fig. 3. This figure illustrates the qualitative results of contrast enhancement algorithm from the original clinical images to the (b) histogram equalization (c) contrast-limited adaptive histogram equalization.

k_{th} eigenvalue, and M is a number of the dimension space. In our experiment, we select the $k_{UNet} = 40$ and $k_{RGB} = 61$ to generate a eigenface with highest accuracy for the U-Net-stream and RGB-stream separately.

3.3 Support Vector Machine

Support Vector Machine is a machine learning technique for classification, regression, and other learning tasks. Support vector classification (SVC) in SVM, map data from an input space to a high-dimensional feature space, in which an optimal separating hyperplane that maximizes the boundary margin between the two classes is established. The hinge loss function is shown as:

$$\frac{1}{n}\left[\sum_{i=1}^{n} max(0, 1 - y_i(\boldsymbol{w} \cdot \boldsymbol{x}_i - b))\right] + \lambda \|\boldsymbol{w}\|^2 \qquad (4)$$

Where the parameter λ determines the trade off between increasing the margin-size and ensuring that the $\boldsymbol{x}_i$ lies on the right side of the margin. We use radial basis function (RBF) and polynomial kernel for SVC, which have been widely discussed [49] as a kernel-based fast SVC for images.

3.4 Contrast Enhancement

Contrast enhancement techniques play a vital role in image processing to bring out the information that exists within a less dynamic range of that image. As a major clinical feature, fundus [50, 51] structure is highly related [52] the image contrast [53]. Here, we use histogram equalization for the contrast enhancement in retinal images. Compare to the original images, images after histogram equalization show the light color detail as lesions in Fig. 3(b). Images after contrast-limited adaptive histogram equalization (CLAHE) give further features as areas of retinopathy in Fig. 3(c).

4 Efforts on Retinal Dataset

Retina Image Bank (RIB) [54] is an international clinical project launched by American Society of Retina Specialists in 2012, which allow retina specialists and ophthalmic photographers around the world to share the existing clinical cases online for medicine-educational proposes for patients and physicians in developing countries lack training resource. Any researcher could join as a contributor for dedicating the retinal images or as a visitor using the medical images and label for non-commercial propose. With the recent success on dataset collection, such as ImageNet [55], we believe that the effort of sorting and mining the clinical labels from RIB is valuable. With a more developer-friendly information pipeline, both Ophthalmology and Computer Vision community could go further on the analytical researches on medical informatics. Our proposed label collection, EyeNet is mainly based on the RIB and following the RIB's using guideline.

5 Experiments

In this section, we describe the implementation details and experiments we conducted to validate our proposed method.

5.1 Label Collection

For experiments, the EyeNet is randomly divided into three parts: 70% for training, 10% for validation and 20% for testing. All the training data have to go through the PCA before SVM. All classification experiments are trained and tested on the EyeNet.

5.2 Setup

The EyeNet has been processed to U-Net to generate a subset with a semantic feature of the blood vessel. For the DNNs and Transfer Learning models, we directly use the RGB images from the retinal dataset. EyeNet will be published online after getting accepted. For the CLAHE processing, we use *adapthisteq* function from the image toolbox in MATLAB.

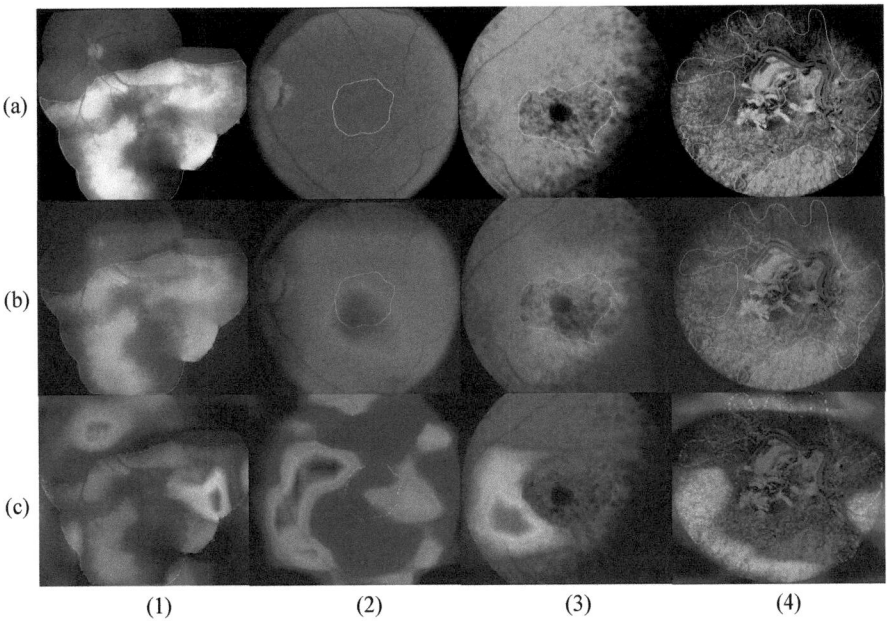

Fig. 4. We use figure (i, j), where $i = a, b, c$ and $j = 1, 2, 3, 4$, to demonstrate that our proposed method can capture the similar lesion areas as the ophthalmologist's manual annotations, i.e., the yellow sketches. (Color figure online)

5.3 Deep Convolutional Neural Networks

CNN has demonstrated extraordinary performance in visual recognition tasks [55], and the state of the art is in a great many vision-related benchmarks and challenges [56]. With little or no prior knowledge and human effort in feature design, it yet provides a general and effective method solving variant vision tasks in variant domains. This new development in computer vision has also shown great potential for helping/replacing human judgment in vision problems like medical imaging [16], which is the topic we try to address in this paper. In this section, we introduce several baselines in multi-class image recognition and compare their results on the EyeNet.

Baseline1-AlexNet

AlexNet [55] brought up a succinct network architecture, with 3 fully connected layers, 5 convolutional layers, and the activation function is ReLU [57].

Baseline2-VGG

The authors of VGG [41] exploit the filters (3×3) repeatedly to replace the large filters ($5 \times 5, 7 \times 7$) in traditional architectures. By increasing depths of the network, it achieved better results on ImageNet with fewer parameters.

Baseline3-ResNet

Residual Networks [58], one of the most popular neural networks today, utilize skip connections or short-cuts to jump over some layers. With skip connections, the network essentially collapses into a shallower network in the initial phase and this makes it easier to be trained, and then it expands its layers as it learns more of the feature space.

Baseline4-SqueezeNet

In real world, medical imaging tasks usually require a small and effective model to adapt to limited resources. As some deep neural networks cost several hundred megabytes to store, SqueezeNet [59] adopting model compression techniques has achieved the accuracy of AlexNet level with around 500 times smaller models.

5.4 Transfer Learning

We use a transfer learning framework from the normalized ImageNet [55] to the EyeNet for solving the small samples issue on the computational retinal visual analytics. With sufficient and utilizable training classified model, Transfer Learning resolves the challenge of Machine Learning in the limit of minimal amount of training labels and it drastically reduces the data requirements. The first few layers of DNNs learn features, similar to Gabor filters and color blobs, and these features appear not to be specific to any particular task or dataset and thus applicable to other datasets and tasks [60]. Our experiments show the significant improvement after we apply the pretrained parameters on our deep learning based models, referring to Tables 3 and 4.

Table 2. Accuracy comparison of the two-streams model with Radial basis function (RBF) and polynomial kernel. We use the hybrid-ratio [61] of the mixed weighted voting between two multi-SVCs trained from images over U-Net and CLAHE.

Hybrid-Ratio	RBF	Polyn.
0%:100%	0.8159	0.8391
40%:60%	0.8371	0.8381
50%:50%	**0.9002**	0.8632
60%:40%	0.8881	**0.9040**
100%:0%	0.8324	0.8241

Table 3. Accuracy comparison of three DNNs baselines on EyeNet.

Model	Pretrained	Random Init.
AlexNet	0.7912	0.4837
VGG11	0.8802	**0.7579**
VGG13	0.8721	0.7123
ResNet18	**0.8805**	0.7250
SqueezeNet	0.8239	0.5625

5.5 Two-Streams Results

All SVM has implemented in Matlab with libsvm [62] module. We separate both the original retinal dataset and the subset to three parts included 70% training set, 20% test set, and 10% validation set. By training two multiple-classes SVM models on both original EyeNet and the subset, we implement a weighted voting method to identify the candidate of retina symptom. We have testified different weight ratio as $Hybrid - Ratio$, SVM model with {Images over CLAHE: Image over U-Net}, with different accuracy at Table 2. We have verified the model without over-fitting by the validation set via normalization on the accuracy with $\tilde{2}.03\%$ difference.

Table 4. Accuracy comparison of three DNNs baselines on EyeNet.

Model	Pretrained	Random Init.
AlexNet	0.7952	0.4892
VGG11	0.8726	0.7583
VGG13	**0.8885**	**0.7588**
ResNet18	0.8834	0.6741
SqueezeNet	0.8349	0.5721

5.6 Deep Neural Networks Results

All DNNs are implemented in PyTorch. We use identical hyperparameters for all models. The training lasts 400 epochs. The first 200 epochs take a learning rate of $1e-4$ and the second 200 take $1e-5$. Besides, we apply random data augmentation during training. In every epoch, there is 70% probability for a training sample to be affinely transformed by one of the operations in {flip, rotate, transpose} × {random crop}. Though ImageNet and our Retinal Dataset are much different, using weights pretrained on ImageNet rather than random ones has boosted test accuracy of any models with 5 to 15%, referring to Table 3. Besides, pretrained models tend to converge much faster than random initialized ones as suggested in Fig. 4. The performance of DNNs on our retinal dataset can greatly benefit from the knowledge of other domains.

5.7 Neuron Visualization for Medical Images

Importantly, we verified the hypothesis that vessel-based segmentation and contrast enhancement are two coherent features to decide the type of retinal diseases. Using techniques of generating class activation maps introduced by [63], we visualized feature maps of the final convolution layer of ResNet18 (which is one of our deep learning model baselines). We notice that the features learned by deep learning models agree with our intuitions about developing the two-stream machine learning model. In fact, in the clinical diagnosis process, "vessel patterns" and "fundus structure" are also the two most crucial features to identify the symptom of different diseases. These two types of features actually cover more than 80% of retinal diseases [50,51].

6 Conclusion and Future Work

In this work, we have designed a novel hybrid model for visual-assisted diagnosis based on the SVM and U-Net. The performance of this model shows the higher accuracy, 90.40%, over the other pre-trained DNNs models as an aid for ophthalmologists. Also, we propose the EyeNet to benefit the medical informatics research community. Finally, since our dataset not only contains images but also text information of the images, image captioning and Visual Question Answering [13–15] based on the retinal images are also the interesting future directions. Our work may also help the remote rural area, where there are no ophthalmologists locally, to screen retinal disease without the help of ophthalmologists in the future.

References

1. Tan, O., et al.: Detection of macular ganglion cell loss in glaucoma by Fourier-domain optical coherence tomography. Ophthalmology **116**, 2305–2314 (2009)

2. Lalezary, M., et al.: Baseline optical coherence tomography predicts the development of glaucomatous change in glaucoma suspects. Am. J. Ophthalmol. **142**, 576–582 (2006)
3. Sharifi, M., Fathy, M., Mahmoudi, M.T.: A classified and comparative study of edge detection algorithms. In: International Conference on Information Technology: Coding and Computing, Proceedings, pp. 117–120. IEEE (2002)
4. Abràmoff, M.D., Garvin, M.K., Sonka, M.: Retinal imaging and image analysis. Rev. Biomed. Eng. **3**, 169–208 (2010)
5. Pizzarello, L., et al.: Vision 2020: the right to sight: a global initiative to eliminate avoidable blindness. Arch. Ophthalmol. **122**, 615–620 (2004)
6. Bhattacharya, S.: Watermarking digital images using fuzzy matrix compositions and (α, β)-cut of fuzzy set. Int. J. Adv. Comput. **5**, 135 (2014)
7. Lin, C.Y., Wu, M., Bloom, J.A., Cox, I.J., Miller, M.L., Lui, Y.M.: Rotation-, scale-, and translation-resilient public watermarking for images. In: Security and Watermarking of Multimedia Contents II, vol. 3971, pp. 90–99. International Society for Optics and Photonics (2000)
8. Cochocki, A., Unbehauen, R.: Neural Networks for Optimization and Signal Processing. Wiley, New York (1993)
9. Hannun, A., et al.: Deep speech: Scaling up end-to-end speech recognition. arXiv preprint arXiv:1412.5567 (2014)
10. Deng, J., Dong, W., Socher, R., Li, L.J., Li, K., Fei-Fei, L.: ImageNet: a large-scale hierarchical image database. In: IEEE Conference on Computer Vision and Pattern Recognition, CVPR 2009, pp. 248–255. IEEE (2009)
11. Rajpurkar, P., Zhang, J., Lopyrev, K., Liang, P.: Squad: 100,000+ questions for machine comprehension of text. arXiv preprint arXiv:1606.05250 (2016)
12. Antol, S., et al.: VQA: Visual question answering. In: Proceedings of the ICCV, pp. 2425–2433 (2015)
13. Huang, J.H., Alfadly, M., Ghanem, B.: VQABQ: visual question answering by basic questions. arXiv:1703.06492 (2017)
14. Huang, J.H., Dao, C.D., Alfadly, M., Ghanem, B.: A novel framework for robustness analysis of visual qa models. arXiv:1711.06232 (2017)
15. Huang, J.H., Alfadly, M., Ghanem, B.: Robustness analysis of visual qa models by basic questions. arXiv:1709.04625 (2017)
16. Esteva, A., et al.: Dermatologist-level classification of skin cancer with deep neural networks. Nature **542**, 115 (2017)
17. Gulshan, V., et al.: Development and validation of a deep learning algorithm for detection of diabetic retinopathy in retinal fundus photographs. JAMA **316**, 2402–2410 (2016)
18. Rajpurkar, P., Hannun, A.Y., Haghpanahi, M., Bourn, C., Ng, A.Y.: Cardiologist-level arrhythmia detection with convolutional neural networks. arXiv preprint arXiv:1707.01836 (2017)
19. Rajpurkar, P., et al.: CheXNet: Radiologist-level pneumonia detection on chest X-rays with deep learning. arXiv preprint arXiv:1711.05225 (2017)
20. Grewal, M., Srivastava, M.M., Kumar, P., Varadarajan, S.: RADNET: radiologist level accuracy using deep learning for hemorrhage detection in ct scans. In: 2018 IEEE 15th International Symposium on Biomedical Imaging (ISBI 2018), pp. 281–284. IEEE (2018)
21. Bejnordi, B.E., et al.: Diagnostic assessment of deep learning algorithms for detection of lymph node metastases in women with breast cancer. JAMA **318**, 2199–2210 (2017)

22. Gale, W., Oakden-Rayner, L., Carneiro, G., Bradley, A.P., Palmer, L.J.: Detecting hip fractures with radiologist-level performance using deep neural networks. arXiv preprint arXiv:1711.06504 (2017)
23. Wang, X., Peng, Y., Lu, L., Lu, Z., Bagheri, M., Summers, R.M.: ChestX-ray8: hospital-scale chest x-ray database and benchmarks on weakly-supervised classification and localization of common thorax diseases. In: 2017 IEEE Conference on Computer Vision and Pattern Recognition (CVPR), pp. 3462–3471. IEEE (2017)
24. Staal, J., Abràmoff, M.D., Niemeijer, M., Viergever, M.A., Van Ginneken, B.: Ridge-based vessel segmentation in color images of the retina. TMI **23**, 501–509 (2004)
25. Gertych, A., Zhang, A., Sayre, J., Pospiech-Kurkowska, S., Huang, H.: Bone age assessment of children using a digital hand atlas. Comput. Med. Imaging Graph. **31**, 322–331 (2007)
26. Rajpurkar, P., et al.: Mura dataset: towards radiologist-level abnormality detection in musculoskeletal radiographs. arXiv preprint arXiv:1712.06957 (2017)
27. Heath, M., Bowyer, K., Kopans, D., Moore, R., Kegelmeyer, P.: The digital database for screening mammography. In: Digital Mammography, pp. 431–434 (2000)
28. Costa, J.A., Hero, A.: Classification constrained dimensionality reduction. In: IEEE International Conference on Acoustics, Speech, and Signal Processing, 2005. Proceedings, (ICASSP'05), vol. 5, pp. 1077. IEEE (2005)
29. Fukunaga, K.: Introduction to Statistical Pattern Recognition. Academic Press, London (2013)
30. Jimenez, L.O., Landgrebe, D.A.: Supervised classification in high-dimensional space: geometrical, statistical, and asymptotical properties of multivariate data. IEEE Trans. Syst. Man Cybern. Part C (Appl. Rev.) **28**, 39–54 (1998)
31. Yang, Z., He, X., Gao, J., Deng, L., Smola, A.: Stacked attention networks for image question answering. In: Proceedings of the IEEE Conference on Computer Vision and Pattern Recognition, pp. 21–29 (2016)
32. Trier, Ø.D., Jain, A.K., Taxt, T.: Feature extraction methods for character recognition-a survey. Pattern Recogn. **29**, 641–662 (1996)
33. Srihari, R., Li, W.: Information extraction supported question answering. Technical report, Cymfony Net Inc., Williamsville NY (1999)
34. Somers, H.: Example-based machine translation. Mach. Transl. **14**, 113–157 (1999)
35. Bahdanau, D., Cho, K., Bengio, Y.: Neural machine translation by jointly learning to align and translate. arXiv preprint arXiv:1409.0473 (2014)
36. Ciresan, D., Giusti, A., Gambardella, L.M., Schmidhuber, J.: Deep neural networks segment neuronal membranes in electron microscopy images. In: Advances in neural information processing systems, pp. 2843–2851 (2012)
37. Hariharan, B., Arbeláez, P., Girshick, R., Malik, J.: Hypercolumns for object segmentation and fine-grained localization. In: Proceedings of the IEEE conference on computer vision and pattern recognition, pp. 447–456 (2015)
38. Seyedhosseini, M., Sajjadi, M., Tasdizen, T.: Image segmentation with cascaded hierarchical models and logistic disjunctive normal networks. In: 2013 IEEE International Conference on Computer Vision (ICCV), pp. 2168–2175. IEEE(2013)
39. Ronneberger, O., Fischer, P., Brox, T.: U-Net: convolutional networks for biomedical image segmentation. In: Navab, N., Hornegger, J., Wells, W.M., Frangi, A.F. (eds.) MICCAI 2015. LNCS, vol. 9351, pp. 234–241. Springer, Cham (2015). https://doi.org/10.1007/978-3-319-24574-4_28

40. Long, J., Shelhamer, E., Darrell, T.: Fully convolutional networks for semantic segmentation. In: Proceedings of the IEEE conference on computer vision and pattern recognition, pp. 3431–3440 (2015)
41. Simonyan, K., Zisserman, A.: Very deep convolutional networks for large-scale image recognition. arXiv:1409.1556 (2014)
42. Khurana, A.: Comprehensive Ophthalmology. New Age International Ltd. (2007)
43. Rezaee, K., Haddadnia, J., Tashk, A.: Optimized clinical segmentation of retinal blood vessels by using combination of adaptive filtering, fuzzy entropy and skeletonization. Appl. Soft Comput. **52**, 937–951 (2017)
44. Turk, M.A., Pentland, A.P.: Face recognition using eigenfaces. In: IEEE Computer Society Conference on Computer Vision and Pattern Recognition, Proceedings CVPR 1991, pp. 586–591. IEEE (1991)
45. Lyons, M.J., Budynek, J., Akamatsu, S.: Automatic classification of single facial images. IEEE Trans. Pattern Anal. Mach. Intell. **21**, 1357–1362 (1999)
46. Wu, J., Zhou, Z.H.: Face recognition with one training image per person. Pattern Recogn. Lett. **23**, 1711–1719 (2002)
47. Moghaddam, B., Wahid, W., Pentland, A.: Beyond eigenfaces: probabilistic matching for face recognition. In: Third IEEE International Conference on Automatic Face and Gesture Recognition, 1998. Proceedings, pp. 30–35. IEEE (1998)
48. Akram, M.U., Tariq, A., Khan, S.A.: Retinal recognition: Personal identification using blood vessels. In: 2011 International Conference for Internet Technology and Secured Transactions (ICITST), pp. 180–184. IEEE (2011)
49. Kuo, B.C., Ho, H.H., Li, C.H., Hung, C.C., Taur, J.S.: A kernel-based feature selection method for SVM with RBF kernel for hyperspectral image classification. IEEE J.Sel. Top. Appl. Earth Observ. Remote Sens. **7**, 317–326 (2014)
50. Crick, R.P., Khaw, P.T.: A Textbook of Clinical Ophthalmology: A Practical Guide to Disorders of the Eyes and Their Management. World Scientific
51. Akram, I., Rubinstein, A.: Common retinal signs. an overview. Optometry Today (2005)
52. Tang, S., Huang, L., Wang, Y., Wang, Y.: Contrast-enhanced ultrasonography diagnosis of fundal localized type of gallbladder adenomyomatosis. BMC Gastroenterol. **15**, 99 (2015)
53. Noyel, G., Thomas, R., Bhakta, G., Crowder, A., Owens, D., Boyle, P.: Superimposition of eye fundus images for longitudinal analysis from large public health databases. Biomed. Phys. Eng. Express **3**, 045015 (2017)
54. : Retina Image Bank: A project from the American Society of Retina Specialists. http://imagebank.asrs.org/about. Accessed 30 June 2018
55. Krizhevsky, A., Sutskever, I., Hinton, G.E.: ImageNet classification with deep convolutional neural networks. In: Advances in NIPS, pp. 1097–1105 (2012)
56. Xie, S., Girshick, R., Dollár, P., Tu, Z., He, K.: Aggregated residual transformations for deep neural networks. In: CVPR, pp. 5987–5995. IEEE (2017)
57. Nair, V., Hinton, G.E.: Rectified linear units improve restricted boltzmann machines. In: Proceedings of the 27th International Conference on Machine Learning (ICML-2010), pp. 807–814 (2010)
58. He, K., Zhang, X., Ren, S., Sun, J.: Deep residual learning for image recognition
59. Iandola, F.N., Han, S., Moskewicz, M.W., Ashraf, K., Dally, W.J., Keutzer, K.: SqueezeNet: AlexNet-level accuracy with 50x fewer parameters and <0.5 MB model size. arXiv:1602.07360 (2016)
60. Yosinski, J., Clune, J., Bengio, Y., Lipson, H.: How transferable are features in deep neural networks? In: NIPS, pp. 3320–3328 (2014)

61. Yang, C.H.H., et al.: A novel hybrid machine learning model for auto-classification of retinal diseases. arXiv preprint arXiv:1806.06423 (2018)
62. Chang, C.C., Lin, C.J.: LIBSVM: a library for support vector machines. TIST **2**, 27 (2011)
63. Zhou, B., Khosla, A., Lapedriza, A., Oliva, A., Torralba, A.: Learning deep features for discriminative localization. In: CVPR (2016)

First International Workshop on Advanced Machine Vision for Real-Life and Industrially Relevant Applications (AMV)

LoANs: Weakly Supervised Object Detection with Localizer Assessor Networks

Christian Bartz[✉], Haojin Yang, Joseph Bethge, and Christoph Meinel

Hasso Plattner Institute, University of Potsdam,
Prof.-Dr.-Helmert Straße 2-3, 14482 Potsdam, Germany
{christian.bartz,haojin.yang,joseph.bethge,christoph.meinel}@hpi.de

Abstract. Recently, deep neural networks have achieved remarkable performance on the task of object detection and recognition. The reason for this success is mainly grounded in the availability of large scale, fully annotated datasets, but the creation of such a dataset is a complicated and costly task. In this paper, we propose a novel method for weakly supervised object detection that simplifies the process of gathering data for training an object detector. We train an ensemble of two models that work together in a student-teacher fashion. Our student (localizer) is a model that learns to localize an object, the teacher (assessor) assesses the quality of the localization and provides feedback to the student. The student uses this feedback to learn how to localize objects and is thus entirely supervised by the teacher, as we are using no labels for training the localizer. In our experiments, we show that our model is very robust to noise and reaches competitive performance compared to a state-of-the-art fully supervised approach. We also show the simplicity of creating a new dataset, based on a few videos (e.g. downloaded from YouTube) and artificially generated data.

1 Introduction

One of the main factors for the success of Deep Neural Networks (DNNs), in the recent years [1–3], is the availability of large-scale labeled datasets like the ImageNet dataset [4]. In the domain of object detection, fully annotated datasets like Pascal VOC [5] enabled several breakthroughs for object detectors [3,6,7]. These methods heavily rely on annotated bounding boxes for each object in an image. Semi-supervised/weakly supervised methods for object detection [8–11] try to overcome the high costs of labeling by using less annotations. We review these and more methods related to our work in Sect. 2. All mentioned methods have in common that they do need some form of annotation for each input image. Creating these annotated datasets incurs a high amount of manual labor that has to be performed in order to label the data and make it available for creating a computer vision model. Having the possibility to get enough annotated training data for a specialized application without the high annotation costs would be ideal. To this end, we propose a novel approach for weakly supervised object detection. We use an ensemble of two independent neural networks that are jointly trained. The first network (localizer) is trained by the second network and learns to perform the task of object localization in a given input image. The second network (assessor) is trained to regress the Intersection over Union (IOU) (also known as Jaccard Index) of the bounding box of an object and an image crop. The assessor is trained in a fully supervised way on purely artificially generated data. We describe the architecture of our system in more detail in Sect. 3. The basic data necessary for generating the training set for the assessor consists of a few template images of the objects that shall be localized and a few different natural background images. In our experiments, we used 25 template images and 8 background images to train an assessor for the task of localizing figure skaters. The localizer, on the contrary, does not need any annotations, as it is entirely trained by the supervision of the assessor. The data used for training the localizer could, for instance, come from a 5 to 10 min long video that has been downloaded from the internet, or especially created for this task. We provide further information about the datasets we used and also the experiments we performed in Sect. 4 and conclude our work in Sect. 5.

The contributions of our work can be summarized as follows: (1) we propose a novel (end-to-end) training method for weakly supervised object detection, based on knowledge transfer between two jointly trained, but independent neural networks. (2) Our proposed model can successfully be trained, even if more than 50% of the images in the train dataset are noisy images (i.e. images that do not contain an object we are looking for, or contain only a partial view of the object). (3) We show that our model reaches competitive performance compared to a state-of-the-art fully supervised object detection system. (4) In our experiments, we show that short video clips, plus a few template and background images that were gathered from the internet, are sufficient to create a new dataset and successfully train a model. (5) We release our code, our models, and the generated data sets to the community.[1]

2 Related Work

Object detection has been intensively studied in the past years. Thanks to the availability of huge amounts of labeled data it is possible to create fully supervised systems that achieve incredible results for object detection and recognition [3,6,7,12,13]. Those methods are fully-supervised, meaning that they need annotations for the location of objects (bounding boxes) and also annotations for the class of each object in the image. Getting fully annotated images is a costly process, especially for applications beyond academic use cases.

Weakly Supervised Localization. Weakly supervised object detection systems try to overcome the annotation problem, by learning to detect objects

---
[1] https://github.com/Bartzi/loans.

with partial bounding box annotations or even without the need for this kind of annotations [8–11]. The approach introduced by Deselaers et al. [8] uses object detectors already trained on certain classes to annotate the locations of objects in new classes. Those labeled images can then be used to train a fully supervised detector on the new class. Liang et al. [9] propose a method that adapts a pre-trained classification model for object detection on new and unseen classes, while needing only a few fully annotated instances and videos that are likely to contain objects of the new class. Misra et al. [10] follow a similar approach by starting with a small set of annotated bounding boxes and iteratively extracting more annotations from unannotated video sequences. Tang et al. [11] propose a system that uses information from fully annotated visually and semantically similar classes to train an object detector on classes that are only partially annotated. Most of these approaches rely on images that at least have a category label, which is in contrast to our proposed method. For training the localizer, we do not need any labels at all, as the localizer is trained by the assessor. The assessor, on the contrary, only needs annotations in form of template images that are placed randomly in natural images.

Knowledge Transfer Between Neural Networks. Knowledge transfer has also been intensively studied in the recent years [14–19]. Existing work mostly concentrates on using one network (the teacher) to teach another network (the student), to perform the same task, but either increasing the performance of the model [17,18], or compressing the model, while keeping the same level of performance [14,15]. Those approaches use a pre-trained model and try to distill or adapt this model into the other. Other approaches train both models at the same time. Jiang et al. [19] make the teacher network behave like a 'real' teacher that provides a curriculum learning strategy for the student. This curriculum helps the student to successfully learn to perform its task on noisy data. In this setting, knowledge transfer is also used for training an image generator, where the teacher acts as an advisor that refines the images generated by the student, while getting additional feeback from the outside world [16]. Apart from the approach by Jiang et al. [19], all knowledge transfer approaches have in common that teacher and student deal with problems from the same domain (i.e. computing the same function, or teacher and student work on image generation). In our proposed method, teacher and student (or assessor and localizer) work in different problem domains. Our assessor is a model that is used to predict the IOU between an image crop and the bounding box of an object in this crop, while the localizer is trained to find and crop objects from an image, by using the feedback of the assessor.

Generative Adversarial Networks. Our approach is, to some extent, inspired by Generative Adversarial Networks (GANs) that have been introduced by Goodfellow et al. [20]. In a GAN, two networks (generator and discriminator) are trained simultaneously, and the goal of both networks is to work against each other. The generator is trying to produce images that are indistinguishable from real-world images. At the same time, the discriminator is trying to decide whether an analyzed sample is a real sample or has been generated by the generator. In our method, the assessor (discriminator in the GAN setting) and localizer (generator in the GAN setting) are two independent networks that are trained simultaneously. The objective of the localizer is not to fool the assessor, but to maximize the output of the assessor. This leads to the situation that the localizer is trained by the supervision of the assessor, while the assessor does not even know that it is used to train another neural network.

3 Proposed System

When humans first see a new object they memorize certain aspects of the object and create a template that is matched against new occurences of the same object class. We mimic a similar behavior, by creating a system that can be trained to localize an object, using only a few template images of the object, which are placed randomly in a natural image and also unlabeled images that are likely to contain the object, which is to be detected (we refer to this kind of object as the "target object" for the remainder of this paper). Our proposed system consists of two independent DNNs (localizer and assessor) that are trained at the same time. In this section, we start with explaining the assessor, followed by an explanation of the localizer, and how both networks are jointly trained.

3.1 Assessor

The first network is the assessor. The assessor receives an input image I_A and produces a value $y \in [0, 1]$. The value y provides a measure of the ratio of an object contained in the image I_A. In other words, the assessor predicts the IOU of the bounding box of an object and the input image. The prediction of this IOU is trained in a fully-supervised fashion based on purely artificially generated data. The assessor consists of a DNN that computes a function $f_{as}(I_A)$. The function computed by the assessor is defined as follows:

$$f_{as}(I_A) = y = \sigma(f_{dnn}(I_A)). \quad (1)$$

$f_{dnn}(I_A)$ is a DNN that produces a scalar value, and σ denotes the logistic sigmoid function, which forces the values of y to be in the interval $[0, 1]$. While training, the assessor minimizes the mean squared error between the prediction y and the groundtruth label $l \in [0, 1]$ (n denotes the batch size used during training):

$$\mathcal{L}_{assessor} = \frac{1}{n} \sum_{i=1}^{n} (f_{as}(I_A^i) - l^i)^2. \quad (2)$$

Fig. 1. Template images of objects used for creating the train dataset of the assessor. These template images have been created by cropping the object from real images.

Data Generation. The assessor is trained on an entirely synthetic dataset. This dataset can be created by using some template images of the target object. For us, a template is an object that has been cropped from a natural image and can be pasted into other natural images. Figure 1 shows some examples of template images that we used for our experiments. The number of template images that are necessary to create a good model depends on the number of pose variants the type of object may have. Besides the template images of the target objects, we also need some background images that do not contain the target object. The template images are pasted onto the background images at random locations, with random sizes. We then select a random box from the image and calculate the IOU of the object bounding box and the random box and save this as annotation for the generated image. Figure 2 shows some generated images that are used for training the assessor.

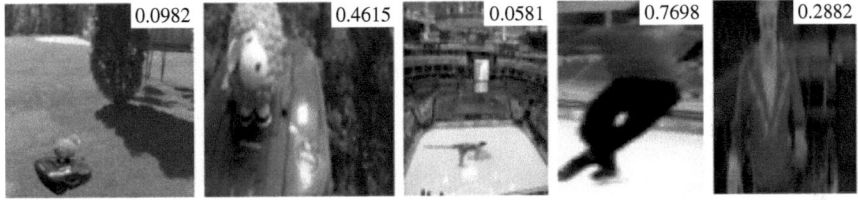

Fig. 2. Sample input images and their corresponding labels for the assessor. Each image contains some portion of an object. The label is the Intersection over Union of the image with the bounding box of the object. In other words, it is the proportion of the object that covers the image.

3.2 Localizer

The second network is the localizer. The localizer receives a natural image as input and tries to crop a region from the input image that is likely to contain an object. The localizer uses a spatial transformer [21] to crop the region from the image. A spatial transformer is a differentiable module for DNNs that applies a spatial transformation on an input feature map I_L and produces an output feature map O. Such a spatial transformer module consists of three different parts: Localization Network, Grid Generator, and Image Sampler.

Localization Network. The localization network is a neural network that computes a set of parameters θ. These parameters define the spatial transformation that is to be applied on the input feature map. These parameters can describe different types of spatial transformations, such as affine or thin plate spline transformations. In our work, we only use affine transformations that allow us to attend to different regions of the input image I_L, by using the transformation to zoom into a region of interest. The localization network learns a function $g_{dnn}(I_L)$ that predicts the parameters θ_i of an affine transformation matrix A_θ that is conditioned on the input image I_L and the parameters of the neural network. The result of this function is defined as follows:

$$g_{dnn}(I_L) = A_\theta = \begin{bmatrix} \theta_1 & 0 & \theta_2 \\ 0 & \theta_3 & \theta_4 \end{bmatrix}. \quad (3)$$

θ_1 to θ_4 are the transformation parameters, regressed by the deep neural network. We constrain the parameters of the affine transformation to only allow cropping, translation, and scaling.

Grid Generator. After the prediction of the affine transformation matrix, the grid generator is used to create a regularly spaced grid consisting of coordinates x_{w_o}, y_{h_o}, with height H_o and width W_o being the spatial size of the output feature map O. The regularly spaced grid is used together with the already predicted transformation matrix to produce a regular grid G of sampling coordinates u_i, v_j, with $i \in [0, \ldots, W_o]$ and $j \in [0, \ldots, H_o]$.

$$\begin{pmatrix} u_i \\ v_j \end{pmatrix} = A_\theta \begin{pmatrix} x_{w_o} \\ y_{h_o} \\ 1 \end{pmatrix} = \begin{bmatrix} \theta_1 & 0 & \theta_2 \\ 0 & \theta_3 & \theta_4 \end{bmatrix} \begin{pmatrix} x_{w_o} \\ y_{h_o} \\ 1 \end{pmatrix}. \quad (4)$$

We can use these coordinates to determine the bounding box of the region of interest, which we want to extract from the image. This bounding box is the intended output of our localizer and is used to display the detection result of the network.

Image Sampler. In order to provide an input image to our assessor, the sampling grid produced by the grid generator is used to sample the input image I_L at the sampling points u_i, v_j of the generated sampling grid G. As the generated sampling grid will not perfectly align with the values in the discrete grid of the input image, we use bilinear sampling and define the values of each pixel i, j ($i \in [0, \ldots, W_o]$ and $j \in [0, \ldots, H_o]$) of the output image O as:

$$f_{loc}(I_L)_{ij} = O_{ij} = \sum_{w}^{W_o} \sum_{h}^{H_o} I_{L_{wh}} \, max(0, 1 - |u_i - w|) \, max(0, 1 - |v_j - h|). \quad (5)$$

This formulation of bilinear sampling is (sub-)differentiable, thus allowing us to propagate error gradients from the assessor to the localization network, using standard backpropagation. The output of the bilinear sampling operation is also the final output of the localizer that represents the function $f_{loc}(I_L)$.

The combination of the three modules *Localization Network*, *Grid Generator*, and *Image Sampler* forms our localizer. During training we extract the output image, produced by the *Image Sampler* and hand it over to the assessor to assess the quality of the detection.

Training Data. We do not need annotated data for training the localizer, as the training of the localizer is supervised by the assessor. This property of the localizer makes it very easy to generate a large scale database of training images. One possibility for getting training data is to extract frames that might contain the target object from a video clip. The frames can directly be used as input to the localizer and creating them does not include any manual labor, except from choosing appropriate videos. Those videos could contain noisy frames, such as frames that do not show any target object, or only some parts of a target object. In our experiments (Sect. 4), we show that a noisy dataset does not necessarily degrade the performance of our approach, it might even improve the performance of our model on a test dataset.

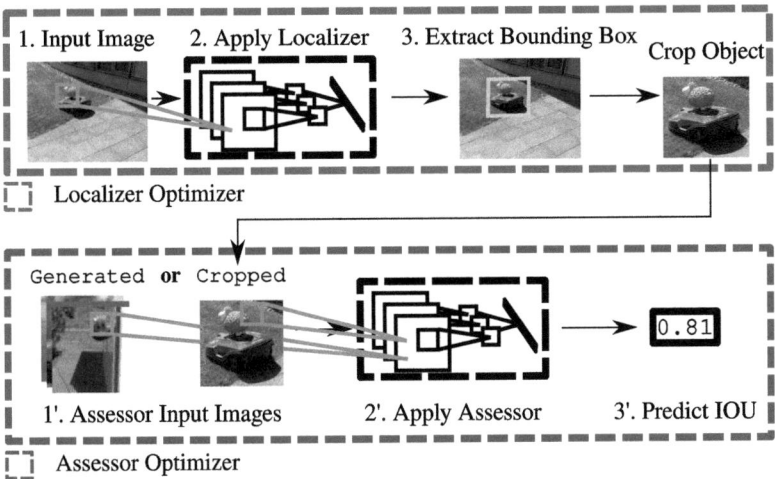

Fig. 3. We use two networks for training our model, each with its own optimizer. The first network is the localizer and the second network is the assessor. The input to the localizer is an image containing the target object. The localizer utilizes a spatial transformer module [21] to crop the object from the image and provide it to the assessor as an input. The assessor predicts the Intersection over Union of the object and the image crop and is used by the localizer to learn its task. The striped lines indicate which parts of the two networks are handled by which optimizer.

3.3 Optimization of Both Networks

The two parts of our model, as such, are independent neural networks. It is possible to train both networks at the same time, but they can also be trained consecutively. It is important that the assessor is at some time able to provide meaningful feedback to the localizer, thus it does not make sense to train the localizer without an assessor that is either pretrained or is learning to regress the IOU of an object and the image crop at the same time. For our experiments (see Sect. 4), we always trained both networks at the same time.

While training both networks at the same time, we use two independent optimizers. One optimizer handles the weight updates of the assessor. The second optimizer handles the weight updates of the localizer. Figure 3 provides a structural overview of our proposed system. The localizer learns to localize objects, by using the assessor to assess the quality of the object that has been localized by the localizer. This means that the cost $\mathcal{L}$ of the localizer is the cost assigned by the assessor to the part of the image cropped by the localizer, plus two localizer specific regularizers:

$$\mathcal{L}_{localizer} = \frac{1}{n}\sum_{i=1}^{n}(f_{as}(f_{loc}(I_L^i)) - 1.0)^2 + \mathcal{L}_{di}(G^i) + \mathcal{L}_{out}(G^i). \quad (6)$$

where $\mathcal{L}_{di}(G)$ is a regularization term based on the direction of the predicted sampling grid G. This regularization term penalizes grids that are mirrored along the x- or y-axis. $\mathcal{L}_{out}(G)$ is a regularization term that penalizes predicted grids with coordinates that lie outside of the image coordinates. The label for the mean squared error loss in Eq. (6) is constant for every input image. We set this constant to 1, as we want our localizer to crop regions of interest that fully contain the target object with as little extra space as possible. It would also be possible to set this value to any other value in the interval $[0, 1]$. Setting this value to 0, for instance, results in a localizer that deliberately chooses regions without the target object.

The most important part of training both networks at the same time, is the actual weight update process. Once we obtain the cost for the assessor (as described in Eq. (2)), we calculate gradients using standard backpropagation and update the weights of the assessor. Updating weights for the localizer works in a similar fashion. Here, we also calculate the gradients with backpropagation and let the gradients flow through the assessor to the localizer and to the first neural network layer. Once we obtained the gradients, we only update the weights of the localizer and leave the weights of the assessor untouched, hence the localizer is trained by the assessor to find a good region of interest.

4 Experiments

In this section we evaluate our proposed system on two different real-world datasets. We performed our experiments, in order to answer the following questions: (1) can we use the error information obtained by one network to train a second network on a different task, while the first network does not know that it is used in such a way? (2) Is it feasible to train the assessor on totally synthetic data, where we do not care whether the samples are realistic or not, and at the same time use unlabeled data for training an object localizer? (3) Can we hold our promise that it is simple to create a new dataset, using our proposed approach? (4) Is our model able to reach competitive performance, compared to a fully supervised model?

In order to answer these questions, we performed experiments on two different datasets, we created ourselves. The first dataset, contains images of an automated lawn-mower that has an orange sheep on top. The second dataset contains images of figure skaters giving a performance, for instance at the Olympic Games.

We begin this section, by introducing the datasets we used throughout our experiments in detail. This description is followed by an explanation of our experimental setup. We conclude the section with showing and discussing the results of our experiments.

4.1 Datasets

We created two challenging real-world datasets, which we tested our method on. In the first dataset we are trying to localize an automated lawn-mower that has an orange sheep on top. This dataset is challenging, because it contains patches where the object is only a few pixels high and wide. We refer to this object for the remainder of the paper as "sheep". In the second dataset we tried to localize figure skaters while they are giving a performance. The figure skater dataset contains a lot of pose variations for each of the skaters, making it challenging for a model to generalize.

Sheep Dataset. We created this dataset by taking 158 different images that we used as background images for the assessor dataset. Besides the backgrounds, we took 10 pictures of the sheep from different angles that are used as template images. We used 8 template images to randomly paste them onto the background images for the assessor dataset. Using this data, we generated 10 000 different images for training the assessor.

Out of the 158 backgrounds, we used 121 randomly chosen backgrounds and the same 8 template images to create a train dataset for the localizer. We pasted the template images onto the background images using positions of hand-crafted bounding boxes, rendering those images as similar to real-world images as possible. We did not use the bounding box information for training the model with our approach, but for training the model with the fully supervised baseline approach. All in all, we have been able to generate 8320 images for training the localizer.

We used the remaining 37 backgrounds and the last two template images to create a test dataset where we also pasted the sheep onto the background images using hand-crafted bounding boxes. Using this approach, we were able to obtain 560 images for testing the localizer.

Figure Skating Dataset. In order to create this dataset we downloaded 5 videos from Youtube, downloaded 8 background images, and created 25 template images. Using the 8 background images and 25 template images, we generated 10000 images for training the assessor.

For the train dataset of the localizer, we took two videos from the Olympic Games in Pyeong Chang 2018 with the performance of Alina Zagitova[2] and Yuzuru Hanyu.[3] We took one video from the Olympic Games of Sochi in 2014 with the performance of Yulia Lipnitskaya.[4] Last, we took the performance of Jason Brown at the US Open in 2014.[5] After extracting all frames from the videos we were left with 68985 images for training the localizer. As these images still contain a lot of noise, where the figure skater is either not entirely, or not at all present in an image, we created a second train dataset without images containing this kind of noise. The second, noise free, dataset contains 33125 images, which is roughly 48% of the original number of images. For testing the localizer, we used the performance of Yuna Kim at the Olympic Games in Sochi 2014.[6] We extracted 100 images from this video that shows Yuna Kim in different positions and manually annotated them with bounding boxes for testing our model.

We were able to very quickly generate the train datasets, for both assessor and localizer, as it only took roughly 1.5 h. This shows that our proposed system makes it possible to create a new dataset for object localization with minimal effort.

4.2 Experimental Setup

In the following we explain the exact configuration of the neural network achitectures that we used during our experiments and also provide some implementation details.

Localizer. We use two different network architectures for training our localizer (ResNet-18 and ResNet-50). Both architectures are based on the ResNet architecture proposed by He et al. [2]. The input to the localizer is the image where the target object shall be localized. Before passing the image to the network, we normalize the image, by subtracting each channel with a mean value obtained from the Imagenet dataset. Before the first residual block of the network, we perform a 3 × 3 convolution with 64 output channels and stride 1, followed by batch normalization [22], ReLU [23], and a 3 × 3 max pooling layer with stride 2. After these layers, 4 residual blocks follow. Each block consists of at least 6 3 × 3 convolutional layers with stride 1, the first convolutional layer of the second, third, and fourth residual block uses a stride of 2. Each convolutional layer is followed by batch normalization and ReLU. The number of convolutional

---

[2] https://www.youtube.com/watch?v=TlXCk1LDlC0.
[3] https://www.youtube.com/watch?v=23EfsN7vEOA.
[4] https://www.youtube.com/watch?v=ke0iusvydl8.
[5] https://www.youtube.com/watch?v=J61k2XjRryM.
[6] https://www.youtube.com/watch?v=hgXKJvTVW9g.

filters is 64, 128, 256, 512, or 256, 512, 1024, 2048 for ResNet-18 and ResNet-50, respectively. We perform global average pooling after the last residual block. The last residual feature map, is fed to a fully connected layer with 6 neurons that predicts the affine transformation parameters that are used to generate the sampling grid. We always set the parameters that are responsible for rotating the input image to zero.

Assessor. We based the architecture of the assessor network on the ResNet architecture, too. We explicitly chose the ResNet architecture in order to mitigate the vanishing gradient problem and keep a strong gradient throughout both of our networks. The input to the assessor is an image that resembles a crop from a larger image, which contains an object. The assessor consists of four residual blocks, where the first and second block consist of three convolutional layers. The first layer, is a 3 × 3 convolutional layer. The last two layers are 4×4 convolutional layers with a stride of 2. The second layer is followed by the ReLU activation function. The last two residual blocks consist of two 3 × 3 convolutional layers, followed by the ReLU activation function, each. The number of convolutional feature maps for each residual block is 128, 128, 128, 128, respectively. A fully connected layer with 1 neuron and the sigmoid activation function σ follows after the residual blocks. We do not use a bias term for any of the layers in the assessor.

Hyperparameters. For all of our experiments, we use Adam [24] as optimizer for both localizer and assessor and set the learning rate (alpha) to 10^{-4}. We use a batch size of 32 for each experiment, and let the training run for 300 epochs. We train the localizer with data augmentation. We apply a random combination of horizontal flipping, color jittering, and random cropping/padding to 50% of the images in each batch.

Implementation. We implemented all of our experiments using Chainer [25] and ChainerCV [26]. We used one NVIDIA 1080Ti GPU for each experiment.

Evaluation Metrics. We follow the evaluation procedure of the Pascal VOC 2012 challenge [27], where we calculate the average precision, based on the IOU of the predicted bounding box and the ground truth bounding box.

4.3 Sheep Experiments

We performed our first experiments on the sheep dataset, which we introduced in Sect. 4.1, to prove that our localizer-assessor concept works. Since we have a fully annotated dataset for training and testing the localizer, we trained a baseline model following the SSD approach of Liu et al. [7], using different input sizes, i.e. images with 300 × 300 and 512 × 512 pixels. We then used the same dataset (without bounding box annotations) for training the localizer, and the

Table 1. Results of our experiments on the sheep dataset. We show the average precision for each model and the respective input sizes. The first row (SSD) shows the results of our trained baseline model. The other rows show the results of our models based on different ResNet architectures.

Method	224 × 224	300 × 300	512 × 512
SSD [7]	-	0.887	0.969
ResNet-18	0.887	0.937	0.967
ResNet-50	0.959	0.958	0.976

dataset we created for the assessor to train different models, based on our approach. We trained models, with different input sizes (224 × 224, 300 × 300, and 512 × 512 pixels), using different network architectures for the localizer (ResNet-18, or ResNet-50), and with an output size of 75 × 75 pixels for the localizer. We always initialized each ResNet model with convolutional layers that have been pre-trained on the Imagenet dataset. Table 1 shows the results of our different experiments. We also show some samples from the dataset including the predictions of our localizer in the left column of Fig. 5. From the results in Table 1 we can clearly see that our model reaches competitive performance compared to a fully supervised model that was trained on the same dataset. This is remarkable, as we do not use any labels for the location of the sheep while training our model. We note, however, that our approach is currently not able to work with multiple objects in one image and also only supports the localization of objects of one class and not multiple classes, yet. Another interesting observation is that our ResNet-18 based model significantly increases its localization performance across the different input sizes, while the ResNet-50 based model only does so in a smaller margin. We think that this is because the ResNet-50 model has a better representational capability, because it is deeper and that this is already enough to extract meaningful features, even at a low spatial resolution.

4.4 Figure Skating Experiments

Following our experiments on the sheep dataset, we performed further experiments on the figure skating dataset, which we introduced in Sect. 4.1. With these experiments, we wanted to achieve the following goals: (1) show that our approach works well across a range of different objects, (2) show that it is easy to create a new dataset for training a model that performs very well, and (3) show that our model is robust to noise in the localization training set. Since we have no fully annotated dataset and also no access to the code of other weakly supervised object localization methods, we were not able to train a baseline model. Instead, we trained a range of different models and examine the influence of different settings for training the model. We trained all models on an input size of 224 × 224 pixels for the localizer, but we varied the following properties of the network: (1) the base model. We use ResNet-18 and a ResNet-50 that was pre-trained on Imagenet. (2) The output size of the localizer/input size of the

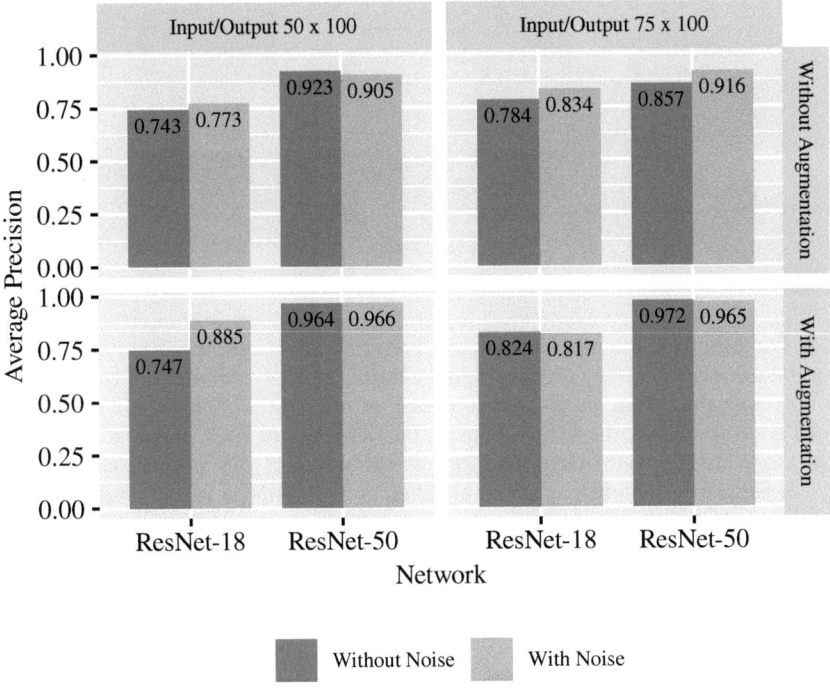

Fig. 4. Results of our experiments on the figure skating dataset. We show the average precision for each model and directly compare the models with and without noise in the train dataset for the localizer. We also compare the results across two different feature extractors and assessors trained with and without augmentation.

assessor (50 × 100 pixels, or 75 × 100 pixels). (3) The input dataset for the localizer. We either used the train dataset without noise, or the dataset with noise, as described in Sect. 4.1. (4) We applied data augmentation on the train images of the assessor, by randomly adding horizontal flipping to 50% of the train images.

Figure 4 shows the results of our experiments with the figure skating dataset, you can also find some samples of the dataset in Fig. 5 in the middle and right columns. From the results, we can see that adding noise to our train dataset does not (necessarily) degrade the performance of the model. Instead, it might even help the model to achieve better performance than before. We argue that this due to the fact that the dataset with noise also contains images that show parts of a figure skater and the model uses this information to learn to localize the figure skater. We also note that using data augmentation in the assessor leads to better results. This shows that the training success of the localizer (student) depends on the assessor (teacher) and also shows us parallels to the behavior of human students and their teachers.

Fig. 5. Samples from our test datasets, including localizations of our network from the sheep dataset (left column) and the figure skating dataset (middle and right column). The bottom-right image shows a failure case of our system, where our model is not able to accurately find the target object. The left part of each image is the input to the localizer and the right part the input to the assessor. The samples show that our model is capable of handling objects of different size, objects in different challenging positions, and also images that contain several distractors.

5 Conclusion and Future Work

In this paper, we presented a novel approach for weakly supervised object detection, based on knowledge transfer between a teacher (assessor) and a student (localizer). We evaluated our approach on two different datasets, showed that we can reach a performance that is on par to a fully supervised model, and that our approach is robust to noise in the training data. Gathering training data for our approach is simple and does not need a lot of time. For training the localizer, we can use real-world training data that has, for example, been extracted from a video. We do not need any further annotation for training the localizer. The train set for the assessor is an entirely synthetic dataset that can be created using a small amount of background and template images. These properties should make it easy to use our approach for specialized object detection systems where it might be very expensive to fully annotate the training data. Instead, taking a video and some pictures suffices for creating a dataset and training a very well performing model.

Our approach has some limitations that we want to address in our future work. Our approach is currently not able to localize more than one object at the same time in an image. We think that it is very important to further develop our idea and make it possible to detect multiple objects of different classes in the same image, in order to be able apply this approach to a broader class of problems. Furthermore, we want to assess whether a model trained with our approach can be trained to work as a general object detector. Preliminary experiments already showed that our model trained on the sheep dataset is able to localize other objects, such as a football. Our model trained on the figure skating dataset works very well in localizing humans that are standing upright in an image, hence we see this as a good starting point to further investigate the generalization capabilities of our approach.

References

1. Krizhevsky, A., Sutskever, I., Hinton, G.E.: ImageNet classification with deep convolutional neural networks. In: Pereira, F., Burges, C.J.C., Bottou, L., Weinberger, K.Q. (eds.) Advances in Neural Information Processing Systems, vol. 25, pp. 1097–1105. Curran Associates, Inc., New York (2012)
2. He, K., Zhang, X., Ren, S., Sun, J.: Deep residual learning for image recognition. In: Proceedings of the IEEE Conference on Computer Vision and Pattern Recognition, pp. 770–778 (2016)
3. Ren, S., He, K., Girshick, R., Sun, J.: Faster R-CNN: towards real-time object detection with region proposal networks. In: Cortes, C., Lawrence, N.D., Lee, D.D., Sugiyama, M., Garnett, R. (eds.) Advances in Neural Information Processing Systems, vol. 28, pp. 91–99. Curran Associates, Inc., New York (2015)
4. Deng, J., Dong, W., Socher, R., Li, L., Li, K., Fei-Fei, L.: ImageNet: a large-scale hierarchical image database. In: 2009 IEEE Conference on Computer Vision and Pattern Recognition, pp. 248–255 (2009)
5. Everingham, M., Gool, L.V., Williams, C.K.I., Winn, J., Zisserman, A.: The Pascal visual object classes (VOC) challenge. Int. J. Comput. Vis. **88**, 303–338 (2010)
6. Redmon, J., Divvala, S., Girshick, R., Farhadi, A.: You only look once: unified, real-time object detection. In: Proceedings of the IEEE Conference on Computer Vision and Pattern Recognition, pp. 779–788 (2016)
7. Liu, W., et al.: SSD: single shot multibox detector. In: Leibe, B., Matas, J., Sebe, N., Welling, M. (eds.) ECCV 2016. LNCS, vol. 9905, pp. 21–37. Springer, Cham (2016). https://doi.org/10.1007/978-3-319-46448-0_2
8. Deselaers, T., Alexe, B., Ferrari, V.: Localizing objects while learning their appearance. In: Daniilidis, K., Maragos, P., Paragios, N. (eds.) ECCV 2010. LNCS, vol. 6314, pp. 452–466. Springer, Heidelberg (2010). https://doi.org/10.1007/978-3-642-15561-1_33
9. Liang, X., Liu, S., Wei, Y., Liu, L., Lin, L., Yan, S.: Towards computational baby learning: a weakly-supervised approach for object detection. In: Proceedings of the IEEE International Conference on Computer Vision, pp. 999–1007 (2015)
10. Misra, I., Shrivastava, A., Hebert, M.: Watch and learn: semi-supervised learning for object detectors from video. In: Proceedings of the IEEE Conference on Computer Vision and Pattern Recognition, pp. 3593–3602 (2015)
11. Tang, Y., Wang, J., Gao, B., Dellandrea, E., Gaizauskas, R., Chen, L.: Large scale semi-supervised object detection using visual and semantic knowledge transfer. In: Proceedings of the IEEE Conference on Computer Vision and Pattern Recognition, pp. 2119–2128. IEEE (2016)
12. Girshick, R.: Fast R-CNN. In: Proceedings of the IEEE International Conference on Computer Vision, pp. 1440–1448 (2015)
13. Singh, B., Najibi, M., Davis, L.S.: Sniper: efficient multi-scale training. arXiv:1805.09300 [cs] (2018)
14. Hinton, G., Vinyals, O., Dean, J.: Distilling the knowledge in a neural network. In: NIPS Deep Learning and Representation Learning Workshop (2015)
15. Tang, Z., Wang, D., Zhang, Z.: Recurrent neural network training with dark knowledge transfer. In: 2016 IEEE International Conference on Acoustics, Speech and Signal Processing (ICASSP), pp. 5900–5904 (2016)

16. Xie, J., Lu, Y., Gao, R., Zhu, S.C., Wu, Y.N.: Cooperative training of descriptor and generator networks. arXiv:1609.09408 [cs, stat] (2016)
17. Chen, T., Goodfellow, I., Shlens, J.: Net2Net: accelerating learning via knowledge transfer. In: International Conference on Learning Representations (2016)
18. Li, Y., Yang, J., Song, Y., Cao, L., Luo, J., Li, L.J.: Learning from noisy labels with distillation. In: Proceedings of the IEEE International Conference on Computer Vision, pp. 1910–1918 (2017)
19. Jiang, L., Zhou, Z., Leung, T., Li, L.J., Fei-Fei, L.: MentorNet: learning data-driven curriculum for very deep neural networks on corrupted labels. In: International Conference on Machine Learning, pp. 2309–2318 (2018)
20. Goodfellow, I., et al.: Generative adversarial nets. In: Ghahramani, Z., Welling, M., Cortes, C., Lawrence, N.D., Weinberger, K.Q. (eds.) Advances in Neural Information Processing Systems, vol. 27, pp. 2672–2680. Curran Associates, Inc., New York (2014)
21. Jaderberg, M., Simonyan, K., Zisserman, A., Kavukcuoglu, K.: Spatial transformer networks. In: Advances in Neural Information Processing Systems, vol. 28, pp. 2017–2025. Curran Associates, Inc. (2015)
22. Ioffe, S., Szegedy, C.: Batch normalization: accelerating deep network training by reducing internal covariate shift. In: Proceedings of The 32nd International Conference on Machine Learning, pp. 448–456 (2015)
23. Nair, V., Hinton, G.E.: Rectified linear units improve restricted Boltzmann machines. In: Proceedings of the 27th International Conference on Machine Learning (ICML-10), pp. 807–814 (2010)
24. Kingma, D.P., Ba, J.: Adam: a method for stochastic optimization. In: Proceedings of the 3rd International Conference on Learning Represenations, San Diego (2015)
25. Tokui, S., Oono, K., Hido, S., Clayton, J.: Chainer: a next-generation open source framework for deep learning. In: Proceedings of Workshop on Machine Learning Systems (LearningSys) in The Twenty-ninth Annual Conference on Neural Information Processing Systems (NIPS) (2015)
26. Niitani, Y., Ogawa, T., Saito, S., Saito, M.: ChainerCV: a library for deep learning in computer vision. In: Proceedings of the 2017 ACM on Multimedia Conference, MM 2017, pp. 1217–1220. ACM, New York (2017)
27. Everingham, M., Van Gool, L., Williams, C.K.I., Winn, J., Zisserman, A.: The Pascal visual object classes challenge 2012 (VOC2012) results (2012)

Reaching Behind Specular Highlights by Registration of Two Images of Broiler Viscera

Anders Jørgensen[1,2](✉), Malte Pedersen[1], Rikke Gade[1], Jens Fagertun[2], and Thomas B. Moeslund[1]

[1] Department of Media Technology, University of Aalborg, Aalborg, Denmark
andjor@create.aau.dk
[2] IHFood A/S, Copenhagen, Denmark

Abstract. The manual postmortem inspection of broilers and their viscera is becoming a bottleneck as the slaughter rate increases. Computer vision can assist veterinarians during the inspection, but specular highlights can hide crucial details when inspecting for diseases on the viscera set. This study aims to restore details behind these specular highlights by capturing two images of the same viscera using shifting light positions. The dataset consists of images captured in-line at a poultry processing plant. The method achieves an average SSIM score of 0.96 over a test set of 100 image sets. The result is visually pleasing images with correct textural information instead of specular highlights.

1 Introduction

The world's production of poultry meat has increased from 8.92 million tons in 1961 to 109.02 million tons in 2013 [13]. This means more processing plants, but also increased production rates. With slaughter rates up to 225 birds per minute [11] on a single line, the task of manual health inspection is becoming difficult. This calls for automation of the inspection task with a computer vision system to aid the veterinarians.

Specular highlights are a well known challenge when designing vision systems, especially when capturing wet and glossy objects. In some cases, it can be enough to detect and discard areas with specular highlights in software, but when inspecting poultry viscera the highlighted areas can hide critical signs of diseases. A simple solution is to change the position of the light source so that its reflection does not shine into the camera, but this will only work on objects with a well defined surface. Another common solution is to use polarizing filters in front of the light source and the camera lens and filter out light reflected directly back from the object. But polarizing filters block at least 50% of the light (by design), so with two filters the camera receives less than 25% of the emitted light. This might be unfavorably in setups with short exposure times, where the light source is already operating at maximum current.

This paper therefore presents a method that restores textural information behind specular highlights by combining two images with different lighting. The goal is to have a single image to use for further analyzing. The scene object is broiler viscera captured in-line at a poultry processing plant during production. Broilers are chickens bred for meat production and the viscera are extracted as the heart, liver and gizzard are sold for consumption. The captured viscera surfaces are wet and uneven, yielding some unpredictable specular highlights. A captured viscera set can be seen in Fig. 1, where the largest organs have been outlined.

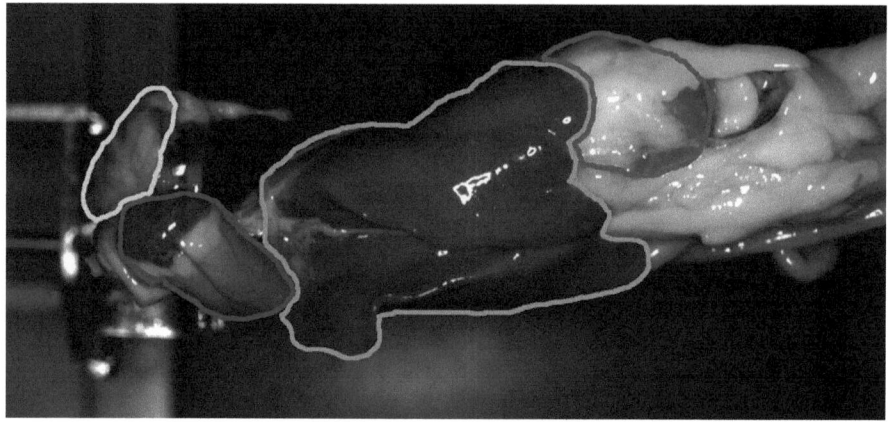

Fig. 1. Example of a captured viscera set. Green marks the livers, blue the heart, yellow a lung and purple the gizzard. Rotated left to fit paper. (Color figure online)

Figure 2 shows two of the most common liver diseases found by the veterinarians during a normal production. In Fig. 2a the broiler is diagnosed with perihepatitis, where the peritoneum get attached the the liver. It is seen as a white membrane on the surface of the liver. Figure 2b shows a liver with necrotic hepatitis. The liver get spotted areas scattered over various parts of the liver. It is clear in this case that the specular highlights can hide texture information crucial for a correct classification of the liver.

2 Related Work

Inspection of broiler viscera have received limited attention from the research community. Work by [17] used UV and color imaging to detect splenomegaly in images of viscera. UV was helpful in segmenting the spleen which appear to have a similar color as the liver in the visible light spectrum. [6] used multi-spectral imaging to classify chicken hearts into four diseases and normal. By selecting four spectral bands from the visible spectrum they achieved classification rates between 84% and 100% for the five classes. Through visible and near infra-red

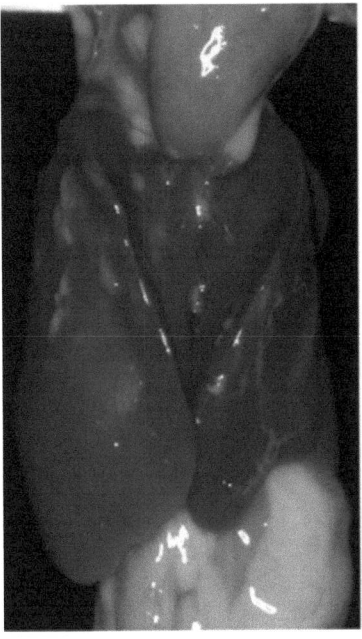 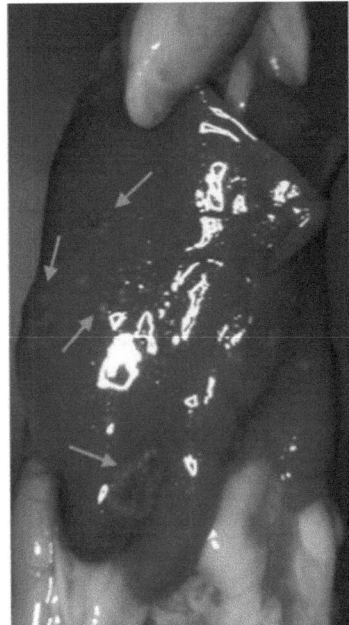

(a) Perihepatitis. (b) Necrotic hepatitis.

Fig. 2. Examples of two common liver diseases.

spectroscopy [8] could separate chicken livers into septicemic and normal birds with 94% and 98% accuracy. All of the above works was done in a controlled lab environment.

More recently [12] proposed a method for segmenting heart, liver and lung in RGB-D images of broiler viscera. [9] used a neural network to classify four liver diagnoses in RGB images and gained an overall true positive rate of 77.6%.

Many different methods exist for the detection of specular highlights. Saturated pixels can be detected by simple intensity thresholding, but more elaborate methods are needed to find specular highlights that are not saturated. [16] proposed a fast method for separating the diffuse and specular components of a single image by using a normalized version of the dichromatic model. Using a physics based approach [2] proposed a method that depends on the Fresnel term of the specular highlight for detection of said highlights.

Saturated specular highlights hide the texture information of the area beneath it. Restoration methods must either inpaint saturated areas or retrieve the data from another image. [7] developed a hardware setup with four flashes connected to the same camera. By combining the four images they are able to generate an image with reduced specular effects. [15] demonstrates a method where a video sequence was used to generate a single image without specular highlights. Using SIFT features the images were registered and for each image set the minimum value for each overlapping pixel were selected. A similar idea was used by [5] who proposed a method for generating a single high quality image of paintings photographed from multiple angles. By getting the median of the gradient from multiple images they use the Poisson equation to recover an image without highlights.

Combining color values from multiple images, in which the object moves, requires a registration. Image registration or alignment generally consists of the following steps: feature detection, feature matching, model estimation and image resampling [14]. SIFT [10] are often used features for finding correspondence points or its speeded up version SURF [4]. [1] have trained a neural network to find and select features and another neural network is trained to generate descriptors.

3 Input Images

The input consists of images of broiler viscera captured in-line at a poultry processing plant during normal operation. Two images are captured per viscera set. The first image is captured with the light shifted to the left, indirect light (IL), and the second image with the light directly from the camera's position, direct light (DL). While this gives different specular highlights between the images, it also means that the right side of the IL image is poorly illuminated. The DL image is the more visually pleasing image with a uniform illumination. The light sources both consists of a red, green and blue ring of LEDs. This generates a white light but some specular highlights appear in one color channel only, due to the spatial distance between the LEDs. An example image set can be seen in Fig. 3.

The viscera is transported at ≈ 0.6 m/s on a conveyor belt and the two consecutive images are captured ≈ 17 ms apart, which mean the viscera move ≈ 1 cm between the captured images. The exposure time is 750 μs to avoid motion blur. The images are captured with a LW-AL-IMX253C-USB3 camera at a resolution of 3000×4096 which is scaled to 1500×2048 through Bayer interpolation.

4 Method

In our dataset the most frequent diseases are present on the liver and heart so these organs will be the focus of this method. The entire viscera set is useful for registration but the color transformation will only be performed on the liver and heart.

The first step is to detect the specular highlights that should be removed. This is done in the DL image as the viscera is more evenly illuminated from this camera's point of view and therefore the image to use for further processing. The next step is to register the images. This happens automatically with out the need for manual registration. The full IL image is resampled to match the DL image. The last step is the color transformation. As the lighting differs greatly in each image this is done individually for each processed highlight. The process is outlined in Fig. 4.

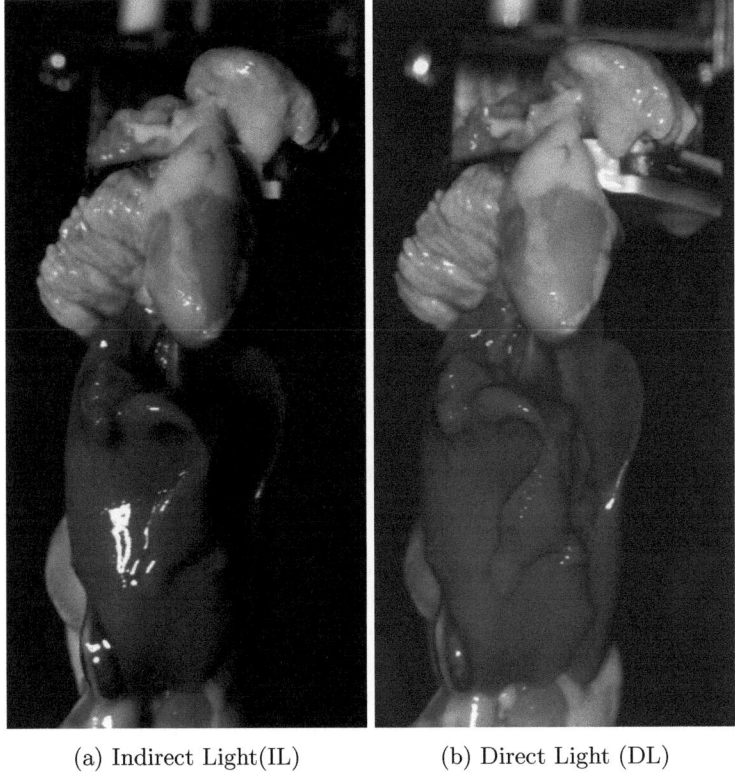

(a) Indirect Light(IL)   (b) Direct Light (DL)

Fig. 3. Example of the two images captured per viscera set. The images have been cropped to better present the important organs. (Color figure online)

Fig. 4. Individual steps in the process.

4.1 Specular Highlight Detection

Specular highlights are detected via a rule based approach. The viscera parts are primarily red with a low response in the green spectrum so pixels with a high response in the green channel are marked as specular highlights. All rules are shown in Eq. 1. The resulting mask is 255 in pixels where a specular highlight is detected, otherwise 0.

$$\begin{aligned} m_{x,y} &= 255 & \text{if} \quad & g_{x,y} > 175 \\ m_{x,y} &= 255 & \text{if} \quad & b_{x,y} \geq r_{x,y} \text{ and } b_{x,y} > 200 \\ m_{x,y} &= 255 & \text{if} \quad & g_{x,y} \geq r_{x,y} \text{ and } g_{x,y} \geq b_{x,y} \\ m_{x,y} &= 0 & \text{else} & \end{aligned} \quad (1)$$

r, g, b are pixel intensities in the red, green and blue color channel of the input image, m is the highlight mask and x, y describes the coordinates of the pixel.

4.2 Image Registration

The viscera are secured with a clamp on the gullet, just behind the lungs and heart. When the viscera moves along the conveyor belt, the vibrations can cause the organs to move independently as they are connected by deformable soft tissue.

In order to investigate the motion of the viscera between the two consecutive images, control points have manually been annotated in 15 viscera image sets, where anatomical landmarks were visible.

Figure 5 shows the control points vertical position (y) plotted with respect to the control point's difference in its x position (Δx) between the two images. Linear regression have been used to fit a line to the control points for each set.

Figure 5 indicates that there is a correlation between Δx and y. The variation in Δx is smallest around $y = 500$, which corresponds to the location of the clamp. As y increases, so does the variation in Δx, yet control points from the same viscera set deviates to the same side. This could indicate that the viscera swings back and forth in the clamp, like a pendulum, when the viscera moves along the conveyor belt. This was also observed at the processing plant. When a viscera set swings to the right the horizontal translation between the images will decrease and vice versa, as the conveyor belt moves to the left seen from the camera.

The difference in the y position (Δy) of the control points with respect to y in DL was also investigated. For all control points Δy was less than 10 pixels and there were no indication of any correlation with y. This means that the viscera does not swing high enough between the two captured images to generate a change in y that is greater than the vibrations from the conveyor belt.

For automatic control point detection it was chosen to use SURF [4] and the resulting matches for a single image set can be seen in Fig. 6a. Most matches are found around the heart or at the intestines with only a few matches found on the liver. For SURF we have used a blob response threshold of 700 and the number of octaves is 3.

Prior knowledge about the transformation, illustrated in Fig. 5, makes it possible to prune matches by looking at their direction. The gray area surrounding the control points in Fig. 5 indicates the area where matches are no longer considered valid. For all matches y must be larger than $y_{\min}$ as the upper part of the image only contains a part of the hanger which is located in a plane further

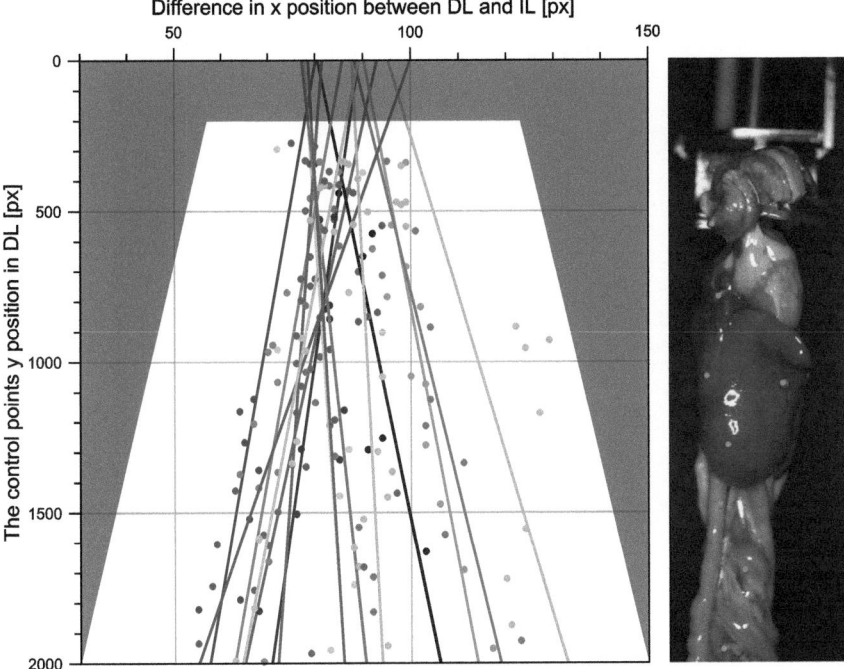

Fig. 5. Manually selected control points plotted as the y position per difference in x position. The gray area indicates invalid matches as described in Sect. 4.2. The green control points are also plotted in the image on the right. (Color figure online)

away from the camera than the viscera set. Matches here will have a very different offset, Δx, compared to the rest of the matches. Matches must also have a Δy less than $\Delta y_{\max}$, otherwise they will be discarded. $\Delta x_{\min}$ and $\Delta x_{\max}$ are calculated from y as per the following formulas, where 60 and 120 are decided from the x-axis in Fig. 5:

$$\Delta x_{\min}(y) = -0.015y + 60 \qquad (2)$$
$$\Delta x_{\max}(y) = 0.015y + 120 \qquad (3)$$

The resulting lines corresponds to the vertical borders between the white and the gray area in Fig. 5. The pruned matches can be seen in Fig. 6b. A total of 35 matches remain. Most are found on the lung and heart, the rest on the intestines and no matches are present on the liver. With so few features it is not possible to apply non-rigid registration methods [21]. Through testing it was found that the best compromise between precision and robustness was an affine transformation. It has the freedom to describe the major transformations between the two images and few enough parameters to be found almost consistently.

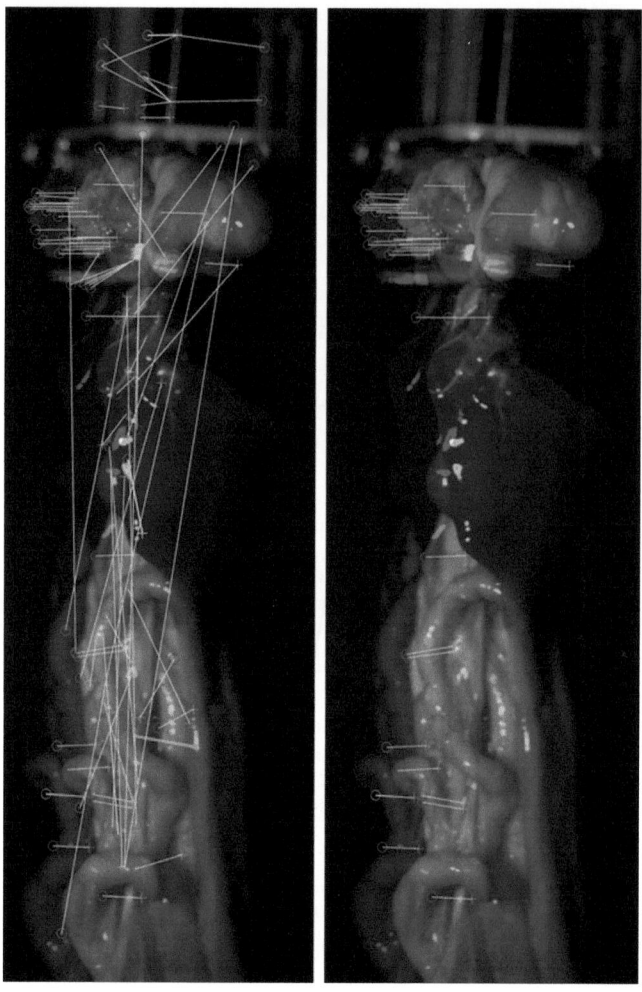

(a) All SURF matches.   (b) Pruned SURF matches.

Fig. 6. Matched SURF features found in the two images.

In some cases the remaining matches are too few and/or too inaccurate. Or the transformation fails because the local transformations are too large to be modelled with an affine transformation. A high amount of shear or rotation indicate a faulty transformation as this should not occur because the viscera are transported in a horizontal direction. This can be detected by inspecting the transformation matrix. The shear and rotation components (index 1,2 and 2,1) should not deviate more than ΔT_{rs} from 0 as this indicates a high amount of shear or rotation. In these cases it was chosen to fall back to a simple horizontal translation. Based on the control points plotted in Fig. 5, the fixed translation have been set to $t_{\mathrm{h}} = 85$ pixels.

4.3 Color Transformation

The color transformation steps are illustrated in Fig. 7. The transformation is calculated by finding the difference in color in the area around a highlight by modelling it with a quadratic polynomial surface. The size of the area depends on the size of the specular highlight. A similar concept have been applied to gray-scale images by [19] to stitch images from an atomic force microscope. The details of each step showed in Fig. 7 will be described in the following. Blob extraction is used on the highlight mask to process the highlights individually. Specular highlights with an area smaller than $A_{\min}$ are ignored. Each blob is dilated with a circular kernel with a radius of r_{dk} to avoid artifacts from color blooming around the specular highlights.

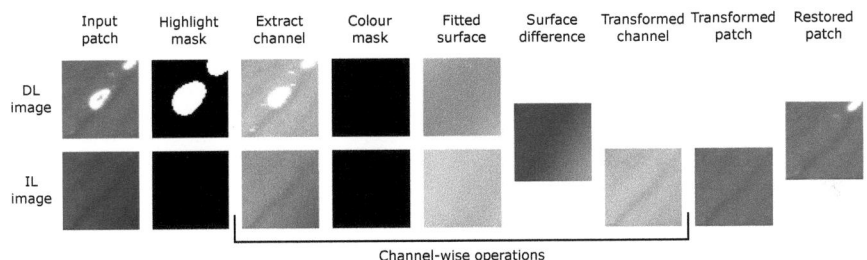

Fig. 7. Steps in the color transformation. Read from left to right.

The dilated blob is extracted from the images DL and IL with a b_{b} wide border around the blob's region of interest (ROI). The extracted image patches can contain other specular highlights so these are found and masked in the same way as described in Sect. 4.1 and dilated the same way.

Each color channel is extracted and smoothed with a Gaussian kernel with a standard deviation of σ. If the highlight is located in an area next to another organ or in an area with a shade, the abrupt change in intensity could result in a non-linearity that is poorly approximated by a polynomial surface. A mask is therefore created that filters pixels that differs from the central region by an intensity change ΔI larger than $\Delta I_{\max}$. As the central region in DL contains a highlight, the reference value for DL is calculated from the pixels surrounding the highlight. The result is a color mask that is white where ΔI is larger than $\Delta I_{\max}$, otherwise black.

The highlight mask and the color mask are used to exclude values when fitting the polynomial surface to the color channel intensities. The surface is fitted using least squares. The resulting surfaces are depicted in Fig. 7, where blue indicates low values and red indicates high values. The surface difference, in this particular example, shows that the lower right corner of the ROI is more different in intensity than the upper left, which can be confirmed by looking at the input images. The difference is added to the IL ROI and the three color channels are combined to a new IL ROI image. Bear in mind that the surface difference can be negative when the IL ROI has a higher intensity than DL ROI. As the last step pixels from the new IL ROI are used to fill the highlight blob in the original image.

5 Results

The results are divided into two parts, qualitative and quantitative. The method has been tested on viscera image sets with specular highlights. As there is no ground truth for these images, the result will be evaluated subjectively. The method will also be tested on image sets with a manually drawn highlight mask. Here the results will be reported with Peak Signal to Noise Ratio (PSNR) and Structural Similarity Index (SSIM) scores [20].

The following settings have been used for the experiments:

$$t_h = 85, \quad b_b = 20, \quad \Delta I_{max} = 80, \quad \sigma = 5, \quad r_{dk} = 5$$
$$y_{min} = 200, \quad \Delta y_{max} = 10, \quad A_{min} = 10, \quad \Delta T_{rs} = 0.05$$

5.1 Qualitative Results

An example of the restoration results can be seen in Fig. 8. Overall it looks good, the large highlights have been removed and pixels on the liver and heart have been restored. Figure 9 displays a close up of the restoration on a liver with necrotic hepatitis. The liver is speckled with bright areas, which are visual

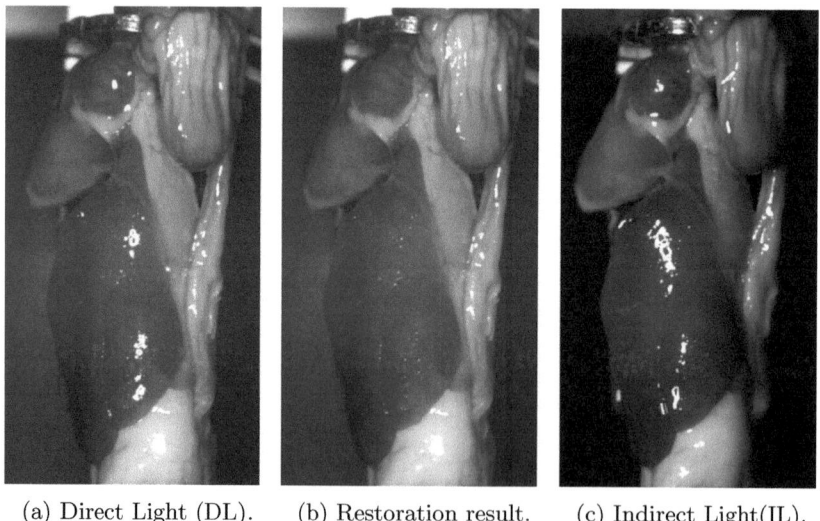

(a) Direct Light (DL). (b) Restoration result. (c) Indirect Light(IL).

Fig. 8. Restoration results in (b), flanked by the two input images in (a) and (c).

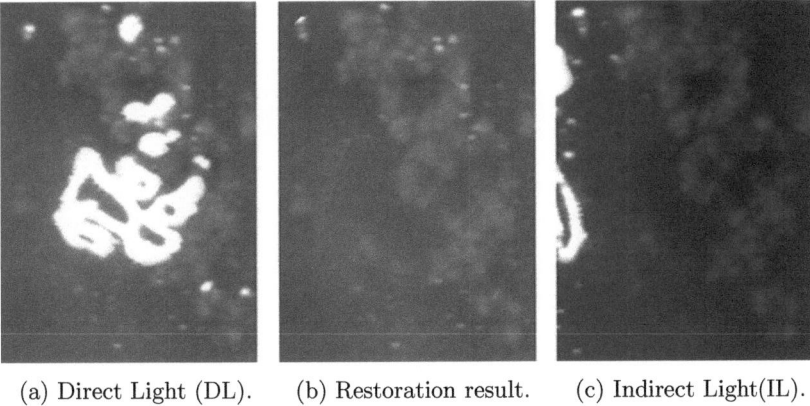

(a) Direct Light (DL). (b) Restoration result. (c) Indirect Light(IL).

Fig. 9. Close up of a liver with necrotic hepatitis. Textural information is correctly imported to the area with specular highlights.

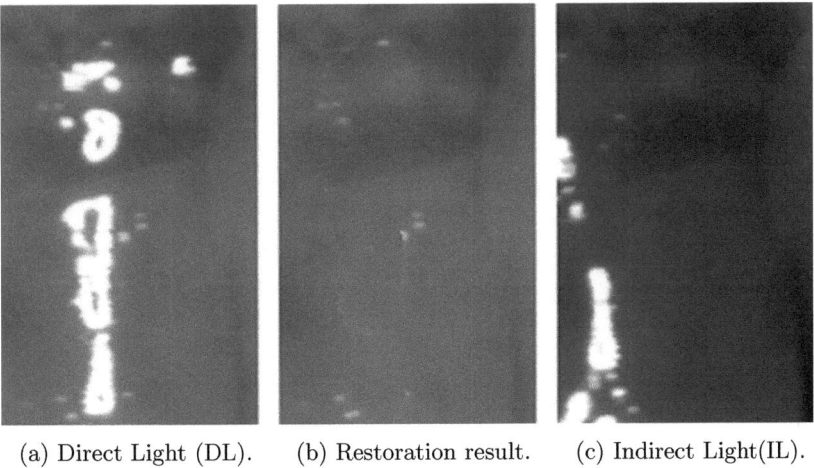

(a) Direct Light (DL). (b) Restoration result. (c) Indirect Light(IL).

Fig. 10. Close up of the restoration of a healthy liver. The dark areas are easily visible in (b).

clues for the diagnosis. The textural information is correctly transferred from image IL into the area in image DL with specular highlights. Figure 10 shows a close up of a healthy liver. The liver has some dark areas, which are damages caused during the evisceration. These damages are of no concern for food safety, but is considered a quality issue. The dark areas are easily visible in Fig. 10b, after the restoration. Figure 11 shows the results of the restoration of highlights in the heart. The veins makes easy to spot if the registration is incorrect, but for this example it is judged to be correct. Figure 12 shows a cut out from another processed viscera set. An issue becomes apparent when looking at the two highlights marked with green in Fig. 12a. The texture information behind

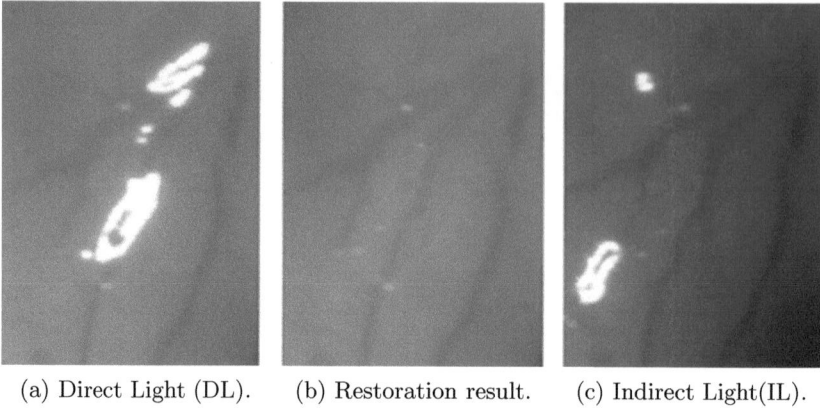

(a) Direct Light (DL). (b) Restoration result. (c) Indirect Light(IL).

Fig. 11. Highlight restoration on the heart. The veins indicate that the registration is correct.

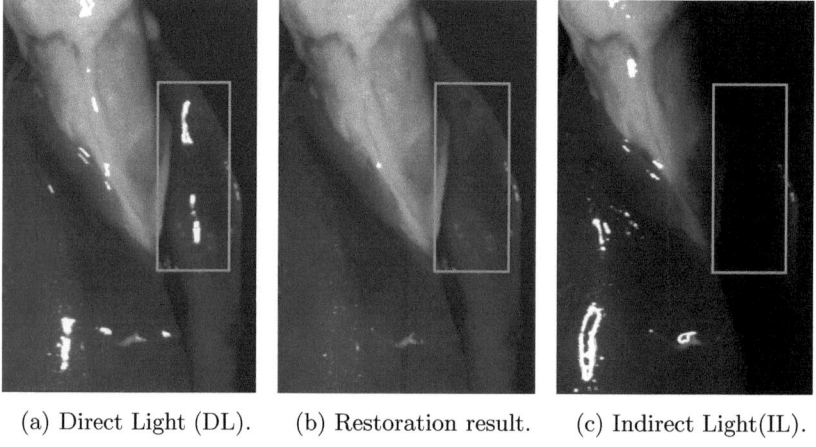

(a) Direct Light (DL). (b) Restoration result. (c) Indirect Light(IL).

Fig. 12. Restoration result for heart and liver. The highlights marked by the green square in (a) requires data from a poorly lit area in (c). (Color figure online)

these highlights should be imported from Fig. 12c, but this area is underexposed and contains little to no information. This means that the method is basically raising noise to fit the color in the DL image.

5.2 Quantitative Results

A total of 100 highlight masks were manually drawn in 30 viscera image sets. The results of the restorations are quantified with PSNR and SSIM scores. Both scores are often used to evaluate the performance of inpaint methods or similar methods where the aim is to restore missing data [3,18,22]. The scores are plotted in Fig. 13. Mean PSNR is 41.80 ± 5.46 and mean SSIM is 0.96 ± 0.03.

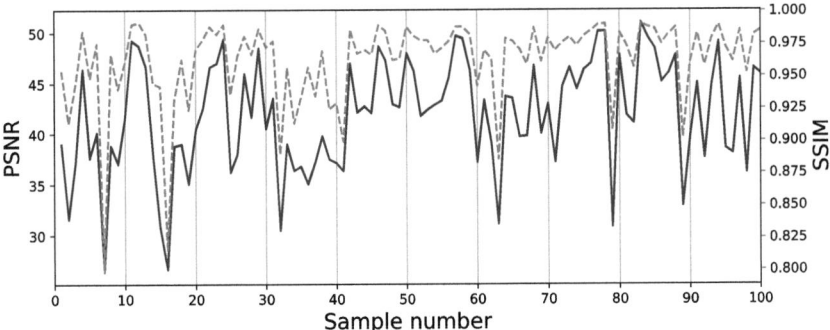

Fig. 13. PSNR and SSIM scores for the 100 manually drawn highlights.

Table 1. Results of manually drawn highlights with PSNR and SSIM Scores.

#	Mask	DL input	Result	IL input	PSNR	SSIM
21					42.57	0.98
3					37.14	0.94
12					48.75	0.99
9					37.05	0.94
79					30.86	0.91
7					26.36	0.80

Table 1 shows the results for a few selected specular highlights. The PSNR and SSIM scores can be compared visually with the resulting image. By looking at sample 7 it is clear that a bad registration will have a negative impact on the result as the restored pixels comes from another area of the image. The inflammation on the liver in sample 9 becomes smaller in the result image due to an incorrect registration, which could be critical for the classification of the liver. Other highlights, like samples 21 and 12 are both registered and color transformed correctly and requires close inspection to detect that pixels have been imported.

6 Conclusion

The proposed method aims to restore pixels behind specular highlights by combining two images into one image without highlights. The method shows good results on a dataset that is far from trivial. In quantitative testing the method scored a mean PSNR of 41.80 ± 5.46 and a mean SSIM of 0.96 ± 0.03. Equally important did it produce visually pleasing images even when zooming in on the restored areas.

The livers contain very few features which together with the different light conditions make the registration a challenge. As the viscera rotates and wobbles as it moves along the conveyor belt there are clear cases were the results would benefit from a non-rigid registration. However as the images are captured just 17 ms apart, the affine transformation is enough to handle most situations, as the results indicate.

This paper did not apply any post processing to beautify the result images. The main purpose is to retrieve data hidden behind highlights and not just detect and discard these areas of the image. Yet one could argue that artifacts along the edge of a corrected region could disturb image processing methods later in the process. It might therefore be beneficial to use some smoothing along these edges to lessen these artifacts while still maintaining an accurate representation of the restored area.

References

1. Altwaijry, H., Veit, A., Belongie, S.: Learning to detect and match keypoints with deep architectures. In: British Machine Vision Conference (BMVC), New York, UK (2016)
2. Angelopoulou, E.: Specular highlight detection based on the fresnel reflection coefficient. In: Proceedings of the IEEE International Conference on Computer Vision (2007)
3. Arumugaperumal, S., Sivagami, B., PazhaniKumar, K.: An advanced scratch removal method for Fingerprint biometrics. In: 2011 3rd International Conference on Electronics Computer Technology, pp. 196–200. IEEE, April 2011. https://doi.org/10.1109/ICECTECH.2011.5941886

4. Bay, H., Ess, A., Tuytelaars, T., van Gool, L.: Speeded-Up Robust Features (SURF). Comput. Vis. Image Underst. **110**(3), 346–359 (2008). https://doi.org/10.1016/j.cviu.2007.09.014
5. Buades, A., Haro, G., Meinhardt-Llopis, E.: Obtaining high quality photographs of paintings by image fusion. Image Process. Line **5**, 159–175 (2015). https://doi.org/10.5201/ipol.2015.49
6. Chao, K., Chen, Y.R., Hruschka, W.R., Park, B.: Chicken heart disease characterization by multi-spectral imaging. Appl. Eng. Agric. Am. Soc. Agric. Eng. **99**(171), 99–106 (2001)
7. Feris, R., Raskar, R., Tan, K.H., Turk, M.: Specular highlights detection and reduction with multi-flash photography. J. Braz. Comput. Soc. **12**(1), 35–42 (2006). https://doi.org/10.1007/BF03192386
8. Hsieh, C., Chen, Y.R., Dey, B.P., Chan, D.E.: Separating septicemic and normal chicken livers by visible/near-infrared spectroscopy and back-propagation neural networks. Trans. ASAE **45**(2), 459–469 (2002)
9. Jørgensen, A., Fagertun, J., Moeslund, T.B.: Diagnosis of broiler livers by classifying image patches. In: Sharma, P., Bianchi, F.M. (eds.) SCIA 2017. LNCS, vol. 10269, pp. 374–385. Springer, Cham (2017). https://doi.org/10.1007/978-3-319-59126-1_31
10. Lowe, D.: Object recognition from local scale-invariant features. In: Proceedings of the Seventh IEEE International Conference on Computer Vision, vol. 2, pp. 1150–1157 (1999). https://doi.org/10.1109/ICCV.1999.790410
11. Marel Poultry: The world of Poultry Processing (2018). https://marel.com/files/pdf/world-of-stork-poultry-en.pdf
12. Philipsen, M.P., Jørgensen, A., Escalera, S., Moeslund, T.B.: RGB-D segmentation of poultry entrails. In: Perales, F.J.J., Kittler, J. (eds.) AMDO 2016. LNCS, vol. 9756, pp. 168–174. Springer, Cham (2016). https://doi.org/10.1007/978-3-319-41778-3_17
13. Ritchie, H., Roser, M.: Meat and seafood production & consumption. In: Our World is Changing (2018). OurWorldInData.org
14. Saxena, S., Singh, R.K.: A survey of recent and classical image registration methods. Int. J. Signal Process. Image Process. Pattern Recogn. **7**(4), 167–176 (2014). https://doi.org/10.14257/ijsip.2014.7.4.16
15. Shah, S.M.Z.A., Marshall, S., Murray, P.: Removal of specular reflections from image sequences using feature correspondences. Mach. Vis. Appl. **28**(3), 409–420 (2017). https://doi.org/10.1007/s00138-017-0826-6
16. Suo, J., An, D., Ji, X., Wang, H., Dai, Q.: Fast and high quality highlight removal from a single image. IEEE Trans. Image Process. **25**(11), 5441–5454 (2016). https://doi.org/10.1109/TIP.2016.2605002
17. Tao, Y., Shao, J., Skeeles, K., Chen, Y.R.: Detection of splenomegaly in poultry carcasses by UV and color imaging. Trans. ASAE **43**(2), 469–474 (2000)
18. Trambadia, S., Mayatra, H.: Image in painting based on Discrete Wavelet Transform (DWT) technique. In: 2016 Online International Conference on Green Engineering and Technologies (IC-GET), pp. 1–6. IEEE, November 2016. https://doi.org/10.1109/GET.2016.7916794
19. Vestergaard, M., Bengtson, S., Pedersen, M., Rankl, C., Moeslund, T.B.: Stitching grid-wise atomic force microscope images. In: Proceedings of the 11th Joint Conference on Computer Vision, Imaging and Computer Graphics Theory and Applications 3 (VISIGRAPP), pp. 110–117 (2016). https://doi.org/10.5220/0005716501100117

20. Wang, Z., Bovik, A.C., Sheikh, H.R., Simoncelli, E.P.: Image quality assessment: from error visibility to structural similarity. IEEE Trans. Image Process. **13**(4), 600–612 (2004)
21. Zagorchev, L., Goshtasby, A.: A comparative study of transformation functions for nonrigid image registration. IEEE Trans. Image Process. **15**(3), 529–538 (2006). https://doi.org/10.1109/TIP.2005.863114
22. Zhang, S., Jiao, L., Liu, F., Wang, S.: Global low-rank image restoration with Gaussian mixture model. IEEE Trans. Cybern. 1–12 (2017). https://doi.org/10.1109/TCYB.2017.2715846

Anomaly Detection Using GANs for Visual Inspection in Noisy Training Data

Masanari Kimura[✉] and Takashi Yanagihara[✉]

Ridge-i Inc., Tokyo, Japan
{mkimura,tyanagihara}@ridge-i.com

Abstract. The detection and the quantification of anomalies in image data are critical tasks in industrial scenes such as detecting micro scratches on product. In recent years, due to the difficulty of defining anomalies and the limit of correcting their labels, research on unsupervised anomaly detection using generative models has attracted attention. Generally, in those studies, only normal images are used for training to model the distribution of normal images. The model measures the anomalies in the target images by reproducing the most similar images and scoring image patches indicating their fit to the learned distribution. This approach is based on a strong presumption; the trained model should not be able to generate abnormal images. However, in reality, the model can generate abnormal images mainly due to noisy normal data which include small abnormal pixels, and such noise severely affects the accuracy of the model. Therefore, we propose a novel anomaly detection method to distort the distribution of the model with existing abnormal images. The proposed method detects pixel-level micro anomalies with a high accuracy from 1024×1024 high resolution images which are actually used in an industrial scene. In this paper, we share experimental results on open datasets, due to the confidentiality of the data.

1 Introduction

The detection and the quantification of anomalies in image data are critical tasks in many industries such as detecting micro scratches on product surfaces, or finding out diseases from medical images. There are many studies dealing with such tasks [1,6,11]. These studies are addressing task-specific problems in detecting anomalies from images.

For such tasks, applying supervised learning method is fairly hard in general due to the difficulty of defining anomalies and collecting enough number of abnormal data. In recent years, research on unsupervised anomaly detection using generative models has attracted attention.

One of the most successful cases regarding generative model research is Generative Adversarial Networks (GANs) [3]. A GAN mimics the given target distribution by simultaneously training typically two networks, a generator G and a discriminator D. The G produces the model distribution and D distinguishes the model distribution from the target. This learning framework has been successful

Fig. 1. Noisy samples included in the MNIST handwritten digits dataset.

in various application fields such as image generation [14], semantic segmentation [10], image translation [20,23], and super resolution [7], among others. In this research, we apply GANs to anomaly detection.

There are several studies on anomaly detection using GANs [15,17,19,22]. In those studies, only normal images are used to train GAN to model the distribution of the normal images. After the training is converged and a target image is queried, G generates the most similar image to the target. When anomalies are included in the target image, there should be some distances between the target and the generated images, since the model only knows the distribution of the normal images. Whether the image is classified as normal or not is decided based on the threshold for the distance. There is one common strong assumption among these approaches; the model G trained with normal images only should generate normal images. In other words, G should not be able to generate abnormal images.

However, in reality, the model can also generate abnormal images mainly due to a small number of abnormal pixels included in some normal images that are used for training. Trained with such noisy data, the generator recognizes them as part of the normal features. In real-world data, immaculate normal data are quite rare and it is virtually impossible to completely remove a few pixels of abnormal or distorted features included in normal images. (See Fig. 1)

Therefore, we propose a anomaly detection method effectively utilizing given abnormal images to resolve the issue. Our main contributions are the following:

- We solve the issues in the failure cases of the earlier studies on anomaly detection using GANs.
- We propose a novel method for anomaly detection using GANs. Our method achieves accurate anomaly detection by utilizing both normal and abnormal images.
- Our method successfully detects pixel-level micro anomalies in 1024 × 1024 high resolution images from an actual industrial scene.

2 Related Works

In this section, we outline two studies referred in our research: Generative Adversarial Networks (GANs) and Anomaly Detection using GANs.

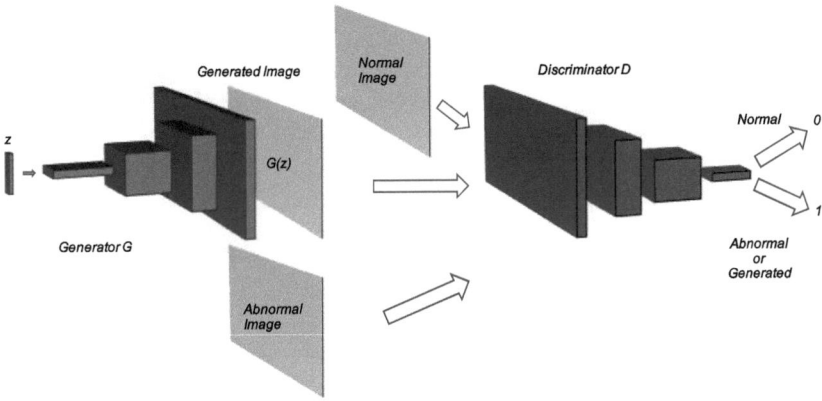

Fig. 2. Anomaly detection using Generative Adversarial Networks. A generator maps noise z onto a real image. A discriminator classifies whether a target image is a normal image, or an abnormal or generated image. The discriminator conducts binary classification; 0 if the input image is normal and 1 if the input image is either abnormal or generated.

2.1 Generative Adversarial Networks

In recent years, GANs [3] have achieved a great success in image generation tasks. A GAN consists of two networks, a generator G and a discriminator D. A generator learns the distribution p_g by mapping noise z, which is sampled from the uniform distribution, to the image space χ. A discriminator learns to distinguish between generated images and genuine images. The discriminator and the generator are simultaneously optimized through the two-player minimax game as follows:

$$\min_G \max_D V(D,G) = \mathbb{E}_{x \sim p_d(x)}[\log D(x)] \\ + \mathbb{E}_{x \sim p_z(z)}[\log(1 - D(G(z)))] \quad (1)$$

Here, p_d is the distribution of real data and p_z is the distribution of noise z. As adversarial training continues, the generator becomes able to generate samples that look similar to the real images, and the discriminator becomes able to identify whether an image is genuine or generated.

Despite of its successful performance in many fields, GANs' instability during the training has always been a critical issue, particularly with complicated images as in a photo-realistic high resolution case. To solve such problems and improve the learning stability of GANs, many studies have been released [2,4,5,12,16] and Karras et al. proposed a method called progressive growing which gradually increases the resolution from low-resolution images throughout the learning phase [5]. This method successfully generates much clearer high-resolution images compared to the existing methods can. We applied the progressive growing framework to our research so that we can accurately detect small anomalies in high-resolution images.

2.2 Anomaly Detection Using GANs

Recently GANs have been used in anomaly detection research and AnoGAN [17] brought a great progress to the field with a simple algorithm that only normal images are used for training a generator to model the distribution of normal images. With the trained G, if a given new query image x is from the normal data distribution, noise $\hat{z}$ must exist in the latent space where $G(\hat{z})$ becomes identical to x. However if x is abnormal, $\hat{z}$ will not exist even though G tries to generate images most similar to x. The algorithm is heavily based on this hypothesis.

To find the noise $\hat{z}$, AnoGAN uses two loss functions: residual loss and discrimination loss.

Residual Loss. The residual loss measures the visual distance between the input image x and the generated image $G(z)$.

$$L_R(z) = \sum |x - G(z)| \qquad (2)$$

If G perfectly learned the distribution of the normal data, L_R should work as follows:

- Input image is normal: $L_R \simeq 0$
- Input image is abnormal: $L_R \gg 0$

From the above, we can formulate visual differences.

Discrimination Loss Based on Feature Matching. In addition to L_R, the discrimination loss is based on feature matching which uses an intermediate feature representation of the discriminator by

$$L_D(z) = \sum |f(x) - f(G(z))| \qquad (3)$$

where the output of the discriminator's intermediate layer $f(\Delta)$ is used to extract the features of the input image and the generated image. For G to learn the mapping to the latent space, overall loss is defined as the weighted sum of both components:

$$L_{Ano}(z) = (1 - \lambda) \cdot L_R(z) + \lambda \cdot L_D(z) \qquad (4)$$

With this differentiable loss function, $\hat{z}$ that makes the image generated by $G(\hat{z})$ most similar to the input image can be searched using back propagation. The trained parameters of the generator G and the discriminator D are kept fixed during the search. This is the fundamental mechanism of using GANs for anomaly detection.

3 Proposed Method

Using GANs for anomaly detection is based on a strong assumption that G trained with normal images cannot generate abnormal images; G should generate normal images only. However, in reality, there are circumstances in which G generates abnormal images due to the following factors:

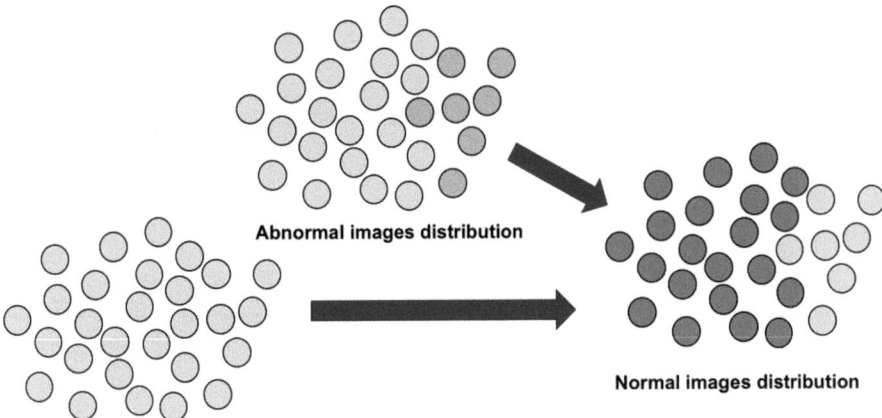

Fig. 3. Visualization of distribution deformation by the proposed method. By using the known abnormal image set as much as possible, the proposed method excludes the distribution of abnormal images from the distribution that G can take.

- The normal images used for training actually included some anomalies, and the generator learns it as normal features. Figure 1 shows the noisy samples included in the MNIST handwritten digits dataset.
- The generator does not have enough representation power or enough training data to learn perfect mapping from z to the image space.

These are the natural behavior of the GAN architecture and we focus on dealing with unavoidable anomalies occurring in the dataset. In real wild data, immaculate normal samples very rare and it is practically unfeasible to completely remove a few pixels of abnormal or distorted features found from the normal dataset.

To solve the problem, we propose a method of helping the generator learn distributions similar to the distribution of the normal data with abnormal images that already exist. Figure 2 shows the overview of our method.

The proposed method reconstructs the learning framework of GANs. The objective function $V(D, G)$ of GANs can be transformed from Eq. 1 to the following equation:

$$V(D, G) = \int_x p_d(x) \log D(x) + p_g(x) \log (1 - D(x)) dx \qquad (5)$$

Algorithm 1. Noisy-AnoGAN Inference

Require: x, the input image, n, the number of iterations, γ, the weight of anomalies loss.
Sample $z \sim p_z$, a noise sample from the uniform distribution.
for $i = t \ldots n$ **do**
    $l \leftarrow L'(z)$
    $z \leftarrow Update(z, l)$
end for
$\hat{z} \leftarrow z$
$anomalyscore \leftarrow L'(\hat{z})$

Here, let $y = D(x)$, $a = p_d(x)$, $b = p_g(x)$,

$$h(y) = a \log y + b \log(1-y) \qquad (6)$$

$$\frac{d}{dy}h(y) = \frac{a}{y} + \frac{b}{y-1} \qquad (7)$$

$$= \frac{a(y-1) + b(y)}{y(y-1)} \qquad (8)$$

$$= \frac{y(a+b) - a}{y(y-1)} \qquad (9)$$

Since $y = \frac{a}{a+b}$ when $\frac{d}{dy}h(y) = 0$ in Eq. 9, the optimum discriminator is derived as below:

$$D^*(x) = \frac{p_d(x)}{p_d(x) + p_g(x)} \qquad (10)$$

Now, we consider Jensen-Shannon divergence (JSD), which is defined as follows:

$$JSD(p_d||p_g) = \frac{1}{2}(KL(p_d||p_A) + KL(p_g||p_A)) \qquad (11)$$

$$KL(p_d||p_g) = \int_x p_d(x) \log \frac{p_d(x)}{p_g(x)} dx \qquad (12)$$

$$p_A = \frac{p_d + p_g}{2} \qquad (13)$$

By combining Eqs. 5, 10, 11 and 12, we obtain the optimum object function below:

$$V(D^*, G) = 2JSD(p_d||p_g) - 2\log 2 \qquad (14)$$

From Eq. 14, we can assume that the generator aims at minimizing the JSD between the real distribution and the generator distribution.

In contrast to the typical objective loss function – Eq. 1 which only takes normal images into consideration, we define an additional loss function to consider abnormal images as well. Our proposed method treats abnormal images as another type of generated images and adds penalty loss $l_{An}(D)$ with penalty weight γ. This can be regarded as distorting the data distribution p_d. The objective loss function is defined as:

$$V'(D,G) = \gamma l_{Adv}(D,G) + (1-\gamma)l_{An}(D), \qquad (15)$$

where

$$l_{Adv}(D,G) = V(D,G) \qquad (16)$$
$$l_{An}(D) = \mathbb{E}_{x \sim p_{an}(x)}[\log(1 - D(x))]. \qquad (17)$$

Here, p_{an} is the distribution of abnormal images and γ is a parameter of (0, 1]. The parameter γ controls the percentage of abnormal images generated. A smaller γ excludes abnormal images from the training data, but at the same time it might even penalize normal features included in abnormal data. Combining Eqs. 14 and 15 and our proposed definition, we obtain the objective function of the generator as:

$$V'(D^*, G) = 2JSD(p_d || p_N) - 2\log 2 \qquad (18)$$
$$p_N = \gamma p_g + (1-\gamma) p_{an}. \qquad (19)$$

Therefore, we can assume that the objective function of G is to minimize the JSD between the real image distribution and the mixed distribution of generated images and abnormal images. Since the JSD becomes the minimum when $p_d = p_N$, the optimum p_g^* for G can be derived as follows:

$$p_N^* = p_d \qquad (20)$$
$$\gamma p_g^* + (1-\gamma) p_{an} = p_d \qquad (21)$$
$$\gamma p_g^* = p_d - (1-\gamma) p_{an} \qquad (22)$$
$$p_g^* = \frac{1}{\gamma} p_d - \frac{(1-\gamma)}{\gamma} p_{an} \qquad (23)$$

where $\frac{1}{\gamma} \geq 1$ and $\frac{(1-\gamma)}{\gamma} = \frac{1}{\gamma} - 1 \geq 1$. From the equations above, we may consider that the proposed method distorts the distribution of real images to remove abnormal images and to make the ideal distribution of normal images. Figure 3 represents the change in the distribution caused by the proposed method.

During the inference, our method uses the following function to search the noise $\hat{z}$ that makes an image most similar to the input.

$$L'(z) = \gamma L_{Ano}(z) + (1-\gamma) L'_{An}(z) \qquad (24)$$
$$L'_{An}(z) = \sum |1 - D(G(z))| \qquad (25)$$

The function $Update(z, l)$ updates the noise z based on the value of l. Algorithm 1 shows the inference algorithm.

After finding the noise $\hat{z}$, we can use *anomaly score* $L'(\hat{z})$ to classify images in to normal and abnormal. Furthermore, we can identify the abnormal pixels in the image by calculating the difference between the generated image $G(\hat{z})$ and the input.

4 Experiments

Our method successfully detects pixel-level micro anomalies in 1024×1024 high resolution images from the real industrial data with a high accuracy. However, we conducted an experiment with open dataset as we cannot disclose the images due to the confidentiality of the data. We use $\gamma = 0.1$, $\lambda = 0.1$ and $n = 500$ as each parameter of the proposed method.

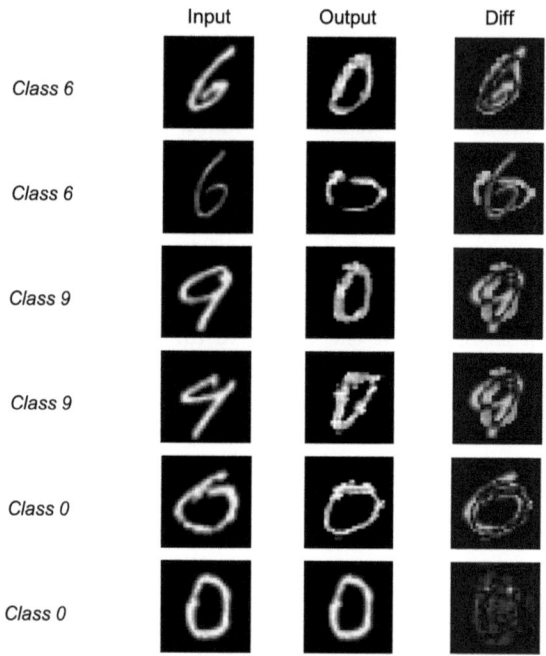

Fig. 4. Experimental results on the MNIST dataset. The output images were generated by the proposed method which trained 0 as a normal class.

4.1 Datasets

We use the following two datasets for experiments. Table 1 shows the list of datasets.

MNIST: This dataset[1] includes 70,000 handwritten digits from 0 to 9. This dataset has a training set of 60,000 examples and a test set of 10,000 examples. The images included in this dataset are unified to the size of 28×28 pixels. We regard one class out of ten classes as a normal data and we consider images of other classes to be abnormal. We select a class as a normal class and allocate

---
[1] http://yann.lecun.com/exdb/mnist/.

70% of it to the training set. In addition to that, 10% from all the classes other than the normal class is added to the training data so that the training data can have both normal and abnormal class. After training, we test with the data that was not used for learning and contains both of the classes. This experiment is repeated for all of the 10 classes.

Caltech-256: This dataset[2] includes 30,607 images of 256 object categories. Each category has at least 80 images. We follow the experimental setup of Sabokrou et al. [15]. In addition, we sample 50 images from all outlying category images, add them to the training data and train the model with the proposed method.

Table 1. An overview of the datasets used for the experiments.

Dataset name	Dataset size	Class
MNIST	70,000	10
Caltech-256	30,607	256
IR-MNIST	6,051	10

IR-MNIST: This dataset[3] is made of MNIST dataset. To create each sample, randomly 121 samples are selected from the MNIST dataset and are put together as a 11 × 11 puzzle. The size of each image is 224 × 224. Training samples are

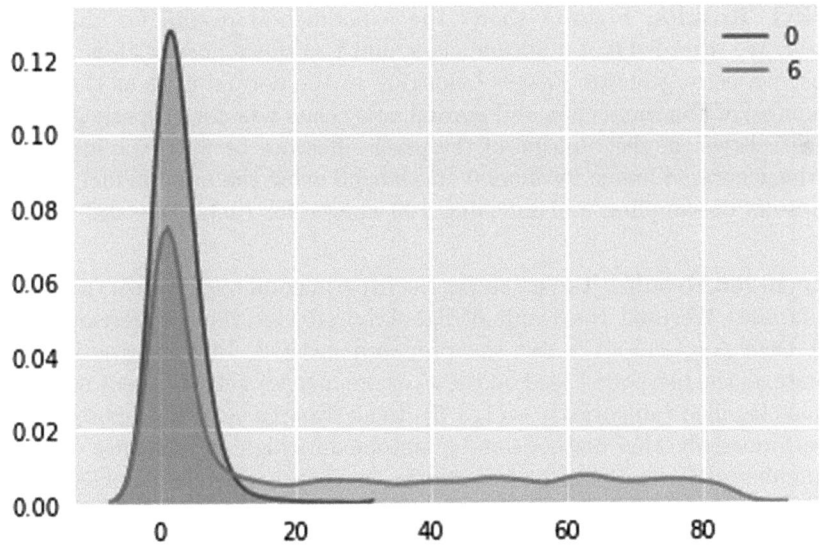

Fig. 5. Distribution of pixel difference between input image and generated image.

[2] http://www.vision.caltech.edu/Image_Datasets/Caltech256/.
[3] http://ai.stanford.edu/~eadeli/publications/data/IR-MNIST.zip.

created without using any images of the digit '3'. Hence, '3' is considered as an abnormal class. We train the proposed method using 5000 normal class data and 50 abnormal class data.

4.2 Network Architecture

We use the progressive growing [5] as a learning framework and further details about the network architecture and the hyper parameters can be found in Table 2 in the corresponding paper.

Table 2. Results on the Caltech-256 dataset. We used the result of Sabokrou [15] for the comparison method other than AnoGAN [17] and the proposed method. We used Karras et al.'s network architecture for AnoGAN and out proposed method. The metric of this table is the $F1$-score, and N is the number of categories of the normal class.

N	CoP [13]	REAPER [8]	LRR [9]	DPCP [18]	R-graph [21]	Sabokrou [15]	AnoGAN [17]	Ours
1	0.880	0.808	0.893	0.785	0.914	0.928	0.956	**0.977**
3	0.718	0.784	0.671	0.777	0.880	0.913	0.915	**0.963**
5	0.672	0.716	0.667	0.715	0.858	0.905	0.887	**0.945**

4.3 Results

We introduce some experimental results on the benchmark dataset.

MNIST Results: Figure 4 shows the experimental results for the MNIST dataset. We regarded 0 as a normal class, and 1 as the abnormal class. We could almost perfectly generate images belonging to the normal class at the bottom, but images of abnormal class and normal noisy class was not properly generated. Figure 5 shows the distribution of the pixel difference between the input image and the generated image for label 0 and label 6 using the same model. We show the results of sampling and inferring 100 images for each class and averaging them.

Caltech-256 Results: Table 2 shows the experimental results with the Caltech-256 dataset. We used the result of Sabokrou [15] for the comparison method other than AnoGAN [17] and the proposed method. In this experiment, we evaluate all the methods based on the F_1-score metrics with different numbers of normal-classified categories $n \in \{1, 3, 5\}$. In all three cases, our proposed method outperformed all other methods and maintained its high performance even when the number of normal-classified categories increased, whereas AnoGAN's score dropped under such a circumstance.

IR-MNIST Results: Figure 6 shows the experimental results with the IR-MNIST dataset. The top images are the original test images. The bottom images are difference images between the outputs of the proposed method and the test samples. In this dataset, '3' does not exist in the normal classes, and it can be seen from the difference image that a large difference is obtained in this class.

Fig. 6. Experimental results on IR-MNIST dataset. The top images are the original test images. In the test image, 3 exists unlike the training image. The bottom images are difference images between the outputs of the proposed method and the test samples. In particular, it can be seen that the difference is large in the portion 3 in the image.

5 Conclusion

In this paper, we proposed a method of detecting anomalies with GANs using both normal images and given abnormal images. By distorting the data distribution and excluding the distribution of the abnormal images, the network can learn more about ideal normal data distributions. This method allows us to make more robust and accurate models to detect anomalies; our model detected smaller than 1% of abnormal pixels in 1024 × 1024 high resolution images. Due to the confidential nature of the data, we share only the results for open datasets, and further validation on various datasets is desirable.

References

1. An, J., Cho, S.: Variational autoencoder based anomaly detection using reconstruction probability. Technical Report, SNU Data Mining Center (2015)
2. Arjovsky, M., Chintala, S., Bottou, L.: Wasserstein generative adversarial networks. In: Precup, D., Teh, Y.W. (eds.) Proceedings of the 34th International Conference on Machine Learning. Proceedings of Machine Learning Research, vol. 70, pp. 214–223. PMLR, International Convention Centre, Sydney, 06–11 August 2017. http://proceedings.mlr.press/v70/arjovsky17a.html
3. Goodfellow, I., et al.: Generative adversarial nets. In: Advances in neural information processing systems, pp. 2672–2680 (2014)

4. Gulrajani, I., Ahmed, F., Arjovsky, M., Dumoulin, V., Courville, A.C.: Improved training of Wasserstein GANs. In: Advances in Neural Information Processing Systems, pp. 5769–5779 (2017)
5. Karras, T., Aila, T., Laine, S., Lehtinen, J.: Progressive growing of GANs for improved quality, stability, and variation. In: International Conference on Learning Representations (2018). https://openreview.net/forum?id=Hk99zCeAb
6. Kim, S.S., Reddy, A.N.: Image-based anomaly detection technique: algorithm, implementation and effectiveness. IEEE J. Sel. Areas Commun. **24**(10), 1942–1954 (2006)
7. Ledig, C., et al.: Photo-realistic single image super-resolution using a generative adversarial network. In: CVPR, vol. 2, p. 4 (2017)
8. Lerman, G., McCoy, M.B., Tropp, J.A., Zhang, T.: Robust computation of linear models by convex relaxation. Found. Comput. Math. **15**(2), 363–410 (2015)
9. Liu, G., Lin, Z., Yu, Y.: Robust subspace segmentation by low-rank representation. In: Proceedings of the 27th International Conference on Machine Learning (ICML-2010), pp. 663–670 (2010)
10. Luc, P., Couprie, C., Chintala, S., Verbeek, J.: Semantic segmentation using adversarial networks. arXiv preprint arXiv:1611.08408 (2016)
11. Quam, L.H.: Road tracking and anomaly detection in aerial imagery. Technical Report, Sri International Artificial Intelligence Center, Menlo Park CA (1978)
12. Radford, A., Metz, L., Chintala, S.: Unsupervised representation learning with deep convolutional generative adversarial networks. arXiv preprint arXiv:1511.06434 (2015)
13. Rahmani, M., Atia, G.K.: Coherence pursuit: fast, simple, and robust principal component analysis. IEEE Trans. Signal Process. **65**(23), 6260–6275 (2017)
14. Reed, S., Akata, Z., Yan, X., Logeswaran, L., Schiele, B., Lee, H.: Generative adversarial text to image synthesis. In: Balcan, M.F., Weinberger, K.Q. (eds.) Proceedings of the 33rd International Conference on Machine Learning. Proceedings of Machine Learning Research, vol. 48, pp. 1060–1069. PMLR, New York, 20–22 June 2016. http://proceedings.mlr.press/v48/reed16.html
15. Sabokrou, M., Khalooei, M., Fathy, M., Adeli, E.: Adversarially learned one-class classifier for novelty detection. In: Proceedings of the IEEE Conference on Computer Vision and Pattern Recognition, pp. 3379–3388 (2018)
16. Salimans, T., Goodfellow, I., Zaremba, W., Cheung, V., Radford, A., Chen, X.: Improved techniques for training GANs. In: Advances in Neural Information Processing Systems, pp. 2234–2242 (2016)
17. Schlegl, T., Seeböck, P., Waldstein, S.M., Schmidt-Erfurth, U., Langs, G.: Unsupervised anomaly detection with generative adversarial networks to guide marker discovery. In: Niethammer, M., et al. (eds.) IPMI 2017. LNCS, vol. 10265, pp. 146–157. Springer, Cham (2017). https://doi.org/10.1007/978-3-319-59050-9_12
18. Tsakiris, M.C., Vidal, R.: Dual principal component pursuit. In: Proceedings of the IEEE International Conference on Computer Vision Workshops, pp. 10–18 (2015)
19. Wang, H.G., Li, X., Zhang, T.: Generative adversarial network based novelty detection using minimized reconstruction error. Front. Inf. Technol. Electron. Eng. **19**(1), 116–125 (2018)

20. Yi, Z., Zhang, H.R., Tan, P., Gong, M.: DualGAN: unsupervised dual learning for image-to-image translation. In: ICCV, pp. 2868–2876 (2017)
21. You, C., Robinson, D.P., Vidal, R.: Provable self representation based outlier detection in a union of subspaces. In: Proceedings of the 2017 IEEE Conference on Computer Vision and Pattern Recognition, pp. 1–10 (2017)
22. Zenati, H., Foo, C.S., Lecouat, B., Manek, G., Chandrasekhar, V.R.: Efficient GAN-based anomaly detection. arXiv preprint arXiv:1802.06222 (2018)
23. Zhu, J.Y., Park, T., Isola, P., Efros, A.A.: Unpaired image-to-image translation using cycle-consistent adversarial networks. In: The IEEE International Conference on Computer Vision (ICCV), October 2017

Integration of Driver Behavior into Emotion Recognition Systems: A Preliminary Study on Steering Wheel and Vehicle Acceleration

Sina Shafaei(✉), Tahir Hacizade(✉), and Alois Knoll(✉)

Technical University of Munich, Munich, Germany
{sina.shafaei,tahir.hacizade}@tum.de, knoll@in.tum.de

Abstract. The current status of the development for emotion recognition systems in cars is mostly focused on camera-based solutions which consider the face as the main input data source. Modeling behavior of the driver in automotive domain is also a challenging topic which has a great impact on developing intelligent and autonomous vehicles. In order to study the correlation between driving behavior and emotional status of the driver, we propose a multimodal system which is based on facial expressions and driver specific behavior including steering wheel usage and the change in vehicle acceleration. The aim of this work is to investigate the impact of integration of driver behavior into emotion recognition systems and to build a structure which continuously classifies the emotions in an efficient and non-intrusive manner. We consider driver behavior as the typical range of interactions with the vehicle which represents the responses to certain stimuli. To recognize facial emotions, we extract the histogram values from the key facial regions and combine them into a single vector which is then used to train a SVM classifier. Following that, using machine learning techniques and statistical methods two modules of abrupt car maneuvers counter, based on steering wheel rotation, and aggressive driver predictor, based on a variation of acceleration, are built. In the end, all three modules are combined into one final emotion classifier which is capable of predicting the emotional group of the driver with 94% of accuracy in sub-samples. For the evaluation we used a real car simulator with 8 different participants as the drivers.

Keywords: Emotion recognition · Multimodality · Driver behavior

1 Introduction

The recognition of emotions has wide implications in the different applications and recently got the attention of the researchers in the field of automotive for the purpose of driver fatigue detection [9,41,45,54], human-car interaction [9,29] and respectively the highly and fully autonomous driving scenarios [21,37]. According to the *7-38-55* Rule, 93% of human communication is performed through nonverbal means, which consist of *facial expressions*, *body language* and *voice tone* [38]. Therefore, a system which aims at automatically analyzing the emotions of humans should mainly focus on these non-verbal channels. This research field respectively is called *Affective Computing* which is an emerging research field in enabling intelligent systems to recognize human emotions. The main challenges in automated affect recognition are *head-pose* variations, *illumination variations*, *registration errors*, *occlusions*, *identity bias* and (subject-independent affect recognition) [47]. The most common approach in the field of affective classification are multimodal methods. The general aim of multimodal fusion is to increase the accuracy and reliability of the estimates. Based on empirical studies and statistical measures, multimodal systems were consistently more accurate than their unimodal counterparts, with an average improvement of 9.83% (median of 6.60%) [14,43]. Fusion of multiple modalities into one single final output is a challenging task. The right fusion method highly depends on the underlying data. Common fusion techniques in the field of affective computing are *feature-level fusion*, *kernel-based fusion*, *model-level fusion*, *score-level fusion*, *decision-level fusion*, and *hybrid* approaches [14,43,44,53]. The most common fusion techniques are feature-level fusion and decision-level fusion. In feature-level fusion the data from separate modalities are first aggregated and then used as a single input into one model. In decision-level fusion each modality has its own trained model, and the predictions are then combined to a single output.

Moreover, most of the state-of-the-art systems have high complexities and are mostly benchmarked in ideal environments and on powerful computers with access to Graphics Processing Units (GPUs) [10,14,39,43]. This limits the applicability of using such systems for in-cabin environments due to the existing limitations regarding computation power in such environments. Considering this, no publicly accessible research, to this date, aims at enabling automated, robust affect recognition for car-drivers on embedded devices. In this work, we propose a system which is designed exclusively for in-cabin environments to tackle the important challenges of affect recognition in automotive and help to increase the emotional awareness of in-cabin environment by investigating the behavior-related modalities of the driver through monitoring the steering wheel for performed maneuvers and the change in acceleration of the car. We study (**RQ1**) the effects of emotions on behavior of the driver while driving, (**RQ2**) modeling the change in acceleration and steering wheel usage by the driver, according to the current emotional status and (**RQ3**) will try to demonstrate the benefits of multimodality in emotion recognition systems for robust predictions.

In the following remainder, we discuss in Sect. 2 relevant state-of-the-art methods in affective computing. Based on this knowledge, we tackle the aforementioned challenges of automatic emotion recognition for in-cabin environments with the help of our proposed approach at Sect. 3. In Sect. 4 we represent the integration of the considered modalities into our system beside the achieved results, and finally, in Sect. 5 we draw an outlook and list the open directions and challenges for future studies.

2 Related Works

Ekman and Friesen [17] proposed 6 universal human emotions (anger, disgust, fear, happiness, sadness, and surprise) and respectively developed the Facial Action Coding System (FACS). Their system interprets one or more facial muscle as Actions Units (AU) and the predefined combination of AUs represents one of the emotions. FACS acts as a basis for most of the automatic facial emotion recognition systems. Similarly, EMFACS (Emotional Facial Action Coding System) [18] which includes only emotion-related action units, is among the widely used systems. Alshamsi et al. [2] proposed a method for real-time emotion recognition on mobile phones. The system has two main parts as feature extraction and emotion classification. In order to extract features, authors label every pixel of a frame as 0 or 1 based on the intensity of pixels using BRIEF binary descriptor [7] a.k.a appearance-based approach. BRIEF differs from its competitors with higher recognition rates. Feature extraction step, can process 15 frames/second on mobile phones and as a result generates the 256-bit feature vector. Authors used the K-Nearest Neighbor (KNN) classification algorithm which uses Euclidean distance to compute the nearest point and requires minimal data distribution information. The trained system could achieve around 85% accuracy on a classification of 6 basic emotions using Cohn-Kanade dataset. Performance of BRIEF feature extractor outperforms previously used methods as *Similarity Normalized Shape Features (SPTS)* and *Canonical Normalized Appearance (CAPP)* [52]. Combination of SPTS and CAPP achieves 83% average detection rate which is still lower than BRIEF.

The majority of the researches in this field are focused on emotion recognition using a combination of several modules, but none of them considered classifying the emotions of driver based on his behavior during the ride. Behavior can be defined as the typical velocity and movements of body parts which then may be used to imply emotions as interest or boredom [4]. Some works with the help of biometric devices try to evaluate the stress, and the distraction level of the driver with the help of biometric devices like electroencephalogram (EEG) checkers [16,23]. Kamaruddin and Wahab [28] investigated the correlation between drivers speech and behavior in order to build a driver emotional indicator system. Their main goal was to identify the behavioral state of the driver through speech emotion recognition. For this purpose, they use the *Mel Frequency Cepstral Coefficient (MFCC)* [8] to extract features from the audio signals of a driver. Then these features were used to classify speech into 4 states of driver behavior, specifically as *talking, sleeping, laughing* and *neutral*. As a classifier, three different methods of *Multi-Layer Perceptron (MLP)* and a fuzzy neural network such as *Adaptive Neuro-Fuzzy Inference System (ANFIS)* and *Generic Self-organizing Fuzzy Neural Network (GenSoFNN)* were considered in their work. Dataset to train models was built from the mix of *Real-time Speech*

Driving Dataset (RtSD) [32], *Berlin Emotional Speech Database (Emo-DB)* [5] and *NAW* dataset [27]. Unlike the previous works, they not only consider words and speech but any vocal voice generated by the driver. A best example is laughing which is the main sign of being happy. There are various implementations of MFCC, but according to the comparison performed by Ganchev et al. [20] and Slaney's implementation [48] considerable improvement in performance was observed by integration of speech modality. However, this approach was not considered as an independent system in emotion recognition, but rather as an add-on to already existing functionality. This was due to the fact that speech is not a regular act while driving especially when the driver is alone in the car. Another complementary module to facial emotion recognition is the identification of head movements. The work of Samanta and Guha [46] shows an impact of head motions in affective recognition. In order to analyze head motions, the authors used *Acted Facial Expression in the Wild (AFEW)* dataset [13] which includes small video clips from 54 movies. All clips are labeled with seven basic emotion categories. After splitting these clips into frames, they consider the head as a 3-D rigid body which is defined by Euler angles (pitch, yaw, and roll) and use *incremental face alignment* method [3] to detect the head in each frame. As the first step of head motion inspection, *root-mean-square (RMS)* values of angular displacement, angular velocity, and angular acceleration are considered. For each emotion class, the nine-time series of RMS values are calculated. Their results show that *anger*, *joy*, and *neutral* states were more distinguishable from the rest. RMS measurements of *sadness* and *surprise* were very similar. In the next stage, they evaluated the impact of RMS measurements in emotion classification. As a classifier k-Nearest Neighbor method was used. After 10-fold cross-validation, overall accuracy of around 34% was achieved which was two times more than random guessing. It was also interesting for the authors to know whether head motions hold information complementary to facial expression. Experiments on AFEW dataset show that accuracy is increased 10% when RMS measurements of head motions are used jointly with facial expression. Findings of Hammal et al. [24] demonstrate that angular velocity and acceleration of head movements are considerably higher during negative affect relative to positive one. Behoora and Tucker [4] were able to find a link between body language and emotional state. By using non-wearable sensors, they tracked human skeletal joints and calculated velocity beside acceleration for each joint. Afterwards, machine learning techniques are applied to quantify body language states. From the perspective of methods, achieved results by previous experiments depict that during classification stage, decision tree based methods (like random forest and IBK) outperform others (like Naive Bayesian and C4.5) and can achieve up to 99% accuracy in recognition of 4 emotions. Vehicle acceleration and deceleration events also have been investigated in similar researches where the aim was to identify the driver and predict the age group [19,34].

The steering wheel is a part of the steering system which is manipulated by the driver. Zhenhai et al. [55] were able to detect driver drowsiness after analyzing time series of steering wheel's angular velocity. As a starting point, steering behavior under the fatigue state was inspected. Then after collecting some portion of data, the sliding window technique was applied and respectively the drowsiness state was recognized after examining high fluctuations in a temporal window. Moreover, the likelihood of eyes holding information about the behavior and emotional state was investigated by Cabrall et al. [6]. With the help of eye tracker apparatus, the authors tried to evaluate the distraction, drowsiness, and cognitive load of the driver during automated driving.

3 Proposed Approach

In order to identify the emotional state, we consider behavior-related data and facial expressions as the sources of input. The modality of facial expression is used as our main input to classify the emotions of driver and in order to increase the confidence and robustness of the predictions, we incorporate the behavior-modality. We model all modalities separately, meaning we use decision-level fusion in order to combine their outcomes. Therefore, each modality needs to be trained separately and then the outcomes need to be weighted and combined together. This architecture is visualized at Fig. 1. The facial expressions is represented by the node *Facial Expressions*. We evaluate this modality by an individual module of *Facial Modality*. The behavior-modality is composed of *Steering Wheel Usage*, and *Change in Acceleration* signals. The variables represent input data to the second module of *Behavior Modality*. Both modules analyze the emotional state individually and are fused on the decision-level to output the final classification of the emotional state.

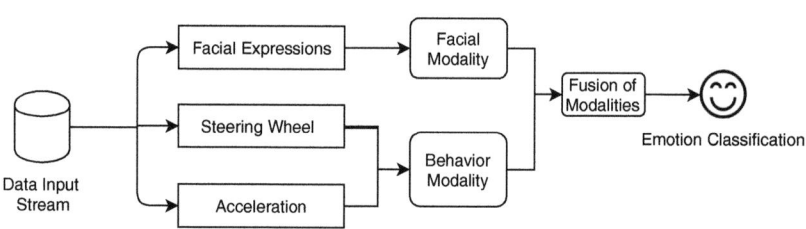

Fig. 1. Different modalities of the proposed system

3.1 Experimental Set Up

We set up a real car simulator for testing and evaluating our approach. On the simulator, driver has almost 180° of view and can easily watch over the cars in other roads at an intersection using the side monitors. Car controlling systems as the steering wheel, accelerator, brake, and transmission are almost identical in size and way of functioning with a real car. Sound system installed in the cabin also helps to convey a real sense of driving. During experiments, 15 drivers have participated, each of drove 36 min on average. Drivers got a chance to drive one route three times. Their attitude was different due to a prehistory condition narrated to them and the predefined situations on the road. Real emotional states of the drivers were collected using a questionnaire organized right after each ride. During the rides, drivers were being recorded using an external camera in a resolution of 960 × 720 and all other internal vehicle parameters as speed, acceleration and steering wheel position were collected by *virtual test drive* software of the simulator.

3.2 Facial Modality

To detect the *Region of Interests* (ROI) we used a facial landmark detector as designed by Kazem et al. [30]. After that, we used *Histogram of Oriented Gradients* (HOG) descriptors by applying a fixed sized sliding window over an image pyramid build upon them. The normalized HOG orientation features make this method capable of reducing false positive rates far better in comparison with *Haar Wavelet-based Detectors* [11]. Support Vector Machines (SVM), Random Forest, and K-Nearest Neighbours (KNN) algorithms are most widely used supervised machine learning techniques for classification tasks. Our model was built based on linear kernel SVM with decision function of *One-vs-Rest*. In order to train our model, k-Fold Cross Validation method was used with a 'k' set to 10. The respective algorithm is represented at Algorithm 1. Facial data is represented by the aggregation of *extended Cohn-Kanade* (CK+) [35] and *Japanese Female Facial Expression* (JAFFE) [36] database.

Algorithm 1. The Facial Emotion Classifier

1: $featureVector \leftarrow$ init list
2: $SVMClassifier \leftarrow$ load model
3: **while** newFrame is exist **do**
4:     $frame \leftarrow FetchVideoStream()$
5:     $grayFrame \leftarrow GrayscaleImage(frame)$
6:     **if** $faceTracker(grayFrame).Score < threshold$ **then**
7:        $face \leftarrow detectFace(grayFrame)$
8:     **else**
9:        $face \leftarrow faceTracker(grayFrame).Position$
10:    **end if**
11:    $ROIarray \leftarrow FetchROI(face)$
12:    **for each** ROI in $ROIarray$ **do**
13:        $hog \leftarrow HOGDescriptor(ROI)$
14:        $featureVector \leftarrow featureVector + hog$
15:    **end for**
16:    $result \leftarrow SVMClassifier(featureVector)$
17: **end while**

3.3 Behavior Modality

Steering wheel angular velocity is one of the primary factors which was considered to be collected during all rides. Due to the fact that some situations like avoiding obstacles may require a sharp steering movement, we should observe the driver usage of steering wheel for some predefined period of time. Later, based on collected initial data, the average of angular velocity in steering wheel is calculated for small fraction of time. This averaged value will be used later as the threshold. Our aim is to detect angular velocity higher than dynamically defined threshold and mark this fraction of time as abnormal and when there is consecutively several abnormal values, the system will identify the emotional state of the driver accordingly. Another measurement factor which infers information about the behavior of driver during a ride, is the intensity of the changes in vehicle acceleration. In order to combine the modalities we use decision-level fusion as it was mentioned earlier. However, since not all of emotions extracted by facial expressions can be reflected in behavior modality, there is a need for high level representation of the emotional state of the driver. This is commonly performed by representing the emotional state with *valence and arousal* [31] as depicted at Fig. 2. Valence is positive or negative affective [22] and defines the description level on a scale from pleasantness/positive emotions to unpleasantness/negative emotions. Similarly arousal measures, is an indicator of how calm or excited the subject is and implies reactiveness of the subject to a stimuli [31].

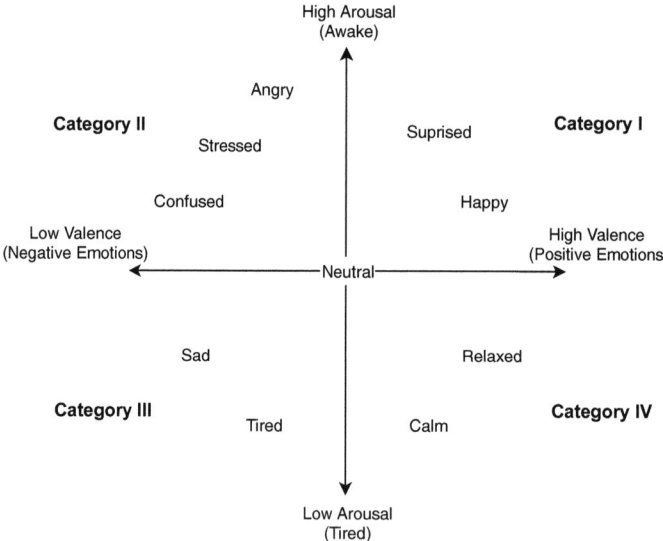

Fig. 2. Different categories of arousal-valence graph

Generally speaking, drivers tend to drive more actively and make more often abrupt movements when they are *angry, happy* or *excited*. Respectively their driving behavior becomes more passive, and most likely don't make eye/body movements as actively as they do when they are *tired* or *sad*. These emotions can exactly match with the emotional categories depicted at Fig. 2. Here we achieve our main pattern based on the fact that active and aggressive driving skills are related to category I and II, whereas category III represents passive driving behavior and category IV depicts a neutral state of the driver.

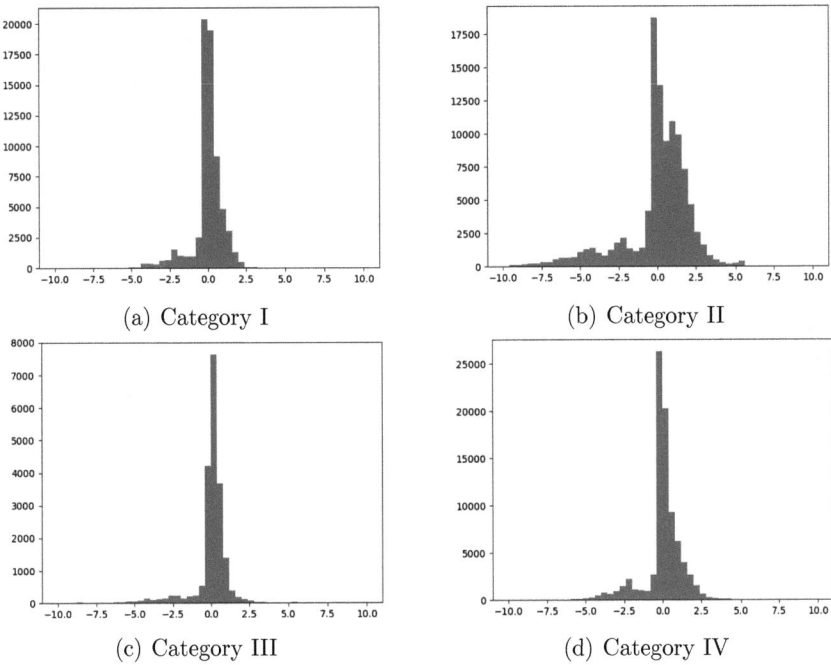

Fig. 3. Frequency distribution of vehicle acceleration in 4 groups of emotional status

In order to compare the vehicle acceleration distribution during different emotional states, the histogram of frequency distribution is plotted at Fig. 3. The vehicle acceleration collection for category I, III and IV are very similar and do not hold much sign of distinction. On the other hand, Fig. 3b shows a wider range of values (−10 to +6) for category II which indicates the angry/stressed/confused drivers tend to accelerate and decelerate faster. We construct a single decision tree using 50 samples and export its flowchart tree at Fig. 4. The result reveals a considerable impact of the vehicle acceleration in prediction of emotions from category II. All 18 samples of category II are grouped using only one condition from vehicle acceleration (VA) which shows the important role of this module in prediction of *anger*, *nervousness* and *stress* of the drivers. The second condition in the decision tree uses the proportion of *sadness* emotion felt by the driver. This feature helps to group all 5 samples from category III. After this step, only samples from category I and IV are left un-grouped. For this purpose, conditions formulated by steering wheel (SW) rotation and *happy*, *neutral* and *sadness* features from the facial expressions module, are considered together. The feature vector is generated from the output of the three modules. The first and second values refer to VA and SW modules, and respectively last 7 values of the vector represent the output of facial expressions module which all are depicted at Table 1. The frequency for generating the feature vector is fixed to 2 min. For this period of time, SW parameter counts a number of abnormal steering wheel rotations, VA parameter makes a decision whether the driver is stressed or not and facial expression parameter counts the occurrences of the driver feeling each one of the seven basic emotions and gets normalized accordingly.

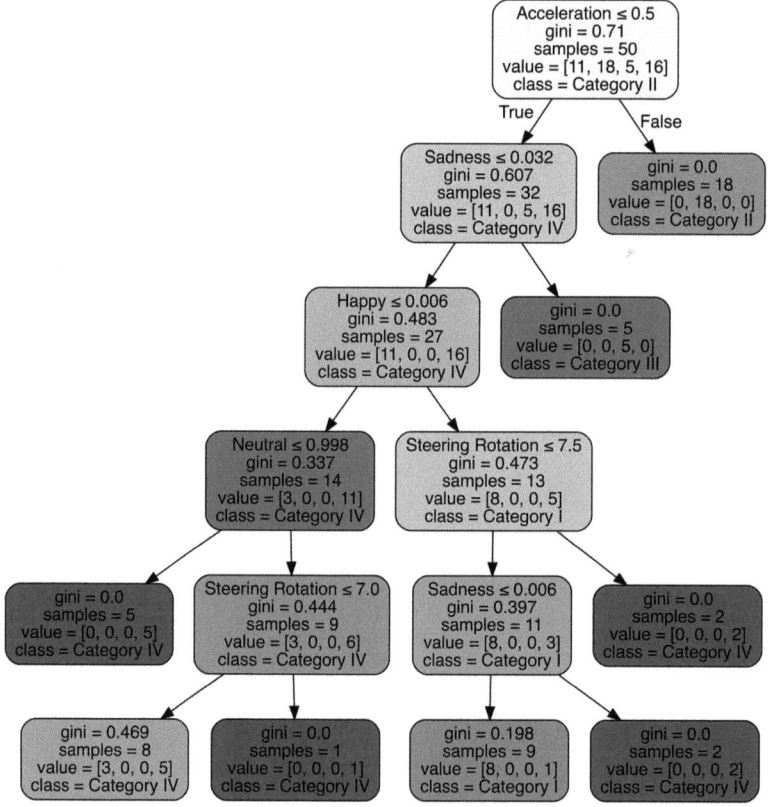

Fig. 4. Decision tree of combining the 3 different modules

After analyzing a single decision tree, we use the same feature vectors from 50 samples to train a random forest classifier (collection of decision trees), in order to achieve higher accuracy while increasing the robustness of the model. Hyper-parameters of the random forest are tuned using grid search and we set the *minimum sample lead* to 2, *maximum depth* to 2, *number of estimators* to 6 and set the *maximum features* variable to 'auto'.

Table 1. Feature vector of final emotion classifier

Module	Vector index	Parameter name	Value
VA	1	Acceleration	0 or 1
SW	2	Steering rotation	0 to ∞
Facial expression	3	Neutral	0 to 1
	4	Anger	0 to 1
	5	Disgust	0 to 1
	6	Fear	0 to 1
	7	Happy	0 to 1
	8	Sadness	0 to 1
	9	Surprise	0 to 1

4 Evaluation and Results

Our proposed method for facial expression-based emotion recognition achieves 93% of accuracy after 10 fold cross-validation. Comparison of achieved result with the state-of-art methods which similarly tested on CK+ dataset is shown at Table 2. Obtained accuracy is higher than most of the previously proposed methods and only 2% less than work of Khan et al. [33], and Donia et al. [15].

Table 2. Comparison of different facial expression-based methods on CK+

Authors	Method	Accuracy
Cohn and Kanade et al. [35]	Active Appearance Models	83%
Alshamsi et al. [2]	BRIEF Feature Extractor	89%
Swinkels et al. [49]	Ensemble of Regression Trees	89.7%
Ouellet [42]	Convolutional Network	94.4%
Khan et al. [33]	HOG-based	95%
Donia et al. [15]	HOG-based	95%
Our Method	**HOG on ROI regions**	**93%**

Confusion matrix of our proposed approach at Fig. 5, demonstrates a nearly perfect performance in detection of *happiness* (100%), *surprise* (96%) and *disgust* (93%). A human face is mostly in a neutral state which is also true in driving situations, therefore it is important to detect the *neutral* state accurately, and in this case, our method achieves 99% of positive predictions. There is slightly

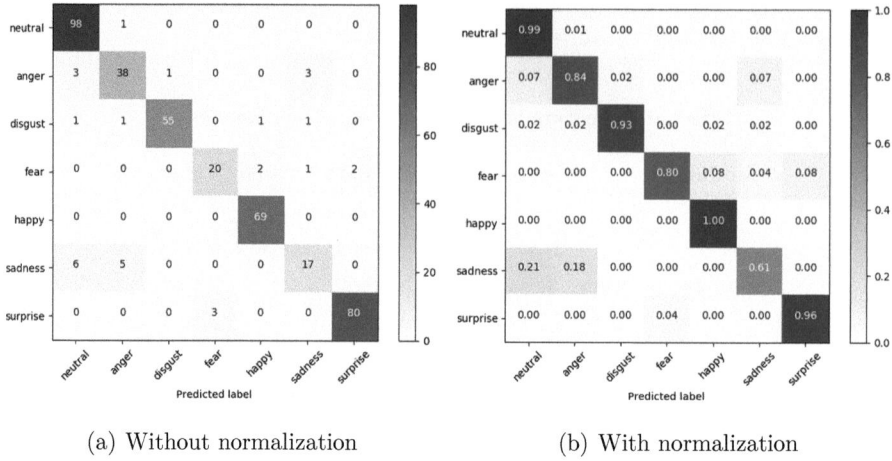

(a) Without normalization (b) With normalization

Fig. 5. Confusion matrix of facial-based emotion recognition classifier

a considerable margin of 20% in recognition of *sad* emotional status which was caused by the low number of samples for this emotion and high level of similarity shared with a neutral state in a human. In total, collected data of 10 rides from 8 different drivers was studied for evaluation of the system. Each ride was divided into sub-samples with the length of 2 min and gave us 79 samples for evaluation. Prediction of the driver emotion in one single ride is obtained from prediction results of its sub-samples. According to Table 3, final outcome of the tests on a single ride, represents that our proposed multi-modal emotion recognition system, achieved better results in comparison with each one of the modules alone. As it was initially considered, facial expression-based module plays the main role in final decision prediction, and SW along with VA are complementary modules.

Table 3. The results of each module in comparison with the fused one, in a single ride

Method	Accuracy	Precision	F1 score	Recall
Facial-based Module	54.54%	54.75%	50.45%	49.86%
SW-based Module	37.5%	10.3%	13.6%	25%
VA-based Module	68.18%	35.51%	37.76%	41.37%
Fusion of All Three Modules	**77.27%**	**73.39%**	**73.59%**	**75.89%**

The 77.27% of accuracy is obtained using multimodal emotion recognition system on data samples with 2 min of length. This condition is prone to errors and false predictions since in real-life situations the 2-min range could be easily falsified by situations like staying behind a red light. In order to cope with

such situations and increase the reliability of the results, we consider the decision taking step at the end of each ride by summarizing the emotion predictions performed for only sub-samples and choosing the most frequently felt emotion. In this way, our multimodal system achieves 94.4% of accuracy for classification into 4 emotional categories. Interestingly, the fusion of only behavioral-based modules (SW + VA) leads to 72.2% of accuracy in the same experiments. This demonstrates that in case of failures in camera(s) used for facial-based emotion recognition or highly illuminated situations, our proposed system is still capable of functioning in an acceptable level by relaying only on behavioral-related factors in order to predict the emotional status of the driver.

Table 4. Comparison of different unimodal and multimodal emotion recognition systems based on accuracy and different number of emotional classes

System	Type	Method	Classes	Accuracy
[40]	Unimodal	Electrodermal Activity (EDA)	3	70%
[51]	Unimodal	Facial Emotion Recognition	6	70.2%
[50]	Unimodal	Speech Emotion Recognition	3	88.1%
[26]	Unimodal	Speech Emotion Recognition	2	80%
[1]	Multimodal	EDA and Skin Temperature	4	92.42%
[12]	Multimodal	Speech & Facial Emotion Recognition	7	57%
[25]	Multimodal	Acoustic & Facial Emotion Recognition	3	90.7%
Our system	Multimodal	Facial and Vehicle Parameters	4	**94.4%**

A brief comparison of the state-of-the-art unimodal and multimodal works is presented at Table 4. Most of the multimodal approaches focus only on the fusion of speech and facial modules where the highest achieved accuracy is 90.7% by Hoch et al. [25]. However, they did consider only 3 classes as neutral, positive and negative emotion. Another notable method was proposed by Ali et al. [1] where they used the combination of EDA and skin temperature parameters of a driver as the input for a convolutional neural network and were able to get 92.4% of accuracy. Our proposed system by using the signals of vehicle controlling systems (steering wheel and acceleration/deceleration), along with the real-time facial expression-based approach achieved the highest accuracy rate of 94.4%.

5 Conclusion and Outlook

Many studies on emotion recognition are based on unimodal approaches where only visual or audio is examined and usually are aimed at classifying relatively basic emotions. There are multiple modalities that can be used to detect emotions. However, context in which the emotion is elicited and what modalities are most likely to be correlated should be taken into account. Various behavioral-based methods show promising results to such an approach. This can be more general in nature, for example head movement, gestures, and eye gaze, or can be specific to the environment of the vehicle. Some behaviors specific to the vehicle context can include acceleration, velocity, speeding, and steering wheel usage. Our main focus in this work was on developing a system with three different modalities of *steering wheel* and *vehicle acceleration* (as behavior modalities) beside the *facial expression* in order to study the correlation between emotional status and in-cabin behavior of the driver during a ride and more importantly, investigate the possibility of increasing the accuracy and robustness of emotion recognition systems by employing such related factors. We were able to represent the advantages of integration of behavior-based modalities into the emotion recognition systems and depict an structure for further developments on different other modalities. Our system was able to achieve relatively high accuracy rate after fusion of the modalities in comparison with each modality alone. Respectively we did demonstrate that our system stands on top of the similar multimodal works in this domain capable of classifying the emotions into 4 main categories with the accuracy of 94.4%. For the future, we plan to extend our system by integration of other different modalities and will try to study the shared models among all of the drivers according to their emotional states.

References

1. Ali, M., Machot, F.A., Mosa, A.H., Kyamakya, K.: CNN based subject-independent driver emotion recognition system involving physiological signals for ADAS. In: Schulze, T., Müller, B., Meyer, G. (eds.) Advanced Microsystems for Automotive Applications 2016. LNM, pp. 125–138. Springer, Cham (2016). https://doi.org/10.1007/978-3-319-44766-7_11
2. Alshamsi, H., Meng, H., Li, M.: Real time facial expression recognition app development on mobile phones. In: 2016 12th International Conference on Natural Computation, Fuzzy Systems and Knowledge Discovery (ICNC-FSKD), pp. 1750–1755. IEEE (2016)
3. Asthana, A., Zafeiriou, S., Cheng, S., Pantic, M.: Incremental face alignment in the wild. In: Proceedings of the IEEE Conference on Computer Vision and Pattern Recognition, pp. 1859–1866 (2014)
4. Behoora, I., Tucker, C.S.: Machine learning classification of design team members' body language patterns for real time emotional state detection. Des. Stud. **39**, 100–127 (2015)
5. Burkhardt, F., Paeschke, A., Rolfes, M., Sendlmeier, W.F., Weiss, B.: A database of German emotional speech. In: Ninth European Conference on Speech Communication and Technology (2005)
6. Cabrall, C., Janssen, N., Goncalves, J., Morando, A., Sassman, M., de Winter, J.: Eye-based driver state monitor of distraction, drowsiness, and cognitive load for transitions of control in automated driving. In: 2016 IEEE International Conference on Systems, Man, and Cybernetics (SMC), pp. 001981–001982. IEEE (2016)
7. Calonder, M., Lepetit, V., Strecha, C., Fua, P.: BRIEF: binary robust independent elementary features. In: Daniilidis, K., Maragos, P., Paragios, N. (eds.) ECCV 2010. LNCS, vol. 6314, pp. 778–792. Springer, Heidelberg (2010). https://doi.org/10.1007/978-3-642-15561-1_56

8. Chauhan, P.M., Desai, N.P.: Mel frequency cepstral coefficients (MFCC) based speaker identification in noisy environment using wiener filter. In: 2014 International Conference on Green Computing Communication and Electrical Engineering (ICGCCEE), pp. 1–5 (2014)
9. Chen, L.l., Zhao, Y., Ye, P.F., Zhang, J., Zou, J.Z.: Detecting driving stress in physiological signals based on multimodal feature analysis and kernel classifiers. Expert Syst. Appl. **85**, 279–291 (2017)
10. Corneanu, C.A., Simón, M.O., Cohn, J.F., Guerrero, S.E.: Survey on RGB, 3D, thermal, and multimodal approaches for facial expression recognition: history, trends, and affect-related applications. IEEE Trans. Pattern Anal. Mach. Intell. **38**(8), 1548–1568 (2016)
11. Dalal, N., Triggs, B.: Histograms of oriented gradients for human detection. In: IEEE Computer Society Conference on Computer Vision and Pattern Recognition CVPR 2005, vol. 1, pp. 886–893. IEEE (2005)
12. Datcu, D., Rothkrantz, L.: Multimodal recognition of emotions in car environments. DCI&I 2009 (2009)
13. Dhall, A., et al.: Collecting large, richly annotated facial-expression databases from movies. IEEE Multimedia **19**(3), 34–41 (2012)
14. D'mello, S.K., Kory, J.: A review and meta-analysis of multimodal affect detection systems. ACM Comput. Surv. (CSUR) **47**(3), 43 (2015)
15. Donia, M.M., Youssif, A.A., Hashad, A.: Spontaneous facial expression recognition based on histogram of oriented gradients descriptor. Comput. Inf. Sci. **7**(3), 31 (2014)
16. Fan, X.A., Bi, L.Z., Chen, Z.L.: Using EEG to detect drivers' emotion with Bayesian networks. In: 2010 International Conference on Machine Learning and Cybernetics (ICMLC), vol. 3, pp. 1177–1181. IEEE (2010)
17. Friesen, E., Ekman, P.: Facial action coding system: a technique for the measurement of facial movement. Palo Alto (1978)
18. Friesen, W.V., Ekman, P., et al.: EMFACS-7: emotional facial action coding system. Univ. Calif. San Francisco **2**(36), 1 (1983)
19. Fung, N.C., et al.: Driver identification using vehicle acceleration and deceleration events from naturalistic driving of older drivers. In: 2017 IEEE International Symposium on Medical Measurements and Applications (MeMeA), pp. 33–38. IEEE (2017)
20. Ganchev, T., Fakotakis, N., Kokkinakis, G.: Comparative evaluation of various MFCC implementations on the speaker verification task. In: Proceedings of the SPECOM, vol. 1, pp. 191–194 (2005)
21. Govindarajan, V., Bajcsy, R.: Human modeling for autonomous vehicles: Reachability analysis, online learning, and driver monitoring for behavior prediction (2017)
22. Guerrero Rázuri, J.F., Larsson, A., Sundgren, D., Bonet, I., Moran, A.: Recognition of emotions by the emotional feedback through behavioral human poses. Int. J. Comput. Sci. Issues **12**(1), 7–17 (2015)
23. Gutmann, M., Grausberg, P., Kyamakya, K.: Detecting human driver's physiological stress and emotions using sophisticated one-person cockpit vehicle simulator. In: Information Technologies in Innovation Business Conference (ITIB) 2015, pp. 15–18. IEEE (2015)
24. Hammal, Z., Cohn, J.F., Heike, C., Speltz, M.L.: What can head and facial movements convey about positive and negative affect? In: 2015 International Conference on Affective Computing and Intelligent Interaction (ACII), pp. 281–287. IEEE (2015)

25. Hoch, S., Althoff, F., McGlaun, G., Rigoll, G.: Bimodal fusion of emotional data in an automotive environment. In: 2005 Proceedings of IEEE International Conference on Acoustics, Speech, and Signal Processing (ICASSP 2005), vol. 2, p. ii–1085. IEEE (2005)
26. Jones, C.M., Jonsson, I.M.: Automatic recognition of affective cues in the speech of car drivers to allow appropriate responses. In: Proceedings of the 17th Australia Conference on Computer-Human Interaction: Citizens Online: Considerations for Today and the Future, pp. 1–10. Computer-Human Interaction Special Interest Group (CHISIG) of Australia (2005)
27. Kamaruddin, N., Wahab, A.: Features extraction for speech emotion. J. Comput. Methods Sci. Eng. **9**(1, 2S1), 1–12 (2009)
28. Kamaruddin, N., Wahab, A.: Driver behavior analysis through speech emotion understanding. In: 2010 IEEE Intelligent Vehicles Symposium (IV), pp. 238–243. IEEE (2010)
29. Katsis, C.D., Rigas, G., Goletsis, Y., Fotiadis, D.I.: Emotion recognition in car industry. In: Emotion Recognition: A Pattern Analysis Approach, pp. 515–544 (2015)
30. Kazemi, V., Sullivan, J.: One millisecond face alignment with an ensemble of regression trees. In: Proceedings of the IEEE Conference on Computer Vision and Pattern Recognition, pp. 1867–1874 (2014)
31. Kensinger, E.A.: Remembering emotional experiences: the contribution of valence and arousal. Rev. Neurosci. **15**(4), 241–252 (2004)
32. Khalid, M., Wahab, A., Kamaruddin, N.: Real time driving data collection and driver verification using CMAC-MFCC. In: Proceeding of the 2008 International Conference on Artificial Intelligence (ICAI 2008), pp. 219–224 (2008)
33. Khan, R.A., Meyer, A., Konik, H., Bouakaz, S.: Human vision inspired framework for facial expressions recognition. In: 2012 19th IEEE International Conference on Image Processing (ICIP), pp. 2593–2596. IEEE (2012)
34. Krotak, T., Simlova, M.: The analysis of the acceleration of the vehicle for assessing the condition of the driver. In: 2012 IEEE Intelligent Vehicles Symposium (IV), pp. 571–576. IEEE (2012)
35. Lucey, P., Cohn, J.F., Kanade, T., Saragih, J., Ambadar, Z., Matthews, I.: The extended cohn-kanade dataset (ck+): a complete dataset for action unit and emotion-specified expression. In: 2010 IEEE Computer Society Conference on Computer Vision and Pattern Recognition Workshops (CVPRW), pp. 94–101. IEEE (2010)
36. Lyons, M., Akamatsu, S., Kamachi, M., Gyoba, J.: Coding facial expressions with gabor wavelets. In: Proceedings of Third IEEE International Conference on Automatic Face and Gesture Recognition, pp. 200–205. IEEE (1998)
37. Mcmanus, A.: Driver Emotion Recognition and Real Time Facial Analysis for the Automotive Industry (2017). http://blog.affectiva.com/driver-emotion-recognition-and-real-time-facial-analysis-for-the-automotive-industry
38. Mehrabian, A., et al.: Silent Messages, vol. 8. Wadsworth, Belmont (1971)
39. Mishra, B., et al.: Facial expression recognition using feature based techniques and model based techniques: a survey. In: 2015 2nd International Conference on Electronics and Communication Systems (ICECS), pp. 589–594. IEEE (2015)
40. Ooi, J.S.K., Ahmad, S.A., Chong, Y.Z., Ali, S.H.M., Ai, G., Wagatsuma, H.: Driver emotion recognition framework based on electrodermal activity measurements during simulated driving conditions. In: 2016 IEEE EMBS Conference on Biomedical Engineering and Sciences (IECBES), pp. 365–369. IEEE (2016)

41. Ooi, J.S.K., Ahmad, S.A., Harun, H.R., Chong, Y.Z., Ali, S.H.M.: A conceptual emotion recognition framework: stress and anger analysis for car accidents. Int. J. Veh. Saf. **9**(3), 181–195 (2017)
42. Ouellet, S.: Real-time emotion recognition for gaming using deep convolutional network features. arXiv preprint arXiv:1408.3750 (2014)
43. Poria, S., Cambria, E., Bajpai, R., Hussain, A.: A review of affective computing: from unimodal analysis to multimodal fusion. Inf. Fusion **37**, 98–125 (2017)
44. Poria, S., Cambria, E., Hussain, A., Huang, G.B.: Towards an intelligent framework for multimodal affective data analysis. Neural Netw. **63**, 104–116 (2015)
45. Salih, H., Kulkarni, L.: Study of video based facial expression and emotions recognition methods. In: 2017 International Conference on I-SMAC (IoT in Social, Mobile, Analytics and Cloud)(I-SMAC), pp. 692–696. IEEE (2017)
46. Samanta, A., Guha, T.: On the role of head motion in affective expression. In: 2017 IEEE International Conference on Acoustics, Speech and Signal Processing (ICASSP), pp. 2886–2890. IEEE (2017)
47. Sariyanidi, E., Gunes, H., Cavallaro, A.: Automatic analysis of facial affect: a survey of registration, representation, and recognition. IEEE Trans. Pattern Anal. Mach. Intell. **37**(6), 1113–1133 (2015)
48. Slaney, M.: Auditory toolbox version 2. interval research corporation. Indiana: Purdue University 2010, 1998-010 (1998)
49. Swinkels, W., Claesen, L., Xiao, F., Shen, H.: SVM point-based real-time emotion detection. In: 2017 IEEE Conference on Dependable and Secure Computing, pp. 86–92. IEEE (2017)
50. Tawari, A., Trivedi, M.: Speech based emotion classification framework for driver assistance system. In: 2010 IEEE Intelligent Vehicles Symposium (IV), pp. 174–178. IEEE (2010)
51. Theagarajan, R., Bhanu, B., Cruz, A., Le, B., Tambo, A.: Novel representation for driver emotion recognition in motor vehicle videos. In: 2017 IEEE International Conference on Image Processing (ICIP), pp. 810–814. IEEE (2017)
52. De la Torre, F., Campoy, J., Ambadar, Z., Cohn, J.F.: Temporal segmentation of facial behavior. In: IEEE 11th International Conference on Computer Vision ICCV 2007, pp. 1–8. IEEE (2007)
53. Zadeh, A., Zellers, R., Pincus, E., Morency, L.P.: Multimodal sentiment intensity analysis in videos: facial gestures and verbal messages. IEEE Intell. Syst. **31**(6), 82–88 (2016)
54. Zhang, Y., Chen, M., Guizani, N., Wu, D., Leung, V.C.: SOVCAN: safety-oriented vehicular controller area network. IEEE Commun. Mag. **55**(8), 94–99 (2017)
55. Zhenhai, G., DinhDat, L., Hongyu, H., Ziwen, Y., Xinyu, W.: Driver drowsiness detection based on time series analysis of steering wheel angular velocity. In: 2017 9th International Conference on Measuring Technology and Mechatronics Automation (ICMTMA), pp. 99–101. IEEE (2017)

Prediction Based Deep Autoencoding Model for Anomaly Detection

Zhanzhong Pang[1(✉)], Xiaoyi Yu[1], Jun Sun[1], and Inakoshi Hiroya[2]

[1] Fujitsu R&D Center Co., Ltd., Beijing, China
{pangzhanzhong,yuxiaoyi,sunjun}@cn.fujitsu.com
[2] Fujitsu Laboratories Ltd., Kawasaki, Japan
inakoshi.hiroya@jp.fujitsu.com

Abstract. Latent variables and reconstruction error generated from auto encoder are the common means for anomaly detection dealing with high dimensional signals. They are exclusively typical representations of the original input, and a plenty of methods utilizing them for anomaly detection have achieved good results. In this paper, we propose a new method combining these two features together to generate proper scores for anomaly detection. As both these two features contain useful information contributing to anomaly detection, good results can be expected by fusion of those two. The architecture proposed in this paper comprises of two networks, and we only use normal data for training. To compress and rebuild an input, a deep auto encoder (AE) is utilized where low dimensional latent variables and reconstruction error can be obtained, and compactness loss is introduced on latent variables to maintain a low intra-variance. Meanwhile, multi-layer perceptron (MLP) network which takes the generated latent variables as input is established aiming at predicting its corresponding reconstruction error. By introducing MLP network, anomalies sharing similar reconstruction error yet different distribution of latent variables to normal data or vice versa can be separated. These two networks, AE and MLP are trained jointly in our model and the prediction error form MLP network is used as the final score for anomaly detection. Experiments on several benchmarks including image and multivariable datasets demonstrate the effectiveness and practicability of this new approach when comparing with several up-to-data algorithms.

Keywords: Anomaly detection · Auto encoder · Prediction mechanism

1 Introduction

The aim of anomaly detection is to identify instances deviating from expected patterns. This job is quite challenging as often the case it's hard or even impossible to obtain adequate knowledge of unknown anomalies beforehand. Most existing methods are on the basis of semi-supervised learning where patterns of normal data are learned without involvement of anomalies, and reconstruction error, density estimation or energy estimation is usually used as scores for anomaly detection. Many related works have been publicized recent years and summarized in the survey of Varun [19] and some state-of-the-art results are reported as well.

Often, given a high dimensional input, learning its low dimensional representation is the first thing to do. Traditionally, methods involving PCA, kernel PCA and robust PCA as shown by Jolliffe [7], Simon [18], and Peter [13] are the common things. With the enormous progress of deep learning, deep neural networks are introduced, and models like auto encoders by Zhou [25], and long short term memory by Aaron [1] are adopted widely. Some also combine deep networks with traditional machine learning methods for anomaly detection where low dimensional features are extracted using deep networks and then fed into conventional classifiers, like SVM, KNN or density estimation used by Scheirer [16], Yang [22], and Arthur [2]. However, the performance of those methods is constrained by the poor reduced features, which are less representative to preserve important information.

Reconstruction models for anomaly detection have been widely adopted in recent years. Zhang [24] learned to get a sparse representation for known class, and used reconstruction error for unknown detection. In the work of Zong [27], auto encoder was utilized to generate a low-dimensional representation and reconstruction error to fit a Gaussian mixture model. Zhai [23] also employed autoencoder for energy evaluation to detect anomalies. Indeed, auto encoder has been proved to be a good baseline for anomaly detection problem.

In this paper, we propose a prediction based deep autoencoding model. Since it has been proved that both reconstruction error and latent variables in auto encoder contains important information for anomaly detection [27], we can expect a better performance by combining these two features for anomaly detection. Also, the attributes of latent variables are key factors influencing the overall performance. For instance, latent variables with large size will contain more information and at the same time contribute to a better reconstruction effect, and adding some constraints on latent variables can lead to more representative features to further separate normal and abnormal data. So in this paper, we'll do some tricks on latent variables to obtain a good anomaly detection model.

Our main contributions may be summarized as: (1) We utilize a relative high dimensional latent variables in auto encoder to preserve more useful information, and jointly use both latent variables and reconstruction error for anomaly detection. (2) Compactness loss is introduced to latent variables to assess its distribution for target class. (3) Multi-layer perceptron is used to combine reconstruction error and latent variables, which we refer as prediction mechanism, where the latent variables will be used as input to predict its corresponding reconstruction error. (4) It is an end-to-end model for anomaly detection, and networks in this model are trained jointly. Thus it's friendly for users.

2 Related Works

Anomaly detection is closely related to rare event detection, outlier detection and novelty detection. Often, techniques in one-class classification can also be employed for anomaly detection. Commonly, all the above issues share the same difficulty – the novel concept is rarely seen and hard to collect. As a result, the prevailing way for these issues is trying to define models only for the target class and reject samples deviating from the defined model as anomalies. There are lots of different models using this core idea for anomaly detection, and here is a brief summarization of the existing popular methods.

Self-reconstruction method learns to form a model to rebuild the input as closely as possible. Zhou [26] and Zhai [23] demonstrated promising performance utilizing auto encoder for self-reconstruction by analyzing the reconstruction error. Some other works like Sabokrou [14] and Cong [4] tried to find sparse representations only for target class, and for anomalies, they would not be sparsely represented. Also, the tail distribution of reconstruction error was evaluated using Extreme Value Theory in the work of Zhang [24] for multi-target classes mission, and have achieved good results. However, the potential problem of these kinds of methods lies in the fact that the reconstruction error often doesn't contain enough useful information. To further enhance the performance, Zong [27] adopted additional information in latent variables besides reconstruction error, whereas due to the less representative latent variables and insufficient capacity of GMM models, plus the curse of dimensionality, the performance is still less satisfying.

Statistical analysis is another way for anomaly detection. It's aiming at discovering the latent distributions for target class, and instances far away from this distribution will be regarded as anomalies. Always, low dimensional features should be first extracted before distribution estimation like the work of Eskin [5] and Markou [11], and density estimation ways including multivariate Gaussian models, Gaussian mixture model and k-means, used by Arthur [2], JooSeuk [9], and Xiong [21], are the common means for statistical analysis. The big challenge in this method is that there are always a lot of hyper-parameters to be predefined, like the number of components in the Gaussian mixture model [27] and the number of clusters in k-means, which increases the burden of training and calls for a lot of efforts to get good results.

GAN-base method is currently the most popular one. As illustrated by Salimans [15] and Schlegl [17], it can also achieve fairly good results in the absence of enough labeled training data. There are two networks, generator for generating realistic data and discriminator for trying to discriminate the real data and the generated one as shown by Goodfellow [6]. Always, the generator or discriminator will be discarded after training, and only one of the trained model will be used. This will also lead to the loss of useful information. If the detection can benefit from both of the two models somehow, the final results could be further enhanced.

3 Proposed Approach

The main framework contains two networks: the deep auto encoder and the multi-layer perceptron. These two networks are jointly trained with semi-supervised manner, only considering normal data for training. The overview of the proposed model is shown in Fig. 1. The auto encoder first performs dimension reduction by encoder to generate low dimensional latent variables for the original input, and then reestablishes the input as closely as possible by decoder, where the reconstruction error between input and output is used as metric for evaluating the reconstruction effect. Then the two features, reconstruction error and latent variables will be fed into the following multi-layer perceptron network. In the multi-layer perceptron network, the latent variables will be used as input, and the reconstruction error will be regarded as the ground truth. This network tries to build connections between latent variables and reconstruction error, and form a model to memorize such connections. The connections in normal and abnormal data should be different, and thus can be used as metric for anomaly detection. To obtain a more robust model, several tricks are employed in each network. Details of each model and training strategy are described in the following sections.

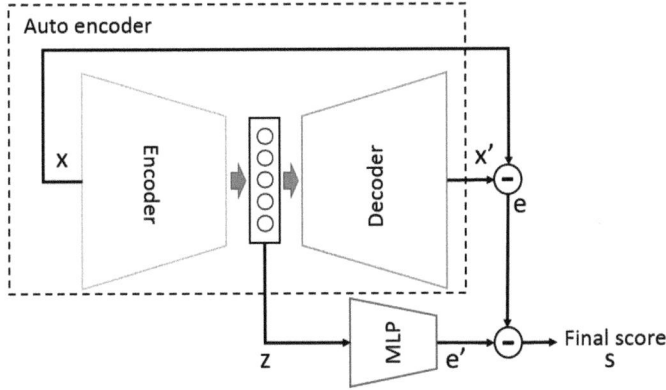

Fig. 1. Overview of the proposed structure

3.1 Auto Encoder

The auto encoder is a useful tool for anomaly detection. It aims at efficiently rebuilding the target class by reducing its reconstruction error as much as possible, while for anomalies, it always performs bad reconstruction effect with the consequence of large reconstruction error. So this model will promote samples sharing similar characters as the target class, and decimates the anomalies.

The auto encoder consists of two parts: encoder and decoder. When an input x is taken in, the encoder will first map it into a low dimensional latent variables z, and then the input will be rebuilt as x' by the decoder from the learned representation z.

$$z = f(W_1 x + b_1), \qquad x' = g(W_2 z + b_2) . \tag{1}$$

where W_1, b_1, W_2, and b_2 are the parameters to be learned, and f and g are activation functions. Usually, the Euclidean distance between x and x' is defined as reconstruction error and will be minimized through training, and the well-learned low dimensional latent variables z is regarded as the compressed features of original input and should be representative.

Several variances of auto encoder have been proposed which make it more robust, including denoising auto encoder (DAE), convolutional auto encoder (CAE) and variational auto encoder (VAE) as shown in the work of Vincent [20], Jonathan [8] and Kingma [10]. According to the type of test dataset, we adopt different variance of auto encoder in our model. Deep convolutional denoising auto encoder (CDAE) and deep auto encoders (AE) are utilized in this paper for image datasets and multi-variable datasets respectively, where several hidden layers are added as we are going to tackle high dimensional datasets. We mainly focus on the discussion of deep convolutional denoising auto encoder in this chapter, since the structure of deep auto encoder is almost the same, except that only fully connected layers exit in AE, and we use the term AE for both of these two models for simplicity.

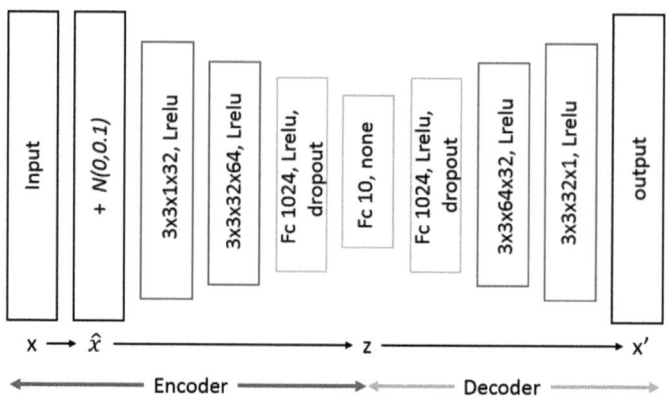

Fig. 2. Deep convolutional denoising auto encoder network architecture. Blue block for convolutional and pooling layers, orange block for fully connected layers. $+N(0, 0.1)$ stands for adding Gaussian noise with mean 0 and std 0.1. Lrelu for leaky relu activation function (Color figure online)

Figure 2 illustrates the main structure of CDAE that we used in our experiments on MNIST dataset. This kind of model is used for dealing with image datasets. Several hidden layers including convolutional, pooling and fully connected layers are stacked to form the network. Feature maps containing spatial information can be learned through convolutional layers, and redundancy of learned feature maps will be removed by the following pooling layers.

To achieve a more robust model with strong generalization, several tricks are employed in our setting. Firstly, as rebuilding the original input x from the corrupted one $\hat{x}$ will force the model to generate more representative features, different kinds of noises are added according to the attributes of input. For example, binomial noise or Gaussian noise is added for input images. Additionally, to prevent overfitting, dropout and regularization are adopted to make the model with good generalization. Also, different kind of activation function are chosen according to the type of test dataset. Detailed implementation for each dataset will be discussed in the following experiment Sect. 4.

3.2 Prediction Mechanism

The low dimensional latent variables z and the reconstruction error e generated from the auto encoder both contain information about the original input, and these two features are always complementary. This prediction mechanism network is designed to efficiently combine those two features together for anomaly detection.

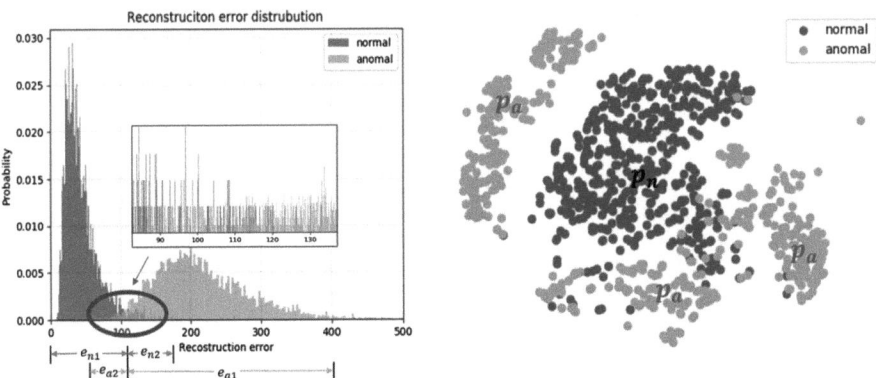

Fig. 3. Distributions of reconstruction error and latent variables on MNIST dataset (class 0 as normal data, and anomalies are randomly chosen from the rest 9 classes): Left one is the distribution of reconstruction error. e_n for reconstruction error from normal data, e_a for anomalies. The reconstruction error can be further divided into two groups for each class according to its corresponding value. Right one is the distribution of latent variables of those samples in the blending area pointed in the left picture (denoted as p)

The complementary attribute between latent variables z and reconstruction error e should be demonstrated first. As for reconstruction error e, the errors from normal data and anomalies always follow some certain distributions. As shown in Fig. 3, most of the reconstruction errors e_{n1} in normal data will be small enough for separation. However, there are still some others e_{n2} that are too large to discriminate from anomalies. Similarly, this situation often occurs for anomalies as well. So e_{n2} and e_{a2} will become useless for separating. As for latent variables z, different patterns of distribution between target class and anomalies also exist. Likewise, there doesn't exist clearly defined distribution patterns to utterly separate normal and abnormal data. However, there are actually some normal samples whose reconstruction errors are relatively large which are useless for discrimination, yet the distributions of their latent variables are quite different from anomalies. As shown in Fig. 3, it's the test results on MNIST dataset. We can notice that, in the region pointed by the red arrow, the reconstruction error is useless for detection. The distribution of latent variables from samples of this blending region is also depicted by TSNE. It's clear that those samples with similar reconstruction error can actually be separated when utilizing their latent variables distribution. So if we could use the latent variables of these samples rather than the reconstruction error for anomaly detection, the overall false positive rate can be greatly reduced, and the opposite is also true. Consequently, these two features are actually complementary to some extent. The behavior behind this main idea can be described as follows:

- For normal data x_n, there are two features generated from the auto encoder network, latent variables z_n and reconstruction e_n. z_n follows the distribution p_n, and e_n can be divided into two groups e_{n1} and e_{n2} for relatively small and large reconstruction error.

$$x_n \rightarrow z_n \sim p_n \rightarrow e_{n1} \; or \; e_{n2} \, . \tag{2}$$

- For anomalies x_a, also two features from the auto encoder network, latent variables z_a and reconstruction error e_a. z_a follows the distribution p_a, and e_a will be divided into two groups e_{a1} and e_{a2} for relatively large and small reconstruction error.

$$x_a \rightarrow z_a \sim p_a \rightarrow e_{a1} \; or \; e_{a2} \, . \tag{3}$$

- For normal and abnormal data whose reconstruction errors can be categorized into e_{n1} and e_{a1}, we can use their reconstruction errors to successfully separate them.

$$e_{n1} \; and \; e_{a1} \rightarrow discrimination \, . \tag{4}$$

- For normal and abnormal data whose reconstruction errors will be categorized into e_{n2} and e_{a2}, we will try to use their latent variables for separation.

$$z_n \; and \; z_a \rightarrow discrimination \, . \tag{5}$$

While we can expect to get better results by utilizing both latent variables and reconstruction error, the only problem is how to combine those two features together for anomaly detection. Here comes the network we propose – MLP network with prediction mechanism.

The main idea behind this prediction mechanism is to build connections between latent variables and reconstruction error. We believe that after training stage, given a certain distribution pattern of latent variables, there will be a corresponding value of reconstruction error. So we construct a multi-layer perceptron for predicting the reconstruction error when given its corresponding latent variables.

$$e' = f_m(W_m z + b_m). \qquad (6)$$

where e' is the prediction of reconstruction error; W_m and b_m are parameters in multi-layer perceptron; f_m is activation function.

Here, MLP works like an automatic cluster. The input of the supposed cluster consists of two components, reconstruction error and latent variables. Training samples with both these similar two components will cluster together. Test samples differ from the learned cluster templates in either the reconstruction error, latent variables, or both will be regarded as anomalies. The metric for measuring such difference is, correspondingly, the prediction error. Since MLP can fit to any nonlinear model, this indicates its strong generalization than GMM [27].

We may predefine a threshold and respectively divide normal data and anomalies into 2 groups according to the value comparison between their reconstruction errors and the threshold. For normal data, the division would be

$$x_n \rightarrow z_n \sim p_n \rightarrow e_{n1}, \qquad x_n' \rightarrow z_n' \sim p_n' \rightarrow e_{n2}. \qquad (7)$$

and for anomalies, the division is

$$x_a \rightarrow z_a \sim p_a \rightarrow e_{a1}, \qquad x_a' \rightarrow z_a' \sim p_a' \rightarrow e_{a2}. \qquad (8)$$

The overall procedures can be described as:

- Training stage:
    1. Only normal data will be used for training. Multi-layer perceptron will learn to connect latent variables with reconstruction error for normal data in two ways, one for small reconstruction error e_{n1}, and the other for large reconstruction error e_{n2}. So there are two modes to learn: $(z_n \rightarrow e_{n1})$ and $(z_n' \rightarrow e_{n2})$.
- Testing stage:
    1. Normal data
        (a) Both the distribution of reconstruction error and latent variables should be seen in training stage. Consequently, good prediction can be guaranteed when given the corresponding latent variables.
    2. Anomalies
        (a) For the group with large reconstruction error e_{a1}. Since this kind of reconstruction error never appears in the training stage, the learned multi-layer perceptron will not correctly predict this kind of error, no matter how the distribution of latent variables is.

(b) For the group with small reconstruction error e_{a2}. The value of this kind of reconstruction error is very close to e_n. However, the distribution of its corresponding latent variables z_a' would be different from its counterpart z_n'. Consequently, with different type of latent variables distribution, it's unlikely for anomalies to output similar reconstruction error close to e_{a2}.

Through the prediction mechanism we propose, we can utilize the information both in latent variables and reconstruction error, and the prediction error can be used as final score for anomaly detection. The whole process can be illustrated in the flowchart as shown in Fig. 4. According to the experiment results, the performance of this model with prediction mechanism is indeed better than the one that only uses reconstruction error for detection.

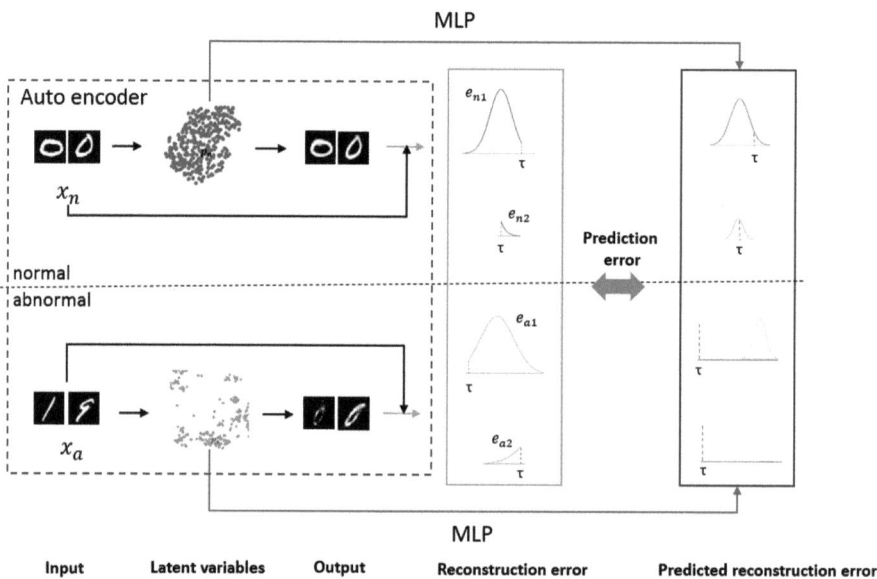

Fig. 4. Flowchart of our proposed model (τ is the chosen threshold for separating normal data and anomalies when only utilizing reconstruction error).

3.3 Compactness Loss

Since we want to utilize the latent variables for anomaly detection, it's preferable to generate representative latent variables. By trial and error, in auto encoder with no constraint on latent variables, the latent variables always makes limited contributions to separate normal samples and anomalies. So we introduce compactness loss on it to obtain more contributing latent variables. The compactness loss is defined as the mean squared intra-bath distance within a given batch [12]. Here, we deploy the Euclidean distance as the basis for compactness loss. For

i-th sample $x_i \in R^k$, the distance between this sample and the rest of the batch d_i can be written as

$$d_i = \|x_i - m_i\|_2, \quad m_i = \frac{1}{n}\sum_{i=1}^{n} x_i. \tag{9}$$

where n is the batch size. Then the compactness loss L_c is defined as the average distance per batch.

$$L_c = \frac{1}{nk}\sum_{i=1}^{n} d_i^T d_i. \tag{10}$$

3.4 Training Strategy

We will pre-train the auto encoder beforehand to guarantee that it functions properly. Then, we deploy joint training to train the two networks simultaneously, and the cost functions of the two networks will be directly added in a certain proportion.

For the AE model, reconstruction error, regularization, and compactness loss are included in its cost function. Suppose a dataset contains N samples, the cost function of this model under this dataset is constructed as

$$J_{AE}(\theta_e, \theta_d) = \frac{1}{N}\sum_{n=1}^{N}\|x_i - x_i'\|_2 + \lambda_1 \sum_{i=1}^{k}\theta_i^2 + \lambda_2 L_c. \tag{11}$$

θ_e and θ_d are network parameters to be trained from encoder and decoder respectively. θ_i is the parameters in fully connected layers. λ_1 and λ_2 are the meta parameter to be set manually, where in our experiments, 1e-4 is used for λ_1.

As for the MLP model, the mean square error of the prediction is used as cost function, and the function can be defined as

$$J_{MLP}(\theta_m) = \frac{1}{N}\sum_{n=1}^{N}\|e_i - e_i'\|_2. \tag{12}$$

θ_m is the network parameters in MLP.

So the overall objective function is defined as:

$$J(\theta_e, \theta_d, \theta_m) = J_{AE}(\theta_e, \theta_d) + \lambda_3 J_{MLP}(\theta_m). \tag{13}$$

where λ_3 is the meta parameter to be set manually beforehand.

In order to fuse the two training stages (pre-training and joint training) into one, we'll first set the meta parameter $\lambda_3 = 0$ to train the auto encoder, then after certain epochs when this model is well trained, the loss function of MLP will be added by setting $\lambda_3 \neq 0$, from which the two networks are jointly trained.

3.5 Evaluation

The prediction error s from MLP network will be used as final score for anomaly detection.

$$s_i = \|e_i - e_i'\|_2 . \tag{14}$$

This prediction error should be much smaller for data from target class than those from anomalies. So the detection scheme can be formulated as

$$prediction = \begin{cases} Target\ class, & if\ s < \tau . \\ Anomaly, & otherwise . \end{cases} \tag{15}$$

where τ is a predefined threshold.

Besides, average precision, recall and F_1 score are considered as indicators to compare performance among different algorithms. The definition of these standards can be found in Zhang [10].

4 Experiments

To illustrate the generalization of our proposed model, we evaluate it on two types of data: image datasets and multivariable datasets. The detailed description of each dataset used in this paper is summarized in Table 1. The test results are analyzed in detail and compared with several up-to-date methods, including DSEBM, DAGMM and OCSVM coming from the work of Zhai [23], Zong [27] and Chen [3] respectively, and also with the baseline auto encoder model AE. Detailed information will be discussed below.

Table 1. Statistics of the benchmark datasets.

	#Classes	#Dimensions	#Instances	Anomaly ratio (ρ)
MNIST	10	28 × 28	70,000	$0.1 \leq \rho \leq 0.4$
CIFAR-10	10	32 × 32	60,000	$0.1 \leq \rho \leq 0.4$
KDDCUP	2	120	494,021	0.2
Thyroid	3	6	3,772	0.025
Arrhythmia	16	274	452	0.15

4.1 On Image Datasets

Two Public Datasets: MNIST and CIFAR-10 are used for this sub task. On MNIST, it contains 70,000 gray images of handwritten digits with 10 classes. One class is randomly chosen as normal data, and anomalies are selected from the remaining 9 classes. Only normal data is used for training, and the training and test set are split by 2:1. On CIFAR-10, this dataset contains 60,000 natural color images with 10 classes. Same as MNIST, we randomly choose one class as normal data, and select anomalies from the remaining 9 classes. The training and test set are also split by 2:1. For both of these two datasets, different number of anomalies is picked in the test set to alter the anomaly ratio ρ from 0.1 to 0.4 for testing the performance of our model under different situation. Since images in CIFAR-10 contain lots of different background information, directly using the original images for reconstruction can not lead to good results. So we'll use the well trained inception V3 net for extracting features, which then, are fed into our model.

Training Strategy: The size of hidden variables we choose is 10 for MNIST and 200 for CIFAR-10. We train the model with mini batch size 200 and learning rate 1e-4. For activation functions, we recommend the leaky relu or relu because of the vanishing gradient problem. The setting of hyper-parameter is dataset dependent since the dimension of different dataset varies. In out test, λ_3 setting as 0.1 and 0.01 for MNIST and CIFAR-10, and λ_2 setting as 20 will generate good results. For training epochs, we assign 700 epochs for pre-training on both datasets, and 200 epochs and 20 epochs for joint training on MNIST and CIFAR-10, respectively. In order to prevent overfitting, MLP with only one layer is deployed.

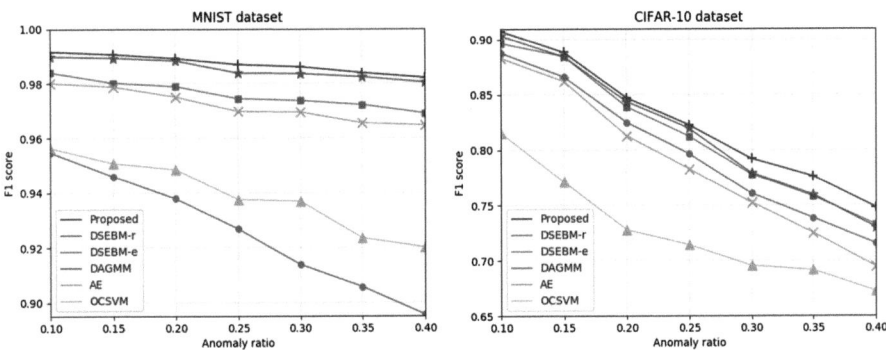

Fig. 5. F_1 scores on two images datasets with different anomaly ratio: MNIST (left), CIFAR-10 (right)

Test Results: The F_1 score vs. anomaly ratio is plotted as shown in Fig. 5, and the detailed average precision, recall and F_1 score with specified anomaly ratio on two datasets are listed in Table 2. As we can see, our method behaves much way better when comparing to the baseline method AE (only use the reconstruction error for detection), which indicates that besides the reconstruction error, our model indeed digs out the useful information in latent variables. Also, in Fig. 5, the results show the predominance of our model over other state-of-the-art methods, and its stably robust performance when the anomaly ratio is changing. However, the result of DAGMM is not quite satisfying, whose score drops greatly when comes to high dimensional image, especially on CIFAR-10. We think the reason may be ascribed to curse of dimensionality related to the latent variables. Although the DAGMM model uses the information carried by the latent variables too, the over-compressed latent variables actually does not bring much useful information due to its low size yet at the same time cause the information loss in the reconstruction error. We also tried to use large size latent variables on DAGMM. The performance actually decreased which may be ascribed to the sparse distribution of high dimensional latent variables. The sparse distribution may be hard to fit into a good GMM model. Also, singularity problem always occurs when we try to use large size on latent variables. That's may be the reason why DAGMM behaves bad on image dataset (The author of DAGMM tested this model only on multivariable dataset with relatively low dimensions).

Table 2. Average scores on two image datasets with different models. The best results are shown in italic.

Method	MNIST ($\rho = 0.3$)			CIFAR-10 ($\rho = 0.3$)		
	Prec	Rec	F_1	Prec	Rec	F_1
OCSVM	0.9131	0.9620	0.9369	0.5833	*0.8610*	0.6954
DSEBM-r	0.8761	0.9552	0.9139	0.7211	0.8041	0.7603
DSEBM-e	0.9645	0.9831	0.9737	0.7364	0.8242	0.7778
DAGMM	0.9814	0.9856	0.9835	0.7481	0.8145	0.7798
AE	0.9675	0.9710	0.9704	0.7205	0.7865	0.7521
Proposed	*0.9860*	*0.9865*	*0.9863*	*0.7556*	0.8315	*0.7912*

4.2 On Multi-variable Datasets

Three Public Datasets: All the three datasets come from UCI repository (Lichman 2013). We use the same data settings as Zong's [27]. On KDD99 10% dataset, it contains 494,021 instances with anomaly ratio 0.2. There are 41 attributes for each sample among which 7 are categorical. We use one-hot representation to encode these categorical attributes and eventually get a 120 dimensional dataset. On Thyroid, there are 3,772 samples with 3 classes. We only treat the hyper function class as anomaly and regard other two classes as normal one. Finally, we obtain the dataset with anomaly ratio 0.025. On Arrhythmia, it contains only 452 instances. Classes with small numbers including 3, 4, 5, 7, 8, 9, 14 and 15 are regarded as anomalies, and under this setting, the anomaly ratio is about 0.15. In all three datasets, the training and test set are split by 1:1.

Training Strategy: The size of hidden variables we choose is 5, 4, and 5 for KDD, Thyroid and Arrhythmia respectively. We train the model with mini batch size 1024, 200 and 64 for the above three datasets and with learning rate 1e-4. For activation functions, we recommend the leaky relu or tanh. The hyper-parameter λ_3 we set for each dataset is 5.0. λ_2 is set as 50.0 for all 3 datasets. The number of pre-training epochs for each dataset is 100, 1000, and 500. For joint training epochs, 100, 300, and 300 are adopted, respectively.

Table 3. Average scores on three datasets with different models. The best results are shown italic.

Method	KDD			Thyroid			Arrhythmia		
	Prec	Rec	F_1	Prec	Rec	F_1	Prec	Rec	F_1
OCSVM	0.7457	0.8523	0.7954	0.3639	0.4239	0.3887	0.6251	0.4545	0.5263
DSEBM-r	0.8521	0.6472	0.7328	0.6715	0.5053	0.5767	0.5789	0.5005	0.5366
DSEBM-e	0.8619	0.6446	0.7399	*0.6811*	0.5054	0.5802	0.6054	0.5294	0.5650
DAGMM	0.9711	0.9414	0.9559	0.6573	0.5054	0.5714	0.6569	0.4697	0.5487
AE	0.9495	0.8897	0.9185	0.6197	0.4731	0.5366	0.6111	0.5012	0.5493
Proposed	*0.9779*	*0.9582*	*0.9679*	0.6760	*0.5161*	*0.5854*	*0.6727*	*0.5606*	*0.6115*

Test Results: Detailed average precision, recall and F_1 score with different outlier ratio on three datasets are listed in Table 3. As we can see, our method achieves comparable or even better performance when compared with the prevailing models. The benefits of additionally introducing latent variables are embodied in the results when comparing with AE model. Also, better performance than DAGMM demonstrates the usefulness of latent variables with high dimensions and under constraint of compactness. The good results on these datasets, to some extent, testify our speculations on latent variables. This indicates that our method are capable of handling datasets with high dimensions.

5 Conclusion

Deep auto encoder with prediction mechanism is proposed in this paper for anomaly detection. The model is comprised of two parts: AE network and MLP network. In the first place, latent variables and reconstruction error are generated from AE with the constraint of compactness. Then, we somehow link these two items together with prediction mechanism using MLP network to learn the hidden connections between these two features. The two networks are trained together, and the prediction error from MLP network will be eventually used as score for anomaly detection. Several experiments are conducted on different kinds of datasets. Comparison with state-of-the-art methods are also done. The overall experiment results demonstrate the superior performance and promising application prospects of our model for anomaly detection.

References

1. Aaron, T.: Recurrent neural network language models for open vocabulary event-level cyber anomaly detection (2017). https://arxiv.org/abs/1712.00557
2. Arthur, Z.: A survey on unsupervised outlier detection in high-dimensional numerical data. Stat. Anal. Data Min. **5**, 363–387 (2012)
3. Chen, Y.: One-class SVM for learning in image retrieval. In: International Conference on Image Processing, vol. 1, pp. 34–37 (2001)
4. Cong, Y.: Sparse reconstruction cost for abnormal event detection. In: Computer Vision and Pattern Recognition (CVPR), pp. 3449–3456 (2011)
5. Eskin, E.: Anomaly detection over noisy data using learned probability distributions. In: Proceedings of the International Conference on Machine Learning (2000)
6. Goodfellow, I.: Generative adversarial nets. In: Advances in Neural Information Processing Systems, pp. 2672–2680 (2014)
7. Jolliffe, I.T.: Principal Component Analysis. Springer, New York (1986). https://doi.org/10.1007/b98835
8. Masci, J., Meier, U., Cireşan, D., Schmidhuber, J.: Stacked convolutional autoencoders for hierarchical feature extraction. In: Honkela, T., Duch, W., Girolami, M., Kaski, S. (eds.) ICANN 2011. LNCS, vol. 6791, pp. 52–59. Springer, Heidelberg (2011). https://doi.org/10.1007/978-3-642-21735-7_7
9. JooSeuk, K.: Robust kernel density estimation. CoRR, abs/1107.3133 (2011)
10. Kingma, D.P.: Auto-encoding variational bayes. In: Proceedings of the International Conference on Learning Representations (2014)
11. Markou, M.: Novelty detection: a review part 1: statistical approaches. Sign. Process. **83**(12), 2481–2497 (2003)
12. Perera, P.: Learning deep features for one-class classification (2018). http://cn.arxiv.org/abs/1801.05365
13. Peter, H.: Robust statistics. Int. Encycl. Stat. Sci. **78**(381), 1248–1251 (2011)
14. Sabokrou, M.: Video anomaly detection and localisation based on the sparsity and reconstruction error of auto-encoder. Electron. Lett. **52**(13), 1122–1124 (2016)
15. Salimans, T.: Improved techniques for training GANs. In: Advances in Neural Information Processing Systems, pp. 2234–2242 (2016)
16. Scheirer, W.J.: Toward open set recognition. IEEE Trans. Pattern Anal. Mach. Intell. **35**(7), 1757–1772 (2013)
17. Schlegl, T., Seeböck, P., Waldstein, S.M., Schmidt-Erfurth, U., Langs, G.: Unsupervised anomaly detection with generative adversarial networks to guide marker discovery. In: Niethammer, M., et al. (eds.) IPMI 2017. LNCS, vol. 10265, pp. 146–157. Springer, Cham (2017). https://doi.org/10.1007/978-3-319-59050-9_12
18. Simon, G.: Fast iterative kernel principal component analysis. J. Mac. Learn. Res. **8**(4), 1893–1918 (2007)
19. Varun, C.: Anomaly detection: a survey. ACM Comput. Surv. **43**(3), 1–58 (2009)
20. Vincent, P.: Extracting and composing robust features with denoising autoencoders. In: Neural Information Processing Systems, NIPS, pp. 1096–1103 (2008)
21. Xiong, L.: Group anomaly detection using flexible genre models. In: Advances in Neural Information Processing Systems, pp. 1071–1079 (2011)
22. Yang, B.: Towards k-means-friendly spaces: simultaneous deep learning and clustering. In: International Conference on Machine Learning (2017)
23. Zhai, S.: Deep structured energy based model for anomaly detection. In: International Conference on Machine Learning, pp. 1100–1109 (2016)

24. Zhang, H.: Sparse representation-based open set recognition. IEEE Trans. Pattern Anal. Mach. Intell. **39**(8), 1690–1696 (2017)
25. Zhou, C.: Anomaly detection with robust deep auto encoders. In: Proceedings of the 23rd ACM SIGKDD International Conference on Knowledge Discovery and Data Mining, pp. 665–674 (2017)
26. Zhou, C.: Anomaly detection with robust deep autoencoders. In: Proceedings of the 23rd ACM SIGKDD International Conference on Knowledge Discovery and Data Mining, pp. 665–674 (2017)
27. Zong, B.: Deep autoencoding gaussian mixture model for unsupervised anomaly detection. In: Sixth International Conference on Learning Representations (2018)

Multimodal Sensor Fusion in Single Thermal Image Super-Resolution

Feras Almasri and Olivier Debeir[✉]

Department LISA - Laboratory of Image Synthesis and Analysis, Université Libre de Bruxelles, CPI 165/57, Avenue Franklin Roosevelt 50, 1050 Brussels, Belgium
{falmasri,odebeir}@ulb.ac.be

Abstract. With the fast growth in the visual surveillance and security sectors, thermal infrared images have become increasingly necessary in a large variety of industrial applications. This is true even though IR sensors are still more expensive than their RGB counterpart having the same resolution. In this paper, we propose a deep learning solution to enhance the thermal image resolution. The following results are given: (I) Introduction of a multimodal, visual-thermal fusion model that addresses thermal image super-resolution, via integrating high-frequency information from the visual image. (II) Investigation of different network architecture schemes in the literature, their up-sampling methods, learning procedures, and their optimization functions by showing their beneficial contribution to the super-resolution problem. (III) A benchmark ULB17-VT dataset that contains thermal images and their visual images counterpart is presented. (IV) Presentation of a qualitative evaluation of a large test set with 58 samples and 22 raters which shows that our proposed model performs better against state-of-the-arts.

Keywords: Super-resolution · Sensor fusion · Thermal images

1 Introduction

In digital images, what we perceive as details greatly depends on the image resolution. The higher the resolution the more accurate the measurement. The visible RGB image has rich information, but objects can occur in different conditions of illumination, occlusion and background clutter. These conditions can severely degrade the system's performance. Therefore visible data is found to be insufficient and thermal images have become a common tool to overcome these problems. Thermal images are used in industrial processes such as heat and gas

---

This work was supported by the European Regional Development Fund (ERDF) and the Brussels-Capital Region within the framework of the Operational Programme 2014–2020 through the ERDF-2020 project F11-08 ICITY-RDI.BRU. The Titan X Pascal used for this research was donated by the NVIDIA Corporation. We are grateful to Thermal Focus BVBA for their help and support.

detecting and they are also used to solve problems such as object detection and the self-driving car.

Integrating captured information from different sensors such as RGB and thermal offers rich information to improve the system performance. In particular, when the nature of the problem requires this integration, and when the environmental conditions are not optimal for a one sensor approach, multimodal sensor fusion methods have been proposed [3,23]. However, thermal sensor cost grows significantly with the increase of its resolution and it is primarily used in low-resolution and in low contrast which introduces the necessity to obtain a higher resolution sensor [4]. As a result, a variety of techniques in computer vision have been developed to enhance thermal resolution given their low-resolution counterpart.

The single super-resolution problem has been widely studied and well-defined in computer vision [1,17,22]. It is defined as non-linear mapping and prediction of a high-resolution image (HR) given only one low-resolution image (LR). However, this is an ill-posed problem since it is a one-to-many problem. Given that multiple HR images it is possible to produce a single LR image, thus mapping from LR to SR is to recover the lost information giving only the information in the LR image. Though they achieved high performance, these methods are limited by their handcrafted features techniques.

Recently with the development of the convolutional neural network (ConvNet), several methods have shown the ability to learn high non-linear transformations. Rather than using handcrafted features, the ConvNet model is capable of automatically learning rich features from the problem domain and adapt its parameters by minimizing the loss function. Most recently, the ConvNet model has been widely used in the SR problem and achieved new high performance. Despite significant progress, the proposed solutions still suffer from the lack of ability to recover high-frequency information.

Most SR conventional methods focus on measuring the similarity between the SR image and its ground truth via pixel-wise distance measurement, although the reconstructed images are blurry by missing sharper edges and texture details. However, this problem is the fault of the objective function, as the classical way to optimize the target is to minimize the content loss by minimizing the mean square error (MSE) loss function. By definition this finds the average values in the HR manifold and consequently maximizes the Peak signal-to-noise ratio (PSNR). By only applying the content loss function, the low-frequency information is restored, but not the high-frequency information. However, MSE is limited in preserving the human visual perception, and PSNR measurement cannot indicate the SR visual perception [17,19].

Different approaches such as perceptual loss [14] and adversarial loss [20], have been proposed to address this drawback, and have shown important progress in recovering high frequency details. Instead of only doing a pixel-wise distance measurement, a mixture of these loss functions could generate high-quality SR images. Also, different model schemes have shown higher image quality such as learning the residual information [15] or by gradually up-sampling [18].

The primary focus of this work was to build a deep learning model that applies multimodal sensor fusion using visible (RGB) and thermal images. The model should integrate the two inputs and enhance the thermal image resolution. The latter part is inspired by the recent advances in RGB super-resolution problem. A thermal GAN based framework is proposed, to enhance the LR thermal image by integrating the rich information in the HR visual image. However, the HR visual sensor price is considerably low compared to the LR thermal sensor and it captures extra information taken from a different domain. We show that HR visual images can help the model fill the missed values and generate higher frequency details in the reconstructed SR thermal image. The model proposed uses the content loss to preserve the low-frequency image content, and the adversarial loss to integrate the high-frequency information.

2 Related Works

Thus far, a number of studies in computer vision and machine learning have been proposed. This discussion focuses on example-based ConvNet methods. Figure 1 depicts the different model architecture schemes, their up-sampling method, and their learning procedure.

A. Resolution Training. The model can be trained to extract features from an up-sampled image in direct mapping using these features to produce SR image as in [6]. The input is either pre-processed, using an interpolation method as shown in Fig. 1(a), or up-sampled using trainable parameters as shown in Fig. 1(d). In another approach, the model can extract features directly from the low-resolution image and map them into high-resolution by using up-sampling techniques at the end of the network as in [26], this model, shown in Fig. 1(c) accelerates the model performance.

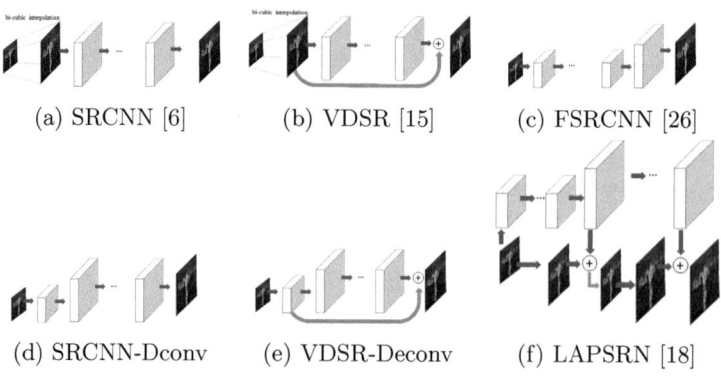

(a) SRCNN [6]   (b) VDSR [15]   (c) FSRCNN [26]

(d) SRCNN-Dconv   (e) VDSR-Deconv   (f) LAPSRN [18]

Fig. 1. Network architecture schemes.

B. Residual Learning and Supervision. Since super-resolution output is similar to the low-resolution input, with the high-frequency information missing, the learning can be made to produce only the residual information. VDSR [15] and DRSN [16] trained a model that learns residual information between LR and HR images. They used a skip connection, that adds the input image to the model residual output, to produce SR image. Lai et al. [18] found that reconstructing the SR image immediately with a high up-sampling scale is a challenging problem. Therefore they addressed the problem in a gradual up-sampling procedure, using deep supervision in each up-sampling scale, and a residual learning as shown in Fig. 1(f).

C. Up-Sampling Procedure. A mixture of network architectures and learning procedures can be used with different up-sampling methods. In SRCNN [6] and VDSR [15], the network takes an interpolated image as input, using either a bilinear or bicubic interpolation, or a Gaussian-Spline kernel [10]. The up-sampling can be learnable and accelerated by using a transposed convolution (deconvolution) layer as in Fig. 1(d) and (e) which is a modified version of SRCNN and VDSR, or added to the end of the network as in FSRCNN Fig. 1(c). A trainable Sub-pixel convolution (Pixelshuffle) ESPCN [24] is also used at the end of the network to up-sample input features as in [20].

D. Optimization Function. The optimization procedure seeks to minimize the distance between the original HR image and the generated SR image. The most used optimization function in the SR problem is the content loss, which is done using the MSE as in [15] or Charbonnier as in [18]. SRGAN [19] instead uses the adversarial loss and [14] uses the perceptual similarity loss to enhance the reconstructed image resolution.

3 Proposed Methods

In this work, the first ConvNet that integrates visual-thermal images to generate thermal image super-resolution is described. Our main contributions are:

- Unlike the RGB-based super-resolution problem, advancement in thermal super-resolution is still relatively low. Therefore, few benchmarks in thermal image SR [22] and they are rarely available. To this end, the authors created a benchmark ULB17-VT multimodal sensors dataset that contains thermal images and their visual images counterparts.
- The model is inspired by the work in [19]. Different modified network architecture schemes, up-sampling methods and optimizing functions are investigated, to verify our model contribution with reference to the current improvement in the super-resolution problem literature.
- Confirmation is given which shows that this thermal SR model, which integrates the visual-thermal fusion, does generate higher human perceptual quality images. This improvement is due to the rich details in the visual images, and the common relation with their thermal image counterpart.

- A qualitative evaluation method based on 58 samples, which is a large qualitative evaluation in the SR problem domain, was also used to test how well the model performed. Twenty-two people were asked to rate the better generated image. The results of study shows that the proposed model performs better against state-of-the-art methods.

3.1 ULB17 Thermal Dataset

A FLIR-E60 camera with multimodal sensors (thermal and color) was used. The thermal sensor produces (320×240) pixel resolution with $0.05\,°C$ thermal sensitivity and $-20\,°C$ to $650\,°C$ which provides good quality thermal images. The color sensor is 3 megapixels and produces (2048×1536) pixels resolution. This device allows capture of both thermal and RGB images aligned with the same geometric information simultaneously. Thermal images were extracted in their raw format and logged in 16-bit float per-pixel in one channel in their raw format, in contrast with [11] in which samples are post-processed and compressed into an uint8 format. All samples in this study are aligned automatically by the device supported software with their associated cropped color images of size (240×320) pixel with the same geometry.

Images in our benchmark were captured inside ULB[1] campus. Each image acquisition process took approximately 3 seconds, which made the data acquisition process rather slow. The acquisition was made in different scenes and different environments (indoor and outdoor, during winter and summer and with static and moving objects) as shown in Fig. 2. Thermal and RGB images were

Fig. 2. Visual-Thermal samples form our ULB17-VT benchmark.

---

[1] Université Libre de Bruxelles.

manually extracted and annotated with a total of 570 pairs. The framework is divided into 512 training and validation samples and 58 test samples.

3.2 Proposed Framework

In this section our model methodology including how different model schemes, up-sampling methods, and optimization function are essential in producing better human perceptual SR images are described.

The aim is to estimate the HR thermal image T^{HR} from its LR counterpart T^{LR} by a 4x factor. The T^{LR} images are produced by first applying Gaussian pyramids to T^{HR} samples and they are then down-scaled by a factor of .25x, from (240×320) pixels to (60×80) pixels.

Our proposed model belongs to the model scheme of FSRCNN shown in Fig. 1(c). The core of our model scheme is to perform feature extraction and feature mapping on the image original size. The model is constructed using X residual blocks with an identical layout inspired by SRGAN [19]. The model then up-samples the feature maps with two sub-pixel convolution layers as proposed by [24]. Starting from the main model as a baseline, the model gain was investigated as follows:

- Instead of up-sampling the features at the end of the network, we tested the model scheme of SRCNN [6] shown in Fig. 1(d). Due to investigation of high-resolution training methods, Sub-pixel layers are removed from this model, and two Deconv layers are added at the beginning of the network by a factor of 2.
- The residual scheme proposed by VDSR as shown in Fig. 1(b) and (e) is tested using (I) bi-linear interpolation, (II) bi-cubic interpolation, and (III) different trainable up-sampling layers.
- Visual images are integrated to investigate whether their texture details can enhance the thermal SR generating process.
- Recently, the Generative adversarial network (GAN) [8] has witnessed creative implementation in several tasks [2,13,25,27,28]. GAN provides a powerful framework which consists of an image transformer and an image discriminator, that can generate images with high human perceptual quality and are similar to the real images distribution. To achieve GAN contribution, our baseline model is re-trained on GAN based model.

3.3 Network Architecture

The generator baseline network thermal SRCNN (TSRCNN) shown in Fig. 3 consists of 5 identical residual blocks, inspired by [19] and follows the layout proposed by [9]. Each block consists of two convolutional layers with 3×3 kernel size, and 64 feature maps each followed by an ELU activation function [5]. Batch-normalization layers [12] were removed from the residual block, since, as indicated in [10,21], they are unnecessary for the SR problem. It is also stated

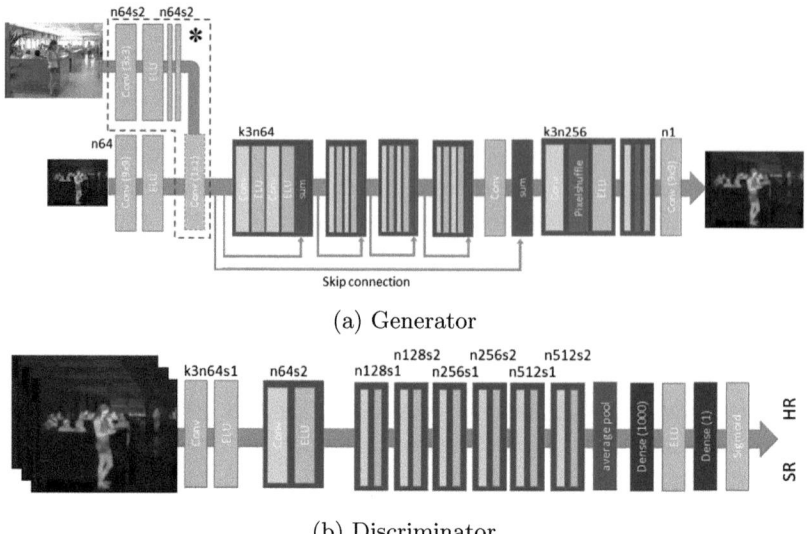

Fig. 3. Architecture of our Generator and Discriminator networks with the corresponding (k) kernel size, (n) number of channels and (s) their stride when it is changed. The highlighted area with (*) indicates the model that merges RGB and thermal channels

that once batch-normalization layers are used, they harm the generated output. To preserve the feature maps size, reflective padding is used around the boundaries before each convolution layer. Feature maps resolution is then increased using two sub-pixel convolution layers [24].

Visual RGB images are integrated into the model using two convolution layers with 3×3 kernel size and 64 feature maps each followed by an ELU activation function. Each convolution layer used a 2-step stride, which reduced the feature maps size to be the same size as the thermal input, before they are fused to form the visual-thermal SRCNN (VTSRCNN) model as shown in Fig. 3 (*). The fusion is handled by concatenating the two feature maps, followed by a convolution layer with 1×1 to reduce channel dimensionality to 64 channels. Due to the high correlation between the visual-thermal modes and the rich texture information in the visual image, the network is supposed to learn these features and fuse them to produce SR thermal images with high perceptual quality. Giving an input thermal image $T \in \mathbb{R}^{H \times W}$ and an input RGB image $X \in \mathbb{R}^{H \times W \times 3}$, the objective function $\hat{Y} = F(T, X)$ seeks to map the LR thermal image to the HR thermal image $Y \in \mathbb{R}^{H \times W}$.

The last two models are re-trained on the GAN based model to form the GAN proposed models (TSRGAN and VTSRGAN). To do this a discriminator network as shown in Fig. 3 is added, to classify generated images from original images. The network architecture is similar to the work in [19], except for the batch normalization layer and ELU activation function. The model consists of eight convolution layers with 3×3 that increase the feature by a factor of 2 from

64 to 512 channels. Image resolution is reduced using a 2-step stride convolution between each layer which doubles the channels number. In this model, adapted average pooling is used on top of the 512 feature maps followed by two dense layers. Finally, a sigmoid activation function is used to produce a probability of the input being an original HR image or a generated SR thermal image.

3.4 Loss Function

Our baseline models (TSRCNN and VTSRCNN) are trained using only the content loss function, which is the mean square error (MSE), while our GAN based models (TSRGAN and VTSRGAN) are trained on a weighted sum of the content loss and the adversarial loss, which is obtained from the discriminator network. By using only the adversarial loss, the models are not able to converge. This is most likely ascribed to the lack of overlap in the distribution supports between original images and generated images. Therefore, the content loss was necessary for the GAN based model. The models that take only thermal images or visual-thermal images are shown in Eq. (1).

$$T^{SR} = \begin{cases} G(T^{LR}), & \text{only thermal model} \\ G(T^{LR}, RGB), & \text{visual-thermal model} \end{cases} \quad (1)$$

Content Loss. MSE in Eq. (2) is the most used optimization function in the SR image problem [6,15,26]. The model is trained on optimizing the Euclidean distance between the constructed T^{SR} and the ground truth T^{HR}. Although the MSE is highly correlated in maximizing the PSNR, it suffers from the lack of high-frequency details, which results in blurred and over-smoothed images. However, it does help the model preserve low-frequency details from the LR image and supports the adversarial loss which could not always ensure convergence.

$$l_{MSE} = \frac{1}{2MN} \sum_{x=1}^{M} \sum_{y=1}^{N} (T^{HR}_{x,y} - T^{SR}_{x,y})^2 \quad (2)$$

Adversarial Loss. To ensure high-frequency details from the original HR distribution, the adversarial loss is added to the content loss. The models are first pre-trained on the content loss MSE and then fine-tuned using the total loss function l^{SR} (Eq. 3), which is a weighted sum of the adversarial loss l_{gen} (Eq. 5) and the content loss l_{MSE} (Eq. 1) where $\lambda = 1e-2$ is a fixed parameter.

$$l^{SR} = l_{gen} + \lambda l_{MSE} \quad (3)$$

The discriminator network is trained using the cross-entropy loss function (Eq. 4) that classifies the original images from the generated images. The generator loss l_{gen} is trained on the recommended equation (Eq. 13 in [7]).

$$J^{(D)} = E_{(T^{HR})} log(D(T^{HR})) + E_{(T^{LR})} log(1 - D(T^{SR})) \quad (4)$$

$$l_{gen} = J^{(G)} = -\frac{1}{2} E_{(T^{LR})} log(D(T^{SR})) \quad (5)$$

3.5 Implementation and Training Details

All of the models are implemented in Pytorch and trained on NVIDIA TITAN Xp using randomly selected mini-batches of size 12, plus 12 RGB mini-batches when the visual-thermal fusion model is used. The generator model uses RMSPROP optimizer with alpha = 0.9. In the GAN based model the discriminator is trained using the SGD optimizer. The baseline model, and all other investigated models, are trained using the content loss for 5000 epochs. The pre-trained baseline model is used to initialize the generator in the adversarial model, where D and G are trained for another 5000 epochs. All models are trained with initial learning rate 10^{-4} and decreased to 10^{-6}.

4 Experiments

4.1 Model Analysis

Resolution Training Size. Attention here is focused on showing the effect of training the model on LR features or on their up-sampled version, which is the difference between the two network schemes (c) and (d) shown in Fig. 1. The first extracts and optimizes features of the original LR image, and up-samples them at the end of the network, while the second up-samples the input features first and then optimizes them along the network. By looking at the trade-off between the computation cost and the model performance, the trained model on the up-sampled features increased the computation cost and did not add a significant improvement to the generated images. Instead, the up-sampled training as shown in Fig. 4, depicts a slight increment in the PSNR/SSIM values compared to our proposed model (TSRCNN) but the model could not generate some fine texture details such as the handbag handle in the second image and the person in the background of the first and third images.

Evaluation with the State-of-the-Arts. Before validating the residual learning model scheme and the up-sampling methods of the proposed models, the proposed baseline model is compared with state-of-the-art: VDSR [15] and LAP-SRN [18] which are based on residual learning. VDSR is implemented in two models, (1) the original VDSR that takes only thermal images as input, and (2) our extended VDSRex that takes visual-thermal images as an input of 4 channels. LAPSRN is trained using only thermal images. The experiment was run on our ULB17-VT benchmark, using the same size model and training procedure explained in the STOA paper. Figure 5 shows that VDSR failed to produce high-frequency details, while the VDSRex produced better results taking advantage of the visual-thermal fusion. However, the proposed baseline model generates images with sharp details and higher perceptual image quality. Table 1 shows that the proposed model also obtained higher PSNR/SSIM value than the STOA.

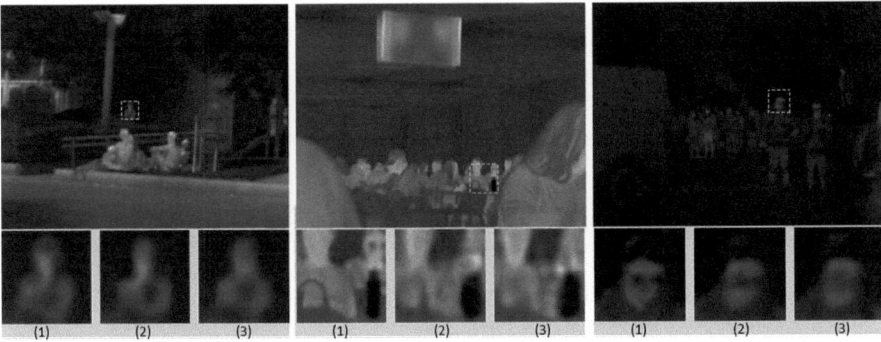

Fig. 4. (1) HR image. (2) Our proposed model TSRCNN trained on LR image features with PSNR/SSIM (52.353/0.9495). (3) The same model trained on the up-sampled features using 2 Deconv layers with PSNR/SSIM (52.656/0.9510)

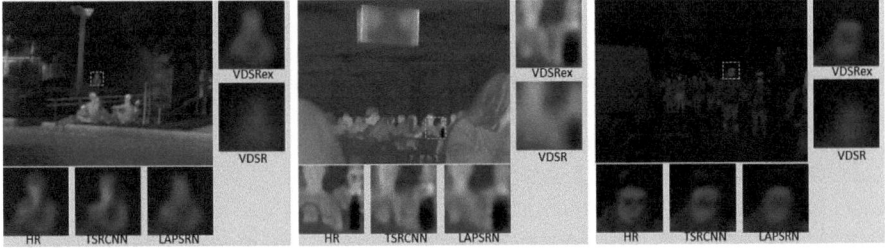

Fig. 5. Comparison between our baseline model TSRCNN and state-of-the-art, LAP-SRN [18], VDSR [15] and our extended VDSRex.

Residual Learning and Up-Sampling Methods. Attention was then focused on adapting and investigating the residual learning model to the thermal SR problem. To use the baseline model, TSRCNN in this model scheme, the input should be rescaled to have the same size as the residual output. We trained four different models with four different up-sampling methods: (1) InpDconv-TRSCNNres that integrates TRSCNN and two deconvolution layers to up-sample the input image; (2) InpBilin-TRSCNNres that up-samples the input using bilinear interpolation; (3) InpBicub-TRSCNNres that uses bicubic interpolation; (4) AllDconv-TRSCNNres which is similar to (1) but the two Pixelshuffle layers at the end of the network are replaced by two deconvolution layers.

Figure 6 shows that the models trained on bilinear and bicubic interpolations methods failed to produce comparable perceptual quality results, and have the lowest PSNR/SSIM values. Models (1) and (4) that use trainable up-sampling methods produced better perceptual results with high PSNR/SSIM values. However, the proposed model produced sharper edges and finer details. Note that the person in the first and third images has sharper details in the proposed model, the bag handle exists only in our model. To this end and to better evaluate the contribution of the models, all models are taken into our qualitative evaluation study.

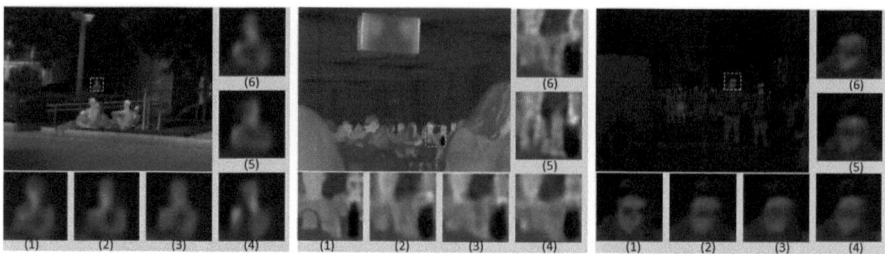

Fig. 6. (1) HR image. (2) Our proposed TSRCNN model with no residual learning and (52.353/0.9495). (3) InpDconv-TSRCNNres with (52.323/0.9491). (4) AllDconv-TSRSCNNres with (52.430/0.9495). (5) InpBilin-TSRCNNres with (51.023/0.9415). (6) InpBicub-TSRCNNres with (51.670/0.9442). Values between brackets are PSNR/SSIM.

Visual-Thermal Fusion. To demonstrate the effect of integrating visual-thermal fusion in the SR problem, and to investigate if the rich information in the visual images can help to produce better thermal SR images, the baseline thermal SR Convnet model (TSRCNN) was trained on only thermal images using the network architecture shown in Fig. 3(a). Also, the model Visual-Thermal SR Convnet (VTSRCNN) model was trained on thermal and visual images using the model shown in Fig. 3(a) which integrate the branch (*). Fusing visual-thermal images added more details to the produced thermal SR images, but also added some artifacts in parts of the images. In particular, these artifacts appear when there is displacement in the objects due to the camera design and image capturing mechanism. The integration enhanced the SR images slightly. Thus the comparison is difficult between them, but it can be seen as sharp and extra details in small regions of the SR images as shown in Fig. 7. Therefore, a qualitative evaluation study was set to validate the contribution of the visual-thermal fusion.

Optimization Function. To investigate the contribution of the adversarial loss on producing high perceptual quality SR images; the two models (TSRGAN that takes only thermal images and VTSRGAN which takes visual-thermal images) are trained using content loss and adversarial loss. Figure 7 shows the proposed models and their contribution to enhancing the thermal SR perceptual quality. Models trained with adversarial loss produced images with high texture details and high-frequency information. Although they added some small artifacts, they produced images that are sharper and less blurry than images generated using only content loss. Table 1 shows the relationship between the mean square error and the PSNR validation measurement, the model TSRCNN has the highest PSNR/SSIM value and also the most blurry images. To better validate the perceptual quality, our four models are added to the qualitative evaluation study.

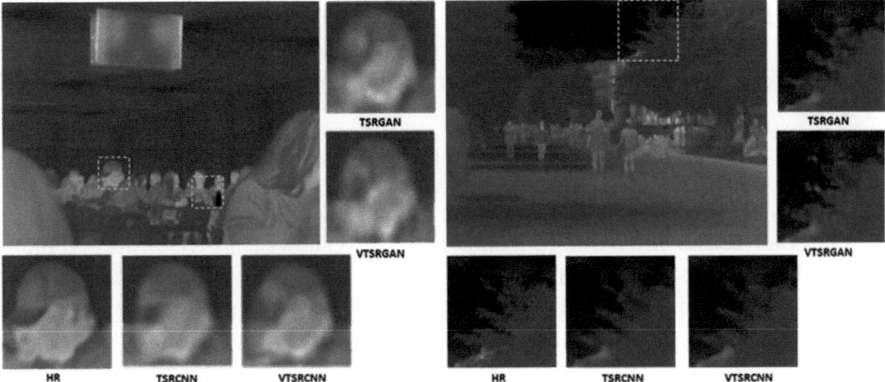

Fig. 7. Our proposed models trained only on thermal or on visual-thermal fusion, using only content loss or with adversarial loss.

Table 1. Quantitative evaluation of the proposed models and the STOA

Our models	TSRCNN	VTSRCNN	TSRGAN	VTSRGAN
PSNR/SSIM	52.353/0.9495	51.727/0.9434	51.094/0.9285	50.979/0.9289
STOA	VDSR	VDSRex	LAPSRN	
PSNR/SSIM	45.557/0.8328	52.027/0.9395	51.936/0.9526	

4.2 Qualitative Evaluation Study

To evaluate the proposed models and the different investigated schemes in comparison with the STOA, a qualitative evaluation study to alleviate the PSNR/SSIM impact and to assist with evaluating the human visual perception was conducted. A website that allows users to choose the most similar image to its original HR counterpart was created. Twenty-two people, with and without computer vision backgrounds, contributed to this evaluation process. They were asked to vote for a large study case, the test set used in the ULB17-VT benchmark with 58 samples. For each image, 9 models were selected for this evaluation process.

Running a qualitative evaluation study on 9 models with 58 images for each is very exhaustive work for the raters. To encourage them and to reduce the overall number of the selections required, three evaluation groups were created. In each group and for each image only three models were presented, these models were selected randomly and not repeated. The evaluation page shows the original HR image and the three selected models output. The user was asked to select the image that was most similar to its original HR image counterpart. For each selection process, a +1 was awarded in favor of the chosen model against the two other models shown. For example, in group 1 image 1 the models [4, 5, 6] outputs are presented. If the user selects the second image, this means the ranking output is +1 for model 5 over model 4 (f_{54}) = +1 and +1 for model

5 over model 6 (f_{56}) = +1. Finally, the total votes for and against the paired models are normalized as shown in Eq. (6), and also normalized by the number of times these paired models were presented in the evaluation process.

$$f_{ij} = \begin{cases} i - j, & \text{if } f_{ij} > f_{ji} \\ 0, & \text{otherwise} \end{cases} \qquad f_{ji} = \begin{cases} j - i, & \text{if } f_{ji} > f_{ij} \\ 0, & \text{otherwise} \end{cases} \qquad (6)$$

The color-coded votes diagram shown in Fig. 8 shows that the proposed models, which integrate visual-thermal fusion, are the highest selected models against almost all the other models. The size of the models to the left of the graph indicates the number of times these models were voted in favor over all the other models, it shows that the model VTSRCNN has 39% and VTSRGAN has 17%. The larger the model to the right of the graph indicates the number of times these models were voted against. The weight of the paths indicates the number of times these models were selected in favor against the opposite model. Our human visual perception study shows that the proposed models with visual-thermal fusion have the highest votes in favor and the lowest votes in disfavor. This highlights the benefits of integrating visual-thermal fusion in the thermal super-resolution problem.

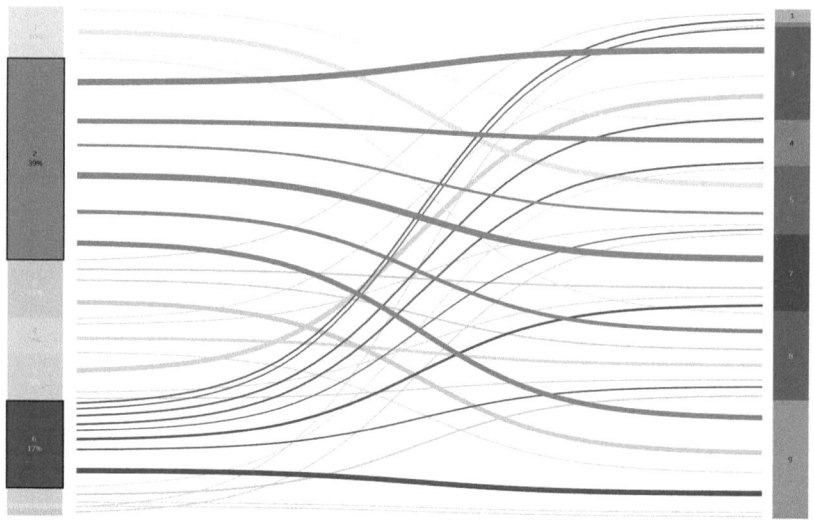

Fig. 8. Color-coded votes flow diagram of models: (1) TSRCNN, (2) VTSRCNN, (3) InpDconv-TRSCNNres, (4) AllDconv-TRSCNNres, (5) TSRGAN, (6) VTSRGAN, (7) VDSR, (8) VDSRex, (9) LAPSRN. Left/right represent the models. Paths in the middle represent the vote in favor between model.

4.3 Limitations

Although the proposed models generate better thermal SR images in human visual perception, some artifacts were noticed in the generated images. These artifacts are most likely caused by the device design or are due to the displacement of the device or the object. The models can preserve the high-frequency details of the visual images, the displacement problem could not be approached simply, and needs a better synchronized device to overcome the problem. Due to this displacement in some samples, the reconstructed versions suffer from artifacts around these objects compared to images with no displacement. We leave this problem open for further study and investigation.

5 Conclusion

In this paper, the problem of thermal super-resolution enhancement using the domain of visual images was addressed. A deep residual network that provides a better solution compared to other network schemes and training methods in the literature was proposed. Our result highlights that visual-thermal fusion can enhance the thermal SR image quality, also by the contribution of GAN based model. Furthermore, a qualitative evaluation study was performed and analyzed. This evaluation indicates a better understanding of the problem evaluation than the widely used PSNR/SSIM measurements. Lastly, a new visual-thermal benchmark in super-resolution problem domain was set.

References

1. Chen, X., Zhai, G., Wang, J., Hu, C., Chen, Y.: Color guided thermal image super resolution. In: Visual Communications and Image Processing (VCIP), pp. 1–4. IEEE (2016)
2. Chen, Z., Tong, Y.: Face super-resolution through Wasserstein GANs. arXiv preprint arXiv:1705.02438 (2017)
3. Cho, H., Seo, Y.W., Kumar, B.V., Rajkumar, R.R.: A multi-sensor fusion system for moving object detection and tracking in urban driving environments. In: 2014 IEEE International Conference on Robotics and Automation (ICRA), pp. 1836–1843. IEEE (2014)
4. Choi, Y., Kim, N., Hwang, S., Kweon, I.S.: Thermal image enhancement using convolutional neural network. In: 2016 IEEE/RSJ International Conference on Intelligent Robots and Systems (IROS), pp. 223–230. IEEE (2016)
5. Clevert, D.A., Unterthiner, T., Hochreiter, S.: Fast and accurate deep network learning by exponential linear units (ELUs). arXiv preprint arXiv:1511.07289 (2015)
6. Dong, C., Change Loy, C., He, K., Tang, X.: Image super-resolution using deep convolutional networks. ArXiv e-prints, December 2015
7. Goodfellow, I.: NIPS 2016 tutorial: generative adversarial networks. arXiv preprint arXiv:1701.00160 (2016)
8. Goodfellow, I., et al.: Generative adversarial nets. In: Advances in Neural Information Processing Systems, pp. 2672–2680 (2014)

9. Gross, S., Wilber, M.: Training and investigating residual nets (2016). https://torch.ch/blog/2016/02/04/resnets.html
10. Huang, Y., Qin, M.: Densely connected high order residual network for single frame image super resolution. arXiv preprint arXiv:1804.05902 (2018)
11. Hwang, S., Park, J., Kim, N., Choi, Y., Kweon, I.S.: Multispectral pedestrian detection: benchmark dataset and baselines. In: Proceedings of IEEE Conference on Computer Vision and Pattern Recognition (CVPR) (2015)
12. Ioffe, S., Szegedy, C.: Batch normalization: accelerating deep network training by reducing internal covariate shift. arXiv preprint arXiv:1502.03167 (2015)
13. Isola, P., Zhu, J.Y., Zhou, T., Efros, A.A.: Image-to-image translation with conditional adversarial networks. arXiv preprint (2017)
14. Johnson, J., Alahi, A., Fei-Fei, L.: Perceptual losses for real-time style transfer and super-resolution. In: Leibe, B., Matas, J., Sebe, N., Welling, M. (eds.) ECCV 2016. LNCS, vol. 9906, pp. 694–711. Springer, Cham (2016). https://doi.org/10.1007/978-3-319-46475-6_43
15. Kim, J., Kwon Lee, J., Mu Lee, K.: Accurate image super-resolution using very deep convolutional networks. In: Proceedings of the IEEE Conference on Computer Vision and Pattern Recognition, pp. 1646–1654 (2016)
16. Kim, J., Kwon Lee, J., Mu Lee, K.: Deeply-recursive convolutional network for image super-resolution. In: Proceedings of the IEEE Conference on Computer Vision and Pattern Recognition, pp. 1637–1645 (2016)
17. Kiran, Y., Shrinidhi, V., Hans, W.J., Venkateswaran, N.: A single-image super-resolution algorithm for infrared thermal images. Int. J. Comput. Sci. Netw. Secur. **17**(10), 256–261 (2017)
18. Lai, W.S., Huang, J.B., Ahuja, N., Yang, M.H.: Deep Laplacian pyramid networks for fast and accurate super-resolution. In: Proceedings IEEE Conference Computer Vision and Pattern Recognition, pp. 624–632 (2017)
19. Ledig, C., et al.: Photo-realistic single image super-resolution using a generative adversarial network. ArXiv e-prints, September 2016
20. Ledig, C., et al.: Photo-realistic single image super-resolution using a generative adversarial network. arXiv preprint (2016)
21. Lim, B., Son, S., Kim, H., Nah, S., Lee, K.M.: Enhanced deep residual networks for single image super-resolution. In: The IEEE Conference on Computer Vision and Pattern Recognition (CVPR) Workshops, vol. 1, p. 4 (2017)
22. Panagiotopoulou, A., Anastassopoulos, V.: Super-resolution reconstruction of thermal infrared images. In: Proceedings of the 4th WSEAS International Conference on Remote Sensing (2008)
23. Qu, Y., Zhang, G., Zou, Z., Liu, Z., Mao, J.: Active multimodal sensor system for target recognition and tracking. Sensors **17**(7), 1518 (2017)
24. Shi, W., et al.: Real-time single image and video super-resolution using an efficient sub-pixel convolutional neural network. In: Proceedings of the IEEE Conference on Computer Vision and Pattern Recognition, pp. 1874–1883 (2016)
25. Wu, B., Duan, H., Liu, Z., Sun, G.: SRPGAN: perceptual generative adversarial network for single image super resolution. arXiv preprint arXiv:1712.05927 (2017)
26. Yang, C., Lu, X., Lin, Z., Shechtman, E., Wang, O., Li, H.: High-resolution image inpainting using multi-scale neural patch synthesis. ArXiv e-prints, November 2016

27. Zhang, H., et al.: StackGAN: text to photo-realistic image synthesis with stacked generative adversarial networks. In: IEEE International Conference on Computer Vision (ICCV), pp. 5907–5915 (2017)
28. Zhu, J.Y., Park, T., Isola, P., Efros, A.A.: Unpaired image-to-image translation using cycle-consistent adversarial networks. arXiv preprint arXiv:1703.10593 (2017)

PCA-RECT: An Energy-Efficient Object Detection Approach for Event Cameras

Bharath Ramesh[(✉)], Andrés Ussa, Luca Della Vedova, Hong Yang, and Garrick Orchard

Temasek Laboratories, National University of Singapore, Singapore 117411, Singapore
bharath.ramesh03@u.nus.edu
http://sites.google.com/view/bharath-ramesh/

Abstract. We present the first purely event-based, energy-efficient approach for object detection and categorization using an event camera. Compared to traditional frame-based cameras, choosing event cameras results in high temporal resolution (order of microseconds), low power consumption (few hundred mW) and wide dynamic range (120 dB) as attractive properties. However, event-based object recognition systems are far behind their frame-based counterparts in terms of accuracy. To this end, this paper presents an event-based feature extraction method devised by accumulating local activity across the image frame and then applying principal component analysis (PCA) to the normalized neighborhood region. Subsequently, we propose a backtracking-free k-d tree mechanism for efficient feature matching by taking advantage of the low-dimensionality of the feature representation. Additionally, the proposed k-d tree mechanism allows for feature selection to obtain a lower-dimensional dictionary representation when hardware resources are limited to implement dimensionality reduction. Consequently, the proposed system can be realized on a field-programmable gate array (FPGA) device leading to high performance over resource ratio. The proposed system is tested on real-world event-based datasets for object categorization, showing superior classification performance and relevance to state-of-the-art algorithms. Additionally, we verified the object detection method and real-time FPGA performance in lab settings under non-controlled illumination conditions with limited training data and ground truth annotations.

Keywords: Object recognition · Neuromorphic vision · Silicon retinas · Low-power FPGA · Object detection · Event cameras

1 Introduction

Through these fruitful decades of computer vision research, we have taken huge strides in solving specific object recognition tasks, such as classification systems

---

Supported by MINDEF grant 9015101332 - PROJECT KENSINGTON.

for automated assembly line inspection, hand-written character recognition in mail sorting machines, bill inspection in automated teller machines, to name a few. Despite these successful applications, generalizing object appearance, even under moderately controlled sensing environments, for robust and practical solutions for industrial challenges like robot navigation and sense-making is a major challenge. This paper focuses on the industrially relevant problem of real-time, low-power object detection using an asynchronous event-based camera [2] with limited training data under unconstrained lighting conditions. Compared to traditional frame-based cameras, event cameras do not have a global shutter or a clock that determines its output. Instead, each pixel responds independently to temporal changes with a latency ranging from a low of tens of microseconds to a high of few milliseconds. This local sensing paradigm naturally results in a wider dynamic range (120 dB), as opposed to the usual 60 dB for frame-based cameras.

Most significantly, event cameras do not output pixel intensities, but only a spike output with a precise timestamp, also termed an event, that signifies a sufficient change in log-intensity of the pixel. As a result, event cameras require lower transmission bandwidth and consume only a few hundred mW vs. a few W by standard cameras [21]. In summary, event-based cameras offer a fundamentally different perspective to visual imaging while having a strong emphasis on low-latency and low-power algorithms [3,4,7,16].

Despite the notable advantages of event cameras, there still remains a significant performance gap between event camera algorithms and frame-based counterparts for various vision problems. This is partly due to a requirement of totally new event-by-event processing paradigms. However, the burgeoning interest in event-based classification/detection is focused on closing the gap using deep spiking neural networks [9,17], something that again entails dependence on powerful hardware like its frame-based counterpart. On the other hand, a succession of frames captured at a constant rate (say 30 Hz), regardless of the scene dynamics and ego-motion, works well with controlled scene condition and camera motion. Frame-based computer vision algorithms have benefited immensely from sophisticated methodologies that reduce the computational burden by selecting and processing only informative regions/keypoints within an image [5,12,23,29]. In addition, frame-based sensing has led to high hardware complexity, such as powerful GPU requirements for state-of-the-art object detection frameworks using deep neural networks [25,26].

In contrast to the above works, this paper introduces a simple, energy-efficient approach for object detection and categorization. Figure 1 illustrates the local event-based feature extraction pipeline that is used for classification using a dictionary-based method. Accordingly, efficient feature matching with the dictionary is required, which is handled by a backtracking-free branch-and-bound k-d tree. This proposed system was ported to a field programmable gate array (FPGA) with certain critical design decisions, one of which demanded a virtual dimensionality reduction method based on the k-d tree, to accommodate very low-power computational needs.

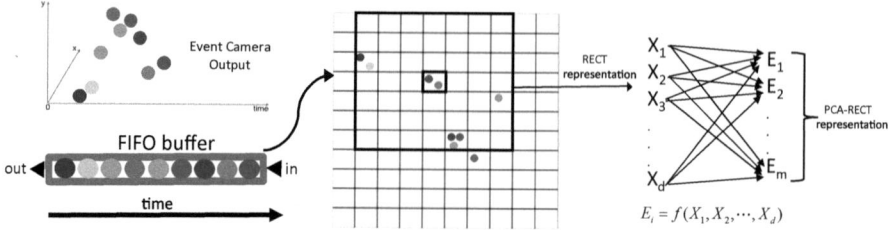

Fig. 1. PCA-RECT representation (best viewed on monitor). Useful events are subsampled and filtered after applying nearest-neighbor temporal filtering and refractory filtering, termed as rectangular event context transform (RECT). The sparser RECT event representation is updated dynamically using a first in, first out (FIFO) buffer. Subsequent feature extraction is carried out by applying principal component analysis (PCA) to project RECT onto a lower-dimensional subspace to obtain the final PCA-RECT feature representation

2 Event Cameras

For real-time experiments, we use the commercial event camera, the Dynamic and Active-pixel Vision Sensor (DAVIS) [2]. It has 240×180 resolution, 130 dB dynamic range and 3 microsecond latency. The DAVIS can concurrently output a stream of events and frame-based intensity read-outs using the same pixel array. An event consists of a pixel location (x, y), a binary polarity value (p) for positive or negative change in log intensity and a timestamp in microseconds (t). In this work, polarity of the events are not considered, and only the event stream of the DAVIS is used.

2.1 Related Work

Since event-based vision is relatively new, only a limited amount of work addresses object detection using these devices [10,11]. Liu et al. [11] focuses on combining a frame-based CNN detector to facilitate the event-based module. We argue that works using deep neural networks for event-based object detection may achieve good performance with lots of training data and computing power, but they go against the idea of low-latency, low-power event-based vision. In contrast, [10] presents a practical event-based approach to face detection by looking for pairs of blinking eyes. While [10] is applicable to human faces in the presence of activity, we develop a general purpose event-based, object detection method using a simple feature representation based on local event aggregation. Thus, this paper is similar in spirit to the recently spawned ideas of generating event-based descriptors, such as histogram of averaged time surfaces [28] and log-polar grids [22,24]. Moreover, the proposed object detection and categorization method was accommodated on FPGA to demonstrate energy-efficient low-power vision.

3 Method

We follow the event-based classification framework proposed in [22], with the following crucial changes: a new descriptor (PCA-RECT), a virtual dimensionality reduction technique using k-d trees (vPCA) and a simplified feature matching mechanism to account for hardware limitations. The framework [22] consists of four main stages: feature extraction, feature matching with a dictionary, dictionary representation followed by a linear classifier. Additionally, we incorporate an object detector in the framework as explained in the following subsections.

3.1 PCA-RECT

Each incoming event, $\mathbf{e}_i = (x_i, y_i, t_i, p_i)^T$ with pixel location x_i and y_i, timestamp t_i, polarity p_i, is encoded as a feature vector $\mathbf{x}_i$. To deal with hardware-level noise from the event camera, two main steps are used: (1) nearest neighbour filtering and (2) refractory filtering. We define a spatial Euclidean distance between events as,

$$D_{i,j} = \left\| \begin{pmatrix} x_i \\ y_i \end{pmatrix} - \begin{pmatrix} x_j \\ y_j \end{pmatrix} \right\| . \qquad (1)$$

Using the above distance measure, for any event we can define a set of previous events within a spatial neighborhood, $N(\mathbf{e}_i, \gamma) = \{\mathbf{e}_i \mid j < i, \; D_{i,j} < \gamma\}$, where $\gamma = \sqrt{2}$ for an eight-connected pixel neighbourhood. When the time difference between the current event and the most recent neighboring event is less than a threshold, Θ_{noise}, the filter can be written as

$$F_{noise}(\mathbf{e}) = \{\mathbf{e}_i \mid N(\mathbf{e}_i, \sqrt{2}) \backslash N(\mathbf{e}_i, 0) \ni \mathbf{e}_j \mid t_i - t_j < \Theta_{noise} \} . \qquad (2)$$

When the neighborhood is only the current pixel, $\gamma = 0$, the set of events getting through the refractory filter F_{ref} are those such that,

$$F_{ref}(\mathbf{e}) = \{\mathbf{e}_j \mid t_i - t_j > \Theta_{ref} \; \forall \, j \mid \mathbf{e}_j \in N(\mathbf{e}_j, 0)\} . \qquad (3)$$

Cascading the filters, we can write the filtered incoming events as,

$$\{\hat{\mathbf{e}}\} = F_{noise}(F_{ref}(\mathbf{e})) . \qquad (4)$$

As shown in Fig. 1, the incoming events $\hat{\mathbf{e}}_i$ are first pushed into a FIFO buffer. The FIFO queue is then used to update an event-count matrix $C \in \mathbb{R}^{m \times n}$, where m and n denote the number of rows and columns of the event camera output.

$$C(x_i, y_i) = C(x_i, y_i) + 1 . \qquad (5)$$

Before pushing the latest event, the FIFO buffer of size s is popped to make space and simultaneously update the count matrix C,

$$C(x_{i-s}, y_{i-s}) = C(x_{i-s}, y_{i-s}) - 1 . \qquad (6)$$

The event-count C is pooled to build local representations, which are further aggregated to obtain the RECT representation of each event. In particular, let A be a $p \times p$ square filter, the 2-D convolution is defined as,

$$R(j,k) = \sum_p \sum_q A(p,q) C(j-p+1, k-q+1) ,\qquad(7)$$

where p run over all values that lead to legal subscripts of $A(p,p)$ and $C(j-p+1, k-p+1)$. In this work, we consider a filter containing equal weights (commonly known as an averaging filter) for simplicity, while it is worth exploring Gaussian-type filters that can suppress noisy events. The resultant 2-D representation is termed as filtered matrix $R \in \mathbb{R}^{(m/p) \times (n/p)}$, where the filter dimensions are chosen to be give integer values for m/p and n/q or conversely C is zero-padded sufficiently. Subsequently, the RECT representation for $\hat{\mathbf{e}}_i$ is obtained as a patch $\mathbf{u}_i$ of dimension d centered at $R(y/p, x/p)$. Subsequently, the filtered event-count patch is projected on-to a lower-dimensional subspace using principal component analysis (PCA) for eliminating noisy dimensions and improving classifier accuracy.

3.2 Feature Selection and Matching Using K-d Trees

The PCA-RECT feature representation for each event is classified using a dictionary type method [22] that can handle the recognition of the desired object categories. However, exhaustive search is too costly for nearest neighbor matching with a dictionary, and approximate algorithms can be orders of magnitude faster than exact search, while almost achieving par accuracy.

In the vision community, k-d tree nearest-neighbor search is popular [14,27], as a means of searching for feature vectors in a large training database. Given n feature vectors $\mathbf{x}_i \in \mathbb{R}^{d'}$, the k-d tree construction algorithm recursively partitions the d'-dimensional Euclidean space into hyper-rectangles along the dimension of maximum variance. However, for high dimensional data, backtracking through the tree to find the optimal solution takes a lot of time.

This paper proposes a simple, backtracking-free branch-and-bound search for dictionary matching, taking advantage of the low-dimensionality of the PCA-RECT representation. The hypothesis is that, in general, the point recovered from the leaf node is a good approximation to the nearest neighbor in low-dimensional spaces, and performance degrades rapidly with increase in dimensionality, as inferred from the intermediate results in [1]. In other words, with $(\log_2 n) - 1$ scalar comparisons, nearest neighbor matching is accomplished without an explicit distance calculation. While the PCA-RECT representation is useful for software implementations, an extra PCA projection step can be computationally demanding on FPGA devices. To this end, we propose a virtual PCA-RECT representation based on the k-d tree, termed as vPCA-RECT.

vPCA-RECT. A key insight is that only a fraction of the data dimensions are used to partition the k-d tree, especially when the dictionary size is only a few times more than the feature dimension. Therefore, instead of using the PCA-RECT representation, an alternative dimensionality reduction scheme can be implemented by discarding the unused dimensions in the k-d tree structure. In other words, the RECT representation is first used to build a k-d tree that selects the important dimensions (projection π), which are then utilized for dictionary learning and classification. It is worth noting that exactly the same k-d tree will be obtained if the RECT data is first projected by π onto a subspace that is aligned with the coordinate axes. Since no actual projection takes place, we refer to this as a virtual projection – the irrelevant dimensions chosen by the k-d tree are discarded to obtain a lower-dimensional feature representation.

3.3 Event-Based Object Categorization and Detection

The Learning Stage: Using either the PCA-RECT or vPCA-RECT event representation, the learning process corresponds to creating a set of K features denoted as $M = \{1, 2, \cdots, K\}$ to form the dictionary. First, a simple sampling process is carried out such that, during training, a large pool of event representations of various categories and at random positions are extracted from a target set of events. In our setup, the dictionary features are learned from the sampled training set using clustering for all the objects jointly.

The learning stage for detection builds on top of the categorization module, in such a way that the learning process corresponds to selecting a subset of features from the dictionary for each object. In contrast to the learning phase of the categorization module, the detector features are selected from the whole training set in a supervised one-vs-all manner.

We propose to evaluate the balanced matches Y_+^k to each dictionary feature f_k from the target events against the matches Y_-^k for all the other events to the respective feature. Mathematically, the ratio

$$D(k) = \frac{\beta_+^k Y_+^k}{\beta_-^k Y_-^k}, \text{ where } \beta_+^k = \frac{|Y_+^k|}{\sum_{k=1}^{K} |Y_+^k|}, \text{ and } \beta_-^k = \frac{|Y_-^k|}{\sum_{k=1}^{K} |Y_-^k|}, \qquad (8)$$

is to be maximized. The balancing component β_+^k denotes the percentage of target events matched to the dictionary feature f_k. Similarly, β_-^k denotes the percentage of non-target events matched to the dictionary feature f_k. Thus, choosing the detector features with the D–largest ratios completes the learning phase.

The Classification/Detection Stage: At runtime, the event representations are propagated through the k-d tree. On the one hand, the distribution of the dictionary features are then extracted and further passed to a simple linear classifier (we experimented with both linear SVM and Kernel Methods). On the other hand, the event representations propagated through the k-d tree are matched with the detector features. Those matched events are used to update a location map for the target object and the region with the highest activation is considered to be the final detection result.

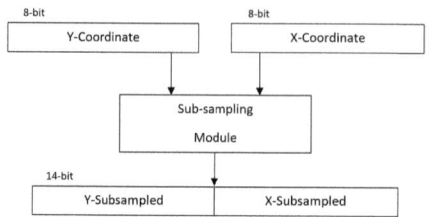

(a) Sub-sampling module

1-bit	12-bit	12-bit	12-bit	6-bit	6-bit
Type	Left Node	Right Node	Index Output	Threshold	Desc. Index

(b) A k-d tree node in hardware

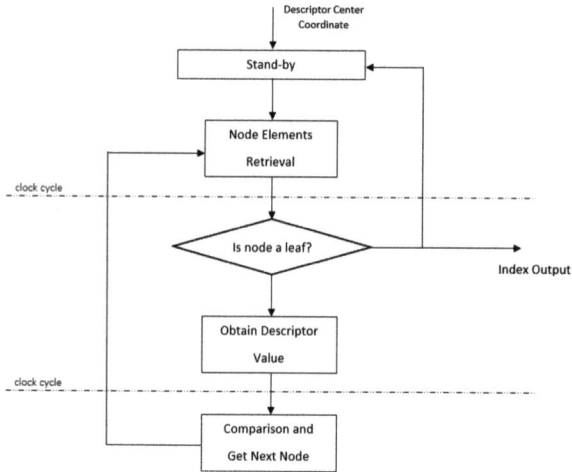

(c) Recursive logic-driven k-d tree implemented in hardware

Fig. 2. FPGA implementation details

4 FPGA Implementation

4.1 Categorization Pipeline

In order to showcase energy-efficient event-based object recognition, the FPGA implementation of the algorithm is designed as a series of four independent hardware units: event sub-sampling, vPCA-RECT generation, a recursive k-d tree and a SVM classifier output on an event-by-event basis, each of which has an independent block design. Generally, these hardware counterparts are not a direct application of the algorithm presented in the earlier section, i.e., certain design decisions were taken for this task, among them, to desist the use of an extra PCA projection along the pipeline.

The sub-sampling block receives the filtered event locations as input values x and y, each 8-bit in size, which are used to update the zero-padded count matrix $C \in \mathbb{R}^{m \times n}$ (Eqs. (5) and (6)). The sub-sampling behavior can be achieved in hardware through a combinatorial module that performs the division by shifting the inputs by one bit, and subsequently adding p and q to that value to obtain the sub-sampled representation (Eq. (7)). This results in two 7-bit values which are then concatenated to output a single memory address (Fig. 2(a)).

The next block uses the cell-count matrix $R \in \mathbb{R}^{(m/p) \times (n/q)}$, created by a block of distributed RAM of depth $((m/p) \times (n/q))$ and $log(s)$-bits width, corresponding to the FIFO buffer size s, initialized to zero for generating the vPCA-RECT representation. To generate a descriptor with respect to the last event received would add a considerable overhead, since each element of the descriptor would have to be read sequentially from the block RAM while being stored by the next module. Instead, the address corresponding to the center of the descriptor is provided, i.e. the input address of the count matrix is passed over to the k-d tree module. This allows to trigger the k-d tree in one clock cycle once the count matrix is updated and later read the descriptor values based on this single coordinate. However, a new issue arises, the count matrix then can not be modified while the k-d tree exploration is being performed. Hence a buffering element is added between the sub-sampling and count matrix modules that will only provide the next address once there is a valid output from the tree.

The k-d tree nodes are represented in a 49-bit number stored in a previously initialized single port ROM of depth equal to the number of nodes. This number is conformed by the elements of a node: type, left node, right node, index output, split value and split dimension; these are concatenated and their width is shown in Fig. 2(b).

The k-d tree module follows a three steps cycle (Fig. 2(c)). The split dimension of a k-d tree node provides the address that needs to be read from the cell-count matrix block RAM to get the relevant descriptor value. Next, the descriptor value is compared to the previously stored split value from the node, taking a path down the tree, left or right, depending on the boolean condition. The corresponding node to get is then retrieved from the respective left or right address element acquired in the retrieval step. This cycle repeats until the node type belongs to a leaf, then the leaf node output is made available for the classifier module. It is worth mentioning that in the software implementation of this algorithm, once the descriptor is formed, it is then normalized before being passed to the k-d tree. A normalization step in hardware would add a big overhead to the pipeline, disturbing its throughput, and it was removed from the FPGA implementation after verifying that the overall performance was not affected harshly.

Algorithm 1. Event-based FPGA Object Detection

Input: Filtered event stream $\{\hat{e}\}$, detector landmarks l, number of events S
Output: Mean object location (x_{obj}, y_{obj})
1: Initialize detector count $D(y, x) = 0_{m,n}$, detector cut-off $threshold = 0$
2: **for** $t = 1 : S$ **do**
3:     For each incoming event $\hat{e}_t = (x_t, y_t, t_t, p_t, \mathbf{x}_t^T)^T$
4:     For $\mathbf{x}_t$ get leaf node index l_t using k-d tree
5:     **if** $l_t \in l$ **then**
6:         $D(y_t, x_t) = D(y_t, x_t) + 1$
7:         **if** $D(y_t, x_t) > threshold$ **then**
8:             $threshold = threshold + 1$
9:             Reset detector mean calculation FIFO
10:         **end if**
11:         **if** $D(y_t, x_t) = threshold$ **then**
12:             Push x_t, y_t into the mean calculation FIFO
13:         **end if**
14:     **end if**
15: **end for**
16: Output the mean of the coordinates in the FIFO as (x_{obj}, y_{obj})

At runtime in a software implementation, the classification is performed by a linear combination of the weights and a feature vector created by the k-d tree after a buffer time of S events. To achieve this in a hardware implementation, the depth of the feature vector would have to be transversed while performing several multiplications which would require a considerable amount of multiplier elements from the FPGA, and would affect the speed of the module. Thus, it was desired to avoid this solution and the following was proposed.

The elements of the linear combination mentioned would be acquired as readily available and would be added to an overall sum vector of length equal to the number of classes to classify, hence performing the dot product operation as one addition per event. Then, after S events, a resulting vector is formed, which is equal to the result of the same linear combination first mentioned in the software implementation. Thus, the final module to perform the classification receives the output index from the k-d tree and adds its corresponding classifier parameter to a sum vector of length equal to the number of classes. In parallel, this index value is stored in another FIFO element. When the queue is full, the oldest value would be passed to the module to be subtracted from the sum. This allows to have a classification output at any point in time, corresponding to the last S events.

4.2 Detection Pipeline

Parallel to the modules performing the classification pipeline, the aim of the detection process is to find the coordinates corresponding to "landmarks" with the highest activation after S events, and then find the most probable location for the object. Again, the algorithm was divided into multiple coherent hardware

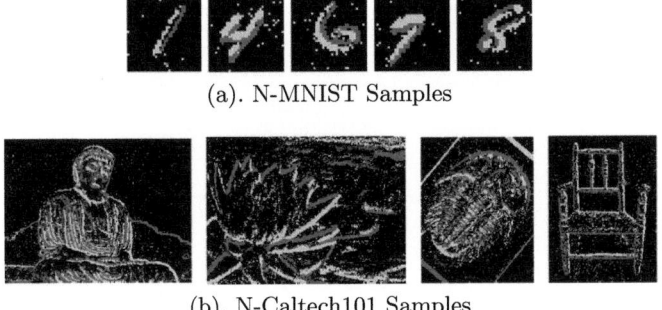

(a). N-MNIST Samples

(b). N-Caltech101 Samples

Fig. 3. Samples from the event-based benchmark datasets

modules that would produce the same results as the original software version. The designed blocks are: landmarks detector, detection heat map and mean calculation.

First, the dictionary features corresponding to the landmarks that were calculated offline are loaded into a binary memory block. This module receives as input the dictionary feature index provided by the k-d tree for the current event. If the feature is found as one of the landmarks, the respective event coordinates x and y are passed as a concatenated address to the next module in the pipeline. Next, a stage corresponding to the heat map is utilized. This module holds a matrix represented as a block RAM of depth $m \times n$, since the coordinates are not sub-sampled and have the ranges $1 \leq x \leq m$ and $1 \leq y \leq n$. For each new input address, its value in memory is incremented.

Since the aim of the detection algorithm is to calculate the average of the coordinates with the highest activation, it would be inefficient to find these event addresses after S events. Therefore, the coordinates with the highest count are stored in a FIFO element while the counting is performed. At the end, this will contain all the x and y coordinates needed for the average calculation. Once the classification flag is triggered, all the coordinates stored in the previous step (which belong to the highest activation) are acquired for calculating the total activation (the divisor). Subsequently, it will calculate the sum of the respective x and y values, and pass these as dividends to hardware dividers that will provide the final coordinates of the detected object. Algorithm 1 summarizes the above object detection hardware pipeline clearly.

5 Experiments and Discussion

5.1 Event-Based Object Categorization

This section compares the proposed object categorization system to state-of-the-art event-based works and thus software implementation is used with double numeric precision. We validated our approach on two benchmark datasets [19],

Table 1. Comparison of classification accuracy on event-based datasets (%).

	N-MNIST	N-Caltech101
H-First	71.20	5.40
HOTS	80.80	21.0
Gabor-SNN	83.70	19.60
HATS	**99.10**	64.20
vPCA-RECT (this work)	98.72	70.25
PCA-RECT (this work)	98.95	**72.30**
Phased LSTM	97.30	-
Deep SNN	98.70	-

namely the N-MNIST and N-Caltech101, that have become de-facto standards for testing event-based categorization algorithms. Figure 3 shows some representative samples from N-MNIST and N-Caltech101.

Parameter Settings. The time thresholds for the nearest neighbour filter and the refractory filter are nominally set as $\Theta_{noise} = 5$ ms and $\Theta_{ref} = 1$ ms respectively, as suggested in [20]. We used a FIFO buffer size of 5000 events for dynamically updating the count matrix as and when events are received. Subsequently, the RECT representation with a 2 by 2 averaging filter without zero padding at the boundaries is used to obtain a 9×9 feature vector for all event locations. We also experimented with other feature vector dimensions using a 3×3, 5×5, 7×7 sampling region and found that increasing the context improved the performance slightly. For obtaining the PCA-RECT representation, the number of PCs can be chosen automatically by retaining the PCs that hold 95% eigenenergy of the training data, which is typically about 60 in our case. For testing on the benchmark datasets, a dictionary size of 3000 was universally used with a k-d tree with backtracking to find precise feature matches.

Results on the Benchmark Datasets. The results on the N-MNIST and N-Caltech101 datasets are given in Table 1. As it is common practice, we report the results in terms of classification accuracy. The baselines methods considered were HATS [28], HOTS [8], HFirst [18] and Spiking Neural Networks (SNN) [9,15] (Gabor-SNN reported in [28]).

On the widely reported N-MNIST dataset, our method is as good as the best performing HATS method. Moreover, other SNN methods are also in the same ballpark, which is due to the simple texture-less digit event streams giving distinct features for most methods. Therefore, it is a good benchmark as long as a proposed method performs in the high 90's. A test on the challenging NCaltech-101 dataset will pave way for testing the effectiveness close to a real-world scenario.

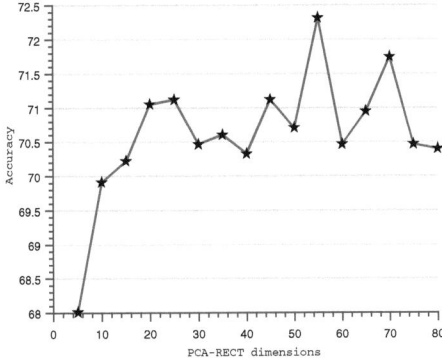

Fig. 4. Number of principal component dimensions vs. accuracy on N-Caltech101

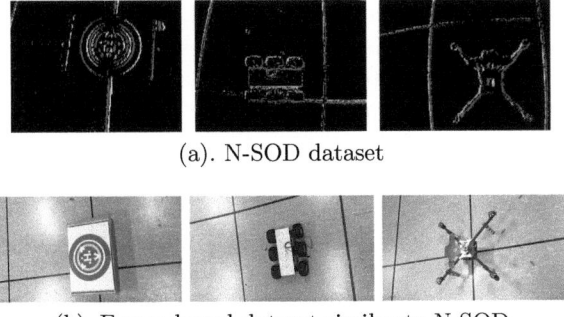

Fig. 5. Dataset samples: landing platform, UAV and Thumper (BG: empty floor).

Our method has the highest classification rate ever reported for an event-based classification method on the challenging N-Caltech101 dataset. The unpublished HATS work is the only comparable method in terms of accuracy, while the other learning mechanisms fail to reach good performance. Figure 4 shows the performance of the PCA-RECT representation as the number of PCs are varied. It is worth noticing that just retaining five dimensions can give better performance compared to available works.

5.2 Event-Based Object Detection

Dataset. The datasets described in the previous section are good for only evaluating the categorization module. In addition, as the benchmark datasets were generated by displaying images on a monitor with limited and predefined motion of the camera, they do not generalize well to real-world situations. To overcome these limitations, we created a new dataset by directly recording objects in lab environment with a freely moving event-based sensor. The in-house dataset, called as Neuromorphic Single Object Dataset (N-SOD), contains three objects

Table 2. Confusion Matrix (%) for the best result on the in-house N-SOD dataset.

	Background	LP	Thumper	UAV
Background	95.4128	0.3058	3.3639	0.9174
LandingPlatform	0	99.2268	0.5155	0.2577
Thumper	0	1.9257	96.9739	1.1004
UAV	0	0	3.1884	96.8116

with samples of varying length in time (up to 20 s). The three objects to be recognized are a thumper 6-wheel ground robot, an unmanned aerial vehicle, a landing platform along with a background class (Fig. 5(a)).

Results on N-SOD. For testing on the N-SOD dataset, we divide the dataset into training and testing, with 80% temporal sequence samples per class for training and the remaining for testing. Using the training features, a dictionary is generated. Since the temporal sequences are of different length, for a fixed number of events, say every 10^5 events, a dictionary representation is extracted and a linear SVM classifier is trained. Similarly for testing, for every 10^5 events, the dictionary representation is classified using the SVM.

Based on the above setup, an accuracy of 97.14% was obtained (Table 2) with a dictionary size of 950, which resulted in a k-d tree with 10 layers. We also experimented with lower dictionary sizes such as 150, 300, 450, etc., and the performance drop was insignificant (>96%). On the other hand, using a k-d tree with backtracking, descriptor normalization, etc., achieved close to 100% accuracy on offline high-performance PCs, which of course does not meet low-power and real-time requirements. In summary, the proposed vPCA-RECT method with a backtracking-free k-d tree implementation mildly compromises on accuracy to handle object detection and categorization using an event camera in real-time.

We report the precision and recall of the detection results by ascertaining if the mean position of the detected result is within the ground truth bounding box. We obtained: (a) *Precision* - (498/727) = 0.685: The percentage of the detections belonging to the object that overlap with the groundtruth (b) *Recall* - (498/729) = 0.683: The percentage of correct detections that are retrieved by the system. The number of "landmarks" were set to 20 in the above experiments while similar results were obtained for values such as five and ten.

Comparison to CNN. In order to compare to state-of-the-art deep neural networks, we recorded a similar dataset to N-SOD using a frame-based camera (Fig. 5(b)) and transfer learning via AlexNet classified the object images. With an equivalent train/test split compared to N-SOD, perfect performance can be achieved on the clearly captured test images, however, when we recorded a frame-based dataset under fast motion conditions (motion blur), an accuracy of only

Table 3. Hardware utilization report for the FPGA running the proposed modules.

	Utilization	Available	Utilization %
LUT	18238	53200	34.28
LUTRAM	12124	17400	69.68
FF	2065	106400	1.94
BRAM	48	140	34.29
DSP	4	220	1.82
IO	102	200	51.00

79.20% was obtained. It was clear that the black UAV frame when blurred looks like the black-stripped background and creates much confusion. This confirms the disadvantage of using frame-based cameras to handle unconstrained camera motion. Note that fast camera motion leads to only an increase in data-rate for event-based cameras and has no effect on the output. In fact, recordings of N-SOD have significant amount of such fast motions.

FPGA Performance. The hardware implementation and performance of the Xilinx Zynq-7020 FPGA running at 100 MHz was evaluated by direct comparison with the results of the algorithm's software version in MATLAB. The time taken for a single event to be classified for the worst possible k-d tree path was 550 ns. The Zynq was interfaced to a down-looking DAVIS camera, onboard an unmanned aerial vehicle flying under unconstrained lighting scenarios. We recommend viewing our submitted video[1] that clearly shows the classification/detection process better than still images.

A summary of utilization of hardware elements can be seen in Table 3. Due to our low hardware requirements, the dynamic on-chip power increased only by 0.37 W while the base FPGA power consumption was in the order of 3 W. As a rough comparison, FPGA-based recognition systems like [6,13,30], which present solutions running at equal or lower clock frequencies, consume more power than our implementation.

6 Conclusions

We have demonstrated object detection and categorization in an energy-efficient manner using event cameras, where the only information that is important for the tasks is how edges move, and the event camera naturally outputs it. The proposed PCA-RECT feature takes advantage of this sparsity to generate a low-dimensional representation. The low-dimensional representation is further exploited for feature matching using a k-d tree approach, capable of obtaining the best performance on the challenging Neuromorphic Caltech-101 dataset

---

[1] https://youtu.be/h3SgXa47Kjc.

compared to state-of-the-art works. Most importantly, real-time FPGA implementation was achieved with several careful design considerations, such as a backtracking-free k-d tree for dictionary matching, a virtual PCA-RECT representation obtained by analyzing the k-d tree partitioning of the feature space, etc. To the best of our knowledge, this is the first work implementing a generic object recognition framework for event cameras on an FPGA device, verified in a lab demo setting under unconstrained motion and lighting setup, thereby demonstrating a high performance over resource ratio.

References

1. Beis, J.S., Lowe, D.G.: Shape indexing using approximate nearest-neighbour search in high-dimensional spaces. In: Proceedings of the Conference on Computer Vision and Pattern Recognition (CVPR). IEEE Computer Society (1997)
2. Brandli, C., Berner, R., Yang, M., Liu, S.C., Delbruck, T.: A 240 x 180 130 db 3 µs latency global shutter spatiotemporal vision sensor. IEEE J. Solid-State Circ. **49**(10), 2333–2341 (2014)
3. Conradt, J., Berner, R., Cook, M., Delbruck, T.: An embedded AER dynamic vision sensor for low-latency pole balancing. In: IEEE International Conference on Computer Vision Workshop, pp. 780–785, September 2009
4. Delbruck, T., Lang, M.: Robotic goalie with 3 ms reaction time at 4% CPU load using event-based dynamic vision sensor. Frontiers Neurosci. **7**, 223 (2013)
5. Galleguillos, C., Rabinovich, A., Belongie, S.: Object categorization using co-occurrence, location and appearance. In: IEEE Conference on Computer Vision and Pattern Recognition, pp. 1–8. IEEE Computer Society (2008)
6. Hikawa, H., Kaida, K.: Novel FPGA implementation of hand sign recognition system with som-hebb classifier. IEEE Trans. Circ. Syst. Video Technol. **25**(1), 153–166 (2015)
7. Kueng, B., Mueggler, E., Gallego, G., Scaramuzza, D.: Low-latency visual Odometry using event-based feature tracks. In: 2016 IEEE/RSJ International Conference on Intelligent Robots and Systems (IROS), pp. 16–23, October 2016
8. Lagorce, X., Orchard, G., Gallupi, F., Shi, B.E., Benosman, R.: HOTS: a hierarchy of event-based time-surfaces for pattern recognition. IEEE Trans. Pattern Anal. Mach. Intell. **1**(99), 1 (2016)
9. Lee, J.H., Delbruck, T., Pfeiffer, M.: Training deep spiking neural networks using backpropagation. Frontiers Neurosci. **10**, 508 (2016)
10. Lenz, G., Ieng, S., Benosman, R.: Event-based dynamic face detection and tracking based on activity. CoRR abs/1803.10106 (2018). http://arxiv.org/abs/1803.10106
11. Liu, H., Moeys, D.P., Das, G., Neil, D., Liu, S.C., Delbruck, T.: Combined frame- and event-based detection and tracking. In: IEEE International Symposium on Circuits and Systems (ISCAS), pp. 2511–2514, May 2016
12. Lowe, D.: Distinctive image features from scale-invariant keypoints. Int. J. Comput. Vis. **60**(2), 91–110 (2004)
13. Mousouliotis, P.G., Panayiotou, K.L., Tsardoulias, E.G., Petrou, L.P., Symeonidis, A.L.: Expanding a robot's life: low power object recognition via FPGA-based DCNN deployment. In: 7th International Conference on Modern Circuits and Systems Technologies (MOCAST), pp. 1–4 (2018)

14. Muja, M., Lowe, D.G.: Fast approximate nearest neighbors with automatic algorithm configuration. In: VISAPP International Conference on Computer Vision Theory and Applications, pp. 331–340 (2009)
15. Neil, D., Pfeiffer, M., Liu, S.C.: Phased LSTM: accelerating recurrent network training for long or event-based sequences. In: Neural Information Processing Systems, NIPS 2016, pp. 3889–3897. Curran Associates Inc. (2016)
16. Ni, Z., Bolopion, A., Agnus, J., Benosman, R., Regnier, S.: Asynchronous event-based visual shape tracking for stable haptic feedback in microrobotics. IEEE Trans. Rob. **28**(5), 1081–1089 (2012)
17. O'Connor, P., Neil, D., Liu, S.C., Delbruck, T., Pfeiffer, M.: Real-time classification and sensor fusion with a spiking deep belief network. Frontiers Neurosci. **7** (2013)
18. Orchard, G., Meyer, C., Etienne-Cummings, R., Posch, C., Thakor, N., Benosman, R.: HFirst: a temporal approach to object recognition. IEEE Trans. Pattern Anal. Mach. Intell. **37**(10), 2028–2040 (2015)
19. Orchard, G., Jayawant, A., Cohen, G.K., Thakor, N.: Converting static image datasets to spiking neuromorphic datasets using saccades. Frontiers Neurosci. **9**, 437 (2015)
20. Padala, V., Basu, A., Orchard, G.: A noise filtering algorithm for event-based asynchronous change detection image sensors on truenorth and its implementation on truenorth. Frontiers Neurosci. **12**, 118 (2018)
21. Posch, C., Serrano-Gotarredona, T., Linares-Barranco, B., Delbruck, T.: Retinomorphic event-based vision sensors: bioinspired cameras with spiking output. Proc. IEEE **102**(10), 1470–1484 (2014)
22. Ramesh, B., Thi, N.A.L., Orchard, G., Xiang, C.: Spike context: a neuromorphic descriptor for pattern recognition. In: IEEE Biomedical Circuits and Systems Conference (BioCAS), pp. 1–4, October 2017
23. Ramesh, B., Jian, N.L.Z., Chen, L., et al.: Soft Comput. **23**, 2429 (2019). https://doi.org/10.1007/s00500-017-2939-2
24. Ramesh, B., Yang, H., Orchard, G.M., Le Thi, N.A., Zhang, S., Xiang, C.: DART: distribution aware retinal transform for event-based cameras. IEEE Trans. Pattern Anal. Mach. Intell. (2019). https://doi.org/10.1109/TPAMI.2019.2919301
25. Redmon, J., Farhadi, A.: YOLOV3: an incremental improvement. CoRR abs/1804.02767 (2018). http://arxiv.org/abs/1804.02767
26. Ren, S., He, K., Girshick, R., Sun, J.: Faster R-CNN: towards real-time object detection with region proposal networks. IEEE Trans. Pattern Anal. Mach. Intell. **39**(6), 1137–1149 (2017)
27. Silpa-Anan, C., Hartley, R.: Optimised KD-trees for fast image descriptor matching. In: IEEE Conference on Computer Vision and Pattern Recognition, pp. 1–8 (2008)
28. Sironi, A., Brambilla, M., Bourdis, N., Lagorce, X., Benosman, R.: HATS: histograms of averaged time surfaces for robust event-based object classification. CoRR abs/1803.07913 (2018). http://arxiv.org/abs/1803.07913
29. Vikram, T.N., Tscherepanow, M., Wrede, B.: A saliency map based on sampling an image into random rectangular regions of interest. Pattern Recogn. **45**(9), 3114–3124 (2012)
30. Zhai, X., Bensaali, F., McDonald-Maier, K.: Automatic number plate recognition on FPGA. In: International Conference on Electronics, Circuits, and Systems (ICECS), pp. 325–328. IEEE (2013)

Unconstrained Iris Segmentation Using Convolutional Neural Networks

Sohaib Ahmad[(✉)] and Benjamin Fuller

University of Connecticut, Storrs, CT 06269, USA
{sohaib.ahmad,benjamin.fuller}@uconn.edu
http://cse.uconn.edu/

Abstract. The extraction of consistent and identifiable features from an image of the human iris is known as iris recognition. Identifying which pixels belong to the iris, known as segmentation, is the first stage of iris recognition. Errors in segmentation propagate to later stages. Current segmentation approaches are tuned to *specific environments*.

We propose using a convolution neural network for iris segmentation. *Our algorithm is accurate when trained on a single environment and tested on multiple environments.* Our network builds on the Mask R-CNN framework (He et al. ICCV 2017). Our approach segments faster than previous approaches including the Mask R-CNN network.

Our network is accurate when trained on a single environment and tested with a different sensors (either visible light or near-infrared). Its accuracy degrades when trained with a visible light sensor and tested with a near-infrared sensor (and vice versa). A small amount of retraining of the visible light model (using a few samples from a near-infrared dataset) yields a tuned network accurate in both settings.

For training and testing, this work uses the Casia v4 Interval, Notre Dame 0405, Ubiris v2, and IITD datasets.

1 Introduction

The extraction of consistent and identifiable features from the human iris is known as iris recognition. Iris recognition algorithms proceed in several phases: (1) segmenting pixels into iris and non-iris (2) extracting features from the iris that are likely to be stable (3) organizing features in a way that enables fast and accurate comparison. We focus on the segmentation phase. Errors in segmentation propagate to later stages of iris recognition [3].

Most segmentation algorithms work best with near-infrared (NIR) images [5, 26]. These algorithms can be used on visible light (RGB) images but their performance degrades [16]. Segmentation algorithms also degrade in unconstrained environments where lighting and each individual's distance, orientation, and stability with respect to the imager vary. Previous algorithms for working in unconstrained environments are dataset centric [28]. *The goal of this work is to design iris segmentation that works in multiple environments.* Prior approaches can be classified into three types:

(a) *Specialized* approaches that use processing techniques developed for the iris. Specialized approaches are fast and require no ground truth data. However, specialized algorithms require hand-crafted features or algorithms. These approaches have limited portability.
(b) *Hybrid* approaches that combine machine learning and specialized iris techniques to improved accuracy. Hybrid approaches may require ground truth data. Hybrid algorithms attempt to enhance portability by pre-processing data to a standard representation before using a specialized approach.
(c) *Learning* approaches that use general techniques for the entire process. Learning based approaches rely on ground truth data to train classifiers. Learning approaches often need a large amount of labeled training data. Previous approaches have been slow without a large accuracy improvement. One advantage of learning approaches is the inheritance of general segmentation advances.

No approach accurately segments irises in diverse environments. We focus on learning based approaches and defer discussion of prior specialized and hybrid approaches to Appendix A.

An important learning based mechanism is the convolutional neural network or CNN which can be used for classification, feature extraction, and segmentation. Hierarchical CNNs and Multi scale CNNs [26] fuse features from images at different scales. CNNs are natively translation invariant. Arsalan et al. propose a two stage segmentation scheme where coarse bounding box around the iris is extracted and used to train a CNN to classify iris pixels [4]. Fully convolutional networks search along the entire image and calculate probabilities of pixels being iris or non-iris. A bounding box around the circular iris can reduce search space reducing complexity and increasing segmentation accuracy.

Our Approach. We propose a new iris segmentation scheme based on convolutional neural networks. Our approach is based on two key ideas:

1. The circular and continuous nature of the iris makes it an ideal candidate for bounding box localization. A recent CNN based segmentation scheme [4] used this idea to detect an ROI (Region of interest) around the iris manually by using edge detection and binarization. Our approach handles this as a learning problem without using specific transforms.
2. Bounding box fitting and classification have been treated as separate problems [13]. It is more intuitive to unify these problems so each each item can be solved in parallel increasing speed and reducing redundancy by sharing features. Mask inference, that is, deciding which bits are iris bits, can now be done more efficiently. The search space has been reduced once the bounding box class has been predicted. Importantly, we use a loss function that is a cumulative of the bounding box, classification and mask inference losses.

To implement these ideas, we start with the recent Mask R-CNN framework [14]. He et al. proposed the Mask R-CNN framework for large scale segmentation involving numerous classes. We find this framework can be adapted to iris segmentation. Importantly, the framework natively produces a per pixel segmentation, a *mask*, ideal for iris mask extraction.

We demonstrate our techniques using four datasets: Casia v4 Interval [34], Ubiris [27], ND-0405 [8], and IITD [23]. We find that Casia v4 and IITD are similar in many aspects. Ubiris is the most difficult and different dataset as it is collected in an unconstrained environment. Jalilian et al. considered Casia v4, Casia v5 aging, and IITD. We believe our dataset collection is more diverse; we directly compare with Jalilian et al. where possible.

Single Dataset Networks. We first train and test our design on images from each dataset. Our scheme achieves comparable segmentation accuracy as previous approaches when trained and tested on an individual dataset. The main advantage of our approach is high accuracy when training and testing on different data sets. As a comparison point, recently Jalilian et al. [20] used *domain adaption* to allow a trained CNN to work in multiple environments. Their approach requires samples from each new environment. Our accuracy is higher than Jalilian et al. [20] without performing explicit domain adaption.

Towards a Universal Network. However, our single network approach demonstrates low accuracy when training on an RGB dataset and testing on an NIR dataset (and vice versa). To remedy this situation, we then develop a second model to segment irises from images across all four datasets used. This single model can segment images from any of the four datasets. We discuss the design of this network further in Sect. 4.

Performance. In addition to segmentation performance we briefly remark on the speed of our implementation. Our implementation speed varies from 8 fps to 20 fps depending on the dataset used. The speed is largely determined by the resolution of the iris image. While this speed is not sufficient to keep pace with video, it is faster than previous learning methods and static methods. Liu et al. [26] report a inference time of 0.2 s for their CNN scheme while our implementation roughly segments in 0.09 s, both works using the Ubiris dataset. Training time can be fine tuned, dependent on the application requirements. We have datasets from different wavelengths and different camera sensors.

Organization. The rest of this work is organized as follows, Sect. 2 describes our overall design (including our single dataset networks), Sect. 3 describes the evaluation methodology and results on single dataset trained model, Sect. 4 describes our tuned network and results, and Sect. 5 concludes. Specialized and hybrid segmentation schemes are discussed in Appendix A.

2 Design

2.1 The Mask R-CNN Framework

The starting point for our network is the recent Mask R-CNN framework [14]. The Mask R-CNN framework augments the region based convolutional neural

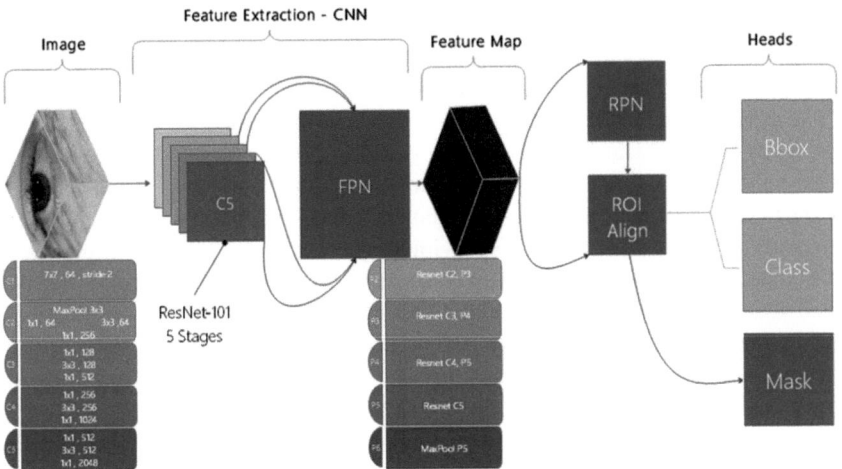

Fig. 1. Simplified overview of the Mask R-CNN framework. Below the five stages of C5/ResNet and FPN are listed below the component. In the FPN stages $C4$ refers to the fourth stage of ResNet while $P4$ refers to the fourth stage of FPN. Note that in MR-CNN bounding box inference, classification, and mask creation are inferred simultaneously.

network (R-CNN). R-CNN takes a two step approach to segmentation. It first finds regions of interest (ROI) using selective search [13]. Then it finds CNN features for these ROI which are classified using a support vector machine (SVM). The Fast R-CNN [12] introduced pooled ROIs while unifying the bounding box and classification heads. The Faster R-CNN [31] speeds up the region proposal process by running a pass of a CNN to obtain feature maps. Proposals are generated from the feature maps by sliding fixed sized anchors to obtain regions with probable objects. A bounding box regressor fits bounding boxes over the regions. Classification of the bounding boxes is handled by a dense layer. MR-CNN adds a third head to the Faster R-CNN, it predicts segmentation masks.

The full MR-CNN framework is summarized in Fig. 1. The MR-CNN framework performs feature extraction using two components: a feature extractor and a feature scaling component. We use ResNet-101 [15] for feature extraction and the FPN (Feature Pyramid Network) [24] for the scaling component.

The MR-CNN has some improvements over previous works. It uses a Resnet backbone for feature extraction. The ResNet has skip connections inside layers which adds previous activations to the current operation allowing for deeper networks. This allows the gradient to flow back into the network which would have otherwise diminished. The feature extractor can thus be trained for longer time periods.

ResNet is a five stage CNN architecture. Each stage has layers of convolution neurons. Each stage produces activation maps at a different scale (decreasing by a factor of 2). The architecture outputs the result of the last four stages of

ResNet. The purpose of outputting multiple stages is to allow the five stage FPN to make the network more resilient to changes in scale. This is done by inferring at five different scales per iris image.

The output of the FPN serves as the feature map. A Region Proposal Network proposes regions in the form of ROIs by sliding anchors of fixed sizes over the feature maps. These ROIs are independently pooled to form fixed dimension (7 × 7) feature maps. The ROI align layer makes the pooled representation of the feature maps aligned with the previous layers by using bilinear interpolation. Classification, bounding box prediction and mask inference is done using the pooled feature maps. A mean binary cross-entropy loss is used to calculate a mask per class so there is no competition among classes for mask inference. The class prediction uses a softmax loss function while the bounding box head uses a smooth L1 loss.

We use the same Intersection over Union threshold and the FPN implementation as the Mask R-CNN paper [14].

2.2 Our Network Design

In this subsection, we discuss the design of our single data set networks building on the Mask R-CNN framework.

Since all four datasets contain iris images without other facial features such as the nose and lips there are fewer candidate bounding boxes accepted for training. As such the bounding box head trains fairly quickly.

We use a pre-trained model for general semantic and instance segmentation for our work, a model trained [36] on the Microsoft COCO dataset [25]. We retrain this model on our datasets.

Our pre-trained model has 80 classes. We expect the complex pre-trained model to port quickly. Since our use case has one class to segment, starting from the pre-trained model should decrease training time.

MR-CNN needs bounding boxes per image, our ground truth has masks only. We create bounding boxes from each mask so that the box encompasses the entire mask with 2 pixels to spare on each side.

Since we are performing binary classification (iris/not-iris), we can further reduce training time by reducing ROIs per image. We reduce ROIs by reducing anchors (the number of different shaped anchor strides that are performed across the image) and using fewer candidate ROIs. Specially, we only use square anchors of 64, 128 and 256 pixels. This reduced number of candidate ROIs only affects the mask accuracy by 2% while speeding up training time by 40%.

Inference (mask extraction) time is a crucial metric for CNN architectures. Ideally, the architecture should infer at camera speed of 30 frames per second. The MR-CNN paper reports a mask inference speed of 5 frames per second. Our implementation of the Mask R-CNN segments an iris in 0.09 s for the Ubiris dataset which roughly equates to 11 frames per second. We attribute this speed improvement to having only one class to segment and lower resolution images.

Instance segmentation is an important aspect of the framework where segmented objects are categorized as instances of a single class. The MR-CNN is an instance-segmentation first framework. This could be useful to segmenting both iris instances from a single image. Iris instance segmentation helps with iris recognition.

For iris segmentation, the main difference between Mask R-CNN and an FCN is the bounding box head. To test this distinction, we trained our models where the bounding was always set to the perimeter of the image. This change degrades the F1 score.

Many iris processing techniques use data augmentation to help in the training of the network. The goal of augmentation is avoiding over-fitting by adding variation to the training dataset. As an example, some schemes blur the image to contrast changes. Although this process adds a pre-processing step it further improves segmentation accuracy by adding additional samples to the training data. Our augmentation is simple, we randomly flip 50% of iris images horizontally during training. We also perform a trivial transform on the grayscale NIR images. We upscale them to RGB by copying the grayscale value in the R,G and B bins. This allows a single network for inference on different datasets (Table 1).

Table 1. Dataset statistics. Each dataset is restricted to images which have segmentation ground truth [16].

Dataset	Resolution	NIR	Realistic	Images
Casia v4 Interval	320 × 280	Y	N	2655
Ubiris v2	400 × 300	N	Y	2250
NotreDame	640 × 480	Y	N	837
IITD	320 × 240	Y	N	2240

Datasets. Our work uses the CASIA, IITD, UBIRIS and the Notre Dame datasets. Since our approach uses supervised learning we restrict to the subset of this datasets where ground truth is available. We utilize segmentation ground truth datasets created by Hofbauer et al. [16].

CASIA Iris Image Database Version 4 [34]. This is an NIR (Near infrared) dataset which consists of 2655 iris images from 249 subjects. The images are of 320 by 280 pixels. Images were collected in an indoor constrained environment using a close up infrared iris camera which leaves an easily distinguishable circular reflection on the pupil across all images due to a circular LED array.

IIT Delhi Iris Database Version 1 [23]. This dataset has NIR images of resolution 320 by 240 taken using a JIRIS JPC1000. Images are taken in a constrained environment with little variation.

ND-IRIS-0405 [8]. The Notre Dame database contains NIR images of resolution 640 by 480 pixels. These images are also taken in a controlled environment with little variation. For the ND dataset we use a small subset of the original dataset where groundtruth is provided by Hofbauer et al. [16].

UBIRIS version 2 [27]. The UBIRIS database has 11101 iris images from 50 different subjects with resolution of 400 by 300 pixels. This dataset has wide variation among images with off-angle, reflections and imaging distance among the varying parameters introducing some realness to the database. The images are also RGB and do not present a clear iris pattern as opposed to the other datasets.

Metrics. We use F-Measure and E1 score from the NICE competition [29] to evaluate segmentation accuracy (see Table 2). The E1 score is the normalized XOR of the binary predicted mask and the ground truth. The E1 score measures what fraction of pixels disagree. The F-measure is the harmonic mean of precision and recall. The E1 rate is normalized by image dimensions making it incompatible between datasets with differing dimensions. We use the F1 score for cross dataset accuracy comparison.

Table 2. Evaluation metrics. TP is true positive: the fraction of pixels that are correctly segment as iris. TN is true negative: the fraction of pixels that are correctly segmented as non-iris. FP and FN are false positive and false negative and are defined in as 1-TP and 1-TN respectively.

Measure	Value
Precision	TP/(TP+TN)
Recall	TP/(TP+FP)
F-Measure	$\frac{2 * Recall * Precision}{Precision + Recall}$
E-Nice1	$\frac{\text{\# pixels that differ from ground truth}}{\text{Image Size}}$

3 Single Dataset Network Results

In this section we describe our performance in training networks for each of the four datasets described above. We use a 3 step training methodology where (1) the heads, (2) stages 4 and up of the ResNet and 3) all stages are trained in sequence. All datasets are split into 40-30-30 disjoint sets for training, testing, and validation respectively. Table 3 which lists performance of the individual datasets with respect to all metrics listed in Table 2.

Performance on individual datasets is competitive with state of the art. Arsalan et al. [5] report slightly better performance on Ubiris than our techniques. We note that Arsalan et al. use ground truth from the NICE competition while we use ground truth provided by Hofbauer et al. [16].

We run adaptability experiments using our four datasets and trained models. We generate a 4 × 4 grid by training on a single dataset and then testing on all four datasets. Table 4 shows the F1 score (the harmonic mean of precision and recall) for each dataset combination. Our system demonstrates portability across

Table 3. Segmentation rates four fold cross validation, trained on 40% and Tested on 30% of the same dataset. Columns present the mean, μ and variance, σ^2, for each metric introduced in Table 2. E1 score should not be compared across datasets as it is scale dependent. The results from 1 fold and 4 fold validation don't differ.

	Prec. %		Rec. %		F1 %		E1 %	
	μ	σ^2	μ	σ^2	μ	σ^2	μ	σ^2
Casia	98.2	0.01	93.6	0.03	95.8	0.01	0.024	0.003
Ubiris	95.9	0.12	93.4	0.08	94.6	0.05	0.77	0.004
ND	97.9	0.02	92.7	0.04	95.2	0.02	0.16	0.005
IITD	98.5	0.01	94.1	0.03	96.2	0.01	0.023	0.002

Table 4. Segmentation rates trained and tested on different datasets - F1 score. The columns list the mean, μ, and variance, σ^2, when the network trained on the dataset in the *column* was tested on the dataset in the *row*. The diagonal represents testing and training on the same dataset.

Dataset	Casia		Ubiris		ND		IITD	
	μ	σ^2	μ	σ^2	μ	σ^2	μ	σ^2
Casia	95.8	0.01	55.5	2.54	95.1	0.01	95.3	0.04
Ubiris	63.5	0.39	94.6	0.05	81.0	2.25	70.4	1.56
ND	93.1	0.11	71.2	1.60	95.2	0.02	93.9	0.05
IITD	95.2	0.03	67.4	2.47	93.7	0.08	96.2	0.01

datasets. As a comparison, Jalilian et al. report an F1 score of .81 when training on Casia v4 Interval and testing on domain adapted IITD images (.71 without domain adaption). Our system achieves an F1 score of .95 for the same pair.

This baseline system achieves adequate performance when moving between IITD and Casia v4 Interval. However, training on just Ubiris (the most difficult and diverse dataset) achieves inadequate performance segmenting on other datasets. Similarly, all models that are not trained on Ubiris demonstrate poor performance on Ubiris.

Segmentation F1 scores of 85% are achieved fairly quickly after training the heads for 2 epochs. After two epochs there is a depreciating accuracy return.

We compare our scheme to recent Ubiris segmentation schemes in Table 5. Our scheme has comparable performance on Ubiris with the benefit of cross dataset portability. The results in Table 3 are from a model trained on 40% of each dataset. Table 6 presents results from testing on a 60-20-20 train-test-validation split for comparison with prior work. The results for the Casia, IITD, Notre Dame dataset show no significant change when trained on 60% of the dataset therefore we only show the results from the Ubiris dataset in Table 6.

Table 5. Recent Ubiris segmentation rates. Bazrafkan et al. [7] infers on only 10% of the dataset while training on 70%, we find 10% of the Ubiris dataset to be too low to show the unconstrained nature of the dataset. The works [4,5,26,38] use the mask dataset from the nice competition (we use ground truth from [16]). They do not report F1 score. Our score is four fold cross-validation, trained on 60% and tested on 20%.

Method	F1 score	E1 score
Ours	94.8	0.74
U-shaped CNN [7]	93.9	0.70
IrisDenseNet [5]	-	0.70
CNN [4]	-	0.82
MFCNN [26]	-	0.90
Total variation [38]	-	1.13
Conv encoder-decoder [19]	86.3	1.87

Table 6. Ubiris model trained on 60% of the dataset. Results are from four-fold cross-validation.

	Prec. %		Rec. %		F1 %		E1 %	
	μ	σ^2	μ	σ^2	μ	σ^2	μ	σ^2
Ubiris	96.2	0.12	93.5	0.08	94.8	0.04	0.74	0.004

4 Universal Model

In the last section we showed our networks trained on a single dataset demonstrated portability especially between NIR datasets. In this section, we show how to tune a model that segments well on all four datasets.

There is an affinity between the CASIA, IITD and Notre Dame datasets with all cross-dataset F1 scores between them being at least 90%. The Ubiris and the Notre Dame dataset have similar *scale* the fraction of the image occupied by the iris. We posit this is the reason by higher F1 scores on the ND-Ubiris pairs (compared to other pairs involving Ubiris).

Ubiris here is the most difficult dataset and its models' capability does not carry over to the the CASIA and IITD datasets. We believe the two most relevant factors for model portability are the scale of the iris and the "hardness" of a dataset. Two factors that contribute to hardness is whether a dataset is NIR or RGB and whether is environmentally constrained.

The Casia and IITD datasets expose the iris wholly and the majority of the image holds the iris relative to the Ubiris and the Notre Dame datasets where the images are from a distance and the iris covers a smaller area. This is an apparent and intuitive problem with any CNN architecture. The FPN component is designed to handle this problem and make the network scale invariant. Scale invariance is further enhanced by training on both Ubiris and Casia.

We choose to train a Ubiris-Casia model to generalize towards all the datasets. Ubiris was chosen as the base dataset due to its hardness and Casia used for retraining due to its NIR nature. Ubiris and Casia also differ in scale by 20.7%. This difference will help in making the model more scale invariant. Additionally, this presents the model with both NIR and RGB features.

We use a 40-30-30 train-test-validation split of the Ubiris dataset to train the generic model. We then use 100 images from the Casia dataset to retrain the model. The effect is to tune it towards the NIR datasets. (We have also provided results from testing on a 60-20-20 train-test-validation split for comparison with prior work.)

We first train the COCO model on the Ubiris training set using the same three stage training regime described Sect. 2. This consists of training the (1) the heads, (2) stages 4 and up of the ResNet and (3) all stages are trained in sequence. We then retrain the heads of the model again on the Casia training set for 2 epochs. We use 100 images from the Casia dataset for tuning. Figure 3 shows examples of where the tuned model performs well on each dataset (top row) and poorly on each dataset (bottom row). This tuned model sees a slight decrease in the Ubiris F1 score (from 94.6% to 93.2%). However, as shown in Table 7, Casia and IITD datasets see a drastic increase in F1 (at least 95%). The model is accurate on both IITD and ND datasets without being trained on samples from these datasets.

Table 7. Model trained on Ubiris with tuning on Casia. This tuned model was then tested on all four datasets. Results are the mean, μ, and variance, σ^2 of F1 Score. Results are from four-fold cross-validation. The second row of the table lists performance of the untuned model as reported in Table 4.

Dataset	Casia		Ubiris		ND		IITD	
	μ	σ^2	μ	σ^2	μ	σ^2	μ	σ^2
Ubiris tuned	95.9	0.01	93.2	0.17	95.2	0.03	95.6	0.04
Ubiris untuned	63.5	0.39	94.6	0.05	81.0	2.25	70.4	1.56

4.1 Discussion

The adaption of the network to the four datasets can be attributed to the FPN and the pixel intensities. The FPN deals with the difference in scales. The Resnet activations are tuned towards the circular nature of the iris and the pupil and are generic towards the four datasets. The NIR images are converted to RGB (for consistency) by pasting the grayscale value in the RGB bins, thus re-training the network on a few samples from one NIR dataset will expose the network to the differing intensity values and will be tuned to segment NIR images. Making the image corners as ground truth for bounding boxes degrades the segmentation accuracy by 3% on average across the datasets. The mask head mimics an FCN except with a different loss function.

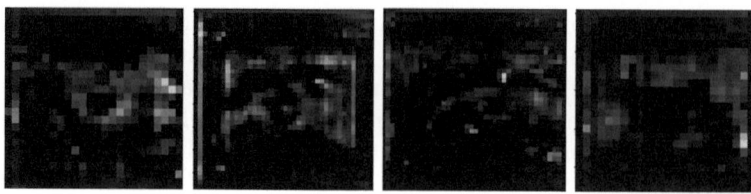

Fig. 2. Activation maps from the fourth layer of the ResNet. The activations show the circular shape of the iris for all four datasets. IITD, Casia, ND and Ubiris in order.

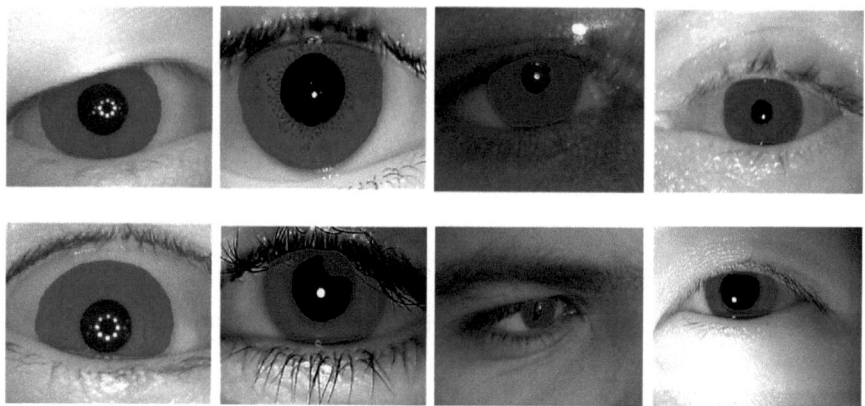

Fig. 3. Segmented Iris Masks from the Casia, IITD, Ubiris and Notre Dame datasets respectively. The final tuned Ubiris-Casia model was used here. The top row shows the Average-Best case masks while the bottom row shows the worst case masks.

We find that we can group datasets based on the scale of the iris. Ubiris has the smallest scale at 6.98% of the image on average. IITD has the largest scale at 30.68%. Notre Dame has 9.4% following closely to Ubiris while the Casia dataset has the scale at 27.7%. It is important to note that Ubiris also has a high variance in its scale. Casia and IITD both being NIR datasets with similar scale are similar F1 scores. They also show similar F1 scores if Casia is used to infer IITD images and vice-versa. ND also follows suit but is less than optimal due to a smaller scale of the iris.

From the Table 4 we see that models trained on IITD, ND and Casia can be used to infer on each other. This can primarily be attributed to the pixel intensity values being close on average and the feature extraction backbone being trained to segment circular irises. An example activation map for the four datasets from the fourth Resnet layer can be seen in Fig. 2. They all show circular activations. The different sized irises between datasets are handled by the FPN with its different scaled outputs. The portability of the model can also be attributed to the mask head being decoupled from the bounding box and classification. This is different from an FCN where class and mask prediction is coupled resulting in segmentation inaccuracy.

The distribution of F1 scores for all four datasets on the tuned model is shown in Fig. 6. Since Ubiris is the worst performing dataset, we separate out the mean F1 score per person for Ubiris in Fig. 5. Furthermore, we present additional instances of poor Ubiris segmentation in Fig. 4. This demonstrates that poor segmentation on Ubiris is a per image phenomena not a per person phenomena.

Inference Speed. The speed of the tuned model varies between 8–20 fps. The primary factor in determining the speed is the resolution of the image, Notre Dame takes 120 ms seconds to segment. Ubiris follows closely at 90 ms while Casia and IITD take 54 ms. All inferences run on a laptop with an i7-7700HQ, 32GB DDR4 RAM, an NVidia GTX 1070. The IrisDenseNet [5] does not report its inference time but their work is based on the SegNet [6] which reports an forward pass time of 422 ms with an image of dimension 360 × 480.

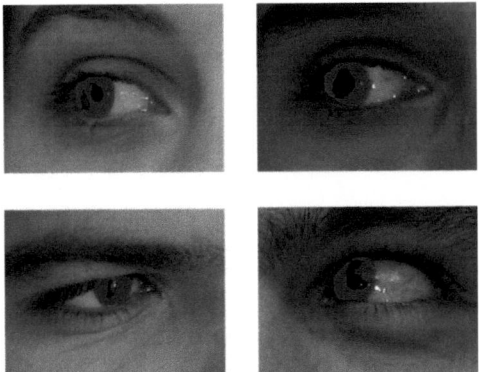

Fig. 4. Some examples of the worst case segmentations. Images have F1 scores below 80%. We define a worst case segmentation as the 5th percentile in the CDF of F1 scores and the average-best case to be F1 scores above the 90th percentile.

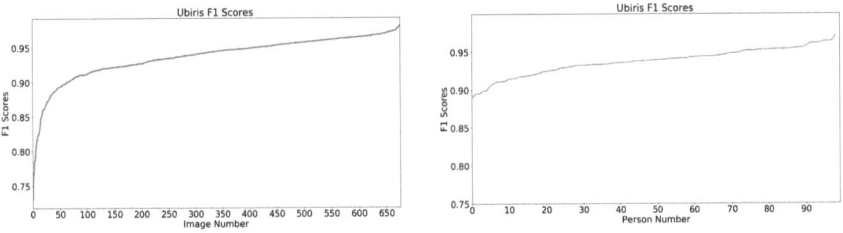

Fig. 5. Cumulative distribution functions of F1 score for Ubiris dataset. Left is a per image distribution function. The right is a per person distribution function. Variance is smaller per person indicating that our network fails to segment particular images rather than performing poorly on individuals. Model trained on just Ubiris is presented here.

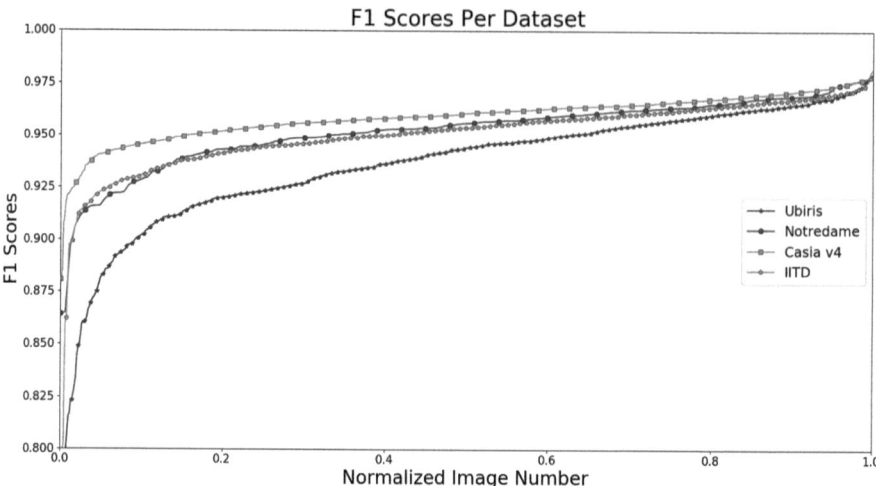

Fig. 6. Sorted F1 scores from all four datasets. The distributions are based on the tuned model described in Sect. 4. Note that our system performs worst on Ubiris.

5 Conclusion

This work presents a new CNN based iris segmentation algorithm whose performance is close to best in class on representative datasets. Our algorithm natively can be used to perform segmentation on a different dataset than was used for training. Datasets where the iris is of similar scale demonstrate high accuracy in cross dataset experiments. To create a "universal" algorithm we need to correct for differing scale of the iris within dataset. Our tuned algorithm primarily trains on Ubiris with a small amount of retraining on Casia. This tuned network is accurate on all four datasets.

In addition to accuracy, our network is fast, segmenting up to 20 frames per second. Our result falls short of a video frame rate but is better than previous learning implementations.

As a *future direction* we suggest using a similar CNN network to perform feature extraction to create a unified learning based iris recognition workflow. An *open question* is whether we can domain adapt between RGB and NIR datasets with fewer samples or global dataset features. The entire segmentation weights could be recycled for iris recognition while simultaneously extracting features improving speed and decreasing redundancy.

Acknowledgement. The authors would like to thank Comcast Inc. and Synchrony Financial for partial support of this research. The authors would like to thank the reviewers for their constructive feedback.

A Additional Related Work

As discussed in the introduction, segmentation algorithms can be classified into specialized, hybrid, and learning. We provide an overview of specialized and hybrid approaches below.

Specialized Approaches. The first generation of segmentation algorithms assumed that the iris and pupil are circular. Under this assumption circle/ellipse fitting techniques are used to find iris and pupil boundaries. Daugman's seminal work uses an integro-differential operator for iris segmentation [9], in essence it tries to fit a circle over an iris exhaustively. Subsequent algorithms are based on integro-differential operators and the Hough transform [10,17,18]. Circle fitting via the Hough transform involves different regions voting for the best circle (which can be seen as an exhaustive search over a possible circle) [37]. New segmentation methods use different techniques to find candidate circles (for example, see Tan and Kumar [33]).

Methods that assume the iris and pupil are elliptical perform well in constrained environments where the individual faces the camera and actively participates in image collection. However, these methods perform poorly in unconstrained environments. As an example, in blurred iris images these algorithms fixate or diverge harshly, converging to edges besides the iris boundary. Substantial pre-processing and post-processing is necessary to use these methods in unconstrained environments.

Improvements to ellipse fitting have come in the form of generalizes structure tensors or GST [2]. GSTs find an iris specific complex circular pattern and convolve this pattern with the collected image to find the iris and pupil. The GST method allows the discovered region to only approximate a circle. Zhao and Kumar first use a total variation model to regularize local variations [38] and then feed this image into circular Hough transform. Interestingly, Zhao and Kumar process the lower half and the upper half of the iris separately.

Active contours [22] are used for general segmentation tasks. Instead of circle fitting, active contours find a high gradient between two sections in an image to indicate a boundary. Abdullah et al. show that with some iris specific modifications, active contours segment well [1]. While active contours do not assume the collected iris is circular they can still fixate on reflections and occlusions.

Hybrid Approaches. Machine learning techniques including neural networks have penetrated into fields that used specialized approaches. Many works segment the iris using a mix of general learning techniques and specialized iris techniques. The common approach is to use learning algorithms to do rough segmentation and post-process via specialized techniques to get the final segmented iris.

Proenca performed coarse iris segmentation using a neural network classifier and refined this segmentation via polynomial fitting [28]. Radman et al. use a HoG (Histogram of Gradients) as input features to train a support vector machine (SVM) [30]. This trained SVM is then used on new images to localize the iris. Subsequent iris segmentation is done by employing the Growcut algorithm [35] which labels pixels based on an initial guess. Adaboost [11] based eye detection is common for identifying the iris region inside a facial image, Joeng et al. [21] refined this technique by adding eyelid and occlusion removal algorithms. Tan and Kumar use Zernike moments as input features to train a neural network and SVM for coarse iris pixel classification [32].

References

1. Abdullah, M.A., Dlay, S.S., Woo, W.L., Chambers, J.A.: Robust iris segmentation method based on a new active contour force with a noncircular normalization. IEEE Trans. Syst. Man Cybern.: Syst. **47**(12), 3128–3141 (2017)
2. Alonso-Fernandez, F., Bigun, J.: Iris boundaries segmentation using the generalized structure tensor. A study on the effects of image degradation. In: 2012 IEEE Fifth International Conference on Biometrics: Theory, Applications and Systems (BTAS), pp. 426–431. IEEE (2012)
3. Alonso-Fernandez, F., Bigun, J.: Quality factors affecting iris segmentation and matching. In: 2013 International Conference on Biometrics (ICB), pp. 1–6. IEEE (2013)
4. Arsalan, M., et al.: Deep learning-based iris segmentation for iris recognition in visible light environment. Symmetry **9**(11), 263 (2017)
5. Arsalan, M., Naqvi, R.A., Kim, D.S., Nguyen, P.H., Owais, M., Park, K.R.: Iris-DenseNet: robust iris segmentation using densely connected fully convolutional networks in the images by visible light and near-infrared light camera sensors. Sensors **18**(5), 1501 (2018)
6. Badrinarayanan, V., Kendall, A., Cipolla, R.: Segnet: A deep convolutional encoder-decoder architecture for image segmentation. IEEE Trans. Pattern Anal. Mach. Intell. **39**(12), 2481–2495 (2017)
7. Bazrafkan, S., Thavalengal, S., Corcoran, P.: An end to end deep neural network for iris segmentation in unconstrained scenarios. Neural Netw. **106**, 79–95 (2018)
8. Bowyer, K.W., Flynn, P.J.: The ND-IRIS-0405 iris image dataset. CoRR abs/1606.04853 (2009)
9. Daugman, J.: How iris recognition works. In: The Essential Guide to Image Processing, pp. 715–739. Elsevier (2009)
10. Duda, R.O., Hart, P.E.: Use of the Hough transformation to detect lines and curves in pictures. Commun. ACM **15**(1), 11–15 (1972)
11. Freund, Y., Schapire, R.E.: A decision-theoretic generalization of on-line learning and an application to boosting. J. Comput. Syst. Sci. **55**(1), 119–139 (1997)
12. Girshick, R.: Fast R-CNN. In: Proceedings of the IEEE International Conference on Computer Vision, pp. 1440–1448 (2015)
13. Girshick, R., Donahue, J., Darrell, T., Malik, J.: Rich feature hierarchies for accurate object detection and semantic segmentation. In: Proceedings of the IEEE Conference on Computer Vision and Pattern Recognition, pp. 580–587 (2014)
14. He, K., Gkioxari, G., Dollár, P., Girshick, R.: Mask R-CNN. In: 2017 IEEE International Conference on Computer Vision (ICCV), pp. 2980–2988. IEEE (2017)
15. He, K., Zhang, X., Ren, S., Sun, J.: Deep residual learning for image recognition. In: Proceedings of the IEEE Conference on Computer Vision and Pattern Recognition, pp. 770–778 (2016)

16. Hofbauer, H., Alonso-Fernandez, F., Wild, P., Bigun, J., Uhl, A.: A ground truth for iris segmentation. In: 2014 22nd International Conference on Pattern Recognition (ICPR), pp. 527–532. IEEE (2014)
17. Hough, P.V.: Method and means for recognizing complex patterns. US Patent 3,069,654, 18 December 1962
18. Illingworth, J., Kittler, J.: A survey of the Hough transform. Comput. Vis. Graph. Image Process. **44**(1), 87–116 (1988)
19. Jalilian, E., Uhl, A.: Iris segmentation using fully convolutional encoder–decoder networks. In: Bhanu, B., Kumar, A. (eds.) Deep Learning for Biometrics. ACVPR, pp. 133–155. Springer, Cham (2017). https://doi.org/10.1007/978-3-319-61657-5_6
20. Jalilian, E., Uhl, A., Kwitt, R.: Domain adaptation for CNN based irissegmentation. In: BIOSIG (2017)
21. Jeong, D.S., et al.: A new iris segmentation method for non-ideal iris images. Image Vis. Comput. **28**(2), 254–260 (2010)
22. Kass, M., Witkin, A., Terzopoulos, D.: Snakes: active contour models. Int. J. Comput. Vis. **1**(4), 321–331 (1988)
23. Kumar, A., Passi, A.: Comparison and combination of iris matchers for reliable personal authentication. Pattern Recogn. **43**(3), 1016–1026 (2010)
24. Lin, T.Y., Dollár, P., Girshick, R., He, K., Hariharan, B., Belongie, S.: Feature pyramid networks for object detection. In: CVPR, vol. 1, p. 4 (2017)
25. Lin, T.-Y., et al.: Microsoft COCO: common objects in context. In: Fleet, D., Pajdla, T., Schiele, B., Tuytelaars, T. (eds.) ECCV 2014. LNCS, vol. 8693, pp. 740–755. Springer, Cham (2014). https://doi.org/10.1007/978-3-319-10602-1_48
26. Liu, N., Li, H., Zhang, M., Liu, J., Sun, Z., Tan, T.: Accurate iris segmentation in non-cooperative environments using fully convolutional networks. In: 2016 International Conference on Biometrics (ICB), pp. 1–8. IEEE (2016)
27. Proenca, H., Filipe, S., Santos, R., Oliveira, J., Alexandre, L.: The UBIRIS.v2: a database of visible wavelength images captured on-the-move and at-a-distance. IEEE Trans. PAMI **32**(8), 1529–1535 (2010). https://doi.org/10.1109/TPAMI.2009.66
28. Proenca, H.: Iris recognition: on the segmentation of degraded images acquired in the visible wavelength. IEEE Trans. Pattern Anal. Mach. Intell. **32**(8), 1502–1516 (2010)
29. Proença, H., Alexandre, L.A.: The NICE. I: noisy iris challenge evaluation-part I. In: 2007 First IEEE International Conference on Biometrics: Theory, Applications, and Systems, pp. 1–4. IEEE September 2007
30. Radman, A., Zainal, N., Suandi, S.A.: Automated segmentation of iris images acquired in an unconstrained environment using HOG-SVM and GrowCut. Digit. Signal Process. **64**, 60–70 (2017)
31. Ren, S., He, K., Girshick, R., Sun, J.: Faster R-CNN: towards real-time object detection with region proposal networks. In: Advances in Neural Information Processing Systems, pp. 91–99 (2015)
32. Tan, C.W., Kumar, A.: Unified framework for automated iris segmentation using distantly acquired face images. IEEE Trans. Image Process. **21**(9), 4068–4079 (2012)
33. Tan, C.W., Kumar, A.: Towards online iris and periocular recognition under relaxed imaging constraints. IEEE Trans. Image Process. **22**(10), 3751–3765 (2013)
34. Tan, T., Sun, Z.: Casia iris v4 interval. http://biometrics.idealtest.org/
35. Vezhnevets, V., Konouchine, V.: GrowCut: interactive multi-label ND image segmentation by cellular automata. In: Proceedings of Graphicon, vol. 1, no. 4, pp. 150–156. June 2005

36. waleedka: Mask R-CNN (2017). https://github.com/matterport/Mask_RCNN
37. Wildes, R.P.: Iris recognition: an emerging biometric technology. Proc. IEEE **85**(9), 1348–1363 (1997)
38. Zhao, Z., Kumar, A.: An accurate iris segmentation framework under relaxed imaging constraints using total variation model. In: 2015 IEEE International Conference on Computer Vision (ICCV), pp. 3828–3836. IEEE (2015)

Simultaneous Multi-view Relative Pose Estimation and 3D Reconstruction from Planar Regions

Robert Frohlich[1] and Zoltan Kato[1,2(✉)]

[1] Institute of Informatics, University of Szeged, Arpad ter 2, Szeged, Hungary
{frohlich,kato}@inf.u-szeged.hu
[2] Department of Mathematics and Informatics, J. Selye University,
Komarno, Slovakia

Abstract. In this paper, we propose a novel solution for multi-view reconstruction, relative pose and homography estimation using planar regions. The proposed method doesn't require point matches, it directly uses a pair of planar image regions and simultaneously reconstructs the normal and distance of the corresponding 3D planar surface patch, the relative pose of the cameras as well as the aligning homography between the image regions. When more than two cameras are available, then a special region-based bundle adjustment is proposed, which provides robust estimates in a multi-view camera system by constructing and solving a non-linear system of equations. The method is quantitatively evaluated on a large synthetic dataset as well as on the KITTI vision benchmark dataset.

Keywords: 3D reconstruction · Pose estimation · Planar regions

1 Introduction

Multi-view 3D reconstruction has an important role in image-based urban HDR mapping and scene reconstruction [1]. New industrial applications are gaining ground in the domain of street level mapping [2], maintenance, autonomous navigation and self localization [3]. A key component in such applications is the simultaneous and efficient solution of 3D reconstruction and pose estimation. Particularly the planar reconstruction of objects like facades, tables, traffic signs is an important task in many applications. Numerous methods already

---

This work was partially supported by the NKFI-6 fund through project K120366; "Integrated program for training new generation of scientists in the fields of computer science", EFOP-3.6.3-VEKOP-16-2017-0002; the Ministry of Human Capacities, Hungary through grant 20391-3/2018/FEKUSTRAT; the Research & Development Operational Programme for the project "Modernization and Improvement of Technical Infrastructure for Research and Development of J. Selye University in the Fields of Nanotechnology and Intelligent Space", ITMS 26210120042, co-funded by the European Regional Development Fund. The authors would like to thank Levente Hajder for the Matlab implementation of the factorization method from [20].

exist for the extraction of *e.g.* traffic signs using CNN [4] and recognition using Deep Learning [5] or facade elements extraction using RNN and MRF [6]. However feature point matching on these surfaces is hard, thus classical reconstruction approaches based on sparse point correspondences [7] will struggle. In contrast our method only relies on the already extracted planar shapes to directly reconstruct (without further processing) the plane parameters that most mapping applications need. Recently, region-based methods have been gaining more attention [8,9], in particular affine invariant detectors [10]. Patch-based scene representation is proved to be efficient [11] and consistent with region-based correspondence-search methods [12].

The importance of piecewise planar object representation in 3D stereo has been recognized by many researchers. Habbecke and Kobbelt used a small plane, called 'disk', for surface reconstruction [13,14]. They proved that the normal is a linear function of the camera matrix and homography. Furukawa proposed using a small patch for better correspondence [11]. The surface is then grown with the expansion of the patches. The piecewise planar stereo method of Sinha *et al.* [15] uses shape from motion to generate an initial point cloud, then a best fitting plane is estimated, and finally an energy optimization problem is solved by graph cut for plane reconstruction. Combining the work by Furukawa and Sinha [11,15], Kowdle *et al.* introduced learning and active user interaction for large planar objects [16]. Hoang *et al.* also started from a point cloud [17] which was subsequently used for creating a visibility consistent mesh. In our approach, planes are directly reconstructed from image region(s) rather than a point cloud. Fraundorfer *et al.* [18] used MSER regions to establish corresponding regions pairs. Then a homography is calculated using SIFT detector inside the regions. Planar regions are then grown until the reprojection error is small. Zhou *et al.* assumed the whole image is a planar object, and proposed a short sequence SFM framework called TRASAC [19]. The homography is calculated using optical flow.

Although the role of planar regions in 3D reconstruction has been noticed by many researchers, the final reconstruction is still obtained via triangulation for most State-of-the-Art methods. Planar objects are only used for better correspondences or camera calibration. However, it is well known that a planar homography between a pair of planar image regions contains information about the camera relative pose as well as the 3D plane parameters, thus plane reconstruction is possible from such a homography [8,9,20–22]. Homography estimation is essential in many applications including pose estimation [23], tracking [24,25], structure from motion [26] as well as recent robotics applications with focus on navigation [27]. In [26], a correspondence-less algorithm is proposed to recover relative camera motion. Although matching is avoided, SIFT features are still needed because camera motion is computed by integrating over all feature pairs that satisfy the epipolar constraint.

In this paper, we will develop a direct method to simultaneously reconstruct whole planar patches and estimate camera relative poses as well as homographies acting between planar region pairs. The proposed homography estimation algorithm, inspired by [28], works directly on segmented planar patches. As a consequence, our method does not need point correspondences. In fact, we do not use any photometric information at all, hence our method can be used even for multimodal sensors. Since segmentation is required anyway in many real-life image analysis tasks, such regions may be available or straightforward to detect. In our experiments, we have used simple interactive segmentations but automatic detection of *e.g.* windows (which are quite common planar regions in urban scenes) is also possible [29]. We reformulate homography estimation as a shape alignment problem, where homography is directly represented in terms of the camera relative pose and the 3D plane parameters, which can be efficiently solved in a similar way as in [28]. The main advantage of the proposed method is the use of regions instead of point correspondence and a generic problem formulation which allows to treat several planes and multi-view camera systems in the same framework. The method has been quantitatively evaluated on a large synthetic dataset and proved to be robust and efficient.

2 Methodology

Given a calibrated camera $\mathbf{P}$ and a 3D scene plane π in the world coordinate frame, the projection of the plane is a 2D region $\mathcal{D}$ in the image plane. A perspective camera matrix $\mathbf{P} = \mathbf{K}[\mathbf{R}|\mathbf{t}]$ consists of the internal calibration matrix $\mathbf{K}$ and the camera pose $[\mathbf{R}|\mathbf{t}]$ w.r.t. the world coordinate frame. A homogeneous 3D point $\mathbf{X}$ is mapped by $\mathbf{P}$ into a homogeneous 2D image point $\mathbf{x}'$ as [21]

$$\mathbf{x}' \cong \mathbf{P}\mathbf{X} = \mathbf{K}[\mathbf{R}|\mathbf{t}]\mathbf{X}, \qquad (1)$$

where '$\cong$' denotes the equivalence of homogeneous coordinates, *i.e.* equality up to a non-zero scale factor. Since we assume a calibrated camera, we can multiply both sides of (1) by $\mathbf{K}^{-1}$ and work with the equivalent normalized image

$$\mathbf{x} = \mathbf{K}^{-1}\mathbf{x}' \cong \mathbf{K}^{-1}\mathbf{P}\mathbf{X} = [\mathbf{R}|\mathbf{t}]\mathbf{X}. \qquad (2)$$

Starting from the above equation, let us formulate the relation between a given scene plane π and its images $\mathcal{D}^0$ and $\mathcal{D}^1$ in two normalized cameras (see Fig. 1). Assuming that the first camera coordinate system $\mathcal{C}_0$ is the reference frame, let us represent π by its unit normal $\mathbf{n} = (n_1, n_2, n_3)^\top$ and distance d to the origin. Furthermore, the relative pose of the second camera frame $\mathcal{C}_1$ is a 3D rigid body transformation $(\mathbf{R}^1, \mathbf{t}^1) : \mathcal{C}_0 \to \mathcal{C}_1$ composed of a rotation $\mathbf{R}^1$ and translation $\mathbf{t}^1$, acting between the camera frames $\mathcal{C}_0$ and $\mathcal{C}_1$. Thus the image in the first and second camera of any homogeneous 3D point $\mathbf{X}$ of the reference frame is given by

$$\mathbf{x}_{\mathcal{C}_0} \cong [\mathbf{I}|\mathbf{0}]\mathbf{X} \quad \text{and} \quad \mathbf{x}_{\mathcal{C}_1} \cong [\mathbf{R}^1|\mathbf{t}^1]\mathbf{X}. \qquad (3)$$

The mapping of 3D plane points $\mathbf{X}_\pi \in \pi$ into the cameras $\mathcal{C}_i, i = 0, 1$ is governed by the same equations, giving rise to a planar homography $\mathbf{H}_\pi^1 : \mathcal{D}^0 \to \mathcal{D}^1$ induced by $\pi = (\mathbf{n}, d)$ between the image regions $\mathcal{D}^0$ and $\mathcal{D}^1$. $\mathbf{H}_\pi^1$ is bijective (unless π is going through the camera center, in which case π is invisible), composed up to a scale factor as

$$\mathbf{H}_\pi^1 \propto \mathbf{R}^1 + \frac{1}{d}\mathbf{t}^1 \mathbf{n}^\top \qquad (4)$$

Thus for any point $\mathbf{X}_\pi \in \pi$, we have the following relation between the corresponding image points $\mathbf{x}_{\mathcal{C}_0}$ and $\mathbf{x}_{\mathcal{C}_1}$:

$$\mathbf{x}_{\mathcal{C}_1} \cong \mathbf{H}_\pi^1 \mathbf{x}_{\mathcal{C}_0} \cong (\mathbf{R}^1 + \frac{1}{d}\mathbf{t}^1 \mathbf{n}^\top)\mathbf{x}_{\mathcal{C}_0} \quad (5)$$

The classical solution is to find at least 4 such point matches and solve for $\mathbf{H}_\pi^1$, then factorize $\mathbf{R}^1$, $\mathbf{t}^1$, and $\mathbf{n}$ from $\mathbf{H}_\pi^1$ (d cannot be recovered due to the free scaling factor) [20]. However, the extraction of point correspondences in urban environment can be challenging due to repetitive structures and textureless facades, while planar regions are easier to segment and matching between frames is not affected by repetitive structures if limited camera movement is assumed. Therefore our solution is inspired by the 2D shape registration approach of Domokos et al. [28], where the alignment of non-linear shape deformations are recovered via the solution of a special system of equations without established point correspondences. In particular, we will show that by identifying a pair of planar regions in two camera images, the relative pose as well as the 3D plane parameters can be solved up to scale without establishing any further correspondences between the regions. Of course, this is just the necessary minimal configuration. The more such regions are available, a more stable solution is obtained. Furthermore, when more cameras are available, then a special region-based bundle adjustment can be constructed within the same algebraic framework.

Since point correspondences are not available, (5) cannot be used directly. However, individual point matches can be integrated out [28] yielding the following integral equation:

$$\int_{\mathcal{D}^1} \mathbf{x}_{\mathcal{C}_1} \, d\mathbf{x}_{\mathcal{C}_1} = \int_{\mathcal{D}^0} \mathbf{H}_\pi^1 \mathbf{x}_{\mathcal{C}_0} |\mathbf{J}_{\mathbf{H}_\pi^1}(\mathbf{x}_{\mathcal{C}_0})| \, d\mathbf{x}_{\mathcal{C}_0}, \quad (6)$$

where the integral transformation $\mathbf{x}_{\mathcal{C}_1} = \mathbf{H}_\pi^1 \mathbf{x}_{\mathcal{C}_0}$, $d\mathbf{x}_{\mathcal{C}_1} = |\mathbf{J}_{\mathbf{H}_\pi^1}(\mathbf{x}_{\mathcal{C}_0})| \, d\mathbf{x}_{\mathcal{C}_0}$ has been applied. Since $\mathbf{H}_\pi^1$ is a 3×3 homogeneous matrix with only 8 degree of freedom, we will set its last element to 1 as in [28]. Note that the above equality is true for inhomogeneous point coordinates $\mathbf{x}_{\mathcal{C}_i}$, which are obtained by projective division. The Jacobian determinant $|\mathbf{J}_{\mathbf{H}_\pi^1}| : \mathbb{R}^2 \to \mathbb{R}$ gives the measure of the transformation at each point [28].

The above equation corresponds to a system of 2 equations only, which is clearly not sufficient to solve for all parameters. It has been previously shown in [28] that applying an appropriate set of functions on both sides of an equality $a = b$ it remains valid for $f(a) = f(b)$, thus enabling us to construct new equations. Indeed, (5) remains valid when a function $\omega : \mathbb{R}^2 \to \mathbb{R}$ is acting on both sides of the equation, yielding the integral equation

$$\int_{\mathcal{D}^1} \omega(\mathbf{x}_{\mathcal{C}_1}) \, d\mathbf{x}_{\mathcal{C}_1} = \int_{\mathcal{D}^0} \omega(\mathbf{H}_\pi^1 \mathbf{x}_{\mathcal{C}_0}) |\mathbf{J}_{\mathbf{H}_\pi^1}(\mathbf{x}_{\mathcal{C}_0})| \, d\mathbf{x}_{\mathcal{C}_0}. \quad (7)$$

Adopting a set of nonlinear functions $\{\omega_i\}_{i=1}^\ell$, each ω_i generates a new equation yielding a system of ℓ independent equations. Hence we are able to generate sufficiently many equations. Although arbitrary ω_i functions could be used, power functions are computationally favorable [28]. In our experiments, we adopted the following functions up to power o:

$$\omega_i(\mathbf{x}) = x_1^{m_i} x_2^{n_i}, \text{ with } 0 \leq m_i, n_i \leq o \qquad (8)$$

The unknown relative pose $(\mathbf{R}^1, \mathbf{t}^1)$ and 3D plane parameters $(\mathbf{n}, d)$ are then simply obtained as the solution of the nonlinear system of Eq. (7). $\mathbf{H}_\pi^1$ has 8 degree of freedom (DoF), because $\mathbf{n}$ is a unit vector with 2 DoF and $\mathbf{t}/d$ can only be obtained up to scale, so it has only 3 DoF. Thus we need 8 equations which can be constructed using ω_i functions from (8) with $0 \leq m_i, n_i \leq 2$ and $m_i + n_i \leq 3$. In practice, however, an overdetermined system is constructed, which is then solved in the *least squares sense* by minimizing the algebraic error via a standard *Levenberg-Marquardt* algorithm.

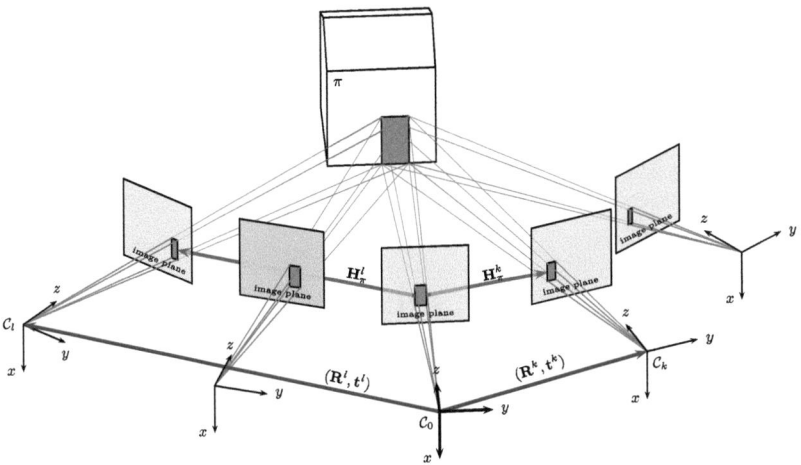

Fig. 1. Projection of a 3D plane π in a multi-view camera system.

2.1 Reconstruction of Multiple Regions

Let us now investigate the case, when a pair of cameras is observing multiple 3D scene planes. Each plane π_i generates a homography $\mathbf{H}_{\pi_i}^1$ between the corresponding image regions $\mathcal{D}_i^0$ and $\mathcal{D}_i^1$. While (5) and (7) remain valid for each of these homographies, note that the relative pose $(\mathbf{R}^1, \mathbf{t}^1)$ of the cameras is the same for all $\mathbf{H}_{\pi_i}^1$, they only differ in the 3D plane parameters $(\mathbf{n}_i, d_i)$. Hence for all $\{\pi_i\}_{i=1}^N$, we have

$$\mathbf{x}_{\mathcal{C}_1} \cong \mathbf{H}_{\pi_i}^1 \mathbf{x}_{\mathcal{C}_0} \cong (\mathbf{R}^1 + \frac{1}{d_i}\mathbf{t}^1 \mathbf{n}_i^\top)\mathbf{x}_{\mathcal{C}_0}, \text{ with } \mathbf{x}_{\mathcal{C}_0} \in \mathcal{D}_i^0 \text{ and } \mathbf{x}_{\mathcal{C}_1} \in \mathcal{D}_i^1 \qquad (9)$$

and (7) becomes a system of N equations in terms of the common camera pose $(\mathbf{R}^1, \mathbf{t}^1)$ and the parameters $(\mathbf{n}_i, d_i)$ of the 3D planes $\{\pi_i\}_{i=1}^N$:

$$\int_{\mathcal{D}_i^1} \omega(\mathbf{x}_{\mathcal{C}_1}) \, d\mathbf{x}_{\mathcal{C}_1} = \int_{\mathcal{D}_i^0} \omega(\mathbf{H}_{\pi_i}^1 \mathbf{x}_{\mathcal{C}_0})|\mathbf{J}_{\mathbf{H}_{\pi_i}^1}(\mathbf{x}_{\mathcal{C}_0})| \, d\mathbf{x}_{\mathcal{C}_0}, \quad 1 \leq i \leq N \qquad (10)$$

For a given ω function, the above equations provide N constraints on the relative pose parameters, but only 1 constraint for each plane π_i, having a total of N equations. Note also, that we have one free scaling factor for the whole system in (10), because a relative d_i parameter for the planes need to be determined, only one of them can be set freely. Therefore the minimal number of equations needed to solve for 2 cameras and $N \geq 1$ planes is $E = 6 + 3N - 1$. In terms of the necessary powers of ω_i functions in (8), o should satisfy $1 + o(o+2) \geq E$.

2.2 Multi-view Reconstruction

When multiple cameras are observing the scene planes, then we can construct a system of equations which contains multiple constraints not only for the camera relative poses but also for each 3D plane. This way, we obtain a region-based bundle adjustment, where all camera pose parameters and all 3D plane parameters are simultaneously solved. Let us have a closer look at these equations. First of all, a reference camera frame $\mathcal{C}_0$ is chosen, which provides the reference coordinate system of the whole camera system: each camera's relative pose is determined w.r.t. $\mathcal{C}_0$ and all planes are reconstructed within $\mathcal{C}_0$. Assuming that all scene planes $\{\pi_i\}_{i=1}^{N}$ are visible in every camera $\{\mathcal{C}_k\}_{k=0}^{M-1}$, each plane π_i generates a homography $\mathbf{H}_{\pi_i}^{k}$ between the corresponding image regions in the reference camera $\mathcal{D}_i^0$ and the kth camera $\mathcal{D}_i^k$:

$$\forall 1 \leq k \leq M-1: \quad \mathbf{x}_{\mathcal{C}_k} \cong \mathbf{H}_{\pi_i}^{k} \mathbf{x}_{\mathcal{C}_0} \cong (\mathbf{R}^k + \frac{1}{d_i}\mathbf{t}^k \mathbf{n}_i^\top) \mathbf{x}_{\mathcal{C}_0}. \quad (11)$$

Hence each camera provides a new constraint on the scene plane parameters $(\mathbf{n}_i, d_i)$, yielding a total of $M-1$ constraints for reconstructing π_i. If a particular plane is not visible in all other cameras, then the number of these constraints is reduced. As long as a particular plane π_i is visible in the reference camera and at least one other camera k, then it is possible to reconstruct it using the equations constructed from the above homography, just like in the minimal case discussed in Sect. 2.

A particular camera pair $(\mathcal{C}_0, \mathcal{C}_k)$ provides N equations in terms of the common camera pose $(\mathbf{R}^k, \mathbf{t}^k)$ and the parameters $(\mathbf{n}_i, d_i)$ of the 3D planes $\{\pi_i\}_{i=1}^{N}$, yielding a system of N equations similar to (7). Therefore we get

$$\int_{\mathcal{D}_i^k} \omega(\mathbf{x}_{\mathcal{C}_k}) \, d\mathbf{x}_{\mathcal{C}_k} = \int_{\mathcal{D}_i^0} \omega(\mathbf{H}_{\pi_i}^{k} \mathbf{x}_{\mathcal{C}_0}) |\mathbf{J}_{\mathbf{H}_{\pi_i}^{k}}(\mathbf{x}_{\mathcal{C}_0})| \, d\mathbf{x}_{\mathcal{C}_0},$$
$$1 \leq i \leq N \text{ and } 1 \leq k \leq M-1 \quad (12)$$

For a given ω function, the above equations provide N constraints on each relative pose $(\mathbf{R}^k, \mathbf{t}^k)$, and $M-1$ constraints for each plane π_i, having a total of $N(M-1)$ equations. The minimal number of equations needed to solve for $M \geq 2$ cameras and $N \geq 1$ planes is $E = 6(M-1) + 3N - 1$. In terms of the necessary powers of ω_i functions in (8), o should satisfy $1 + o(o+2) \geq E$.

Algorithm 1. The proposed multi-view algorithm.

Input: $M \geq 3$ 2D image masks with $N \geq 1$ corresponding planar regions
Output: Relative pose of the cameras w.r.t. $\mathcal{C}_0$, reconstruction $(\mathbf{n}_i, d_i)$ of the N planes
1: **Pairwise step:** For each $M - 1$ neighboring camera pair:
2: Initialize pose parameters with $[\mathbf{I}|\mathbf{0}]$ and plane parameters with $n = (0, 0, -1)^T$, $d = -7$
3: Construct $\mathbf{H}_\pi$ using (9) and divide it by its last element
4: Construct and solve the system of equations of (10)
5: **Multi-view step:** Choose reference camera $\mathcal{C}_0$
6: Write up relative poses w.r.t. $\mathcal{C}_0$ as (14) and transform reconstruction $(\mathbf{n}_i, d_i)$ parameters into $\mathcal{C}_0$ reference frame using (13)
7: Initialize reconstruction based on the filtered camera pairs
8: Write up $\mathbf{H}_{\pi_i}^k$ (devided by its last element) for each camera pair $(\mathcal{C}_0, \mathcal{C}_k)$ using (11)
9: Construct and solve the system of equations of (12) for M cameras and N planes simultaneously

2.3 Algorithmic Solution

The algorithmic summary of the proposed method for an arbitrary ($M \geq 3$) multi-view camera system is presented in Algorithm 1. The first part of the algorithm is to solve for each neighboring camera pair, that will provide the initial parameters for the second part. This step does not require any specific initialization of the parameters, except that $d_i = 0$ should be avoided. Since plane distance is expressed as the distance from the origin along the surface normal vectors direction, it is a negative number, it can be initialized with an arbitrary value, in our tests we used $d_i = -7$. Since plane normal has only 2 DoF the third parameter is always calculated with the criteria that the normal should point towards the camera. Since each solution provides a reconstruction in one of the cameras, these have to be transformed into the common reference frame of $\mathcal{C}_0$, that is practically chosen the middle camera. Plane parameters $(\mathbf{n}_i^0, d_i^0)$ are obtained from $(\mathbf{n}_i^k, d_i^k)$ as

$$\mathbf{n}_i^0 = \mathbf{R}^{kT} \mathbf{n}_i^k \quad \text{and} \quad d_i^0 = d_i^k - (\mathbf{n}_i^k)^T \mathbf{t}^k \quad (13)$$

Relative poses also have to be expressed in the $\mathcal{C}_0$ reference frame. For any camera $\mathcal{C}_l$ that has a relative pose $(\mathbf{R}^{k,l}, \mathbf{t}^{k,l})$ defined to its neighbor C_k, whose relative pose $(\mathbf{R}^{0,k}, \mathbf{t}^{0,k})$ w.r.t. $\mathcal{C}_0$ is already known, then the relative pose of C_l in the reference frame will be

$$(\mathbf{R}^{0,l}|\mathbf{t}^{0,l}) = (\mathbf{R}^{k,l}|\mathbf{t}^{k,l})(\mathbf{R}^{0,k}|\mathbf{t}^{0,k}), \quad (14)$$

where $(\mathbf{R}|\mathbf{t})$ denote the homogeneous 4×4 matrix constructed from $\mathbf{R}$ and $\mathbf{t}$.

Since multiple camera pairs will provide alternative initializations for the reconstruction, and some pairs might be solved less precisely than others, we have to filter the camera pairs. Comparing the algebraic error of the pairwise reconstructions we filter out the pair with the highest error if it's above the experimentally determined threshold of $5e^{-9}$, and if it's bigger than 3 times the median errors of the camera pairs. The reconstruction parameters of the unfiltered pairs are simply averaged out and together with the relative poses expressed w.r.t. $\mathcal{C}_0$ (14) provide the input for the multi-view step.

For the numerical implementation of the equations we also included the alternative forms of the equation using the inverse transformation and the reverse integral transformation as described in [28]. These mathematically redundant forms don't provide extra constraints for the parameters, but increase the numerical stability of the method.

3 Evaluation on Synthetic Data

For the quantitative evaluation of the proposed approach, a benchmark dataset is generated with a greatly simplified real world urban environment in mind. The synthetic data is not metric, but we can interpret it as having the planar shapes in the 3D scene represent $1\,\text{m} \times 1\,\text{m}$ regions, which scales everything into a metric interpretation for easier understanding. A scene was created by placing 3 different planar shapes in 3D space having $\pm 20°$ relative rotation around the vertical or horizontal axis and translated by 1..2 m in the horizontal and vertical direction, while 1..3 m in depth. The scene is then captured by a 1Mpx virtual camera placed at the initial distance of 4 m from the middle plane, then moved into 5 different random positions, in such a way that the resulting positions form a movement trajectory (see Fig. 1). Between each frame there is a random relative movement of up to 0.5 m and a rotation of $\pm 5°$ around the vertical axis, and $\pm 2°$ around the other two axes. The binary images captured by the camera are the input parameters of our algorithm, having the correspondence between the regions provided. Practically there is no limitation on the size difference of the projections. The results were quantitatively evaluated in the pose and

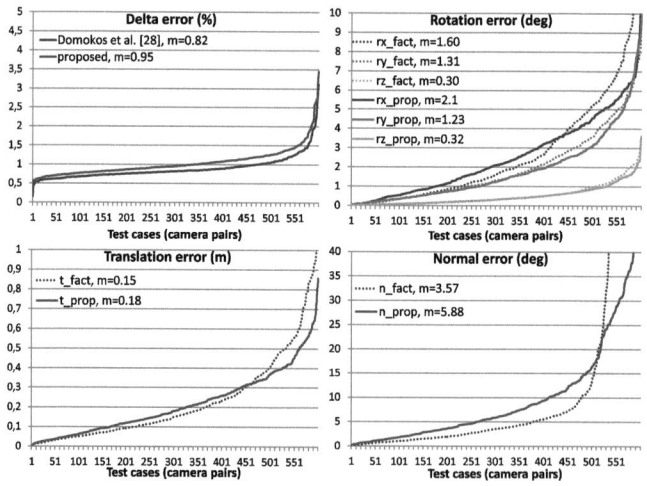

Fig. 2. Comparison to homography estimation method of [28] in terms of δ error of the projections, and relative camera pose and plane parameters (factorized from **H** by [28], provided directly by proposed). (m stands for median).

reconstruction parameters, as well as in terms of the aligning homography, which is characterized by the percentage of the non-overlapping areas between the aligned regions (denoted here as δ error).

3.1 Minimal Case

The minimal case consists of one plane seen by two cameras, where we have to estimate a single homography aligning the planar image regions. First of all, we compared our method to the homography estimation method of [28] that solves a similar system of equations but it is parameterized in terms of 8 elements of $\mathbf{H}_\pi^1$, while our method uses the $\mathbf{R}^1$, $\mathbf{t}^1$, $\mathbf{n}$, d parameterization. In Fig. 2, the first plot shows that despite having a different parameterization, the stability of the proposed method remains similar. All synthetic plots are sorted based on the error values. We have to highlight here that while the first method only estimates a homography matrix with 8 DoF, the proposed method estimates the parameters of the relative pose $\mathbf{R}^1$, $\mathbf{t}^1$, the 3D plane reconstruction $\mathbf{n}$, d, as well as the composed aligning homography $\mathbf{H}_\pi^1$ simultaneously, up to a scale factor.

Of course, we can decompose the homography matrix computed by the method of [28] in terms of $(\mathbf{R}, \mathbf{t})$ and $(\mathbf{n}, d)$ using the standard decomposition of [20] which uses the singular value decomposition (SVD) of the homography. In Fig. 2, we compare these decomposed parameters with our results. We can observe that while the pose parameters are obtained with similar precision, the plane reconstruction has slightly higher error in median, but also shows increased robustness in the last part of the plots. These results match well with the slightly higher δ errors shown on the first plot in Fig. 2. We should highlight here, that while this was a fair comparison to the baseline method [28], our method's advantage is the ability to handle multiple regions and camera images, since it will provide an optimized solution for the camera group with a common scale, instead of having independent solutions for each region and camera pair.

3.2 Multi-view Reconstruction

As it was shown in Sect. 2, multiple cameras theoretically provide more constraints for the reconstruction, while more planes on the pose parameters. To confirm this, we evaluated the proposed method with 5 cameras in two different setups: First solving a pairwise reconstruction for each neighboring camera pair, then in the second setup solving for all 5 cameras, using the full algorithm as presented in Algorithm 1. In both cases, 3 planes were used and the results were compared to the synthetic reference values, that were also used to correctly scale the translation and plane distance parameters that are estimated only up to a scale factor. The relative pose parameters are evaluated as absolute errors in the rotation angles, and the difference in the total translation (see first row of Fig. 3). We can observe, that the relevant improvement of the multi-camera setup is not necessarily visible in the median error levels, but more so in the number of correct solutions. The number of camera pairs solved with a relative pose error lower than 0.5° in rotation and 5 cm in translation is increased from 75% to above 90%.

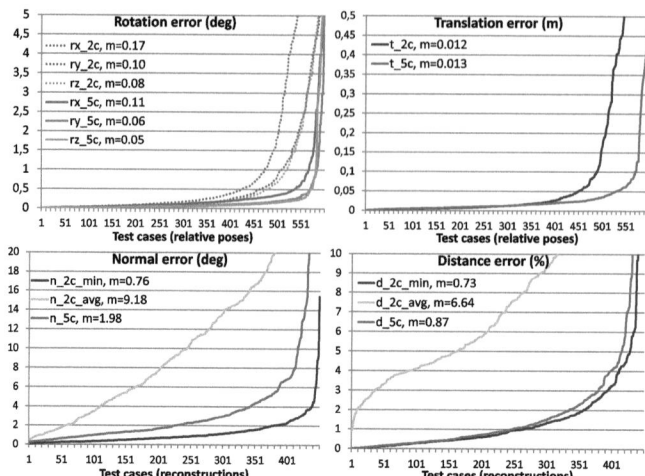

Fig. 3. Bundle adjustment refinement over 5 cameras compared to a pairwise solution, both with 3 regions (m stands for median).

Since the 4 camera pairs in each test case were reconstructed separately in the 2-camera pairwise setup, the reconstruction they provide will be 4 different ones for the same plane, thus in the second row of Fig. 3 we show both the minimum and average errors in $(\mathbf{n}, d)$ for the 2-camera setup. In contrast, the 5-camera setup provides one single reconstruction in the reference camera frame. We can see, that the bundle adjustment step greatly reduces the mean errors that the pairwise solution had, approaching to the minimal errors. Note that d is evaluated as the difference of the scaled result and the reference distance, expressed as a percentage of the ground truth.

Single Plane Reconstruction. An interesting scenario is a multi-view setup with only one plane available, therefore the method was evaluated for the $M = 5$ and $N = 1$ setup. Results were compared to those obtained on the full dataset using 3 planar regions in each test case, to evaluate the improvements given by the higher number of planes. As can be seen in the first row of Fig. 4, the rotation and translation parameters of the relative pose are greatly improved due to multiple different planes. In more than 90% of the cases, all rotation errors were well below 0.5° in the 3 region setup, while in the single region case the errors are below 1° in half of the test cases only. The translation parameters show the same improvement: from a median error of 8 cm reducing errors to below 5 cm in 88% of the cases.

The reconstruction error plots in the second row of Fig. 4 show the errors in the normal vector angle, and the plane distance. While in the first row on the horizontal axis, the number of camera pairs were depicted which (having a reference dataset of 150 test cases each with 5 consecutive frames of a scene with 3 regions) consists of a total of 600 relative poses; in case of the reconstruction parameters we only have to refer to the separate test cases since in each test case

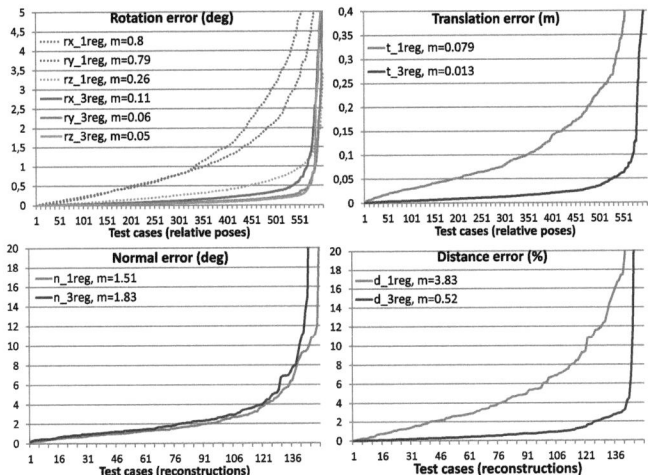

Fig. 4. 5 camera results with 1 region compared to 3 regions evaluated in terms of the pose errors (first row) and reconstruction parameters (second row), that were evaluated on the same regions for the 1 and 3 region test cases.

multiple cameras estimate one common reconstruction of the scene. According to the plots in Fig. 4, we can observe that the plane normal is less affected by the reduced number of planes, while the plane distance parameter is affected in a quantity comparable to the pose parameters, which is expected, since up to a point these parameters are able to compensate each other if not enough constraints are given. But using only two extra regions, the results can drastically improve: in 85% of the test cases, the distance of the plane is estimated with a relative error less then 2% instead of 10%.

3.3 Robustness Against Segmentation Errors

In order to evaluate the robustness of the proposed algorithm against the inevitable errors occuring in image segmentation, we simulated segmentation errors by randomly changing pixels around the contour of the regions by an amount of 2% and 5% of the size of the region. Herein, all tests were run in the $M = 5$ cameras and $N = 3$ planes setup.

The errors in the estimated relative pose on these specific datasets can be seen in the first row of Fig. 5, where first the rotation errors of all the relative poses are plotted, grouped by the axes, then the translation errors are shown next. All plots are sorted in a best to worst sense by each parameter separately, and the results are compared to the base dataset which uses perfect segmentations. In the second row of Fig. 5, the reconstruction errors are shown, that were estimated simultaneously with the relative pose by the proposed algorithm. Both plane normal and distance errors are evaluated in light of the segmentation errors.

Analyzing the pose and reconstruction parameters together, one can observe that the segmentation errors have a similar impact on all the parameters, but still the median rotation errors don't go over 0.5° except the rotation around the

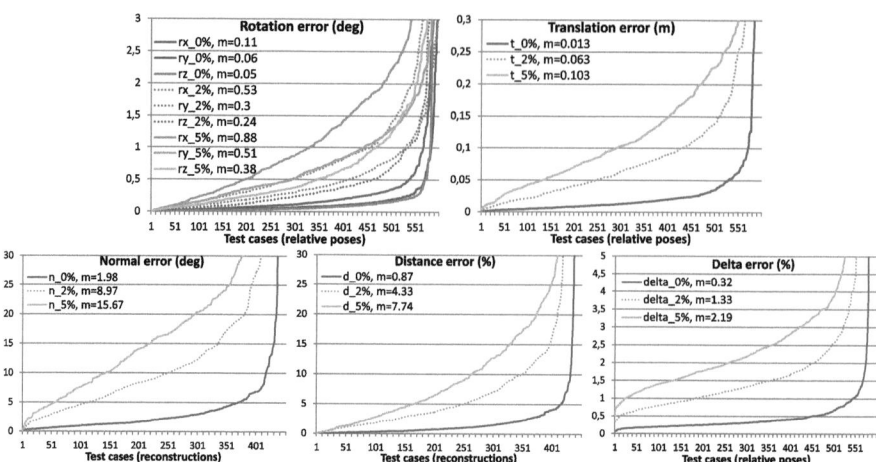

Fig. 5. Segmentation error test results in terms of pose and reconstruction parameter errors both in the case of perfect regions and regions with simulated segmentation errors of 2% and 5%. δ error measured on the perfect regions.

vertical X axis in the 5% segmentation error case. Based on the relative pose results, 5% segmentation error could be acceptable in many applications, where 10 cm translation errors are acceptable, but due to the reconstruction being more sensitive to these, we would say a segmentation error of less than 2% would be desirable in most applications. On the last plot in Fig. 5, the δ errors are shown. We can see that in about 66% of the cases, a δ error less than 3% is achieved even in the presence of segmentation error. Based on our previous experiences, in many applications a δ error of up to 5% is considered a correct solution.

4 Real Data Experiments

In the first real data test case, we present the results on a high resolution 2D-3D dataset, that contains ground truth pointcloud data, 4K resolution UAV video frames and also reference 3D position of special markers placed in scene, which enabled the calculation of reference camera poses with UPnP [30] for each frame used, resulting a forward projection error of the markers of only 1–2 cm median. In urban environments the automatic segmentation of planar structures, windows, doors, facades or boards could be solved with different methods [29]. In our tests the segmentation of the corresponding planar regions on each frame was performed in a semi-automatic way using region growing segmentation method available in commercial image editing programs, requiring only a few clicks of user intervention. The segmented 2 regions are marked with red in Fig. 6 on the first and last image frame. We used 5 frames of the video sequence, at 1–2 s distance from each other. The estimated parameters were compared to the ground truth values (plane parameters were calculated from the point cloud data). The relative camera pose rotations were estimated with a mean error of $0.72°$, $0.2°$, $0.59°$ around the X, Y, Z axes, the maximum rotation

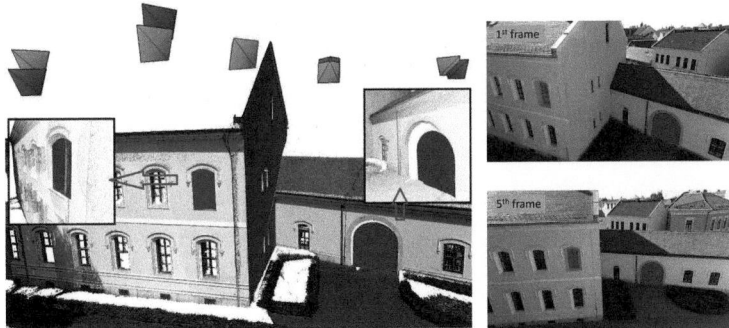

Fig. 6. Right: first and last image of the sequence, with the 2 segmented corresponding regions marked in red. Left: the reference camera positions (green), the estimated camera positions (red) and the reconstructed 3D planar regions are shown (also including a side view of both). (Color figure online)

errors being below 1°. The relative translation was evaluated as the difference of the reference value and the correctly scaled up estimated translation, that can be interpreted as a position displacement in the metric space. These errors are between 12 cm and 33 cm. The difference in the orientation of the plane normals was 2° and 2.95° respectively, while the error of the plane distance from the origin is 0.38 m and 0.77 m. For a different perspective over the plane distance parameter, we also calculated the distance from the camera to the center of the reference 3D region and the reconstructed 3D region, since this might be more useful in many applications. At camera distances of 14.1 m to 21.4 m these errors represent 3% and 7% differences, respectively. These results comply with the synthetic test results in Fig. 5, where we found that with higher segmentation error the plane distance error can go above 7%. Using all segmentable regions in the same sequence the mean pose errors reduced to 0.12°, 0.18°, 0.13° rotation and (2.7–16) cm translation; and the median reconstruction errors were 5° and 65 cm, thus we considered test cases with less regions are more interesting to show, since more regions obviously increase the stability of the algorithm.

Comparison on KITTI Dataset. To test the applicability of the proposed method to urban road-scene applications we used the KITTI [31] dataset. Having a camera attached to a car that is only capable of forward motion and turns is a more challenging problem for pose estimation and reconstruction. A region based plane reconstruction method can be applied in such an environment for example for the reconstruction of traffic signs as planar objects. Unfortunately in the KITTI dataset not all traffic signs are visible in the 3D pointclouds, due to their different height and the position and orientation of the Velodyne scanner, thus we selected all the traffic signs with available 3D data from the first 9 sequences resulting in 41 different test cases. In each test case the segmented traffic signs on 5 consecutive frames were extracted using the tool described in the previous section, while automatic segmentation of these objects is also a well researched topic with many solutions, *e.g.* [4] also provides the boundary of the signs.

	solved	inBB	norm.(deg)	obj_dist(m)	R(deg/m)	T(%)	time
COLMAP	28/41	11/28	11.07	**0.46**	**0.13**	**2.35**	46
Proposed	**41/41**	**34/41**	**8.63**	0.47	0.17	4.53	**15**

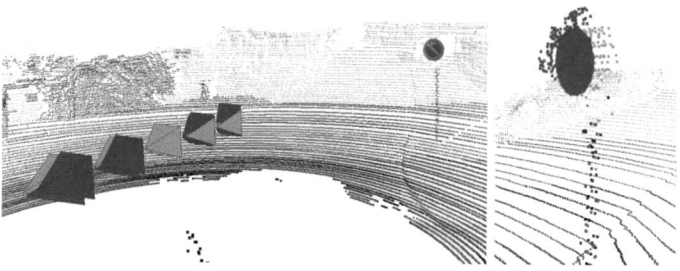

Fig. 7. Quantitative results of the proposed method and COLMAP [33,34] on the KITTI dataset, evaluated only on test cases where reconstruction was inside the reference bounding box. Camera poses (left) and a traffic sign reconstruction (right) shown in green (ground truth), red (proposed), and blue (COLMAP). (Color figure online)

The proposed method was tested both on the minimum number of 3 frames, and on 5 frames per test case (using only one small segmented region from each frame) where the latter showed slightly better reconstruction results, the individual relative poses showed similar median errors but more robustness for the 3 camera setup. This is caused by the traffic signs moving out of the frame too fast, thus the more frames we try to use, the segmentation of the regions becomes less precise and lower resolution. Nevertheless, 80% of the cases were solved with reconstruction errors below 20° in normal vector, and 1 m in the object centers distance with 5 frames. Evaluating our results in a similar way as the official KITTI Visual Odometry benchmark, but only on the above described test cases with traffic signs using 5 frames, we get a median translation error of 5.28% and rotation error of $0.2126(deg/m)$, that is comparable to the published benchmark results of State-of-the-Art methods (e.g. VISO2-M [32] is only better in rotation [T= 11.94%, R=$0.0234(deg/m)$], but it cannot reconstruct traffic signs).

A direct comparison with feature based multi-view reconstruction methods can only be performed using the full images as inputs instead of just the segmented traffic signs, since those typically wouldn't provide enough image features. For this we used the State-of-the-Art Structure from Motion and multi-view reconstruction library COLMAP [33,34] that was recently rated the best of the tested 15 reconstruction methods by [35]. We used the C++ implementation with CUDA and reconstructed each test case from the same 5 frames. The median errors of the estimated camera poses and the reconstructed plane parameters are given in Fig. 7. Note that COLMAP fails to find good initial image pairs in 13 cases, thus providing no solution at all, while less then half of the solved cases provided a correct reconstruction of the traffic sign that can be identified inside the 1 m bounding box of the reference. For a fair comparison we only evaluated the test cases where the traffic sign was reconstructed inside the bounding box. Not only the proposed algorithm runs faster with a native

Matlab implementation, but it solves all test cases and reconstructs inside the bounding box in 34 test cases. An example result of frame 220 of Sequence 03 is shown in Fig. 7.

5 Conclusions

In this paper, a simultaneous multi-view reconstruction, relative pose and homography estimation method has been proposed for perspective cameras, which works directly on segmented planar regions without the need for point matches. It constructs a system of non-linear equations, whose solution directly provides the relative poses of the cameras, the reconstruction of the 3D planes, as well as the aligning homographies between the image regions. It has been shown that with more than two cameras, a special region-based bundle adjustment provides robust results in a multi-view camera system. Quantitative evaluation on various synthetic tests confirm the performance and robustness of the method, while comparisons with recent methods on the KITTI dataset prove the State-of-the-Art performance of the approach.

References

1. Musialski, P., Wonka, P., Aliaga, D.G., Wimmer, M., van Gool, L., Purgathofer, W.: A survey of urban reconstruction. In: EUROGRAPHICS 2012 State of the Art Reports, Eurographics Association, pp. 1–28 (2012)
2. Micusik, B., Kosecka, J.: Piecewise planar city 3D modeling from street view panoramic sequences. In: Proceedings of International Conference on Computer Vision and Pattern Recognition, IEEE (2009)
3. Levinson, J., et al.: Towards fully autonomous driving: systems and algorithms. In: Proceedings of Intelligent Vehicles Symposium, IEEE (2011)
4. Lee, H.S., Kim, K.: Simultaneous traffic sign detection and boundary estimation using convolutional neural network. IEEE Trans. Intell. Transp. Syst. **19**, 1652–1663 (2018)
5. Arcos-García, Á., Álvarez-García, J.A., Soria-Morillo, L.M.: Deep neural network for traffic sign recognition systems: an analysis of spatial transformers and stochastic optimisation methods. Neural Networks **99**, 158–165 (2018)
6. Martinović, A., Mathias, M., Weissenberg, J., Van Gool, L.: A three-layered approach to facade parsing. In: Fitzgibbon, A., Lazebnik, S., Perona, P., Sato, Y., Schmid, C. (eds.) ECCV 2012. LNCS, vol. 7578, pp. 416–429. Springer, Heidelberg (2012). https://doi.org/10.1007/978-3-642-33786-4_31
7. Hartley, R.I., Zisserman, A.: Multiple View Geometry in Computer Vision, 2nd edn. Cambridge University Press, ISBN: 0521540518 (2004)
8. Molnar, J., Huang, R., Kato, Z.: 3D reconstruction of planar surface patches: a direct solution. In: Jawahar, C.V., Shan, S. (eds.) ACCV 2014. LNCS, vol. 9008, pp. 286–300. Springer, Cham (2015). https://doi.org/10.1007/978-3-319-16628-5_21
9. Tanács, A., Majdik, A., Hajder, L., Molnár, J., Sánta, Z., Kato, Z.: Collaborative mobile 3D reconstruction of urban scenes. In: Jawahar, C.V., Shan, S. (eds.) ACCV 2014. LNCS, vol. 9010, pp. 486–501. Springer, Cham (2015). https://doi.org/10.1007/978-3-319-16634-6_36
10. Mikolajczyk, K., et al.: A comparison of affine region detectors. Int. J. Comput. Vision **65**, 43–72 (2005)

11. Furukawa, Y., Ponce, J.: Accurate, dense, and robust multiview stereopsis. IEEE Trans. Pattern Anal. Mach. Intell. **32**, 1362–1376 (2010)
12. Tanács, A., Majdik, A., Molnár, J., Rai, A., Kato, Z.: Establishing correspondences between planar image patches. In: Proceedings of International Conference on Digital Image Computing: Techniques and Applications, Wollongong, Australia, pp. 1–7. IEEE (2014). Best Paper Award
13. Habbecke, M., Kobbelt, L.: Iterative multi-view plane fitting. In: VMV 2006 (2006)
14. Habbecke, M., Kobbelt, L.: A surface-growing approach to multi-view stereo reconstruction. In: IEEE Conference on Computer Vision and Pattern Recognition, CVPR 2007, pp. 1–8 (2007)
15. Sinha, S., Steedly, D., Szeliski, R.: Piecewise planar stereo for image-based rendering. In: IEEE International Conference on Computer Vision, pp. 1881–1888 (2009)
16. Kowdle, A., Chang, Y.J., Gallagher, A., Chen, T.: Active learning for piecewise planar 3D reconstruction. In: Proceedings of the 2011 IEEE Conference on Computer Vision and Pattern Recognition, CVPR 2011, pp. 929–936. IEEE Computer Society, Washington (2011)
17. Hiep, V.H., Keriven, R., Labatut, P., Pons, J.P.: Towards high-resolution large-scale multi-view stereo. In: IEEE Conference on Computer Vision and Pattern Recognition, CVPR 2009, pp. 1430–1437 (2009)
18. Fraundorfer, F., Schindler, K., Bischof, H.: Piecewise planar scene reconstruction from sparse correspondences. Image Vision Comput. **24**, 395–406 (2006)
19. Zhou, Z., Jin, H., Ma, Y.: Robust plane-based structure from motion. In: Proceedings of the 2012 IEEE Conference on Computer Vision and Pattern Recognition (CVPR), pp. 1482–1489. IEEE Computer Society, Washington (2012)
20. Faugeras, O., Lustman, F.: Motion and structure from motion in a piecewise planar environment. Technical Report RR-0856, INRIA, Sophia Antipolis, France (1988)
21. Hartley, R., Zisserman, A.: Multiple View Geometry in Computer Vision. Cambridge University Press, Cambridge (2004)
22. Frohlich, R., Tamás, L., Kato, Z.: Homography estimation between omnidirectional cameras without point correspondences. In: Buşoniu, L., Tamás, L. (eds.) Handling Uncertainty and Networked Structure in Robot Control. SSDC, vol. 42, pp. 129–151. Springer, Cham (2015). https://doi.org/10.1007/978-3-319-26327-4_6
23. Sturm, P.: Algorithms for plane-based pose estimation. In: Proceedings of International Conference on Computer Vision and Pattern Recognition, vol. 1, pp. 706–711(2000)
24. Mei, C., Benhimane, S., Malis, E., Rives, P.: Efficient homography-based tracking and 3-D reconstruction for single-viewpoint sensors. IEEE Trans. Robot. **24**, 1352–1364 (2008)
25. Caron, G., Marchand, E., Mouaddib, E.M.: Tracking planes in omnidirectional stereovision. In: International Conference on Robotics and Automation, pp. 6306–6311. IEEE (2011)
26. Makadia, A., Geyer, C., Daniilidis, K.: Correspondence-free structure from motion. Int. J. Comput. Vision **75**, 311–327 (2007)
27. Saurer, O., Fraundorfer, F., Pollefeys, M.: Homography based visual odometry with known vertical direction and weak Manhattan world assumption. In: IEEE/IROS Workshop on Visual Control of Mobile Robots (ViCoMoR) (2012)
28. Domokos, C., Nemeth, J., Kato, Z.: Nonlinear shape registration without correspondences. IEEE Trans. Pattern Anal. Mach. Intell. **34**, 943–958 (2012)
29. Recky, M., Leberl, F.: Window detection in complex facades. In: Proceedings of European Workshop on Visual Information Processing, pp. 220–225 (2010)
30. Kneip, L., Li, H., Seo, Y.: UPnP: an optimal $O(n)$ solution to the absolute pose problem with universal applicability. In: Fleet, D., Pajdla, T., Schiele, B., Tuytelaars, T. (eds.) ECCV 2014. LNCS, vol. 8689, pp. 127–142. Springer, Cham (2014). https://doi.org/10.1007/978-3-319-10590-1_9

31. Geiger, A., Lenz, P., Urtasun, R.: Are we ready for autonomous driving? the KITTI vision benchmark suite. In: Proceedings of International Conference on Computer Vision and Pattern Recognition, IEEE (2012)
32. Geiger, A., Ziegler, J., Stiller, C.: StereoScan: dense 3d reconstruction in real-time. In: Proceedings of Intelligent Vehicles Symposium, IEEE (2011)
33. Schonberger, J.L., Frahm, J.M.: Structure-from-motion revisited. In: Proceedings of International Conference on Computer Vision and Pattern Recognition, IEEE (2016)
34. Schönberger, J.L., Zheng, E., Frahm, J.-M., Pollefeys, M.: Pixelwise view selection for unstructured multi-view stereo. In: Leibe, B., Matas, J., Sebe, N., Welling, M. (eds.) ECCV 2016. LNCS, vol. 9907, pp. 501–518. Springer, Cham (2016). https://doi.org/10.1007/978-3-319-46487-9_31
35. Knapitsch, A., Park, J., Zhou, Q.Y., Koltun, V.: Tanks and temples. ACM Trans. Graph. **36**, 1–13 (2017)

WNet: Joint Multiple Head Detection and Head Pose Estimation from a Spectator Crowd Image

Yasir Jan[✉], Ferdous Sohel, Mohd Fairuz Shiratuddin, and Kok Wai Wong

Murdoch University, Perth, Australia
{Y.Jan,F.Sohel,F.Shiratuddin,K.Wong}@murdoch.edu.au

Abstract. Crowd image analysis has various application areas such as surveillance, crowd management and augmented reality. Existing techniques can detect multiple faces in a single crowd image, but small head/face size and additional non facial regions in the head bounding box makes the head detection (HD) challenging. Additionally, in existing head pose estimations (HPE) of multiple heads in an image, individual cropped head image is passed through a network one by one, instead of estimating poses of multiple heads at the same time. The proposed WNet, performs both HD and HPE jointly on multiple heads in a single crowd image, in a single pass. Experiments are demonstrated on the spectator crowd S-HOCK dataset and results are compared with the HPE benchmarks. WNet proposes to use lesser number of training images compared to number of cropped images used by benchmarks, and does not utilize transferred weights from other networks. WNet not just performs HPE, but joint HD and HPE efficiently i.e. accuracy for more number of heads while depending on lesser number of testing images, compared to the benchmarks.

Keywords: Head detection · Head pose estimation · Crowd analysis

1 Introduction

Research in crowd analysis is focused on various aspects of crowd such as crowd counting [9,26], face detection [15,16], body detection [5,19] and HPE [1,2,15,16, 19]. These tasks become more challenging with the increasing number of people in the crowd, body occlusions and the low resolution features [26]. This paper focuses on joint multiple HD and multiple HPE of small sized heads present in a crowd image.

Previously, research has aimed towards single task of face detection [8], HD or HPE, while others propose joint HD and HPE [1,2,15,16,22,24] but with few limitations. Some techniques can do face alignment and HPE in a joint manner [24] but are applicable for images with single heads only. Other techniques do multiple HD but do not perform multiple HPE [15,16,19]. Multiple HPE is done by cropping individual faces/heads and then individually estimating the pose of each face/head one by one. Head dimensions is also an issue for some techniques [15]. They can detect faces of varying dimensions but perform weakly in small sized faces, because they are dependent on other pretrained networks [6]. To detect small sized faces upscaling of low resolution images to high resolution images is proposed [6], which also increases computation. Yet these architectures are only applicable for single HPE at a time. Therefore, as far as we know, there is no existing technique which performs joint HD and HPE of multiple small sized heads.

The proposed WNet architecture, consists of two cascaded UNets [7,17], followed by a grouping module. Previously, UNets have been used for image transformation techniques such as image de/colorization, sketch to image conversion, aerial image to map generation, facades generation, image de-noising/de-snowing, image segmentation and vice versa [7,17,23]. In tasks such as aerial to map generation and facades generation, detailed aerial and facade images are transformed into simplified unicolor regions. Based on these previous ideas, in the proposed architecture, UNets are first used to transform cluttered crowd images into simplified color blocks based images. These simplified images give a better visual understanding of the scene rather than the original cluttered scene. Therefore, using the transformed simplified images, simple color search and euclidean distance based techniques can be utilized to do HD and HPE.

The main contributions in this paper are as follows:

- To the best of our knowledge, this is the first CNN based technique to perform joint HD and HPE of multiple heads.
- It does not need each head to be cropped and passed to the network individually for HPE.
- WNet generates intermediate secondary output images, which reduces the complete black box effect of the end to end network pipeline.

The rest of the paper is organized as follows. Section 2 discusses the previous work related to head detection and head pose estimations. Section 3 discusses our methodology, as well as architecture. Section 4 discusses the S-HOCK dataset. Section 5 explains our experimental protocol while in Sect. 6 the results are shown. Section 7 concludes the paper, while Sect. 8 discusses the future possible improvements in this work.

2 Related Work

There are various CNN based approaches for face detection [15,16]. Some techniques are focused on single person face datasets [13], and do not target crowd images. For multiple face datasets, such as WIDER Face [25], CNN based networks trained on the Imagenet dataset, are used for face detection. Since Imagenet have dimensions larger than 40 pixels [6], therefore, these networks cannot successfully locate and identify objects of smaller dimensions [6,10]. For detecting images with tiny faces, image upscaling [6] is proposed, so that smaller faces become bigger in size and are then detected. Another solution is to have a network which can detect small dimensional objects, rather than images scaled to higher dimension and then detecting. Instead of upscaling, "super-resolved" CNN features [10] can be used to detect small objects. Super-resolving convolves small object CNN features and makes them similar to large object CNN features. Other than HD, some techniques do body detection as well, in which network can locate center of body parts, including heads [3]. Such body detection techniques may locate heads but are not aimed for HPE.

HPE is achieved using hand crafted features as well as deep learning based approach [11,14,15]. Deep learning based approaches in this aspect are very scarce as research is focused on facial landmark detection which indirectly is used for HPE [16,18]. In low resolution images, the techniques depending on facial landmarks fail [18]. Therefore, HPE techniques should be independent of facial landmark detection. Existing HPE techniques have various other limitations. They are applicable to single person images, or they focus on multiple persons by individually cropping each face for pose estimations [15,16]. Multiple faces pose estimations are not performed in a single forward pass of the network.

The network [15] proposes to fuse intermediate layer features and train separate sub networks for face detection, landmark localization and pose estimation. Similarly, [18] proposes to train a separate sub network for each head angle separately. Both these networks are aimed to calculate single head angles at a time, therefore cannot perform multiple HPE at the same time. UNets have also been used previously in a cascaded/stacked manner [4,20], but for different applications.

3 Method

In the proposed WNet method, we follow a 3 step approach, as shown in Fig. 1. First step is to transform a crowd image into a less cluttered image. Aim is to remove all the non head pixels from the image, because they may cause clutter and errors in further steps. Therefore at first step a UNet [7] converts a crowd image to a head-region-masked (HRM) image. The generated HRM image will have all the non head pixel values suppressed to 0, while other head region pixels remain unaffected. Second step is to have an image with color markers. To reduce the effect of color variation in HRM heads, the HRM image is first converted to grayscale and then passed onto second UNet block. The second UNet generates a color coded head (CCH) image from grayscaled HRM image. In CCH image individual head regions and their centers are marked with different colors. The centers are marked with 3 × 3 white pixels, while the head regions are colored based on their pose. In the third step, CCH image is used and based on colors and euclidean distance, the head centers and the head regions are identified. Based on the color of the head region head poses are also identified. The details of the architecture is explained below.

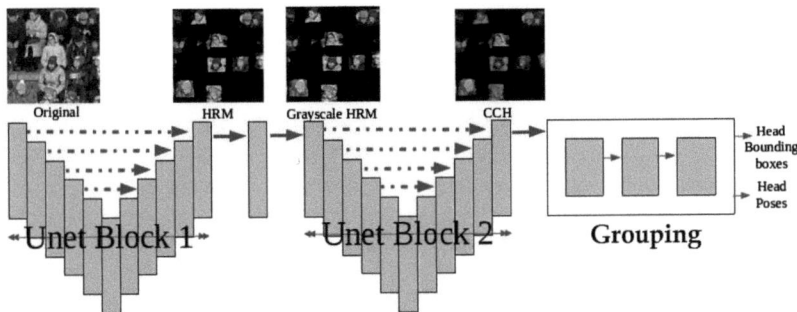

Fig. 1. The proposed WNet architecture, consists of two UNet blocks [7], followed by a grouping block. The UNet blocks transform the original image to a color coded head image. The grouping block locates the marked head centers, then bounding boxes and then head poses. (Best viewed in color)

3.1 WNet Architecture

The proposed WNet architecture, is composed of two UNet blocks, followed by a grouping module, as shown in Fig. 1. Each UNet block layers are similar to [7]. Each block consists of 8 encoder and 8 decoder layers. The number of output filters at each encoder layer are in the sequence: 64, 128, 256, 512, 512, 512, 512. There are skip connections between encoder and corresponding decoder layers. Therefore at each decoder layer input, the output from previous layer is concatenated with the corresponding encoder layer output. The number of filters in the decoder are in the sequence: 512, 512, 512, 512, 256, 128, 64, 3. Encoder layers are activated with LeakyReLU while decoder has ReLU activation functions. At all layers filter size is 4×4, with stride 2 and padding 1 in each direction. Both UNets are trained separately, using conditional Generative Adversarial Networks (cGANs), similar to [7].

UNet block 1: The first UNet block is trained to convert a cluttered RGB crowd image into a simplified HRM RGB image. The output HRM image is generated by suppressing all R, G, B channel values of the background and body part pixels, and making them 0. The head region pixels remain unchanged. The HRM image is then converted to grayscale by averaging all R, G and B channel values. As a result the inter channel color variation is finished and all the heads become almost similar in color, irrespective of their original color shades. This reduces the negative effect caused due to skin or hair color.

UNet block 2: The second UNet block takes the grayscaled HRM image as input, and an output CCH image is generated. In CCH image different head pose will be represented by activating only a combination of RGB color channels, and suppressing the rest to value 0. For example, a right pose head region will have only R channel activated, while G and B channels are suppressed to 0. Similarly, a left head pose will have only G channel activated and rest of the channels will be suppressed to 0. Therefore, for the five head poses i.e. right, left, front, away and down, the respective activated color channel combinations used are R, G,

B, RG and GB respectively. Additionally, a 3 × 3 white pixel block is created in the middle of each head region, which is later used to identify the head center. Therefore, each head's pixels in the input image are replaced with the channel selected head's pixels with an additional white pixel block in the center of head.

Grouping: The CCH image generated from the previous UNet block is used to extract the head centers and head pose. This step can be divided into 3 sub steps. (*i*) The mid positions of 3 × 3 white pixels in the image are extracted. It identifies the head centers. Noise correction is done, by averaging head centers within the half head size range. (*ii*) Group all the head pixels, which are around their centers within the average half head size range. The minimum and maximum pixel positions of each group gives the bounding box values of that head. (*iii*) Identify head poses of each head. In a CCH image, all the pixels within the head bounding box are color coded based on the pose. Therefore, the color codes of all the pixels within the head region are aggregated, and the maximum color is chosen to identify the head pose.

WNet generates simplified uncluttered crowd images at intermediate steps in the pipeline before calculating head bounding boxes, while other techniques first generates numerical values for head bounding boxes and then mark the head boundaries. These simplified images can be useful in applications where exact head locations are not required but a clear visual understanding of the scene e.g. crowd surveillance, augmented reality, is required. This intermediate step also reduces the full blackbox effect of the networks. Each intermediate step of the network can be fine tuned for further improvement.

4 Dataset

The Spectator Hockey (S-HOCK) dataset [19] is used for the experiments. It is the only publicly available dataset for spectator crowd with small heads annotated with head bounding boxes and head poses. It has a total of 75 videos (5 camera views × 15 different matches). Video from only a single camera has been annotated with head bounding box and head pose values. Each videos is of 31 s duration is split into 930 annotated frames. Out of the 15 matches, 2 are used for training, 2 for validation and 11 for testing. Each frame has a resolution of 1280 × 1024 pixels with the dense crowd.

5 Experiments

S-HOCK has a total of 1860 annotated training frames (930 frames of 2 training videos) and 10230 annotated testing frames (930 frames of 11 testing videos). To reduce redundancy and also reduce the number of frames, 9 frames out of 10 are skipped. A total of 93 frames are extracted from each 930 frame video (5 : 10 : 930). Therefore the interval between two consecutive frames is approx 1/3 of a second. It should be observed that only 186 frames are used for training which is far lesser number than the thousands of ImageNet data, and 1023 frames are used for testing. In 1023 testing frames there are a total of 155085 people, with average head dimensions of width 36.46 pixels and height 40.69 pixels. The range of head dimensions in testing images is shown in Fig. 2.

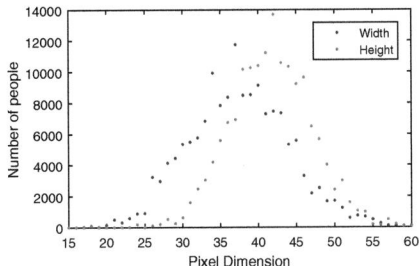

Fig. 2. Head dimensions of people in testing images.

Each frame is further sliced into 20 subframes to maintain a resolution of 256 × 256. The proposed WNet architecture consists of 2 UNets, each one of them trained separately. Both UNets are trained with their own input output image pair as discussed below.

UNet block 1: All the 186 frames are sliced into 20 each subframe (totaling 3720 subframes). Input 3720 subframes are paired with output 3720 HRM subframes, for generating input output training pairs. Training of UNEt block 1 with these input output pairs is done for 30 epochs.

UNet block 2: Block 2 is trained using the grayscaled HRM and respective RGB CCH frames of the 186 training frames of the dataset. Input HRM subframes are grayscaled and paired with respective RGB CCH subframes, for generating input output training pairs. But there is a class imbalance problem regarding the head pose i.e. left pose heads in the dataset are more than the right pose heads. Therefore, to solve the class imbalance issue, horizontally flipped 3720 sub frames are added into the training data. It makes a total of 7440 training subframes. Flipped and grayscaled HRM subframes are paired with respective flipped CCH subframes, for generating additional input output training pairs. For flipped images, the color of left and right pose will also be swapped. The 7440 input output pairs are used for training the UNet2 block with 10 epochs.

6 Results

The proposed WNet technique is tested using 1023 testing frames sliced into resolution 256 × 256. The technique first detects heads and generates the bounding box. Then based on the bounding box it identifies the head pose of each detected head. After frame slicing, the heads at the edges of the subframes get sliced as well. HD and HPE results are generated by ignoring the sliced heads. Generally the Intersection over Union (IoU) of detected head bounding box region and

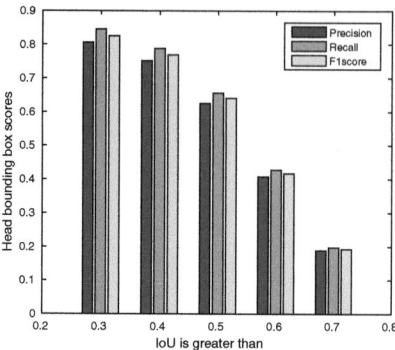

Fig. 3. Head bounding box accuracy.

Table 1. S-HOCK dataset benchmark HPE average accuracy compared with WNet HPE accuracy. Benchmarks are tested on 34949 cropped heads images. While WNet is tested on only 1023 full scene frames (155085 heads). For IoU = (0.3, 0.4, 0.5, 0.6, 0.7), $HD \approx 0.8, 0.7, 0.6, 0.4, 0.2$.

Method	Avg Acc.	Acc HPE headcount	Method type
Orozco [12]	0.368	$\approx$ 12861	Only single HPE
WArCo [21]	0.376	$\approx$ 13140	Only single HPE
CNN [19]	0.346	$\approx$ 12092	Only single HPE
SAE [19]	0.348	$\approx$ 12162	Only single HPE
WNet (IoU = 0.3)	0.321	$\approx$ **39825**	Joint multiple HD and HPE
WNet (IoU = 0.4)	0.323	$\approx$ **35064**	Joint multiple HD and HPE
WNet (IoU = 0.5)	0.325	$\approx$ **30241**	Joint multiple HD and HPE
WNet (IoU = 0.6)	0.337	$\approx$ **20905**	Joint multiple HD and HPE
WNet (IoU = 0.7)	0.34	$\approx$ 10545	Joint multiple HD and HPE

ground truth head bounding box region greater than 0.5 is accepted as correct. Experiments are performed for multiple HD IoUs i.e. IoU greater than 0.3, 0.4, 0.5, 0.6, 0.7. The precision, recall and f1score of HD for varying IoU is given in the Fig. 3. It achieves more than 0.6 precision, recall and F1 score for HD (IoU greater than 0.5).

The HPE benchmarks mentioned in the dataset paper [19] performs HPE on 34949 single head instances. An individual head is cropped and then head pose is estimated. Therefore, it takes 34949 cropped head images to generate the results of 34949 heads. Their accuracy ranges between 0.3 and 0.4, as shown in Table 1. In contrast, the proposed WNet architecture was tested with fewer number of frames (1023 frames/20460 subframes). Although in these lesser testing frames, the total number of heads is 155085 which is $\approx$ 4.4 times more than the benchmark number of heads (34949). Therefore, WNet can do HPE for more heads with lesser frames. Additionally, this technique also performs HD, not just HPE. HPE accuracy is dependent on the HD accuracy. Therefore, the Table 1 shows the accuracy for correctly estimated head poses with respect to correctly detected heads.

The accuracy of different IoU values is greater than 0.32. Our focus is on the number of accurately detected heads and head poses which is greater for WNet compared to other techniques. Results should be compared keeping in view that the benchmarks do not perform HD and can perform HPE on single cropped head. While proposed WNet jointly performs HD and HPE on multiple heads. Therefore, WNet uses lesser testing data frames and calculates higher number of accurate head poses.

7 Conclusion

Proposed WNet architecture, can perform joint multiple HD and HPE in a single forward pass. The technique is based on image to image transformation. First sub blocks of the architecture transforms the cluttered crowd images into color marked simplified images. Using the simplified images, head bounding box and head pose information are extracted. The proposed technique has been tested on S-HOCK spectator crowd dataset. Results of HD and HPE show that the proposed WNet technique uses lesser number of frames and accurately estimates pose of more number of heads. WNet is an image to image transformation technique, which is also useful for applications where exact head dimensions are not required but simplified crowd images may be useful for a better visual understanding. E.g. crowd surveillance.

8 Future Work

This technique currently aims towards spectator crowd dataset, but it could b extended for heads/faces in the wild. It could benefit from heads segmented datasets, which could improve HD accuracy. This may result in sharper head extraction. Additionally a range of colors maybe assigned for a range of head poses which can be correlated. Instead of image to image transformation, head bounding box values can be extracted using other techniques, which can be further used for pose estimation.

Acknowledgment. This work was partially supported by an Australian Research Council grant DE120102960 and Murdoch University grant.

References

1. Asteriadis, S., Karpouzis, K., Kollias, S.: Face tracking and head pose estimation using convolutional neural networks. In: Proceedings of the SSPNET 2nd International Symposium on Facial Analysis and Animation, FAA 2010, p. 19. ACM, New York (2010). https://doi.org/10.1145/1924035.1924046

2. Bao, J., Ye, M.: Head pose estimation based on robust convolutional neuralnetwork. Cybern. Inf. Technol. **16**(6), 133–145 (2016). https://doi.org/10.1515/cait-2016-0083
3. Cao, Z., Simon, T., Wei, S., Sheikh, Y.: Realtime multi-person 2D pose estimation using part affinity fields. In: 2017 IEEE Conference on Computer Vision and Pattern Recognition (CVPR), pp. 1302–1310, July 2017. https://doi.org/10.1109/CVPR.2017.143
4. Christ, P.F., et al.: Automatic liver and lesion segmentation in CT using cascaded fully convolutional neural networks and 3D conditional random fields. In: Ourselin, S., Joskowicz, L., Sabuncu, M.R., Unal, G., Wells, W. (eds.) MICCAI 2016. LNCS, vol. 9901, pp. 415–423. Springer, Cham (2016). https://doi.org/10.1007/978-3-319-46723-8_48
5. Felzenszwalb, P.F., Girshick, R.B., McAllester, D., Ramanan, D.: Object detection with discriminatively trained part-based models. IEEE Trans. Pattern Anal. Mach. Intell. **32**(9), 1627–1645 (2010). https://doi.org/10.1109/TPAMI.2009.167
6. Hu, P., Ramanan, D.: Finding tiny faces. In: 2017 IEEE Conference on Computer Vision and Pattern Recognition (CVPR), pp. 1522–1530, July 2017. https://doi.org/10.1109/CVPR.2017.166
7. Isola, P., Zhu, J.Y., Zhou, T., Efros, A.A.: Image-to-image translation with conditional adversarial networks. In: 2017 IEEE Conference on Computer Vision and Pattern Recognition (CVPR), pp. 5967–5976 (2017)
8. Jiang, H., Learned-Miller, E.: Face detection with the faster R-CNN. In: 2017 12th IEEE International Conference on Automatic Face Gesture Recognition (FG 2017), pp. 650–657, May 2017. https://doi.org/10.1109/FG.2017.82
9. Kang, D., Ma, Z., Chan, A.B.: Beyond counting: comparisons of density maps for crowd analysis tasks - counting, detection, and tracking. CoRR abs/1705.10118 (2017). http://arxiv.org/abs/1705.10118
10. Li, J., Liang, X., Wei, Y., Xu, T., Feng, J., Yan, S.: Perceptual generative adversarial networks for small object detection. In: 2017 IEEE Conference on Computer Vision and Pattern Recognition (CVPR), pp. 1951–1959, July 2017. https://doi.org/10.1109/CVPR.2017.211
11. Murphy-Chutorian, E., Trivedi, M.M.: Head pose estimation in computer vision: a survey. IEEE Trans. Pattern Anal. Mach. Intell. **31**(4), 607–626 (2009). https://doi.org/10.1109/TPAMI.2008.106
12. Orozco, J., Gong, S., Xiang, T.: Head pose classification in crowded scenes. In: Proceedings of the British Machine Vision Conference, pp. 120.1–120.11. BMVA Press (2009). https://doi.org/10.5244/C.23.120
13. Parkhi, O.M., Vedaldi, A., Zisserman, A.: Deep face recognition. In: Proceedings of the British Machine Vision Conference (BMVC), pp. 41.1–41.12. BMVA Press, September 2015. https://doi.org/10.5244/C.29.41
14. Patacchiola, M., Cangelosi, A.: Head pose estimation in the wild using convolutional neural networks and adaptive gradient methods. Pattern Recogn. **71**(Supplement C), 132–143 (2017). https://doi.org/10.1016/j.patcog.2017.06.009. http://www.sciencedirect.com/science/article/pii/S0031320317302327
15. Ranjan, R., Patel, V.M., Chellappa, R.: HyperFace: a deep multi-task learning framework for face detection, landmark localization, pose estimation, and gender recognition. IEEE Trans. Pattern Anal. Mach. Intell., 1 (2018). https://doi.org/10.1109/TPAMI.2017.2781233

16. Ranjan, R., Sankaranarayanan, S., Castillo, C.D., Chellappa, R.: An all-in-one convolutional neural network for face analysis. In: 2017 12th IEEE International Conference on Automatic Face Gesture Recognition (FG 2017), pp. 17–24, May 2017. https://doi.org/10.1109/FG.2017.137
17. Ronneberger, O., Fischer, P., Brox, T.: U-net: convolutional networks for biomedical image segmentation. In: Navab, N., Hornegger, J., Wells, W.M., Frangi, A.F. (eds.) MICCAI 2015. LNCS, vol. 9351, pp. 234–241. Springer, Cham (2015). https://doi.org/10.1007/978-3-319-24574-4_28
18. Ruiz, N., Chong, E., Rehg, J.M.: Fine-grained head pose estimation without keypoints. CoRR abs/1710.00925 (2017). http://arxiv.org/abs/1710.00925
19. Setti, F., et al.: The s-hock dataset: a new benchmark for spectator crowd analysis. Comput. Vis. Image Underst. **159**(Supplement C), 47–58 (2017). https://doi.org/10.1016/j.cviu.2017.01.003. Computer Vision in Sports. http://www.sciencedirect.com/science/article/pii/S1077314217300024
20. Shah, S., Ghosh, P., Davis, L.S., Goldstein, T.: Stacked U-nets: a no-frills approach to natural image segmentation. CoRR abs/1804.10343 (2018). http://arxiv.org/abs/1804.10343
21. Tosato, D., Spera, M., Cristani, M., Murino, V.: Characterizing humans on riemannian manifolds. IEEE Trans. Pattern Anal. Mach. Intell. **35**(8), 1972–1984 (2013). https://doi.org/10.1109/TPAMI.2012.263
22. Vu, T., Osokin, A., Laptev, I.: Context-aware CNNs for person head detection. In: International Conference on Computer Vision (ICCV) (2015)
23. Wang, C., Xu, C., Wang, C., Tao, D.: Perceptual adversarial networks for image-to-image transformation. IEEE Trans. Image Process. **27**(8), 4066–4079 (2018). https://doi.org/10.1109/TIP.2018.2836316
24. Xu, X., Kakadiaris, I.A.: Joint head pose estimation and face alignment framework using global and local CNN features. In: 2017 12th IEEE International Conference on Automatic Face Gesture Recognition (FG 2017), pp. 642–649, May 2017. https://doi.org/10.1109/FG.2017.81
25. Yang, S., Luo, P., Loy, C.C., Tang, X.: Wider face: a face detection benchmark. In: IEEE Conference on Computer Vision and Pattern Recognition (CVPR) (2016)
26. Zhang, C., Li, H., Wang, X., Yang, X.: Cross-scene crowd counting via deep convolutional neural networks. In: 2015 IEEE Conference on Computer Vision and Pattern Recognition (CVPR), pp. 833–841, June 2015. https://doi.org/10.1109/CVPR.2015.7298684

Markerless Augmented Advertising for Sports Videos

Hallee E. Wong[1(✉)], Osman Akar[2], Emmanuel Antonio Cuevas[3], Iuliana Tabian[4], Divyaa Ravichandran[5], Iris Fu[5], and Cambron Carter[5]

[1] Williams College, Williamstown, USA
hew1@williams.edu
[2] University of California Los Angeles, Los Angeles, CA, USA
osmanakar1123@hotmail.com
[3] Universidad de Guanaquatro, Guanajuato, Mexico
emmanuel.antonio@cimat.mx
[4] Imperial College London, London, UK
iuliana.tabian15@imperial.ac.uk
[5] GumGum Inc., Santa Monica, USA
{dravi,iris,cambron}@gumgum.com

Abstract. Markerless augmented reality can be a challenging computer vision task, especially in live broadcast settings and in the absence of information related to the video capture such as the intrinsic camera parameters. This typically requires the assistance of a skilled artist, along with the use of advanced video editing tools in a post-production environment. We present an automated video augmentation pipeline that identifies textures of interest and overlays an advertisement onto these regions. We constrain the advertisement to be placed in a way that is aesthetic and natural. The aim is to augment the scene such that there is no longer a need for commercial breaks. In order to achieve seamless integration of the advertisement with the original video we build a 3D representation of the scene, place the advertisement in 3D, and then project it back onto the image plane. After successful placement in a single frame, we use homography-based, shape-preserving tracking such that the advertisement appears perspective correct for the duration of a video clip. The tracker is designed to handle smooth camera motion and shot boundaries.

Keywords: Augmented reality · Virtual advertisement insertion · Overlay video advertising

1 Introduction

Advertisements traditionally occur in between breaks during the broadcast of a live sporting event. These breaks interfere with the viewing experience enough to

---

Supported by the Institute for Pure and Applied Mathematics (IPAM) at the University of California Los Angeles, GumGum Inc. and U.S. National Science Foundation Grant DMS-0931852.

motivate the advent of Digital Video Recording (DVR). This technology allows viewers to skip through commercial breaks, which negates the impact of the advertising altogether. This work motivates a system which integrates advertising seamlessly into a live sports broadcast without diverting too much attention from the main focus in the stream – namely the action taking place on the field, court, rink, etc.

Different approaches have been attempted to blend an advertisement, which we will refer to as "asset", into video content. The goal is to place an asset such that augmentation has a minimal impact on the viewing experience. Manual solutions exist but require the expertise of a graphic artist. While effective, this approach is laborious and expensive. Alternative methods such as visual attention [6] and visual harmony [21] have been used to reduce human dependency while achieving similar computational aesthetics. In contrast to common video asset overlays that consistently reside in the same position, often resulting in occluding important content information, the work by Mei et al. [25] detects non-salient regions in the video before overlaying relevant assets based on textual descriptions. Similarly, Chang et al. [5] devise an algorithm to identify regions with high viewer interest and insert assets exhibiting color harmony with the content to stay visually consistent. While both of these methods strive to minimize the lack of coherence between the asset placement and the video content, the final asset can be argued to take away from the focus of the content despite the intended purpose [26]. In the examples provided by [5] and [15], the asset placement is on the tennis court itself because the system heavily relies on the court lines for obtaining camera information. However, this asset placement can interfere with the focus of the video - which is the tennis ball in the game.

Placing assets in and nearby the focus of the video can compromise the viewing experience. We take an alternative approach: we leverage underutilized virtual real estate which we can automatically detect. In this work, we identify "virtual real estate" as the crowded sections of a sporting arena and use those regions for asset insertion. We argue that the latter are good candidates for asset placement because they are of less relevance to the focus of the broadcast [19,29].

In this work, we propose a novel system that:

1. Automatically identifies viable "crowd" regions through spatio-temporal analysis in a video clip
2. Places the asset in a "natural" fashion, respecting the physical constraints of the real world scene
3. Is fully automatic

The rest of this work is organized as follows: Sect. 2 discusses some relevant work on the topic, Sect. 3 discusses our system and each of its parts in detail, and we conclude with the results and discussions in Sect. 4.

2 Related Work

Various systems and pipelines have been proposed for the insertion of assets in video. Ideally, the asset should integrate seamlessly without occluding any pertinent video content. The asset should be apparent but not disruptive. ImageSence [26] solves this problem by choosing insertion content according to visual consistency. The authors in [6] work around the problem by harmonizing the asset to be visually consistent with the original content. Liu et al. in [21] define intrusiveness as follows: (a) if the inserted asset covers the Region of Interest (ROI), it is truly very intrusive, and (b) if the asset distracts audience attention from the original attending point, it is also very intrusive. They use these metrics to insert assets "gently" into the target content.

One of the challenges in achieving augmented advertising is constraining the overlaid asset to the physical boundaries of the real world scene. Xu et al. [30] rely on static regions (e.g. ground) in a soccer field and make use of strong and reliable field boundary markings so that the final asset could be placed appropriately. Wan et al. [29] use the geometry of the candidate regions derived from known markers to decide whether a text, image or animation type of asset is more suitable. Chang et al. [5] represent the asset in the chosen video frame by color-harmonizing it with the background. Given the known landmarks, and calibration parameters, derived 3D camera pose is used to project the asset onto the region of interest. They also use a visual attention model to find the most "attention-grabbing" region to place the asset. However, it can make the final asset placement very intrusive to the viewing experience, since in their specific use case of tennis matches, the highest attention region is around the player.

Our biggest challenge was to achieve the goal of virtual asset placement in compliance with the conditions of (a) non-intrusiveness, and (b) conformity to real world scene constraints, while requiring minimal manual intervention. Usually, advertisers hire professional editors to manually implement virtual ads. It usually is very labor-intensive and inefficient for rapid productions on monetizing sports videos. We approach the problem with the intention of having a fully automatic pipeline. The authors in [29] aim to automate the pipeline for sports highlights; however, there is an initial manual step of segmenting out the highlights in the video. They also model their virtual reality around the boundaries of a single game event, so they manually remove the replays from the broadcast videos as well. The work done in [24] is similar in attempting to construct a system with a fundamental requirement being that the system performs on-line in real-time, with no human intervention and no on screen errors. Prior assumption that the billboard to be substituted in the target video is known beforehand reduces the problem to one of template matching.

It must be noted that a lot of the work briefly reviewed in this section are built around certain very specific use cases (tennis [5,6], soccer [30], baseball [19]), relying heavily on the presence of known, reliable markings on the ground and a rigid sporting-ground structure enabling assets to be integrated seamlessly into the scenery.

We aim to be independent of such assumptions while focusing on the crowds and the surrounding areas at sporting events. Our approach also completely removes the manual component from the entire system, presenting an end-to-end pipeline for the overlay of ads in a non-intrusive, engaging fashion.

3 Setup

The assumptions that are made for the proposed system are detailed in the following list:

- the input video is captured from a single viewpoint with a monocular RGB camera
- intrinsic parameters about the camera may not be known
- the texture we aim to overlay on will be a crowd of people in a sports stadium
- the asset to be overlayed in the video will be a 2D image/video and not a 3D object
- the shot need not be static, i.e., the camera may change location or angle
- the video may contain multiple camera shots

The following sections describe the system in detail and the above assumptions are addressed in more detail. Figure 1 illustrates a conceptual diagram of our proposed pipeline.

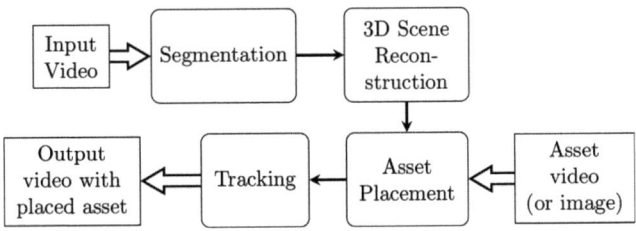

Fig. 1. Our proposed automated pipeline for augmentation.

3.1 Segmentation and Seed Frame Selection

To augment the input video efficiently, we first attempt to isolate and overlay augmentation on the most ideal frame. Once this frame is determined, we track our asset through subsequent frames. We are primarily concerned with whether the seed frame contains the texture of interest (e.g. crowds in sport stadium imagery) and if the textured area is large enough for the asset to be adequately overlayed.

Semantic segmentation decomposes a scene into its various components at the pixel level. Our system requires pixel-level in order to adequately overlay an asset onto the scene. This work makes use of a convolutional neural network (CNN) based segmentation technique called Pyramid Scene Parsing network (PSPNet) [32], which has been shown to be competitive in various scene-parsing challenges (e.g. ImageNet 2016 [27], PASCAL VOC 2012 [12], and CityScapes 2016 [8] benchmarks).

We make use of a PSPNet model trained on the ADE20K [33,34] dataset subset to identify our textures of choice: "person" and "grandstand". We refer to this combination of classes as "crowd". Figure 2 shows an example segmentation using PSPNet.

 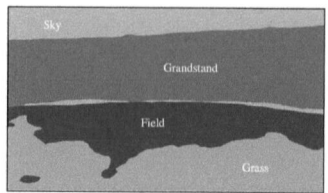

(a) Input image   (b) Image segmented by PSP-Net

Fig. 2. The input image of a baseball game is segmented by PSPNet's ADE20K trained model into sky (*blue*), grandstand (*red*), wall (*gray*) fence (*orange*), field (*purple*), and grass (*green*) [33,34]. (Color figure online)

This segmentation technique is computationally expensive to carry out on every frame. To reduce the computational overhead, we sample the video at one frame per second and only segment those frames. Alternative segmentation techniques could be explored to alleviate computation time but we will restrict our focus to accuracy using this method. Once we have identified a seed frame, we discontinue segmentation until tracking fails, which will be discussed in Sect. 3.4.

Measuring Segmentation Quality. Due to errors in judgment in classifying the image at the pixel level (segmentation), the segmentation mask can be far from ideal, containing holes, fragmentation etc. We aim to ensure that (a) the asset only covers the crowd region of the image and (b) the crowd region of the image is large enough and contiguous enough such that further processing has a higher likelihood of succeeding. Thus we define an ideally segmented region to be one which:

- Is connected
- Contains no holes
- Is compact

To evaluate the binary segmentation images of the sampled frames with respect to these three conditions, we propose a metric called the Segmentation Quality Score (SQS). The SQS is defined as the product of three subscores,

$$SQS = S_{cp}\ S_{cl}\ S_{sp} \qquad (1)$$

where S_{cp} is the component score, S_{sp} is the completeness score and S_{sp} is the shape score. Low values are associated with good segmentation and large values are associated with poor segmentation. The minimum possible SQS score is 1.

Component Score. To evaluate the connectedness of the segmented crowd region, we calculate the component score S_{cp} as

$$S_{cp} = \frac{a}{max_i a_i}, \quad (2)$$

where a is the area of the entire crowd region and a_i is the area of the ith connected component in the crowd region. The image is divided into disjoint connected components and the largest component is identified. Next, the ratio of the area of this largest component with respect to the entire crowd region in the binary image is computed. This value will always be larger than or equal to 1 (which will be the case when there is only one major component).

Completeness Score. The completeness score S_{cl}, defined as

$$S_{cl} = \frac{a'}{a} \quad (3)$$

where a' is the total area of the crowd region with all holes filled in, quantifies the size of hole(s) in the segmented area. This score is close to 1 when the total area of holes in the larges crowd segmented crowd component is small.

Shape Score. The shape score, defined as

$$S_{sp} = \frac{p_j}{2\sqrt{\pi\, a_j}} \quad (4)$$

where p_j and a_j are the perimeter and area of the largest connected crowd component respectively, quantifies the regularity of the shape of the largest connected crowd component. If the crowd region has a large boundary relative to the area it covers, it is indicative of an irregular shape (Fig. 3). The denominator (Eq. 4) contains the $\sqrt{a_j}$ term to make the score invariant under scaling and a factor of $2\sqrt{\pi}$ so that the minimum value of $S_s p$ is 1 (when the shape is circular). We assume that the crowd will be seated or standing in a regularly shaped area in the images, so if the crowd segmentation is highly irregular, we conclude that the segmentation is not suitable for an asset placement and likely to be erroneous.

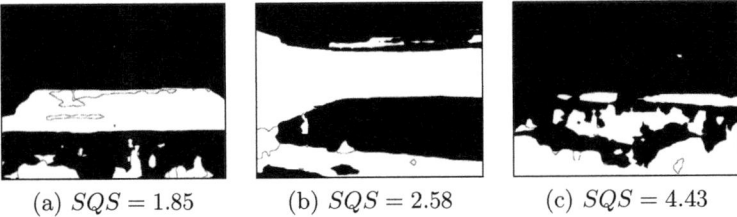

(a) $SQS = 1.85$ (b) $SQS = 2.58$ (c) $SQS = 4.43$

Fig. 3. Segmented images and the SQS associated with the quality of the segmentation. The smaller the SQS value, the better the quality

For some frames with small SQS, the detected crowd area is significantly small. To eliminate the chance of trying to further process such cases, the algorithm first runs through all selected frames and finds the maximum detected crowd area, then disregards all frames with detected crowd area less than the half of the maximum area. The frame with the lowest SQS (Eq. 1) is then chosen from the remaining frames as the best-suited frame for asset placement.

3.2 3D Reconstruction

After deciding on a keyframe for asset placement, we estimate the depth of locations in the scene relative to the camera. This will facilitate in identifying the dominant plane coinciding with the crowd region and placing the asset on this plane in a perspective-correct way.

Depth Estimation. To create a 3D reconstruction of the scene, we must first estimate the distance between the camera and points in the scene. To estimate depth for each pixel in the image, we use MegaDepth [20], a CNN for predicting a dense relative depth map from a single monocular RGB image (see Fig. 4). Let $MD(u, v)$ be the relative depth estimated by MegaDepth for the pixel at image coordinates (u, v).

(a) Input image   (b) Inverse depth map

Fig. 4. An example of a crowd image and a inverse depth map visualization of the relative depth values predicted by MegaDepth. In (b) dark pixels have large predicted relative depths and light pixels have small relative predicted depth values.

Pinhole Camera Projection. The output from MegaDepth is not usable for our purposes as is, and for this reason we create a 3D point cloud from the dense relative depth map. To convert the relative depth values $(MD(u, v))$ estimated by MegaDepth to absolute depth values (z), we multiply by an empirically determined scale factor s. We transform the depth map of points $(u, v, MD(u, v))$ to a 3D point cloud of points (x, y, z) following the pinhole camera model.

To simplify the projection between the world coordinate system and the image coordinate system, we assume that the world coordinate system be centered on the camera sensor with the x and y axes aligned with the sides of the sensor plane and the z axis perpendicular to image plane. We assume that the optical center of the camera (c_x, c_y) is at the center of the image and let the world coordinate system origin $(0,0,0)$ be located at the image coordinates origin $(0,0)$.

Given a relative depth map of points $(u, v, MD(u,v))$ and parameters s and f, we create a 3D point cloud of points (x, y, z) by letting

$$x = c_x + (u - c_x)\frac{z}{f} \quad (5)$$

$$y = c_y + (u - c_y)\frac{z}{f} \quad (6)$$

$$z = s\ MD(u,v) \quad (7)$$

where f is the focal length of the camera and s is a chosen scaling factor. The next section presents methods for estimating the focal length (f) from an image without prior knowledge of the camera used to take the photo.

Focal Length Estimation. To convert a depth map to a 3D point cloud, we need to know the focal length of the camera. We estimate the focal length from the image using a method based on vanishing point detection from Li et al. [18]. Li et al. detect lines in the image and use the distribution of the orientations of those lines to estimate vanishing points and then calculate the focal length.

To identify the dominant plane within the crowd area, we use the segmentation mask provided by PSPNet [32] to identify points in the 3D reconstruction pertaining to the largest connected crowd component and then apply the RANSAC algorithm [13].

3.3 Asset Placement

For the asset to look "natural", we would like it to appear aligned with the intersection of the crowd plane and the adjacent class (in our case, the ground) plane. In Fig. 5, both the asset placements are technically correct, but only one of them (Fig. 5b) provides a harmonious viewing experience. With this consideration in mind, we aim to align the asset parallel to the dividing line between the crowd and ground planes.

Orienting the Asset. We experimented with RANSAC [13] to fit planes to both the crowd and ground regions with information obtained from the segmentation mask and the depth map. The resulting planes intersect at a 3D line; however, due to noise issues with the depth map, when this line is projected back into the image plane for asset placement, the asset looks "unnatural". To uniquely specify the orientation of the asset, we need a vector v that is parallel to the surface of the 3D crowd plane to serve as the bottom edge of the rectangular asset. We turned to edge and line detection methods to identify a line to align the asset with.

We will first find an alignment line in 2D image coordinates, and then transform it into a 3D plane of points that can be inserted into our 3D reconstruction

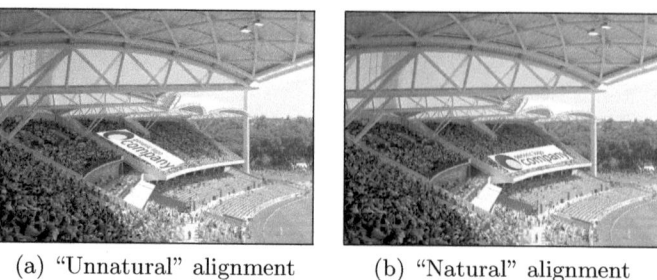

(a) "Unnatural" alignment (b) "Natural" alignment

Fig. 5. Perspective correct asset placement with "unnatural" and "natural" orientation relative to the scene.

and used to calculate the alignment vector $\boldsymbol{v}$. To first identify the edges of the crowd region, we apply Canny edge detection [4] to the binary segmentation image (Fig. 6a) that identifies the largest connected crowd component. Having identified the edges of the target crowd area, we now use Hough line detection [9] to identify straight line segments. We choose the longest line segment to be our alignment line with equation $y = ax + b$ in image coordinates (Fig. 6b).

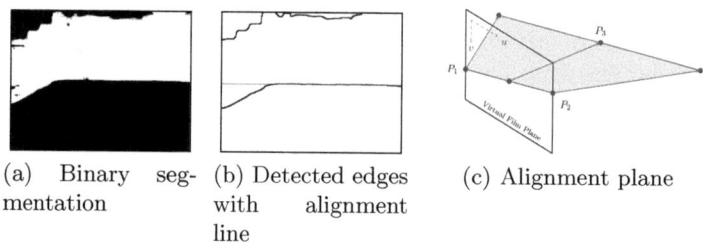

(a) Binary segmentation (b) Detected edges with alignment line (c) Alignment plane

Fig. 6. Illustration of asset placement procedure using Fig. 8a as input: (a) The largest crowd component (*white*) identified by segmentation (b) Canny edge detection [4] is applied and the longest line found by Hough line detection [9] is selected as the alignment line (*red*). (c) The points P_1 and P_2 in the image plane are used with a point P_3 to compute the equation of the alignment plane. (Color figure online)

To align the asset such that is appears parallel to this 2D alignment line in the final image, we must place the asset in 3D parallel to the plane of points which project to the 2D alignment line. We calculate the equation of the 3D alignment plane (Fig. 6c) by choosing three arbitrary points (P_1, P_2, P_3) on the 2D alignment line in the image plane. We assume that points P_1 and P_2 in our image have depths of 0, and point P_3 has an arbitrary (non-zero) depth of z in the real world relative to the camera. We can then reconstruct these three sets of image coordinates in 3D following the pinhole camera model as described in Eqs. 5–7. Our 3D reconstruction consists of three points (P_1, P_2, P_3), which uniquely determine the alignment plane of points which project to the alignment line in the 2D image.

To make the placed asset appear parallel to the alignment line, we find the intersection of the alignment plane and the dominant crowd plane in the 3D reconstruction. Let vector component of this intersection line be the alignment vector v. We place the asset in the reconstruction such that it is on the surface of the dominant crowd plane and one of its edges is parallel to the alignment vector (v).

Sizing the Asset. With considerations to maximize the asset size without covering any non-crowd pixels, we fit a convex hull to the inliers of the crowd plane and require all corners of the asset to be inside the hull. The aspect ratio of the overlaid asset in the 3D reconstruction is equivalent to the original aspect ratio of the asset. Finally, we use a homography transformation [16] to transform the coordinate system of the asset to the coordinate system of the target image, i.e. onto the identified crowd plane.

3.4 Asset Tracking Across Video

To reduce computation time we augment a seed frame and then employ a tracker to place the asset in all frames. The asset should appear stabilized in a perspective-correct way in subsequent frames, in the face of smooth camera motion and across shot boundaries.

Empirically, we found tracking to be far more accurate if we use four anchor quadrilateral tracks around the asset rather than track the points within the asset boundary. We use a combination of of SIFT [22], SURF [3] and KAZE [2] feature descriptors to obtain key points at each of the corners of the asset's updated location. To track multiple features at once, we make use of the work by Lucas-Kanade on optical flow-based tracking [23].

Shot Change Detection. Since we will be overlaying assets on crowd regions in videos of sporting events, we recognize that these events are commonly filmed using multiple cameras, from various vantage points. The resulting shot changes can occur rapidly and frequently throughout. We detect shot changes per the process in [31]. When a shot change is detected, tracking is suspended but features used for tracking just prior to the shot change are saved. As the video advances, new features are extracted and matched with the stored features to determine if the previously tracked feature points are back in view. If an excessive amount of frames pass and no match is found, the entire system is restarted. We leave the definition of excessive up to the preference of the user.

Improving Robustness. Tracking fails when one or more corners of the quadrilateral can no longer be matched with the previous frame. This generally occurs when said corner goes out of frame. To avoid this, we try to predict the position of the corner which is out of frame using: (a) the locations of the remaining corners and, (b) prior knowledge about the quadrilateral positioning of the corners using the Kalman filter [17]. First, we identify features to track around each corner of the quadrilateral. For example, in Fig. 7, we have four groups of features, illustrated by red points. Each group is inside a circle with radius $r = 50px$ centered at each corner of the quadrilateral. For each group of features we calculate the average velocity vector, then set the velocity vector for each corner of the quadrilateral to be

$$v_{corner_i} = \alpha v_i + (1-\alpha) \frac{v_1 + v_2 + v_3 + v_4}{4} \qquad (8)$$

where v_i is the computed average velocity vector for each corner i, and $\alpha \in (0, 1)$ is a parameter chosen empirically. We found that $\alpha \geq 0.8$ works best, because the motion of the features in the group centered at a particular corner are more indicative of that corner's movement than the motion of features from the other corner groups.

To calculate the new position of the points which are out of frame, we compute the Kalman Filter [17] prediction on that corner and then use v_{corner_i} from Eq. 8 to update the error estimation.

Fig. 7. Features (*red points*) to be tracked are identified within a 50 px radius (*yellow circles*) of the corners (*large green points*) of the quadrilateral. (Color figure online)

4 Conclusion

4.1 Results

Examples of the intermediate results of all of the steps in the pipeline on a single image are illustrated in Fig. 8. We have in place two pipelines, one for a single image, and one for a video. The pipeline for the single image is the same as the video pipeline but excludes the tracking as well as the SQS (Sect. 3.1) calculation.

An example of the system's output for a video is provided online[1]. In this demonstration, the asset is also a video, thus augmenting the target crowd region with a video overlay. Video assets appear aesthetically pleasing as long as their

[1] https://youtu.be/ugZ-08c6IWY.

framerate matches that of the target video. The entire pipeline was assembled and tested on a 64-bit CPU (Intel Core i7-6800K, 3.40 GHz). PSPNet [32] was run on a GPU (Nvidia GTX 1080, with 8GB RAM). Table 1 outlines the time taken per step (approximately) to select and augment a seed image of size 1920 × 1080 px from a series of 25 video frames.

Table 1. Timing per step in pipeline.

Time (secs)	Process, coding platform/language
11.491	PSPNet on GPU, Python and Tensorflow [1]
0.374	SQS on 25 segmented frames (only in video pipeline), Python
12.159	MegaDepth, Python and Torch [7]
0.922	Segment image to select "crowd" region, Python
1.117	Identify alignment line, Python
6.627	Estimate focal length using vanishing points, Octave [11]
8.664	Create 3D reconstruction and place asset in 3D, C++
0.008	Display inliers (only for visualization purposes), C++
0.090	Warp asset using homography, C++

4.2 Limitations

Many steps need to succeed in order for the system to work. The pipeline performs best on daytime scenes with a single crowd plane. Night-time scenes are challenging for MegaDepth [20] due to the bright overhead lighting often used by sporting arenas. Scenes in which the crowd is covered by an awning are also challenging for MegaDepth as problematic shadows are cast. The focal length estimation method (detailed in Sect. 3.2) was designed for images that contain clear orthogonal axes, such as present in a Manhattan world. We observed that the error in estimated focal length was smaller for images taken with small focal lengths. Perpendicular lines will appear more acute when captured with small focal lengths as compared to larger focal lengths which have a wider field of view.

4.3 Future Work

Success of the pipeline relies on accurate depth estimation and image segmentation. Improving these steps may allow for more robust behavior in a wider range of scenarios. Our pipeline utilizes both MegaDepth [20] and PSPNet [32] without any major modifications. An alternative technique for depth estimation would be to follow the method of Sturm et al. [28]. Producing more reliable and complete camera intrinsic estimates would also allow for the usage of self-localization techniques such as Simultaneous Localization and Mapping (SLAM) [10] to extract depth information. As SLAM is not a learned procedure, its depth estimation will likely be less prone to error in situations where MegaDepth fails to produce adequate results.

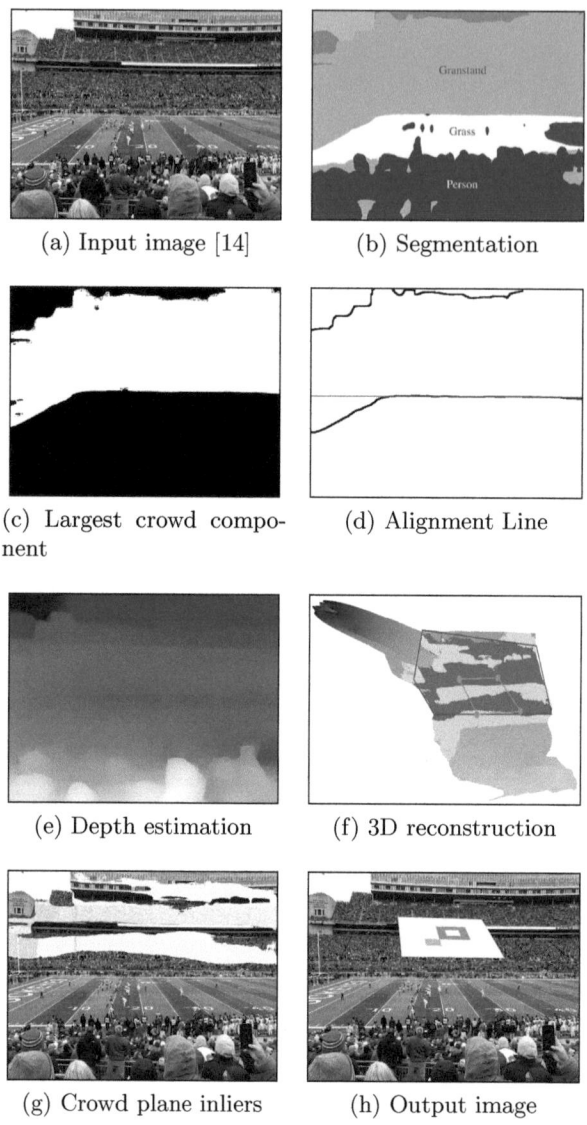

Fig. 8. Example of the pipeline's intermediate outputs running on a single image. The pipeline was run with a depth scaling factor of 1,000,000 and RANSAC tolerance of 10,000. In the 3D point cloud (f) created from the MegaDepth depth map (e) a convex hull (*blue*) is fit to the inliers (*dark red*) of the dominant plane in the segmented crowd region (*light red*). The rectangle (*green*) in the 3D reconstruction (f) corresponds to the final placement of the asset in the output image (h). (Color figure online)

The method of segmentation may be improved upon by overcoming sensitivity to highly non-homogeneous textures. Accurate segmentation of our target texture, crowd, is sensitive to scale and lighting. Exploring a segmentation approach which better accounts for texture information may be beneficial. With the exception of focal length estimation (Sect. 3.2) and the SQS score (Sect. 3.1), few steps in the pipeline can be assessed quantitatively. Developing a method for quantitatively assessing the quality of an asset placement would make it easier to evaluate the performance of the pipeline in different use cases.

Our primary method of benchmarking for perspective correctness has been manual inspection of augmented video. This could be improved by finding a qualitative benchmark to compare against. Additionally, conducting a study in which human participants are asked to assess whether an image asset is perspective correct could reveal viewers' tolerance for imperfect asset placement.

References

1. Abadi, M., et al.: TensorFlow: Large-scale machine learning on heterogeneous systems (2015). https://www.tensorflow.org/, tensorflow.org
2. Alcantarilla, P.F., Bartoli, A., Davison, A.J.: KAZE features. In: Fitzgibbon, A., Lazebnik, S., Perona, P., Sato, Y., Schmid, C. (eds.) ECCV 2012. LNCS, vol. 7577, pp. 214–227. Springer, Heidelberg (2012). https://doi.org/10.1007/978-3-642-33783-3_16
3. Bay, H., Ess, A., Tuytelaars, T., Van Gool, L.: Speeded-up robust features (surf). Comput. Vis. Image Underst. **110**(3), 346–359 (2008). https://doi.org/10.1016/j.cviu.2007.09.014
4. Canny, J.: A computational approach to edge detection. IEEE Trans. Pattern Anal. Mach. Intell. **8**(6), 679–698 (1986). https://doi.org/10.1109/TPAMI.1986.4767851
5. Chang, C.H., Hsieh, K.Y., Chiang, M.C., Wu, J.L.: Virtual spotlighted advertising for tennis videos. J. Visual Commun. Image Represent. **21**, 595–612 (2010)
6. Chang, C.H., Hsieh, K.Y., Chung, M.C., Wu, J.L.: Visa: virtual spotlighted advertising. In: Proceedings of the 16th ACM International Conference on Multimedia, pp. 837–840 (2008). https://doi.org/10.1145/1459359.1459500
7. Collobert, R., Kavukcuoglu, K., Farabet, C.: Torch7: a matlab-like environment for machine learning. In: BigLearn, NIPS Workshop (2011)
8. Cordts, M., et al.: The cityscapes dataset for semantic urban scene understanding. In: Proceedings of the IEEE Conference on Computer Vision and Pattern Recognition (CVPR) (2016)
9. Duda, R.O., Hart, P.E.: Use of the hough transformation to detect lines and curves in pictures. Commun. ACM **15**(1), 11–15 (1972). https://doi.org/10.1145/361237.361242
10. Durrant-whyte, H., Bailey, T.: Simultaneous localization and mapping: Part i. IEEE Robot. Autom. Mag. **13**, 99–110 (2006). https://doi.org/10.1109/MRA.2006.1638022
11. Eaton, J.W.: GNU Octave Manual. Network Theory Limited, Bristol (2002)
12. Everingham, M., Van Gool, L., Williams, C.K.I., Winn, J., Zisserman, A.: The PASCAL Visual Object Classes Challenge 2012 (VOC2012) Results (2012). http://host.robots.ox.ac.uk/pascal/VOC/voc2012/

13. Fischler, M.A., Bolles, R.C.: Random sample consensus: a paradigm for model fitting with applications to image analysis and automated cartography. Commun. ACM **24**(6), 381–395 (1981). https://doi.org/10.1145/358669.358692
14. Guzzo, N.: Michigan15 (2016). https://flic.kr/p/QeVPEJ. Accessed 21 Sept 2018
15. Han, J., de With, P.H.N.: 3-D camera modeling and its applications in sports broadcast video analysis. In: Sebe, N., Liu, Y., Zhuang, Y., Huang, T.S. (eds.) MCAM 2007. LNCS, vol. 4577, pp. 434–443. Springer, Heidelberg (2007). https://doi.org/10.1007/978-3-540-73417-8_52
16. Hartley, R., Zisserman, A.: Multiple View Geometry in Computer Vision, 2nd edn. Cambridge University Press, New York (2003)
17. Kalman, R.: A new approach to linear filtering and prediction problems. J. Basic Eng. (ASME) **82D**, 35–45 (1960)
18. Li, B., Peng, K., Ying, X., Zha, H.: Simultaneous vanishing point detection and camera calibration from single images. In: Bebis, G., et al. (eds.) ISVC 2010. LNCS, vol. 6454, pp. 151–160. Springer, Heidelberg (2010). https://doi.org/10.1007/978-3-642-17274-8_15
19. Li, Y., Wan, K.W., Yan, X., Xu, C.: Real time advertisement insertion in baseball video based on advertisement effect. In: Proceedings of the 13th Annual ACM International Conference on Multimedia, pp. 343–346 (2005). https://doi.org/10.1145/1101149.1101221
20. Li, Z., Snavely, N.: Megadepth: learning single-view depth prediction from internet photos. In: Proceedings of the IEEE Conference on Computer Vision and Pattern Recognition (CVPR) (2018)
21. Liu, H., Qiu, X., Huang, Q., Jiang, S., Xu, C.: Advertise gently - in-image advertising with low intrusiveness. In: 16th IEEE International Conference on Image Processing (ICIP), pp. 3105–3108 (2009)
22. Lowe, D.G.: Distinctive image features from scale-invariant keypoints. Int. J. Comput. Vis. **60**(2), 91–110 (2004). https://doi.org/10.1023/B:VISI.0000029664.99615.94
23. Lucas, B.D., Kanade, T.: An iterative image registration technique with an application to stereo vision. In: Proceedings of the 7th International Joint Conference on Artificial Intelligence. IJCAI 1981, vol. 2, pp. 674–679. Morgan Kaufmann Publishers Inc., San Francisco (1981). http://dl.acm.org/citation.cfm?id=1623264.1623280
24. Medioni, G., Guy, G., Rom, H., François, A.: Real-time billboard substitution in a video stream. In: De Natale, F., Pupolin, S. (eds.) Multimedia Communications, pp. 71–84. Springer London (1999). https://doi.org/10.1007/978-1-4471-0859-7_6
25. Mei, T., Guo, J., Hua, X.S., Liu, F.: Adon: toward contextual overlay in-video advertising. Multimedia Syst. **16**(4–5), 335–344 (2010)
26. Mei, T., Hua, X.S., Li, S.: Contextual in-image advertising. In: Proceedings of the 16th ACM International Conference on Multimedia, pp. 439–448. ACM (2008). https://doi.org/10.1145/1459359.1459418
27. Russakovsky, O., et al.: ImageNet large scale visual recognition challenge. Int. J. Comput. Vis. (IJCV) **115**(3), 211–252 (2015). https://doi.org/10.1007/s11263-015-0816-y
28. Sturm, P., Triggs, B.: A factorization based algorithm for multi-image projective structure and motion. In: Buxton, B., Cipolla, R. (eds.) ECCV 1996. LNCS, vol. 1065, pp. 709–720. Springer, Heidelberg (1996). https://doi.org/10.1007/3-540-61123-1_183

29. Wan, K.W., Xu, C.: Automatic content placement in sports highlights. In: 2006 IEEE International Conference on Multimedia and Expo, pp. 1893–1896 (2006)
30. Xu, C., Wan, K.W., Bui, S.H., Tian, Q.: Implanting virtual advertisement into broadcast soccer video. In: Aizawa, K., Nakamura, Y., Satoh, S. (eds.) PCM 2004. LNCS, vol. 3332, pp. 264–271. Springer, Heidelberg (2004). https://doi.org/10.1007/978-3-540-30542-2_33
31. Yildrim, Y.: Shotdetection (2015). https://github.com/yasinyildirim/ShotDetection
32. Zhao, H., Shi, J., Qi, X., Wang, X., Jia, J.: Pyramid scene parsing network. In: Proceedings of the IEEE Conference on Computer Vision and Pattern Recognition (CVPR) (2017)
33. Zhou, B., Zhao, H., Puig, X., Fidler, S., Barriuso, A., Torralba, A.: Scene parsing through ade20k dataset. In: Proceedings of the IEEE Conference on Computer Vision and Pattern Recognition (CVPR) (2017)
34. Zhou, B., et al.: Semantic understanding of scenes through the ade20k dataset. Int. J. Comput. Vis. (2018). https://doi.org/10.1007/s11263-018-1140-0

Visual Siamese Clustering for Cosmetic Product Recommendation

Christopher J. Holder[1(✉)], Boguslaw Obara[1], and Stephen Ricketts[2]

[1] Department of Computer Science, Durham University, Durham, UK
c.j.holder@durham.ac.uk
[2] Walgreens Boots Alliance, Nottingham, UK

Abstract. We investigate the problem of a visual similarity-based recommender system, where cosmetic products are recommended based on the preferences of people who share similarity of visual features. In this work we train a Siamese convolutional neural network, using our own dataset of cropped eye regions from images of 91 female subjects, such that it learns to output feature vectors that place images of the same subject close together in high-dimensional space. We evaluate the trained network based on its ability to correctly identify existing subjects from unseen images, and then assess its capability to find visually similar matches amongst the existing subjects when an image of a new subject is input.

1 Introduction

Recommender systems that make use of large amounts of data about a person to predict their preferences have been an effective method for businesses to increase customer engagement and retention since they were first proposed in the 1990s [1]. With the advent of big data and deep learning, sophisticated models capable of highly accurate predictions have been deployed within numerous industries [2, 3], however these approaches still require large numbers of datapoints for each customer, which are often not available to traditional bricks-and-mortar retail businesses.

For certain product types however, such as cosmetics or clothing, visual information, such as that captured by in store cameras or a customer's mobile device, may be all that is needed to make accurate product recommendations. Color Match [4] is mobile cosmetic advisory system, that uses a colour-based statistical analysis of a calibrated mobile photograph to recommend a foundation product. McAuley et al. [5] propose an approach to matching clothing and accessories based on human notions of complementarity by computing an embedding that places the output vectors of a pretrained convolutional neural network (CNN) for two products close together if online shopping data demonstrates a correlation between interest in the two products.

In the broader area of visual matching, the concept of the Siamese network was first proposed by Bromley et al. in [6], applied to the problem of signature verification, with the feature vector generated from a signature being compared with the stored feature vector corresponding to a given signer to determine whether the signature is genuine or not. Siamese, along with related Triplet network [7], based approaches have since been proposed for solving a broad array of problems including facial recognition [8], unsupervised learning [9], one-shot image recognition [10] and image retrieval [11].

In this work, we propose a vision-based recommender system for the cosmetics retail industry, which uses a CNN to recommend products to new customers based on the preferences of other people deemed to be similar based only on learned visual features. Focusing on mascara products, our objective is to create a model that, given an image of a person's eye, will output the products most preferred by those people whose eyes are visually similar.

We achieve this by collecting data from 91 women and training a Siamese network such that it optimises to match images of visually similar eyes. Given an input image of a new customer, the model outputs the most similar samples from the 91 people it has already seen, whose product preferences can then be made known to the new customer as recommendations. Figure 1 shows some example eye input images (top row) and the closest matches found by our model for those images (bottom row).

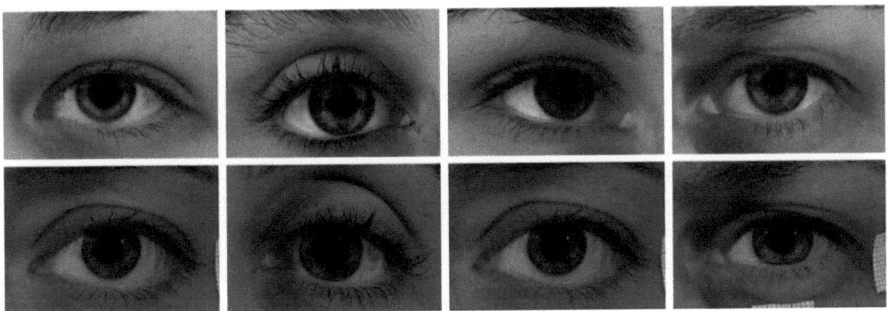

Fig. 1. Example eye images from our dataset (top) along with images of the subjects determined by our model to be the closest matches (bottom)

2 Method

The problem we are attempting to solve in this work is the recommendation of cosmetic products based on the visual similarity between a customer's features and those of a set of people whose preferences are already known. We first collect a set of facial images as well as data about the mascara product preferences of a group of women. From these images we use a Histogram of Oriented Gradients (HOG) [12] based detector to crop out each subject's eyes, which are then used as input for the training of a Siamese network which aims to learn to cluster together images of eyes belonging to the same person based on similarity of visual features. The aim of clustering these images in this manner is that the network will learn a latent embedding of eye images based on visual similarity that can be used to match new subjects to the samples with the highest similarity of visual features out of those already seen.

2.1 Dataset

We have compiled a dataset comprising frontal facial images of 91 Caucasian women between the ages of 18 and 60, along with quantitative and qualitative data about their experiences of 8 different mascara products. For each subject, 4 photographs were taken on consecutive days using a digital SLR camera while the subject was not wearing any make up. Mascara was then applied to each subject's eyelashes, which were measured before and after application to provide a quantitative measure of how each product affected each subject's lashes. Measurements taken were the length of the longest lash, average degree of lash curl, number of visually distinct lashes, and lash surface area. Each subject was then asked to complete a questionnaire to give a subjective account of their experience with each product.

We use only the image data in training our CNN model, while product preference data is used to make recommendations once a customer has been matched to their most similar subjects.

From each image we generate two crops, one for each eye, giving us eight eye images per subject, seven of which we use for training with one withheld for testing of the trained network model.

2.2 Eye Detector

The initial input is a set of images of whole faces, however we are only interested in the region surrounding each of the eyes. Manually cropping every image in our dataset would consume a lot of time and may not be an option if a system like this were deployed into a retail environment, so we use a histogram of oriented gradients (HOG) [12] feature descriptor and support vector machine (SVM) [13] classifier to identify the two regions of interest in each image for cropping.

We manually locate the eyes in a small subset of our training data, which we subsequently crop and scale to dimensions of 48×32 pixels from which HOG features are computed and used to train an SVM classifier. Each HOG descriptor comprises a 540-dimensional vector encoding a 9-bin histogram describing the gradient features present in an 8×8 pixel cell computed within a 16×16 sliding window with a stride of 8.

This vector is used as input to a one-class linear SVM, which during training attempts to determine the optimum boundary between observed samples and the rest of the feature space. Training continues until either a predetermined number of iterations have been completed or the magnitude of an error function computed over the training data is below a predetermined tolerance threshold, whichever is sooner.

Images from which we want to extract the eyes are resized to 128×128 pixels, and HOG features are computed in a sliding window of 48×32 pixels with a stride of 1. We assume that each input image is closely cropped to a single face, that this face contains two eyes which are open, and that human eyes are of a consistent size relative to the rest of the face. The HOG descriptor computed at each position is used as input to our trained SVM which outputs the signed distance between a sample and the learned decision boundary, which we interpret as a confidence value that the given window is centred on an eye.

These values are used to create a heatmap H where each pixel value is the accumulated confidence scores computed for all HOG descriptor windows that contain it, as shown in Eq. 1. For every sliding window position Ri a confidence value Ci is computed, and the value of a heatmap pixel $H_{x,y}$ is the sum of all those Ci for which the corresponding Ri includes the point (x, y).

$$H_{x,y} = \sum_{i=0}^{n} \begin{cases} C_i \text{ if } (x,y) \in R_i \\ 0 \text{ otherwise} \end{cases} \quad (1)$$

We find the highest scoring regions within the heat map using a sliding 48 × 32 pixel window with a stride of 1. For each window location we sum the heat of each contained pixel, and the two highest scoring non-overlapping locations are determined to give us the locations of the subject's eyes, as illustrated in Fig. 2.

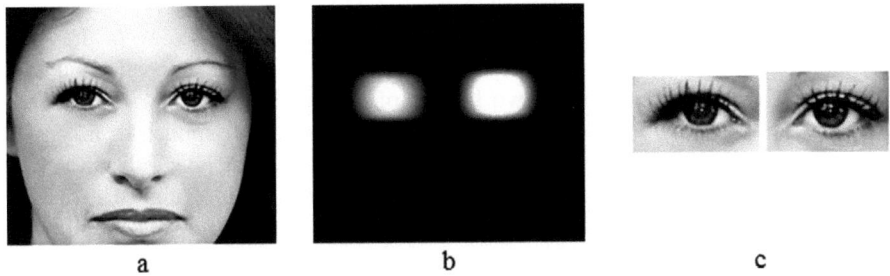

a b c

Fig. 2. Our eye detector uses HOG features and an SVM classifier to detect and crop eye regions from an image of the whole face (a). A heatmap (b) is generated from the confidence values output by a trained SVM, and the regions with the highest response are cropped (c) to give two eye images.

We use our approach to crop the eyes from the remainder of our dataset, manually checking the output cropped images for accuracy and determining a crop to be successful if an eye is fully contained within it. Successful crops were output for 97% of the unseen images in our dataset, leaving 3% that required manual cropping. Failure cases included images of subjects with prominent eyebrows, which would appear to give a similar HOG response to eyes, and images where a subject's eyes were closed, which we subsequently removed from the dataset. Some example failure cases are shown in Fig. 3, demonstrating a closed eye, (although in this case the detector found the correct region it still had to be removed from the dataset), a prominent eyebrow that appears to have confused the detector, and an image where the subject's nose was mistaken for an eye.

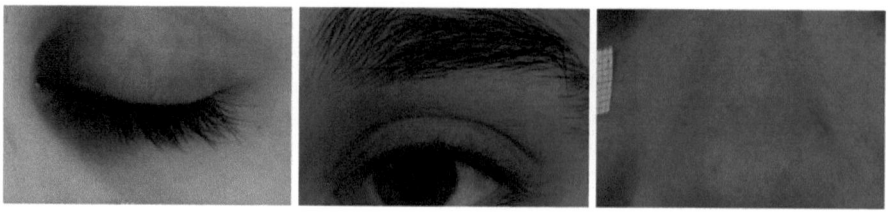

Fig. 3. Examples of failure cases of our HOG based eye region detector

2.3 Siamese Network

We use our HOG detector to crop the eye regions from the images in our dataset, which are subsequently used to train a Siamese network. First proposed in [6], a Siamese network comprises two identical neural networks which share weights and are optimised such that when a pair of input samples belong to the same category, the output is similar by some distance metric, and when an input pair do not belong to the same category the output vectors are dissimilar. In our case, the network is optimised such that output vectors are similar for two images of the same person's eyes (either one image of each eye or two separate images of the same eye) and dissimilar for images of different people's eyes, with similarity being determined by Euclidean distance. Our reasoning behind using this method is that the network should optimise to a state whereby input images of visually similar eyes lead to similar output vectors, allowing us to match unseen people to those whose features are visually similar.

The network model we use is VGG16 [14], first proposed by Simonyan et al. in 2014 for the purpose of large-scale image recognition, which is shown in a Siamese configuration in Fig. 4. The network comprises thirteen 3×3 convolutions interspersed with five 2×2 max-pooling layers, followed by three fully-connected layers, the last of which outputs the final n-dimensional output vector. Batch normalisation is used between convolutions, rectified linear units provide non-linearity and dropout is used during training to reduce the likelihood of overfitting. We use RGB input images with dimensions of 384×256 pixels, and test network models giving output vectors of dimensionality between 8 and 64.

During a training iteration using input image X_1, it is decided at random with equal probability whether the second input image X_2 will be selected at random from the set of different images of the same subject or selected at random from the set of images that contain different subjects. To introduce greater variety into the data, we also mirror each input image at random with a probability of 0.5. X_1 and X_2 are each used as input for one forward pass of the network, generating two n-dimensional vectors, Y_1 and Y_2. We compute the Euclidean distance, D, between Y_1 and Y_2 and use a contrastive loss function similar to that of [15] (Eq. 2) which gives us loss l with respect to label t, where if X_1 and X_2 are images of the same subject $t = 0$, otherwise $t = 1$. A margin $m = 2$ is used such that the loss is 0 in cases where $t = 1$ and D is greater than m, as in cases where both samples come from different subjects we are only interested in ensuring that the distance between Y_1 and Y_2 is greater than or equal to m.

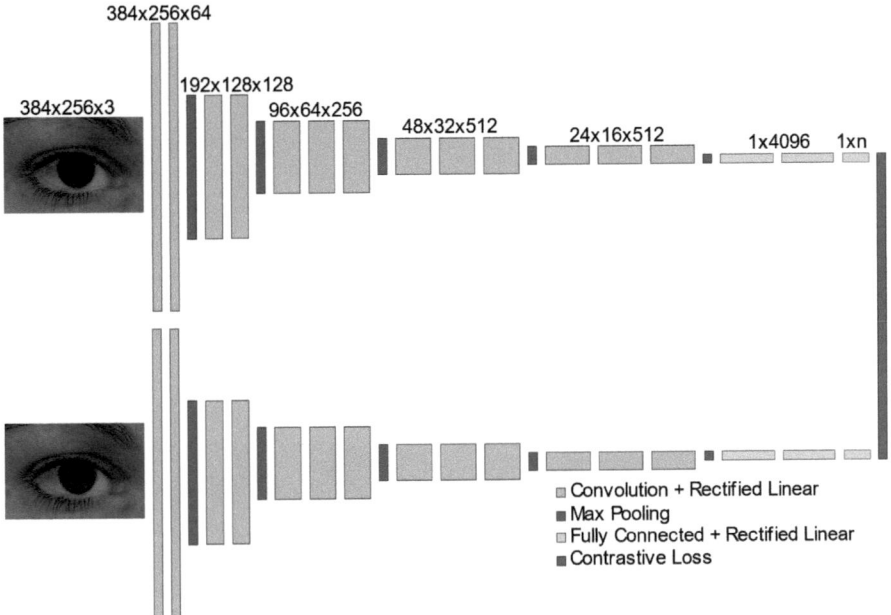

Fig. 4. The configuration of our Siamese network during training.

$$l = (1-t) * D^2 + t * \max\{0, m - D\}^2 \qquad (2)$$

We use backpropagation to optimise network parameters using the Adam optimiser [16] with weight decay to regularise parameters and learning rate decay to improve network convergence as training progresses. We train for 1000 epochs (an epoch being a period of training during which every training sample has been used as X_1 input once, although this may not be the case for X_2 due to it being selected at random), and save the model state at every 100 epochs so that we can evaluate network performance throughout the training process.

2.4 Clustering

Once the network model is trained, we perform one forward pass for each of our training images, along with mirrored versions, and record the output vector, from which we compute the mean and standard deviation in each dimension for each subject. In this case we are creating clusters for the 91 subjects whose data was used to train the model, however clusters could be added for new subjects if required without the model undergoing any additional training.

When matching a new image, X_1, to these clusters, X_1 and its mirror, X_2, are each input to the network and the mean vector Y of the two output vectors, Y_1 and Y_2, is computed. We calculate a distance metric d from Y to each subject s as shown in Eq. 3, whereby we compute the Euclidean distance between Y and μ_s, the mean of cluster s, proportional to the standard deviation of the cluster, σ_s, in each dimension. This distance is then used to identify the k nearest clusters, from which product recommendations can be made based on the preference data recorded for these subjects.

$$d = \left\| \frac{\mu_{s-Y}}{\sigma_s} \right\| \tag{3}$$

We visualise our dataset within the created n-dimension feature space using the T-distributed Stochastic Neighbour Embedding (t-SNE) method of van der Maaten and Hinton [17], as shown in Fig. 5. This takes the high-dimensional vectors output by our model and creates a low-dimensional embedding of our dataset that allows us to assess how well visually similar samples are being clustered.

Fig. 5. The clustering of our training dataset visualised by the t-SNE approach of van der Maaten and Hinton [17]

3 Results

The overall goal of this work is to create a model capable of matching images of new subjects based on visual similarity, however this is difficult to assess quantitatively. In order to quantify the performance of our model, we instead input an unseen image from each of the 91 subjects in our training dataset and note whether the correct subject cluster is identified by our matching algorithm within the output k nearest clusters for $k = 1$, $k = 5$ and $k = 10$.

The rationale behind this is that a model capable of accurately matching new subjects will also be capable of matching existing subjects correctly, as the visual similarity should always be high between two images of the same subject. However, as this is not a pure classification task but a metric of similarity, we would not expect the same subject to always return the same single closest cluster, and so by taking account of the nearest 5 and nearest 10 we can better evaluate the model's performance at the task it was designed for.

3.1 Effect of Vector Dimensionality

We evaluate eight trained models with output vectors of dimensionality between 8 and 64 in order to observe the effect that output dimensionality has on matching performance. In each case we tested the model at every 100 training epochs and selected the instance that demonstrated the best performance.

Results are shown in Table 1 and Fig. 6, showing that the best performance was demonstrated by the model with an output vector of 24 dimensions. It would appear that an output vector with dimensionality of less than 24 is insufficient to encode the information needed to adequately perform this task, however the additional complexity introduced with dimensions greater than 24 seems to negatively affect performance. These results are consistent when evaluation is based on the top 1, top 5 and top 10 nearest clusters. The top performing configuration, with an output vector of 24 dimensions, identifies the correct subject within its top 10 closest matches for 97% of samples, and as the top 1 closest match for 59% of samples, which considering this is essentially a 91-class problem for which our model has only seen 7 training samples per class, would seem to be quite a good result.

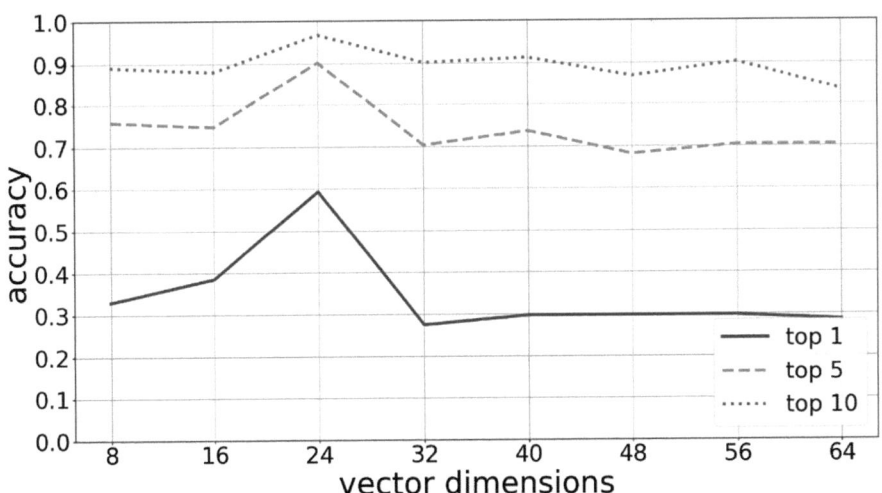

Fig. 6. Plot of results shown in Table 1 demonstrating the effect of output vector dimensionality on matching performance.

Table 1. Best performance demonstrated by models of different output vector dimensionality. In each case the probability of the correct subject being identified in the top k nearest clusters for $k = 1$, $k = 5$ and $k = 10$ is shown.

Dimensions	8	16	24	32	40	48	56	64
Top 1	0.33	0.38	**0.59**	0.27	0.30	0.30	0.30	0.29
Top 5	0.76	0.75	**0.90**	0.70	0.74	0.68	0.70	0.70
Top 10	0.89	0.88	**0.97**	0.90	0.91	0.87	0.90	0.84

3.2 Effect of Training Duration

For each model we save the parameters after every 100 epochs of training so that the effect of training duration on performance can be assessed. In Table 2 and Fig. 7 results are shown for the training process of our 24-dimension output model, which demonstrated the best overall performance. We can see that the model was able to reliably identify the correct subject within the top 10 nearest clusters very quickly, reaching an

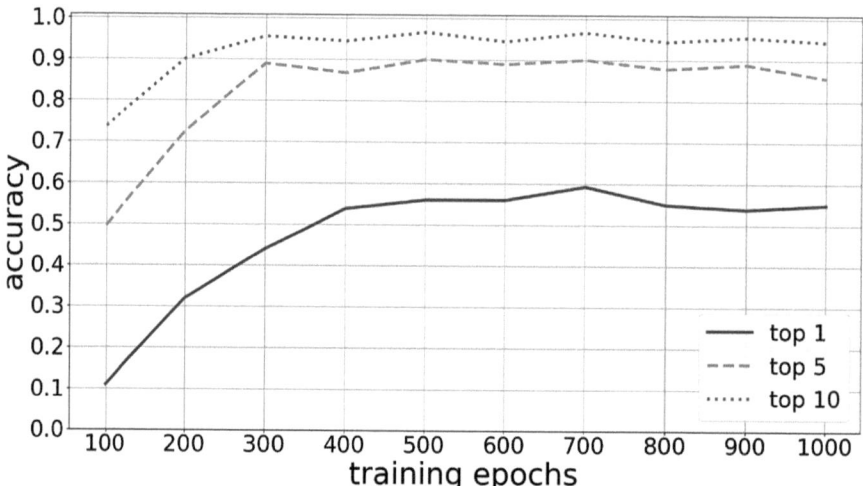

Fig. 7. Plot of the results shown in Table 2 demonstrating how our 24-dimension output model performed after different amounts of training.

Table 2. Performance of our 24-dimension output model during the training process. In each case the probability of the correct subject being identified in the top k nearest clusters for $k = 1$, $k = 5$ and $k = 10$ is shown.

Epochs	100	200	300	400	500	600	700	800	900	1000
Top 1	0.11	0.32	0.44	0.54	0.56	0.56	**0.59**	0.55	0.54	0.55
Top 5	0.49	0.73	0.89	0.87	**0.90**	0.89	**0.90**	0.88	0.89	0.86
Top 10	0.74	0.90	0.96	0.95	**0.97**	0.95	**0.97**	0.95	0.96	0.95

accuracy of 0.9 after just 200 epochs. After 300 epochs, top 5 performance appears to be nearly optimised, while top 1 performance continued to slowly improve until 700 training epochs, after which performance degraded slightly.

The best performance is observed after 700 epochs, at which point there are only 3 test samples for which the correct subject is not included in the top 10 nearest clusters. These 3 failure cases are displayed in Fig. 8 along with a subset of the training images of the same subject that form the correct cluster, and a subset of the training images of the subject whose cluster was incorrectly identified as the closest match. In the top two examples, it would appear that a change in lighting between training and test images may have caused the mismatch, as the incorrectly matched cluster and the input test image both appear slightly darker than the correct cluster. In the third example there appears to be a large amount of variability amongst training samples that may have caused the error, however unlike the other two examples there is little visual similarity between the input test image and the incorrectly matched cluster.

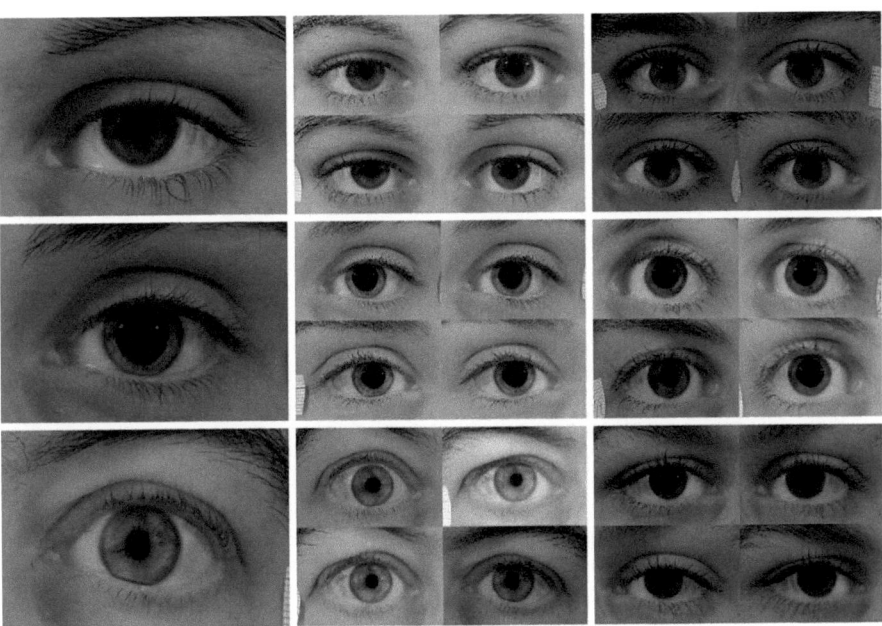

Fig. 8. Three examples where our model failed to identify the correct subject. The left column shows the input test image, in the centre are some of the training images of the correct subject, the right column contains some of the training images of the subject that was incorrectly identified as the closest match.

3.3 Qualitative Evaluation

We have demonstrated the ability of our model to correctly match unseen images to their subjects, however the aim of this work is to match images of new subjects to the most visually similar of the set of subjects the model has already seen. To assess the

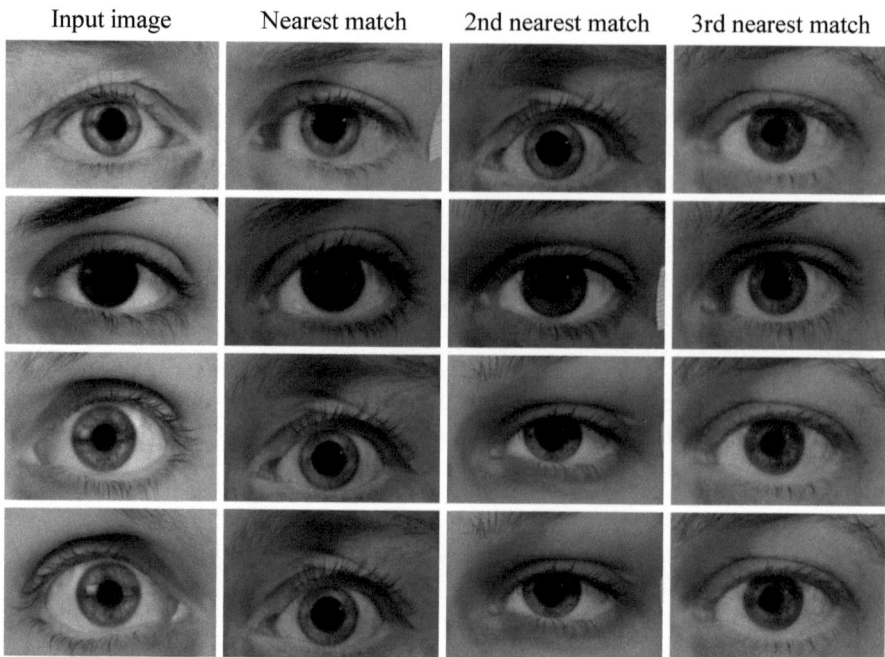

Fig. 9. Some example test images of unseen subjects shown next to images of the 3 closest matches found by our model.

ability of the model to do this, we input images of subjects not included in the initial training set, captured under the same conditions and cropped using the same HOG/SVM method described above. For each input image we output the top 3 closest matches from the clusters created from our training data. Figure 9 shows some example images along with an image from each of the top 3 nearest clusters. In all cases we use the model which performed best in our quantitative evaluation, which has an output vector of 24 dimensions and was trained on our training data set for 700 epochs.

Comparing the input images to those of the closest matched subjects, there appears to be quite a high level of visual similarity in terms of skin tone, eye colour and eye shape, as well as the appearance of eyelashes, eyebrows and eyelid. The two bottom rows of Fig. 9 show the left and right eyes of the same subject, each of which gave the same matches as expected.

There does however seem to be a higher reliance on skin tone and eye colour than on other features, so one potential direction for expanding on this work may be to adapt the model to work without this information, for example by using gradient images as input.

4 Conclusions

The problem we are addressing is to make cosmetic product recommendations based on the preferences of visually similar people. We generate our own dataset comprising facial images of 91 women, from which we automatically crop eye regions using an effective HOG feature and SVM classifier approach. We then train a Siamese network such that it optimises to cluster together images of the same subject in high-dimensional space, and evaluate its ability to do this using unseen images. We then assess the ability of this trained network to place images of new subjects within the same high-dimensional feature space such that they are near to the stored clusters pertaining to existing subjects that are visually similar.

We evaluate Siamese networks with different output feature vector lengths throughout the training cycle to identify the best-performing configuration, and demonstrate capabilities both in matching new images of seen subjects to the correct clusters, and in matching images of new subjects to clusters that are visually similar.

References

1. Resnick, P., Varian, H.: Recommender systems. Commun. ACM, 56–58 (1997)
2. Gomez-Uribe, C.A., Hunt, N.: The Netflix recommender system: algorithms, business value, and innovation. ACM Trans. Manag. Inf. Syst. **6**(4), 13 (2016)
3. Smith, B., Linden, G.: Two decades of recommender systems at Amazon.com. IEEE Internet Comput. **21**(3), 12–18 (2017)
4. Bhatti, N., et al.: Mobile cosmetics advisor: an imaging based mobile service. In: SPIE 7542 Multimedia on Mobile Devices (2010)
5. McAuley, J., Targett, C., Shi, Q., Van Den Hengel, A.: Image-based recommendations on styles and substitutes. In: International ACM SIGIR Conference on Research and Development in Information Retrieval (2015)
6. Bromley, J., Guyon, I., LeCun, Y., Säckinger, E., Shah, R.: Signature verification using a "siamese" time delay neural network. In: Advances in Neural Information Processing Systems, pp. 737–744 (1994)
7. Wang, J., et al.: Learning fine-grained image similarity with deep ranking. In: IEEE Conference on Computer Vision and Pattern Recognition (2014)
8. Chopra, S., Hadsell, R., Lecun, Y.: Learning a similarity metric discriminatively, with application to face verification. In: IEEE Conference on Computer Vision and Pattern Recognition (2005)
9. Wang, X., Gupta, A.: Unsupervised learning of visual representations using videos. In: IEEE International Conference on Computer Vision (2015)
10. Koch, G., Zemel, R., Salakhutdinov, R.: Siamese neural networks for one-shot image recognition. In ICML Deep Learning Workshop (2015)
11. Yu, Q., et al.: Sketch me that shoe. In: IEEE Conference on Computer Vision and Pattern Recognition (2016)
12. Dalal, N., Triggs, B.: Histograms of oriented gradients for human detection. In: IEEE Computer Society Conference on Computer Vision and Pattern Recognition, pp. 886–893 (2005)
13. Cortes, C., Vapnik, V.: Support vector networks. Mach. Learn. **20**(3), 273–297 (1995)

14. Simonyan, K., Zisserman, A.: Very deep convolutional networks for large-scale image recognition. In: International Conference on Learning Representations (2015)
15. Chopra, S., Hadsell, R., LeCunn, Y.: Dimensionality reduction by learning an invariant mapping. In: Computer Vision and Pattern Recognition, pp. 539–546 (2005)
16. Kingma, D.P., Ba, J.L.: Adam: a method for stochastic optimization. In: 3rd International Conference on Learning Representations (2014)
17. van der Maaten, L., Hinton, G.: Visualizing data using t-SNE. J. Mach. Learn. Res. **9**, 2579–2605 (2008)

Multimodal Deep Neural Networks Based Ensemble Learning for X-Ray Object Recognition

Quan Kong[1](✉), Naoto Akira[1], Bin Tong[1], Yuki Watanabe[2], Daisuke Matsubara[1], and Tomokazu Murakami[1]

[1] R&D Group, Hitachi, Ltd., Tokyo, Japan
{quan.kong.xz,naoto.akira.vu,bin.tong.hh,daisuke.matsubara.ba,
tomokazu.murakami.xr}@hitachi.com
[2] R&D Group, Hitachi, Ltd., Santa Clara, USA
yuki.watanabe.dv@hitachi.com

Abstract. X-ray object recognition is essential to reduce the workload of human inspectors regarding X-ray baggage screening and improve the throughput of X-ray screening. Traditionally, researchers focused on single-view or multiple views object recognition from only one type of pseudo X-ray image generated from X-ray energy data (e.g., dual-energy or mono-energy X-ray image). It is known that different types of X-ray images represent different object characteristics (e.g., material or density). Thus, effectively using different types of X-ray images as multiple modalities is promising to achieve more reliable recognition performance. In this paper, we explore different stage of ensemble approaches for X-ray object-recognition and propose an approach that exploits a classifier ensemble by using the multimodality information of X-ray images on a single-view object. We use a deep neural network to learn a good representation for each modality, which is used to train the base classifiers. To ensure high overall classification performance, the reliabilities of the base classifiers are estimated by taking the inherent features (e.g., color and shape) of an object in an X-ray image into consideration. We conducted experiments to evaluate the competitive performance of our method using a 15 classes dataset.

1 Introduction

X-ray imaging technology has been widely applied to baggage inspection at security checkpoints in public areas such as airports. Although there has been remarkable progress in X-ray imaging technology, this technology serves only to assist human inspectors, and manual screening is still extremely demanding due to the high priority of security. Manually screening over a long time is tedious, and detection accuracy by human inspectors is only about 80–90% [1]. To better assist human inspectors, baggage screening using computer vision techniques has been extensively investigated [2–4]. Such studies focused on recognizing dangerous or prohibited objects based on a limited number of categories (commonly three to six classes) such as 'handgun', 'camera, and 'laptop'. In fact, very few bags actually contain dangerous objects, but human inspectors are still required to confirm if all objects are dangerous or prohibited even in baggage considered safe, which may increase the burden of identifying. In this study, we extended the number of recognizable categories to daily objects that are safe to pass X-ray testing. Safe-object recognition is expected to relieve the stress of identifying a wide range of objects in baggage, allowing human inspectors to concentrate more on suspicious areas and improve human-detection accuracy. Motivated by the above reasons, we collected X-ray baggage images with 15 classes of objects, which contains 13 classes for daily use such as smartphones, umbrellas, and wallets.

The X-ray image used in the recognition task is a pseudo color or greyscale image generated using a dual-energy or mono-energy image. Traditionally, researchers attempt to recognize objects only from one type of the above X-ray images. It is known that different types of X-ray images represent different object characteristics [5], in which a dual-energy image reflects the material of an object and a mono-energy image reflects the density of an object. In previous researches [6,7], only one type of X-ray image was used to recognize an object. Moreover, we empirically found that the different types of generated X-ray images have different misclassified categories. Inspired by the above observations, we use different types of X-ray images as multimodal information of X-ray images to achieve reliable recognition performance. We use a deep neural network (DNN) to learn a good representation for each modality and apply it to train a base classifier for each modality. An novel ensemble method is proposed by considering the reliability of each classifier with utilizing the characteristics of X-ray image. We compute the reliability of each base classifiers by taking the context feature of an X-ray image into account, which improves the overall classification performance by assigning different weights according to the context feature of each input data for base classifiers. The context feature used in our approach is the inherent information reflected by the object in an X-ray image, which consists of color and shape. We choose color and shape as the context feature is because that the belt conveyor and the X-ray emitter is fixed during scanning, the color and shape of the same object in X-ray image is relatively invariant. To the best of our knowledge, this is the first study that used multimodal information to recognize X-ray images, and our experimental results of proposed method are significantly superior to those from the existed approaches on single-view X-ray image.

Contribution

(1) We proposed a new X-ray imaging algorithm by considering both the characteristics of material and density into one image, and utilize it as a new modality of X-ray image for ensemble learning. (2) We explored the ensemble architectures for X-ray image recognition and propose an X-ray object-recognition approach that uses multimodal information generated from X-ray energy raw data with DNN. Our ensemble method aggregates the results of the base classifiers to boost the recognition performance by considering the reliability of classifiers according

to the context feature of each X-ray image modality. (3) We conducted extensive experiments on our dataset to evaluate our approach on different popular DNN architectures for 15 categories recognition. We found that the recognition accuracy significantly improved (8 points higher than single modality on F-measure).

2 Related Works

DNNs for X-Ray Object Recognition. There are some contributions in computer vision for X-ray testing last decade such as [2,7,8] with local descriptors based methods. Deep neural networks have been used to obtain state-of-the-art results on a number of generic benchmark generic-image challenges [9]. To exploit deep learning for X-ray object recognition, Akcay et al. [10] used a fine-tuned DNN for the entire feature-extraction, representation, and classification process on X-ray-image object recognition and achieved good performance on their own single modality dataset. Mery et al. [11] also used fine-tuned GoogleNet [12] and AlexNet [13] to be carried out on their single modality X-ray image dataset called GDXray [14]. They focus on how to efficiently perform a DNN on a single kind of X-ray images, and only validate their approach on only limited number of categories such as 4 [11] and 6 [10]. Our proposed approach also uses DNNs to learn a good representation of X-ray images. We show a promising ensemble way for using multimodal X-ray images with a classifier level based ensemble to achieve better recognition performance by utilizing the characteristics of X-ray images than using a single network on 15 categories.

Multimodal Learning with DNNs. It is an essential challenge for utilizing multimodal learning on vision problems. Recent years, within the context of data fusion applications, deep learning methods have been shown to be able to bridge the gap between different modalities and produce useful joint representations [15,16]. For utilizing different image modalities cases, Simonyan *et al.* [17] proposed two-stream Covnets that incorporated spatial and temporal information on video action recognition. Use RGB and depth data as two modalities processed in two separate CNN based streams, then combined with a late fusion network for object recognition [18] has been proposed. Zhu *et al.* [19] introduced a novel multi-modal fusion framework for RGB-D scene recognition by using a feature level fusion, that the feature is regularized to be discriminative and compact with consideration of the correlation of modalities. However, multimodal image data source for baggage inspection through computer vision technology has not been studied thoroughly. It is worth mention that different X-ray imaging algorithm leads to different type of X-ray image generated, which can be used as different modalities, as for they focus on different characteristics of the objects.

3 X-Ray Image Data

3.1 Overview

We collected about 7063 images of baggage by using the Hitachi BIS-X-C7555A X-ray machine. All X-ray energy data were transferred into two types of X-ray images with different characteristics, i.e., material and density, and a custom image representing both material and density information. There are 19,198 manually cropped object images from the X-ray baggage images labelled with 15 classes. To illustrate our dataset, a random selection of 36 X-ray images (material images) are shown in Fig. 1.

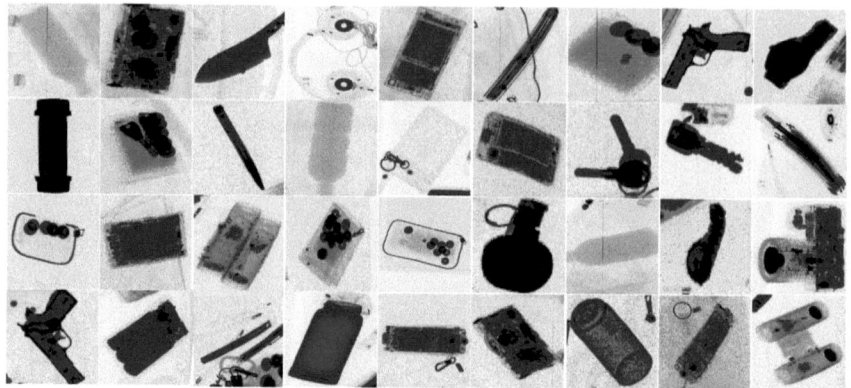

Fig. 1. The illustration of our data set.

3.2 X-Ray Image Data Generation

X-ray radiation is passed through a test object, and an X-ray image is captured using a detector corresponding to the radiation intensity attenuated by the test object. According to the principle of photoelectric absorption [20]: $I = I_0 e^{-\mu z}$, where the transmitted intensity I depends on the incident radiation intensity I_0, thickness z of the object, and energy-dependent linear attenuation coefficient μ associated with the material. Based on the above theory, generally there are three types of generated X-ray images as follows from X-ray energy data.

Material Image. By using dual-energy, it is possible to calculate the ratio: $R_m = ln(\frac{I_{hi}}{I_0})/ln(\frac{I_{lo}}{I_0})$, where I_{lo} and I_{hi} are the transmitted I obtained using low and high energies E_{lo} and E_{hi}, respectively [21]. Base on the computed R_m, an image can usually represent the material of an object by using a look-up-table that produces pseudo color information [22].

Density Image. As mentioned above, when we irradiate E_{hi} to an object, the absorbed energy mainly depends on the density of the test object. The calculated $R_d = ln(I_{hi}/I_0)$ can be used for representing the density of a test object, the material of which the image does not take into account. A grey-scale image is generated by scaling R_d into intensity information.

Composite Image. A composite image takes both the material and density information into account by combining the R_m and R_d and converting them into the hue-saturation-value (HSV) color space. The R_m is converted into hue

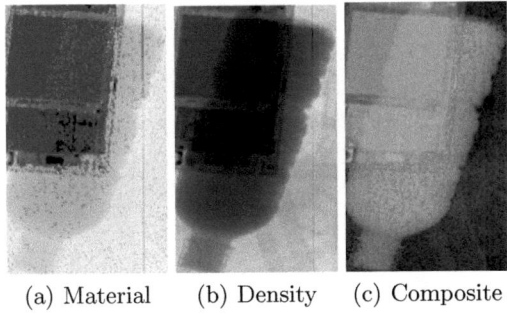

(a) Material (b) Density (c) Composite

Fig. 2. Examples of generated X-ray images used in our approaches (smartphone and bottle). (a) Material image. (b) Density image. (c) Our composite image both reflects material and density information.

H by using a look-up-table that produces pseudo hue information. Saturation S is acquired by $S = R_m$ after clamping R_m to a fixed box $[0, 1.0]$. Value V (also brightness) is calculated as $V = 1 - R_d$. In the above principle, we can generate a composite image that reflects both material and density information of a test object in the HSV color space.

3.3 Characteristics of Generated X-Ray Image

The three types of X-ray images are shown in Fig. 2. The material image shows the materials of the objects by different colors, but the edge patterns are not clear enough. The density image shows the density of the objects from intensity information. Clear edges of the objects enables us to easily find irregularities in the surface texture of the bottle. From the composite image, we can observe that the material information can be represented, but the details (e.g., smartphone's edge and body) and surface texture of the bottle are not the same as those of the material and density images.

Intuitively, material, density and composite images provide auxiliary visual information to each other in x-ray object recognition. To study the diversity potential among the three type of images, we trained three separate x-ray object classifier with material and density images only, based on the same network architectures as VGG [23] which is pre-trained on ILSVRC dataset [9]. The training set is 70% from our collected data was used in fine-tuning of the above DNNs. The classification result is validated on the remained parts as test images. We use a disagreement measure [24] to measure the diversity of the base classifiers in our approach. The diversity of misclassified samples between classifiers C_j and C_k is thus computed as,

$$Dis_{jk} = \frac{N^{10} + N^{01}}{N} = \frac{N^{10} + N^{01}}{N^{11} + N^{10} + N^{01} + N^{00}}, \quad (1)$$

Table 1. Pair-wise recognition result.

Classifier pair	N^{10}	N^{01}	Diversity
(Material, Density)	1,839	1,724	0.185
(Density, Composite)	1,977	2,101	0.212
(Composite, Material)	2,526	2,245	0.248

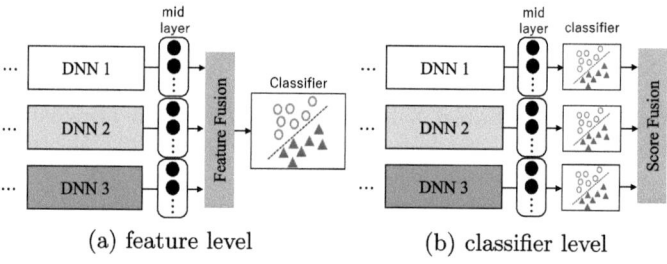

(a) feature level   (b) classifier level

Fig. 3. Fuse DNNs at different stage. Feature level ensemble: concatenate the feature extracted from multimodal DNNs to a single classifier. Classifier level ensemble: combine the score from each classifier's.

where $N = N^{11} + N^{10} + N^{01} + N^{00}$, N^{00} and N^{11} is the number of samples misclassified and correctly classified by both, N^{10} denotes the number of samples that were correctly classified by C_j but misclassified by C_k, and N^{01} denotes the number of samples misclassified by C_j but correctly classified by C_k. The diversity between each two classifier pair are shown in Table 1. Obviously, that each type of images provide complementary information and it is a promising way to improve the overall classification performance by fusing the above three types of images as different modalities.

4 Methodology

For a single modality, our x-ray object recognition approach composed of three steps: x-ray image generation, feature extraction and classification. Based on the observation in Table 1, ensemble is a promising way to improve the classification performance. However we think ensemble at different stages would lead to different classification results. Therefore, we explored two approaches to fuse the material, density and composite images for x-ray image classification. Basically, they are three-branch DNNs used that perform ensemble at different stages, denoted as feature level ensemble and classifier level ensemble, as shown in Fig. 3. Besides, we proposed a third ensemble method that can obtain superior results than the above two considerable ensemble approaches, which was also based on classifier level ensemble. However, instead of simply fusing the classification score, we developed a multimodal X-ray object-recognition approach with a reliability estimator for each classifier by utilizing the characteristics of generated X-ray images. The color and shape of an object in an X-ray image are

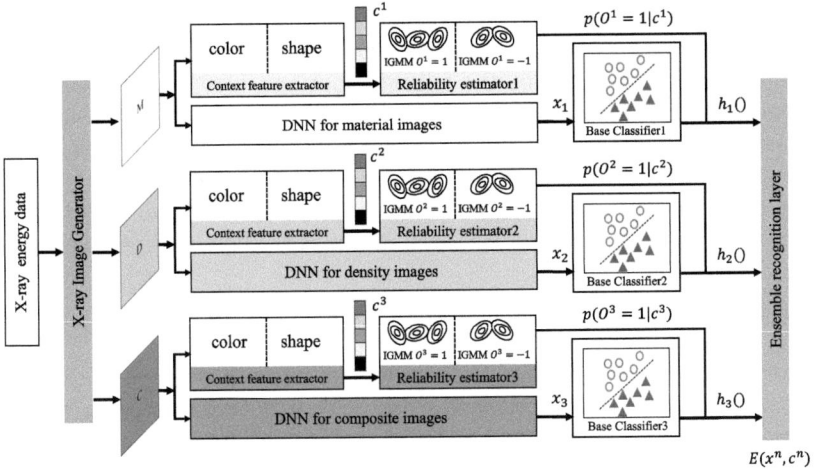

Fig. 4. Overview of our proposed method.

mainly constrained to the radiation intensity for the object of the same class (thickness and material is similar). Thus, the color and shape of an object of the same class is inherent information when the X-ray source maintains a fixed position during the X-ray test. We used color and shape as the image context feature to predict the reliability of a base classifier.

4.1 Proposed Method Overview

The overview of our proposed approach is shown as in Fig. 4. It consists of three components: multimodal DNN-based classifiers, classifier reliability estimators, and a classifier-based ensemble-recognition layer. To use the different characteristics of an X-ray image generated from energy data we described in Sect. 3, our approach has four distinct process stages, as shown in Fig. 4. First, we prepare a DNN to learn a good representation for each modality image. When we have N training instances $\{x_i^n \in X\}_{i=1}^{N}$, x_i^n means the ith instance feature extracted with the DNN of the nth modality. Second, the extracted x_i^n is applied to train the base classifier f_n for the nth characteristics of the X-ray image to predict the classification scores $h_n = f_n(x_i^n)$. Third, $h_n(x_i^n)$ are weighted by the nth reliability estimator that is prepared for each base classifier to estimate the reliability r_i^n of $h_n(x_i^n)$ for the ith instance when the context feature c_i^n is given. Finally, the base classifiers with their output reliability are incorporated by classifier-level ensemble to ensure high overall classification performance.

4.2 Feature Extraction

We explored several DNNs as feature extractor, e.g., AlexNet [13], GoogleNet [25] VGG [23] and ResNet [26]. The DNNs we used are pre-trained on the ILSVRC dataset and fine-tune the DNNs by using our dataset to optimize it for X-ray object images. The input of the DNNs is a 256 × 256 X-ray image. Data augmentation is randomly executed by the following options. (1) Use the entire original input image. (2) Randomly sample a 224 × 224 batch and adjust the aspect ratio to between 1/2 to 2. The second fully connected layer (fc7) has been selected for feature extraction in AlexNet, VGG-16 and VGG-19 networks. For GoogleNet, feature is extracted from pool5/7x7s1 layer. The features from the ResNet-50, ResNet-101 are extracted from the res4f and res4b22 layers respectively.

4.3 Base Classifier

The extracted features are used to train the classifier that is constructed based on the one-vs.-rest SVM for each category with a decision function written as $f_n(x) = a^T \cdot k(x) + b$, where a and b are the vector of the weights assigned to each training instance and the bias. Also, $k = [k(x_1, x) \ldots k(x_N, x)]^T$, where $k(\cdot, \cdot)$ is a kernel function that calculates the distance (similarity) between two instances. We use a polynomial kernel for the SVM, which is usually used for image classification. For each base classifier $f_n(x)$, the output label is $y = \arg\max f_{n,l}(x)$, where $f_{n,l}(x)$ is the predictive score returned by the classifier f_n when the input x is labelled with l. The score is the margin of test instance for the trained SVM. The classification score $h_n(x) = \{f_{n,1}(x), \ldots, f_{n,j}(x), \ldots, f_{n,L}(x)\}$, where $f_{n,j}(x)$ is the predictive scores returned by the nth base classifier for the class label j for $1 < j < L$, and L is the number of classes.

4.4 Learning for Reliability Estimator

We use a classifier-based ensemble by taking the reliability of the base classifier into account to optimize the weight of each base classifier. The reliability r_i^n can be defined as the following equation: $r_i^n = p(O^n = 1|c_i^n)$, where $O^n \in \{-1, +1\}$ shows whether the nth base classifier's prediction is correct, c_i^n is the image's context feature, which is compact and lite, by compressing the color and edge-pattern histogram [27] into a 200-dimensional features with Principal Component Analysis (PCA), N is the number of characteristics of an X-ray image, and $p(O^n = 1|c_i^n)$ is the probability with which the nth base classifier's predicted result is correct when the ith instance with nth characteristics whose context feature vector c_i^n is given. That is, we estimate the reliability of the nth base classifier by using the image's context feature and incorporate it into our ensemble recognition layer. We can compute the probability as follows by using Bayes' theorem.

$$p(O^n = 1|c_i^n) = \frac{p(c_i^n|O^n = 1)p(O^n = 1)}{p(c_i^n|O^n)p(O^n = 1) + p(c_i^n|O^n = -1)p(O^n = -1)}, \quad (2)$$

where $p(O^n)$ is the prior density of the nth base classifier's reliability computed from its classifier's prediction by using the validation data. The term $p(c_i^n)$ is the prior density of the image's context feature c_i^n, and $p(c_i^n|O^n)$ is the likelihood of

O^n for c_i^n. We use a Gaussian mixture model (GMM) to model O^n. That is, we prepare two models, one for $O^n = 1$ and the other for $O_n = -1$, and each model shows the distribution of context features c_i^n corresponding to its prediction result (1 or -1). To construct the model by using the GMM, a fitting number of the GMM's components should be better to model the distribution. Therefore, we obtain such components based on non-parametric Bayesian methods. We achieve non-parametric unsupervised clustering with an infinite GMM (IGMM), which is a GMM with a Dirichlet process prior defined over mixture components [28]. We can compute the likelihood of the IGMM of $O^n = 1$ (or $O^n = -1$) for c_i^n as follows: $p(c_i^n|O^n) = \sum_i \pi_i \mathcal{N}(c_i^n, \mu_i, \sigma_i)$, where π_i is the mixture weight of the ith multivariate Gaussian distribution of the IGMM, and μ_i and σ_i are the mean vector and covariance matrix of the Gaussian distribution, respectively.

4.5 Ensemble

A classifier-level ensemble is used to ensure high overall classification performance. Considering the reliability of a base classifier and compatibility issues arising from different fine-tuned DNNs, the ensemble-recognition layer in our approach is defined as the following equation:

$$E(x_i, c_i) = \sum_{n=1}^{N} \alpha_n r_i^n h_n(x_i^n) \tag{3}$$

where α_n is the weight of the nth base classifier. The weight corresponds to the prediction accuracy of the nth classifier computed from training data with a cross validation approach. We choose the class that classifies a test instance with the greatest ensemble scores, $argmax E(x_i, c_i)$ for the ith instance as the final prediction result, i.e., the recognized object.

5 Evaluation

We present the experiments to evaluate the proposed method as follows. Firstly, we describe the experimental datasets and methods we used. Secondly, we investigate the impact of our multimodal architecture on the classification performance. Thirdly, experiments are further conducted to show the whether reliability estimator benefits the performance of X-ray object recognition. Finally, we discuss the effect of the amount of training data and validation data on our proposed method.

5.1 Data Set

Our evaluation dataset is constructed with 19,198 instance of X-ray energy data. Three types of X-ray image are generated from each energy data. There are 60% data used for training data, 20% for validation data and 20% for test data in our evaluation with cross validation as default. 15 categories are used for evaluating our proposed method. Each category contains 500–2000 images. There 13 classes for our daily used safe objects. "danger" class contains the objects such as "gun", "bomb" and "plastic explosive". "other" contains the objects with a small number other than "danger" and 13 safe categories.

5.2 Evaluation Methods

We evaluated the performance of our method based on the average F-measure ($\frac{2 \cdot precision \cdot recall}{precision + recall}$). To investigate its effectiveness, we tested the performance of six different methods as follows on different DNNs to confirm the effectiveness of our proposed method.

- **Single(m)** and **Single(d)**: uses a single DNN trained by material or density images as feature extractor to classifier as previous works.
- **Single(c)**: uses a single DNN trained by composite images as feature extractor to classifier. *Single(c)* also can be seen as a data level ensemble method.
- **Multi(ft)**: Feature level ensemble, concatenate the feature extracted from mid-layer's output of multimodal DNNs trained with material, density and composite images respectively with the same architecture to a single classifier.
- **Multi(cl)**: Multimodal DNNs based classifier level ensemble without the reliability estimator, one classifier for one modality.
- **Multi(cl)+R**: Multimodal DNNs based classifier ensemble with reliability estimator.

We used SVM as classifier, which is trained using grid-search for the best hyper-parameters. The DNNs are used for feature extraction: AlexNet, GoogleNet, VGG and ResNet follow the same architecture of [13,23,25] and [26], respectively.

5.3 Results of X-Ray Object Recognition

Effects of Different Level Ensemble. Table 2 shows the F-measures about the six methods on different DNN architectures. Generally speaking, classifier with single image modality (material or density) obtained inferior results than ensemble methods on all the DNNs we used. *Single(m)* obtains 0.811–0.884 F-measure on material images across different DNNs while working similar as the *Single(d)*, which obtained a F-measure from 0.828–0.892 on density images. On the other side, we focus on the *Single(c)*, that is our data level ensemble result. Compared to *Single(m)* and *Single(d)*, by considering both the material and density information, the F-measure related to each architecture of DNN achieved a slight improvements about 2 points on average. Besides, the diversity of composite image was confirmed on Table 1, that utilize the composite image as another modality independent of material and density is a considerable efficient way on late stage ensemble.

Table 2 also shows results about feature level ensemble *Multi(ft)* and classifier level ensemble without using reliability estimators *Multi(cl)*. Feature level

Table 2. Classification results for all compared methods.

	Methods					
	Single(m)	Single(d)	Single(c)	Multi(ft)	Multi(cl)	Multi(cl)+R
AlexNet	0.811	0.828	0.833	0.847	0.873	**0.895**
GoogleNet	0.821	0.833	0.853	0.860	0.878	**0.901**
VGG-16	0.881	0.877	0.894	0.907	0.928	**0.957**
VGG-19	0.879	0.863	0.898	0.903	0.921	**0.948**
ResNet-50	0.884	0.892	0.903	0.895	0.925	**0.951**
ResNet-101	0.868	0.874	0.886	0.880	0.913	**0.943**

ensemble obtained inferior results than classifier ensemble across all the DNNs, and data level ensemble *Single(c)* on ResNet. As for fusing multiple modalities in the feature level would weaken the utility of other modality features, which could undermine the ensemble performance. On the other side, *Multi(cl)* fused the high level semantic information, confidence score. However, in some cases, it would be difficult for these three classifiers to adjust decision mistake of one image modality. *Multi(cl)+R* solved this problem by introducing a reliability estimator for each classifier and achieved the best performance among all the methods.

Effects of Reliability Estimators. *Multi(cl)+R* has the best overall performance among all the methods on F-measure across all the architectures of DNNs, and achieved a very good accuracy, the highest F-measure 0.957 when using VGG-16 as the backbone networks as shown in Table 2. Compared to single modality methods, *Multi(cl)+R* was 6.3 points–8.0 points higher than each single modality method on VGG-16. *Mutil(cl)+R* also performed 5.0 points and 2.9 points higher than feature and classifier ensemble method, under the same network backbone VGG-16, showing the most effective multimodal synergy for x-ray image recognition.

Figure 5 shows the visual confusion matrix of each method on VGG-16. As shown in the matrix, "plastic bottle", "spray", "wallet" and "watch" were relatively poor in *Single(m)* compared to *Single(d)*, "battery", "binoculars", "water bottle" and "umbrella" were relatively poor in *Single(d)* compared to *Single(m)*, showing the distinguishable categories of *Single(m)* and *Single(d)* are different and complementary to each other. "danger", "umbrella" and "pass case" were improved by *Single(c)*. It achieved the performance similar to the better one between *Single(m)* and *Single(d)*, showing our composite image reflects both characteristics of material and density successfully. *Multi(ft)* performs slightly better than single modality methods. However, since feature level would weaken the utility of other modality features, such as "key" became poorer than single modality. Obviously, *Multi(cl)+R* achieved further improvements on most of categories compared to *Multi(cl)*, especially for the categories were relatively poor

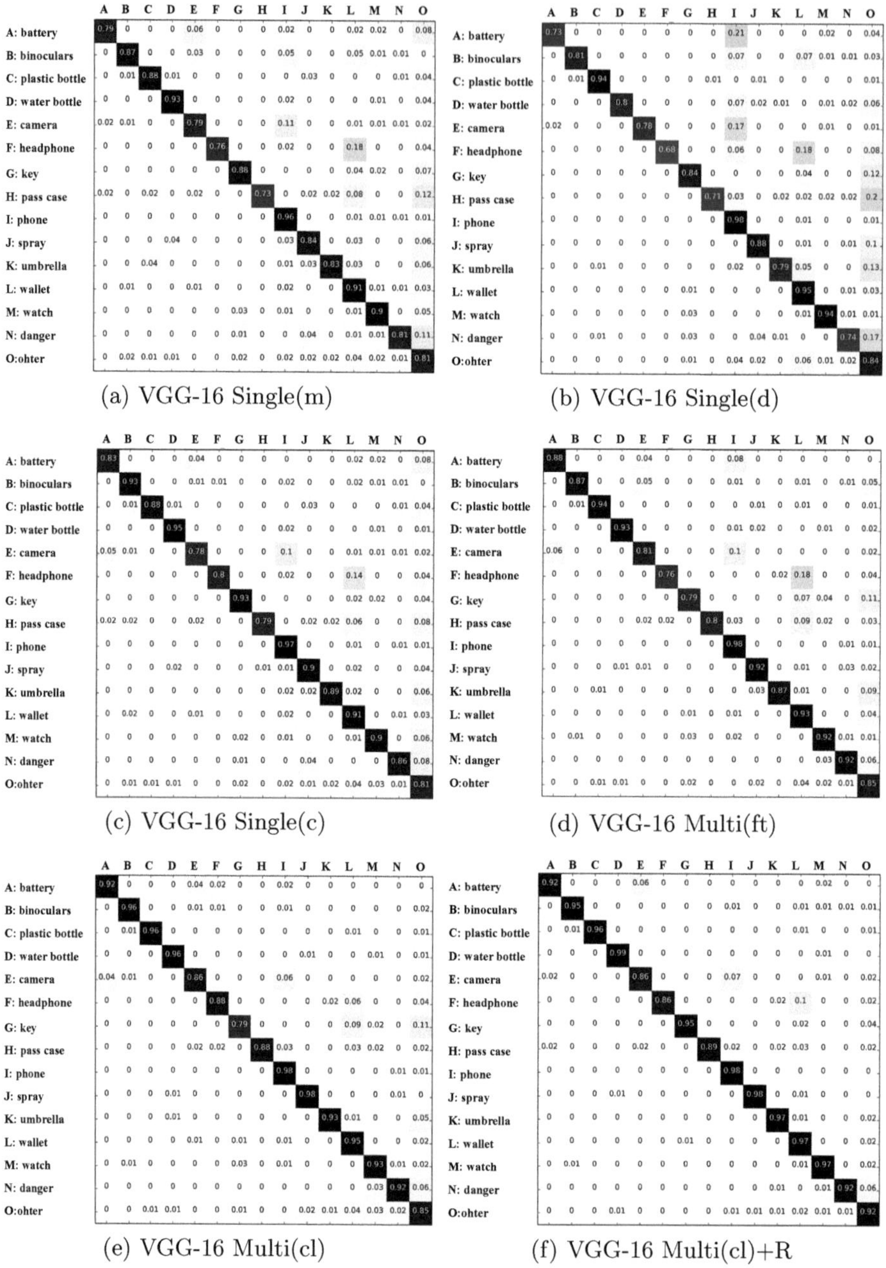

Fig. 5. Visual confusion matrix of each method on VGG-16.

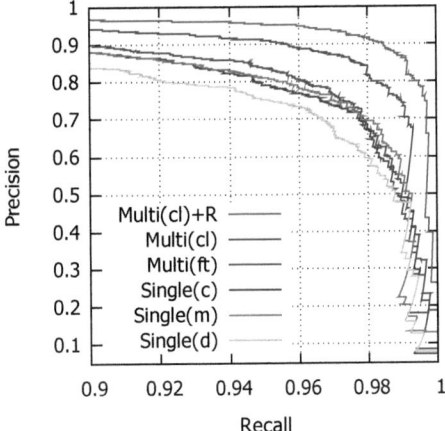

Fig. 6. Precision-Recall curve on VGG-16 for each method.

in *Single(m)* and *Single(d)*. "O:other" was improved greatly compared to the other ensemble methods. The performance of "O:other" was improved small in the other ensemble methods, since "O:other" is the negative samples collection contains the samples except of the other 14 categories, it is hard to abstract a stable pattern for it. *Multi(cl)+R* exploited the image context information, shape and color, to model the reliability estimator that the likelihood of error prediction for the input image without a stable pattern would be high, thus the reliability of the related classifier would be low, to avoid mistake decision.

We also assessed the precision in *Multi(cl)+R* on VGG-16, with regard of recalls. Figure 6 shows the precision-recall curve of each method on VGG-16. As for our safe X-ray object recognition is expected to relieve the stress of identifying a wide range of objects in baggage for human inspectors, the precision is required to be as high as possible when recall was high enough. Figure 6 shows *Multi(cl)+R* achieved about 97% precision when recall was 90%, compared to other methods around 85%–94% precision. Moreover, *Multi(cl)+R* achieved 86% precision with 99% recall, which was 22 points higher than *Multi(cl)* (74%) and 32 points higher than *Single(m)* (54%), showing the robustness of our *Multi(cl)+R* method.

Amount of Training Data. The reliability estimator used in *Multi(cl)+R* is trained from its classifier's prediction by using the validation data. The reliability estimator is highly related to the base classifier's performance and amount of validation data. Classifier's performance is also effected by amount of training data used for training classifier.

Figure 7 shows the average F-measure when amount of training and validation data were changed on VGG-16. To investigate the performance of *Multi(cl)+R* when the amount of training data was changed. We fixed the validation and test data as 20% respectively, and trained the classifiers with different percentage

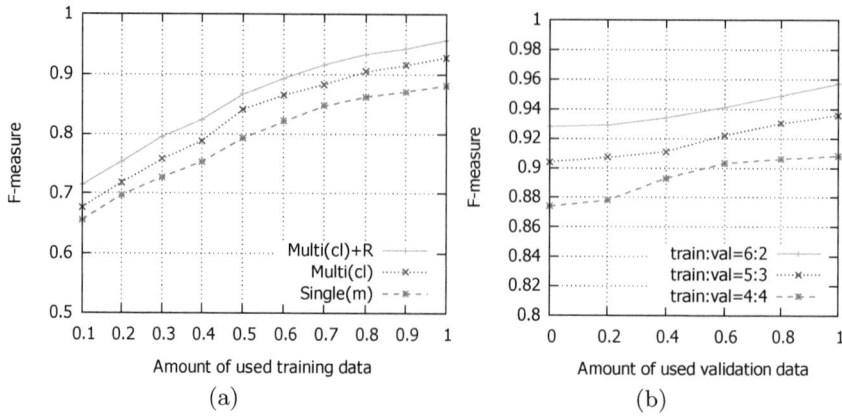

Fig. 7. Transitions of average F-measures for *Multi(cl)+R* on VGG-16. (a) train:val:test = 6:2:2, F-measure for each method when amount of used training data was changed. (b) (train+val):test = 8:2, F-measure for *Multi(cl)+R* when amount of used validation data was changed with different ratios of train to val.

of remained parts of 60% data. Figure 7(a) shows as amount of training data increases, the F-measure of *Multi(cl)+R* also increases. Besides, the average of difference between *Multi(cl)+R* and *Multi(cl)* was about 3.5 points when amount of training data was less than 50%, and 3.0 points when amount of raining data was more than 50%. In other words, *Multi(cl)+R* is effective when the base classifiers trained with scant training data. To investigate the performance of *Multi(cl)+R* when amount of validation data was changed, we used three ratios of training to validation data, and increased the amount of validation data with a fixed amount of training data. Figure 7(b) shows the F-measure of *Multi(cl)+R* on VGG-16 when amount of validation data increases. The improvements of *Multi(cl)+R* was small when validation data was insufficient, which could be confirmed on "train:val = 4:4" in Fig. 7(b). However, when validation data was large enough, the improvements was also small, since the bottleneck was transferred from reliability estimator to the base classifier's performance. In this scenario, we conclude that reliability estimator could work well with adequate validation data, and the ratio of training to validation data, according to the above observation, "train:val = 3:1" could be recommended as a default setting.

5.4 Conclusion

We explored different stages of ensemble on X-ray image and proposed a multi-modal X-ray object recognition approach exploiting the classifier ensemble based on DNNs. Inspired by the diversity of classifiers constructed from single-view X-ray images, our approach exploits three types of X-ray images, one for each modality. We utilize a classifier level ensemble by considering the context feature of the X-ray image to achieve high accurate recognition.

References

1. Michel, S.: Computer-based training increases efficiency in X-ray image interpretation by aviation security screeners. In: 41st Annual IEEE International Carnahan Conference on Security Technology, Ottawa, ON, Canada, pp. 201–206 (2007)
2. Bastan, M., Byeon, W., Breuel, T.M.: Object recognition in multi-view dual energy X-ray images. In: British Machine Vision Conference (BMVC) (2013)
3. Mery, D.: Active X-ray testing of complex objects. Insight Non Destruct. Testing Cond. Monit. **54**(1), 28–35 (2012)
4. Mery, D.: Inspection of complex objects using multiple-X-ray views. IEEE/ASME Trans. Mechatron. **20**(1), 338–347 (2015)
5. Mery, D.: X-ray testing: The state of the art. J. Departement Comput. Sci.-Pontificia Univ. Catolica de Chile Av. Vicuna Mackenna. Santiago de Chile **18**(9), 1–12 (2013)
6. Uroukov, I., Speller, R.: A preliminary approach to intelligent X-ray imaging for baggage inspection at airports. Signal Process. Res. **4**, 1–11 (2015)
7. Mery, D., Riffo, V., Zuccar, I., Pieringer, C.: Automated X-ray object recognition using an efficient search algorithm in multiple views. In: IEEE Conference on Computer Vision and Pattern Recognition Workshops, pp. 368–374, June 2013
8. Turcsány, D., Mouton, A., Breckon, T.P.: Improving feature-based object recognition for X-ray baggage security screening using primed visualwords. In: IEEE International Conference on Industrial Technology (ICIT), pp. 1140–1145 (2013)
9. Russakovsky, O., et al.: ImageNet large scale visual recognition challenge. Int. J. Comput. Vision (IJCV) **115**(3), 211–252 (2015)
10. Akcay, S., Kundegorski, M.E., Willcocks, C.G., Breckon, T.P.: Using deep convolutional neural network architectures for object classification and detection within X-ray baggage security imagery. IEEE Trans. Inf. Forensics Secur. **13**, 2203–2215 (2018)
11. Mery, D., Svec, E., Arias, M., Riffo, V., Saavedra, J.M., Banerjee, S.: Modern computer vision techniques for X-ray testing in baggage inspection. IEEE Trans. Syst. Man Cybern. Syst. **47**(4), 682–692 (2017)
12. Szegedy, C., et al.: Going deeper with convolutions. In: Computer Vision and Pattern Recognition (CVPR) (2015)
13. Krizhevsky, A., Sutskever, I., Hinton, G.E.: Imagenet classification with deep convolutional neural networks. In: Pereira, F., Burges, C.J.C., Bottou, L., Weinberger, K.Q. (eds.) Advances in Neural Information Processing Systems 25, pp. 1097–1105. Curran Associates Inc. (2012)
14. Mery, D., et al.: GDXray: the database of X-ray images for nondestructive testing. J. Nondestr. Eval. **34**(4), 1–12 (2015)
15. Ngiam, J., Khosla, A., Kim, M., Nam, J., Lee, H., Ng, A.Y.: Multimodal deep learning. In: Getoor, L., Scheffer, T. (eds.) ICML, pp. 689–696. Omnipress (2011)
16. Srivastava, N., Salakhutdinov, R.: Multimodal learning with deep Boltzmann machines. J. Mach. Learn. Res. **15**, 2949–2980 (2014)
17. Simonyan, K., Zisserman, A.: Two-stream convolutional networks for action recognition in videos. In: Ghahramani, Z., Welling, M., Cortes, C., Lawrence, N.D., Weinberger, K.Q. (eds.) Advances in Neural Information Processing Systems 27, pp. 568–576. Curran Associates Inc. (2014)
18. Eitel, A., Springenberg, J.T., Spinello, L., Riedmiller, M.A., Burgard, W.: Multimodal deep learning for robust RGB-D object recognition. CoRR, abs/1507.06821 (2015)

19. Zhu, H., Weibel, J.-B., Lu, S.: Discriminative multi-modal feature fusion for RGBD indoor scene recognition. In: IEEE Conference on Computer Vision and Pattern Recognition (CVPR), pp. 2969–2976 (2016)
20. Als-Neielsen, J., McMorrow, D.: Elements of Modern X-ray Physics, 2edn. (2011)
21. Heitz, G., Chechik, G.: Object separation in X-ray image sets. In: IEEE Computer Society Conference on Computer Vision and Pattern Recognition (CVPR), pp. 2093–2100, June 2010
22. Baştan, M., Yousefi, M.R., Breuel, T.M.: Visual words on baggage X-ray images. In: Real, P., Diaz-Pernil, D., Molina-Abril, H., Berciano, A., Kropatsch, W. (eds.) CAIP 2011. LNCS, vol. 6854, pp. 360–368. Springer, Heidelberg (2011). https://doi.org/10.1007/978-3-642-23672-3_44
23. Simonyan, K., Zisserman, A.: Very deep convolutional networks for large-scale image recognition. CoRR, abs/1409.1556 (2014)
24. Kuncheva, L.I., Whitaker, C.J.: Measures of diversity in classifier ensembles and their relationship with the ensemble accuracy. Mach. Learn. **51**(2), 181–207 (2003)
25. Szegedy, C., et al.: Going deeper with convolutions. In: IEEE Conference on Computer Vision and Pattern Recognition (CVPR), pp. 1–9, June 2015
26. He, K., Zhang, X., Ren, S., Sun, J.: Deep residual learning for image recognition. CoRR, abs/1512.03385 (2015)
27. Subrahmanyam, M., Maheshwari, R.P., Balasubramanian, R.: Local maximum edge binary patterns: a new descriptor for image retrieval and object tracking. Signal Process. **92**(6), 1467–1479 (2012)
28. Rasmussen, C.E.: The infinite Gaussian mixture model. In: Advances in Neural Information Processing Systems 12, pp. 554–560. MIT Press (2000)

Author Index

Adachi, Shoto 251
Ahmad, Sohaib 450
Akar, Osman 494
Akira, Naoto 523
Almasri, Feras 418
Alonso-Caneiro, David 215
Animesh 159
Argyriou, Vasileios 39
Arthur, Edmund 261

Banerjee, Rajdeep H. 75
Bartz, Christian 341
Belaïd, A. 144
Belaïd, Y. 144
Bellemo, Valentina 282, 289, 309
Bethge, Joseph 341
Bressler, N. M. 303, 316
Burlina, Philippe 289, 303, 316
Bušta, Michal 127

Cabrera DeBuc, Delia 261, 316
Carter, Cambron 494
Chen, Fred K. 215
Cheng, Ching-Yu 309
Choi, Chankyu 202
Chowdhury, Arindam 159, 186
Collins, Michael J. 215
Cuevas, Emmanuel Antonio 494

Debeir, Olivier 418
Deguchi, Daisuke 15

Fagertun, Jens 357
Fajtl, Jiri 39
Frohlich, Robert 467
Fu, Iris 494
Fujita, Koji 31
Fuller, Benjamin 450

Gade, Rikke 357
Garcia-Franco, Renata 309

Hacizade, Tahir 386
Hamwood, Jared 215
Hamzah, Haslina 282, 309
Hirayama, Takatsugu 15
Hiroya, Inakoshi 402
Ho, Jinyi 282, 309
Holder, Christopher J. 510
Hsu, Wynne 276, 282, 309
Huang, Jia-Hong 235, 323
Huck Yang, C.-H. 235, 323

Ide, Ichiro 15
Ienaga, Naoto 31
I-Hung Lin, M. D. 323
Ito, Seiya 64

Jan, Yasir 484
Jha, Nilpa 75
Jørgensen, Anders 357
Joshi, N. 303, 316

Kairanbay, Magzhan 110
Kaneko, Naoshi 64
Kashino, Kunio 15
Kato, Zoltan 467
Kawai, Wataru 31
Kawanishi, Yasutomo 15
Kim, Junseok 202
Kimura, Masanari 373
Knoll, Alois 386
Kodama, Yuki 15
Kong, Quan 523
Kugelman, Jason 215

Lamoureux, Ecosse 309
Lee, Junsu 202
Lee, Mong Li 276, 282, 309
Lee, Xin Qi 282, 309
Li, Hongdong 3
Lim, Gilbert 276, 282, 309
Lim, Zhan Wei 282
Liu, Fangyu 323
Liu, T. Y. Alvin 316

Liu, Yi Chieh 323
Liu, Yi-Chieh 235
Lohani, D. 144

Makihara, Yasushi 55
Masumoto, Hiroki 229, 251
Matas, Jiri 127
Matsubara, Daisuke 523
Meinel, Christoph 341
Menon, Geeta 309
Mittal, Samarth 159
Miyata, Natsuki 31
Moeslund, Thomas B. 357
Monekosso, Dorothy 39
Morikawa, Hiromasa 235, 323
Murakami, Tomokazu 523
Muramatsu, Daigo 55
Murase, Hiroshi 15

Nagano, Hidehisa 15
Nagasato, Daisuke 251
Nakakura, Shunsuke 229, 251
Narusawa, Atsushi 100
Nguyen, Quang Duc 309
Noguchi, Asuka 229

Obara, Boguslaw 510
Ohsugi, Hideharu 251
Orchard, Garrick 434

Pang, Zhanzhong 402
Patel, Yash 127
Patro, Arun 75
Pedersen, Malte 357
Pekala, M. 316

Quang, Nguyen Duc 282

Rahul, Rohit 159, 186
Rajagopal, Anoop 75
Rajan, Aruna 75
Ramesh, Bharath 434
Ravichandran, Divyaa 494
Read, Scott A. 215
Remagnino, Paolo 39
Ricketts, Stephen 510
Robles-Kelly, Antonio 3

Saito, Hideo 31
Sakata, Atsuya 55
See, John 110
Sehgal, Gunjan 186
Shafaei, Sina 386
Sharma, Monika 174, 186
Shimoda, Wataru 100
Shiratuddin, Mohd Fairuz 484
Shroff, Gautam 186
Sohel, Ferdous 484
Sokeh, Hajar Sadeghi 39
Srinivasan, Ashwin 186
Sugiura, Yuta 31
Sugiyama, Yu 88
Sumi, Kazuhiko 64
Sun, Jun 402
Sun, Xiaoming 3
Swati 186

Tabian, Iuliana 494
Tabuchi, Hitoshi 229, 251
Takemura, Noriko 55
Tanabe, Hirotaka 229
Tegnèr, Jesper 235, 323
Tian, Meng 235, 323
Ting, Daniel Shu Wei 282, 289, 309
Tong, Bin 523
Tsai, Yi-Chang James 235

Ussa, Andrés 434

Vedova, Luca Della 434
Verma, Abhishek 174
Vig, Lovekesh 159, 174, 186
Vincent, Stephen J. 215
Vishwanath, D. 186

Wang, Qing 3
Watanabe, Yuki 523
Wong, Hallee E. 494
Wong, Kok Wai 484
Wong, Lai-Kuan 110
Wong, Tien Yin 282, 289, 309

Xie, Yuchen 282, 309
Xu, Dejiang 309

Yagi, Yasushi 55
Yamada, Kaho 64
Yanagihara, Takashi 373
Yanai, Keiji 88, 100
Yang, Hao-Hsiang 235, 323
Yang, Haojin 341
Yang, Hong 434

Yip, Michelle Yuen Ting 282, 309
Yong, Liu 289
Yoon, Youngmin 202
Yu, Xiaoyi 402

Zhang, Qi 3
Zhu, Hao 3

MIX
Papier aus verantwortungsvollen Quellen
Paper from responsible sources
FSC® C105338

If you have any concerns about our products,
you can contact us on
ProductSafety@springernature.com

In case Publisher is established outside the EU,
the EU authorized representative is:
**Springer Nature Customer Service Center GmbH
Europaplatz 3, 69115 Heidelberg, Germany**

Printed by Libri Plureos GmbH
in Hamburg, Germany